Bunnie Engstrom   1977

Bunnie Engstrom   1977

The Leading Ladies

BY JAMES ROBERT PARISH

As Author
THE FOX GIRLS*
THE RKO GALS*
THE PARAMOUNT PRETTIES*
THE SLAPSTICK QUEENS
GOOD DAMES
HOLLYWOOD'S GREAT LOVE TEAMS*
ELVIS!
GREAT MOVIE HEROES
GREAT CHILD STARS
GREAT WESTERN STARS
FILM DIRECTORS GUIDE: WESTERN EUROPE
FILM ACTORS GUIDE: WESTERN EUROPE
THE JEANETTE MacDONALD STORY
THE TOUGH GUYS*

As Co-author
THE EMMY AWARDS: A PICTORIAL HISTORY
THE CINEMA OF EDWARD G. ROBINSON
THE MGM STOCK COMPANY: THE GOLDEN ERA*
THE GREAT SPY PICTURES
THE GEORGE RAFT FILE
THE GLAMOUR GIRLS*
LIZA!
THE DEBONAIRS*
HOLLYWOOD PLAYERS: THE FORTIES*
THE SWASHBUCKLERS*
THE ALL-AMERICANS*
THE GREAT GANGSTER PICTURES
THE GREAT WESTERN PICTURES
HOLLYWOOD PLAYERS: THE THIRTIES*
FILM DIRECTORS GUIDE: THE U.S.
THE GREAT SCIENCE FICTION PICTURES

As Editor
THE GREAT MOVIE SERIES
ACTORS' TELEVISION CREDITS: 1950-1972 and SUPPLEMENT

As Associate Editor
THE AMERICAN MOVIES REFERENCE BOOK
TV MOVIES

BY DON E. STANKE

As Co-author
THE GLAMOUR GIRLS*
THE DEBONAIRS*
THE SWASHBUCKLERS*
THE ALL-AMERICANS*

*Published by Arlington House

The Leading Ladies

James Robert Parish
and Don E. Stanke

EDITOR:
T. Allan Taylor

RESEARCH ASSOCIATES:
John Robert Cocchi • Florence Solomon
Richard Wentzler

INTRODUCTION BY:
Gerald Weales

ARLINGTON HOUSE·PUBLISHERS
NEW ROCHELLE, NEW YORK

Library of Congress Cataloging in Publication Data

Parish, James Robert.
    The leading ladies.

    Includes index.
    1. Moving-picture actors and actresses—United States—Biography.
I. Stanke, Don E., joint author. II. Title.
PN1998.A2P393   791.43'028'0922 [B]   77-24565
ISBN 0-87000-388-7

For MARTIN GROSS

A Most Gracious and Efficient Editor

Key to the Abbreviations

AA	Allied Artists Picture Corporation
AIP	American International Pictures
AVCO EMB	Avco Embassy Pictures Corporation
C	Color
BV	Buena Vista Distribution Co., Inc.
CIN	Cinerama, Inc.
COL	Columbia Pictures Industries, Inc.
EL	Eagle Lion Films, Inc.
EMB	Embassy Pictures Corporation
FN	First National Pictures, Inc. (later part of Warner Bros.)
FOX	Fox Film Corporation (later part of Twentieth Century-Fox)
LIP	Lippert Pictures, Inc.
MGM	Metro-Goldwyn-Mayer, Inc.
MON	Monogram Pictures Corporation
PAR	Paramount Pictures Corporation
PRC	Producers Releasing Corporation
RKO	RKO Radio Pictures, Inc.
REP	Republic Pictures Corporation
20th	Twentieth Century-Fox Film Corporation
UA	United Artists Corporation
UNIV	Universal Pictures, Inc.
WB	Warner Bros., Inc.

Acknowledgments

RESEARCH MATERIAL CONSULTANT:
DOUG McCLELLAND

RESEARCH VERIFIER:
EARL ANDERSON

John R. Adams
DeWitt Bodeen
Ronald Bowers
Bill Culp
Howard Davis
Charlie Earle
Robert A. Evans
Morris Everett, Jr.
Film Favorites
Filmfacts (Ernest Parmentier)
Films and Filming
Films in Review
Focus on Film
Charles Forsythe
Connie Gilchrist
Mrs. R. F. Hastings
Carol Herbst
Hollywood Revue of Movie Memorabilia
David Johnson
Ken D. Jones
Miles Kreuger

Joseph Lehman
William T. Leonard
David McGillivray
Albert B. Manski
Alvin H. Marill
Mrs. Earl Meisinger
Peter Miglierini
Norman Miller
Movie Star News (Paula Klaw)
Richard Picchiarini
Michael R. Pitts
H. Richardson
Jerry Rowland
Screen Facts (Alan G. Barbour)
Bob Smith
Charles Smith
Mrs. Peter Smith
Madolin Stanke
Roz Starr Service
Charles K. Stumpf
Evelyn Thompson

And special thanks to Paul Myers, curator of the Theatre Collection at the Lincoln Center Library for the Performing Arts (New York City), and his staff: Monty Arnold, David Bartholomew, Rod Bladel, Donald Fowle, Maxwell Silverman, Dorothy Swerdlove, Betty Wharton, and Don Madison of Photo Services.

Contents

Introduction

by Gerald Weales

Tradition tells us that when Fay Templeton sang "Yesterdays" on the opening night of *Roberta* (November 18, 1933), there was not a dry eye in the house.

Legend tells us that when Ethel Griffies sang "Only for Americans" on the opening night of *Miss Liberty* (July 15, 1949), she permanently upstaged Irving Berlin, Robert E. Sherwood, Emma Lazarus, and all the other stars, offstage and on, who helped create that very expensive show.

Brooks Atkinson, less lachrymose than tradition, was choked up enough to write in his *New York Times* review of *Roberta,* "Theatregoers are sentimental folk, praise be to God," and to go on to say of Templeton that "it is hard to know whether she or the audience is more deeply moved." Fay Templeton was only in her late sixties when *Roberta* opened, but her years in show business and her great size (by 1933, she weighed 250 pounds and had to play most of *Roberta* sitting down) made her a monument of America's great theatrical past. Through their tears, the audience presumably saw her as some kind of Barbarossa, risen from her nostalgia cave, to unify Broadway past and pres-

ent. In fact, it was not a return; she had never really been away. Fay Templeton was one of those stars who go in and out of retirement the way railroads go in and out of bankruptcy court. After stirring up a scandal in London in the 1880s—by dressing too skimpily and singing "I Like It, I Do" with too naughty an intonation—she left the stage only to emerge in the 1890s, when she was often compared with her friend Lillian Russell, as a headliner at the Weber and Fields Music Hall. A decade later, George M. Cohan wrote *Forty-Five Minutes from Broadway* expressly for her, and in the year I was born she was playing the Palace in an all-star line-up of old timers. Two years before *Roberta* opened, she was singing—and not for the first time—"Poor Little Butterfly" in the Civic Light Opera production of *H.M.S. Pinafore.*

Ethel Griffies was never a star as Fay Templeton was. She was simply a remarkably efficient English character actress, constantly busy on stage, in England and America, and in films. American moviegoers will remember her, tight-lipped, sharp-faced, starchily softhearted, doing housekeeperly things in the background of movies like *Anna Karenina* and *Jane Eyre* or, if they are lucky, as the venomous grandmother in *Billy Liar.* Unless these tired old eyes deceive me (to use a locution particularly favored by drama critics of the Alexander Woollcott school who dote on legendary moments like those I used to open this essay), I saw her on television the other afternoon, done up in her head-nurse costume, being both austere and understanding with Carole Lombard in a 1940 weeper, *Vigil in the Night.* By 1949, when she was in her early seventies, Griffies had developed such authority that it was inevitable that her number should stand out in *Miss Liberty,* which by all accounts was at once overstuffed and ambiguous, a well-meant but unwelcome valentine to the Statue of Liberty. Her inspired croak (catch it on the original cast recording if you can find a copy) so stirred warm-hearted audiences that their journalistic counterparts starting building return-of-Ethel-Griffies myths. In a Sunday column on the show, Atkinson, who liked little of it aside from Griffies, said, somewhat laconically, that the actress "retired two years ago and has been particularly busy ever since."

Why—to introduce a book about six long-playing records of the silver screen—do I go on at such length about Fay Templeton and Ethel Griffies? Sheer happenstance, I'm afraid. When I sat down at this typewriter, planning to talk about theatrical durability and what nostalgia does to simple professionalism, I reached for images to illustrate my case, and my mind, which is stuffed with odds and ends like the drawer in which my mother used to keep bits of cloth she thought might come in handy, sent *Roberta* and *Miss Liberty* to the surface. I could have been more *au courant,* chosen almost anyone in the cast of *Follies* or *70 Girls 70* or any of the actresses who have *schlepped Hello, Dolly* and *Mame* through the boondocks. How I do harp on musical comedy, but then musical performers —even more than movie stars—are notorious carriers of the virulent nostalgia virus. "They usually sing 'I'm Still Here,'" wrote Arthur Bell, reviewing Vivian Blaine's new club act for the *Village Voice* (June 9, 1975), "and

usually three men in the audience cry." He is talking specifically about performers who package their past (he mentions Dolores Gray and Margaret Whiting, but he could have pointed to Judy Garland, who never got away from that damned rainbow, or the exquisite automaton which has been passing itself off as Marlene Dietrich for the last ten years) and "sell one-hour survival kits to an audience who in turn applauds what was, rather than what is."

What never was, in some cases. After all "I'm Still Here" is Carlotta's song from *Follies,* and it was Yvonne De Carlo who regularly stopped the show with that number. Although Parish and Stanke give De Carlo seventy pages and a number of kind words in another one of their compendiums, *The Glamour Girls,* I never really believed that she had an audience outside the publicity room at Universal—at least until *The Munsters.* I think fondly of *Salome, Where She Danced* from time to time, but only because of one wonderful line; was it Marjorie Rambeau who opened the door to the theatrical troupe with "Show folks, ain't ya, come on in"? That line has less to do with either the character or the performer who spoke it than with indulgent audiences in general. Although Bell was pretty brutal to Vivian Blaine in the review I quoted above, I suspect that most of the audience tried to be friendly. If a performer has been around for a long time, we want to like what he/she is doing because, by God, the performer is a trouper. The other night I sat through great stretches of Bing Crosby's Christmas television special because I did not really believe that he and Fred Astaire could be as mediocre and foolish as the incredibly awful script made them look. But Crosby and Astaire have real performing histories; and Vivian Blaine was once a wonderful Adelaide in *Guys and Dolls.* If the *is* is weak, there's always the aura of the *was.* If the *was* is weak, but the performer is in there punching—as De Carlo certainly did in *Follies*—we'll reinvent the past. Alice Faye and John Payne were impossible in the recent revival of *Good News,* but they tried so hard that I found myself wanting to believe that John Payne was once a good actor and that there was a time when Alice Faye was a real singer; and I could almost do so because I remember that, when I was thirteen, I accepted the unlikely premise of *Alexander's Ragtime Band*, that Alice Faye was a better singer than Ethel Merman.

This impulse to rewrite history goes beyond "show folks," of course, as the retirement of any senator over seventy will show. Let me take a literary example, however. In the *New York Times Book Review* for June 15, 1975, Evelyn Ames, reporting on the celebrations in England for J. B. Priestley's eightieth birthday, commented—apparently with a straight face—on "a surge of recognition among the English that living quietly in their midst was a great master of letters." A good popular novelist, an efficient playwright, a hard-working hack journalist, Priestley is "a great master of letters" in the way that Yvonne De Carlo is a star. What was being celebrated at Priestley's birthday party was sheer survival and—although she is more than a quarter of century younger than the dramatist—that was what De Carlo was singing about and embodying in "I'm Still Here." Hume Cronyn made a joke about it the last time I saw him on stage. He and Jessica Tandy came to the university where I teach (where, in fact, I once tried to teach Jim Parish) to do an evening of readings. When they walked on stage, the audience gave them such an enthusiastic round of applause that Cronyn smiled at Tandy and then, wryly, at the audience and delivered what I suspect was a well-practiced ad lib: "It's wonderful what longevity does for you."

The whole business of nostalgic revival, then, has something to do with physical survival, but the admirable thing about P. G. Wodehouse is not that he lived into his nineties, but that he raced death to get one last Bertie Wooster to the printers. I read in the paper the other day about a 104-year-old blind man who had been robbed, and what came through the article was not the pathos of his situation, but the marvelous sense of vital-

ity in the old man. Yet, I was struck by the fact that he had retired—or so he remembered —in 1929, and a man, however active, who has been in retirement for almost fifty years cannot have quite the same appeal as a woman who can evoke the past by singing "Yesterdays" and at the same time reassert her claim on the present. I know, I know, the blind centenarian was not in show business, and domestic service does not have the same traditions, except in fiction (think of the character of Firs in *The Cherry Orchard*). The point of all this—in case you had begun to think there was no point at all—is that existence is not enough. Even ripeness is not all, whatever Lear said, unless it's ready to slip on tap shoes when the follow spot comes on.

I have let the word *nostalgia* creep occasionally into the *mélange* above. In its purest sense that word is inappropriate to a book which celebrates six indestructible actresses; it denotes a withdrawal into the past, an escape from the present. One crouches behind a wall of Big Little Books, studying one's Little Orphan Annie decoder ring, and imagines that one is safe from attack by Sonny and Cher, Tony Orlando and Dawn. A great deal of what goes on in movie-memory books these days is nostalgic in that sense, but the nostalgia implicit in the reception of Fay Templeton in *Roberta*—or Yvonne De Carlo in *Follies*, for that matter—is informed not by retreat, but by continuity. The performer making a triumphal return (Sarah Bernhardt is the classic example) is like the Fifth Avenue shopkeeper, selling overpriced handkerchiefs to tourists behind a window plastered with signs (FIRE SALE, GOING OUT OF BUSINESS, EVERYTHING MUST GO) which have been there so long that one feels another should be added: TWENTIETH SUCCESSFUL YEAR.

The operative image—the most romantic, the most sentimental figure in show business mythology—is the old trouper. "Don't look at us like we are, sir," says the ancient Shakespearean actor in *The Fantasticks*, "But see me in a doublet! . . . try to see me under light!" The Sunshine Boys never really retire; they are only between engagements. If a booking is not quite up to the performer's greatest days—the superannuated Hamlet of *The Fantasticks* reduced to a bit-part in a mock-rape—or if the performer is not quite up to the job at hand, there is always one's professional bag of tricks to fall back on ("Indians are always off left"). If I were to try to list all those show-business shows in which the old-timer insists on going on, I would use up even more paper than this book has done to give you Bette Davis' credits. One of the most persistent of the breed is that wheezy old favorite, *The Royal Family*, perhaps because the Cavendish family in full cry sets up echoes of real American theatrical families like the Drews and the Barrymores. "I've been a trouper all my life, and I'm going to keep on trouping," says Fanny early in the play, and only death—a tearful curtain after three acts of frenetic comedy—can keep her from taking to the road again. The Bicentennial season, which has sent so many artistic directors scurrying back to the library shelves, has already turned up several productions of *The Royal Family*. Fittingly enough, one of them has Eva Le Gallienne playing Fanny. Le Gallienne, the youthful founder of the Civic Rep, was already by way of becoming a theatrical institution when George Kaufman and Edna Ferber gave birth to Fanny Cavendish.

Although there are plenty of show-must-go-on films that peddle the old-trouper legend (where, after all, is W. C. Fields going at the end of *The Old-Fashioned Way* but back on the boards?), it is a story that seems really to belong to the stage. In the movies, oddly enough, the more popular story is the one about how the show is never going on again. Or how it stopped years ago. Two favorite Hollywood images of the performer—actresses in both cases—are the woman who gives up her career for love and the recluse, closeted—often in splendor—with her memories. Bette Davis has played both. Margo Channing is the famous version of the former, of course, although Margaret Elliot of *The Star* is a more conventional one since, unlike the old trouper, she decides not to hit the comeback trail but scurries off to "real life" in a marina with an ex-leading man who has long since seen the light. *What Ever Happened to Baby Jane?* is the macabre variation on the great-ladies-in-retirement film, with both Davis' Baby Jane and Joan Crawford's Blanche as cartoon variations on the kind of character that we all know best in Norma Desmond, Gloria Swanson's memorable creation in *Sunset Boulevard*. The assumption behind such characters is that stardom is based on evanescent qualities such as beauty—which fades—or style—which becomes dated—and that all an actress can do is cut and run when her antennae tell her her powers are going. "There's no more valuable knowledge than knowing the right time to go," says Tennessee Williams' Alexandra Del Lago in *Sweet Bird of Youth*. "I went at the right time to go. RETIRED! Where to? To what? To that dead planet the moon. . . ." There are real figures moving behind the fictional facades of the Norma Desmonds and the Alexandra Del Lagos. Greta Garbo and Luise Rainer—to give just two glorious examples—and how we do hate to let them go. Walking the East 50s in Manhattan, intent on one kind of editorial business or another, I cannot help looking twice at every elegant woman in dark glasses just in case it turns out to be Garbo off to the drugstore for an orange stick; after the tenth person had asked me if I had noticed that Luise Rainer was sitting on the couch in one of the scenes in *La Dolce Vita*, I became convinced that I had seen the lady when all I had really seen—and that in my mind's eye—was Anna Held's delight in the gift of flowers in *The Great Ziegfeld*.

Garbo and Rainer may be quite content in retirement, leading busy and fascinating lives (although Garbo stories, like the one in Tennessee Williams' *Memoirs*, keep insisting that such is not the case). As Alexandra's "Where to? To what?" indicates, their fictional counterparts find precious little peace of mind. Baby Jane may be an extreme case of going batty down memory lane—the generic demands of the horror film—but Norma Des-

14

mond is not exactly granny in a cottage, baking cookies for the neighborhood children. She is as clear a negative image as Fanny Cavendish is a positive one. It may seem a little odd at first glance, but I suspect that our two chief show-business *schmaltz* stories are really underground messages from the Protestant work ethic, saying, stick to your job and have a full life like Fanny Cavendish or turn your back on your work and settle for isolation, emptiness, madness. The other retirement story is a touch more optimistic. When, just before the final fade-out, the star chooses love over art, the movie is heading for a conventional happy ending; and we must accept it as such, even though, having read Molly Haskell, we know that it is just another example of Hollywood's co-opting a strong female character for a supporting role in a male-oriented society. Besides, the production of the movies, the casting of the roles, the whole artistic process deny the stories being told. Bette Davis must have known that the end of *The Star* was not the end of the story, that Margaret Elliot—had she been made of the flesh, blood, and ambition of the woman who played her—would have had to go beyond the marina to whatever new role lay ahead; after all, Davis tried marriage often enough and found it no cure for career and—as an act of defiance and celebration—she called her first autobiography *The Lonely Life*. Women who do not choose love over work play women who do, and women like Davis, Crawford, Swanson—indestructibles, all—are necessary to give form to the fictional ladies who hide away. Even Alexandra Del Lago, who may have begun in Garbo withdrawal, knows by the end of the play that she belongs in the other camp: "Out of the passion and torment of my existence, I have created a thing that I can unveil, a sculpture, almost heroic." Williams, the eternal sentimentalist about loss, denies that Alexandra has a future to go to, but we know better than he does. She is the vitality that makes the play work (in so far as it does) and, besides, Williams, who is a kind of Alexandra Del Lago in drag, refuses to stop writing. "Say,

Yes," sang Mildred Natwick and a whole overage chorus at the end of *70 Girls 70.*

"But I have survived. I always survive; that is my major accomplishment." The quotation comes from a gushy article, "A Breathtaking Visit with Bette Davis," which Gail Cameron did for *McCall's* (November 1974). The actress was talking about the dissolution of her marriage to Gary Merrill and the distress that followed the divorce, but the words would serve as well to summarize her whole career. Yet, there are a number of ways of surviving and the way that a performer chooses depends a great deal on her sense not only of self but of the whole profession of acting. What set me thinking about the variations within the survival ritual was a photograph that I came across a few weeks ago as I leafed through some nostalgia book or other. It was from the famous garden scene in *Dark Victory*, with Geraldine Fitzgerald, a look of understanding and pain on her face, kneeling beside an almost radiant Bette Davis. I found myself thinking not so much of the movie, over which I no longer cry, as of the two women and what a distance they have traveled since 1939. And by what different ways. The thoughts came, I suppose, because both Fitzgerald and Davis had played Philadelphia the season before and a juxtaposition—very different from the one in *Dark Victory*—was fresh in my mind. In late 1974, Davis opened in *Miss Moffat,* an idiotic musical that Emlyn Williams, Joshua Logan, and Albert Hague had carpentered out of *The Corn Is Green.* No one would suggest, I suppose, that either the Williams play or the movie based on it is a classic, but its schoolteacher heroine provides a good strong role that gives a Tallulah Bankhead or a Bette Davis elbow room in which to build a performance. The Miss Moffat of the musical turned out to be only a skeleton of her former self, a character whose strength and vitality, whose whole existence depended on the audience's memory of Davis in the role thirty years earlier. That memory turned out to be a great deal dimmer than the producers of the musical expected. The show was awful, Davis was embarrassing and, after the Philadelphia run, *Miss Moffat* folded quietly. If Davis was disappointed, she should not have been; at least, she was spared a New York opening. A few months later, Geraldine Fitzgerald came to town to play Mary Tyrone in a production of *Long Day's Journey into Night* put on by the Philadelphia Drama Guild, a local company that tries—with mixed success—to do good plays with interesting performers. The O'Neill play was one of the best productions the company has done, and Fitzgerald was a fine Mary Tyrone.

Why should Davis, the star, have been talk-singing her way through a lifeless retread of an old part, while Fitzgerald, never a star in the Davis sense, was playing one of the best dramatic roles for a woman that the American stage provides? The question carries its own answer. In his *Bette Davis,* Jerry Vermilye quotes the actress: "Hell, I could do a million of those character roles. But I'm stubborn about playing the lead. I'd like to go out with my name above the title." She had another pre-departure hope in the Cameron interview, in which she said that her last wish "is *not* to leave this planet doing junk." That, she explained, was why she was doing *Miss Moffat.* It is possible that Davis just does not know junk when she sees it—particularly well-intentioned, high-principled junk of the Emlyn Williams variety—but the real problem, I think, is that the two last dreams of Davis are in deep conflict. Katharine Hepburn, the most obvious indestructible leading lady missing* from this book, seems to have been the only one of the female stars of the 1930s who managed to hang on to star status and to do quality work at the same time. She has had her share of fragile goods from *Spitfire* to *Rooster Cogburn*—not her fair share if one looks at the credits of Davis and Crawford—but she has also had access to roles like the lead in Enid Bagnold's new play, *A Matter of Gravity,* in which she is currently giving one of the best performances of her life. For most stars, like Davis, keeping one's name above the title calls for too frequent de-

*Editor's note: see *The RKO Gals* (Arlington House, 1974) by James Robert Parish.

scents into—to use her own word—junk. Fitzgerald, not having to worry about stardom, has been able to take interesting small parts, like the one in *The Pawnbroker,* and more important to become just another member of the company—at the Drama Guild, at the Long Wharf in New Haven—and has been able to build a career that lacks the flamboyance of Davis' but—from the outside, at least—looks a great deal more rewarding. In *The Lonely Life,* Davis speaks fondly of Laura Hope Crews, with whom she had acted in summer theater back in 1928, and sadly comments on the fact that the last role of her distinguished career was a bit in *The Man Who Came to Dinner* and that it ended on the cutting-room floor. Perhaps Davis is haunted by this image, but surely the salient point in the story is that Crews continued to perform long after she had ceased to be the star who evoked from Sidney Howard, whose *The Silver Cord* had given her one of her most famous roles, a celebration of "the brave, ephemeral, beautiful art of acting." Some might say that it is better to risk the cutting-room floor as a character actress than to star oneself onto a motorcycle with Ernest Borgnine in *Bunny O'Hare,* but every survivor has to decide the terms which keep her on stage or in front of the camera. As I write this, Geraldine Fitzgerald is back in Philadelphia, this time playing Amanda in *The Glass Menagerie,* and Bette Davis has just finished shooting *Burnt Offerings,* still another horror flic, which, according to Rex Reed's column, provoked her to say, "This film has been amateur night in Dixie."

I may be as star-touched as any movie buff, but the critic in me joins hands with the sentimentalist to applaud a performer like Geraldine Fitzgerald, like Valli, like Valentina Cortesa, like Alexis Smith, like Shelley Winters, who continues to grow—or at least to find opportunities in which growth is a possibility. Of the six women whose careers make up this book, it is Joan Blondell, oddly enough, who belongs in this company. I may cling to the girl who tapped, sang, and wisecracked her way into my heart in *Gold Dig-*

gers of 1933, but that heart goes out to the actress who was willing to risk following Sada Thompson as Beatrice in the off-Broadway production of *The Effect of Gamma Rays on Man-in-the-Moon Marigolds.* Still, I spent too many happy or tearful hours in the three movie houses in downtown Connersville, Indiana, to let the austerity of artistic purpose obscure the grandeur implicit in simply becoming one of the indestructible leading ladies. Let's have a chorus of "I'm Still Here." Better still, let's hear it from Fanny Cavendish: "I've been a trouper all my life, and I'm going to keep on trouping."

PHILADELPHIA
DECEMBER 1975

17

Starlet, 1931-style.

CHAPTER 1

Joan Blondell

5'3"
115 pounds
Blonde hair
Gray eyes
Virgo

"I've had a very long career with not very good material under me. I've never had a favorite role. None of them was that good. I play Joan Blondell, and I play her the best I can." This is the appraisal of the saucy, saucer-eyed actress who has survived vaudeville, the Warner Bros. filmmaking assembly line, assorted TV series, and three broken marriages.

Most people fondly recall Joan Blondell as the flippant, shapely, blondized doll of assorted Busby Berkeley screen musicals and Depression-era movie comedies and dramas. In the Thirties, she typified the spirit of a woman who had taken the worst the Depression could dish out, but was still game. Her characters always seemed to suggest that although times were tough, one could lick the Depression by working hard and playing it "on the square."

Her cinema prototype in the Thirties had seen hard times but had lost none of her dignity. She knew a raw deal when she saw one and would stand up and call it what it was with plenty of sauce. "There's two things I haven't any use for, and jail is both of 'em." Her voice was low-pitched, nasal, and gave the impression that there was a marble rolling around in her mouth somewhere. But she always conveyed her point to audiences. She could equal James Cagney in toughness and Glenda Farrell or Pat O'Brien in rapid-fire delivery, and was a surprising match for Margaret Sullavan in the vulnerability department.

If anything diluted Joan's opportunity for screen stardom of the highest rank, it was her firm stand that her domestic life came above anything, especially career. She was a conscientious, willing worker at the studio. In fact, she was too amenable to the studio system. Unlike her confreres—Bette Davis, James Cagney, et al.—she never said "no" to a bad picture, but worked herself to a frazzle to fulfill the letter of her contractual obligation.

Honest and gutsy, both on and off the screen, Joan displayed a very human vulnerability in the marital sweepstakes. Thrice married (cinematographer George Barnes, screen-crooner Dick Powell, and Broadway entrepreneur Mike Todd) and the mother of two children, she readily admits that her three divorces prove something went wrong along the way. What she does not emphasize is that these relationships sapped her energy to promote her career; in some instances her spouses seemed bent on diverting the momentum of her screen popularity.

But this earthy lady continually picked up the pieces of her life and career and moved onward with typical Blondell verve. No longer the ingenue, she gave new dimension to the role of the blowsy character lead. Repeatedly, on screen (and in rare stage appearances), she would demonstrate that she could be a fine dramatic actress and not *just* a brassy, snappy comedienne with a wonderful flair for wisecracks. In this capacity, she shone in *A Tree Grows in Brooklyn* (1945) as Aunt Cissy and later was Oscar-nominated for Best Supporting Actress for playing the show business mother in *The Blue Veil* (1951).

In the Seventies, endurable Joan starred off-Broadway in *The Effect of Gamma Rays on Man-in-the-Moon Marigolds,* was author of a well-received autobiographical novel (*Center Door Fancy*), and continues to bolster often mediocre movies and telefeatures with her forceful presence.

According to Joan, "I'm a staunch lover in every sense of the word. I love people, husbands, children, grandchildren, dogs. I'm a great appreciator of good things—the veins in a leaf, roses, the look of morning, the smell of babies. . . . [Of course] there's a lump inside you always, lumps of sorrow, griefs, failures. But with a little effort you can keep them in the background."

She was born on Monday, August 30, 1909, at two minutes to midnight in a large New York City apartment on 91st Street near Central Park West. Joan did not know it yet, but her parents were enjoying a period of financial and popular success as vaudeville performers. Her father, Ed Blondell, once achieved nationwide fame as the original Katzenjammer Kid and now had another winning routine, the "Lost Boy" act with his wife and partner Katherine (or Kathryn or Kath-

run) Cane. An ancestor named Blondell had been the favorite minstrel of King Richard the Lion-Hearted of England, purportedly cheering up the monarch when the battles were going badly during the Crusades.

It was a maxim of the vaudeville life that money should be spent "as fast as you can earn it." And that unpropitious life-style was the foundation of the Blondells' existence. Their fashionable apartment was equipped with two servants while Joan and her two-year-older brother, Edward Jr., ate, dressed, and traveled in style.

The Blondell family was an extremely close-knit unit. Rather than leave their offspring at home in the care of a servant, Ed insisted that they be backstage during performances. This meant that, even before she could comprehend what they were, little Joan would be bombarded with the garish sights and sounds of the vaudeville stage for many uninterrupted hours of each day. For her, bright lights and gaudy music became the rule rather than the exception. When the Blondells were busy onstage, the duty of minding the children fell on the other performers. This brought an endless stream of magicians, singers, dancers, clowns, jugglers, animal trainers, and acrobats parading before the Blondell toddlers.

Joan became the recipient of hundreds of brightly colored, glittering adornments from the many elaborate stage costumes that passed her way. To her growing collection she added whatever beads and trinkets she could scavenge from the stage floor when an act had finished. As time went on, this box of sundries became more and more a central possession in her bohemian life.

In the Blondell household there was nothing more sure than travel. Before she was two weeks old, little Joan was whisked off to Germany. The Blondells traveled first class, staying in the best hotels and dining at the best restaurants. Joan's first birthday was celebrated in Paris; before she was four, her parents would have played engagements in nearly every capital of the Continent. During this hectic period, Joan saw virtually no children her own age, her older brother being her sole playmate. Her other companions were the vaudevillians and stage hands.

It might seem that such a background would be an ideal way to train a child to go onstage with her parents' act. But her father had no such intention. Mr. Blondell dearly loved his profession but he had no intention of forcing the trade on his children. "Our father always kept us away from the show business routine," Joan would recall later.

Thus, it was without her father's consent

that Joan made her unofficial vaudeville debut at the age of fourteen months. Ed and Katherine were doing their act at a theatre in Sydney, Australia, when the audience suddenly burst into laughter. Mr. Blondell could not understand such an enthusiastic response coming at that particular point in the routine. Then he noticed that his daughter had sauntered onstage and upstage clad in nothing more than a flannel strip around her waist. Burlesque was to figure importantly in Joan's later career, but never again would she be this unclad onstage.

Her fifth birthday was the first one she could celebrate in her native America. And by the time of her sixth, she and her family were traveling to Australia. Also aboard ship were the Polish pianist Ignace Paderewski, Al Jolson, and Fred Niblo who would direct such distinguished silent features as *Mark of Zorro* (1920) and *Ben-Hur* (1926). The outgoing Jolson made Joan a present of a manicure set. With this gift the youngster rushed about the passenger deck, soliciting customers at the bargain rate of five cents. From Down Under they departed by cattle boat to fulfill an engagement in China.

Back in New York, a year or so later, the Blondell troupe took an enforced holiday from show business as Katherine gave birth to a third child, Gloria. Meanwhile, Joan and her brother had their first extensive exposure to the cinema and enjoyed the local matinees. It was during this period that Joan's attitude toward Ed became increasingly maternal. In an apparent imitation of her mother's rapport with her boy, Joan began treating her older brother more like a son. (Interestingly enough, in her semi-autobiographical novel *Center Door Fancy* [1972], the heroine's brother is *younger*.)

In the meantime, Ed Sr. was performing a single act on the vaudeville circuit and was experiencing the repercussions of the gradual decline of the medium. The movies were now the attention-grabbers. Many theatre owners were converting their facilities to accommodate motion pictures, and acts were becoming harder to book as the bottom began dropping out of the stage show market. The Blondells would no longer ride, eat, or sleep first class. The knock-out blow, however, came in 1918, when it was discovered that the San Diego real estate in which Mr. Blondell had placed most of his life savings—sight unseen—was found to be worthless. In fact, two-thirds of the property was under water.

Once sister Gloria had reached a reasonably advanced age, Mrs. Blondell rejoined the act. It was decided at this point that Joan's education should not be limited to the occasional lesson which her parents could provide in their spare time. Her father wanted to ensure that she had proper training. Realizing that the family was going to be in a different town every week, he obtained a certificate from the governor of New York which permitted Joan to attend a school for a minimum period of one week in any part of the country.

Almost invariably, Joan would enter a classroom full of children who had known each other for years. The stranger would be treated coldly by her companions. However, she was able to add dignity to her exile by telling wild and fanciful stories of her show business upbringing. Frequently, she would demonstrate a few of the entertaining stunts her folks had taught her.

By the time Joan was ten, the family's increasingly desperate financial situation forced the Blondells into incorporating cute little Joan into the act. They made use of her proven ability to mimic other performers, a talent she had demonstrated at an early age. This ability became the foundation of her own act, with a gypsy dance and some vocalizing tossed in for good measure. Her official debut in vaudeville, though, was with an old family standby, the "Lost Boy" routine.

Now that the entire family was getting into the act, the Blondells became even more closely knit and Joan loved it. "When I look back on it all I don't see how it is possible for people to be any happier than theatre folks."

Joan's ability to perform onstage depended on local union regulations which varied from town to town. Some places were much more tolerant than others concerning child labor. The Blondells were also constantly on their guard against a nationwide organization, the Geary Society, who took it upon themselves to make sure children were in schools, not performing in front of the footlights. Johnny —the affectionate nickname Joan used for her father—always hoped that Joan would have a chance for a proper education. Finally, he had to give way to the many pressures upon him, and he arranged with friends in Brooklyn for Joan to board with them. Thus, she was to have her first full year of schooling in Flatbush's P.S. 139.

It was little wonder that Joan was initially confused as to the correct deportment of a girl her age. At least in the area of sports she felt no self-consciousness. Although she also enjoyed football and swimming, she was never more at home than when she was tossing fast balls from the pitcher's mound. It was baseball that won Joan the camaraderie and respect of the boys in her class.

For her second full school year, thirteen-year-old Joan had another change of scenery. The Blondell act had been scheduled for an extensive tour of California during the coming months. So Joan was transferred to the Venice School in the town of the same name, where her parents could occasionally supervise their mischievous teen-age daughter, whose only academic interest seemed to be in sports and pranks.

Very shortly, romance brought a change to Joan's life. Her growing interest in Johnny Kenny, president of the eighth grade class, led her to eliminate many of the tomboyish mannerisms from her repertoire. As it happened, it would be Johnny who would tell Joan the facts of life, a subject her mother had carefully avoided mentioning. The two amateur lovebirds developed a routine whereby Johnny would borrow his father's car, drive two or three blocks, and park. Once the car had safely come to rest by the roadside, Joan and Johnny would venture a few hesitant kisses and then return home. The routine had almost become a habit when a sudden flash of "insight" put a fast end to these afternoons of innocent adventure.

The untutored Joan believed, as her movie-watching seemed to confirm, that a kiss led directly to having babies. Thus, one afternoon while experimenting with Johnny, Joan dashed out of the car and ran home. Once there, she decided to ask her girlfriend whose father was a doctor. After Joan had confided her predicament to her, the two drew up a diet that seemed appropriate for an expectant mother. She would require a good deal of food that was "good for her," including that awful-tasting spinach. Eventually, it was a patient Johnny who explained to Joan the real facts of life.

Even when she was not thinking about Johnny, Joan did not take much interest in academics. Mathematics was the subject she liked least, with English and science next on her hate list. The only thing she liked about school were the occasional classes in music and theatre. One of her habits was bringing itching powder to class, which had the expected results on her neighbors. For lunch, nothing pleased Joan more than a diet of pickles and ice cream. Her stated ambition in life was to drive a fire engine or be a sergeant in the Marines on a battleship. One of her teachers, a Miss Whitsett, predicted that she would wind up in reform school. But this was not to be the case.

Her encounter with California academics was suddenly cut short when she won an argument with a schoolmate by knocking out her two front teeth with a baseball bat. Joan was not upset about being expelled; at least she would not have to read any more books.

During a stay in Denton, the home of Texas State University, Ed Jr. became enamored of a co-ed. He said he was in love and married the girl. Unfortunately, the entire Blondell stage act had been written around their eighteen-year-old son. Hiring another adolescent would have been painful for the family unit, and to prepare another act would mean a loss of time and salary while it was being tried out.

Mr. Blondell decided it was now time to try to settle down. He gathered the family's savings of around $200 and rented a small store in Denton. Thus, Blondell's Clothing Shop, located across the street from the University, depended mostly on student trade. Girls' clothing was chosen as the store's specialty since Joan and Gloria were available as full-time models. When they were not mannequins, the girls entertained the customers with singing and dancing, the latter being Joan's particular forte.

Considering the store's unique qualities, it is not surprising that the Blondells' business became a thriving enterprise. But then the college passed a minor regulation requiring all its students to wear uniforms, which the school would provide. Once again the Blondells were forced to tread the vaudeville circuit.

When the family car collapsed in Dallas, that city became the spot for the family's return to show business. However, their act never seemed to materialize. Without money, friends, or prospects, the Blondells seemed beaten. But not Joan. She went out searching for a job and found one with a stock company, and her eighteen-dollar-per-week salary helped her family to survive. Then Helen Dodger, a close high school acquaintance, turned up in town. She was caring for someone's apartment in lieu of rent and wanted Joan to keep her company there.

The Blondells had misgivings, but their desperate financial situation persuaded them to see the practical side of the move. After three weeks at her new residence, Joan felt secure enough to take a long shot. Helen noticed a newspaper ad for entrants to a local beauty contest. Joan did not at first share Helen's enthusiasm for the idea, but Helen planned to enter, regardless, so Joan tagged along. It cost nothing to enter and the $2,000 prize was a strong inducement to register for the competition. Joan entered the contest under the name Rosebud (her middle name) Blondell.

Joan's familiarity with beauty contests was minimal. She felt awkward parading before a jury with no special talent to demonstrate. Both she and Helen were among the twenty finalists. There would be three more elimination rounds before the winner was selected. On studying the *real* competition, Joan felt she had little chance in the finals. Like the other competitors, she wore a pink and baby blue one-piece bathing suit, white high-heeled shoes, and a little striped cap. Her hair had been allowed to return to its natural shade for the time being. Her legs were a little on the heavy side, but that was a plus in those days. Helen was among the next ten to be eliminated, but Joan found herself among the three finalists.

Hoping to bolster her chances, Joan reached into her vaudeville grab bag of tricks and pulled out a southern accent that was better than genuine. While the other two finalists were ill at ease in front of the judging audience, Joan was in her element. She had a chance to make use of her show business background, and her stage presence never deserted her for an instant. During her interview with the judges, she inventively painted a perfect picture of the girl the selectors were seeking.

Joan won the contest. As it happened, "There was a judge on the committee from Kentucky, so I proceeded to 'indeedy' and suh' him to death. He later told me it was a real relief ma'am to hear a real southern accent after all this Texas twang!'" Joan Blondell, who had lived in Texas less than a year, was now "Miss Dallas" and on her way to a national competition in Atlantic City, New Jersey.

Suddenly a girl whose last taste of luxury had been in infancy was showered with prizes. A group of local stores sponsored a complete wardrobe for her. Once in the city of the Steel Pier and salt water taffy, Joan won the title of runner-up in the Southwest Division. The title of Miss Dallas earned her a part in a touring vaudeville act. But Joan longed to escape the limelight for a while and spend some time with her family—this pattern of reaction to public adulation became typical of her whole approach to show business as a career.

When the traveling act of local winners finally reached Dallas, Joan was glad to join them onstage in her own special number. It was here that she would learn something about the lower depths of theatrical life. A sly Oklahoma millionaire, who derived a perverse pleasure from treating showgirls roughly, spotted Joan. Through a ruse he en-

ticed Joan out on a date and when he finally agreed to take the nervous girl home, he exploded in a drunken rage. He attempted to rape her and when she screamed he beat her incessantly. Later, she managed to escape from his moving vehicle. In the course of the fall, she dropped fourteen feet and hit adjacent rocks. With two broken ankles and a battered body, Joan crawled a mile on her hands to a gas station where she received first aid and a doctor was summoned.

For three months thereafter, Joan walked on crutches or not at all. A lawyer offered to help her prosecute the assailant but Joan refused, "It would have meant having to *see* him again, and I felt I couldn't stand that." In a further effort to put the horrible experience behind her, Joan urged her parents to move to New York where she might obtain a fresh start in show business. Still grateful for the $2,000 prize money that had been a godsend, Ed and Katherine were happy to oblige.

Leaving Ed Jr. behind with his wife, the Blondells relocated to 84th Street and Lexington Avenue in Manhattan. Ed Sr. found employment in the dying vaudeville arena as a single act. Eventually, mother and even little sister would be working to support the family.

In the meantime, Joan sought a job in the chorus line of a Broadway show. Each morning she made the rounds seeking work. Stage directors would quickly notice her good looks and sharp personality, but had to refuse her reluctantly when they auditioned her dancing. The healing bones of her ankles had left thick calcium deposits in the joint, making them stiff. But still Joan forced herself to make the rounds of casting offices.

In an early audition for the *Ziegfeld Follies*, Joan tried to impress veteran (casting) director Sammy Lee. She informed him that she was Miss Dallas. "I don't care if you're Miss Manhattan Transfer!" he snapped. When she later learned of a forthcoming production of *Rosalie* starring Marilyn Miller, she returned to the Ziegfeld offices. She was one of the first girls to show up for the audition. After a brief try-out she was selected for the show.

She was to report back the next day for

rehearsal. But her present physical condition, she knew, would not bear up under the strain of a full day of grueling dance steps. All the exercises she tried seemed useless; her ankles would not respond to therapy. Finally, in her frustrated desperation, she tore a leg muscle. Thus, her hopes of landing a chorus job were shattered and her heart was broken. Only years later, when reviewing this turn in her career, could Joan appreciate that it was a blessing in disguise. Becoming a chorine would most likely never have led her to her eventual success.

Having lost her pride, Joan decided to take whatever job came along. Unsuccessfully, she tried being a waitress and was even a circus hand. For fifteen minutes, she was a clerk at Macy's department store, before being fired as too inexperienced. She attempted to learn employable skills at the College of Industrial Arts but soon abandoned that time- and money-consuming idea. Finally, she met an employer, the owner of a stationery store, with whom she was compatible. Her name was Mrs. Wright and, after witnessing the industrious way Joan had tidied and decorated the store window, she put the young girl to work operating the circulating library which accounted for half of the store's business.

Joan, a blonde once more, soon was making her employer a tidy profit, luring customers into the store. As Mrs. Wright once recalled, "She was a good clerk on account of she would not let boys have dates with her unless they joined my circulating library. One night there were seventeen boys lined up to join." Joan would write the men's phone numbers on the wall, which soon became a one hundred-entry telephone directory of local available males.

Meanwhile, her dad had returned home. He was too ill to continue working. Joan's salary, unfortunately, was the same as it had been in Dallas, eighteen dollars weekly. Whatever free time she had was devoted to making the rounds at theatres, this time seeking a straight dramatic role. Her first "find" was a part in a sleazy farce, *My Girl Friday*, at the Provincetown Theatre in Greenwich Village. She worked gratis there for coffee and cake money. After its brief run, she was offered a scholarship at John Murray Anderson's Drama School. Unable to quit her daytime job because her parents were depending on the income, Joan had to refuse the scholarship.

Three weeks later, her first break came when producer Al Woods gave her a part in the road company of *The Trial of Mary Dugan*. Along with her role as a lisping chorus girl, Joan understudied the title role. The tour lasted seven months and then she returned to Mrs. Wright's Library at 2428 Broadway. (Joan also worked at several other branches owned by Mrs. Wright.) But the eighteen-dollar salary from the shop was insufficient for the growing needs of her family, and Joan was constantly on the alert for opportunities on the stage.

Unemployed and discouraged, Ed Blondell finally convinced his wife to join him in a trek to California. Once there, they found they were still dependent on the few dollars Joan was able to send them weekly. Gloria remained behind with her sister, but she was still too young to earn a substantial income. Soon after their parents' departure, Gloria developed a dangerous fever. In her delirium, she babbled of missing her parents and hating New York City. The moment she was well enough to travel Gloria found herself being hustled into a car bound for California by thoughtful Joan, who had borrowed one hundred dollars from Al Woods to pay for the car, driver, and road expense.

In order to send more of her eighteen-dollar weekly salary to the Blondells in California, Joan was forced to vacate her modest apartment and depend on friends for accommodations. When even her friends deserted her, she seemed to have hit rock bottom. Of times such as these, she has recalled, "I've known what it is to wonder where I was going to sleep when night came. I've been at a stage of pocketbook flatness when half a sandwich, shared with another girl in the same predicament, was a banquet."

In spite of her own problems, Joan had an unending concern for her parents' well-being.

One day she was seized by an urge to contact them. She entered the Park Central Hotel but soon realized that a telephone call was beyond her resources. She decided to write her family then and there. As she approached the desk clerk to purchase a stamp, a young man smiled at her. It reassured her to know there was still warmth left in the world. She did not yet know who the man was.

Not long thereafter, Joan was sitting in a cafeteria near Broadway wishing her cup of coffee was a lunch. A breathless young man rushed in and sat down next to her. She took him for an aspiring actor and asked him what was happening. The news was that none other than George Kelly was casting his new play right across the street.

Five minutes later, Joan opened the office door to find wall-to-wall people. The situation looked discouraging but a red-haired fellow who was jammed next to her suggested that she should come back later since casting would continue well into the evening. On her return, Joan found only a few bedraggled aspirants still there. A few minutes later she was ushered into Mr. Kelly's office. To start the audition, he read her the part of Etta and closely observed her reactions. By doing no more than laughing in the right places Joan Blondell had won the female lead in one of the most desirable shows of the season!

Critical response to *Maggie the Magnificent,* which opened on October 21, 1929, at the Cort Theatre, was not up to that given to Kelly's earlier *The Show-Off* or *Craig's Wife.* But even the notoriously cynical reviewers such as Robert Benchley and George Jean Nathan singled out Joan as a promising actress, and Brooks Atkinson pinpointed the play's mainstay, "Joan Blondell—inclining toward caricature but highly amusing in a drama that needs tangible vitality."

Kelly had selected Joan not because she could *play* Etta but because to him she *was* Etta. During their four weeks of rehearsal, Joan, who had never had a drama coach or drama lesson, was taught the A to Z of acting fundamentals. Still, once onstage before an audience, her vaudeville instincts led her to ham up her performance, and the critics noted

it. Joan took their criticism constructively and thereafter tried to curb her penchant for overemphasis. The role of Etta was, incidentally, her first exposure to the wisecracking blonde character for which she would later be stereotyped.

As it happened, *Maggie* opened the week of the stock market crash, and the audiences were anything but in a jubilant mood. Joan's dreams and ambition to "make good for my family, and maybe buy a new dress" evaporated. As she phrased it, "No one was going to the theatre . . . too busy jumping out windows," but "you don't have what it takes to be a real star unless you've had flops as well as successes."

Although the public had little opportunity to see Joan onstage during *Maggie's* short run of thirty-two performances, her reputation in the trade was made, and parts now were being offered to her. Until she selected one, however, she remained a librarian at 2428 Broadway. Her family required her constant help, especially since vaudeville had died. Ed Jr. had made a very shaky start in his marriage, with jobs suddenly being hard to find and a wife and two children to support. It was no time for Joan to be complacent.

Yet Joan still found time for romance. Her amour was an actor then performing onstage in *Coquette.* The man was almost a personification of a certain type of person: the genuinely talented individual who takes it upon himself, as if no one else could, to destroy his life. His world-weary cynicism would not allow him to take seriously the love that young and naïve Joan offered. Her efforts to save him were futile because he would not let her help. However, she did not have the strength to leave him. It was a miserable romantic start, but she learned something from the traumatic experience that helped her through a similar experience much later in her life.

Her next part was in George M. Cohan's *Sporting Blood* (1930). While the play was on the road in Hartford, Connecticut, an agent named Mary Bohner was busy digging up a real part for Joan. The result was the female lead in *Penny Arcade,* a show which had another relative newcomer named James Cagney in the cast. Joan had met the fellow before, the red-haired man in George Kelly's office. She would encounter him again and again in the years to come.

Six rehearsing weeks later, on March 10, 1930, Marie Baumer's play opened at the Fulton Theatre to wildly enthusiastic reviews and an audience that hungered for escape from thoughts of the Depression. Cagney received most of the critics' attention but Joan was typed as a perfect foil for his rollicking sassiness. Again she was playing a wisecracking gal fresh off the streets, though this time as a photographer's assistant in Coney Island.

Al Jolson, in one of his seemingly rare charitable moods, so liked the youngsters in *Penny Arcade* that he persuaded some talent scouts from his studio, Warner Bros., to see the fresh young talents performing on stage. (Joan could also be viewed in a 1930 Vitaphone short subject, *Broadway's Like That*. The ten-minute item starred Ruth Etting and featured Humphrey Bogart and Mary Phillips, with Joan as a "burlesque cutie.") These scouts brought the news of their "discovery" back to Hollywood. Only when the studio had decided to purchase the film rights to the play did they learn that Jolson had a controlling interest in the show and they would have to negotiate with him.

As a favor to that long-ago child on the Australia-bound boat, the one who would *not* grow up to be a manicurist, Jolson pulled for Blondell and Cagney to be signed for the movie version. Before long, both were on their way to Hollywood. Director William Keighley, who had helmed *Penny Arcade*, would follow them but would have a less heralded arrival. The excited New York performers were signed to three-week contracts, just enough time, according to the Warner Bros. production schedule, to churn out a film version of *Penny Arcade*.

For what was to be her 392nd cross-country trip, Joan invested in a second-hand 1927 Ford. Her thoughts were not entirely on Hollywood as she traveled westward. She was leaving behind the suicidal Broadway lover who had made a shambles of her last year.

But for this unexpected break in pictures, she might never have summoned the courage to leave him.

There was no need to give Joan a screen test as long as the studio was being persuaded to use her in their version of *Penny Arcade*. But there was no guarantee at all that an actress, however captivating on a stage, would prove photogenic in appearance or character. The rushes of her first day's work, then, became an unofficial screen test.

When the executives saw the rushes, they decided quickly to place her under contract. Their offer was a $200-per-week, five-year pact with annual raises of ten dollars a week in all years but the fourth, culminating in a $500 weekly salary. For Joan, this meant security and comfort for her destitute family. With the Warners' deal, the Blondells were able to be reunited under one roof; even Ed Jr. soon abandoned his multiple problems in the Midwest and moved to California with his family. Joan was able to obtain for him a steady, well-paying job at Warner Bros. (and later at other studios) as a lighting technician. It provided him with an income right up to the days of television.

Once Joan, Gloria, Katherine, and Ed Sr. were settled into their North Hollywood home, the budding movie star began making her daily treks to the Burbank lot via her battered Ford. Her schedule began at 4:30 A.M. which was far from being a nuisance for lively blonde Joan as it has always been her favorite time of the day. She adores rising with the sun.

According to magazine accounts, after changing out of her nightgown—she almost always wore one to bed—she would limber up her face muscles by making grotesque faces in the mirror before having a light breakfast. What she ate in the morning depended on what diet, if any, she was currently pursuing. While not a health addict, Joan has always been a firm believer in the value of three square meals a day.

She was expected at the studio by 8:00 A.M. Once there, her first stop was usually the makeup department where she spent from one to three hours, and then she would make a stop at wardrobe which required another hour or so. When unoccupied on the lot, she could be seen lounging around the facilities, usually in her favorite casual outfit, a sweatshirt and white duck pants. Her favorite lunch—when she could get it—was a hamburger and apple cider, a combination she has relished since childhood.

Since contract players in the Thirties were virtually studio property, the company made sure that it got its money's worth. With no union to protect the actors, performers worked a typical twelve-hour day, six days a week. Under a schedule like this, Joan's first year's salary came down to an hourly rate of about two dollars an hour.

Of the major studios, efficient Warner Bros. probably had the tightest shooting schedules. Whenever possible, the studio cut corners by starting new films before the old ones even were finished to cover any scheduling gaps. That is why Joan wound up in *The Office Wife* (1930) whose release managed to precede *Sinner's Holiday* (1930), the new title for *Penny Arcade*.

But *Sinner's Holiday* (a rather irrelevant title) was the first of Joan's many Hollywood features. Before production began, studio production chief Darryl F. Zanuck conferred with Joan and Cagney and asked if they *really* thought they could handle the leading roles of the film. "We both said 'no' in unison without looking at one another. So Zanuck gave Grant Withers the male lead and Evalyn Knapp got my part." In her part as a hardboiled floozie named Myrtle, she (along with Cagney) managed to steal many scenes from her more experienced co-workers, Grant Withers, Evalyn Knapp, and Noel Madison. At one point in the story a police captain questions her about the gangster (Cagney) whom she is protecting with her fibs.

> *He:* Was you in the sand with Johnny? . . . Think of your reputation!
> *Joan:* [in what was already her trademark flip style] You think about it. You worry about it more than I do. Sure I was on the beach with Johnny last night.

Only once in the course of the film does she betray her cinema inexperience, when she can be seen looking directly into the camera. For her screen debut, her hair was kept in a dusty blonde shade and she wore the same brown checked dress throughout the proceedings.

Because Joan proved to be a quick study on the set and acted natural onscreen, she was well-liked by her directors. Her friendly nature also evidenced itself with the technicians on the sets, to whom she often gave tickets to football games. Thirty years later, Joan would find that her friends did not forget her.

About this time, Joan began to mingle with the higher echelons of Hollywood society and she made some observations about them. "Picture people aren't like stage people. They're so tense. They can't laugh at themselves as we vaudeville folk used to do." This simple, not particularly ambitious girl was sorry to find that among performers "the truth of the matter is, you don't have real friends in Hollywood, there's too much competition."

As Joan began to become more aware of her screen image, she grew more uncomfortable with her celluloid persona. Her first glimpses of herself on the big screen made her realize that the person America was starting to adore was not the real Joan Blondell. Instead, it was the bastard child of the imaginations of a score of Warner Bros. staff writers and the nonsense spread by sensation-hungry Hollywood columnists. Contrary to her budding reputation of brassiness, guts, and self-assurance, Joan was actually quite shy and insecure. And as she has often said, "the shyness only leaves me when I work."

Fearful that too much self-examination of her screen work would be detrimental, Joan stopped going to see her rushes and completed films. In fact, Joan became somewhat uncooperative with the studio publicity department on these matters. While she was glad to grant interviews and discuss with open honesty her feelings and her background, she found not the slightest temptation to make up little lies here and there that would help spice up the writing in the fan magazines and ad copy. However, the studio was not to be derailed from its publicity objectives. The PR people fabricated their own fantasies about Joan's background and present activities, knowing that sweet, demure Joan would never have the heart to take them to court.

While Joan was slowly building up her box-office appeal, occasionally on loan-out as in RKO's *Millie* (1931) starring Helen Twelvetrees and Robert Ames, Jimmy Cagney had become one of the studio's hottest properties. Warners had quickly realized that oncamera Cagney and Blondell were ideally suited. Joan was the perfect damper for Jimmy's ebullient energy and the studio used her on all of his really major screen projects.

The fortuitous foursome of Cagney and Blondell as actors and Kubec Glasmon and John Bright as writers met each other head-on when the immortal film, *The Public Enemy* (1931), was conceived. The authors had poured many years of first-hand experience with the underworld into their first movie script and it showed. The film's brutal realism was typical of the studio's penchant for yarns yanked from the headlines. The film almost single-handedly turned the screen gangster into a hero. While Joan was but one of three women in the brutal life of Cagney's Tom Powers, she displayed a resilience and naturalness that outshone Jean "Hell's Angels" Harlow or Mae Clarke, the lass who suffered a grapefruit being ground into her face.

In these films, it was Joan's character who was the "soul" of the stories. She was the sole reason for the audience to maintain faith in law and order and the natural tendency for a person to do the right thing. In the end, it was Joan Blondell's character who kept these underworld yarns from degenerating into pessimistic anarchy.

The Blondell-Cagney and Glasmon-Bright teams were reunited professionally twice more, in *Blonde Crazy* (1931) and Howard Hawks' *The Crowd Roars* (1932), but never again did they hit the public with such a forceful impact. Joan and Jimmy played off one another without Glasmon and Bright in the later *Footlight Parade* (1933) and *He Was Her Man* (1934) until it seemed that Cagney's film image had outgrown Joan's and he went on to super-stardom alone. Joan was amazed to see her spunky New York friend, whom she remembered from the Manhattan days as "a wonderful ballet dancer," turn into such a Hollywood success. But there is every reason to believe that perhaps Joan too could have hit the real heights *if* fame had been her primary concern.

She had watched James Cagney as he simply walked off the soundstage set when he thought he was being treated in a matter unbefitting his talents. She had witnessed her former New York acquaintance Bette Davis fight hard for every salary raise she thought she deserved and who managed to avoid being handed the same silly properties all the time. Joan knew very well what these confreres were doing and how; she admired them for it. But she was so security-conscious that she dared not jeopardize her salary for the chance of bettering her career. Nothing was more important to her than the well-being of her family.

If Joan was not being aggressive on the lot, the public nonetheless had grown very fond of her and their preferences could be measured in dollars and cents. In grateful recognition of this fact, and the profits that accrued therefrom, Joan was named one of the WAMPAS (Western Association of Motion Picture Advertisers) Baby Stars of 1931. Her screen career was blossoming, but she remained faithful to her first love (the theatre) whenever she had the opportunity. She played her fifty-sixth vaudeville engagement before making *The Crowd Roars,* a stage turn she much preferred to the seemingly endless personal appearance tours required by the Warners publicity department.

Her growing prestige—enhanced by her remarkable number of appearances yearly oncamera—caused her to be coveted increasingly by other studios. Paramount, the home of Marlene Dietrich, Claudette Colbert, Nancy Carroll, and Sylvia Sidney, borrowed her to play opposite Stuart Erwin in a new screen version of *Merton of the Movies*, called *Make Me a Star* (1932). It was a frivolous,

With Eddie Woods, James Cagney, and Mae Clarke in *Public Enemy* ('31).

In *Blonde Crazy* ('31). →

With Dorothy Mackaill in *The Office Wife* ('30).

IT'S A MATTER OF LIFE and DEATH!

CROWD ROARS

Starring!

James CAGNEY
Joan BLONDELL

with

ANN DVORAK
ERIC LINDEN
GUY KIBBEE

Story by
Howard Hawks and
Seton I. Miller

Dialogue by
Glasmon and Bright

Direction by
HOWARD HAWKS
of "Dawn Patrol" fame

Speed demons with goggled eyes glued on glory . . . Grinning at death . . . laughing at love! . . . Breaking necks to break records—while the Crowd Roars—FOR BLOOD! . . . Never —never—never has the screen shown such nerve-racking ACTION—lifted right off the track of the world's greatest speedway! It's the thrill epic of all time—the talk of every town that's seen it . . . Forty men risked death to film it. Miss it at your own risk!

12 of the world's greatest race drivers in the most thrilling action pictures ever shown!

She fought for her man— with every trick love knows!

THE HIT of the YEAR - FROM WARNER BROS.

←
Advertisement for *The Crowd Roars* ('32).

With Douglas Fairbanks, Jr., in *Union Depot* ('32).

With Stuart Erwin in *Make Me a Star* ('32).

33

jocular on-the-lot account of carefree movie-making days with guest appearances by such Paramount luminaries as Tallulah Bankhead, Clive Brook, Fredric March, and Maurice Chevalier.

Much more important to Joan's professional future was her loan-out to Samuel Goldwyn at United Artists. The property was *The Greeks Had a Word for Them* (1932) based on Zöe Akins' Broadway show, *The Greeks Had a Word for It.* Co-starring with Joan in this sophisticated account of three gold-diggers (who wear Chanel gowns) were Madge Evans (an incongruous replacement for Carole Lombard) and Ina Claire, with dapper Lowell Sherman both directing the vehicle and playing the key role of Boris Feldman, the famed pianist.

Sam Goldwyn was perhaps more conscious of the importance of craft in his films than any Hollywood producer before or since. He surrounded himself with the finest technicians available. He was particularly careful when choosing his director of photography, the man who lit the set and made the decisions regarding exposure, focus, filtering, and the like. Goldwyn was very proud of his latest discovery, and retained him at a salary of approximately $2,500 weekly. His name was George Barnes (born 1893) and he had begun his career as a still photographer. In this capacity he became an expert at soft-focus lensing and was much sought-after for his ability to make any woman look like a goddess. This skill was of course very useful in the movies, where a cameraman's future depended more than anything else on whether the leading lady liked the "mirror" into which she was looking.

While at Warners, Joan's cinematographers and directors aimed at making each celluloid shot as real as possible, however brutal or unflattering it might be. Joan's reaction to viewing herself in Warners products had been, "while it didn't exactly frighten me, certainly [it] never thrilled me. I had always watched myself on the screen with a sinking feeling in the pit of my stomach."

In contrast, Goldwyn strove for exoticism, romance, and glamour in his productions.

Not only did Joan look and do better under Barnes camera, but she did these things to an extent that she had never dreamed possible. She had never considered herself to be a glamour girl but now she looked as beautiful as any of them, and she was beginning to understand how stars got that way.

There was something indefinable about Barnes that caused Joan to get romantically interested in him almost immediately. He was tall, dark, and handsome, with a trim, black moustache. His warm, paternal smile had a familiar quality that Joan did not comprehend, and, for that reason, she found him all the more enchanting. They dated quite a few times and soon Joan felt she was in love with Mr. Barnes.

Suddenly Hollywood was a friendly place for her and, for the first time, she felt at home there. She and George would spend countless evenings at the home of his close friend (through Goldwyn's productions) Ronald Colman. Among their company were some of the "magic people" Joan had always heard about, but had given up hope of really finding. They included Richard Barthelmess, Clive Brook, William Powell, and Warner Baxter.

"I had been one of those kid fans of Ronald Colman. To me, Ronnie's home was the most homey I'd seen. The evenings were fabulous there. He and his friends were so distinguished, and he had divine humor. We'd all tell stories, and sometimes he'd get up and act them out while we'd all be sitting crosslegged on the floor and couch. Those were beautiful, wonderful evenings. I'll never forget he set up a security for me, a life insurance policy, whereby at the age of forty I would never have to work again. And another policy, so that if I ever had an accident, whatever I was being paid at that moment, I'd get for the rest of my life." Despite all her affection for Colman, Leslie Howard was Joan's favorite actor.

In many ways, though, Joan never really belonged to Hollywood's upper crust. Nothing that happened to her ever did, or ever could, change the fact that she was a simple girl with uncomplicated needs. Her car was the same second-hand Ford she had purchased three years previously. For all her traveling, she had never been in an airplane (not unusual in the Thirties). Her character was reflected in her clothing: she dressed as simply as possible. She disliked jewelry, and did not wear makeup or hats.

Pets were an integral part of her life, and would continue to play an increasingly large part in her affairs as time went on. It seemed that dogs were the only companions on which she could truly depend. In 1932, she owned a Boston Bull terrier named Abadaba.

Joan overcame her juvenile distaste for reading and did quite a bit of it in her spare moments. Her favorite book was Justin Huntley McCarthy's *If I Were King* and John V. A. Weaver was her favorite modern poet. She also was greatly attracted by the works of Shaw and Hemingway.

If there was one thing that separated Joan from the cream of Hollywood society, it was her dislike of "ritzy" people. Joan was anything but a social climber and one of her other distinctive marks was was that she did not (and does not) play bridge.

One of her most significant productions of 1932 featured a Glasmon-Bright story and a Lucien Hubbard scenario. It was Joan's first and only film opposite Bette Davis. *Three On a Match* was the first of her four features under the aegis of the studio's hottest director, Mervyn "Little Caesar" LeRoy. In this case, Joan could observe the studio publicity department at its silliest and small-minded best. Rather than promote the compact, sixty-three-minute feature on its many merits, the public was enticed into the theatre with the prospect of playing a match game built around photos of the stars: Blondell, Davis, Warren William, Ann Dvorak, Lyle Talbot, and Humphrey Bogart, cut horizontally into three strips which an audience would supposedly delight in trying to piece together.

Theatre managers were forever encouraged by distributor/exhibitor chains to arrange phony stunts, skits, and demonstrations on the neighboring street corners to try to get the pedestrians into the theatre to see the latest film wonder. *Central Park* (First National,

1932), which reunited Joan with director John Adolfi of *Sinner's Holiday*, did not need any big push from the publicity department. The film's author, a New York columnist named Ward Morehouse, concocted all sorts of parades, parties, and stunts to publicize the otherwise unspectacular premiere. The production-line film fell on its ear, and it could have done that without any help from Morehouse.

Meanwhile, Joan made up her mind to take life on the lot a bit easier. In her first three years as "a studio dame," she made an average of nine features a year—high by any standards. Often Joan was called to work on more than one film at a time; there would not be time for her to learn lines properly or even, on occasion, read the script. It was a fairly common practice on a tight production schedule for the actors and director to make up the dialogue and plot as they proceeded.

In January of 1933, Joan left Hollywood to perform a week of vaudeville in Chicago. The previous summer she had badly wanted to return to New York, but an unexpected illness had changed her plans. She was determined that nothing would interfere in the following summer. In April, she went to Oregon to spend a much-needed vacation fishing and enjoying life in the rough. Her secret, if fan magazine releases can be believed, for preserving her skin and hair in the great outdoors was frequent washing of both with kerosene. By May of that year, she was revisiting the old circulating library at 2428 Broadway. Mrs. Wright was still there and so were the telephone numbers scribbled on the walls so long ago. While in Manhattan, she made an appearance on the New York vaudeville stage.

With Joan and George Barnes being seen in public so frequently and continuing their professional association (as in Fox's 1933 *Broadway Bad*), the fan magazines were touting them as an engaged couple. When reporters queried her in regard to whether a career or matrimony was more essential to her happiness, Joan voiced, "We would be happy in a little store or some business somewhere else if Hollywood wouldn't let us make a go of our marriage. This town hasn't gotten into my

With George Brent
in *Miss Pinkerton* ('32).

With Ann Dvorak in *Three on a
Match* ('32).

blood." Joan's choice between career and personal life would never be in doubt, not at this time nor in the future.

Yet there was a more practical reason why Joan and George, the perennial twosome about town, were not yet wed. Barnes had not received his final divorce from his wife. When the final legal technicalities were settled, Joan and her cinematographer beau were wed on Saturday, August 5, 1933. It was a simple, private California ceremony, and Joan wore an equally simple red gown and dark glasses. Present were Joan's family and witnesses Arlen Vincent and Liz Wilson, the latter a motion picture magazine writer.

It was only after she was wed that it occurred to Joan just why George had looked so familiar to her when they met on the United Artists soundstage. Long before coming to Hollywood, back at the Park Central Hotel, he had been that tall man at the hotel desk with the friendly smile.

Before long, more of the fantasy and mystery about George vanished. Joan slowly realized that it was her exotic image of Barnes that she knew and loved and not the man himself. George was the type of man who made women particularly susceptible to this kind of self-deception. He talked as little as possible, allowing them to form all kinds of assumptions. Although he was kind and considerate to the point of giving at least minimal response to the needs of his wife, he almost never showed real concern or excitement for her. But these truths were slow to dawn on Joan who, at this juncture, was too busy picking up her career where she had left off.

While her previous films had all provided exposure to the public, it was not until *Blondie Johnson* (First National, 1933) that Joan had her first solo starring part. The script by Earl Baldwin had been written with her in mind. This film was an important step in the direction of liberation of the usual female screen type, and Joan was cast as a tough, independent gangstress who does not need any help from the many men in her life. "I play a feminine Little Caesar" is how Joan described this role. While Mae West might have been more tantalizing in the part, Joan's

softer image was aimed at making the rugged story more acceptable to filmgoers. Even though her characterization was not an endearing one, the *New York Daily Mirror* found that the Blondell of *Blondie Johnson* "never was lovelier." (Joan in particular was quite aware that the dependence on beauty for the success of a film career was a dangerous path to follow; she even by-lined a few magazine articles on this thesis—one of them was entitled "Lucky for Me I'm Not So Pretty.")

In 1933, a man entered Joan's life who would accomplish more for her career in a purely professional and unintentional way than even Cagney, and who would take her with him to the summit of her fame. The prodigious talent of Busby Berkeley almost defies description. Working behind the camera and only on short sequences of musicals to which he was assigned, he helped to lift the screen song-and-dance films out of their pre-gangster era slump. At the same time, he revolutionized the genre and, to a certain extent, changed the craft of filmmaking itself.

On the strength of a staggering box-office record at Sam Goldwyn's studio at United Artists in the early Thirties, Berkeley could command huge sums of money to accomplish his extravagant film excursions into fantasyland. And Joan Blondell had the good fortune of becoming the oncamera hallmark of his films. Something in Joan's open, wide-eyed charm allowed her, above the many performers who graced his extravaganzas, to be identified with those early, landmark Warner musicals.

The first one was *Gold Diggers of 1933*. The story derived from David Balasco's stage production *The Gold Diggers* (1919), which had starred Ina Claire and Lilyan Tashman. Harry Beaumont's silent film version of 1923 featured Hope Hampton and Louise Fazenda, and the property was revitalized in 1929 as *The Gold Diggers of Broadway* with Winnie Lightner, Miss Tashman, and Conway Tearle. So the story was hardly fresh, and neither was Joan's part as gold digger Carol King, but the film certainly was.

Ironically, the picture's release immediately followed America's abandonment of the gold standard. Simultaneously, the film destroyed Warner Bros.' image of frugality. To help mock in a joyous tone the tight-money woes of the Depression, Berkeley had fifty-four luscious chorus girls parading about in coin outfits for the "We're in the Money" routine, stationed on a staircase of gold piece replicas against a backdrop of silver dollars.

While Ginger Rogers, who sang some of the lyrics in pig Latin, had the featured spot in that routine, it was Joan, Aline MacMahon, and Ruby Keeler who comprised the trio of money-hungry chorines who reveal themselves as having hearts of gold. While tap-dancing Keeler wins song-composer Dick Powell (continuing the teaming from 1933's *42nd Street*), it is Joan who romances, rejects, and reaccepts Warren William (the stuffy Boston banker brother of easygoing Powell) who provides the real story thread of this musical revue. The *New York Times* in assessing the virtues of this money-making film noted that Joan is "lively."

If anything, that adjective is an understatement of the pert performance turned in by Blondell as the chorine who refuses to be bought off by aristocratic William. More importantly, this film paid a tribute to Joan that is about the highest Hollywood could have offered: Busby Berkeley built an entire production number around her.

The "Remember My Forgotten Man" number by Harry Warren and Al Dubin is exceptional beyond the gymnastics involved, for its socio-political overtones recalled the Bonus Army's march on Washington, D.C., a few years prior. Though all her vaudeville experience could not hide her untrained voice, Joan's brief characterization in that plaintive number remains one of her finest sophisticated interpretations oncamera.

Berkeley would later admit, "I knew Joan couldn't sing when I decided to use her. . . . But I knew she could act the song, talk it, and put over its drama for me." Warner Bros. got the best of both worlds by dubbing over the unique Blondell image with the impressive voice of black songstress Etta Moten. In some refrains of the song, Joan does her own talk-singing. The mammoth number with its sil-houette and third-dimensional parading of ex-GIs has become a classic of the Thirties' cinema. Frequently when documentaries of the period are assembled, as in *Brother, Can You Spare a Dime?* (1975), the "My Forgotten Man" number, which so gloriously showcases a trim, flinty Joan, is considered a *must* inclusion.

The success of *Gold Diggers of 1933* (with a record-breaking ten-week Broadway run) led Warner Bros. to give Busby Berkeley the go-ahead for *Footlight Parade* (1933). The studio assigned many of the lot's stock company (Guy Kibbee, Ruth Donnelly, Claire Dodd, Hugh Herbert, Frank McHugh) to pepper the proceedings and, for good measure, allowed James Cagney to dance in his first screen musical. Joan played Nan Prescott, the ever-wise, faithful girl Friday who stands by her stage director beau (Cagney) through thick and thin. For additional marquee insurance there was dimpled crooner Dick Powell and winsome Ruby Keeler once more playing the ingenues both onstage and offstage. The central production number of this extravaganza was "By a Waterfall" which utilized some 200 girls on an incredible round, terraced tower.

The Warner Bros. publicity department promoted a 150-man parade to coincide with the opening of *Footlight Parade,* while a chain of countless bonfires stretched across the country in an apparent attempt to equal Berkeley's imagination. Flabbergasted audiences still lined up for tickets but there were warning signs of a coming box-office slump for musicals.

Productive, non-complaining Joan made other entries at the Warners' factory in addition to her musicals. Typical of the period was *Havana Widows* (1933) which reunited her with her studio counterpart, snappy Glenda Farrell. Like the equally talented Aline MacMahon, Miss Farrell was as adept as Joan at the saucy double entendre and double take, but it was Blondell who received most of the breaks at the studio during this period. By the time of *I've Got Your Number* (1934) with Pat O'Brien and Allen Jenkins and *Kansas City Princess* (1934) with Robert

Armstrong and Hugh Herbert, it was Joan and not co-star Glenda Farrell who was receiving the prime screen time.

The next Berkeley-Blondell-Powell musical would, unfortunately and unbeknownst to the trio, also be the last. *Dames* (1934) was the film that gave Berkeley the damning "Million-Dollar Dance Director" reputation he so much hated. The central number of the film, which was one more backstage musical story, was the immortal "I Only Have Eyes for You." The six-figure budget for this number included salaries for some 500 workmen, working in four shifts of six hours each. Less ostentatious and far more titillating was Joan's solo routine "The Girl at the Ironing Board" where she delivers a song of romance and woe as a laundress ironing a pair of men's pajamas which seemed to have a life of their own on or off the clothes line. It showed that Joan, unlike film co-star Ruby Keeler, could handle any type of sophisticated number for the demanding Berkeley.

Powell, a young actor (who did not much care for acting) and singer (who *hated* vocalizing), was a frequent guest at Joan's house through his friendship with George Barnes. Although Joan was always cordial to the rising star, she had mixed feelings about him.

In between her array of Berkeley musicals, Joan continued with her seemingly endless stream of routine films for the studio. Her image evolved from lingerie lounge-about to gangster to reporter to whatever the public seemed most ready to pay for at the time. Determined professionalism led her to follow orders to the best of her abilities, but, even without dissipating her energy after hours, Joan at times found it impossible to cope with her grueling work schedule. "There was no way humanly possible of knowing your lines, being on time, working steadily, and looking right if you went out at night. . . ."

When signs of the strain caught up with her, she tried to ignore them. An important part of her screen character was built around one of these telltale signals. Joan's protruding eyes were striking enough (in the Betty Boop tradition) without her constant fluttering of the eyelashes. However, the fluttering was

neither an idea of hers, the makeup man's, nor the director's. "That was because I was exhausted and couldn't keep my eyes open!" When she began to stutter, Joan finally walked off the set and into a doctor's office. After about two days of sleep, she returned to work, compliant and congenial as ever.

If there was any one element in Joan's background which enabled her to survive the Warner Bros. sweat factory, it was more likely her old vaudeville ready-for-anything attitude than all the instruction in emotional nuance taught to her by George Kelly.

Even if Hollywood failed to find the time to teach her much about the art of highly emotional acting, it made up the loss in other areas. Among the skills Joan was forced to acquire through crash courses from imported technical advisors were process serving (for the "We're in the Money" sequence of *Gold Diggers of 1933*), nursing (*Night Nurse*), wrestling (*Miss Pinkerton*), business law (*Lawyer Man*), truck driving, small yacht navigation, cement mixing and spreading, basic flying, high-pressure salesmanship, French, Spanish, and taking a fall from a flight of stairs (not quite as practical as the rest).

But there was one skill (besides being a true professional) that Joan had that was the envy of many a young starlet. She could cry most effectively on cue. While even the more accomplished screen stars would have to call in the makeup man to encourage some tears with onions, or camphor spray, or fake them with glycerine, Joan would just cry! And she had been doing it instinctively since she was a kid so she really did not know *how* she did it.

Besides, in the mid-Thirties there were a good many things for Joan to cry about. In an intended gesture of confidence in her spouse, Joan let it be known that she wanted her named changed to Joan Barnes on the marquees. When he recovered from the initial shock, studio boss Jack L. Warner soberly tried to explain to her that such an action would cost the studio thousands of dollars in publicity, as well as jeopardize her career. At the start of her Warner Bros. tenure, the studio had tried to pressure her into adopting the

With Toshia Mori, Olin Howland, Donald Kirke, and
Mae Busch in *Blondie Johnson* ('33).

With Spencer Charters (behind desk) and Phil Tead in
Broadway Bad ('33).

40

With Claire Dodd and
James Cagney in *Footlight
Parade* ('33).

With Warren Hull in *Miss
Pacific Fleet* ('35).

41

more alluring Inez Holmes as her professional name, but she had refused.

While Joan was deciding to relent on her name change, in November 1933 her house caught fire. Working together, Joan and Barnes got the blaze under control with the aid of a garden hose. No sooner had the air been cleared than Joan was whisked off to a hospital with appendicitis. Her illness interrupted the shooting of *I've Got Your Number* (1934) for which Joan had already shot too much footage to be replaced. Her operation

In *Dames* ('34).

took place on November 25th. She was then sent home, ordered to rest in bed, and told not to laugh for at least three weeks. In order to finish the film, the studio had the scenario rewritten so that Joan could complete her role from bedside at home. But the additional footage did not quite wrap up the film, so frustrated studio heads waited impatiently for three weeks until Joan's return to the soundstages.

Joan was no sooner through with her convalescence than it was learned that legal technicalities concerning Barnes' most recent divorce (of three) had called his marriage with Joan into question. They had a hasty and unceremonious remarriage on Thursday, January 4, 1934.

After the final completion of *I've Got Your Number*, Joan went to Death Valley for a real rest as well as for thought and contemplation. At this time she explored many of her inner feelings, though no public display was made of these thoughts. "I've wanted to be a mother since before I even thought of going on the stage. And I come from a theatrical family." She was concerned about her desire because Barnes had no interest in being a father, and he had made that quite clear when she had experienced a false alarm pregnancy on a prior occasion. Barnes had his reason: a tumultuous childhood had made him an almost pathological craver of quietness. A child, he knew, would disrupt the coveted peace he treasured. Nevertheless, early in February 1934 Joan became pregnant and resolved to keep the baby.

Pregnancy did not interrupt her career. "They kept shooting me higher and higher. They had me in back of everything—desks, barrels, anything." One of those "bust shot" pictures was *Smarty* (1934), directed by Robert Florey and co-starring Warren William, Edward Everett Horton, Frank McHugh, and Claire Dodd. Her role as Vicki, a woman who seeks a dominant lover, gave her ample opportunity to express her views on romance. "I'd like to see a man try to hold me by treating me rough! It's the attentiveness, the courtesy, the consideration, with which European men are taught from childhood to treat women, that is one reason why European marriages last so much longer than American ones."

In addition, pregnancy did not dim Joan's box-office appeal either. She was awarded the WAMPAS Achievement Trophy for the WAMPAS Baby Star who had made the most progress in her career in two years. Among the disappointed losers were: Ginger Rogers, Constance Cummings, Gloria Stuart, Frances Dee, Karen Morley, Sidney Fox, and Mary Carlisle. The trophy, also known as the Nash Prize, was of solid silver.

By mid-1934, Joan's marriage was becoming very shaky. Ever more certain that the child would compete with his love for Joan, Barnes began to withdraw more and more into his private world, becoming sullen and irritable. Joan could not understand his attitude, but she was determined to have this child. The "troublemaker" was born on Friday, November 2. George managed to be on hand when she gave birth to a son that they would name Norman Scott. Joan would later admit, "No thrill I ever experienced on the stage or screen has matched the thrill of holding my first baby. No applause ever touched my heart like his smile."

The Barneses spared no effort to ensure the safety of their child. The nursery wing of the house was made earthquake-proof with the installation of steel girders to anchor it firmly to the ground beneath. The recent sensational kidnapping of the child of Charles A. Lindbergh spread waves of paranoia throughout Hollywood. There were steel bars at the entrance to Norman's room and burglar alarms everywhere. Watchmen stood a round-the-clock watch in the garden and a trained attack-dog slept at the north entrance.

To keep her figure trim, Joan abandoned an old taboo and put herself on a diet, drinking juice between meals to curb her appetite. She ate no sweets or starches, allowed herself one meat course per week, and survived on salads, plenty of water, and two cups of tea per day.

Meanwhile, the domestic rapport between Joan and Barnes was deteriorating again. Barnes finally took an apartment of his own.

Although he still photographed many of her films—he developed a new camera for her film *The Traveling Saleslady* (1935)—and they got along well on the set, both knew that divorce was inevitable. Joan was miserable, but felt powerless to do anything about the situation. She must have thought back enviously to the lobby cards that billed her character in *Public Enemy* as the girl who "fought for her man with every trick love knows." In real life, Joan did not rely on guile.

Divorce finally came later in 1935 on grounds of incompatibility. An out-of-court settlement climaxed Joan's short (ten-minute) in-court recital of charges. She stated, "He wouldn't take any responsibility for business matters and the bills would go unpaid because he wouldn't take time to find out what was due." Barnes did not contest. The cinematographer who went on to win an Oscar for his work on *Rebecca* would marry three more times. His last wife (number seven), Margaret Atkinson, held him until his death in 1953 at the age of sixty.

After the divorce, Joan found herself "a nervous and physical wreck." Sister Gloria, who had joined the Warner Bros. payroll as an actress (her biggest role at the studio would be opposite Ronald Reagan in a programmer, *Accidents Will Happen,* 1938), came to the rescue. She prevented her older sister from eating herself into obesity by supervising her diet and doing her chores (Joan never had maids) when she was too distressed to work.

The recovery was miraculous, so much so in fact that a reporter who knew Joan well saw her dancing with Dick Powell and wrote the next day that Powell had been "dancing with a gorgeous new blond." Powell was born Richard E. Powell in Mountain View, Arkansas, on November 14, 1904. He was educated at Little Rock College and sang in church choirs. Later, he was employed by a telephone company. With his facility for playing instruments, he joined various bands and toured with them as both an instrumentalist and a vocalist. Still later, he was the master of ceremonies for the Stanley and Enright Theatres in Pittsburgh. A Warner Bros.

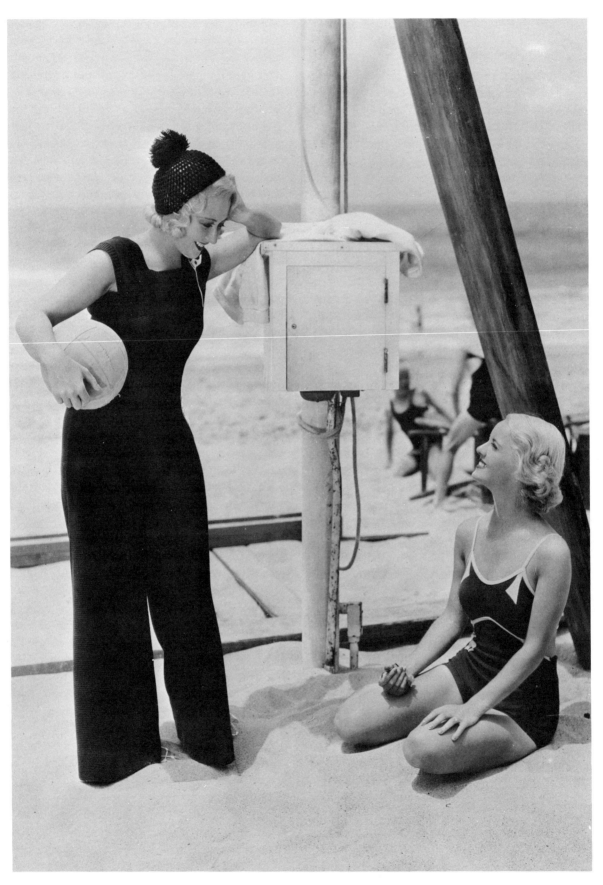

With Bette Davis, sunbathing
for the press department
(August 1936).

With Hobart Cavanaugh and
Dick Powell in *Stage Struck*
('36).

talent scout spotted him and Powell went to California, allegedly to play the title role in *Crooner* (1932), a role that went to David Manners. Instead, the studio cast him in *Blessed Event* (1932). It was his co-starring role with Ruby Keeler in *42nd Street* (1933) that set the mold for Powell's career at Warner Bros. as the resident crooner and obliging young leading man.

Congenial Powell became a regular at Joan's house and was of invaluable help in putting her stagnating financial affairs in order. They were seen together in public with increasing frequency, which met with approval from the studio hierarchy. When Dick proposed to the distraught divorcée, she found it only natural to accept.

The private wedding took place on Saturday, September 19, 1936, aboard the luxury liner *San Paula* while it was moored in San Pedro harbor. Actor Regis Toomey served as best man. The ship then took the pair on a seventeen-day honeymoon to the Atlantic via the Panama Canal. During a stopover at Ha-

vana, the newlyweds attended a costume ball as guests of Luis J. "Daiquiri" Bacardi. Joan came as a Tahitian maid and Dick as a beachcomber. Aboard the *San Paula* Dick proved to be the skeet-shooting champion with a score of twenty-three out of twenty-five tries. When the ship reached New York, the couple found that publicity-conscious Warner Bros. had chartered a plane to fly over the harbor trailing a banner "WELCOME DICK AND JOAN." An astrologer named Norvell predicted an unhappy end for the new marriage, but Joan was light-hearted. "I'm still waiting for that million bucks a seer promised me years ago!" For the newsreel cameras, Joan smiled and said, "I got him, girls!"

The home that awaited them was not the one they left behind. Powell had sold it at a tidy profit as the first in a long series of real-estate coups that would see Joan moving out of house after house before she could get accustomed to them. In place of the old homestead, Powell had contracted builders to construct an old English cottage, a house that would not require much furniture or heavy operating expenses. Dick also initiated the paperwork for adoption of Norman. Barnes was cooperative, and Powell was grateful.

Meanwhile, back at the studio the bosses were seeking another Busby Berkeley–type dance director to take the place of the high-priced and temperamental Berkeley. In Bobby Connolly, they thought they had their man. Joan worked with him in the musical *Colleen* (1936). Connolly's rigorous routines forced Joan, like all the other girls, into a restricted life-style. Dance numbers involving ping pong and hurdles required the girls to be asleep by 9:00 P.M., and smoking, drinking, and dieting were forbidden (if one can believe the publicity releases). Wisecracking Jack Oakie was imported from Paramount to be teamed with Joan. Much to Miss Blondell's chagrin, it was once more the love pair of Powell and Ruby Keeler who were the focus of this less than brilliant musical. However, professional as always, Joan shone as her smart-mouthed screen self and enjoyed the film's sole highlight when she joined with Oakie in strutting through the satirical talk-song, pseudo-ballroom number, "A Boulevardier from the Bronx." *Colleen* would be the final Powell-Keeler screen teaming. Both screen formats and favorite actors and actresses on the Warner Bros. lot were changing fast as Joan would later discover.

In fairness to the studio, Joan was given a wide variety of roles during 1936, yet none of the parts individually was enough to make the industry or public believe that she was still a top personality on the lot. In *Sons O' Guns,* with wide-mouthed Joe E. Brown, Joan was the very appealing tart, Yvonne. For *Bullets or Ballots,* in which Edward G. Robinson is on the right side of the law and Humphrey Bogart on the wrong side, Joan's *Penny Arcade* director William Keighley, now a top Warner Bros. director, was at the helm. Joan, who could add conviction to almost any kind of proceeding, was cast as Lee Morgan, Robinson's loyal girl. The thrust of the plot had the latter posing as a thug to gain evidence on Barton MacLane and his boys (including Bo-

gart). The climactic shoot-out in which both Robinson and Bogart were killed and MacLane's arrest assured may have been the film's high point, but it was the presence of such pros as Joan, Frank McHugh, Louise Beavers, Henry O'Neill, George E. Stone, and Joseph Crehan which provided the feature with its mobility and stability. The feature was based on a screen story by Martin Mooney, who had once served a thirty-day jail sentence for refusing to disclose information from confidential sources regarding New York racketeering.

The underrated Busby Berkeley feature *Stage Struck* has one of Joan's most memorable performances. It opened at Warner Bros.' flagship theatre in New York, the Strand, one week after Dick and Joan's marriage. The film attempted to copy the formula of *42nd Street:* temperamental stage star Peggy Revere (Joan) with too little talent but lots of pluck clashes with director George Randall (Powell). Later, they are professionally reunited by producer Harris (Warren William) for a new Main Stem production. Dapper Harris manages to match the uncooperative Peggy with the all-business Randall by playing up to her illusions of sophistication and intellectual stamina. The film's four songs were composed by E. Y. Harburg and Harold Arlen. While each of them was an above par number, none of them became a standard (despite Powell plugging them on his popular radio program, "Hollywood Hotel"). Joan did her valiant best to boost this production into a higher category of filmmaking, but the script and its *deja vu* (of even the lampoon) defeated even versatile Joan. Perhaps the worst ignominy of the film was that a soppy new studio ingenue, Jeanne Madden, was the girl who won Powell's heart within the storyline. It is to the inept Miss Madden that the crooner sang the love song "Fancy Meeting You," staged in a museum setting. One can only imagine how Joan felt about losing Powell oncamera to such inferior competition. Evidentally Warner Bros. had no plans for a professional Powell-Blondell love team.

The inferior *Gold Diggers of 1937* was the

With Frank McHugh and Carol Hughes in a publicity pose for *Three Men on a Horse* ('36).

With Errol Flynn in *The Perfect Specimen* ('37).

Promotional duty ('38).

last time she would work with either Berkeley or Glenda Farrell and the film was unworthy. Fortunately, the Mervyn LeRoy-directed *Three Men on a Horse* (1936) was a different story. Adapted from the very popular Broadway play by John Cecil Holm and George Abbott, the madcap farce concerns three desperate, daring graspers (Allen Jenkins, Sam Levene, Teddy Hart) who discover that inebriated Frank McHugh is a whiz at picking racehorse winners—that is, as long as he never attends any equestrian competition. Joan cavorts through the wild proceedings as Mabel, the cover girl of *Film Fun* magazine.

Producer-director Mervyn LeRoy would utilize Joan's services again in *The King and the Chorus Girl* (1937), a film based on a rather tame idea by Norman Krasna and Groucho Marx. French import Fernand Gravet was the royalty and Joan the commoner with whom he falls in love. Just as twenty years later Laurence Olivier and Marilyn Monroe could instill little fresh life into a similarly plotted concoction, *The Prince and the Showgirl*, so Gravet and Joan struggled against adverse odds. The studio then dumped Joan into *Back in Circulation* (1937), a quickie with Pat O'Brien and Margaret Lindsay. Much more infectious was the Michael Curtiz-directed *The Perfect Specimen* (First National, 1937) in which a chipper Joan indoctrinates sheltered rich-boy Errol Flynn in the ways of the world and love.

Having recovered from a bout of neuritis in her right shoulder that had her hospitalized, Joan was loaned to United Artists at Leslie Howard's request to co-star with him and a similarly borrowed Humphrey Bogart in *Stand-In* (1937). Although the part of Lester Plum, the stand-in for Colossal Pictures' big star Thelma Cheri (Marla Shelton), was her typical, all-knowing blonde role, Joan imparted such dimension to her characterization that even her most loyal adherents were impressed by her presentation. As is evident on the screen, *Stand-In* proved to be one of her most enjoyable working experiences. She got along extremely well with director Tay Garnett. "I love Tay. He knows what he wants

48

and he lets you *go*." Unfortunately, she would never work with Garnett again, nor would Warner Bros. ever understand that Joan was anything more than a workhorse, gold-digger screen type.

Perhaps if Joan had possessed a more realistic attitude toward her professional self, Warner Bros. would not have felt so inclined to step on, and over, her so frequently. When her contract had come due in 1937, she had re-signed with the studio, fearful of losing the all-important security. Then, too, unlike Bette Davis who rushed off to England to fight the studio because it was stagnating her career, Joan was too intimidated to bolt. As she would later explain, "I wasn't such a tremendous star I could afford to revolt." Her new studio pact called for six pictures a year, one more than even compliant Joan thought she should be required to produce within a twelve-month period.

Her second child, a daughter named Ellen, was born on Friday, July 1, 1938. Earlier that year (February 2), Dick Powell's adoption of Norman had become official. When the studio learned that Joan was pregnant, they tried to intimidate her into an abortion by putting her on suspension. Joan laughed at the idea. "I'm a mother first. Nothing else in my life is as important as my children. No part of my career is as vital to me as the role of actual mother." Up until the birth of Norman, Joan had been getting a $500 weekly bonus for allowing the studio to keep her on the soundstages past 5:00 P.M. When he was born, she relinquished this added salary so as to spend as much time as possible with her child.

While Warner Bros. was busily building up other contract players or importing Carole Lombard to co-star with Fernand Gravet in *Fools for Scandal* (1938), Joan was loaned to Columbia for *There's Always a Woman* (1938). Her co-star was the debonair Melvyn Douglas and, with the help of the artful director Alexander Hall, this spin-off of MGM's *The Thin Man* evolved as a delightful exercise. It was yet another entry in the cycle of husband-and-wife zany detective yarns, with Douglas and Blondell involved in a double

With Melvyn Douglas in *There's Always a Woman* ('38).

49

murder case with chic Mary Astor and slick Jerome Cowan as devious killers. Perhaps the highlight of the eighty-two-minute comedy is the sequence in which ebullient Joan is being grilled by the police. Under the hot lights she remains impervious to the third degree. In fact, she stays bright and cheerful while the police dissolve into tattered inquisitors. The following year Columbia would make a sequel entitled *There's That Woman Again*, this time replacing Blondell with a more available Virginia Bruce as lawyer and sleuth Douglas' ever-helpful spouse.

Just as Warner Bros. had decided to allow high-toned Kay Francis to work out the remainder of her contract in ill-conceived *B* pictures, so the studio felt no scruples about tossing Joan into the cheapie *Off the Record* (1939). She was matched yet again with that stable workhorse Pat O'Brien in a slim newspaper yarn that was barely worth its sixty-two minutes of screen time.

Even Joan had a limit to her tolerance and she was fast approaching it with such treatment by the home lot. She openly told the press that she would adore playing the title role in a screen version of *May Flavin*. As she explained, "I'd like to show that I can do things besides girl reporters and girl detectives." But nothing came of this project and instead she was loaned to Universal for Bing Crosby's *East Side of Heaven* (1939). Of this vehicle, the *New York Times* enthused, "a comedy which, though it shamelessly exploits several other well-known public weaknesses, including Joan Blondell, Mischa Auer, and C. Aubrey Smith, is much too ingratiating to be missed in these truculent and sour times." While Joan bounced through the romantic scenes at her bubbling best and Baby Sandy, the newest tiny tyke discovery, stole the limelight, crooner Crosby sang "Sing a Song of Moonbeams" and "East Side of Heaven," as well as other pleasing tunes by Johnny Burke and James V. Monaco. It was a clever piece of maneuvering on the part of the studio to have the spouse of a leading screen crooner (Dick Powell) play opposite one of his strongest cinema competitors.

If anything could be said to be the final blow to Joan's ego, it was being sandwiched into *The Kid from Kokomo* (1939) at Warner Bros. Yet another cheapie, the film matched her with Pat O'Brien and Wayne Morris in what was supposed to be a follow-up to Morris' *Kid Galahad* (1937), that semi-classic that had featured Bette Davis, Edward G. Robinson, and Humphrey Bogart.

Since Warner Bros. was giving a big buildup to Ann Sheridan and planned to do the same for Jane Wyman, yet another wisecracking screen type, Joan could perceive that her future at the studio would never improve. Since both her and Powell's contracts were due to expire at the end of the year (December 11, 1938), Dick, forever straining at the company's insistence to retain him in musical comedies, advised Joan to leave the lot with him. She followed her husband, though on her own she would probably never have summoned up enough courage to leave her employers. It was yet another entry in the passing of an era, but Joan was too content doing what Dick told her to do to realize that her movie-starring days were coming quickly to an end.

Since Joan had worked so well with Melvyn Douglas and director Alexander Hall in the past, Columbia hired her to star in two more features with dapper Douglas. The first of these comedy gems was *Good Girls Go to Paris* (1939). Originally the film was entitled *Good Girls Go to Paris, Too*, but the censors objected and the final word was eliminated from the release title. In one scene, Hall had Joan sneaking up a flight of stairs. To make the character more nervous, he wanted one of the stairs to creak as she stepped on it. Nothing they tried would produce the desired effect. Finally a studio technician was called in. "Why didn't you tell me?" he asked. He pulled a "creak" out of his pocket, inserted it under the stair and the scene was accomplished in one take. Hollywood had provisions for everything, or so it seemed.

Joan and director Hall got along fine during the making of *Good Girls* and their other joint vehicles. Of her, he said in his usual arch

50

way, "I think the habitual wideness and roundness of her eyes plays an important factor in her responsive expression. . . . Most persons are afraid their eyes will give away their real thoughts. . . . Miss Blondell has nothing to hide." This last remark was most definitely intended as a compliment.

The team of Blondell, Douglas, and Hall, was reunited yet again for *The Amazing Mr. Williams* (1939). Here suave Douglas is an ambitious detective, while Joan is an employee in the mayor's office. To bolster the proceedings, there are Clarence Kolb as the straight-laced police captain, Ed Brophy as a pleasant convicted murderer, and Donald MacBride as Lieutenant Bixler, your more than average harassed, nitwit, angered cop.

Now that she was away from Warner Bros., Joan also broke away from the image they had conceived for her. She now wore her hair in a freer, more feminine style, and used much less makeup. Of this period, though, she said, "Believe me, my mind wasn't on acting at that time. I'd do a romantic scene with a leading man with my thoughts on the babies at home, and what to give them for dinner, and how the drapes should hang, and why my current marriage wasn't working out." The fact that her brother Ed had divorced in August of 1938 was probably also on her mind. For the time being, however, things were going passably well (on most occasions) with Dick. At home she called him "Pa Powell," and he called her "Rosebud."

Two Girls on Broadway (1940), a remake of the Oscar-winning *Broadway Melody* (1929), was Joan's first screen work at MGM. Eye trouble kept her out of the shooting for a while, but the major problem for the production was Adolphe Menjou, whose recurring illness finally caused his removal from the cast after several weeks of postponement. Metro was more anxious in building budding sex goddess Lana Turner, and it was she who received top billing over Joan in this pleasant but unexceptional exercise which also featured George Murphy and Kent Taylor.

In the summer of 1940, Joan was voted by a mothers' organization as "The Most Glamorous Mother in Hollywood," a title she did not relish. She felt that glamour and motherhood were mutually exclusive. In a statement to the press, she confided that "the greatest penalty of screen success is a familiar face" which often times conflicted with the type of life and things that one treasured.

Although Joan generally eschewed blatantly commercial work, she occasionally took fees for full-page magazine ads for cosmetics and similar products (often tied in to her latest film release). In one for Calox Tooth Powder, she "claimed" that "One of the Big Hollywood Things movie life teaches you is to keep your teeth spic and spruce. . . . Yes, I'm another Calox user."

Little Norman, now officially adopted by the Powells, received straight A's on his first school report card. Dick ran movies for the youth several times a week in the Powells' home screening room. The features that were selected were ones which did not star Joan or Dick, for the couple believed that work and home life should be separated.

Then Dick and Joan decided they wanted to do a film together. He was under contract to Paramount where his best film to date, Preston Sturges' *Christmas in July,* had done nicely at the box-office. The studio agreed to teaming Powell and Blondell in *I Want a Divorce* (1940), a prophetically and badly titled project. The picture was to be a serious drama on the evils of divorce, and a kind of test of the Powells' real-life relationship. (Joan had starred on radio with John Deering in an NBC network, thirty-minute show during 1939-1940 entitled *I Want a Divorce.*) Evidently the studio could not decide what this picture was to be, a heavy melodrama or a breezy comedy, for it advertised the project as "funnier than 10,000 mother-in-laws."

When *I Want a Divorce* opened at the Paramount Theatre in New York on October 2, 1940, Bosley Crowther took the occasion to offer a little essay in his *New York Times'* review:

Miss Joan Blondell of Hollywood once solemnly informed this de-

With George Murphy and
Lana Turner in *Two Girls on
Broadway* ('40).

With Jerome Cowan in *East
Side of Heaven* ('39).

In *I Want a Divorce* ('40) with Dick Powell.

With the cast of *The Kid from Kokomo* ('39): Ed Brophy, Sidney Toler, Wayne Morris, Pat O'Brien, Stanley Fields, Jane Wyman, and May Robson.

With Roland Young in *Topper Returns* ('41).

With John Wayne in *Lady for a Night* ('41).

partment that she would like very much to break away from the frivolous type of films she had been playing for several years and really get her teeth into something nice and dramatic. Well she has had her wish. . . . And now, with the kindest intentions, we would like to suggest that she consider a reconciliation and return to her old bed and board. . . . Now, we don't say Miss Blondell is not a dramatic actress; we simply say she isn't in *I Want a Divorce.*

Personally, the Powells sailed through *I Want a Divorce* with general contentment but professionally the film set back both of their careers by several notches. Joan would not return to Paramount for any kind of film production for another twenty-five years.

If Joan seemed the model of health and frivolity oncamera, off the soundstages she was subject to the same vulnerabilities as any more obviously delicate screen player. In June 1940, she had returned to the stage in Sheldon Davis' *Goodbye to Love.* It was produced by her old boss, Al Woods, and financed by Dick Powell. Although Joan had the top billing, sister Gloria had the lead role. It received horrible notices when it played San Francisco at the Geary Theatre. It closed there and Joan was hospitalized for a week due to exhaustion, postponing plans she had of venturing back into other show-business fields.

When she recovered, Joan was used as a replacement for the high-priced Constance Bennett in the third of the *Topper* films. *Topper Returns* (1941), produced by Hal Roach for United Artists release, brought back Roland Young and Billie Burke as Cosmo and Henrietta Topper, this time involved with the curvaceous apparition Gail Richards (Joan) who seeks their help in cornering the culprit who stabbed her to death in the Carrington mansion. Patsy Kelly as the maid and Eddie "Rochester" Anderson as the Toppers' chauffeur provided very broad doubletake humor.

Young and Burke were their bumbling selves, Carole Landis and Dennis O'Keefe were the attractive romantic interest, and overtaxed Joan tried to make something airy and entertaining out of a heavy-handed dud.

At Universal, where Powell suffered through *In the Navy* (1941) with Abbott and Costello and the Andrews Sisters, Joan and Dick were teamed in *Model Wife* (1941). Dick, Joan, producer-director Leigh Jason, packager Charles K. Feldman, and scripters Charles Kaufman, Horace Jackson, and Grant Garrett each had a percentage-of-the-profits deal on this picture. Cast as a couple who are secretly wed (they are employed by a company which forbids interoffice marriages), the comedy load falls on Ruth Donnelly, Charles Ruggles, and Lucile Watson. Some five weeks after the film opened to mild reviews, Joan and Dick recreated their roles on Cecil B. DeMille's "Lux Radio Theatre."

From his "Hollywood Hotel" and other radio chores, Powell was adept at the medium, but Joan felt adrift. "It seemed as if I could read only one word at a time." But she soon mastered the new format. "You have got to be alert; you have to prepare as well as expect whatever evolutions the script calls for." She had begun to find screen work a disappointment. "The startling performance I had hoped to give some day seems to matter less now and I content myself with being adequate." Thus, she welcomed the greater variety of roles that radio provided her.

Three Girls about Town (1941) completed her Columbia chores as she, Binnie Barnes, and Janet Blair sought to enliven a rather shallow bit of big-city sophistication. Leigh Jason, who had handled the less than stellar *Model Wife,* was the director on this modest vehicle as well.

Joan and Dick went to New York on a business-pleasure trip late in 1941. Thirty-two-year-old Joan met there with an enterprising young Broadway producer, a friend of her husband's, to discuss a play project that never developed. His name was Mike Todd. Meanwhile, Dick took time off to see George Abbott's new Broadway musical, *Best Foot*

Forward, at the Ethel Barrymore Theatre. He was attracted by one of the young performers and went backstage to talk to her. Her name was June Allyson.

Before the trek to the East, Joan had completed *Lady for a Night* (1941) for Republic. Once again her guiding force through the production was Leigh Jason and here she was top-billed over studio star John Wayne in one of the year's corniest vehicles. Bosley Crowther (*New York Times*) warned the public, "Before you drop around to see . . . [it]—we suggest that you sniff some wisteria and check your wits outside. For this costly (for Republic) concoction whipped up in 'Old Southern' costumes by a company of well-known actors out of a badly dog-eared script is as fuzzy and stereotyped a picture as you're likely to encounter in these times." The turgid proceedings had Joan decked out in black net tights, an uplifted hair-do, and a syrupy Dixie accent, and hoping to marry into quality, as she ties her future to loutish "gentleman" Ray Middleton.

Much more constructive was Joan's contribution to the morale of the troops. Her USO-sponsored tour of military bases enabled her to entertain over 3.5 million lonely troops, sometimes appearing before 30,000 a day. Her routine lasted fifteen minutes: eight of them devoted to topical jokes and the other seven to a strip tease. Joan would begin to remove her clothes, but just when the soldiers started to sit up and take notice, her zippers would become stuck. She would throw up her hands in a "Sorry fellas, but what can I do?" expression and leave the stage to an always enthusiastic applause.

On her tours, she was shocked to discover how many GIs did not receive letters from home, a morale-booster she knew they badly needed. When she returned to the States, she made some 1,500 phone calls to servicemen's families, often urging them to write to their homesick sons.

When she was not engaged in such patriotic activities, Joan took an interest in music, with George Gershwin being her favorite composer, and she frequently played the piano. She liked football but was crazy about boxing. According to the fan magazines, her favorite dishes those days were chop suey and hamburgers with almonds chopped into them. In addition, she still took dancing lessons.

While the war had created a shortage of actors available for filmmaking, such was not the case with actresses and Joan found it increasingly difficult to find assignments that were suitable to her maturing standards. One bit of "type casting" was her role in *Cry Havoc* (1943), MGM's answer to Paramount's *So Proudly We Hail* (1943). As Grace, Joan is an ex-strip teaser (her service act had many admirers), one of many refugees caught on Bataan after the capture of Manila by the Japanese. The *New York Times* credited Joan for putting "a rough-and-ready humor into the role." But at times during the proceedings it was difficult to differentiate either physically or characteristically between Joan's part and that of Ann "Maisie" Sothern, who performed within the film as a tough ex-waitress who now appreciates the grim realities of life. Margaret Sullavan, in a part originally planned for Joan Crawford, was the valiant nurse who keeps the varied girls in the dugout sane and constructive.

Early in 1943, Joan went east again at the urging of Powell and Todd. Ever since meeting her, the producer had been digging around for a suitable property to justify their working together. The one which he had found was called *The Naked Genius.* Only a devout showman like Todd could have put across a show with such a debilitating title. Written (and rewritten and re-rewritten) by ace craftsman George S. Kaufman, the play was loosely based on the career of burlesque star Gypsy Rose Lee. The strip-tease queen, who had constructed the original comedy premise, even chipped in to help finance the production (which Kaufman had wanted to close out of town—he refused to attend the opening).

Late in March, while Joan was on the East Coast, she received a telegram from California. Her father was gravely ill. Though she wrangled a priority pass to be on the next available plane west, she did not arrive in time. He passed away on March 29 at the age of seventy-seven. The simple, quiet funeral services were attended by several of his old vaudeville cronies as well as the Blondell clan.

Recovering from her grief, Joan returned to New York, *The Naked Genius,* and Mike Todd. Mike Todd was born Michael Hirsch Goldbogen in Minneapolis, Minnesota, on June 22, 1907. Later the family had moved to Chicago, where he grew up in a poor Jewish section of town, attending Tuley High School. After an assortment of odd jobs, including working as an assistant pharmacist and a trunk boy for a shoe salesman, he turned to various get-rich-quick schemes. These included the founding of a College of Bricklaying when it seemed as if there might be a demand for one (he was the president). Like most of his other brainstorms, it was short-lived. He finally made a profit in Hollywood by soundproofing the stages during the talkie revolution, but lost it all during the stock market crash of 1929. When he began again, it was in show business, and he emerged at the Chicago World's Fair (1933) with a highly touted "Flame Dance." His first New York production was *Call Me Ziggy* (1936) and thereafter he was involved with *The Man from Cairo* (1938), *The Hot Mikado* (1939), *Gay New Orleans, Dancing Campus,* and *The Streets of Paris,* the latter trio given at the New York World's Fair (1939). Next came *Star and Garter* (1942), and the following year *Something for the Boys* with Ethel Merman.

It was not very long into rehearsal time when it became obvious that Mike had become smitten with perky Joan. His courtship, like his showmanship, was violent, impetuous, and demanding. He lavished incredible sums of money on gifts and niceties to satisfy her every whim, and any whim she *might* formulate. He was at her side every possible moment. If she so much as sneezed twice in succession, he would promptly hire a personal physician to tend her. No excuse was over-looked for expending extravagant funds on the movie star. All this was in direct contrast to the simplistic, parsimonious existence she shared with economy-minded Powell. Stocky, but dapper, Todd spent money as though it was not his, which it mostly was not. At first, Joan held her ground against his impetuous advances, but her resistance deteriorated rapidly. After all, she had never had such a motivated lover before. He literally swept her off her feet.

Long before *The Naked Genius,* Todd had learned well every possible trick of publicizing a property regardless of its intrinsic quality. *The Naked Genius* was no exception. It underwent a shakedown, pre-Broadway tour that only substantiated everyone's belief that the project did not, could not, and should not jell. In early October the comedy was struggling through a run in Pittsburgh when word was "leaked" to New York that both Gypsy Rose Lee and George S. Kaufman wanted to close the show. Rather than fight these rumors, Todd embellished upon them, promoting his production with "guaranteed not to win the Pulitzer Prize."

On Thursday, October 21, 1943, the production debuted at the Plymouth Theatre. As Burton Rascoe reported in the *New York World-Telegram,* there was "a silently abashed audience, each member of which must have been grieving with shame at the embarrassment of some favorite in the huge cast, that he or she should be caught dead in so stupid and witless a mess." The slender plot concerned burlesque performer Honey Bee Carroll (Joan) who has hired a ghost writer to compose a novel for her, leading to her matrimonial debacle with her publisher. Others in the big cast included Millard Mitchell, Phyllis Povah, and Doro Merande. Summing up the critical reaction to Joan in her thankless role was Louis Kronenberger's observation for *PM,* "Joan Blondell plays the culture-loving Honey Bee Carroll as well, I suppose, as she can: but the effect, for me, is curiously unexciting."

Crafty Todd had already induced Twentieth Century-Fox to invest $150,000 in the

With Ella Raines,
Heather Angel,
Frances Gifford, and
Ann Sothern in *Cry
Havoc* ('43).

With Peggy Ann
Garner, Ted
Donaldson, and
Martha Wentworth in
*A Tree Grows in
Brooklyn* ('45).

With Greer Garson
and Clark Gable in
Adventure ('45).

With Mike Mazurki,
Tyrone Power, and
Coleen Gray in
Nightmare Alley ('47).

59

production, with an option for the film company to sign over another $200,000 for the movie rights if the show played for at least thirty-five performances on Broadway. Thanks to Todd's ingenuity, the gargantuan show was playing to near-capacity houses— it was wartime and any diversion was acceptable to many money-spenders—when after thirty-six performances Todd closed the show. In a grand face-saving move, Todd announced "I am closing the show despite the fact it is earning a substantial profit. I believe the money I might be losing as a result is not as important as the good will of the people who might not like the show." Almost needless to say, Todd did not bother to mention that he exercised the screen rights clause and Fox turned over the balance of payment required. The studio produced the property as *Doll Face* (1945) with Perry Como, Vivian Blaine, and Carmen Miranda, and the results were almost as bad as the Broadway version.

That her attraction to Todd blinded Joan to much of Todd's dubious working procedures was obvious, but during the brief run of *The Naked Genius*, Joan the homemaker constantly voiced her wish to return to California to see her children. Her desire to end the show gave rise to a little routine. Whenever she would hint that she wanted to see her children again, Todd instantly called over a crew to begin taking down the marquee. Every time she brought up the subject again, it was the same story. The only element that varied was the number of letters the workmen could remove from "JOAN BLONDELL" before she relented, agreeing to continue with the three-ring-circus show.

Even before *The Naked Genius* had closed, Todd was busy with his next extravaganza, *Mexican Hayride,* which he vowed would be the biggest, splashiest musical Broadway had yet seen. He proved to be right this time; the show debuted in early 1944 and would run for over 500 successful performances.

Meanwhile, Joan returned to California to be reunited with her family. A subsequent illness kept her on the West Coast longer than she had anticipated. In the weeks that followed, she saw "Pa Powell" in a completely new light, and wondered how she had ever lived with him. Dick was similarly antagonistic. Now that they both had new romantic interests, there was no question but that their marriage was coming to an end. During Joan's absence, Powell had spent many an evening at the home of June Allyson, now a rising MGM contractee. In the event of a divorce between Joan and Dick, there was little room for speculation as to Powell's domestic future: June had been eager to wed him for years and he was the sort who needed to be married. On the other hand, the future was not clear for Joan.

At a tender age, Todd had married Bertha Freshman whose major achievement and reason for being was her marriage. She had driven him from their house way back in his Chicago days and since then their only occasion for communicating to one another was the continuing dispute over the care of their child, Mike Jr. Seemingly, nothing could shake this woman's iron grip on her husband. Obviously, no divorce was forthcoming from her.

Meanwhile, Joan returned to film work with a series of character roles, the traditional fate of the talented actress who no longer has all of her beauty. "I think I rushed things a bit, I could have had some extra gauzes put on the camera instead of going from young girl to old girl roles in one leap." But those roles also won Joan her first serious recognition as a cinema actress.

One of them was a part that had originally been planned for Alice Faye, that of Aunt Sissy in *A Tree Grows in Brooklyn* (1945), a film with which Joan felt an obvious and deep personal identity. "My uncle had one in his side yard and if we chopped it down once, we chopped it down fifty times. But the darn thing always grew right back." She got along extremely well with director Elia Kazan, who was handling his first feature film. The Twentieth Century-Fox producers were severely restricted by the U.S. government wartime rationing board which put a $5,000 ceiling on the amount supposedly to be spent on new sets. Against their will, the *A Tree Grows in Brooklyn* company was forced to use some actual locations, which greatly enhanced this flavorful piece of Americana.

Based on Betty Smith's warm novel of life in the shadow of the Williamsburg Bridge and of a slum family struggling for existence, the picture abounds with wonderful performances. James Dunn, once a star at the old Fox Pictures in the early Thirties, returned to his alma mater (and won an Oscar in the process) for his touching performance as the dreamy Johnny Nolan whose best intentions were lost in booze. Peggy Ann Garner won a special (juvenile) Oscar for her interpretation of little Francie, the light of her father's eye, who after his death must give up her promising schooling to help her mother (Dorothy McGuire) and brother (Ted Donaldson) survive the jungle of life. There is also Lloyd Nolan as McShane, the cop on the beat who offers to wed Katie Nolan after she has become a widow.

And then there was Joan as Katie's sister Sissy, pleasingly plump and always anxious to keep up everyone's spirits. As Bosley Crowther (*New York Times*) reported, "Joan Blondell's performance of Aunt Sissy, the family's problem, is obviously hedged by the script's abbreviations and the usual 'Hays office restraints, but a sketchy conception of a warm character is plumply expanded by her." John T. McManus of *PM* insisted, "Joan Blondell, in the frequent times she is onscreen as Aunt Sissy, swipes the show from them all." Joan's Aunt Sissy was a distant cousin of the gold diggers the actress portrayed in the Thirties but, like those characterizations, her brassy dame has a heart of gold.

The industry spoke of Joan's performance as a comeback bid and in a way it was. She should have been Oscar-nominated, but sadly was not. (At a later date, the real Aunt Sissy turned up demanding from the studio a modest quarter million dollars in damages. An out-of-court settlement was reached.) Meanwhile, at Fox, Joan joined William Bendix in the cheapie *Don Juan Quilligan* (1945),

a silly farce that provided Bendix with a one-man show as a barge captain who finds himself wed to a girl at both ends of his canal trek: to Margie (Joan) in Brooklyn and to Lucy (Mary Treen) in Utica. It was announced that this entry, directed by Frank Tuttle, would be the first of a series, but the idea was dropped after the picture's release.

Joan's descent from true stardom was signified by her below-the-stars billing in *Adventure* (1946), the MGM debacle that provided Clark Gable with his first post-World War II service role. Greer Garson was his co-lead, but it was saucy Joan, as schoolmarm Garson's breezy friend, who stole the notices. "Only Miss Blondell ever manages to sound like a human being and not a talking book," noted Eileen Creelman of *The New York Sun*.

Meanwhile, the expected divorce with Powell came in mid-July 1945. In a typical gesture, Joan shortened the miserable formalities by acceding to all of her husband's numerous demands. He had somehow accounted for every nickel she spent, going back to 1935, and now applied the total against her share of the estate. Frances Marion would recall walking unannounced into the Blondell-Powell home, finding the couple in the basement, and hearing Joan saying "one for you, one for me." She was dividing up the inventory of canned fruit. Then she heard Joan saying, "You can have all of this, I don't need it." The item in question was a case of toilet tissue. Three weeks later Powell and June Allyson were wed.

After Todd had launched a failure, *Around the World in 80 Days* (1946), and a success, *Up in Central Park* (1945), he proceeded westward to begin a filmmaking-producing phase of his career. One-track Bertha, his wife, followed and no amount of persuasion could gain him the necessary divorce. Thus, he and Joan had to be as discreet as possible. Then on August 12, 1946, Bertha Todd died at St. John's Hospital in Santa Monica. She had entered the facility for a simple operation on her hand and a short time later that tremendously vital woman was dead under the anesthesia. Todd was concerned for the effect the turn-of-events would have on his son, but overjoyed that he could now wed Joan.

But Joan's relationship with mercurial, high-pressure Todd had become a living nightmare. He was fanatically possessive. At the slightest suspicion of infidelity he would beat her terribly, more than once landing her in a hospital. Nevertheless, there were good times too, and he always came back crying, begging at her feet for forgiveness. In one such peak of tenderness the two were married. It happened just before midnight on Saturday, July 5, 1947, at Nevada's hotel El Rancho Vegas. The Reverend R. V. Carpenter performed the ceremony in the presence of Joan's two children. She wore a flowered afternoon dress with orchids. Joan insisted on a clause in the marriage contract in which Todd promised to be home every night by 7:30.

If it had not been for Joan's financial assistance ($80,000 worth), the Todds could not have lived on the luxury level that Mike preferred. Despite Todd's Hollywood interest, his financial base was still in New York. At least Joan was able to insist on a country home, a magnificent thirty-acre Hudson River estate in Irvington, New York. Among the multi-millionaires they shared fences with was Averell Harriman. If Ellen, Norman, and Mike Jr. ever tired of playing in their eleven-room home, there was always the six-room guest house, or the six-room apartment atop their private stables.

Additional financing for the estate purchase came through Todd's flair for obtaining loans. People seemed almost to feel good about losing their money, knowing Todd had spent it so joyously. Other expenses for the Todd ménage included round-the-clock guards and detectives on the estate to assuage Joan's obsessive fear of kidnappers. The three children got along well together and Joan joined the local PTA to be closer to their education.

Her film career during the Todd years was at best erratic, the diamond-in-the-mud being *Nightmare Alley* (1947) at Twentieth Century-Fox. This film was a haunting and circuitous tale of destiny at work among a carni-val's riff-raff. Its big attraction was Tyrone Power in a strictly dramatic role, aided by two contrasting females—the lovely, young Coleen Gray as Molly and Joan as Zeena the mindreader. "I play a seeress with a heart like an artichoke, a leaf for every man." As had become customary with Joan's secondary film parts, she offered the most seasoned and rewarding performance in the film.

During this time, Joan worked mostly in summer stock (where her name still meant something) and paid serious attention to her kids. She spent most of her free time on the beaches of Long Island with them. When little Norman got restless seeing his bustling parents and having nothing to do himself, Joan took it upon herself to get him a job at a local drug store. When Todd would return home after a grueling day, Joan would console him with her expert back massage, an experience Todd treasured.

Summer stock began for Joan in 1949 when she joined the Fairhaven, Connecticut, run of *Happy Birthday,* during the course of which she was able to celebrate her own birthday in a gala backstage party. The production traveled to Princeton for that community's annual drama festival at the McCarter Theatre. Mike was along to assist her, and Mike Jr. was the assistant stage manager.

Todd was continually frustrated, trying to top his last show business exploit with a bigger success, and a good deal of his confusion and indecision was directed towards Joan and resulted in unpleasant scenes. He made life unbearable for the usually bubbly Joan with his unpredictable violent mood changes. She insisted he see a psychiatrist of her choosing but was not satisfied with the results. In May 1950, she executed the most courageous decision of her life, one which she has never regretted. She traveled to Las Vegas to file for divorce from Todd. She charged cruelty and asked no alimony. The divorce was granted on Thursday, June 8, 1950.

Not that Todd was completely out of Joan's life. He kept her up-to-date on all his current projects, sometimes calling her ten times a day. By November of that year, he even was taking her out socially and introducing her as "the former and future Mrs. Todd." But Joan could not tolerate the situation for very long, and their soirees ended. It got so that his presence would so upset her that he had to be barred from the set when she was filming.

Todd had gone bankrupt just recently and Joan did not have the heart to sue him for the $80,000 he still owed her. She felt he had troubles enough. He would marry Elizabeth Taylor in May 1957 and their child Elizabeth Frances would be born that year. He died at the height of a new fame in movies (*Around the World in 80 Days*) in an airplane crash (March 22, 1958). Joan was not bequeathed anything in the will, nor did she contest it.

Joan made two more films, *For Heaven's Sake* (1950) at Twentieth Century-Fox and *The Blue Veil* (1951) at RKO, before beginning a five-year routine of stage and TV work. The latter film, starring Jane Wyman, won Joan a Best Supporting Actress nomination for her heart-felt portrayal of Annie Rawlins, a show business mother. Although she lost the Oscar bid to Kim Hunter (*A Streetcar Named Desire*), her brief but telling performance indicated that Joan's years of trouping had paid back dividends. But, ironically, Joan has always played-down this assignment. In fact, on one occasion she would say, "That was the worst piece of trash I ever made. I did it in a day and a half in New York."

In November 1950, Joan sold the Irvington estate and rented a trailer when she interrupted her work for a reunion with the children. Later, she decided to live in the East until her children had completed high school. Norman went on to receive a B.A. in economics from Cornell University. Ellen would later marry and give Joan a granddaughter of the same name. For the sake of that little girl, Joan began keeping a scrapbook for the first time in her life.

Some of her stage work was not that prestigious. She starred in a show which dealt light-heartedly with the sexual behavior of the human female, based in part on the work of Dr. Kinsey. Taking the form of a panel discussion, this Texas-based show had considerable difficulty finding stages across the country once the local Bible societies got to work. Then Joan traveled with William Inge's *Come Back, Little Sheba,* inheriting in stock the role that Shirley Booth played on Broadway and in films. But a contractual dispute with the producer ended this tour. The International Brotherhood of Electrical Workers formed a touring company of *Gypsy,* a musical very loosely based on the exploits of stripper Gypsy Rose Lee. Evidently, recalling Joan's part in *The Naked Genius,* the actress was hired to appear in the revue-like show before various units of the Bell Telephone System during the summer of 1952. There was bad news in November of that year when her mother Katherine died at age sixty-eight. The elder Blondell had resumed her stage career after the war, first appearing in *I Give You My Husband.*

Some of Joan's other stage work in this period included replacing Ethel Merman (if anyone can) in *Call Me Madam.* Then Joan took over another Shirley Booth Broadway role (but one this time that had been created by Joan), that of Aunt Sissy in a musical version of *A Tree Grows in Brooklyn.* Around this time, Joan, who had been making frequent acting forays into live and filmed TV (she was especially memorable in *Burlesque* on CBS-TV's "Shower of Stars" in March 1955), thought that she might like to direct a production in this, her newest favorite medium. But she never exerted enough pressure to break out of acting and launch a career as a director. Sister Gloria, who unlike Joan had retained her shape and rather youthful verve, was having a professional crest playing Honeybee, the Gilleses' neighbor on "The Life of Riley" TV series. Gloria also proved to be an accomplished painter.

Though Joan did not achieve much new fame in this period, she certainly spared no effort in her professional work. During a rehearsal for a TV "Comedy Hour" in 1954, she fainted from exhaustion on the set. Her condition was complicated by a long history of overwork and a fever of 102°. Betty Furness

With Sammy Ogg,
Katharine Hepburn, Dina
Merrill, and Sue Randall
in *Desk Set* ('57).

With Harry Von Zell,
Joan Bennett, Robert
Cummings, Jack LaRue,
and Clifton Webb in *For
Heaven's Sake* ('50).

64

completed the episode which was entitled *Let's Face It*. Among other video performances Joan was outstanding in a one-hour special drama called *White Gloves* in which she portrayed an aging stage actress. Ironically, Joan frequently received condescending critical reviews from TV columnists who insisted that because she had so often played brassy dames before, her current high-level performances of the same ilk had to be discounted.

While Mike Todd was beginning to ride the crest of success again in the mid-Fifties, Joan found herself burdened with old debts engendered by him. In 1954 she was sued by a Canadian plaintiff regarding a $12,000 loan made in 1948 to her when she was desperate for funds to help Todd out of his difficulties. The next year found Joan being linked romantically by columnists with millionaire architect and sportsman Hal Hayes. She seemed excited and there was much talk of marriage, though not from Joan. The relationship finally dissolved.

With rare exception, television has remained the hidden medium. For example, a performer might do an outstanding piece of characterization, but unless the performance wins an Emmy or the role is part of a sustaining series, viewers and critics alike quickly forget the acting in question. Such was frequently the case with Joan. In the mid-Fifties, she offered an exceedingly fine performance on a drama entitled *Snow Job,* playing the silly, harassed wife of a doorman and the mother of a thirteen-year-old son.

Unlike Joan Crawford, Bette Davis, and Rosalind Russell, Joan had no qualms about lessening her professional status if the part were right for her. She was a trouper of the old school and the most important thing for Joan was giving the audience a decent show, not maintaining her show business ego. But, as stated before, even Joan had a limit to her tolerance. In August 1955, she was cast in the lead of *A Palm Tree in a Rose Garden.* But the play producers insisted upon tinkering with her characterization so much that she left the production and was replaced in the stock tour by Dorothy Stickney. More often than not

As Annie Rawlins of *The Blue Veil* ('51).

65

Joan had a good perspective on her talents and limitations. She was offered a stage script in which she played straight woman to Cara Williams' comic lead. She rejected it with, "A good script, but not for me."

There had been many rumors during the Forties that Joan's screen career had taken a nosedive not so much because of her maturing years, but because of her relationship with Todd. Some gossip followers insisted that meddlesome Todd had even tried to have Joan blacklisted at several studios, wishing her to remain in the background while he promoted his own moviemaking ventures. At any rate, by the mid-Fifties, both Joan and Hollywood were ready for one another again.

She returned to movieland with three films at MGM. The first was *The Opposite Sex* (1956), a musical remake (to use the word loosely) of *The Women,* Clare Boothe's play of 1936. Joan's character was Edith Potter, the part played by Phyllis Povah in the stage and film versions. Actually, Joan had been considered for a role in the 1939 MGM picture adaptation but had rejected the offer by George Cukor, as she had that of Belle Watling in MGM's *Gone with the Wind* the same year. *The Opposite Sex,* shot in CinemaScope and color, might have been fun, but the material seemed outdated and director David Miller failed to take proper advantage of his intriguing cast: June Allyson, Joan Collins, Dolores Gray, Ann Sheridan, Ann Miller, Agnes Moorehead, and Charlotte Greenwood. Also, the addition of oncamera males to the bitchy proceedings did nothing to enhance Miss Boothe's original concept. If Hollywood onlookers expected Miss Allyson and Joan to come to blows on the sets, they were disappointed. Both actresses remained cool but civil to one another. In her Helen Rose outfits, while playing a pregnant wife, Joan looked her most becoming in years.

Then came *Lizzie* (1957), which some movie chroniclers have termed the road version of *The Three Faces of Eve* (Twentieth Century-Fox, 1957). The latter psychological study featured Joanne Woodward in an Oscar-winning performance of a woman with a tri-split personality, while *Lizzie* focused on Eleanor Parker's interpretation of a disturbed woman with a dual personality. Joan played Aunt Morgan, and considered this black-and-white film her best since *A Tree Grows in Brooklyn.* In the Robert Wise-directed *This Could Be the Night,* a nightclub musical starring the strange trio of Jean Simmons, Paul Douglas, and Anthony Franciosa, Joan was Crystal, a bubbly stage mother.

Joan had much better luck at Twentieth Century-Fox where she joined with Katharine Hepburn and Spencer Tracy in their eighth of nine co-starring vehicles, *Desk Set* (1957). Joan thoroughly enjoyed the making of this comedy—mainly for one reason, Katie. "If I ever come back to this life," Joan later said, "I want to be Katharine Hepburn. She is the most resourceful woman I know. . . . I've never seen her equal." The two veteran performers got along together beautifully. Joan might well have been replaced due to an illness but Katharine saw to it that the shooting was rescheduled to save her part, and, incidentally, during Joan's convalescence, she took care of Miss Blondell's brindle pup, Bridie Murphy. So well did the two actresses get along that one suspects some of their oncamera dialogue was repeated from their coffee-break conversation.

At one point in the scenario, Katharine says to Joan that if she can't find a worthwhile husband soon, "We'll move in together and keep cats." Joan's answer was the story of her life, "I don't like cats, I like men. And so do you." She did not like cats, but, in the absence of men, Joan was always willing to settle for one or more dogs. Bridie Murphy was so named because when she found him, the search for a friend was over.

While on the Fox lot, Joan joined with Jayne Mansfield, Tony Randall, and Betsy Drake in a rather tame version of *Will Success Spoil Rock Hunter?* (1957). A plump Joan was on hand as curvaceous, breathy Miss Mansfield's secretary, confidante, and masseuse, and, as usual, managed to make far more of her part than the script or director required.

While Joan's return foray into motion pictures garnered her renewed interest with the public, events in her private life managed to put her name back on the front pages of newspapers. On Sunday, July 22, 1956, her son Norman married Ann McDowell, a story which split the front page of national newspapers with the latest news of President Eisenhower. Norman and Ann had attended high school together at Irvington. In fact, Norman had courted her since he was thirteen! But Dick Powell out in Hollywood was upset over the match. He sent two telegrams: one to Hedda Hopper stating his dissatisfaction, and another to the wedding, sending his adopted son his best wishes. The ceremony took place in Joan's new Manhattan apartment at 2 Sutton Place, and her gift to the newlyweds was a new car with two signs on it: "Ann and Norm" and "Just Dunn It!"

When Joan was offered a co-starring role in a new musical, *Copper and Brass,* she thought it was too nice a deal to pass up. She later regretted her decision. The show starred Nancy Walker as a rookie New York cop who is assigned the job of curbing juvenile delinquency at a jazz dive across from a public school. In the true Judy Holliday tradition, she makes a botch of it. Joan was cast as Miss Walker's mother, a former vaudeville trouper who has wonderful memories of the past. The show tried out in Philadelphia to moderate response, but by the time it reached New Haven, Joan's show-stopping song-and-dance number had been removed, and she left the faltering production. She was replaced by Benay Venuta; the show opened on Broadway on October 17, 1957, and lasted thirty-six performances.

But Joan did not sit back and take the defeat lightly. Instead, she accepted an offer to join Siobhan McKenna and Art Carney in a grim drama entitled *The Rope Dancers.* The drama centers on the tragic life of an eleven-year-old girl (Beverly Lunsford) and opened at the Cort Theatre on Wednesday, November 20, 1957. While the other performers received their critical dues, it was Joan who received the best notices. "Real warmth comes onto the stage whenever the tenant from the floor below comes up—Joan Blondell, as hearty and messy a woman as you ever saw" (*New York Daily News*). ". . . Gives a wonderfully exhilarating and at times affecting performance" (*New York Times*). "Joan Blondell stands out vividly as an amiable, sluttish neighbor" (*New York Daily Mirror*). John McClain of the *New York Journal-American* offered the finest tribute to Joan: "The most rewarding part in the play is that allotted Joan Blondell, the heart-of-gold neighbor, and she scores consistently. She has almost all the laugh lines, and she is one character that I understood all the way." Because of its morose ambiguities, the play did not appeal to a wide enough audience and closed after 189 performances. Many fans thought Joan should have won a Tony Award for her well-etched characterization. (She lost to Anne Bancroft of *Two for the Seesaw*.)

Undaunted by her bad luck on Broadway, Joan joined Tallulah Bankhead and Estelle Winwood in an extensive road tour of *Crazy October.* The trio were directed by the play's author, James Leo Herlihy. "I play a gal who's passed forty so successfully I still think I'm thirty-two," Joan said at the time. Also that year Joan did one of her several unsold TV pilot shows, this one entitled "The Jacksons." Others over the years included "Mrs. Thursday" in 1968, and "Bobby Parker & Co." in 1971.

Her other stage work of this period included *The Dark at the Top of the Stairs, Time of the Cuckoo,* and *New Girl in Town.* She also opened in San Francisco in a national tour of *Bye Bye Birdie* in May 1961, playing the role of the over-reacting mother. But by February of the following year, she went before the appropriate union arbitration board complaining about director Gower Champion and the way her role had been reinterpreted.

Joan's film work in the Sixties was spotty. *Angel Baby* (1961) for Allied Artists was a poor man's version of *Elmer Gantry* (1960) with Joan and Henry Jones as tipsy members of an evangelistic group. MGM's *Advance to the Rear* (1964) was a period war comedy in

With her girls in *Advance to the Rear* ('64).

← With Henry Jones in *Will Success Spoil Rock Hunter?* ('57).

With Jack Weston and Karl Malden in *The Cincinnati Kid* ('65).

With Harry Davis in
Waterhole # 3 ('67).

←

The star of TV's "Here
Come the Brides" ('68).

With James Garner in
Support Your Local Sheriff
('71).

which nobody gets killed for a change. Joan was type-cast, playing a heart-of-gold madam in this misfire which reunited her with Melvyn Douglas. Perhaps Joan's best role of the decade was in *The Cincinnati Kid* (1965) at MGM in which Joan (as cardsharp Lady Fingers) and Edward G. Robinson (as Lancey Howard) stole the show from the film's new wave of stars, Steve McQueen, Ann-Margret, and Tuesday Weld. With *Waterhole No. 3* (1967), Joan celebrated her fiftieth production (thirty-seven on the screen) in show business. In this rollicking satire of greed in the Old West, she was again cast as a matronly, bouncy madam. (Along the way, Joan dropped out of the 1964 production of *Straight-Jacket,* a William Castle horror yarn, and was eventually replaced by Joan Crawford.) *Kona Coast* (1968) had originally been intended as a teleseries pilot, but was released by Warner Bros.-Seven Arts as a full-length feature. Joan played Kittibelle Lightfoot, the operator of a broken-down resort for alcoholics. The muddled drama was shot on location in Honolulu where star Richard Boone had set up his home.

In Hollywood, as in other walks of life, the past continues to haunt people. Over the years there were many roles that Joan could have played on the various series produced for television by Four Star Enterprises, a video producing corporation partially controlled by Dick Powell; but for personal reasons Joan remained unasked. Ironically, she did appear on "The Dick Powell Theatre" on Christmas Day 1962 in an episode entitled *The Big Day.* But by this point her ex-husband was near death from his bout with cancer. The only Blondell that was allowed to be at the dying man's bedside was adopted son Norman. Powell died on January 4, 1963. Joan seems to have been scarcely mentioned in the wealthy man's will. Norman and Ellen, however, each received 3,000 shares of Four Star Television, equivalent to about $31,500 in cash.

Although Joan still got occasional movie roles and parts in telefeatures, it was to be a teleseries that played the biggest part in her

career after 1967. In that year, before making *Kona Coast* and the Elvis Presley *Stay Away, Joe* (1968), Joan said, "I still like motion pictures best of all and a good role will always prevail over pressure-cooker TV." But afterwards came, "I find making features dull; hopefully this series will run twelve years and I won't have to worry about films to keep busy." Did she still want to direct? "I certainly do, but don't let them hear it around here."

The series she was referring to was "Here Come the Brides" produced by Screen Gems. Set in Seattle, Washington, in the 1870s, the show continued a story developed in the 1954 MGM musical *Seven Brides for Seven Brothers,* with Joan playing Lottie, a high-powered saloon owner. Although she joined the series late in the initial production, her scenes (rushed into the completed segments) proved popular and she was Emmy-nominated in 1969. Her co-star was Robert Brown, "the first real hunk of man I've seen since Errol Flynn." "One of the reasons I decided to do this series was because Bridie and Fresh are getting too old to be bounced around from job to job. I thought it looked like an elegant set-up. I liked Robert. Not everyone is psychelic these days, thank God. . . . Funny thing about a series though, a little girl came up to me the other day. 'I know you,' she said, 'you're Lottie.' You know she was right? Joan Blondell no longer exists. I'm somebody named Lottie. That's—what do they say?— that's where it's at nowadays." The hour-long color series lasted for two seasons on the ABC-TV network.

Since then, Joan has not stopped working professionally but is not always visible to the mass public. She has become a frequent source of first-hand material for TV documentaries on the history of Hollywood in the Golden Era, but she much prefers living for today. Like many other veteran screen actresses, she regrets that "women are almost extinct in pictures now. It's the man's era of stardom. While I think they're divine creatures, I think there's too much of them in front of the camera." She remains very loyal to her co-workers in front of, and behind, the scenes. When Paramount artist Dottie Ponedel landed in Mount Sinai Hospital, Joan was her only visitor, bribing the attendants with forty pounds of chocolates to get Dot special attention.

When Joan's two pug dogs died, she uprooted herself from the Sherman Oaks area of California to accept the replacement lead in the off-Broadway production of *The Effect of Gamma Rays on Man-in-the-Moon Marigolds*. Earthy Joan, with never any pretensions of high intellect, made no show at comprehending the intricacies (if there were any) of Paul Zindel's Pulitzer Prize–winning drama which had originally starred Eileen Heckart on TV and then Sada Thompson on the stage. But she told Ronald Bowers in an interview for *Films in Review,* "My whole day, waking and sleeping, is spent trying to make the character of the mother explicable, so I guess inside I'm quite a serious actress. At least I want audiences to get their money's worth. The character of the mother I play is demented and the long monologues have no clues or other helps. Each night I try to make it make sense."

On Tuesday, September 28, 1971, at The New Theatre on East 54th Street, Joan made her bow in the role of Beatrice. As Marjorie Gunner would evaluate in *Events* newspaper, it was not a role that Blondell should have tackled. "Joan Blondell misinterprets the part for reasons explained by the actress in the playbill interview better than any critic could have imagined. . . . 'It's awfully difficult to be something you just ain't. . . . She's [Beatrice] brutal to those kids, but I love children!' And so, in true Judith Anderson tradition, . . . [Miss Blondell] kicks her little foot as if in plea that the audience disregard her behavior and hark back to *Golddiggers of 1935.* . . . But Miss Blondell's desire for audience sympathy evokes only condolences for the play." Joan grew to dislike the part so much that she was glad when she came down with the mumps and had to relinquish her part in the production.

Unlike many of her contemporaries, who have fallen by the wayside professionally and emotionally, Joan has always remained part of the "now" generation. On her sixty-second birthday, she was persuaded to try marijuana. Although an unpleasant reaction made it her last contact with the drug, she is glad that she at least experimented. However Joan refuses to try any kind of cosmetic surgery. "I feel if my heart lifts, my face will go with it."

On Friday, November 15, 1972, she debuted in another series, this hour show was "Banyon" on NBC-TV. It starred Robert Forster as a 1930s detective, with Joan as the head of a secretarial school that supplied girls for Forster's office. Very little of Joan was seen in the short-lived series, but the role brought her back to the Warner Bros. studio. Plenty of the old crew members were around and they would come up to her and ask, "Joanie, where ya been?"

Also in 1972, Joan became an author. Rather than write an autobiography, she chose to put her career into fictional form. It was the result of ten years of hard work and the final book shows this. In fact she was so reluctant to complete it—she could not think how to end it properly—that she finally conceded to her publisher's request and wrote a hasty finale. Delacorte published *Center Door Fancy,* and a year later, its paperback subsidiary, Dell Publishing, released the softcover edition. The *New York Times* labeled it "a warm, lively novel. . . . What never appeared in fan magazines." *Publishers Weekly* enthused, "Genuine, marvelous, thoroughly entertaining!" The plotline follows very closely Joan's own life and through the chapters one can interpret just how she felt about George Barnes, Dick Powell, June Allyson, and Mike Todd. As the publicity release for the book detailed, "Nora Marten grew up as a kid playing the vaudeville circuit with her family in big cities and hick towns across the country. She came to Hollywood in the golden days and made it big in movies. She also made a few marriages that didn't exactly pan out. One husband was a famous cameraman, another a star crooner-actor, a

With Quentin Dean and Elvis Presley in *Stay Away, Joe* ('68).

← With stepson Mike Todd, Jr., at the opening of her off-Broadway run in *The Effect of Gamma Rays on Man-in-the-Moon Marigolds* (September 29, 1971).

Being directed by son Norman Powell on "The New Dick Van Dyke Show" (November 1973).

third the greatest showman of his time. And in-between there were other men and fellow stars and hard work and raising kids and a lot of other things that never made the columns."

On another occasion, Joan said of her marriages, "Barnes provided my first real home and Powell was my security man and Todd was my passion. Each was totally different. If you could take a part of each one of them and put them into one man, you'd have a helluva husband." As a matter of fact, Joan still thinks about those three husbands. "When I was married—all *three* times—I put everything I had into it. . . . I tried to be the best. I guess that's why I was so shaken each time one of my marriages broke up. I was ashamed of divorce. . . . After my third divorce, I knew I couldn't go through it again, so I haven't been near marriage since.

"I always had one leg on the movie set and [one] leg at home. . . . If my career *ever* threatened to interfere with my personal life, I'd fix it up instantly. The things that hurt my personal relationships were the things that were most devastating, not the ups and downs of my career. . . . I'd be a far bigger star today if I had concentrated on my career . . . . [My three husbands] all represented chunks of my life and I had put so much into each one of them. I can't tell you the blood that ran out of me with their deaths."

Besides her dog, she has other company, "I'm a great believer in God and His presence and help. I'd never even be here without it." Now living in California again, Joan endured the grief of her brother's death on July 8, 1974. Thereafter she plunged back into acting work. She has made several telefeature appearances, including *The Dead Don't Scream* (1975) with George Hamilton and Ray Milland, *Winner Take All* (1975) with Shirley Jones and Sylvia Sidney; and the misguided *Death at Love House* (1976) in which Joan, Sylvia Sydney, and Dorothy Lamour were wasted. (Of this latter TV movie quickie, the location filming at the Harold Lloyd estate emerged as the only notable item.) Just as Joan had lent her name and presence to *The Phynx* (1970), so she joined the array of

"name" personalities who decorated *Won Ton Ton, the Dog Who Saved Hollywood* (Paramount, 1976). It was a lackluster spoof on the rise of canine star Rin Tin Tin in 1920s Hollywood. Thankfully, Joan was onscreen only momentarily as the landlady in the mini-saga.

In early 1977, when Joan was filming her latest film, *Opening Night,* co-starred with Gena Rowlands, Ben Gazzara, and John Cassavetes (also the writer-director), the still saucy actress admitted, "I've done over ninety movies, but none of them has been like this. You never know where the camera is; Cassavetes follows you around the corner, into the phone booth, under the bed, everywhere. I couldn't tell when the actors were having a private conversation and when they were actually changing the lines of the script. They were always so natural. I must say, it's lovely not having to stick to all the author's ifs, ands, and buts." Ironically, within the film, Blondell interprets the role of a playwright who becomes frantic when a determined actress improvises on her stage dialogue. "The play I've written is on the serious side," says Joan of her onscreen role, "but the girl is putting in her own words and making a comedy out of what is not meant to be funny. And that irks me." "But," she continues, "don't ask me if *Opening Night* is supposed to be a comedy or a drama. I'll have to see it before I can tell."

Regarding her own catalogue of films, Joan admits, "Some of my movies I haven't even seen yet; I figure I'll catch up with them on the late show. Mostly, I remember the movies I did by what was happening *offscreen*—who I was married to, what child I had, which house I was living in. I look back on a movie like *Nightmare Alley* with fondness because of my affection for Ty Power. He was a darling guy. And I got to work with Clark Gable in *Adventure.* You never heard *anyone* say a bad word about Gable. Hell, he was so damned nice to everybody.

"I've worked with such wonderful people. It was fun working with directors like Mervy LeRoy, Tay Garnett, and even crazy Mike

Curtiz. I'm so tickled that Bette Davis . . . [got] that award from the American Film Institute; I just love that feisty gal—she *fought* her way up, a real Miss Gutsy. I miss Glenda Farrell so much; she was one gal I kept close to—she and Joannie Bennett. I do see Ruby Keeler once in a while, and Alice Faye and Patsy Kelly, and occasionally Jim Cagney and I will talk on the phone. You don't keep up all the old friendships, though; there are people you love and there's nothing that's going to shake that love, but that doesn't mean you're roommates."

Of present day Hollywood, the still very earthy, feisty Joan reflects, "*Nobody* ever imagined it'd be a ghost town. It was so beautifully run, by such genuinely capable people. There were silly ones, I admit, but the majority knew their business and protected it."

Facing the realities, Joan looks to television to supply most of her current show business income. (Son Norman recently turned TV film producer. Previously in mid-1975 he was named CBS-TV director, comedy program development. He had joined the network in Hollywood a year prior. Earlier he had created and co-produced "The Bob Crane Show," been executive in charge of "The New Dick Van Dyke Show," and had been associated with Four Star International for twelve years.)

As for her many years in show business, Joan states, "No matter what happens to the world, people want to be taken out of themselves, to be entertained. . . . I take pride in being in a profession that isn't going down the drain."

77

FILMOGRAPHY

THE OFFICE WIFE *(Warner Bros., 1930)* 59 min.

Director, Lloyd Bacon; based on the novel by Faith Baldwin; screenplay, Charles Kenyon; camera, William Rees; editor, George Marsh.

Dorothy Mackaill (Anne Murdock); Lewis Stone (Lawrence Fellows); Hobart Bosworth (Mr. McGowan); Blanche Frederici (Kate Halsey); Joan Blondell (Catherine Murdock); Natalie Moorhead (Linda Fellows); Brooks Benedict (Mr. Jameson); Dale Fuller (Miss Andrews); Walter Merrill (Ted O'Hara).

SINNER'S HOLIDAY *(Warner Bros., 1930)* 55 min.

Director, John Adolfi; based on the play *Penny Arcade* by Marie Baumer; screenplay, Harvey Thew; camera, Ira Morgan; editor, James Gibbon.

Grant Withers (Angel Harrigan); Evalyn Knapp (Jennie); James Cagney (Harry); Lucille La Verne (Ma Delano); Noel Madison (Buck); Otto Hoffman (George); Warren Hymer (Mack); Ray Gallagher (Joe); Joan Blondell (Myrtle); Hank Mann (Happy); Purnell Pratt (Sykes).

ILLICIT *(Warner Bros., 1931)* 81 min.

Director, Archie Mayo; based on the play by Edith Fitzgerald, Robert Riskin; screenplay, Harvey Thew; costumes, Earl Luick; camera, Robert Kurrie; editor, Bill Holmes.

Barbara Stanwyck (Anne Vincent); James Rennie (Dick Ives); Ricardo Cortez (Price Baines); Natalie Moorhead (Margie True); Charles Butterworth (Evans); Joan Blondell (Helen "Duckie" Childers); Claude Gillingwater (Ives Sr.).

MILLIE *(RKO, 1931)* 85 min.

Director, John Francis Dillon; based on the novel by Donald Henderson Clarke; screenplay, Charles Kenyon; dialogue, Kenyon, Ralph Murphy; camera, Ernest Haller.

Helen Twelvetrees (Millie); Robert Ames (Tommy Roche); James Hall (Jack Maitland); Lilyan Tashman (Helen Riley); John Halliday (Jimmy Daimer); Joan Blondell (Angie); Anita Louise (Connie); Edmund Breese (Attorney); Frank McHugh (Holmes); Charlotte Walker (Mrs. Maitland).

MY PAST *(Warner Bros., 1931)* 83 min.

Director, Roy Del Ruth; based on the novel *Ex-Mistress* by Dora Macy; screenplay, Charles Kenyon; camera, Chick McGill; editor, Ralph Dawson.

Bebe Daniels (Doreee Macy); Ben Lyon (Robert Byrne); Lewis Stone (John Thornley); Joan Blondell (Marion Moore); Natalie Moorhead (Consuelo Byrne); Virginia Sale (Lionel Reich); Daisy Belmore (Mrs. Bennett).

GOD'S GIFT TO WOMEN *(Warner Bros., 1931)* 71 min.

Director, Michael Curtiz; based on the play *The Devil Was Sick* by Jane Hinton; screenplay, Joseph Jackson, Raymond Griffith; camera, Robert Kurrie; editor, James Gibbons.

Frank Fay (Jacques Duryea); Laura La Plante (Diane); Joan Blondell (Fifi); Charles Winninger (Mr. Churchill); Arthur Edmund Carewe (Mr. Dumont); Alan Mowbray (Auguste); Louise Brooks (Florine); Tyrrell Davis (Basil); Billy House (Cesare); Yola d'Avril (Dagmar); Margaret Livingston (Tania).

THE PUBLIC ENEMY *(Warner Bros., 1931)* 74 min.

Director, William A. Wellman; based on the story *Beer and Blood* by John Bright; screenplay, Kubec Glasmon, Bright; adaptor/dialogue, Harvey Thew; art director, Max Parker; music director, David Mendoza; costumes, Earl Luick; makeup, Perc Westmore; camera, Dev Jennings; editor, Ed McCormick.

James Cagney (Tom Powers); Jean Harlow (Gwen Allen); Edward Woods (Matt Doyle); Joan Blondell (Mamie); Beryl Mercer (Ma Powers); Donald Cook (Mike Powers); Mae Clarke (Kitty); Mia Marvin (Jane); Leslie Fenton (Nails Nathan); Robert Emmett O'Connor (Paddy Ryan); Murray Kinnell (Putty Nose); Ben Hendricks, Jr. (Bugs Moran); Rita Flynn (Molly Doyle); Clark Burroughs (Dutch); Snitz Edwards (Hack); Frank Coghlan, Jr. (Tommy as a Boy); Frankie Darro (Matt as a Boy); Adele Watson (Mrs. Doyle); Robert E. Homans (Officer Pat Burke); Dorothy Gee (Nails' Girl); Purnell Pratt (Officer Powers); Lee Phelps (Steve, the Bartender); Helen Parrish, Dorothy Gray, Nanci Price (Little Girls); Ben Hendricks, III

(Bugs as a Boy); George Daly (Machine Gunner); Eddie Kane (Joe, the Headwaiter); William Strauss (Pawnbroker); Sam McDaniel (Black Headwaiter); Douglas Gerrard (Assistant Tailor).

British release title: *Enemies of the Public.*

OTHER MEN'S WOMEN *(Warner Bros., 1931)* 70 min.

Director, William A. Wellman; story, Maude Fulton; screenplay, Fulton, William K. Wells; music director, Leo F. Forbstein; makeup, Perc Westmore; camera, Chick McGill; editor, Edward McDermott.

Grant Withers (Bill); Mary Astor (Lily); Regis Toomey (Jack); James Cagney (Ed); Fred Kohler (Haley); J. Farrell MacDonald (Pegleg); Joan Blondell (Marie); Walter Long (Bixby); Bob Perry, Lee Moran, Kewpie Morgan, Pat Hartigan (Railroad Workers).

BIG BUSINESS GIRL *(First National, 1931)* 79 min.

Director, William Seiter; story, Patricia Reilly, Harold N. Swanson; screenplay, Robert Lord; camera, Sol Polito; editor, Peter Frisch.

Loretta Young (Claire McIntyre); Frank Albertson (John Saunders); Ricardo Cortez (Ralph Clayton); Joan Blondell (Pearl); Frank Darion (Luke Winters); Dorothy Christy (Mrs. Emery); Mickey Bennett (Joe); Bobby Gordon (Messenger Boy); Nancy Dover (Sarah Ellen); Virginia Sale (Sally Curtis); Oscar Apfel (Walter Morley).

NIGHT NURSE *(Warner Bros., 1931)* 73 min.

Director, William A. Wellman; based on the novel by Dora Macy; screenplay, Oliver H. P. Garrett; additional dialogue, Charles Kenyon; art director, Max Parker; costumes, Earl Luick; camera, Barney McGill; editor, Edward M. McDermott.

Barbara Stanwyck (Lora Hart); Ben Lyon (Mortie); Joan Blondell (Maloney); Charles Winninger (Dr. Bell); Charlotte Merriam (Mrs. Richey); Edward Nugent (Eagan); Allan Lane (Intern); Blanche Frederici (Mrs. Maxwell); Vera Lewis (Miss Dillon); Ralf Harolde (Dr. Ranger); Clark Cable (Nick); Walter McGrail (Drunk); Betty May (Nurse); Marcia Mae Jones (Nanny Richey); Betty Jane Graham (Desney Richey).

MAKE ME A STAR *(Paramount, 1932)* 83 min.

Director, William Beaudine; based on the book *Merton of the Movies* by Harry Leon Wilson and the play by George S. Kaufman, Marc Connelly; adaptors, Sam Wintz, Walter De Leon, Arthur Kober; sound, Earle Hayman; camera, Allen Siegler; editor, LeRoy Stone.

Stuart Erwin (Merton Gill); Joan Blondell (Flips Montague); ZaSu Pitts (Mrs. Scudder); Ben Turpin (Ben); Charles Sellon (Mr. Gashwiler); Florence Roberts (Mrs. Gashwiler); Helen Jerome Eddy (Tessie Kearns); Arthur Hoyt (Hardy Powell); Dink Templeton (Buck Benson); Ruth Donnelly (The Countess); Sam Hardy (Jeff Baird); Oscar Apfel (Henshaw); Frank Mills (Chuck Collins); Polly Walters (Doris

Randall); Victor Potel, Bobby Vernon, Snub Pollard, Billy Bletcher, Bud Jamison, Nick Thompson (Actors); Tallulah Bankhead, Clive Brook, Maurice Chevalier, Claudette Colbert, Gary Cooper, Phillips Holmes, Fredric March, Jack Oakie, Charles Ruggles, Sylvia Sidney (Guest Stars).

THE RECKLESS HOUR *(First National, 1931)* 70 min.

Director, John Francis Dillon; based on the play *Ambush* by Arthur Richman; screenplay, Florence Ryerson, Robert Lord; camera, James Van Trees; editor, Harold Young.

Dorothy Mackaill (Margaret Nichols); Conrad Nagel (Edward Adams); Joan Blondell (Myrtle Nichols); H. B. Warner (Walter Nichols); Helen Ware (Harriett Nichols); Walter Byron (Allan Crane); Joe Donahue (Harry Gleason); William House (Jennison); Dorothy Peterson (Mrs. Jennison); Ivan Simpson (Stevens); Claude King (Howard Crane); Mae Madison (Rita); Robert Allen (Friend).

BLONDE CRAZY *(Warner Bros., 1931)* 73 min.

Director, Roy Del Ruth; story/screenplay, Kubec Glasmon, John Bright; music director, Leo F. Forbstein; songs, E. A. Swan; Gerald Marks and Buddy Fields; Roy Turk and Fred Ahlert; Sidney Mitchell, Archie Gottler, and George W. Meyer; makeup, Perc Westmore; camera, Sid Hickox; editor, Ralph Dawson.

James Cagney (Bert Harris); Joan Blondell (Ann Roberts); Louis Calhern (Dapper Dan Barker); Noel Francis (Helen Wilson); Guy Kibbee (A. Rupert Johnson, Jr.); Ray Milland (Joe Reynolds); Polly Walters (Peggy); Charles Lane (Four-Eyes, the Desk Clerk); William Burress (Colonel Bellock); Peter Erkelenz (Dutch); Maude Eburne (Mrs. Snyder); Walter Percival (Lee); Nat Pendleton (Hank); Russell Hopton (Jerry); Dick Cramer (Cabbie); Wade Boteler (Detective); Ray Cooke, Edward Morgan (Bellhops); Phil Sleeman (Con Artist).

British release title: *Larceny Lane.*

UNION DEPOT *(First National, 1932)* 75 min.

Director, Alfred E. Green; story, Joe Laurie, Gene Fowler, Douglas Durkin; screenplay, Kenyon Nicholson, Walter De Leon; dialogue, John Bright, Kubec Glasmon; camera, Sol Polito; editor, Jack Killifer.

Douglas Fairbanks, Jr. (Chic); Joan Blondell (Ruth); Guy Kibbee (Scrap Iron); Alan Hale (The Baron); George Rosener (Bernardi); Dickie Moore (Little Boy); Ruth Hall (Welfare Worker); Mae Madison (Waitress); Polly Walters (Mabel); David Landau (Kendall); Lillian Bond (Actress on Train); Frank McHugh (The Drunk); Junior Coghlan (A Ragged Urchin); Dorothy Christy (Society Woman); Adrienne Dore (Saide); Eulalie Jensen (Cafe Proprietress); Virginia Sale (Woman on Platform); George McFarlane (Train Caller); Earle Foxe (Parker); Mary Doran (Daisy); Walter McGrail, Ed Brody (Bits).

THE GREEKS HAD A WORD FOR THEM *(United Artists, 1932)* 79 min.

Director, Lowell Sherman; based on the play *The Greeks Had a Word for It* by Zöe Akins; screenplay, Sidney Howard; gowns, Mlle. Chanel; sound, Frank Maher; camera, George Barnes; editor, Stuart Heisler.

Madge Evans (Polaire); Joan Blondell (Schatze); Ina Claire (Jean Lawrence); David Manners (Dey Emery); Lowell Sherman (Boris Feldman); Phillips Smalley (Justin Emery); Sidney Bracy (The Waiter).

THE CROWD ROARS *(Warner Bros., 1932)* 85 min.

Director, Howard Hawks; story, Seton I. Miller, Hawks; screenplay, Kubec Glasmon, John Bright, Niven Busch; art director, Jack Okey; music director, Leo F. Forbstein; assistant director, Dick Rossen; makeup, Perc Westmore; camera, Sid Hickox; editor, John Stumar.

James Cagney (Joe Greer); Joan Blondell (Anne); Ann Dvorak (Lee); Eric Linden (Eddie Greer); Guy Kibbee (Dad Greer); Frank McHugh (Spud Connors); William Arnold (Bill Arnold); Leo Nomis (Jim); Charlotte Merriam (Mrs. Spud Connors); Regis Toomey (Dick Wilbur); Harry Hartz, Ralph Hepburn, Fred Guisso, Fred Frame, Phil Pardee, Spider Matlock, Jack Brisko, Lou Schneider, Bryan Salspaugh, Stubby Stubblefield, Shorty Cantlon, Mel Keneally, Wilbur Shaw (Drivers); James Burtis (Mechanic); Sam Hayes (Ascot Announcer); Robert McWade (Counterman); Ralph Dunn (Official); John Conte (Announcer); John Harron (Red—Eddie's Pitman).

THE FAMOUS FERGUSON CASE *(First National, 1932)* 70 min.

Director, Lloyd Bacon; based on the story *Circulation* by Granville Moore, Courtney Terrett; screenplay, Terrett, Harvey Thew; camera, Dev Jennings; editor, Howard Bretherton.

Joan Blondell (Maizie Dickson); Tom Brown (Bruce Foster); Adrienne Dore (Tony Martin); Walter Miller (Cedric Works); Leslie Fenton (Perrin); Vivienne Osborne (Mrs. Marcia Ferguson); J. Carroll Naish (Claude Wright); Purnell Pratt (George M. Ferguson); Russell Hopton (Rusty Callahan); Kenneth Thomson (Bob Parks); Grant Mitchell (Martin Collins); Leon Ames (Judd Brooks); Miriam Segar (Mrs. Brooks); Willard Robertson (The Sheriff); George Meeker (Jigger Bolton); Russell Simpson (Craig); Mike Donlin (Photographer); Fred Burton (Bridges); Spencer Charters (Fire Chief).

MISS PINKERTON *(First National, 1932)* 66 min.

Director, Lloyd Bacon; based on the novel by Mary Roberts Rinehart; screenplay, Lillian Hayward, Niven Busch; camera, Barney McGill; editor, Ray Curtiss.

Joan Blondell (Miss Adams [Miss Pinkerton]); George Brent (Inspector Patten); Mae Madison (Nurse); John Wray (Hugo); Ruth Hall (Paula Brent); Allan Lane (Herbert Wynne); C. Henry Gordon (Dr. Stewart); Donald Dillaway (Charles Elliott); Blanche Frederici (Mary); Mary Doran (Florence Lenz); Holmes Herbert (Arthur Glenn); Eulalie Jensen (Miss Gibbons); Treva Lawler, Luana Walters (Other Nurses); Lucien Littlefield (Henderson); Nigel de Brulier (The Coroner).

BIG CITY BLUES *(Warner Bros., 1932)* 65 min.

Director, Mervyn LeRoy; based on the unproduced play *New York Town* by Ward Morehouse; screenplay, Morehouse, Lillie Hayward; art director, Anton Grot; music director, Leo F. Forbstein; camera, James Van Trees; editor, Ray Curtiss.

Joan Blondell (Vida); Eric Linden (Bud Reeves); Inez Courtney (Faun); Evalyn Knapp (Jo-Jo); Guy Kibbee (Hummel); Lyle Talbot (Sully); Gloria Shea (Agnes); Walter Catlett (Gibbony); Jobyna Howland (Serena); Humphrey Bogart (Adkins); Josephine Dunn (Jackie); Grant Mitchell (Station Agent); Thomas Jackson (Quelkin); Ned Sparks (Stackhouse); Sheila Terry (Lorna); Tom Dugan (Red); Betty Gillette (Mabel); Edward McWade (Baggage Master); J. Carrol Naish (Bootlegger); Voice of Dick Powell (Radio Announcer); Clarence Muse (Nightclub Singer); Dennis O'Keefe (Dice Spectator); Herman Bing, Torben Meyer (Waiters); Selmer Jackson (Joe).

THREE ON A MATCH *(First National, 1932)* 63 min.

Associate producer, Samuel Bischoff; director, Mervyn LeRoy; story, Kubec Glasmon, John Bright; screenplay, Lucien Hubbard; art director, Robert Haas; camera, Sol Polito; editor, Ray Curtiss.

Joan Blondell (Mary Keaton); Warren William (Bob Kirkwood); Ann Dvorak (Vivian Revere); Bette Davis (Ruth Westcott); Grant Mitchell (School Principal); Lyle Talbot (Michael Loftus); Sheila Terry (Naomi); Glenda Farrell (Mrs. Black); Clara Blandick (Mrs. Keaton); Buster Phelps (Junior); Humphrey Bogart (The "Mug"); John Marston (Bikerson); Patricia Ellis (Linda); Hale Hamilton (Defense Attorney); Edward Arnold (Ace); Allen Jenkins (Dick); Jack LaRue, Stanley Price (Mugs).

CENTRAL PARK *(First National, 1932)* 57 min.

Director, John Adolfi; story, Ward Morehouse; screenplay, Morehouse, Earl Baldwin; songs, Cliff Hess; camera, Sid Hickox; editor, Bert Levy.

Joan Blondell (Dot); Wallace Ford (Rick); Guy Kibbee (Charley); Henry B. Walthall (Eby); Patricia Ellis (Vivian); Charles Sellon (Luke); Spencer Charters (Sergeant Riley); John Wray (Smiley); Harold Huber (Nick); Holmes Herbert (Chairman of Casino Ball); DeWitt Jennings (Police Lieutenant); Henry Armetta (Tony); Willard Robertson (Captain of Detectives); Harry Holman (Police Captain); William Pawley (Hymie); Wade Boteler (Barney); Edward LeSaint (Police Commissioner); Irving Bacon (Oscar); George Collins (Spud); Lee Shumway (Police Lieutenant); Ted Oliver (Joe, the Cop); Larry Steers (Headwaiter); Dennis O'Keefe (Casino Diner); William Norton Bailey (Hood); Harry Seymour (Hood-Guard); Rolfe Sedan (Casino Patron); Morgan Wallace (Commissioner).

LAWYER MAN *(Warner Bros., 1932)* 72 min.

Director, William Dieterle; based on the novel by Max Treel; screenplay, Rian James, James Seymour; camera, Robert Kurrle.

William Powell (Anton Adam); Joan Blondell (Olga); Helen Vinson (Barbara Bentley); Alan Dinehart (Granville Bentley); Allen Jenkins (Issy Levine); David Landau (Gilmurry); Claire Dodd (Virginia); Sheila Terry (Flo); Kenneth Thomson (Dr. Gresham); Jack LaRue (Spike); Rockliffe Fellows (Kovak); Roscoe Karns (Merritt); Dorothy Christy (Chorus Girl); Ann Brody (Mrs. Levine); Curley Wright (Guiseppi); Edward McWade (Moyle); Tom Kennedy (Jake, the Iceman); Sterling Holloway (Olga's Dining Friend); Vaughn Taylor (Reporter); Wade Boteler (Court Officer); Hooper Atcheley (Anton's Aide); Irving Bacon (Court Guard); Frederick Burton (Judge); Henry Hall (Juryman); Wilfred Lucas (Jury Foreman); Dewey Robinson (Client).

BLONDIE JOHNSON *(First National, 1933)* 67 min.

Director, Ray Enright; story/screenplay, Earl Baldwin; camera, Tony Gaudio; editor, George Weeks.

Joan Blondell (Blondie Johnson); Chester Morris (Curley Jones); Allen Jenkins (Louie); Claire Dodd (Gladys La Mann); Earle Foxe (Scannell); Mae Busch (Mae); Joseph Cawthorn (Jewelry Store Manager); Sterling Holloway (Red Charley); Olin Howland (Eddie); Arthur Vinton (Max Wagner); Donald Kirke (Joe); Tom Kennedy (Hype); Sam Godfrey (Freddie); Toshia Mori (Lulu).

BROADWAY BAD *(Fox, 1933)* 59 min.

Director, Sidney Lanfield; story, William R. Lipman, A. W. Pezet; screenplay, Arthur Kober, Maude Fulton; art director, Gordon Wiles; camera, George Barnes; editor, Paul Weatherwax.

Joan Blondell (Tony Landers); Ricardo Cortez (Craig Cutting); Ginger Rogers (Flip Daly); Adrienne Ames (Aileen); Allen Vincent (Bob North); Phil Tead (Joe Flynn); Francis McDonald (Charley Davis); Spencer Charters (Lew Gordon); Ronald Cosbey (Big Fella); Frederick Burton (Robert North, Jr.); Margaret Seddon (Bixby); Donald Crisp (Darrall); Max Wagner, Harold Goodwin (Reporters); Eddie Kane (Jeweler); John Davidson (Prince); Larry Steers (Business Associate); Matty Roubert, Eddie Berger (Newsboys); Henry Hall (Bailiff).

GOLD DIGGERS OF 1933 *(Warner Bros., 1933)* 96 min.

Director, Mervyn LeRoy; based on the play *Gold Diggers* by Avery Hopwood; adaptors, Erwin Gelsey, James Seymour; dialogue, David Boehm, Ben Markson; art director, Anton Grot; gowns, Orry-Kelly; choreography, Busby Berkeley; songs, Harry Warren and Al Dubin; camera, Sol Polito; editor, George Amy.

Warren William (J. Lawrence Bradford); Joan Blondell (Carol King); Aline MacMahon (Trixie Lorraine); Ruby Keeler (Polly Parker); Dick Powell (Brad Roberts [Robert Treat Bradford]); Guy Kibbee (Faneuil H. Peabody); Ned Sparks (Barney Hopkins); Ginger Rogers (Fay Fortune); Clarence Nordstrom (Gordon); Robert Agnew (Dance Director); Sterling Holloway (Messenger Boy); Tammany Young (Gigolo Eddie); Ferdinand Gottschalk (Clubman); Lynn Browning (Gold Digger Girl); Charles C. Wilson (Deputy); Billy Barty ("Pettin' in the Park" Baby); Fred "Snowflake" Toones, Theresa Harris (Black Couple); Joan Barclay (Chorus Girl); Wallace MacDonald (Stage Manager); Charles Lane, Wilbur Mack, Grace Hayle (Society Reporters); Hobart Cavanaugh (Dog Salesman); Bill Elliott (Dance Extra); Dennis O'Keefe (Extra during Intermission); Busby Berkeley (Call Boy); Fred Kelsey (Detective Jones); Frank Mills (First Forgotten Man); Etta Moten ("Forgotten Man" Singer); Billy West (Medal of Honor Winner).

GOODBYE AGAIN *(First National, 1933)* 65 min.

Director, Michael Curtiz; story, George Haight, Allan Scott; screenplay, Ben Markson; camera, George Barnes; editor, Thomas Pratt.

Warren William (Kenneth Bixby); Joan Blondell (Anne); Genevieve Tobin (Julie Wilson); Helen Chandler (Elizabeth); Ruth Donnelly (Maid); Wallace Ford (Arthur Westlake); Hugh Herbert (Harvey Wilson); Hobart Cavanaugh (Clayton); Jay Ward (Theodore); Ray Cooke (Bellboy).

FOOTLIGHT PARADE *(Warner Bros., 1933)* 102 min.

Producer, Darryl F. Zanuck; director, Lloyd Bacon; screenplay, Manuel Seff, James Seymour; dances staged by Busby Berkeley; songs, Harry Warren and Al Dubin; music director, Leo F. Forbstein; dialogue director, William Keighley; art director, Anton Grot; costumes, Milo Anderson; makeup, Perc Westmore; camera, George Barnes; editor, George Amy.

James Cagney (Chester Kent); Joan Blondell (Nan Prescott); Ruby Keeler (Bea Thorn); Dick Powell (Scotty Blair); Guy Kibbee (Silas Gould); Ruth Donnelly (Harriet Bowers Gould); Claire Dodd (Vivian Rich); Hugh Herbert (Charlie Bowers); Frank McHugh (Francis); Arthur Hohl (Al Frazer); Gordon Westcott (Harry Thompson); Renee Whitney (Cynthia Kent); Philip Faversham (Joe Farrington); Juliet Ware (Miss Smythe); Herman Bing (Fralick, the Music Director); Paul Porcasi (George Appolinaris); William Granger (Doorman); Charles C. Wilson (Cop); Barbara Rogers (Gracie); Billy Taft (Specialty Dancer); Marjean Rogers, Pat Wing, Donna La Barr, Marlo Dwyer, Donna Mae Roberts (Chorus Girls); Dave O'Brien (Chorus Boy); George Chandler (Drugstore Attendant); Hobart Cavanaugh (Title Thinker Upper); William V. Mong (Auditor); Lee Moran (Mac, the Dance Director); Billy

Barty (Mouse in "Sittin' on a Backyard Fence" Number/Little Boy in "Honeymoon Hotel" Number); Harry Seymour (Desk Clerk in "Honeymoon Hotel" Number); Sam McDaniel (Porter); Fred Kelsey (Hotel Detective); Jimmy Conlin (Uncle); Roger Gray (Sailor-Pal in "Shanghai Lil" Number); John Garfield (Sailor behind Table in "Shanghai Lil" Number); Duke York (Sailor on Table in "Shanghai Lil" Number).

HAVANA WIDOWS (First National, 1933) 67 min.

Director, Ray Enright; story, Earl Baldwin; dialogue, Stanley Logan; camera, George Barnes; editor, Clarence Kolster.

Joan Blondell (Mae Knight); Glenda Farrell (Sadie Appleby); Guy Kibbee (Deacon Jones); Lyle Talbot (Bob Jones); Allen Jenkins (Herman Brody); Frank McHugh (Duffy); Ruth Donnelly (Mrs. Jones); Ralph Ince (Butch O'Neill); Maude Eburne (Mrs. Ryan); George Cooper (Mullins); Charles Wilson (Timberg); Garry Owen (Wheelman).

CONVENTION CITY (First National, 1933) 69 min.

Director, Archie Mayo; story, Peter Milne; adaptor, Robert Lord; camera, William Reese; editor, Owen Marks.

Joan Blondell (Nancy Lorraine); Adolphe Menjou (T. R. Kent); Dick Powell (Jerry Ford); Mary Astor (Arlene Dale); Guy Kibbee (George Ellerbe); Frank McHugh (Will Goodwin); Patricia Ellis (Claire Honeywell); Ruth Donnelly (Mrs. Ellerbe); Hugh Herbert (Hotstetter); Hobart Cavanaugh (Orchard); Grant Mitchell (J. B. Honeywell); Gordon Westcott (Phil Lorraine); Johnny Arthur (Tavia); Huey White (Bootlegger).

I'VE GOT YOUR NUMBER (Warner Bros., 1934) 68 min.

Director, Ray Enright; story, William Rankin; screenplay, Warren Duff, Sidney Sutherland; camera, Arthur Todd; editor, Clarence Kolster.

Joan Blondell (Maria Lawson); Pat O'Brien (Terry); Glenda Farrell (Bonnie); Allen Jenkins (John); Eugene Pallette (Flood); Gordon Westcott (Nicky); Henry O'Neill (Mr. Schuyler); Hobart Cavanaugh (Dooley); Renee Whitney (Loretta); Robert Ellis (Turk); Louise Beavers (Crystal); Milton Kibbee (Dispatcher); Bess Flowers (Miss Banks); Tom Costello (Ed); Selmer Jackson (Joe).

SMARTY (Warner Bros., 1934) 64 min.

Director, Robert Florey; story, F. Hugh Herbert; screenplay, Herbert and Carl Erickson; art director, John Hughes; gowns, Orry-Kelly; music director, Leo F. Forbstein; dialogue director, Frank McDonald; camera, George Barnes; editor, Jack Killifer.

Joan Blondell (Vicki Wallace Thorpe); Warren William (Tony Wallace); Edward Everett Horton (Vernon Thorpe); Frank McHugh (George Lancaster); Claire Dodd (Anita); Joan Wheeler (Bonnie); Virginia Sale

(Edna); Leonard Carey (Tilford); Dennis O'Keefe (Dancing Extra); Lester Dorr (Court Recorder); Bert Moorhouse (Clerk); Frederick Burton (Judge); Camille Rovelle (Mrs. Crosby); Frank Darien (Court Spectator); Sarah Edwards (Mrs. Crosby's Mother); Lester Dorr (Court Recorder).

HE WAS HER MAN (Warner Bros., 1934) 70 min.

Director, Lloyd Bacon; story, Robert Lord; screenplay, Tom Buckingham, Niven Busch; art director, Anton Grot; music director, Leo F. Forbstein; song, Sidney Mitchell and Lew Pollack; costumes, Orry-Kelly; camera, George Barnes; editor, George Amy.

James Cagney (Flicker Hayes); Joan Blondell (Rose Lawrence); Victor Jory (Nick Gardella); Frank Craven (Pop Sims); Harold Huber (J. C. Ward); Russell Hopton (Monk); Ralf Harolde (Red Deering); Sarah Padden (Mrs. Gardella); John Qualen (Dutch); Bradley Page (Dan Curly); Samuel S. Hinds (Gassy); George Chandler (Waiter); James Eagles (Whitey); Gino Corrado (Fisherman); Willard Robertson (Police Captain); Sidney Bracy (Waiter); Lee Shumway (Detective); Billy West (Chick); Samuel E. Hines (Desk Clerk); Dennis O'Keefe (Reporter).

DAMES (Warner Bros., 1934) 90 min.

Producer, Darryl F. Zanuck; director, Ray Enright; story, Robert Lord, Delmer Daves; adapted screenplay, Daves; dances staged by Busby Berkeley; art directors, Robert Haas, Willy Pogany; music director, Leo F. Forbstein; songs, Harry Warren and Al Dubin; costumes, Orry-Kelly; camera, Sid Hickox, George Barnes; editor, Harold McLernon.

Joan Blondell (Mabel Anderson); Dick Powell (Jimmy Higgens); Ruby Keeler (Barbara Hemingway); ZaSu Pitts (Mathilda Hemingway); Hugh Herbert (Ezra Ounce); Arthur Vinton (Bulger); Sammy Fain (Buttercup Baumer); Phil Regan (Johnny Harris); Arthur Aylesworth (Conductor); Leila Bennett (Laura, the Maid); Berton Churchill (H. Elsworthy Todd); Patricia Harper, Ruth Eddings, De Don Blunier, Gloria Faythe, Diana Douglas (Chorus Girls); Lester Dorr (Elevator Starter); Eddy Chandler (Guard); Harry Holman (Spanish War Veteran); Fred "Snowflake" Toones (Porter); Frank Darien (Druggist); Eddie Kane (Harry, the Stage Manager); Charlie Williams (Dance Director).

KANSAS CITY PRINCESS (Warner Bros., 1934) 64 min.

Director, William Keighley; story, Sy Bartlett; screenplay, Manuel Seff, Bartlett; camera, George Barnes; editor, William Clemens.

Joan Blondell (Rosy); Glenda Farrell (Marie); Robert Armstrong (Dynamite); Hugh Herbert (Junior Ashcraft); Osgood Perkins (Marcel Duryea); Hobart Cavanaugh (Sam Waller); Gordon Westcott (Jimmy, the Dude); Ivan Lebedeff (Dr. Sascha Pilnikoff); T. Roy Barnes (Jim Cameron); Renee Whitney (Mrs. Ashcraft); Arthur Hoyt (Greenway); Eddie Shubert (Shooting Gallery Proprietor); Arthur Housman (Salesman); Harry Seymour (Waiter); Edward Keane (Captain); Lorena Layson (Cashier); Jack Wise (Soda Clerk); Lillian Harmer (Scout Mistress); Maxine Doyle (Dumb Girl); Henry Otho (Policeman); Jack Richardson (Porter); Alphonse Martell (Officer); Andre Cheron, Leo White (French Stewards); Edith Baker (Saleslady); John Binnet (French Clerk).

TRAVELING SALESLADY (First National, 1935) 64 min.

Producer, Sam Bischoff; director, Ray Enright; story, Frank Howard Clark; screenplay, F. Hugh Herbert, Manuel Seff, Benny Rubin; camera, George Barnes; editor, Owen Marks.

Joan Blondell (Angela Twitchell); William Gargan (Pat O'Connor); Glenda Farrell (Claudette Ruggles); Hugh Herbert (Elmer Niles); Grant Mitchell (Rufus K. Twitchell); Ruth Donnelly (Millicent Twitchell); Al Shean (Schmidt); Johnny Arthur (Melton); Mary Treen (Miss Wells); Bert Roach (Harry); Joseph Crehan (Murdock); James Donlan (McNeill); Harry Holman (O'Connor); Carroll Nye (Burroughs); Selmer Jackson (Scovil); Gordon "Bill" Elliott (Freddie); Milton Kibbee (Stenographer); Frances Lee (Secretary); Bill May (Announcer); Hattie McDaniel (Black Woman); Harry Seymour (Buyer); Olive Jones (Miss Henry); Gertrude Sutton (Secretary); Ferdinand Schumann-Heink (Clerk).

BROADWAY GONDOLIER (Warner Bros., 1935) 98 min.

Director, Lloyd Bacon; story, Sig Herzig, Hans Kraly, E. Y. Harburg; screenplay, Herzig, Warren Duff, Jerry Wald, Julius J. Epstein; songs, Al Dubin and Harry Warren; camera, George Barnes; editor, George Amy.

Dick Powell (Dick Purcell); Joan Blondell (Alice Hughes); Adolphe Menjou (Professor Eduardo de Vinci); Louise Fazenda (Mrs. Flagenheim); William Gargan (Cliff Stanley); George Barbier (Hayward); Grant Mitchell (E. V. Richards); Hobart Cavanaugh (Gilmore); Joe Sawyer (Red, the Cabby); Rafael Storm (Ramon); Bob Murphy (Singing Cop); James Burke (Uncle Andy); Don Turner (Cabby); June Travis (Hatcheck Girl); Ted Fiorito and his Band, Four Mills Brothers (Themselves); Judy Canova (Annie); Zeke Canova (Pete, the Hillbilly); Sam Ash (Singer); Leo F. Forbstein (Orchestra Leader); Milton Kibbee (Cabby); Mary Treen (Mother); Leo White (Listener); Rolfe Sedan (Mrs. Flagenheim's Secretary); Gino Corrado (Venetian Merchant); Georges Renavent (Dancing Extra—Venice); Jack Norton, Emmett Vogan, William Elliott, George Chandler (Reporters); Selmer Jackson (Announcer).

WE'RE IN THE MONEY (Warner Bros., 1935) 65 min.

Director, Raymond Enright; story, George R. Bison;

screenplay, F. Hugh Herbert, Brown Holmes, Edwin Gelsey; music director, Leo F. Forbstein; songs, Allie Wrubel and Mort Dix; camera, Arthur Todd; editor, Owen Marks.

Joan Blondell (Ginger Stewart); Glenda Farrell (Dixie Tilton); Ross Alexander (C. Richard Courtney); Hugh Herbert (Homer Bronson); Henry O'Neill (Stephen Dinsmoor); Hobart Cavanaugh (Max); Anita Kerry (Claire LeClaire); Phil Regan (Phil Ryan); Lionel Stander (Butch); Man Mountain Dean (Himself); Edward Gargan (O'Rourke); Joseph King (Mr. Blank); E. E. Clive (Jevons); Myron Cox (Chief Pontiac); Virginia Sale (Maid); Sam McDaniel (Attendant); Gene Morgan (Band Leader); Frank Moran, John Kelly (Mugs); Joseph Crehan, Mayo Methot (Bits); Walter Brennan (Wedding Witness); Al Hill (Bodyguard); Billy Wayne (Process Server); Frank Marlowe (Sailor); Edwin Mordant (Judge); Harlan Briggs (Justice of the Peace).

MISS PACIFIC FLEET (Warner Bros., 1935) 66 min.

Producer, Earl Baldwin; director, Ray Enright; story, Frederick Hazlitt Brennan; screenplay, Lucille Newmark, Peter Milne; camera, Arthur Todd; editor, Clarence Kolster.

Joan Blondell (Gloria Fay); Glenda Farrell (Mae O'Brien); Allen Jenkins (Kewpie Wiggins); Hugh Herbert (Mr. Freitag); Minna Gombell (Sadie Freitag); Eddie Acuff (Clarence); Marie Wilson (Virgie Matthews); Guinn "Big Boy" Williams (Nick); Anita Kerry (Annie); Mary Green (Violet); Marie Astaire, Lucille Collins (Girls); Eddy Chandler (Chief Petty Officer); Paul Irving (Mr. Winch); Mary Doran (Miss LaMay); Sam Rice (Proprietor); Ben Hendricks (Cop); Paul Fix, James Burtis (Sailors); Louis Natheaux, Nick Copeland, Joe Bordeaux (Mugs); Harrison Greene (Jackson); Douglas Fowley (Second); Allen Wood (Hay); Emmett Vogan, Harry Seymour (Announcers); Jack Norton (Radio Official); Tom Manning (Judge); Stuart Homes (Conductor); Claude Peyton (Caretaker).

COLLEEN (Warner Bros., 1936) 89 min.

Director, Alfred E. Green; story, Robert Lord; screenplay, Peter Milne, Hugh Herbert, Sig Herzig; production numbers staged by Bobby Connolly; art director, Max Parker; music director, Leo F. Forbstein; songs, Harry Warren and Al Dubin; gowns, Orry-Kelly; camera, George Barnes; editor, Byron Haskin.

Dick Powell (Donald Ames); Ruby Keeler (Colleen Riley); Jack Oakie (Joe Cork); Joan Blondell (Minnie Mawkins); Hugh Herbert (Cedric Ames); Louise Fazenda (Alicia Ames); Paul Draper (Paul); Luis Alberni (Carlo); Marie Wilson (Mabel); Mary Treen (Miss Hively); Hobart Cavanaugh (Noggin); Berton Churchill (Logan); J. M. Kerrigan (Pop Riley); Spencer Charters (Dr. Frothingham); Addison Richards (Schuyler); Charles Coleman (Butler); Colleen Colman (Lois); Herbert Evans (Footman); Viola Lowry (Receptionist); Emmett Vogan (Official); Cyril Ring (Client);

Harry Depp (Assistant); Shirley Lloyd (Girl); Bob Murphy, Ward Bond (Cops); Alma Lloyd (Nurse); Sarah Edwards, Laura Pierpont (Society Women); John Albright (Page Boy); Alphonse Martel (Head Waiter); Andre Cheron (Waiter); Iris March (Miss Graham); Edward Keane (Edwards); George Andre Beranger (Jeweler); Pauline Caron (Maid); Antonio Filauri (Bartender); Charles E. Delaney (Ship's Radio Operator); Joan Barclay (Cafe Guest).

SONS O' GUNS (Warner Bros., 1936) 82 min.

Producer, Harry Joe Brown; director, Lloyd Bacon; story, Fred Thompson, Jack Donahue; screenplay, Jerry Wald, Julius J. Epstein; music director, Leo F. Forbstein; songs, Harry Warren and Al Dubin; musical numbers staged by Bobby Connolly; camera, Sol Polito; editor, James Gibbons.

Joe E. Brown (Jimmy Canfield); Joan Blondell (Yvonne); Beverly Roberts (Mary Harper); Winifred Shaw (Bernice Pearce); Eric Blore (Hobson); G. P. Huntley, Jr. (Lieutenant Archibald Pensonby-Falcke); Joseph King (Colonel Harper); David Worth (Arthur Travers); Craig Reynolds (Lieutenant Burton); Robert Barrat (Pierre); Michael Mark (Carl); Frank Mitchell, Bert Roach, Hans Joby (German Prisoners); Mischa Auer, Otto Fries (German Spies); Max Wagner, Don Turner, Leo Sulky, Bill Dagwell (Soldiers); James Eagles (Young Soldier); Milton Kibbee, Allen Matthews (Military Policemen); Robert A'Dair, Olaf Hytten (Sentries); Pat Flaherty, Sol Gorss, Henry Otho (Apaches).

BULLETS OR BALLOTS (First National, 1936) 81 min.

Associate producer, Louis F. Edelman; director, William Keighley; story, Martin Mooney, Seton I. Miller; screenplay, Miller; music, Heinz Roemheld; assistant director, Chuck Hansen; art director, Carl Jules Weyl; sound, Oliver S. Garretson; special effects, Fred Jackman, Fred Jackman, Jr., Warren E. Lynch; camera, Hal Mohr; editor, Jack Killifer.

Edward G. Robinson (Johnny Blake); Joan Blondell (Lee Morgan); Barton MacLane (Al Kruger); Humphrey Bogart (Nick "Bugs" Fenner); Frank McHugh (Herman); Joseph King (Captain Dan McLaren); Richard Purcell (Driscoll); George E. Stone (Wires); Joseph Crehan (Grand Jury Spokesman); Henry O'Neill (Bryant); Henry Kolker (Hollister); Gilbert Emery (Thorndyke); Herbert Rawlinson (Caldwell); Louise Beavers (Nellie); Norman Willis (Vinci); William Pawley (Crail); Ralph Remley (Kelly); Frank Faylen (Gatley); Gordon "Bill" Elliott, Anne Nagel (Bank Secretaries); Jack Goodrich (Cigar Clerk); Howard Mitchell (Police Official); Saul Gorss (Young Man); Ben Hendricks, Eddy Chandler, Ralph Dunn, Hal Craig (Policemen); Harrison Greene (Man at Counter); Alma Lloyd, Frances Morris (Beauty Attendants); Guy Kingsford (Hotel Clerk).

STAGE STRUCK (First National, 1936) 91 min.

Director, Busby Berkeley; story, Robert Lord; screenplay, Tom Buckingham, Pat C. Flick; songs, E. Y. Harburg and Harold Arlen; music director, Leo F. Forbstein; camera, Byron Haskin; editor, Tom Richards.

Dick Powell (George Randall); Joan Blondell (Peggy Revere); Warren William (Harris); Jean Madden (Ruth Williams); Frank McHugh (Sid); Carol Hughes (Grace Randall); Hobart Cavanaugh (Wayne); Spring Byington (Mrs. Randall); Johnny Arthur (Oscar Freud); Craig Reynolds (Gilmore Frost); Andrew Tombes (Burns Haywood); Lulu McConnell (Toots O'Connor); Ed Gargan (Riordan); Eddy Chandler (Heney); Thomas Pogue (Dr. Stanley); Libby Taylor (Yvonne); George Offerman, Jr. (Wilbur); Irene Coleman (Brunette); Henry Martin (Chauffeur); Herbert Ashley (Bartender); George Riley (Drunk); Leo White (Waiter); Mary Treen (Clerk); Kathrin Clare Ward (Landlady); Iris Adrian (Miss DeRue); Rosalind Marquis (Miss LaHenc); Jane Wyman (Bessie Funfnick); Val and Ernie Stanton (Marley & Cooper); John Alexander (Red Cap); Mary Gordon (Mrs. Cassidy); Glen Cavender, Walter Clyde (Stagehands); Baldy Belmont (Doorman); Sarah Edwards (Spinster School Teacher at Aquarium).

THREE MEN ON A HORSE (First National, 1936) 88 min.

Director, Mervyn LeRoy; based on the play by John Cecil Holm, George Abbott; screenplay, Laird Doyle; camera, Sol Polito; editor, Ralph Dawson.

Frank McHugh (Erwin Trowbridge); Joan Blondell (Mabel); Carol Hughes (Audrey Trowbridge); Allen Jenkins (Charley); Guy Kibbee (Mr. Carver); Sam Levene (Patsy); Teddy Hart (Frankie); Edgar Kennedy (Harry); Paul Harvey (Clarence Dobbins); Margaret Irving (Gloria); George Chandler (Al); Harry Davenport (William); Eddie Anderson (Moses); Virginia Sale (Chamber Maid); Charles Lane (Cleaner); Mickey Daniels (Delivery Boy); Cliff Saum (Bus Conductor); Harry Hayden (Man on Bus); Tola Nesmith (Head Nurse); Eily Malyon (Nurse); Edith Craig, Irene Colman (Women Bettors); John Sheehan, Pat West (Male Bettors); Ted Bliss (Radio Announcer).

GOLD DIGGERS OF 1937 (First National, 1936) 100 min.

Producer, Hal B. Wallis; associate producer, Earl Baldwin; director, Lloyd Bacon; story, Richard Maibuam, Michael Wallach, George Haight; screenplay, Warren Duff; music director, Leo F. Forbstein; songs, Harry Warren and Al Dubin; Harold Arlen and E. Y. Harburg; dance numbers staged by Busby Berkeley; camera, Arthur Edeson; editor, Thomas Richards.

Dick Powell (Rosmer Peek); Joan Blondell (Norma Parry); Glenda Farrell (Genevieve Larkin); Victor Moore (J. J. Hobart); Lee Dixon (Boop Oglethorpe); Osgood Perkins (Morty Wethered); Charles D. Brown

(John Huge); Rosalind Marquis (Sally); Irene Ware (Irene); William Davidson (Andy Callahan); Joseph Crehan (Chairman at Insurance Convention); Susan Fleming (Lucille Bailey); Charles Halton (Dr. Warshoff); Olin Howland (Dr. McDuffy); Paul Irving (Dr. Henry); Harry Bradley (Dr. Bell); Fred "Snowflake" Toones (Snowflake); Pat West (Drunken Salesman); Iris Adrian (Verna); Cliff Saum (Conductor); Jane Wyman, Irene Coleman, Shirley Lloyd, Betty Mauk, Naomi Judge, Betty McIvor, Sheila Bromley, Lois Lindsay, Marjorie Weaver, Lucille Keeling, Virginia Dabney, Jane Marshall (Girls); Wedgwood Nowell (Penfield); Tom Ricketts (Reginald); Bobby Jarvis (Stage Manager); Myrtle Stedman, Jacqueline Saunders (Nurses); Gordon Hart (White).

THE KING AND THE CHORUS GIRL (Warner Bros., 1937) 94 min.

Producer/director, Mervyn LeRoy; story/screenplay, Norman Krasna, Groucho Marx; music director, Leo F. Forbstein; songs, Werner Richard Heymann and Ted Koehler; dances staged by Bobby Connolly; camera, Tony Gaudio; editor, Thomas Richards.

Fernand Gravet (Alfred); Joan Blondell (Dorothy); Edward Everett Horton (Count Humber); Alan Mowbray (Don Ald); Mary Nash (Duchess Anne); Jane Wyman (Babette); Luis Alberni (Gaston); Kenny Baker (Singer); Shaw and Lee (Specialty); Ben Welden (Waiter); Adrian Resley (Concierge); Lionel Pape (Professor Kornish); Leonard Mudie (Footman); Ferdinand Schumann-Heink (Chauffeur); Torben Meyer (Eric); Armand Kaliz (Theatre Manager); Georgette Rhodes (Hatcheck Girl); George Sorel, Alphonse Martel (Servants); Sam Ash, Lee Kohlmar (Violinists); Carlos San Martin (Policeman); Gaston Glass (Junior Officer); Jacques Lory (Waiter); Robert Graves (Captain of Ocean Liner); Adele St. Maur (Stewardess); Georges Renavent (Yacht Captain).

BACK IN CIRCULATION (Warner Bros., 1937) 82 min.

Producer, Hal B. Wallis; associate producer, Sam Bischoff; director, Ray Enright; story, Adela Rogers St. John; screenplay, Warren Duff; art director, Hugh Reticker; music director, Leo F. Forbstein; camera, Arthur Todd; editor, Clarence Kolster.

Pat O'Brien (Bill Morgan); Joan Blondell (Timothea Blake); Margaret Lindsay (Arlene Wade); John Litel (Dr. Forde); Eddie Acuff (Murphy); Regis Toomey (Buck); George E. Stone (I. R. Daniels); Craig Reynolds (Si Rothwell); Ben Welden (Sam Sherman); Walter Byron (Carleton Whitney); Granville Bates (Dr. Evans); Herbert Rawlinson (Stephen A. Saunders); Raymond Brown (Bottsford); Anderson Lawler (Butch Jason); Frank Faylen (James Maxwell); William Hopper (Pete Edington); Milton Kibbee (Pink Thomas); Edward Price (Sid Roark); Veda Ann Borg (Gertrude); Howard Hickman (Judge); Willard Parker (Ben); Spencer Charters (Sheriff); Loia Cheaney (Enid); Robert Darrell (Assistant Dispatcher); Emmett Vogan (Chief Dispatcher); Eddy Chandler (Chief Officer); Patsy "Babe" Kane (Switchboard Operator); Zelda Bennett, Myrtle Stedman (Women); Tom Brower (Foreman); Davison Clark (Court Clerk).

THE PERFECT SPECIMEN (First National, 1937) 97 min.

Executive producer, Hal B. Wallis; associate producer, Harry Joe Brown; director, Michael Curtiz; based on the story by Samuel Hopkins Adams; screenplay, Norman Reilly Raine, Lawrence Riley, Brewster Morse, Fritz Falkenstein; music, Heinz Roemheld; assistant director, Frank Heath; dialogue director, Gene Lewis; art director, Robert Haas; gowns, Howard Shoup; sound, Everett A. Brown; special effects, Byron Haskin; camera, Charles Rosher; editor, Terry Morse.

Errol Flynn (Gerald Beresford); Joan Blondell (Mona Carter); Hugh Herbert (Killigrew Shaw); Edward Everett Horton (Mr. Grattan); Dick Foran (Jink Carter); Beverly Roberts (Alicia); May Robson (Mrs. Leona Wicks); Allen Jenkins (Pinky); Dennie Moore (Clarabelle); Hugh O'Connell (Hotel Clerk); James Burke (Snodgrass); Granville Bates (Hooker); Harry Davenport (Carl Carter); Tim Henning (Briggs); Spencer Charters (Station Master); Lee Phelps (Head of State Patrol); Al Herman (Copy Reader); James Burtis, Hal Craig (Cops); Wilfred Lucas (Deputy Sheriff); Tom Brewer (Sheriff); Larry McGrath (John Phillips); Cliff Saum, Jack Kenney (Spectators); Frank Mayo, Harry Hollingsworth (Detectives); Evelyn Mulhall (Sarah).

STAND-IN (United Artists, 1937) 90 min.

Producer, Walter Wanger; director, Tay Garnett; based on the serialized story by Clarence Budington Kelland; screenplay Gene Towne, Graham Baker; music, Heinz Roemheld; assistant director, Charles Kerr; art directors, Alexander Toluboff, Wade Rubottom; costumes, Helen Taylor; sound, Paul Neal; camera, Charles Clarke; editors, Otho Lovering, Dorothy Spencer.

Leslie Howard (Atterbury Dodd); Joan Blondell (Lester Plum); Humphrey Bogart (Douglas Quintain); Alan Mowbray (Koslofski); Marla Shelton (Thelma Cheri); C. Henry Gordon (Ivor Nassau); Jack Carson (Potts); Tully Marshall (Pennypacker, Sr.); J. C. Nugent (Pennypacker, Jr.); William V. Mong (Pennypacker).

THERE'S ALWAYS A WOMAN (Columbia, 1938) 82 min.

Producer, William Perlberg; director, Alexander Hall; story, Wilson Collison; (uncredited) screen treatment, Joel Sayre, Philip Rapp; screenplay, Gladys Lehman, (uncredited) Morrie Ryskind; art directors, Stephen Goosson, Lionel Banks; music director, Morris Stoloff; gowns, Kalloch; camera, Henry Freulich; editor, Viola Lawrence.

Joan Blondell (Sally Reardon); Melvyn Douglas

(William Reardon); Mary Astor (Lola Fraser); Frances Drake (Anne Calhoun); Jerome Cowan (Nick Shane); Robert Paige (Jerry Marlowe); Thurston Hall (District Attorney); Pierre Watkin (Mr. Ketterling); Walter Kingsford (Grigson); Lester Matthews (Walter Fraser); Rita Hayworth (Ketterling's Secretary); Wade Boteler (Sam, the Radio Car Driver); Arthur Loft (Radio Patrolman); William H. Strauss (Rent Collector); Marek Windheim (Head Waiter); Bud Jamison (Jim, the Bartender); George Davis (Waiter); Robert Emmett Keane (*Dispatch* City Editor); John Gallaudet (Reporter); Eddie Fetherston (Photographer); Josef De Stefani (Cigar Stand Clerk); Ted Oliver (Cop); Gene Morgan (Officer Fogarty); Tom Dugan (Detective Flannigan); Bud Geary (D. A. Assistant); Billy Benedict (Bellhop); Lee Phelps (Police Broadcaster); Eddie Dunn, George McKay (Cops).

OFF THE RECORD (Warner Bros., 1939) 62 min.

Director, James Flood; story, Saul Elkins, Sally Sandlin; screenplay, Niven Busch, Lawrence Kimble, Earl Baldwin; camera, Charles Rosher; editor, Thomas Richards.

Pat O'Brien (Thomas "Breezy" Elliott); Joan Blondell (Jane Morgan); Bobby Jordan (Mickey Fallon); Alan Baxter (Joe Fallon); William Davidson (Scotty); Morgan Conway (Lou Baronette); Clay Clement (Jaeggers); Selmer Jackson (Detective Mendall); Addison Richards (Brand); Pierre Watkin (Barton); Joe King (Brown); Douglas Wood (J. W.); Armand Kaliz (Chateau); Sarah Padden (Mrs. Fallon); Howard Hickman (Doctor); Mary Gordon (Mrs. Finnegan); Lottie Williams (Woman); David Durand (Blackie); Norman Phillips, Jr. (Nick); Tommy Bupp (Boy); Wade Boteler (Deputy); Sibyl Harris (Woman); Stanley Fields (Big Bruiser); Emmett Vogan (Priest); Al Hill, Jr. (Kid); Frank Coghlan, Jr. (Copy Boy); William Gould (Swede Captain); Emory Parnell (Policeman); Guy Usher (Inspector); Barbara Pepper (Flossie, the Telephone Operator); Charles Seel (Veterinary).

EAST SIDE OF HEAVEN (Universal, 1939) 90 min.

Associate producer, Herbert Polesie; director, David Butler; story, Butler, Polesie; screenplay, William Conselman; art director, Jack Otterson; music director, Charles Previn; orchestrators, Frank Skinner, John Scott Trotter; songs, Johnny Burke and James V. Monaco; camera, George Robinson; editor, Irene Morra.

Bing Crosby (Danny); Joan Blondell (Mary); Mischa Auer (Nicky); Irene Hervey (Mona); Jerome Cowan (Claudius De Wolfe); Robert Kent (Cyrus Barrett, Jr.); C. Aubrey Smith (Barrett, Sr.); Jackie Gerlich (Bobbie); Douglas Wood (Fisher); Arthur Hoyt (Loftus); Brandon Hurst (Butler); Sandra Lee Henville (Baby Sandy); Raymond Parker (Messenger); Jack Powell (Happy Jack Powell); Jane Jones, Rose Valyda, Helen Warner (Trio); J. Farrell MacDonald, (Doorman); Russell Hicks (Winkle); Chester Clute (Phil); Phyllis Kennedy (Mamie); Clarence Wilson

(Telegraph Operator); Joe King (Detective); Dorothy Christy (Mrs. Henry Smith); Wade Boteler (Detective); Jane Goude (Landlady); Emory Parnell (Doorman); Leyleh Tyler (Woman); Edward Earle (Mr. Henry Smith); Frank Coglan, Jr. (Messenger Boy); Harry Depp, Lloyd Ingraham (Executives); Lillian West (Nurse); Frank Moran (Workman); Billy Wayne (Garage Man).

THE KID FROM KOKOMO (Warner Bros., 1939) 95 min.

Director, Lewis Seiler; story, Dalton Trumbo; screenplay, Jerry Wald, Richard Macaulay; camera, Sid Hickox; editor, Jack Killifer.

Pat O'Brien (Bill Murphy); Wayne Morris (Homer Baston); Joan Blondell (Doris Harvey); Jane Wyman (Miss Bronson); May Robson (Ma "Maggie" Martin); Maxie Rosenbloom (Curly Bender); Ed Brophy (Eddie Black); Stanley Fields ("Muscles"); Sidney Toler (Judge Bronson); Winifred Harris (Mrs. Bronson); Morgan Conway (Louie); John Ridgely (Sam); Frank Mayo (Durb); Al Hill (Lippy); Clem Bevans (Jim); Ward Bond (Klewicke); Olin Howland (Stan); Paul Hurst, Tom Wilson, Frank Hagney, Bob Perry (Old Men); Reid Kilpatrick, John Harron (Radio Announcers); Cliff Saum (Boy); Frederick Clark (Black Butler); Nat Carr (Court Clerk); Jack Mower (Hotel Clerk); Dick Wessel (Mug).

GOOD GIRLS GO TO PARIS (Columbia, 1939) 75 min.

Producer, William Perlberg; director, Alexander Hall; story, Lenore Coffee, William Joyce Cowen; screenplay, Gladys Lehman, Ken Englund; art director, Lionel Banks; music director, Morris W. Stoloff; camera, Henry Freulich; editor, Al Clark.

Melvyn Douglas (Ronnie); Joan Blondell (Jenny); Walter Connolly (Olaf); Alan Curtis (Tom); Joan Perry (Sylvia); Isabel Jeans (Caroline); Stanley Brown (Ted); Alexander D'Arcy (Paul); Mary Field (Ada); George McKay (Chauffeur); John Maurice Sullivan (Minister); Walter Sande (Ticket Agent); Jack Daley (Train Conductor); Catherine Courtney, Jane Loffbourrow (Old Maids); Ray Turner (Red Cap); George Lloyd (Schultz); Leon Belasco (Violinist).

THE AMAZING MR. WILLIAMS (Columbia, 1939) 80 min.

Producer, Everett Riskin; director, Alexander Hall; story, Sy Bartlett; screenplay, Dwight Taylor, Bartlett, Richard Maibaum; art director, Lionel Banks; music director, Morris W. Stoloff; camera, Arthur Todd; editor, Viola Lawrence.

Melvyn Douglas (Kenny Williams); Joan Blondell (Maxine Carroll); Clarence Kolb (Captain McGovern); Ruth Donnelly (Effie); Edward S. Brophy (Buck Moseby); Donald MacBride (Lieutenant Bixler); Don Beddoe (Deever); Jonathan Hale (Mayor); John Wray (Stanley); Robert Middlemass (Police Commissioner);

Maurice Cass (Little Man); Barbara Pepper (Muriel); Luis Alberni (Rinaldo); Peggy Shannon (Kitty); Richard Lane (Reagan); Maude Eburne (Landlady); Ralph Peters (Tobacco Store Proprietor); Walter Miller (Browning); William Hall (Jamieson); William Forrest (Anderson); Sidney D'Albrook (Fat Pedestrian); John Locke (Shop Keeper); Tommy Mullins, Wyndham Standing, Frank Jaquet, Robert Dudley (Men); Stanley Brown, Robert Sterling (Elevator Boys); William Newell, Herbert Clifton (Waiters).

TWO GIRLS ON BROADWAY (MGM, 1940) 71 min.

Producer, Jack Cummings; director, S. Sylvan Simon; story, Edmund Goulding; screenplay, Joseph Fields, Jerome Chodorov; songs, Gus Kahn and Walter Donaldson; Arthur Freed, Nacio Herb Brown, and Roger Edens; Bob Wright, Chet Forrest, and Walter Donaldson; Ted Fetter and Jimmy McHugh; camera, George Folsey; editor, Blanche Sewell.

Lana Turner (Pat Mahoney); Joan Blondell (Molly Mahoney); George Murphy (Eddie Karns); Kent Taylor (Chat Chatsworth); Richard Lane (Buddy Baker); Wallace Ford (Joe Marlowe); Otto Hahn (Ito); Chester Clute (Salesman); Lloyd Corrigan (Judge); Don Wilson (Announcer); George Meader (McChesney); May McAvoy (Secretary); Charles Wagenheim, Cyril Ring (Assistants); Adrienne d'Ambricourt (Miss Apricots); Arthur O'Connell, Lester Dorr, J. Anthony Hughes, Harry Lash (Reporters); Jimmy Conlin (Poem Vendor); Jessie Arnold (Secretary); Ed Peil, Sr. (Man); George Lollier (Chauffeur); Lee Murray (Newsboy); Maxine Conrad (Chorus Girl); Daisy Bufford (Maid); Jack Gardner (Messenger Boy); Hillary Brooke, Carole Wayne (Girls).

British release title: *Choose Your Partner*.

I WANT A DIVORCE (Paramount, 1940) 75 min.

Producer, George Arthur; director, Ralph Murphy; story, Adela Rogers St. John; screenplay, Frank Butler; art directors, Hans Dreier, Ernst Fegte; camera, Ted Tetzlaff; editor, LeRoy Stone.

Joan Blondell (Geraldine "Jerry" Brokaw); Dick Powell (Alan MacNally); Gloria Dickson (Wanda Holland); Frank Fay (Jeff Gilman); Jessie Ralph (Grandma Brokaw); Harry Davenport (Grandpa Brokaw); Conrad Nagel (David Holland, Sr.); Mickey Kuhn (David Holland, Jr.); Dorothy Burgess ("Peppy" Gilman); Sidney Blackmer (Erskine Brandon); Louise Beavers (Celestine); George Huntley (Michael); Brandon Tynan (Judge); Herbert Rawlinson (Lan Howard); Natalie Moorhead (Mrs. Tyrell); George Meader (Murietta); Charles McAvoy (Captain of Detectives); Roscoe Ates (Process Server); Elizabeth Valentine (Maid); Byron Foulger (Secretary); Edward Earle, Ed Stanley (Ministers); Frank Austin (Taxi Driver); Isabel Withers (Secretary); Frank Wayne (Bailiff); Fred "Snowflake" Toones (Porter); Paco Moreno (Peppy's Father); Eva Puig (Peppy's Mother); Archie Twitchell, Frances

Morris (Couple); Ruth Cherrington (Dowager); John Kelly (Marine).

TOPPER RETURNS (United Artists, 1941) 85 min.

Producer, Hal Roach; director, Roy Del Ruth; based on the characters created by Thorne Smith; screenplay, Jonathan Latimer, Gordon Douglas; camera, Norbert Brodine; editor, James Newcom.

Joan Blondell (Gail Richards); Roland Young (Cosmo Topper); Carole Landis (Ann Carrington); Billie Burke (Mrs. Topper); Dennis O'Keefe (Bob); Patsy Kelly (Maid); H. B. Warner (Mr. Carrington); Eddie "Rochester" Anderson (Chauffeur); George Zucco (Dr. Jeris); Donald MacBride (Sergeant Roberts); Rafaela Ottiano (Lillian); Trevor Bardette (Rama).

MODEL WIFE (Universal, 1941) 78 min.

Producer/director, Leigh Jason; screenplay, Charles Kaufman, Horace Jackson, Grant Garrett; camera, Norbert Brodine; editor, Arthur Hilton.

Dick Powell (Fred Chambers); Joan Blondell (Joan Keating Chambers); Ruth Donnelly (Mrs. Everett); Charles Ruggles (Mr. Milo Everett); Lucile Watson (J. J. Benson); Lee Bowman (Ralph Benson); Kathryn Adams (Salesgirl); John Qualen (Janitor); Frank Faylen (Master of Ceremonies); Dale Winter (Anna); Mary Kelley (Miss Kendall); Ferdinand Munier (Mr. Howard); George Chandler (Joe); Henry Roquemore (Perry); Vera Lewis (Mrs. Leahy); Gloria Blondell (Gloria); Grace Stafford (Miss Manahan); Virginia Carroll, Catherine Lewis (Salesgirls); Jack Gwynne (Prestidigitator); Charles Sherlock, Mervin Williams (Players); Tom Seidel (Stage Door Johnnie); Irene Colman (Miss Smith); Ray Cooke (Mailman); Dick Wessel (Laundry Man); Mary Carr (Servant).

THREE GIRLS ABOUT TOWN (Columbia, 1941)

Producer, Samuel Bischoff; director, Leigh Jason; screenplay, Richard Carroll; art director, Lionel Banks; music director, Morris W. Stoloff; camera, Franz F. Planer; editor, Charles Nelson.

Joan Blondell (Hope Banner); Robert Benchley (Wilburforse Paddle); John Howard (Tommy Hopkins); Binnie Barnes (Faith Banner); Janet Blair (Charity Banner); Hugh O'Connell (Chief of Police); Paul Harvey (Fred Chambers); Frank McGlynn (Josephus Wiegal); Eric Blore (Charlemagne); Una O'Connor (Maggie O'Callahan); Almira Sessions (Tessie Conarchy); Dorothy Vaughan (Mrs. McDougall); Walter Soderling (Charlie); Ben Taggart (Doorman); Chester Clute, Eddie Laughton, Dick Elliott (Magicians); Charles Lane (Mortician); Bess Flowers (Mortician's Wife); Minna Phillips (Martha); Alec Craig (Samuel); Larry Parks, Ray Walker, Bruce Bennett, Lloyd Bridges, John Tyrrell, Lester Dorr (Reporters); William Newell (Laundry Man); George Hickman (Bellhop); Arthur Aylesworth, Arthur Loft, Harrison Greene (Poker Players); Vera Lewis, Jessie Arnold, Sarah Edwards, Barbara Brown (Club Women).

LADY FOR A NIGHT (*Republic, 1941*) 87 min.

Producer, Herbert J. Yates; associate producer, Albert J. Cohen; director, Leigh Jason; screenplay, Isabel Dawn, Boyce DeGaw; art director, John Victor Mackay; music, David Buttolph; music director, Cy Feuer; camera, Norbert Brodine; editor, Ernest Nims.

Joan Blondell (Jenny Blake); John Wayne (Jack Morgan); Ray Middleton (Alan Alderson); Blanche Yurka (Julia Alderson); Edith Barrett (Katherine Alderson); Leonid Kinsky (Boris); Philip Merivale (Stephen Alderson); Hattie Noel (Chloe); Dorothy Burgess (Flo); Patricia Knox (Mabel); Montagu Love (Judge); Lew Payton (Napoleon); Guy Usher (Governor); Margaret Armstrong (Governor's Wife); Ivan Miller (Mayor); Carmel Myers (Mayor's Wife); Betty Hill (Governor's Daughter); Marilyn Hare (Young Girl); Corinne Valdez (Can-Can Dancer); Pierre Watkin (Prosecutor); Jac George (Orchestra Leader); Gertrude Astor (Woman); Minerva Urecal (Spinster); Dudley Dickerson, Paul White (Black Specialty Dancers); Dolores Gray (Dolores); Dewey Robinson (Horse Dealer); Hall Johnson Choir (Choir).

CRY HAVOC (*MGM, 1943*) 97 min.

Producer, Edwin Knopf; director, Richard Thorpe; based on the play by Allan R. Kenward; screenplay, Paul Osborne; art directors, Cedric Gibbons, Stephen Goosson; set decorators, Edwin B. Willis, Glen Barner; music, Daniele Amfitheatrof; assistant director, Rollie Asher; sound, Frank B. MacKenzie; camera, Karl Freund; editor, Ralph E. Winters.

Margaret Sullavan (Lieutenant Smith); Ann Sothern (Pat); Joan Blondell (Grace); Fay Bainter (Captain Marsh); Marsha Hunt (Flo Norris); Ella Raines (Connie); Frances Gifford (Helen); Diana Lewis (Nydia); Heather Angel (Andra); Dorothy Morris (Sue); Connie Gilchrist (Sadie); Gloria Grafton (Steve); Fely Franquelli (Luisita).

A TREE GROWS IN BROOKLYN (*Twentieth Century-Fox, 1945*) 128 min.

Producer, Louis D. Lighton; director, Elia Kazan; based on the novel by Betty Smith; screenplay, Tess Slesinger, Frank Davis; music, Alfred Newman; orchestrator, Edward Powell; assistant director, Saul Wurtzel; art director, Lyle Wheeler; set decorators, Thomas Little, Frank E. Hughes; sound, Bernard Freericks; special effects, Fred Sersen; camera, Leon Shamroy; editor, Dorothy Spencer.

Dorothy McGuire (Katie); Joan Blondell (Aunt Sissy); James Dunn (Johnny Nolan); Lloyd Nolan (McShane); Peggy Ann Garner (Francie Nolan); Ted Donaldson (Neeley Nolan); James Gleason (McGarrity); Ruth Nelson (Miss McDonough); John Alexander (Steve); B. S. Pully (Christmas Tree Vendor); Ferike Boros (Grandma Rommely); Charles Halton (Mr. Barker); J. Farrell MacDonald (Carney, the Junk Man); Adeline DeWalt Reynolds (Mrs. Waters); George Melford (Mr. Spencer); Mae Marsh, Edna

Jackson (Tynmore Sisters); Alec Craig (Warner); Virginia Brissac (Miss Pilford); Art Smith (Ice Man); Francis Pierlot (Priest); Harry Seymour (Floorwalker); Walt Robbins (Junk Man); Joyce Tucker (Girl); Robert Tait (Street Singer); Nick Ray (Bakery Clerk); Patricia McFadden (Sheila); Robert Malcolm (Doctor).

DON JUAN QUILLIGAN (*Twentieth Century-Fox, 1945*) 75 min.

Producer, William LeBaron; director, Frank Tuttle; story, Herbert Clyde Lewis; screenplay, Arthur Kober, Frank Gabrielson; art directors, Lyle Wheeler, Ben Hayne; set decorators, Thomas Little, Frank E. Hughes; music, David Raskin; music director, Emil Newman; orchestrator, Maurice de Packh; assistant director, Tom Dudley; sound, Alfred Bruzlin; special camera effects, Fred Sersen; camera, Norbert Brodine; editor, Norman Colbert.

William Bendix (Patrick Quilligan); Joan Blondell (Marjorie Mossrock); Phil Silvers (MacDenny); Anne Revere (Mrs. Rostigaff); B. S. Pully (Ed Mossrock); Mary Treen (Lucy); John Russell (Howie Mossrock); Veda Ann Borg (Beattle); Thurston Hall (Judge); Cara Williams (Salesgirl); Richard Gaines (Defense Attorney); Hobart Cavanaugh (Mr. Rostigaff); Renee Carson (Annie Mossrock); George Macready (District Attorney); Helen Freeman (Mrs. Blake); Charles Cane (Artie); Anthony Caruso (One-Eyed Fagen); Eddie Acuff (Customer); Joel Friedkin (Judge); Charles Marsh (Court Clerk); Emmett Vogan (Minister); James Flavin (Police Sergeant); Genevieve Bell (Dowager); Byron Foulger, Frank Johnson (Men); Brick Sullivan (Detective).

ADVENTURE (*MGM, 1945*) 126 min.

Producer, Sam Zimbalist; director, Victor Fleming; based on the novel *The Strange Adventure* by Clyde Brian Davis; screenplay, Frederick Hazlitt Brennan, Vincent Lawrence; adaptors, Anthony Veiller, William H. Wright; art directors, Cedric Gibbons, Urie McCleary; set decorator, Edwin B. Willis; music, Herbert Stothart; orchestrator, Murray Cutter; assistant director, Marvin Stuart; sound, Douglas Shearer; special effects, Warren Newcombe; camera, Joseph Ruttenberg; editor, Frank Sullivan.

Clark Gable (Harry Patterson); Greer Garson (Emily Sears); Joan Blondell (Helen Melohn); Thomas Mitchell (Mudgin); Tom Tully (Gus); John Qualen (Model T); Richard Haydn (Limo); Lina Romay (Maria); Philip Merivale (Old Ramon); Harry Davenport (Dr. Ashlon); Tito Renaldo (Young Ramon); Pedro De Cordoba (Felipe); Chef Joseph Milani (Rudolfo); Martin Garralaga (Nick, the Bartender); Dorothy Granger (Cashier); Elizabeth Russell, Barbara Billingsley, Rebel Randall, Sue Moore (Dames); Esther Howard (Blister); Florence Auer (Landlady); Eddie Hart (Milkman); Lee Phelps (Bartender); Morris Ankrum (Mr. Ludlow); Dorothy Vaughan (Mrs. Ludlow); Martha Wentworth (Woman); Byron Foulger (Rico); Audrey Totter (Littleton); Rex Ingram (Black Preacher); Kay Medford (Red); Stanley Andrews (Officer); Bess Flowers (Modiste); Tom Kingston (Chip Man); Sayre Dearing (Roulette Man); Claire McDowell (Bit in Library).

THE CORPSE CAME C.O.D. (Columbia, 1947) 87 min.

Producer, Samuel Bischoff; director, Henry Levin; based on the novel by Jimmy Starr; screenplay, George Bricker, Dwight Babcock; art directors, Stephen Goosson, George Brooks; set decorators, Wilbur Menefee, James Crowe; music, George Duning; music director, Morris Stoloff; songs, Allan Roberts and Doris Fisher; assistant director, Carl Hiecke; sound, Jack Haynes; montage, Donald W. Starling; camera, Lucien Andriot; editor, Jerome Thoms.

George Brent (Joe Medford); Joan Blondell (Rosemary Durant); Adele Jergens (Mona Harrison); Jim Bannon (Detective Mark Wilson); Leslie Brooks (Peggy Holmes); John Berkes (Larry Massey); Fred Sears (Detective Dave Short); William Trenk (Fields); Grant Mitchell (Mitchell Edwards); Una O'Connor (Nora); Marvin Miller (Rudy Frasso); William Forrest (Lance Fowler); Mary Field (Felice); Cliff Clark (Emmett Willard); Wilton Graff (Maxwell Kenyon); Cosmo Sardo (Hector Rose); Judy Stevens (Specialty Singer); Lane Chandler (Prison Guard); Robert Kellard, Myron Healey, Paul Bryar, Michael Towne (Reporters); Martha West (Cigarette Girl).

NIGHTMARE ALLEY (Twentieth Century-Fox, 1947) 111 min.

Producer, George Jessel; director, Edmund Goulding; based on the novel by William Lindsay Gresham; screenplay, Jules Furthman; art directors, Lyle Wheeler, J. Russell Spencer; set decorators, Thomas Little, Stuart Reiss; music, Cyril Mockridge; orchestrator, Earle Hagen; music director, Lionel Newman; assistant director, Gaston Glass; sound, E. Clayton Ward, Roger Heman; special effects, Fred Sersen; camera, Lee Garmes; editor, Barbara McLean.

Tyrone Power (Stan Carlisle); Joan Blondell (Zeena); Coleen Gray (Molly); Helen Walker (Lilith Ritter); Taylor Holmes (Ezra Grindle); Mike Mazurki (Bruno); Ian Keith (Pete); Julia Dean (Mrs. Peabody); James Flavin (Hoatley); Roy Roberts (McGraw); James Burke (Town Marshal); Maurice Navarro (Fire-Eater); Leo Gray (Detective); Harry Hays Morgan (Headwaiter); Albin Robeling (Captain); George Beranger (Geek); Marjorie Wood (Mrs. Prescott); Harry Chesire (Mr. Prescott); Edward Clark (Farmer); Eddy Waller (Old Farmer); Mike Lally (Charlie); George Davis (Waiter); Hollis Jewell (Delivery Boy); Laura Treadwell (Woman); Nina Gilbert (Woman); Bill Free (Man in Spode Room); Henry Hall (Man); John Wald (Radio Announcer); Oliver Blake, George Chandler, Emmett Lynn, Jack Raymond, George Lloyd (Hobos).

CHRISTMAS EVE (United Artists, 1947) 90 min.

Producer, Benedict Bogeaus; director, Edwin L. Marin; stories, Laurence Stallings, Richard H. Landau; screenplay, Stallings; art director, Ernst Fegte; set decorator, Eugene Redd; music, Heinz Roemheld; music director, David Chudnow; assistant director, Joseph Depew; sound, William Lynch; camera, Gordon Avil; editor, James Smith.

George Raft (Mario Torio); George Brent (Michael Brooks); Randolph Scott (Jonathan); Joan Blondell (Ann Nelson); Virginia Field (Claire); Dolores Moran (Jean); Ann Harding (Matilda Reid); Reginald Denny (Phillip Hastings); Carl Harbord (Dr. Doremus); Clarence Kolb (Judge Alston); John Litel (FBI Agent); Joe Sawyer (Gimlet); Douglass Dumbrille (Dr. Bunyan); Dennis Hoey (Williams); Molly Lamont (Harriett); Walter Sande (Hood); Konstantin Shayne (Reichman); Claire Whitney (Dr. Bunyan's Wife); Andrew Tombes (Auctioneer); Soledad Jimenez (Rosita); Marie Blake (Girl Reporter); Ernest Hilliard (Assistant Bartender); Al Hill (Bartender); John Indrisano (Gateman).

Reissue title: Sinners' Holiday.

FOR HEAVEN'S SAKE (Twentieth Century-Fox, 1950) 92 min.

Producer, William Perlberg; director, George Seaton; based on the stories May We Come In? and Windy by Harry Segall, Dorothy Segall; screenplay, Seaton; art directors, Lyle Wheeler, Richard Irvine; music, Alfred Newman; camera, Lloyd Ahern; editor, Robert Simpson.

Clifton Webb (Charles); Joan Bennett (Lydia); Robert Cummings (Jeff Bolton); Edmund Gwenn (Arthur); Joan Blondell (Daphne); Gigi Perreau (Item); Jack La-Rue (Tony); Harry Von Zell (Tex); Tommy Rettig (Joe); Dick Ryan (Michael); Charles Lane (Tax Agent); Robert Kent (Joe's Father); Whit Bissell, Ashmead Scott (Doctors); Dorothy Neumann (Western Union Woman); Perc Launders (Doorman); Albert Pollett, Sid Fields (Waiters); Jack Daly, Bob Harlow, Richard Thorne (Bits).

THE BLUE VEIL (RKO, 1951) 113 min.

Producers, Jerry Wald, Norman Krasna; director, Curtis Bernhardt; based on the story by Francois Campaux; screenplay, Norman Corwin; art directors, Albert S. D'Agostino, Carroll Clark; music director, C. Bakaleinikoff; camera, Franz Planer; editor, George J. Amy.

Jane Wyman (Louise Mason); Charles Laughton (Fred K. Begley); Joan Blondell (Annie Rawlins); Richard Carlson (Gerald Kean); Agnes Moorehead (Mrs. Palfrey); Don Taylor (Dr. Robert Palfrey); Audrey Totter (Helen Williams); Cyril Cusack (Frank Hutchins); Everett Sloane (District Attorney); Natalie Wood (Stephanie Rawlins); Vivian Vance (Alicia); Carleton Young (Mr. Palfrey); Alan Napier (Professor Carter); Warner Anderson (Bill); Les Tremayne (Joplin); Dan Seymour (Pelt); Dan O'Herlihy (Hugh Williams);

Henry "Harry" Morgan (Charles Hall); Gary Jackson (Robert Palfrey as a Boy); Gregory Marshall (Harrison Palfrey); Dee Pollack (Tony); Miles Shepard (Guard); Ann Moore (Sarah); Jane Liddell (Denis' Wife); Richard Norris (Denis); Torben Meyer (Photographer); Lillian Albertson (Mrs. Lipscott); Lewis Martin (Archbishop); Jim Hawkins (Tommy); Sammy Shack (Cabbie); Sylvia Simms (Miss Quimby); Joy Hallward (Miss Golub).

THE OPPOSITE SEX (MGM, 1956) C-117 min.

Producer, Joseph Pasternak; director, David Miller; based on the play *The Women* by Clare Boothe; screenplay, Fay and Michael Kanin; art directors, Cedric Gibbons, Daniel B. Cathcart; music supervisor, George Stoll; music, Nicholas Brodszky; songs, Brodszky and Sammy Cahn; orchestrators, Albert Sendrey, Skip Martin; choreography and dance numbers staged by Robert Sidney; costumes, Helen Rose; assistant director, George Rheim; camera, Robert Bronner; editor, John McSweeney, Jr.

June Allyson (Kay); Joan Collins (Crystal); Dolores Gray (Sylvia); Ann Sheridan (Amanda); Ann Miller (Gloria); Leslie Nielsen (Steve Hilliard); Jeff Richards (Buck Winston); Agnes Moorehead (Countess); Charlotte Greenwood (Lucy); Joan Blondell (Edith); Sam Levene (Mike Pearl); Bill Goodwin (Howard Fowler); Alice Pearce (Olga); Barbara Jo Allen [Vera Vague] (Dolly); Sandy Descher (Debbie); Carolyn Jones (Pat); Jerry Antes (Leading Male Dancer); Alan Marshal (Ted); Jonathan Hale (Phelps Potter); Harry James, Art Mooney (Themselves); Dick Shawn (Singer); Jim Backus (Psychiatrist); Celia Lovsky (Lutsi); Harry McKenna (Hughie); Janet Lake (Girl on Train); Jo Gilbert (Woman Attendant); Don Dillaway (Box Office Man); Dean Jones (Assistant Stage Manager); Joe Karnes (Pianist); Barrie Chase, Ellen Ray (Specialty Dancers); Juanita Moore (Maid); Vivian Marshall (Girl).

LIZZIE (MGM, 1957) 81 min.

Producer, Jerry Bresler; associate producer, Edward Lewis; director, Hugo Haas; based on the novel *The Bird's Nest* by Shirley Jackson; screenplay Mel Dinelli; art director, Rudi Feld; music/music director, Leith Stevens; assistant director, Leon Chooluck; wardrobe, Norman Martien, Sabine Manela; songs, Hal David and Burt Bacharach; camera, Paul Ivano; editor, Leon Barsha.

Eleanor Parker (Elizabeth Richmond); Richard Boone (Dr. Neal Wright); Joan Blondell (Aunt Morgan); Hugo Haas (Walter Brenner); Ric Roman (Johnny Valenzo); Dorothy Arnold (Elizabeth's Mother); John Reach (Robin); Marion Ross (Ruth Seaton); Johnny Mathis (Nightclub Singer); Jan Englund (Helen Jameson); Carol Wells (Elizabeth at Age Thirteen); Karen Green (Elizabeth at Age Nine); Gene Walker (Guard); Pat Gordon (Man in Bar); Dick Paxton (Waiter); Michael Mark (Bartender).

THIS COULD BE THE NIGHT (MGM, 1957) 103 min.

Producer, Joe Pasternak; director, Robert Wise; based on the short stories by Cordelia Baird Gross; screenplay, Isobel Lennart; choreography, Jack Baker; assistant director, Ridgeway Callow; music supervisor, George Stoll; orchestrators, Billy May, Skip Martin, Robert Van Eps, Don Simpson; camera, Russell Harlan; editor, George Roemler.

Jean Simmons (Anne Leeds); Paul Douglas (Rocco); Anthony Franciosa (Tony Armotti); Julie Wilson (Ivy Corlane); Neile Adams (Patsy St. Clair); Joan Blondell (Crystal); J. Carroll Naish (Leon); Rafael Campos (Hussein Mohammed); ZaSu Pitts (Mrs. Shea); Tom Helmore (Steve Devlin); Murvyn Vye (Waxie London); Vaughn Taylor (Ziggy Dawlt); Frank Ferguson (Mr. Shea); William Ogden (Bruce Cameron); James Todd (Mr. Hallerby); Ray Anthony and His Orchestra (Themselves); John Harding (Eduardo); Percy Helton (Charlie); Richard Collier (Homer); Edna Holland (Teacher); Betty Uitti (Sexy Girl); Lew Smith (Waiter); June Blair (Chorus Girl); Harry Hines, Gregg Martell, Matty Fain (Guests); Archie Savage, Andrew Robinson, Walter Davis (Archie Savage Trio).

DESK SET (Twentieth Century-Fox, 1957) C-103 min.

Producer, Henry Ephron; director, Walter Lang; based on the play *The Desk Set* by William Marchant; screenplay, Phoebe and Henry Ephron; art directors, Lyle Wheeler, Maurice Randsford; set decorators, Walter M. Scott, Paul S. Fox; assistant director, Hal Herman; music, Cyril J. Mockridge; music director, Lionel Newman; orchestrator, Edward B. Powell; costumes, Charles LeMaire; makeup, Ben Nye; sound, E. Clayton Ward, Mary M. Leonard; special camera effects, Ray Kellogg; camera; Leon Shamroy; editor, Robert Simpson.

Spencer Tracy (Richard Sumner); Katharine Hepburn (Bunny Watson); Gig Young (Mike Cutler); Joan Blondell (Peg Costello); Dina Merrill (Sylvia); Sue Randall (Ruthie); Neva Patterson (Miss Warringer); Harry Ellerbe (Smithers); Nicholas Joy (Azae); Diane Jergens (Alice); Merry Anders (Cathy); Ida Moore (Old Lady); Rachel Stephens (Receptionist); Sammy Ogg (Kenny); King Mojave, Charles Heard, Harry Evans, Hal Taggart, Jack M. Lee, Bill Duray (Board Members); Dick Gardner (Fred); Renny McEvoy (Man); Jesslyn Fax (Mrs. Hewitt); Shirley Mitchell (Myra Smithers).

British release title: *His Other Woman*.

WILL SUCCESS SPOIL ROCK HUNTER? (Twentieth Century-Fox, 1957) C-94 min.

Producer/director, Frank Tashlin; based on the play by George Axelrod; screenplay, Tashlin; art directors, Lyle Wheeler, Leland Fuller; music, Cyril J. Mockridge; song, Bobby Troup; music director, Lionel Newman; orchestrator, Edward B. Powell; wardrobe designer, Charles Le Maire; assistant director, Joseph E. Rickards; special camera effects, L. B. Abbott; camera, Joe MacDonald; editor, Hugh S. Fowler.

Jayne Mansfield (Rita Marlowe); Tony Randall (Rock Hunter), Betsy Drake (Jenny); Joan Blondell (Violet); John Williams (Le Salle, Jr.); Henry Jones (Rufus); Lili Gentle (April); Mickey Hargitay (Bobo); Georgia Carr (Calypso Number); Groucho Marx (Surprise Guest); Dick Whittinghill (TV Interviewer); Ann McCrea (Gladys); Lida Piazza (Jr.'s Secretary); Bob Adler, Phil Chambers (Mailmen); Larry Kerr (Mr. Ezzarus); Sherrill Terry (Annie); Mack Williams (Hotel Doorman); Patrick Powell (Receptionist); Carmen Nisbit (Breakfast Food Demonstrator); Richard Deems (Razor Demonstrator); Don Corey (Voice of Ed Sullivan); Benny Rubin (Theatre Manager); Minta Durfee, Edith Russell (Scrub Women).

ANGEL BABY (Allied Artists, 1961) 97 min.

Producer, Thomas F. Woods; associate producer, Francis Schwartz; director, Paul Wendkos; based on the novel *Jenny Angel* by Elsie Oaks Barber; screenplay, Orin Borsten, Paul Mason, Samuel Roeca; music/ music director, Wayne Snaklin; orchestrator, Henry Beau; art director, Val Tamelin; set designer, Sid Clifford; costumes, Marjorie Corso; makeup, Stanley E. Campbell, Guy Del Russo; assistant director, Leonard Kazman; sound, Al Overton, Kay Ross; camera, Haskell Wexler, Jack Marta; editor, Betty J. Lane.

Salome Jens (Jenny Brooks [Angel Baby]); George Hamilton (Paul Strand); Mercedes McCambridge (Sarah Strand); Joan Blondell (Mollie Hays); Henry Jones (Ben Hays); Burt Reynolds (Hoke Adams); Roger Clark (Sam Wilcox); Dudley Remus (Otis Finch); Victoria Adams (Ma Brooks); Eddie Firestone ("Blind" Man); Barbara Biggart (Farm Girl); Davy Biladeau (Little Boy); Harry Swoger (Big Cripple).

ADVANCE TO THE REAR (MGM, 1964) 97 min.

Producer, Ted Richmond; director, George Marshall; suggested by the story *The Company of Cowards* by William Chamberlain; screen story, Jack Schaefer; screenplay, Samuel A. Peeples, William Bowers; art directors, George W. Davis, Eddie Imazu; set decorators, Henry Grace, Budd S. Friend; makeup, William Tuttle; assistant director, William McGarry; music, Randy Sparks; music adaptor/conductor, Hugo Montenegro; sound, Franklin Milton; special camera effects, J. McMillan Johnson; camera, Milton Krasner; editor, Archie Marshek.

Glenn Ford (Jared Heath); Stella Stevens (Mary Lou Williams); Melvyn Douglas (Colonel Brackenby); Jim Backus (General Willoughby); Joan Blondell (Easy Jenny); Andrew Prine (Private Selous); Jesse Pearson (Corporal Geary); Alan Hale (Sergeant Davis); James Griffith (Hugo Zattig); Yvonne Craig (Ora); Whit Bissell (Captain Queeg); Michael Pate (Thin Elk); Chuck Roberson (Monk); Frank Mitchell (Fulton); Preston Foster (General Bateman); Harlan Warde (Major Hayward); Linda Jones (Junie); Paul Langton (Major For-

sythe); Barnaby Hale (Lieutenant); Ken Wales (Lieutenant Aide); Peter Ford (Townsman); Gregg Palmer (Gambler).

British release title: *Company of Cowards.*

THE CINCINNATI KID (MGM, 1965) C-113 min.

Producer, Martin Ransohoff; associate producer, John Calley; director, Norman Jewison; based on the novel by Richard Jessup; screenplay, Ring Lardner, Jr., Terry Southern; assistant director, Kurt Neumann; art directors, George W. Davis, Edward Carfagno; set decorators, Henry Grace, Hugh Hunt; music, Lalo Schifrin; camera, Philip H. Lathrop; editor, Hal Ashby.

Steve McQueen (The Cincinnati Kid); Edward G. Robinson (Lancey Howard); Ann-Margret (Melba); Karl Malden (Shooter); Tuesday Weld (Christian); Joan Blondell (Lady Fingers); Rip Torn (Slade); Jack Weston (Pig); Cab Calloway (Yeller); Jeff Corey (Hoban); Theo Marcuse (Felix); Milton Selzer (Sokal); Karl Swenson (Mr. Rudd); Emile Genest (Cajun); Ron Soble (Danny); Irene Tedrow (Mrs. Rudd); Midge Ware (Mrs. Slade); Dub Taylor (Dealer); Joyce Perry (Hoban's Wife); Claude Hall (Gambler); Olan Soule (Desk Clerk); Barry O'Hara (Eddie); Bill Zuckert, Pat McCaffrie, John Hart, Sandy Kevin (Poker Players); Robert Do Qui (Philly); Hal Taggert (Bettor); Andy Albin (Referee).

RIDE BEYOND VENGEANCE (Columbia, 1966) C-100 min.

Producer, Andrew J. Fenady; director, Bernard McEveety; based on the novel *The Night of the Tiger* by Al Dewlen; screenplay, Fenady; music, Richard Markowitz; song, Markowitz and Fenady; art director, Stan Jolley; set decorator, William Calvert; makeup, Fred B. Phillips; assistant director, Lee H. Katzin; sound, Terry Kellum, Joel Moss; special effects, Lee Varque; camera, Lester Shorr; editor, Otho Lovering.

Chuck Connors (Jonas Trapp); Michael Rennie (Brooks Durham); Kathryn Hays (Jessie); Joan Blondell (Mrs. Lavender); Gloria Grahame (Bonnie Shelley); Gary Merrill (Dub Stokes); Bill Bixby (Johnsy Boy Hood); Claude Akins (Elwood Coates); Paul Fix (Hanley); Marrisa Mathes (Maria); Harry Harvey, Sr. (Vogan); William Bryant (Bartender); Jamie Farr (Pete); Larry Domasin (Mexican Boy); William Catching (Drunk); *Prologue Characters:* James MacArthur (Census Taker); Arthur O'Connell (Narrator); Ruth Warrick (Aunt Gussie); Buddy Baer (Mr. Kratz); Frank Gorshin (Tod Wisdom); Robert Q. Lewis (Hotel Clerk).

WATERHOLE NO. 3 (Paramount, 1967) C-95 min.

Executive producer, Owen Crump; producer, Joseph Steck; director, William Graham; screenplay, Steck, Robert R. Young; music, Dave Grusin; song, Grusin and Robert Wells; art director, Fernando Carrere; set decorators, Reg Allen, Jack Stevens; costumes, Jack Bear; assistant directors, Daniel J. McCauley, Mickey

McCardle; sound, Joseph Edmondson; camera, Robert Burks; editor, Warren Low.

James Coburn (Lewton Cole); Carroll O'Connor (Sheriff John Copperud); Margaret Blye (Billee Copperud); Claude Akins (Sergeant Henry Foggers); Timothy Carey (Hilb); Bruce Dern (Deputy); Joan Blondell (Lavinia); James Whitmore (Captain Shipley); Harry Davis (Ben); Roy Jenson (Doc Quinlen); Robert Cornthwaite (Hotel Clerk); Jim Boles (Corporal Blyth); Steve Whittaker, Ted Markland (Soldiers); Rupert Crosse (Prince); Jay Ose (Bartender); Buzz Henry (Cowpoke).

WINCHESTER '73 *(Universal, 1967)* C-100 min.

Producer, Richard E. Lyons; director, Herschel Daugherty; teleplay, Stephen Kandel, Richard L. Adams; based on the screenplay by Borden Chase, Robert L. Richards; art director, Frank Arrigo; music, Sol Kaplan; camera, Bud Thackery; editor, Richard G. Wray.

Tom Tryon (Lin McAdam); John Saxon (Dakin Mc-Adam); Dan Duryea (Bart McAdam); John Drew Barrymore (The Preacher); Joan Blondell (Larouge); John Dehner (High-Spade); Barbara Luna (Meriden); and John Doucette, David Pritchard, Paul Fix, John Hoyt, Jack Lambert, Jan Arvan, Robert Bice, Ned Romero, George Keymas.

STAY AWAY, JOE *(MGM, 1968)* C-101 min.

Producer, Douglas Laurence; director, Peter Tewksbury; based on the novel by Dan Cushman; screenplay, Burt Kennedy, Michael A. Hoey; music, Jack Marshall; songs, Jerry Reed; art directors, George W. Davis, Carl Anderson; set decorators, Henry Grace, Don Greenwood, Jr.; assistant director, Dale Hutchinson; sound, Franklin Milton; camera, Fred Koenekamp; editor, George W. Brooks.

Elvis Presley (Joe Lightcloud); Burgess Meredith (Charlie Lightcloud); Joan Blondell (Glenda Callahan); Katy Jurado (Annie Lightcloud); Thomas Gomez (Grandpa); Henry Jones (Hy Slager); L. Q. Jones (Bronc Hoverty); Quentin Dean (Mamie Callahan); Anne Seymour (Mrs. Hawkins); Angus Duncan (Lorne Hawkins); Douglas Henderson (Congressman Morrissey); Michael Lane (Frank Hawk); Susan Trustman (Mary Lightcloud); Warren Vanders (Hike Bowers); Buck Kartalian (Bull Shortgun); Del "Sonny" West (Jackson He-Crow); Jennifer Peak (Little Deer); Brett Parker (Deputy Sheriff Hank Matson); Michael Keller (Orville Witt).

KONA COAST *(Warner Bros.-Seven Arts, 1968)* C-93 min.

Executive producer, Richard Boone; producer/director, Lamont Johnson; based on the story *Bimini Gall* by John D. MacDonald; screenplay, Gil Ralston; music, Jack Marshall; assistant director, Michael Glick; sound, Burdick S. Trask; camera, Joseph La Shelle; editor, Alec McCombie.

Richard Boone (Captain Sam Moran); Vera Miles (Melissa Hyde); Joan Blondell (Kittibelle Lightfoot); Steve Ihnat (Kryder); Chips Rafferty (Charlie Lightfoot); Kent Smith (Akamal); Sam Kapu, Jr. (Kimo); Gina Villines (Mim Lowry); Duane Eddy (Tigercat); Scott Thomas (Tate Packer); Erwin Neal (Junior Packer); Doris Erickson (Doris); Gloria Nakea (Dee); Lucky Luck (Kunewa); Kaai Hayes (Butler); Dr. Mark Thomas (Macklin); Red Kanuha (Bartender); Sue Paishon (Sue).

THE PHYNX *(Warner Bros., 1970)* C-91 min.

Producer, Bob Booker; director, Lee H. Katzin; story, Booker; screenplay, Stan Cornyn; assistant director, Les Sheldon; production designer, Stan Jolley; music, Mike Stoller; songs, Stoller and Jerry Leiber; sound, John Kean; camera, Michel Hugo; editor, Dann Cahn.

A. Michael Miller, Ray Chippeway, Dennis Larden, Lonny Stevens (The Phynx); Lou Antonio (Corrigan); Mike Kellin (Bogey); Michael Ansara (Colonel Rostinov); George Tobias (Markvitch); Joan Blondell (Ruby); Martha Raye (Foxy); Larry Hankin (Philbaby); Teddy Eccles (Wee Johnny Urlso); Ultra Violet (Herself); Pat McCormack (Father O'Hoolihan); Joseph Grazel (Yakov); Bob Williams (Number One); Barbara Noonan (Bogey's Secretary); Rich Little (Voice in Box); Sue Bernard, Ann Morrell, Sherry Mills (Girls); Patty Andrews, Busby Berkeley, Xavier Cugat, Fritz Feld, John Hart, Ruby Keeler, Joe Louis, Marilyn Maxwell, Maureen O'Sullivan, Harold Sakata, Ed Sullivan, Rona Barrett, James Brown, Cass Daley, Leo Gorcey, Louis Hayward, Patsy Kelly, Guy Lombardo, Butterfly McQueen, Richard Pryor, Colonel Harland Sanders, Rudy Vallee, Johnny Weissmuller, Edgar Bergen, Dick Clark, Andy Devine, Huntz Hall, George Jessel, Dorothy Lamour, Trini Lopez, Pat O'Brien, Jay Silverheels, Clint Walker (Themselves); Sally Ann Struthers (No. 1 Fan).

SUPPORT YOUR LOCAL GUNFIGHTER *(United Artists, 1971)* C-92 min.

Executive producer, Burt Kennedy; producer, William Finnegan; director, Kennedy; screenplay, James Edward Grant; music, Jack Elliott, Allyn Ferguson; art director, Phil Barber; set decorator, Chester L. Bayhi; costumes, Lambert Marks, Pat Norris; makeup, Tom Tuttle; assistant director, Al Jennings; sound, Chuck Wilborn; special effects, A. D. Flowers; camera, Harry Stradling, Jr.; editor, Bill Gulick.

James Garner (Latigo Smith); Suzanne Pleshette (Patience Barton); Jack Elam (Jug May); Joan Blondell (Jenny); Henry "Harry" Morgan (Taylor Barton); Marie Windsor (Goldie); Henry Jones (Ez); John Dehner (Colonel Ames); Chuck Connors (Swifty Morgan); Dub Taylor (Mrs. Perkins); Ellen Corby (Abigail); Dick Curtis (Bud Barton); Herb Vigran (Fat); Mike Wagner (Bartender); Ben Cooper (Colorado); Willis Bouchey (McLaglen); Grady Sutton (Storekeeper);

Walter Burke (Morris); Terry Wilson (Thug); Roy Glenn (Headwaiter).

THE DEAD DON'T SCREAM *(NBC-TV, 1975)* C-75 min.

Executive producers, Douglas S. Cramer, Wilford Lloyd Baumes; producer, Henry Colman; director, Curtis Harrington; teleplay, Robert Bloch; costumes, Oscar Rodriquez, Betsy Cox; camera, James Crabe; editor, Ronald Fagan.

George Hamilton (Don Drake); Ray Milland (Jim Moss); Linda Cristal (Vera La Valle); Ralph Meeker (Lieutenant Reardon); James McEachin (Frankie Specht); Joan Blondell (Levenia); Reggie Nalder (Perdido); Jerry Douglas (Ralph Drake); Milton Parsons (Undertaker); William O'Connell (Priest).

WINNER TAKE ALL *(NBC-TV, 1975)* C-100 min.

Executive producer, Gerald I. Isenberg; producer, Nancy Malone; director, Paul Bogart; teleplay, Caryl Ledner; music, David Shire; camera, Terry K. Meade; editor, Folmar Blangsted.

Shirley Jones (Eleanor Anderson); Laurence Luckinbill (Bill Anderson); Sam Groom (Rick Santos); Joan Blondell (Beverly Craig); Sylvia Sidney (Anne Barclay); Joyce Van Patten (Edie Gould); John Carter (Leonard Fields); Lori Busk (Stacy Anderson); Wynn Irwin (Arnie); Al Lantieri (Man at Track).

WON TON TON, THE DOG WHO SAVED HOLLYWOOD *(Paramount, 1976)* C-92 min.

Producers, David V. Picker, Arnold Schulman, Michael Winner; director, Winner; screenplay, Schulman, Cy Howard; art director, Ward Preston; set director, Ned Parsons; assistant director, Charles Okun; makeup, Philip Rhodes; music, Neal Hefti; dogs trained by Karl Miller; sound, Bob Post; camera, Richard H. Kline; editor, Bernard Gribble.

Dennis Morgan (Tour Guide); Shecky Greene (Tourist); Phil Leeds, Cliff Norton (Dog Catchers); Madeline Kahn (Estie Del Ruth); Teri Garr (Fluffy Peters); Romo Vincent (Short-Order Cook); Bruce Dern (Grayson Potchuck); Sterling Holloway (Old Man on Bus); William Benedict (Man on Bus); Dorothy Gulliver (Old Woman on Bus); William Demarest (Studio Gatekeeper); Art Carney (J. J. Fromberg); Virginia Mayo (Miss Battley); Henny Youngman (Manny Farber); Rory Calhoun (Philip Hart); Billy Barty (Assistant Director); Henry Wilcoxon (Silent Film Director); Richard Arlen, Ricardo Montalban (Silent Film Stars); Johnny Weissmuller, Jackie Coogan (Stage Hands); Jack La Rue (Silent Film Villain); Joan Blondell (Landlady); Yvonne De Carlo (Cleaning Woman);

Ethel Merman (Hedda Parsons); Aldo Ray (Stubby Stebbins); Broderick Crawford (Special Effects Man); Dorothy Lamour (Visiting Film Star); Phil Silvers (Murray Fromberg); Nancy Walker (Mrs. Fromberg); Gloria De Haven, Ann Miller, Janet Blair, Cyd Charisse (President's Girls); Stepin Fetchit (Dancing Butler); Ken Murray (Souvenir Salesman); George Jessel (Awards' Announcer); Rudy Vallee (Autograph Hound); Dean Stockwell (Paul Lavell); Dick Haymes (James Crawford); Tab Hunter (David Hamilton); Ron Leibman (Rudy Montague); Fritz Feld (Rudy's Butler); Robert Alda (Richard Entwhistle); Dennis Day (Singing Telegraph Man); The Ritz Brothers (Cleaning Women); Jesse White (Rudy's Agent); Carmel Myers (Woman Journalist); Jack Carter (Male Journalist); Victor Mature (Nick); Barbara Nichols (Nick's Girl); Fernando Lamas, Zsa Zsa Gabor (Stars at Premiere); Huntz Hall (Moving Man); Doodles Weaver (Man in Mexican Film); Edgar Bergen (Professor Quicksand); Peter Lawford (Slapstick Star); Morey Amsterdam, Eddie Foy, Jr. (Custard Pie Stars); Alice Faye (Secretary at Gate); Ann Rutherford (Grayson's Studio Secretary); Milton Berle (Blind Man); Patricia Morison, Guy Madison (Stars at Screening); John Carradine (Drunk); Walter Pidgeon (Grayson's Butler); Keye Luke (Cook in Kitchen); Pedro Gonzales-Gonzales (Mexican Projectionist); Army Archerd (Premiere M.C.).

DEATH AT LOVE HOUSE *(ABC-TV, 1976)* C-75 min.

Executive producers, Aaron Spelling, Leonard Goldberg; producer, Hal Sitowitz; director, E. W. Swackhamer; teleplay, Jim Barnett; music, Laurence Rosenthal; art director, Paul Sylos; camera, Dennis Dalzell; editor, John Woodcock.

Robert Wagner (Joel Gregory Jr./Joel Gregory Sr.); Kate Jackson (Donna Gregory); Sylvia Sydney (Mrs. Josephs); Marianna Hill (Lorna Love); Joan Blondell (Marcella Geffenhart); John Carradine (Conan Carroll); Dorothy Lamour (Denise Christian); Bill Macy (Oscar); Joe Bernard (Bus Driver); John A. Zee (Eric Herman); Robert Gibbons (Director); Al Hansen (Policeman); Croften Hardester (Actor in Film).

OPENING NIGHT *(Faces Distribution, Inc., 1977)*

Producer, Al Ruban; director/screenplay, John Cassavetes; art director, Bryan Ryman; assistant directors, Foster H. Phinney, Edward Ledding; music/sound, Bo Harwood; camera, Ruban.

With: John Cassavetes, Gena Rowlands, Ben Gazzara, Joan Blondell, Paul Stewart, Zohra Lampert, Angelo Grisanti, John Tuell.

In *This Modern Age* ('31).

CHAPTER 2

Joan Crawford

5'4"
125 pounds
Brown hair
Blue eyes
Aries

For some reason, a segment of the film industry and the moviegoing public always held it against Joan Crawford for being the ultimate example of what Hollywood created best—a most digestible fantasy confection. Yet, when the history of the twentieth-century American cinema is one day put into proper perspective, undoubtedly Joan Crawford will remain as the incredible, real-life illustration that anything was possible in Hollywood during the Golden Age.

Miss Crawford herself once insisted, "A Star will last always, as in the heavens. A personality will go down just as quick as it appears." And she knew it full well. In the annals of American cinema, few came close to equalling her unique blend of glamour, persistence, and magnetism. Through labor, perseverance, and a sharpening knowledge of audience taste, she bulldozed a promising career as a 1920s MGM starlet into the realm of being an enduring legend.

The late columnist Louella O. Parsons once noted, "Joan Crawford manufactured herself. While others have of course changed themselves and their personalities, Joan created herself and her personality, drawing up a blueprint, deciding what she wanted to look and sound like, and then putting that person into existence." Always her own severest critic, Crawford admitted on one occasion, "The people who resent the pressures of life are the ones who grow old. I love life, and when you love life, the biggest and the smallest chores are fascinating." This last observation may well explain Joan's perennial, almost fanatical, devotion to the smallest detail of her everyday life—whether to her duties as a big MGM star in the Thirties, as a dynamic spokeswoman for Pepsi-Cola in the late Fifties and Sixties, or as the individual thereafter.

In his analysis of the superstar in *Joan Crawford* (1974), Stephen Harvey wrote, "Everything about Miss Crawford has always been triumphantly outsized: her luxuriant eyebrows, sensuous half-melon mouth, granite promontory jaw, those jutting, contoured cheekbones, and of course her trademarked hyperthyroid eyes and shoulders of near quarterback proportions. Even those physical traits that were more or less to scale were made to seem superhuman through Crawford's forcefulness and discipline. Though only of ordinary height, like [even shorter] fellow screen star Gloria Swanson, Crawford was able to maintain the illusion of extraordinary height and presence through a combination of imperial carriage and the sort of self-assurance on screen that implied that even if her stature was bested by some, she was otherwise bigger and more impressive than anyone else and she knew it."

A popular game among movie addicts of the Thirties, Forties, Fifties, and Sixties was to compare the virtues and vices of the performing Joan Crawford to those of Bette Davis. It was usually the case that the individual who admired Crawford had far less good to say about Davis, and vice versa. This long-time rivalry, which the two luminaries judged first-hand in the Forties when both worked at Warner Bros., reached its apex when they co-starred in *What Ever Happened to Baby Jane?* (1962). For many filmgoers, there was a good deal of real-life enthusiasm as the two onscreen ex-stars challenged, baited, and tormented one another, each anxious to gain the maximum of attention, sympathy, and power. Another rematch, *Hush . . . Hush, Sweet Charlotte* (1965), was short-circuited when illness forced Crawford to relinquish her role co-starring with Davis to Olivia de Havilland.

From Roaring Twenties' flapper to Thirties' shopgirl-making-good to Forties' career woman (her Oscar-winning *Mildred Pierce*, 1945) to Fifties' high-strung neurotic, and onward into recent years, Crawford always instilled her characterizations with tremendous self-belief. No matter how clichéd the part, how contrived the film, or how unrealistically glamorous the celluloid exercise, she never let the viewer forget that this was the ultimate testimony of honest entertainment. It is an acting trait that has salvaged many of her lesser vehicles.

Perhaps the best summation of the now late Miss Crawford, the full-time superstar, was offered by gossip reporter Hedda Hopper, "She's courageous and thinks like a man. She labors twenty-four hours a day to keep her name in the pupil of the public's eye."

She was born in San Antonio, Texas, on Wednesday, March 23, 1904 (some sources claim 1903). Named Lucille Fay, she was the second child (her brother Hal was five years older) born to Anna Johnson Le Sueur who had divorced her husband, Thomas Le Sueur, before Lucille was born. Six weeks after Lucille's arrival, Anna married Henry Cassin who owned a vaudeville theatre in Lawton, Oklahoma. It was there that the girl spent the first seven years of her life. Because of her tomboyish ways, Cassin called her "Billie" and she became known in the neighborhood as Billie Cassin. The little girl grew up thinking that Cassin was her father and she would not learn the truth until she was eight years old.

She got along better with boys than with girls and adopted some boyish habits such as climbing trees. She hated to have her hair combed or braided into pigtails. One of her favorite pastimes was playing "show" in a barn behind the house where Daddy Cassin stored costumes, props, and scenery. When she was old enough, her constant habit was to stand backstage at the theatre during performances and watch the dancers. Her little feet worked in unison with those of the players onstage and soon she perfected several of their intricate routines. By the time Billie was six, she had decided to become a ballet dancer, but this dream was shattered when, dancing on the lawn, she stepped on a broken bottle. The doctor at first feared that she might never walk again on that foot. However, after months of intensive care, she was able to place her weight on it. Ballet dancing was now out of the question, but she found that she could still dance and her dreams continued to grow.

When Billie was seven-and-a-half years old, her stepfather sold his theatre and leased a Kansas City hotel which became the home of the Cassin clan. Six months later, Henry Cassin deserted his wife. Unable to supervise the hotel by herself and with two children to support, Anna took over a laundry next door to the hotel and moved her family into its back room. Hal got a job as a soda jerk, while Billie, who had been a tuition-paying student at St. Agnes Academy, was forced to work her way through school waiting on tables and making beds.

The other school girls, who had been friendly toward her when her status matched theirs, now treated her like a domestic. She boarded at the school but spent the weekends with her mother. On finishing the sixth grade at St. Agnes, she transferred to another school, Rockingham, which was located in a fourteen-room mansion and was operated by a hulking woman whose treatment of Billie was far from humane. Billie was the sole working student at Rockingham and it was up to her to clean the entire institution, make beds, wash dishes, and wait on tables. If one small detail was overlooked, the head mistress would lumber up to Billie's attic room and beat her. Once, when Billie attempted to run away from the school, she was beaten, kicked, and thrown down a flight of stairs by the cruel woman. Little wonder that in later years Joan would become noted for her perfectionism in housekeeping.

With all of this housework, Billie had little time for studies. From an academic point of view, she learned almost nothing at Rockingham. She did, however, learn to hate. Again, the girl students shunned her, but the boys liked her and when some of those from wealthy families took her out dancing, the head mistress dared not forbid it for fear of losing the boys as paying students. By this time Anna Johnson Le Sueur Cassin had found another husband, a man named Hough who disliked Billie's sullenness. Because of her new stepfather's animosity Billie seldom went home to visit.

When the requisite number of years were completed at Rockingham, Billie was handed a letter from the head mistress claiming that she had satisfactorily passed her studies through high school level. She then obtained a job as a sales clerk in a department store earning twelve dollars weekly. She was now able to purchase a few pieces of clothing, but her tastes, understandably, were cheap and her makeup gaudy. She continued to dream of earning money as a dancer, and was encouraged in this fantasy by winning a Charleston contest at a spot called the Jack O'Lantern Cafe in Kansas City.

For three months, she attended St. Stephen's High School at Columbia, Missouri, where she tried to support herself as a dining-room helper. But she was scholastically so far behind the other students that she felt that she could never catch up to them and so she quit. She moved in with her mother and stepfather and continued working at the department store notions counter. She acquired something of a steady boyfriend in the person of Ray Sterling. In 1938, he told writer Katherine Albert of *Liberty* magazine, "When Billie came into a room, every boy sat up and took notice. She weighed too much and her face was freckled. Her clothes were terrible, but there was something electric about her. I loved her with all the devotion of a puppy, but being in love with Billie was trying, because I had to defend her reputation so often. She was running wild and I understand why. . . ." Life's greatest joy to Billie Cassin was dancing, and to her male friends she became known as "the Charleston kid."

When she learned one day that interviews were being conducted at the Hotel Baltimore by the promoter of a stage revue that was supposed to be bound for Broadway, enterprising Billie lost little time in rushing to the hotel. She auditioned and told the man that her name was Lucille Le Sueur. "Well, kid, you sure picked a fancy one," he told her. She won a job as one of the sixteen chorus girls who would back the show's star, Katherine Emerine. The revue got as far as Springfield, Missouri, where it closed one week after its opening. The kind Miss Emerine liked Lucille and advised her to contact her should she ever get to Chicago.

With money obtained from Ray Sterling, Lucille returned to Kansas City and her sales job, this time in the ladies' dress department. Soon after returning, she had a serious quarrel with her mother and stepfather and decided it was now time to go to Chicago to find Miss Emerine. "Restless, eager, full of energy, I packed my bags," she remembered in *Woman's Home Companion* of January 1955. "I was fifteen [sic]. I was through being Billie Cassin. I was going to be Lucille Le Sueur."

The stage-struck girl reached Chicago with less than four dollars, but an elderly gentleman at the train station—so legend has it—offered to share a cab with her to the vicinity of Miss Emerine's apartment. She managed to avoid paying half of the taxi fare, but found that dancer Emerine was out of town on tour. With no one to turn to, she remembered suddenly the name of Ernie Young, a producer-friend of Emerine's, and located his office address in the Chicago telephone directory. She took several streetcars to get to his place of business, and was grossly disappointed to discover his office waiting room filled with slim, pretty girls, all of whom hoped for the chance to become famous dancers.

Knowing that she did not stand a chance in competition with them, she dashed boldly into Young's inner office when the door opened. "I'm not tall or pretty," she cried, "but I *have* to have a job." Young's wife took pity on her, bought her a dinner, and found her a singing-dancing job at a local nightclub for "what looked like an enormous paycheck —twenty-five dollars a week." Two weeks later she was sent to replace an ailing dancer at Detroit's Oriole Terrace where thirty-two girls danced eight routines each night. Again, she was disliked by many of the girls (they called her "Squirt") and was relegated to using a broom closet as a dressing room. She was not bothered by this—she was dancing, receiving a salary, and what else mattered?

One night, as she twirled before the audience—so the legend continues—her skirt accidentally knocked a glass of liquid from a table top which spilled into the lap of master showman J. J. Shubert. "There have been suggestions," she has said, "that I knocked the glass on purpose. I didn't have that much sense. I didn't even know who J. J. Shubert was." The great Shubert sought her out that night after the performance. He asked to see the "little fat girl with the blue eyes." The end result of their meeting was a chorus job in New York in Shubert's latest revue, *Innocent Eyes,* which opened on Tuesday, May 20, 1924. Also in the dance line-up was jocular Jack Oakie, who became Lucille's pal and confidante. Together, they discovered the sights of New York and talked of the days when they would each be famous.

During the revue's run, Lucille also worked as a singer-dancer at Harry Richman's nightclub, Club Richman. When *Innocent Eyes* closed in August 1924, the chorus was shifted to Shubert's *The Passing Show of 1924* which opened at the Winter Garden on Wednesday, September 3, 1924. In this satirical topical revue, which utilized forty-five chorines, Lucille enacted a beaded bag in a "living curtain" segment and appeared as "Miss Labor Day" in the "Holiday" portion of the revue.

In December 1924, she was selected to make a screen test for Harry Rapf, a talent scout from Hollywood's Metro-Goldwyn Studios. She knew nothing about movies nor did she particularly care to know. But she did know that salaries were higher in the glossy world of southern California, so she agreed to a test. An associate of Rapf's, named Ruben, would later recall the pre-test interview with, "When she walked in, her eyes looked just like a cow's—wide open and scared. We couldn't get a word out of her." After the screen test, which Ruben stated "had possibilities," Lucille took a train to Kansas City to spend Christmas with her mother and brother. (Anna, by this time, had shed husband Hough.) On Christmas Day, she received a telegram from Rapf stating, "You are put under a five-year contract at a salary of seventy-five dollars a week. Leave immediately for California. Contact Kansas City office for transportation."

On Thursday, January 1, 1925, plump (145 pounds) Lucille Le Sueur, measuring 5'4" in height and possessing thick reddish-brown hair, broad shoulders, big blue eyes, a wide mouth, and tremendous energy, boarded a Los Angeles-bound train. Her traveling outfit was a loose-fitting gray suit, a big hat atop her too-curly hair, and shoes with bows on them.

Allegedly never having read a movie magazine (she did not even read newspapers then), she had no criteria by which to judge Hollywood on her arrival a few days later. She was met at the train station by Rapf's secretary who had secured a hotel room for her, and escorted to the studio for a second screen test. The cameraman for the audition, Johnny Arnold (later to become head of Metro's camera department), told her, "You don't look like anybody else. You're athletic-looking and your face is *built*."

Contrary to Arnold's assessment that she did not resemble anyone else, her first screen job was to double for Norma Shearer (des-

tined to become one of the studio's most popular stars) in *Lady of the Night* (1925). Shearer played dual roles as a society lady and a tough woman, and Lucille substituted for her in the long shots and in some over-the-shoulder set-ups. While there was no visible resemblance between the two ambitious women, their profiles (prominent nose, strong chin) were similar. The film was released on March 15, 1925, with Lucille receiving no credit mention.

Along with posing for the standard cheesecake publicity photos, Lucille was put to work as a party guest in *Proud Flesh* (1925) starring Eleanor Boardman, and as a chorus girl in *Pretty Ladies* (1925). For the latter picture starring ZaSu Pitts, Lucille and fellow newcomer Myrna Loy were seated on dry ice floats wearing scanty maribou costumes while imitation snow flakes filtered through their hair. Lucille played young Lady Catherine in *The Circle* (1925), a screen version of the Somerset Maugham play. (There is also some evidence that she had a bit walk-on in the studio's lushly-mounted *The Merry Widow*.) However, "my first real part was in *Old Clothes*" (1925), released before *The Circle*.

For *Old Clothes*, directed by Edward Cline, she claimed to have been one of 150 Metro-Goldwyn ingenues who auditioned for the part of Mary Riley, a poor-but-honest girl befriended by a youth (Jackie Coogan) and a middle-aged man (Max Davidson) who are partnered in the second-hand clothing business. The film's producer, Jack Coogan, Sr., chose Lucille for the role. In the motion picture, after the partners give Mary a place in their home, she falls in love with a Wall Street tycoon (Alan Forrest) whose mother (Lillian Elliott) is completely against her son's interest in the common girl. Through a ploy involving a Wall Street stock deal, the hero is able to salvage his business, and he and Mary find happiness together.

That the budding actress was still very unsophisticated, has been described incisively by Hollywood chronicler Adela Rogers St. John. Miss St. John wrote, "The first time I saw Lucille Le Sueur was a memorable one to

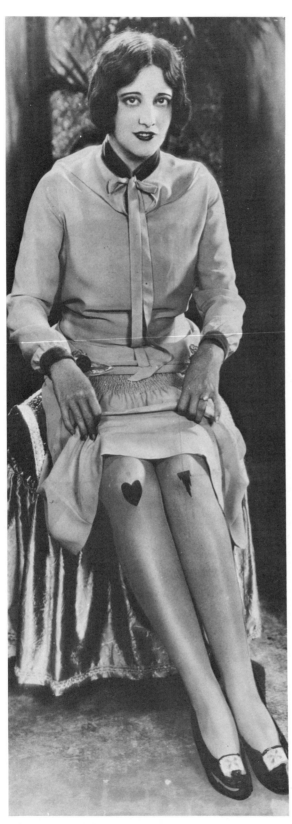

The starlet at Culver City in 1925.

me. . . . I was knocked off my feet by her resemblance to Pauline Frederick, to me the most all-around attractive woman of her generation. So when I walked out on the M-G-M lot one bright morning and saw crossing the sweep of a lawn a young girl who, in some uncanny fashion, turned back the clock to the days when Pauline Frederick conquered New York, I got tremendously excited. Here was the same beauty . . . winged feet and hidden fire . . . [and] air of pride that had thrilled theatre and movie audiences of Miss Frederick.

"The disappointment in meeting Miss Le Sueur was correspondingly great and, I realize now, correspondingly unfair. Obviously, it wasn't fair to expect an untrained, inexperienced kid only a short time out of the chorus to have the full-fledged beauty and mentality, culture and poise, wit and wisdom that time, contacts, and hard work had given Pauline Frederick." In *This Modern Age* (1931), Miss Frederick would portray Joan's oncamera mother.

That her studio was most anxious to alter Lucille's image was indicated by the order given to the publicity department to give the newcomer a fresh, more appropriate screen name and a more glamorous background. The obliging public relations department set out to construct a new person for the girl. It inaugurated a publicity campaign through the auspices of *Movie Weekly* to find the proper professional name for the new contract player. According to the magazine, "She is an auburn-haired, blue-eyed beauty and is of French and Irish descent. Second only to her career is her interest in athletics, and she devotes much of her spare time to swimming and tennis." The magazine also reported, "Her parents would not consider a theatrical career for their only daughter, and as all her pleadings were in vain, Miss Le Sueur took matters into her own hands last spring and ran away from school, landing in Chicago with just two dollars." The Metro publicists also suggested that Lucille "was a popular subdeb in Kansas City and gave up a promising social career to further her acting ambitions." Much to her chagrin, Lucille had to go

With ZaSu Pitts in *Pretty Ladies* ('25).

With Constance Bennett and Sally O'Neil in *Sally, Irene and Mary* ('25).

along with the ruse. The winning name in the contest was Joan Arden, but a short time later it was discovered that there was a real Joan Arden on the Metro lot, so the second choice name was selected. It was Joan Crawford. "I hated it then," the star would later say. "'Crawford, Crawford!—it sounds like Crawfish,' I mourned." So it was that the credit lines heralding *Old Clothes* listed Joan Crawford in the cast. Of her role in that film, reviewer Louella Parsons wrote, "She is very attractive, and shows promise."

Along with the new name (she persisted in pronouncing it Jo-Anne) and her sudden acceptance by her studio as a potential starlet, Joan Crawford underwent various glamorizing treatments. Her eyebrows were thinned, her wide mouth was narrowed by lipstick to more closely resemble the bow of Cupid (*a la* the bee-sting lipstick shape of the lot's star Mae Murray). A tutor gave Joan instructions in the art of walking like a lady, and she was placed on a crash diet to dissolve at least fifteen pounds.

She literally fell in love with the business of making movies and became a regular fan. ("I could have looked at movies eighteen times a day.") She had the run of the studio lot where she practiced her dancing on an empty sound stage and watched the big stars at work. William Haines, one of the top names during the era, became her closest friend; it was a relationship that would endure until his death in December 1973. His pet name for her was "Cranberry." Almost every evening the vivacious Joan would dance at the Cocoanut Grove (located in Hollywood's Ambassador Hotel), which was the hub of the town and popular with all the screen stars and would-be cinema personalities. Joan's steady dance partner was Michael Cudahy, heir to the Chicago meat-packing wealth, whose mother was reportedly unhappy with his choice of social team-mate.

Studio advisors alerted Joan that an early-to-bed schedule would be more advantageous to keeping her face youthful but she shrugged off such advice. Louella Parsons was to later recall Joan's terpsichorean activities with, "It was remarkable to watch the abandon with which she threw herself into the dance." Joan fell in love with Cudahy because "he was terribly romantic, tall, dark, and a magnificent dancer." She once admitted to having wished to marry him, but he was too much the professional playboy. For her dancing talents, she won more than a hundred cups performing the athletic Charleston.

In his admirable picture and text study, *Four Fabulous Faces* (1970), author Larry Carr vividly depicts Joan Crawford throughout the years. However, he is at his best in his picture of the starlet in the mid-Twenties. "During her first few years as a stock contract player, among the assets Joan Crawford had going for her was the fact that she was extremely likable, frank, fun, and good-natured. Most of all, she was cooperative. Just ask Joan and before you could say Metro-Goldwyn-Mayer, she would pose for anything you could dream up. The result was that she quickly became a favorite of the publicity department and began appearing with increasing rapidity in every magazine in the country. (This was at the same period when Garbo wouldn't pose for *any* publicity.) . . . But Joan would and did! She posed winning Charleston dancing cups; racing whippets, autos, and trains; reading papers, poetry, and pamphlets; fondling dolls, dogs, and diaries. She posed as a pirate, a Spanish senorita, as Hamlet, and a sailor's sweetheart; she christened battleships, joined the marines, met visiting dignitaries. . . . Her unquenchable vitality is apparent in every picture."

Onscreen, Joan was a dancer in a Broadway revue, the Irene of *Sally, Irene and Mary* (1925). The film was adapted and directed by sensitive Edmund Goulding from a 1922 musical play by Eddie Dowling and Cyrus Woods. It depicts the backstage lives and loves of three showgirls. Sally (Constance Bennett) is the self-confident one who wants and gets a sugar daddy (Henry Kolker); Irene is the romantic one who takes up with a slick heel (Douglas Gilmore) and learns that he is interested in her only for sex; Mary (Sally O'Neil) is a spunky little Irish lass who settles for a poor plumber (William Haines). After being dropped by cad Gilmore, Irene finds true love with another man (Ray Howard) but they are killed when his car is hit by a train. *Photoplay* magazine credited Joan with giving "a good performance."

When Joan, ever anxious to please and attract movie executives and new fans, was not altering the color and style of her hair, or trying out an exotic eye or mouth makeup, she was formulating—often with subconscious lack of guile—the latest real Joan Crawford. Whereas in others it might have seemed coldly calculating, with Joan it was the case of an overly ambitious newcomer thirsting for a better way of life and seeking a set—any set—of values to guide her through these overwhelming changes in her lifestyles. While other aspiring stars created publicity around their own sense of self, Joan adapted herself around almost every plausible aspect of the press releases being turned out about her. Thus it was inevitable that she should become the ultimate living Hollywood legend, literally being a complete product of the film industry.

Next, oncamera, Joan was a prohibition agent in *The Boob* (1926). George K. Arthur, a cherubic little comedian, played the title role of a Wyoming farm boy who uncovers a gang of rumrunners near his home and joins the Federal agents. This low-budget entry was directed by William Wellman who, like Joan, was destined for much finer celluloid projects. Proving her growing value to the film industry, First National borrowed Joan for Harry Langdon's first feature-length film, *Tramp, Tramp, Tramp* (1926). Unfortunately, as Betty Burton, she plays "a nice leading lady with little to do" (*Variety*).

During the filming of *Tramp, Tramp, Tramp*, Joan added the word claustrophobia to her vocabulary and discovered that she suffered from this condition. In one of the comedy's chase scenes, the script dictated that Langdon find a manhole, shove Joan into it, and slam down the lid. "I've never been more terrified in any picture," she would recall. "I wasn't so sure I wanted to be in movies." At the same time as she was learning new words and more about herself, she eagerly learned

techniques from her directors and co-workers. For example, in the course of making *Paris* (1926) with co-star Charles Ray, director Edmund Goulding gave this advice to Joan at the start of a dramatic scene, "Take off your shoes. Now . . . stand with your feet apart and grip the earth firmly with your feet. Draw the strength of the earth right into you!" Due to this tip, Joan confessed, "I've played many big scenes shoeless since then." She also learned about placing male co-stars on boxes when they were shorter than she.

Joan was selected as a WAMPAS Baby Star in 1926 (along with Mary Astor, Janet Gaynor, Fay Wray, and Dolores Del Rio). She had moved from the Washington Hotel in Culver City to a furnished house on Ogden Drive in Los Angeles. The purpose of this transition was to make room for her brother Hal and her mother Anna, both of whom also hoped to find work and happiness in the sun of southern California. Joan's happiness consisted of grinding out hastily made movies and then dancing at nightclubs after work. The latter habit earned her the reputation around Hollywood as the "Hot-Cha Girl." "I got more publicity than any Wampas Baby Starlet," she was to later remember. Of her acting in those halcyon days, she once said, "I overacted terribly but I learned and I never [sic] imitated anyone else." F. Scott Fitzgerald called her "the best example of the flapper —the girl you see at smart clubs . . . dancing deliciously, laughing a great deal, with wide, hurt eyes. . . ."

As in *Paris*, which had cast her as an apache dancer, *The Taxi Dancer* (1927) took the opportunity to display her dancing talents. *Winners of the Wilderness* (1927), which boasted some Technicolor sequences, paired Joan with Colonel Tim McCoy under W. S. Van Dyke II's direction. The Western was set during the French and Indian War in the American colonies and featured Joan as Renee Contrecoeur, the daughter of the French Commander. (Anything was possible in silent films!) The feature was better on atmosphere than on plot construction. In *The Understanding Heart* (1927), Joan was paired with Francis X. Bushman, Jr., son of the famed matinee idol. This production-line picture offered Joan as a fire spotter for the Forest Rangers. (Eleven years later, Bushman would be playing a bit in one of Joan's starring vehicles, *The Shining Hour*. Such was the way of Hollywood popularity.)

One of Hollywood's top stars of the decade was Lon Chaney, the master of makeup and of excellence in character definition. The MGM hierarchy (Louis B. Mayer, Irving Thalberg, and Paul Bern) thought enough of Joan's potential to showcase her opposite the great Chaney, knowing that his popularity could only bring favorable attention to any leading lady. The film was *The Unknown* (1927), a bizarre tale written and directed by Tod Browning which dealt with Alonzo (Chaney), a circus performer who pretends to be armless to cover up a crime he has committed. He ties his arms to his sides and hides them beneath his clothing while he tosses knives with his feet. The sharp blades are tossed at his pretty assistant, Estrellita (Joan), with whom he is in love. Regarding this film, the *New York Evening World* reported that Joan is "one of the screen's acknowledged artists and each picture seems to merely justify this characterization." Of her one-picture liaison with the talented Chaney, Joan once observed, "[He] was my introduction to acting. The concentration, the complete absorption he gave to his characterization filled me with such awe I could scarcely speak to him. . . . Watching him gave me the desire to be a real actress."

Another headliner of the Roaring Twenties was John Gilbert of whom Joan played opposite in *Twelve Miles Out* (1927). During the filming of this turgid drama, Gilbert had no time to take notice of pert Joan except in the line of business. At the time, his sole preoccupation was with MGM's top female star, Greta Garbo. Gilbert did a lot of pacing when offcamera while grumbling about his problematic affair with the Swede. For *Spring Fever* (1927), Joan donned the wardrobe of a rich girl who is sold on golf as a pastime. At an exclusive country club she meets and marries a golf pro (William Haines) with whom she fights and later becomes reconciled.

In *The Unknown* ('27).

Joan and the very congenial Haines were professionally reunited again for *West Point* (1928). She was no more than the big-eyed, decorous, and obligatory love interest, while he was the smart-alecky West Point football star. At the time of making *West Point*, Ann Sylvester of *Picture Play* magazine interviewed the ingenue and had these observations: "She has a little habit of making engagements and forgetting them. . . . She gets a frightful bill from some impatient creditor and on the same day entertains ten girls at a high-priced restaurant. . . . Her mind is quicker than a trigger, but uncultivated. . . . One moment she is broadly sounding her vowels, the next she's racking herself with a laugh that can be heard beyond the city limits. She's a funny kid alright."

On October 17, 1927, while attending a performance of the play *Young Woodley* at the Majestic Theatre in Los Angeles, Joan became entranced with the show's young star. Douglas Fairbanks, Jr., was trying very hard to prove that he was more than just his father's son. As the actress later remembered, he "was the most exciting thing I had ever seen—sensitive, colorful, a great talent." After the Los Angeles engagement, the play moved to San Francisco. When he returned to the movie capital, handsome young Doug met Miss Crawford. As Joan would relate to Brian Connell in *Knight Errant: A Biography of Douglas Fairbanks, Jr.* (1955), "He was charming, with a divine sense of humor. He liked me, too, and understood my serious attitude towards my work and life."

By the end of 1927, Joan's almost constant escort around Hollywood was Doug Jr. His father, the senior Fairbanks, married to America's sweetheart, Mary Pickford, did not approve of his son's relationship with the older (Doug Jr. was born on December 12, 1909), uneducated Miss Crawford, but the fans did. The couple soon became the favorite love targets of the fan magazines with nearly everyone guessing as to when or where they would marry. There were those people about Hollywood who insisted that Fairbanks Sr. and Miss Pickford's primary fear was that Doug Jr. would make them grandparents.

However, the conflicts between senior and junior Fairbanks ran much deeper, and Joan was only one more source of irritation. The more the swashbuckler of the screen urged his son to drop her, the more the youth determined to wed her. It certainly helped his decision that, through Joan's encouragement, he was now receiving better screen roles, parts that relied on his personality rather than just being the famous son of a celebrity.

Meanwhile, Joan replaced Renee Adoree as the "silent" heroine of *Rose-Marie* (1928), playing an independent, fiery French-Canadian lass. Taken from the Otto Harbach-Oscar Hammerstein II-Rudolf Friml-Herbert Stothart operetta, this first screening,* due to the lack of sound, was without any musical scoring. The plot developed as a suspenseful drama of Rose-Marie—pursued by others—falling in love with Jim (James Murray), a soldier of fortune accused of murdering a Canadian Mountie. Eventually, after many breathtaking and hazardous scenes of near-calamity, Jim is proved innocent and free to woo Rose-Marie. Following this feature, the Ben Ames Williams novel *All the Brothers Were Valiant* provided the basis for *Across to Singapore* (1928). The brothers of the piece are Ramon Novarro and Ernest Torrence who fight over Priscilla Crowninshield (Joan). MGM would remake the seafaring yarn under Williams' original title in 1953 with Ann Blyth as the fair damsel and Robert Taylor and Stewart Granger as the brothers.

A pair of brothers also figure prominently in Joan's next picture, *The Law of the Range* (1928). In this Western of no distinction, the good one is Tim McCoy, while the sinister one is Rex Lease. Much more box-office worthy was *Four Walls* (1928) in which Joan was teamed again with John Gilbert. She "simply walks off with it" (*New York Evening World*) as Frieda, the no-nonsense, hardhearted gun moll who, when her underworld lover (Gilbert) is sent to prison, takes up with his second-in-command (Louis Natheaux).

If any film can be considered the turning point in the meteoric career rise of Joan Craw-

---

* The property would be remade twice again by MGM: in 1936, with Jeanette MacDonald; in 1954, with Ann Blyth.

357

106

Returning to Los Angeles from
New York with husband
Douglas Fairbanks, Jr. (June
1929).

←

With her leading man before
being replaced in *Tide of
Empire* ('28).

With Gwen Lee (second) and
Mary Doran (fifth) in *Our
Modern Maidens* ('29).

ford, it is *Our Dancing Daughters*. Josephine Lovett fashioned the story of the true jazz age. Joan appears as Diana Medford, a high-spirited gal whose feet are never still for long. She is a good girl but her wild ways lead Ben (John Mack Brown), the man in her life, to believe that she is much too promiscuous to wed. The two other dancing daughters are Bea (Dorothy Sebastian—a real-life friend of Joan's) who has become branded because of a pre-marital sexual experience, and Anne (Anita Page) who is everything that Diana is purported to be, but masks it with sweetness and light.

"I'd never before so enjoyed making a picture," Joan would say in retrospect. "*Our Dancing Daughters* was my big turning point. None of us was starred in this movie but the moment the film was released, reviews and fan letters began to pour in." Everyone was enchanted and intrigued by Joan's big scene in which she madly dances the Charleston, exhibiting her trademark vitality and verse. Joan claimed that exhibitors were the ones responsible for giving her top status by placing her name on the marquees along with the film's title. This so pleased her that she took to driving her white Ford convertible about the Los Angeles area to take box-camera snapshots of the marquees.

The film, with sets by Cedric Gibbons and wardrobe by David Cox, was an instant hit. Joan was pronounced the personification of the Jazz Age, and became overnight a severe threat to Paramount's "It" girl, Clara Bow. Joan's position as a Metro-Goldwyn-Mayer star was assured when her salary rose to $500.00 a week. The fan mail poured in and she excitedly replied to each letter in her own handwriting. She later said, "In the house on Roxbury Drive [in Beverly Hills] my light burned late. There was no bedtime for me until every letter was answered." With the advent of fan and critical recognition as a star, Joan began to "study and observe myself." She established career goals for herself, one of which was to do something dramatically worthwhile that would require acting instead of dancing or maintaining the fixed smile of a pretty backdrop for the film's leading man.

On Friday, December 28, 1928, Joan and Doug Jr. announced their engagement, little to the surprise of anyone. Just as Joan was enjoying a wave of professional success,* so was Doug. Warner Bros.-First National was embarking upon a series of features that would establish him as a leading man of the cinema. On Monday, June 3, 1929, Joan married Douglas Elton Fairbanks, Jr., in New York City at St. Malachy's Catholic Church. They wed on the East Coast to avoid any possible embarrassment to his family since there was still friction between father and son. Doug was then only nineteen and had to obtain permission to marry from his mother, Beth Sully Fairbanks, who would soon marry stage-star Jack Whiting. Doug Sr. sent a telegram of congratulations proving, on the surface, that peace was restored in the Fairbanks family. Within a week after the ceremony, the honeymoon couple returned to California and their soundstage obligations.

The microphone had entered Hollywood's world in 1927 (with Warner Bros.' part-talkie *The Jazz Singer*) and by 1929 all the major studios were experimenting with sound. Joan later recalled, "Everybody panicked at Metro, and I mean everybody. . . . When I first heard my voice recorded I said, 'That's not me, that's a man.'" Her voice, which did not sound mannish to the public, was first heard singing "I've Got a Feeling for You" in *Hollywood Revue of 1929* (1929). For the song number, she lounged across the top of a grand piano in the style of Helen Morgan, and then later danced to the music supplied by the Biltmore Quartet. Bits of this sequence appear in *That's Entertainment* (1974). Other MGM personnel who were seen in the revue-style film (and a not very good one at that) were Norma Shearer, John Gilbert, Marie Dressler, Polly Moran, and William Haines.

It was inevitable after Joan and Doug's return to Hollywood that they must be entertained at Pickfair, the royal seat of Doug Sr. and his regal consort, Mary Pickford. If Joan had played to perfection the liquor-drinking,

---

* *Dream of Love* (1928) required little of Joan and was a ridiculous story with the actress cast as a gypsy singer who falls in love with a prince (Nils Asther). After being replaced by Renee Adoree in *Tide of Empire* (1929), she was William Haines' college-gal love interest in *The Duke Steps Out* (1929).

dance–mad flapper with a tousled bob in *Our Dancing Daughters,* she appeared the model of decorum as the deferring daughter-in-law the night when she and her nervous spouse drove up to the mansion on Summit Drive. As Joan ascended the flight of stairs to the main floor entrance of Pickfair, her shoe came undone. In perhaps the one moment of unforced graciousness throughout the evening, Doug Sr. gallantly bent down at her feet to redo it. Many later would insist this was a calculated situation by Joan to win at least one point of recognition. According to the other dinner guests, the hosts and guests spent a strained evening, with each generation of diners viewing the others with distrust. It was a deflating scene that Joan would and could not forget. It made her all the more anxious to achieve more fame and power through her screen career.

Although talking pictures were well established by the fall of 1929, there were those studios which were not totally prepared to gear every production toward sound and those not yet equipped with the up-to-date equipment. Therefore, a few silent films were allowed to pass through, such as MGM's *Our Modern Maidens* (1929), a follow-up (not a sequel) to *Our Dancing Daughters.* Written by Josephine Lovett, as was the earlier film, it had the bonus element of uniting Joan and Doug Jr. oncamera, the only time during their careers that they would appear together in a film. A more complicated story than *Our Dancing Daughters,* the film nevertheless allowed plenty of footage of scantily clad Joan's dancing abilities. Her fans were not disappointed. In addition, the film represented the start of a professional and personal relationship with fashion designer Adrian that would last many years. The man was a pace-setter whose designs affected women's styles all over the nation. "I frankly don't remember any 'fashions' before Adrian," Joan once said. "My style had been bows—everywhere. Adrian toned me down—not in color but in line."

Joan's next scheduled film was *Great Day,* a musical talkie set to Vincent Youmans' music. She was asked to play an ingenue role for which she felt too old, and after ten days' shooting she told Louis B. Mayer that she wanted out. "I can't talk baby talk," she said. "I can't play an ingenue." The film was shut down (after expending $280,000) never to be re-vitalized.

In a gargantuan effort to fit in with the lordly inhabitants of Pickfair, Joan devoted as much time as she could to reading the prose and poetry works of the masters and to learning what she could about classical music. She addressed the senior Fairbanks as "Uncle Douglas," but could not bring herself to calling Miss Pickford by her first name. Although Fairbanks and Miss Pickford made some attempt to accept Joan as a member of their special family, they found it difficult to relax with her because she was ill-at-ease in their presence. Louella Parsons reported some years later, "There was always a barrier between them and it never came down during the period that Joan and Doug Jr. were married." Unkind Hollywood gossips hinted that the main reason Joan had married Douglas Jr. was to further her own career by association.

At the studio, Joan continued to ask for better roles and borrowed all the scripts she could carry from the various piles that were to be sent out to producers and stars. "I'd pull one off the bottom and go and read it on my lunch hour. I knew every picture that was being made. That's how I discovered what I wanted to do." At the same time, she convinced her bosses to get rid of the Cupid's bow lips and she was permitted to show her whole mouth when oncamera. After all, Joan had changed her image in private life. No longer was she the frivolous dancing madcap. Now she was the devoted, intense housewife, hooking rugs, sewing some of her own clothes, and being very domestic and serious.

It is doubtful that she selected *Untamed* (1930); she *must* have been forced into it. It is considered her sound debut film. (*Hollywood Revue* had not been a fair measure of her voice quality because she did not have dialogue; she only sang.) Of her diction in this acting film in which she played Bingo, a wild young thing raised in the South American jungle, the Brooklyn *Daily Eagle* rated it "clear and unaffected." Her romantic interest in the picture is Andy (Robert Montgomery), aristocratic, charming, and poor. In real life,

With Ernest Torrence and
Robert Montgomery in
Untamed ('29).

→
With choreographer Sammy
Lee on the set of *Hollywood
Revue of 1929*.

With John Miljan in *Paid* ('31).

Montgomery and Doug Jr. were very good friends.

Irving Thalberg's sister Sylvia was responsible for the story and continuity of *Montana Moon* (1930), Joan's next screen venture. She is the rich rancher's daughter who meets a cowboy named Larry (John Mack Brown) on her way to New York. They later wed, fight, and then patch up their differences. During these events, she is briefly romanced by ex-Latin lover Ricardo Cortez.

It was obvious to nearly everyone on the Metro lot that Garbo, Shearer, and Crawford (in that order) represented the triumvirate of leading actresses. Each had her own special audience, studio defenders, and particular talents. While others might have conceded to these two screen giants, dynamic Joan pursued her career with a near-vengeance, determined to push herself to the pinnacle of success.

For Joan's second of her three 1930 releases, the studio assigned her to *Our Blushing Brides,* rematching her with Dorothy Sebastian, Anita Page, and Robert Montgomery. There is a good deal of autobiography in this diverting feature in which Joan is gorgeously photographed by Merritt B. Gerstad. She is Jerry Marsh from Simpkinsville, New York, who works in Manhattan's Jardine Department Store. For a weekly salary of $22.50, she toils in the women's lingerie section and is frequently called upon to model female finery. She is eyed by cynical Tony Jardine (Montgomery), the thirty-year-old department store heir. He thinks Jerry is nifty, admiring her "delicate carriage and poise," and would not mind setting up housekeeping with her—without benefit of clergy. But Jerry has loftier ideals. She wants a life where "there's plenty of air to breathe and everything you look at is beautiful." Later, at his family's country home, Tony attempts to seduce Jerry but she cautions him, "When a man begins to talk about inhibition, it's time to start looking at the view." A still later moment in the scenario reveals the essence of the Joan Crawford screen prototype of this period. A dejected, rebuffed Tony says of prim Jerry, "What charming innocence."

With utter conviction (Joan's trademark quality), she responds mysteriously, "No . . . something else you wouldn't understand." The story concludes with Tony proposing to her, proving to distaff filmgoers that success and morality were still possible in depression-plagued 1930. One can only wonder how Dorothy Sebastian and Anita Page, her screen equals only a brief two years ago when they all appeared in *Our Dancing Daughters,* felt about the good fortunes of Joan Crawford, bona-fide star.

One individual who knew very well, or thought he did, the Crawford of this period put his observations on paper for the public to read. Between film assignments Doug Jr. appeared in two other stage plays, larked about the countryside with his pals Robert Montgomery and Laurence Olivier, tried his hand at sculpturing and painting, and wrote several short stories that appeared in assorted periodicals. *Vanity Fair* magazine hired Doug Jr. to prepare a series of profiles of movietown celebrities, which he illustrated with self-drawn caricatures. Of his wife he reported, "[she] has temperament without being temperamental. She demands the things to which she knows she has the right, and will ask for no more until she knows with all sincerity she is worthy of it. When she meets with disappointment she has a tendency towards bitterness rather than remorse, which, no doubt, is a throwback from an acute memory of less happy days. She is extremely sensitive to surroundings and instantly conscious of any discord. . . . She is intolerant of people's weaknesses. Jealousy is not in her makeup, but she resents those who have become successful without serving the same trying apprenticeship that she herself experienced. She is a ten-year-old girl who has put on her mother's dress—and has done it convincingly."

Joan's first bona-fide dramatic part was one she fought to get. Norma Shearer was set originally to star in *Paid* (1930) but the part went begging when Shearer's pregnancy forced her to withdraw. Joan urged Mayer and director Sam Wood to give her a chance, and they finally relented. The film was

112

adapted from the 1912 play by Bayard Veiller called *Within the Law* which had brought Broadway stardom to Jane Cowl. It had been previously filmed in 1917 with Alice Joyce and in 1923 with Norma Talmadge and Lew Cody. Joan played Mary Turner, a department store clerk who is sent to prison on a criminal charge of which she is innocent. While serving three years behind walls, she becomes embittered and swears revenge. Joan wore no glamorous makeup for the prison sequences. *Variety* accoladed Joan with, "Histrionically, she impresses us as about ready to stand up under any directorial assignment."

A pattern was now established for Joan which led her happily away from portraying the "flaming youth" type of roles. *Paid* proved that she was capable of doing more than the Charleston and the studio quickly cast her as another worldly soul in *Dance, Fools, Dance* (1931). The title is misleading in that it is an underworld tale rather than one of show business. In this Harry Beaumont-directed feature, Joan is Bonnie Jordan who is forced to abandon the carefree playgirl life when her father loses his wealth. As a cub reporter on a metropolitan newspaper, she is given an assignment to become chummy with gangland leader Jake Luva (Clark Gable) whom, it is surmised, was responsible for the death of star reporter Bert Scranton (Cliff Edwards). Adding to Bonnie's problems are her reckless brother (William Bakewell) and her love for wealthy Bob Townsend (Lester Vail) who thinks she's empty-headed. The film was a hit due to Joan's enormous box-office popularity and marked the first real acting job of the Crawford-Gable combination that would generate so much excitement in future years. Gable received sixth billing but his rugged role was impressive and his scenes with Joan created a good deal of audience interest. Joan would admit that their initial meeting "was like an electric current went right through my body. There was a thing that went through the two of us like dynamite."

Joan had finished *Complete Surrender*, based on Kenyon Nicholson's play *Torch Song* (on Broadway in 1930 with Mayo Methot), in which she played opposite John Mack Brown, but she was displeased by the previewed film. Her main objection was that the lack of chemistry between her and Brown was making the product dull. She went to Mr. Mayer and put her arms around his thick neck ("He always responded to that," she once said, "and he never touched my boobs or pinched my butt"). She asked that the picture be re-shot, but with Clark Gable instead of Brown. Mayer agreed.

In the production, renamed *Laughing Sinners* (1931), Joan plays blonde-haired Ivy Stevens, a small-town entertainer. In the early scenes, she dances and sings "What Can I Do?—I Love That Man" to emphasize her feelings for a traveling salesman (Neil Hamilton). When he brushes her off, she contemplates suicide but is saved from ending her life by a Salvation Army man (Gable). She regresses once more to an immoral life, but her idealistic suitor forgives her and asks Ivy to become his wife. The *New York Times* found Joan to be "better than usual in a film that is less than average in its overall scheme. It doesn't live up to its publicity."

This screen teaming also resulted in an offscreen love affair, with Clark Gable in love with Joan. Gable was still legally wed to the older Josephine Dillon, while Joan, of course, was the wife of Fairbanks Jr. When Louis B. Mayer became aware of the matter, he ordered Gable to remove himself from Joan's private life. Gable and Dillon were later divorced, and on June 19, 1931, the actor wed Ria Langham, seventeen years his senior, which stilled some of the wagging tongues of the Hollywood gossips.

For *This Modern Age* (1931), Joan was very blonde but not platinum. *Silver Screen* magazine informed its readers, "You'll like the new blonde Joan and bear with the picture for her sake." As Valentine Winters, she is a socialite who travels to Paris to see her mother (Pauline Frederick) where she meets a dissolute playboy (Monroe Owsley), but falls in love with rich, young Bob Blake (Neil Hamilton). One of the "shocking" sequences occurs when Valentine learns that her mother is the mistress of a wealthy French gentleman (Albert Conti).

Joan's tresses were back to their natural shade in *Possessed* (1931) in which she is an employee in a small-town box factory. Being the virtuous optimist, she knows there is more to life than what she is doing. Later, in New York, she encounters Mark Whitney (Clark Gable), a married man who aspires to a career in politics. Because of these ambitions he dare not attempt a divorce, and he persuades the heroine to become his mistress. The sweet-faced girl from the box factory now becomes a somewhat jaded lady. When Mark slaps her and calls her a tramp (this was the day of the double standard), the hearts of thousands of feminine movie fans beat a little faster. The film ends happily, in spite of the earlier heavy proceedings. Mordaunt Hall (*New York Times*) credited Joan with adding "another excellent performance to her list. . . ."

While Joan was competing for better vehicles at Metro, Doug Jr. had signed a new contract with Warner Bros.-First National. In 1931 he earned $72,791.67 compared to Joan's $145,750 salary from MGM. Within another year, the very enterprising Fairbanks had risen in status to match Joan's annual income. Beyond the growing career rivalry and Joan's amorous defection, the Fairbanks Jrs. suffered from the exhaustive scrutiny of the press who detailed and enlarged upon their every joint and separate activity. The fourth estate demanded more of the couple than either could offer. Then, too, Doug had more varied outlets than Joan. He cared about the fine arts, politics, sports, and life, while Joan was almost exclusively devoted to her film career. Socially, they gravitated toward different types of people and when entertaining at home their guest lists were often the subject of arguments.

With good cause, Joan had come to think of herself as the glamour arbiter of the Culver City lot. She found it hard to accept her spot as just one of many stars in *Grand Hotel* (1932). Directed by her pal Edmund Goulding, the project glittered with a cast of notables including Greta Garbo, Wallace Beery,

John and Lionel Barrymore, and Lewis Stone. It has been reported that an angry, sullen Joan demonstrated her disaffection at being subordinated to Garbo in the project by delaying her entrances on the set and playing Marlene Dietrich recordings in her dressing room. Though Joan and Garbo shared no scenes in the lavishly mounted film, Miss Garbo undoubtedly perceived Joan's turntable message.

In *Grand Hotel,* Joan is Flaemmchen, a hotel stenographer who is after a rich lover or husband. She enters into an affair with Preysing (Beery), a gruff industrialist, whom she finds repulsive but who presents an excellent opportunity for acquiring wealth. She is also pursued by an elderly bookkeeper (Lionel Barrymore) suffering from an incurable disease who wants a few joyous escapades before death claims him. Interwoven in this glossy picture are the relationships between Grusinskaya (Garbo), a famed but fading ballerina, and Baron von Geigern (John Barrymore), an adventurer in need of funds. At the story's end, Flaemmchen departs with the bookkeeper (the Baron has been killed by Preysing) for a Parisian holiday. The *Motion Picture Herald* astutely noted, "Joan Crawford puts all of her wiles into the stenographer who is out on the make."

Motion Picture Herald in selecting the ten "Biggest Money Making Stars of 1931-1932," based on the results of its poll of U.S. exhibitors, revealed Joan to be in third position, following Metro's Marie Dressler and Fox's Janet Gaynor, but ahead of Garbo, Shearer, Beery, and Will Rogers (Gable was number eight).

Joan's reputation as a "fashion plate" was probably initiated with the release in May 1932 of *Letty Lynton.* Adrian designed the coats, furs, gowns, and dresses worn by Joan in the title role and she had never looked lovelier or more glamorous onscreen. In the Clarence Brown-directed vehicle, Joan is a socialite from Manhattan who proves that crime does pay, at least for her. Her co-stars were Robert Montgomery, Nils Asther, Lewis Stone, and May Robson. Most of the critics focused their reviews on Joan's wardrobe.

Motion Picture Herald, for example, reported, "The gowns . . . will be the talk of your town for weeks after . . . and *how* she wears them!" The *New York Times* simply called Joan "Efficient." But lawyers were to have the last word on *Letty Lynton.* A complex copyright infringement suit was filed against the studio and the film was forced to be withdrawn from release, and to this day it is still unavailable for theatrical or TV showings.

Always anxious to prove that she could top her rivals, Joan was alerted that a planned remake of *Sadie Thompson* (which had won Gloria Swanson an Oscar nomination in 1928) was being prepared at United Artists. Joan begged to play the lead from Somerset Maugham's popular short story which had been turned into a stage vehicle for Jeanne Eagels. Joan insisted to her MGM bosses that she was ready and capable of portraying the hardened prostitute and apparently producer Joseph M. Schenck and director Lewis Milestone agreed. With Louis B. Mayer's agreement, Joan became Sadie Thompson in the film (retitled *Rain*), stranded for fourteen days on the island of Pago Pago where the rains never seem to stop (the actual shooting took place on Catalina Island by night). Her first onscreen word is "Boys!" as she emerges from her seedy hotel room after the camera travels from the bracelets of her right arm to her left arm to her shoes and then settles on her face.

Joan is hardly recognizable beneath the heavy makeup job. Her eyes are darkened, her mouth is a blotch, and a shock of hair hides the top portion of her face. The boys she is addressing are U.S. Marines assigned to the island's military installation. "How long am I booked for this joint, do you know?" When told it will be more than two weeks, she shrugs and says that she won't mind because "I like the boys here." She takes a particular liking to Marine Sergeant O'Hara (William Gargan), which leads to her confrontation with "Reverend" Alfred Davidson (Walter Huston), a determined missionary. Within a few days, Davidson has converted Sadie into a funless, Bible-quoting creature. But when

he later steals into her room one night to make love, the conversion ends and so does Davidson's life. He commits suicide and his body is found on the beach the next morning. At the end, back in her San Francisco finery, Sadie admits, "I'm sorry for everybody in the world, I guess."

Rain's Sadie Thompson was Joan's first major cinematic mistake. She overacted and many of her scenes, especially those dealing with her conversion, are quite unbelievable. She would say in retrospect, "Oh, who am I kidding? I just gave a lousy performance!" *Variety* agreed: "It shows her off unfavorably."

In mid-1932, Joan and Doug agreed to a two-month trip to Europe, hoping to restore some harmony in their unsettled domestic life. They crossed the Atlantic on the *Bremen* and were met at the English dockside by Doug's friend Noël Coward who introduced them to the enticing social life of London. At one of the parties arranged for the couple by Coward, Prince George was in attendance. While Doug thrived on the airy surroundings, Joan felt very ill at ease. Later, when it was arranged for the movie celebrities to attend a garden party at Buckingham Palace, Joan grew afraid and refused to attend. Thereafter the couple spent two weeks in Paris and returned to Hollywood. By now it was clear to them that their marriage was doomed.

On Monday, March 13, 1933, Doug Jr. was the defendant in a $50,000 alienation of affection lawsuit instigated by Jorgen Dietz. Joan told the press, "There's nothing for me to say except I have known all about this from the start. We've discussed these flagrant charges together. It is an outrageous injustice and there is no truth in them whatever." It was the contention of Dietz, a Danish mechanical engineer, that Fairbanks Jr. had alienated his divorced wife Solveig's "maliciously debauched" affections. While Solveig Dietz announced from Copenhagen that Doug would obtain a Paris divorce and marry her, Fairbanks said, "Joan is the only woman for me."

But the conflicting reports of various news media were bringing their own consequences to the occupants of 426 North Bristol Avenue. Joan had confided to a fan magazine reporter of her growing estrangement from Doug. Since this story was given to the publication before the Dietz flare-up, Joan would indeed be placed in a contradictory spot if she did not admit the pending separation to the Hollywood press. Louella Parsons of the Hearst newspaper syndicate was invited to Joan's house and informed of the future course of the Fairbanks Jr.-Crawford union.

In April 1933, by which time the Dietz case had failed to come to a courtroom hearing (dropped by the plaintiff), the *London Sunday Express* was publishing a serialized version of "The Love Story of Joan Crawford," highlighting the break-up of her marriage. One of the installments in the British paper was entitled "Why I Left My Husband," and was allegedly written by Joan. Although Fairbanks had told pressmen that he intended to re-woo his wife, the couple was divorced in Los Angeles on Friday, May 12, 1933, after almost four years of marriage. It was immediately rumored about Hollywood that Joan would marry Franchot Tone, who played her brother in her next film.

The picture *Today We Live* (1933) teamed her opposite Paramount's Gary Cooper for the first and only time. Set in rural England during World War I, the scenario (based on a William Faulkner story) miscasts Joan as regal Diana Boyce-Smith, the ever-so-noble daughter of a titled Britisher who has died at the front. "Just when I think I have no tears left, I surprise myself," says the saintly Diana to the local padre. It develops that American aviator Richard Bogard (Cooper) enters her life and supplants childhood sweetheart Claude (Robert Young) in Diana's affection. Later, when Diana is told that Bogard has died in action, she returns to live with Claude at the French front. One would not think that such a fickle girl (who wears such divine Adrian concoctions) would be given more chances, but Bogard returns unhurt and she agains wavers in her affection. Then Claude is blinded in battle and, not wanting to be a burden to anyone, sets off with Ronnie (Tone) on a suicide mission that has been

scheduled for Bogard. This, then, leaves Diana with only one choice. While Howard Hawks was able to instill some interest in the aerial and sea combat scenes, the interaction of the people on land was forced, trite, and embarrassing. Even the more devout Crawford fans could not accept Joan as a "ver-ee" British aristocrat.

In late 1933, *Liberty* magazine published a full-page ad of Joan holding a Coca-Cola bottle and smiling over it. (During the Forties, she would promote Royal Crown Cola in media ads.) In December 1933, MGM proceeded with a remake of *The Merry Widow* but could not decide whether it should be a musical or a straight drama. If the latter, Joan was to be starred. As it developed, the property was made as a musical with Jeanette MacDonald as the widow.

Where she lost popularity with *Rain* and *Today We Live,* Joan regained and augmented it with *Dancing Lady* (1933). This was MGM's and David O. Selznick's answer to Warner Bros. *42nd Street* (1933). Billed above the title, Joan is Janie Barlow, a burlesque performer who is fed up with her scruffy lot and announces: "I'm through with burlesque. I'm goin' up-uptown and on my own. I'm goin' up to where it's art—uptown." In the course of her transformation into a Broadway musical comedy star, she scraps with Main Stem director Patch Gallegher (Clark Gable) and is romanced by wealthy Tod Newton (Franchot Tone). After launching herself successfully on the Great White Way, Janie relinquishes her hold on Tod and returns to the waiting arms of Patch. The film's production was delayed at the outset while Gable underwent an appendectomy. William Gargan was mentioned as a likely replacement, but Joan refused to work with him again because he had publicly criticized her *Rain* performance.

The public was even more enthusiastic than the critics about *Dancing Lady,* which featured interludes of Joan, once again blonde, dancing and singing with Fred Astaire and Nelson Eddy. In the 1933 *Motion Picture Herald's* box-office poll, Joan showed up in tenth spot. She was now preceded by

Shearer, Gable, Harlow, Beery, and Dressler, all of whom were MGM stablemates.

Even in its day, *Sadie McKee* (1934) was glossy kitsch. In the title role, Joan was a maid in a wealthy small-town home where Michael (Franchot Tone) is the heir apparent. Sadie's mother (Helen Ware) hopes that Michael will take a shine to Sadie, but the girl has designs of her own on a factory worker named Tommy (Gene Raymond). Later Sadie loses Tommy to a show business performer (Esther Ralston), becomes an entertainer, and meets an alcoholic millionaire (Edward Arnold) and marries him. All this time she harbors the abiding notion that Tommy will re-enter her life, which he does, but it is only as he lies dying in a hospital. Her true love dead, she is bereft and fed-up with Brennan (Arnold). Out of the past comes Michael and she decides that she now loves him. The Nacio Herb Brown-Arthur Fred song "All I Do Is Dream of You" became the film's popular theme song. Scenes from *Sadie McKee* would be spliced into Joan's later *What Ever Happened to Baby Jane?* (1962).

MGM was always on the prowl for screen material in which to showcase their popular, fashion-conscious star. But, in true Hollywood fashion, many of the projects fell by the wayside. Joan and Clifton Webb (taken to Hollywood on the heels of his Broadway success in *As Thousands Cheer*) rehearsed dance sequences for *Elegance* in which Webb was to befriend a dancehall girl (Joan), teach her to become a lady, and spur her on to stage stardom. Not only did the two very contrasting artists dislike one another throughout rehearsals, but the studio soon decided the story premise was outmoded and shelved the project. Screen writer P. J. Wolfson was assigned to write a scenario for Joan and Gable under the title of *The Christian,* but this too was abandoned. The studio purchased a *McCall's* magazine story, "There Goes Romance," as a possible Crawford venture, but it was also dumped. In the autumn of 1934, it was reported that Gus Kahn had designed a new dance which he called the Carioca for use in a projected Crawford-William Powell musical *Reckless* (1935) in which Jean Harlow (as

she had on several previous occasions) replaced Joan. The dance number was not used on the Metro soundstages, as it had been to advantage at RKO for *Flying Down to Rio* with Ginger Rogers and Fred Astaire. Joan was later considered for the title role of *Outcast Lady* (1934), but Constance Bennett accepted this less than stellar property, and it would be Ann Harding who starred in *Biography of a Bachelor Girl* (1935) when it was decided that Joan was not suited for that role.

Thanks to the carry-over effects from the long-running *Dancing Lady* and her popular 1934 releases, the *Motion Picture Herald* box-office list for 1934 promoted Joan to the number six position, following Will Rogers, Gable, Janet Gaynor, Wallace Beery, and Mae West. *Vanity Fair* magazine, in compiling the ideal American beauty, superimposed the portraits of nine of the screen's loveliest women, one over another. Joan was one of the nine ladies, together with Norma Shearer, Marlene Dietrich, Ruth Chatterton, Helen Hayes, Greta Garbo, Peggy Shannon, Dorothy Jordan, and Joan Bennett. (Joan Crawford's beau, Franchot Tone, was one of nine males selected to exemplify the handsomeness of American men.)

In 1934, cartoonist Milton Caniff created the comic strip "Terry and the Pirates" which was destined to gain much popularity with adults and children. An important and sexy character in the strip was The Dragon Lady, whom Caniff patterned after Joan. He did not reveal his model's name until early in 1973 when the strip came to an end. Said Caniff, in explaining why Joan had been his unwitting model, "In appearance only, not personality. I saw her in some movie in which she played a siren. She had her hair parted in the middle and wore a high-collared cape. And that became The Dragon Lady."

The film of which Caniff spoke was *Chained* (1934) in which Joan wore the Adrian-designed cape during a shipboard romance scene with Clark Gable. The gossamer plot of the melodrama centers about lovely Diane Lovering (Joan), the secretary and mistress to steamship mogul Richard Field (Otto Kruger). Field's wife (Marjorie Gateson) re-

In *Dancing Lady* ('33).

With Clark Gable,
Frank Conroy, and
Skeets Gallagher in
Possessed ('31).

fuses to divorce him and he sends Diane on a cruise to South America while he tries to reason with his unyielding spouse. On the luxury liner, Diane meets Mike Bradley (Gable) and the expected happens. In the finale, Field steps aside, like a gent, so that the two lovers may find happiness. *Photoplay's* review stated that "Joan Crawford in the moonlight on the open sea appears quite seductive and Clark Gable seems to agree."

With Robert Montgomery, Joan and Clark Gable enacted the eternal love triangle in the comedy-drama *Forsaking All Others* (1934). Within the film, the three grew up together with both Jeff (Gable) and Dill (Montgomery) in love with Mary Clay (Joan). For one of the first times oncamera, Joan participated in some broad slapstick as she jockeyed back and forth between the two appealing leads, finally selecting Jeff as the man in her life. *Variety's* estimation was: "In the performances of Crawford, Gable, and Montgomery there is scarcely a shade of preference. All three are superb."

While, offscreen, Joan had safety glass installed in her home shower (a 1934 earthquake had damaged the original glass door), onscreen, she was the first to immerse her shapely form in the newly constructed aquatic facility on MGM's stage twenty-three. The pool was made to be easily converted from a modest swimming area to an enormous tank for water ballet numbers (it was later used for the Esther Williams aquatic extravaganzas). The pool's debut was in *No More Ladies* (1935), a frothy photoplay directed by Edward H. Griffith and George Cukor in which well-dressed, well-coiffed Joan loves philanderer Robert Montgomery who seemingly cannot change his women-loving ways. She attempts to make her dapper husband jealous by leading him to believe that she has had an affair with smooth Franchot Tone, but she is too much the moralist to do such a thing. Montgomery eventually comes around to her way of thinking, but it is hard to say for how long.

Joan's next released feature (which underwent several title changes: *Claustrophobia, If You Love,* and *Glitter*) emerged as *I Live My Life* (1935). In this pedestrian vehicle, she is an extrovert society gal who toys with the affections of an archeologist (Brian Aherne) whom she meets while on a visit to Greece. The serious young artifacts digger takes her at her word and becomes deeply infatuated and trails her back to Manhattan. He does not fit in with her society friends whom she in turn soon finds uninteresting. Ultimately she realizes that she is capable of abandoning the fun life of cafe society in favor of digging for historical remnants with the handsome, blue-eyed Aherne. Adrian designed twelve costume changes for Joan which she copied for her personal wardrobe because they were "the same general type that I would choose for my own use." *Movie Classic* magazine pointed out that the two "outstanding things" designed for the film were an evening coat of metallic cloth and a coat of black galyak fur with a six-inch belt.

On Friday, October 11, 1935, the predictable happened. Joan and Franchot Tone were wed in Englewood Cliffs, New Jersey, at the home of his parents, Mr. and Mrs. Frank J. Tone. The elder Tone, president of Carborundom Company, was the 1935 winner of the Electro-Chemical Society's International Medal. Franchot was a Cornell graduate and the possessor of a Phi Beta Kappa key. He was thirty years old; Joan was thirty-one. The newlyweds honeymooned at the Waldorf-Astoria in New York City where their suite was festooned with gifts of gardenia plants, long-stemmed red roses, and orchids. They were mobbed by fans whenever they elected to leave the hotel on a day's outing and Joan revealed to inquiries concerning her stylish wardrobe that she wore a size 4-B shoe. One newspaper published, "She breathes luxury and extravagance." The happy Tones returned to California and to a new home in Brentwood Heights complete with swimming pool, stables, and a movie theatre. Married again to an urbane gentleman of wit and intellect, Joan increased her knowledge by reading and delving into the finer arts. "It was what the role demanded," Louella Parsons once observed, "and she could not help living the role; it was her life."

119

Joan took voice lessons every day and told an interviewer in 1935 that she wanted to sing in opera as well as dance ballet. She also said that she was interested in starring in a Broadway show.

Dodd, Mead, and Company in September 1935 published *Memory Room,* a book of verses written by Don Blanding. One of the poems called "The Little Girl across the Street" was dedicated to Joan.

The Gorgeous Hussy (1936) had been a novel by Samuel Hopkins Adams. RKO bought the screen rights in 1934 as a vehicle for Katharine Hepburn, but MGM, in turn, bought it for Jean Harlow. Consistent with Joan's persistent fight for mature dramatic roles, she persuaded producer Joseph L. Mankiewicz to cast her in the role when it became apparent that Miss Harlow had neither the time nor the talent for such heavy histrionics. The character of the title is Peggy O'Neal, an innkeeper's (Gene Lockhart) daughter who becomes a pet of the politicians of Washington, D.C. Her major admirer is Andrew Jackson (Lionel Barrymore), the nation's President, who finds her vivacious and entertaining. During her brief stay in Washington, she loves a prospective senator (Melvyn Douglas) who rejects her. She marries a Navy lieutenant (Robert Taylor) who is later killed, and then weds a cabinet member (Franchot Tone). The women of Washington resent her for her lowly beginnings and ostracize her, but the men flock about her and find the young woman to be refreshingly comfortable company. Jackson adopts her as his "niece" and confidante, which shocks the more conservative Washingtonians. Peggy eventually leaves the city when it becomes obvious, even to her, that her presence is an embarrassment to the administration. The *New York Herald-Tribune's* Howard Barnes found Joan to be "handsome, although century-old costumes do not go well with the pronounced modernity of her personality." The fans felt the same and avoided seeing their favorite modern swinger in a costume piece. When she was asked the next year to join

In a pose for *The Gorgeous Hussy* ('36).

Clark Gable in the historical entry *Parnell*, she refused and Myrna Loy replaced her in this MGM disaster.

Back in the contemporary groove, Joan made *Love on the Run* (1936) which attempted to showcase her in a screwball comedy. She is the heiress and Gable the newspaperman who dash about Europe in pursuit of and escaping from spies and her one-time fiancé (Ivan Lebedeff). Franchot Tone, in a role that must have created offcamera disharmony between him and Joan, was once again the other man, a rival to Gable in both love and profession and who loses in both departments. At one point, Joan and Gable wind up at the palace of Fontainbleau where the polished floors provide an excellent base for a dance scene in which Joan does a miniature bump 'n' grind.

In May 1937, when 6,000 painters, makeup men, and scenic artists went on strike against the major studios for union recognition and closed shops, the Screen Actors' Guild debated whether or not to strike for higher salaries for 4,500 low-paid (less than $250 per week) extras and bit players. Guild president Robert Montgomery held late evening meetings with other Guild officers Fredric March, Chester Morris, Franchot Tone, Edward Arnold, Jean Muir, and Joan (second vice-president). They met every evening with producers in the hope of reaching an agreeable decision. *Time* magazine recorded the meetings while Joan "knitted away like a Madam Defarge, occasionally stiffening the men's backbones with her cry: 'We Strike!'" A strike was averted when Joseph M. Schenck (Twentieth Century-Fox's chairman) and Louis B. Mayer (MGM's vice-president) agreed to the Guild's demands on behalf of RKO, Paramount, MGM, Columbia, Universal, and Fox. Warner Bros. joined their brethren a day later.

Since *Love on the Run* redeemed Joan with her public, she was not anxious at the moment to break too far away from that mold. She replaced Myrna Loy and co-starred with Robert Montgomery for the sixth and final time in *The Last of Mrs. Cheyney* (1937), adapted for a second go-round onscreen (first done in 1929 with Norma Shearer) from the Frederick Lonsdale play seen on Broadway in 1925 with Ina Claire. Fay Cheyney (Joan) is a fake British aristocrat who robs her "friends" of their jewels. Her accomplice is Charles (William Powell) who masks his activities in the guise of a butler. During their sojourn into British aristocracy, the two thieves discover that their intended victims are much looser in their morals than they. One of these is Lord Arthur (Montgomery) who is revealed to be a real cad. The two thieves eventually retire from their careers and expect to find bliss at more honest professions. The public was not overly enthused by *The Last of Mrs. Cheyney*.

Whereas her box-office draw for 1936, according to the *Motion Picture Herald*, was recorded to be in seventh place, the following year she had drastically slipped to fortieth. *The Bride Wore Red* (1937) had not helped matters. As a jaded cabaret singer, Joan is paid by a prankster (George Zucco) to impersonate a wealthy debutante at a Tyrolean resort. In Adrian creations, she bedazzles the resort crowd and attracts a rich young man (Robert Young) as well as the village mailman (Franchot Tone) who is anti-establishment. The talky script did not appeal to moviegoers or critics. Howard Barnes (*New York Herald-Tribune*) wrote, "Your enjoyment of it will depend on how much of Miss Crawford you can take at a stretch." The Cinderella-type theme, heavy-handedly directed by Dorothy Arzner, was of too serious a nature to be widely entertaining. It was another professional setback for Joan. She even admitted to her favorite confidante, the fan magazine, that after viewing herself oncamera lately, ". . . I wish I could crawl away and die. Because it appears to me that I haven't given a thing—that not the faintest spark of emotion has been picked up."

Meanwhile, just as her relationship with Doug Fairbanks, Jr., had floundered over professional rivalry and cultural gaps, so the bliss between Joan and Franchot Tone had long ago departed. He would be at his happiest when his pals from New York's Group Theatre were in town and he could indulge in long conversations on serious drama. Joan's primary concern still was her film career.

With her Metro contract about to expire, the studio rushed her into *Mannequin* (1938), her only co-starring vehicle with Spencer Tracy. It is a very typical rags-to-riches tale slickly handled by director Frank Borzage. Joan is the beautiful model who falls in love with businessman Spencer Tracy after she has wed sweetheart Alan Curtis, a small-time chiseler. Her ex-husband later tries to blackmail upright Joan, but does not succeed. She remains steadfast to Tracy who is engulfed in industry labor problems. It is a familiar plotline, but the cast did its best to overcome the bad writing. It was films such as these which placed Joan on that infamous box-office poison list published by exhibitors in 1938. She was in fine company: Katharine Hepburn, Greta Garbo, Marlene Dietrich, and Mae West, among others.

But, by this point, her new MGM contract had been signed and called for five pictures a year over a five-year period. She was scheduled to earn over $1.5 million. (In 1938 Joan earned $305,384 in comparison to studio boss Mayer's $680,369 and Garbo's $270,000.) The initial project under the fresh and secure pact was to be *Infidelity*, an F. Scott Fitzgerald script wherein a husband commits adultery while his wife suffers long and hard to forgive and forget. Due to the still-in-force production code, such subjects as adultery were considered distasteful; the script was locked away.

In July 1938, while at work on *The Shining Hour*, Joan separated from Franchot Tone charging that he objected to her studio (super)activities and was angry and sullen for days when she was too tired to go out socially with him. In actuality what bothered Franchot Tone the most was being Mr. Joan Crawford.

As Olivia Riley in *The Shining Hour* (1938), she is a nightclub dancer who weds suave Henry Linden (Melvyn Douglas), a country squire, and goes with him to live in the family home. There she is opposed by his strong-willed sister Hannah (Fay Bainter) and brother David (Robert Young). The lat-

ter's wife Judy (Margaret Sullavan) is sympathetic and becomes her only friend. Within a short time, David's dislike turns to fascination and he encourages her to indulge in a game of coquetry. Later Hannah sets fire to the home in which Judy is trapped but she is saved by Olivia. It is then that David realizes that he cannot jeopardize his marriage to Judy. As he professes unending loyalty to his wife, Olivia returns to benevolent husband Henry. In *Variety's* estimation, "[the] picture is a confused jungle of cross-purpose motivations and situations that fail entirely to arouse interest."

In February 1939, in Los Angeles, Joan sued Tone for divorce on grounds of "extreme mental cruelty." Despite these charges, they remained friends and in March 1939 they dined and danced together at Club 21 in Manhattan. The following morning Joan appeared before New York Judge Benjamin Scheinman. She sought to obtain a divorce by "proxy," but he informed her that "the courts in this state look with disfavor on mail-order divorces," and ordered her to return to Los Angeles where her deposition had been filed. When Judge Scheinman asked for an explanation regarding her amicability toward Tone, she responded, "I hope that I am intelligent enough to be friendly with my husband." On Tuesday, April 11, 1939, in Los Angeles, she received her divorce. Louella Parsons was to write some years later, "I watched as that marriage ended. The divorce was without bitterness. Joan did not cease being Mrs. Franchot Tone because she was divorced. How could she?"

In February 1939, along with signing a divorce deposition, Joan added her name to the Hollywood "Declaration of Democratic Independence," instigated by director Herbert Biberman as a petition to President Franklin D. Roosevelt and the Congress to cease all trade relations with Germany. Joan was one of the original fifty-six signers of the document which also included Melvyn Douglas, Edward G. Robinson, Joan Bennett, Bette Davis, and Myrna Loy.

MGM elected to enter the new sweepstakes film category encompassing ice skating.

Since Sonja Henie was a box-office draw for Twentieth Century-Fox, there seemed no reason why Joan Crawford could not do the same for MGM. There was one very important consideration that stood in the way—Joan was not a trained ice skater. *The Ice Folllies of 1939* in final release was devoid of her skating inabilities and the on-ice sequences were handled by the company of skaters belonging to The International Ice Follies. Wearing a jet black wig parted in the middle (Hedy Lamarr did *not* sense competition in this area), Joan is an actress wed to an ice skater (James Stewart) who yearns to produce a follies on ice. Later, when she becomes a success in movies, her boss (Lewis Stone) solves her domestic separation by hiring the husband to produce skating movies. Crawford was the first to admit that these shenanigans produced a box-office turkey that demanded a great deal of loyalty from her indulgent fans. There was a certain amount of bleak irony in Joan's professional situation at this point. David Shipman notes in his *The Great Movie Stars: The Golden Years* (1970), "The executives started believing the fan magazines which persisted in the cry that Crawford was through, which was poetic justice, because she had always ardently believed in them."

Early in March 1939, Joan, who had spent untold hours and dollars studying with vocal coaches to improve her singing, recorded selections for Victor Records. On a seventy-eight rpm record, she sang "I'm in Love with the Honorable Mr. So and So" and "It's All So New to Me." Two other selections ("Tears from My Inkwell" and "I Never Knew Heaven Could Speak") would not be released by Victor at this time, but would later turn up in LP form on compilation nostalgia albums.

Of the next important phase of her screen career, Joan would state in her autobiography (co-authored with Jane Ardmore), *A Portrait of Joan* (1962), that "at this critical moment I set my sights on the part of Crystal, the hard-boiled perfume clerk who uses every wile to catch another woman's husband in *The Women.*" Joan let her desire be known to both George Cukor (director) and Hunt Stromberg (producer). Although she was eager to change her image, they were not so sure that her public would accept her as the blatant husband stealer. It was finally Cukor who took a chance and cast her as Crystal.

Advance advertisements for this film version of Clare Boothe's Broadway hit exclaimed, "135 women with nothing on their minds but men" and at the head of the all-female line-up was Norma Shearer, the darling of MGM and one whom Joan had envied in her early days for acquiring the best roles the studio had to offer. Now that Norma Shearer's protector and husband, Irving Thalberg, was dead, the actress was in a far more vulnerable position and both she and Joan knew it. Those who worked on *The Women* (1939) were not sure what to expect from the two major leads during production. While Norma tried to be more subtle about her envy and dislike of Joan, such as suggesting on several occasions that Miss Crawford's wardrobe was clashing with hers, Joan with her own brand of method acting seemed to assume the characteristics of Crystal both on and off the set. According to some observers on the set, director George Cukor more than once had to deal severely with Joan's behavior.

Perhaps the high point of the oncamera competition between Joan's Crystal and Norma Shearer's Mary Haines occurs at a high-fashion dress shop. Mary confronts Crystal with her blatant affair with her husband. The catty Crystal slyly remarks, "When Stephen doesn't like something I'm wearing, I just take it off." This is enough to send sweet Mary to Reno where she mingles with other gals (Rosalind Russell, Mary Boland, Joan Fontaine, Paulette Goddard) all of whom are likewise obtaining divorces. Back in New York, Crystal marries Stephen but finds him a bore and is soon dallying with Boland's young cowboy husband. Mary hears of this and shows her mettle in winning back Stephen.

Frank S. Nugent of the *New York Times* liked *The Women* and "we believe every studio in Hollywood should make at least one thoroughly nasty picture a year." He found Joan to be "hard as nails in the Crystal Allen

With Spencer Tracy and
Alan Curtis in a pose for
Mannequin ('38).

With Franchot Tone,
Mona Barrie, and
Reginald Owen in *Love
on the Run* ('36).

With James Stewart and
Lew Ayres promoting
The Ice Follies of 1939.

With Fay Bainter,
Robert Young, Melvyn
Douglas, and Margaret
Sullavan in *The Shining
Hour* ('38).

role, which is as it should be." The picture bolstered Joan's screen career greatly. It proved that the thirty-five-year-old star was by no means washed up in Hollywood.

In 1940, Joan adopted a three-month-old baby girl whom she named Christina. After two luckless marriages and four miscarriages, she still had enough faith to desire a family of her own. She was devoted to the little girl who quickly became the center of her life. A nurse cared for the child when Joan worked, but after studio hours, she rushed home to be with and play with Christina.

Her eighth and last starring film with Clark Gable was *Strange Cargo* (1940). Adapted by Lawrence Hazard from Richard Sale's novel *Not Too Narrow, Not Too Deep,* the film offered Joan as Julie, an immoral cabaret entertainer in a town near a New Guinea penal colony. She later finds herself aboard a sloop with several escaping prisoners. Andre Verne (Gable) challenges the authority of the convict Moll (Albert Dekker) and soon takes over as commander of the vessel. One of the escapees, Cambreau (Ian Hunter), is a strange, Bible-toting figure whose spiritual being has influence on every one of the prisoners as they die, one by one. With just the three (Gable, Hunter, and Joan) remaining alive on the boat, Verne rejects Cambreau and pushes him overboard. But he has second thoughts about drowning the man and drags him back to safety. It is then that Julie's prayers are answered, for Verne decides to return to the penal colony, serve his time, and return to her a free man. Reformed through love, Julie could not be happier.

For the first time in nine years, Joan performed through most of the film's running time with a minimum of makeup. Also her customarily sumptuous wardrobe was reduced to three garments (not designed by Adrian). With reviews like "The acting is high grade with Joan Crawford giving her best performance to date" (*Film Daily*), the feature should have been a box-office bonanza. It was not, however, because the Legion of Decency and other groups condemned it for its anti-Christ aspect and lustful situations. As a result, many Catholic churches forbade parishioners to see the movie and some cities refused to book it. Such actions were their misfortune, for this Frank Borzage-directed picture has a good deal to recommend it.

Offcamera it was reported that Clark Gable, now married to Carole Lombard, felt "uncomfortable" about working opposite Joan again. Although Miss Lombard did not consider Joan as a threat to her marriage, she jokingly threatened to pounce onto the set with a loaded shotgun if she were to hear any rumors about them. (However, it was Gable's newer screenmate, Lana Turner—of *Honky Tonk,* 1940—that Miss Lombard had better cause to fear.)

It was obvious now to most everyone that Joan was more than just a motion picture personality; she was developing into a good actress. Another step in that direction was the George Cukor-directed *Susan and God* (1940). Anita Loos adapted for the screen the Rachel Crothers play which had been a popular Broadway comedy of 1937 starring Gertrude Lawrence as Susan. Joan became the giddy, selfish, insensitive society matron onscreen after Norma Shearer rejected the role because she did not want to play the mother of a teen-age daughter. Joan wanted the role and Cukor and Mayer knew it. When Shearer declined, Mayer telephoned Joan in New York, where she was sojourning, and asked, "Will you be willing to play a mother?" Joan replied without hesitation, "I'll play Wally Beery's grandmother if it's a good part."

Susan Trexel returns home from Europe with a new enthusiasm—a religious movement that involves a lot of Pollyanna dogoodism. She tries to convert her chic Long Island friends but they are too jaded to respond and she succeeds only in causing trouble with her meddlesome ways. Her husband (Fredric March) has long ago abandoned hope of saving their marriage and has turned to liquor for solace. He initially thinks that Susan's religious viewpoint indicates a mature involvement, but he soon discovers that it is no more than another shallow fad. Their daughter (Rita Quigley), an introverted, neglected girl, finds no friendship with her mother and sympathizes with her father.

Eventually Susan comes to realize that her family needs her and that she should begin crusading at home rather than upsetting her friends' status. It is also during this transition that the film ceases being a comedy and joins all the rest of the slick and glamorous MGM offerings.

According to the *New York Daily Mirror,* however, "Joan Crawford's first appearance as a stellar comedienne is a spectacular success. . . ." *Variety* noted that the role of Susan "provides the studio with the key to future assignments for its star, which might bring her back considerably as a box-office personality." Unfortunately, *Susan and God* was not the public's cup of tea and Joan suffered another career reversal.

On Joan's first film *(The Women)* with George Cukor, it is reported that after she performed a particularly difficult initial scene, he said, "Miss Crawford, that was very nice. You knew your lines real well and you didn't make a single mistake. Now, let's get down to some *acting.*" It was while making *A Woman's Face* that the star and director worked together at their professional best. The picture was a remake of a Swedish film, *En Kvinnas Ansikte* (1938), which had starred Ingrid Bergman. The story's premise required that, for a good deal of the proceedings, Joan's famed, glamorous countenance be distorted by a scar or covered in bandages. Ironically, Joan offered what many consider her finest performance, proving that her remarkable face was not her only key to stardom.

She is Anna Holm, living in Stockholm with a heart filled with fear and hatred and a purse containing funds obtained through her chosen profession—blackmail. As a child, Anna was burned on the right side of her face in a fire that was accidentally started by her drunken father. Consequently, she grew up with a hideous scar for which she blamed fate and the world at large. Blackmail is her means of getting even. She meets Torsten Barring (Conrad Veidt at his scoundrelly best) who inveigles her into a dastardly scheme that requires her to arrange for the death of his nephew so that Torsten will in-herit the family fortune. Meanwhile, she encounters Dr. Gustav Segert (Melvyn Douglas), a famed plastic surgeon who persuades her to undergo an operation to remove the scar. The surgery is a success and Anna emerges a strikingly beautiful woman—on the outside. It takes a while before she also becomes beautiful inside and finds love with the doctor who has divorced his faithless wife (Osa Massen).

Audiences sufficiently familiar with the Joan Crawford film canon pick out one supreme moment in *A Woman's Face* as the height of the Crawford mystique. Veidt's Torsten Barring asks her, "Do you like music? . . . Symphonies? Concertos?" With determined seriousness, Joan's Anna responds, "Some symphonies, most concertos." Screenwriter Donald Ogden Stewart, one of Hollywood's best, obviously was having a devilishly good time with his scenario assignment.

A Woman's Face is, nevertheless, a *tour de force* for Joan who was aided by cameraman Robert Planck, the music of Bronislau Kaper, and a superb supporting cast. Among the latter was Connie Gilchrist in her third film who today, on recalling that production, describes Joan as "wonderful." Miss Gilchrist remembers that Joan often served coffee and small cakes on the set and although the atmosphere was friendly and warm, Connie, out of respect for a star, could not bring herself to address Joan by anything but "Miss Crawford." After several attempts to persuade Connie to call her by her first name, Joan finally said sternly, "My name is Joan! If you don't call me Joan, I'm going to call you 'Miss Kill-Christ.'" That was it. "After that," Connie says, "it was strictly a first-name basis."

A Woman's Face was slow to win audience acceptance, largely due to MGM's publicizing it as though it were another Crawford glamour picture and "a psychological study of a woman's soul." This did not particularly arouse prospective filmgoers. When the film opened in Detroit, a local theatre manager devised his own promotional campaign, exploiting Joan's Anna as "A Scarred She-Devil,"

"A Female Monster," "A Soulless Woman." That type of advertising sold tickets and MGM used the same form of advertising thereafter. *Photoplay* gave the film a rating as "Outstanding," and reported, "You'll find yourself completely held by the gripping intensity of this. Joan Crawford is magnificent." *Variety* noted, "Miss Crawford has a strongly dramatic and sympathetic role . . . which she handles in top-notch fashion."

If Greta Garbo and Norma Shearer had been Joan's chief rivals throughout the late Twenties and the Thirties, Joan had a new set to cope with in the Forties: Hedy Lamarr, Katharine Hepburn, Greer Garson, and Lana Turner. It would be Miss Garson, Louis B. Mayer's new favorite, who would prove the largest threat to Joan's continued reign at Metro. And when the studio chose to remake Rachel Crothers' play *When Ladies Meet,* Joan was matched oncamera with Greer Garson. As Stephen Harvey would write in *Joan Crawford* (Pyramid, 1974), "Crothers' perennial trump card was to toy with daring ideas while undermining them with cozy platitudes, and this hypocrisy is particularly in evidence throughout *When Ladies Meet.* Fabricated with the usual Metro polish, *When Ladies Meet* sports plenty of attitudinizing but scarcely a single genuine human emotion. In keeping with the scenario, Crawford conveys little of the sincerity she had displayed in *A Woman's Face.* Audiences admired her array of high-Forties [Adrian] frocks but little else about the film."

In this talky entry, Joan is Mary Howard (played in 1933 by Myrna Loy and on the 1932 Broadway stage by Frieda Inescort), a novelist in love with her publisher, Rogers Woodruff (Herbert Marshall). The publisher has a comely wife (Garson) but Mary assumes she is a stodgy individual or why else would the husband dally? Jimmie Lee (Robert Taylor) is a fun-loving guy who has set his sights on Mary but appears to be indifferent. The crux of the drama occurs when Mary and Claire (Garson) meet at the home of a mutual friend (Spring Byington) and have a lengthy talk that is most notable for allowing the viewer to carefully study the looks and mannerisms of these two studio rivals.

With Ian Hunter in *Strange Cargo* ('40).

If anything, the years had whetted Joan's appetite for better screen assignments rather than dulled her ambition. She continued to request assignments that required acting rather than vapid glamour, but was turned down as the lead in *Random Harvest* (1942) opposite Ronald Colman (the role went to Greer Garson). Joan later asked to do *Madame Curie* (1943), a project once considered for Irene Dunne or Greta Garbo, but Garson also got that one. Joan refused to play in *Her Cardboard Lover* (1942), which proved disastrous for Norma Shearer, and was placed on brief suspension. MGM would not release her from the contract. Then she was sent on her first loan-out in ten years, to Columbia to re-

With Melvyn Douglas in
A Woman's Face ('41).

With Roland Young in
*They All Kissed the
Bride* ('42).

place Carole Lombard who had died on a bond-selling tour in January 1942. During his period of grieving over Lombard's death, Gable relied on Crawford's friendship a good deal.* There were skeptical souls in Hollywood who insisted that Joan seized upon the tragedy to win the meaty role in *They All Kissed the Bride.*

For her work in *They All Kissed the Bride* (1942), Joan was paid $112,500, all of which was turned over to the American Red Cross and other charitable causes that would help end the war. In the P. J. Wolfson screenplay, Joan is Margaret J. Drew, a typical Rosalind Russell-type liberated woman who runs a business (trucking), runs her family (Billie Burke, Helen Parrish), and tries to run a nosey newspaper reporter (Melvyn Douglas) off the premises. The latter scheme backfires, and she falls in love with him, thus beginning the thawing-out process which leaves her utterly feminine and dependent on him. One can imagine how Miss Russell, Jean Arthur, or the late Carole Lombard would have handled this trifling soufflé. As it was, Joan was just a bit too earnest and practical for such capers.

While Joan was struggling (some insisted fumbling) with her screen career, she continued to remain an active force on the social scene. One of her escorts in early 1942 was actor Phillip Terry who had several supporting roles at MGM in the late Thirties before moving on to bigger parts in lesser films at minor studios. On Tuesday, July 21, 1942, Joan married Terry at Hidden Valley Ranch near Ventura, California. Joan was thirty-eight; her groom was thirty-three. He had been born Frederick H. Kornmann, on March 7, 1909, in Sacramento, California. He grew up in Glendale, California, and was a graduate of Stanford University.

Fledgling director Jules Dassin was assigned to guide Joan through her next Metro vehicle, *Reunion in France* (1942), which was anything but a wedding bouquet for the en-

during star. "You are France. . . . Whenever I think of France I think of you," Philip Dorn says of Joan's Michele de la Becque. This is after the heroine, one of the bubbly Parisian gadabouts, has a change of heart about the Nazi occupation of her homeland. No longer does she think only of her (Irene) wardrobe for now she has become a patriot involved with the Resistance. One of her missions is to lead Pat Talbot (John Wayne), a Yank with the RAF, out of the danger zone. Along the arduous way the couple fall in love, but she realizes her mission is to remain with loyal Dorn and to further aid her beleaguered country. The *New York Times* dryly found, "Miss Crawford, as usual, makes an elegant mannequin for a series of ensembles that probably will excite more female comment than the role itself."

In retrospect, it almost seems as if such artless ploys—shoving the studio's once top female stars into sub-standard vehicles and then "graciously" allowing them to leave the studio—were deliberate. After *Two-Faced Woman* (1941), Greta Garbo went on a temporary leave of absence that became permanent. After *We Were Dancing* and *Her Cardboard Lover,* both 1942 releases, Norma Shearer abdicated her berth at Metro. For Joan, the deciding factor was *Above Suspicion* (1943), a feckless espionage caper. It derived from a good source—Helen MacInnes' novel—but the transplant to screen was embarrassing. It dealt with newlywed Americans who become involved with the British Secret Service in Germany. The couple, Frances (Joan) and Richard (Fred MacMurray), are to obtain vital information from British agents in Germany, but are hounded by a determined Gestapo chief (Basil Rathbone). Later Frances is captured and imprisoned in an old palace. She is rescued by her angry husband and a handful of agents and escapes to freedom through the underground. As the *New York Herald-Tribune* delicately assessed it, "Unfortunately, neither Joan Crawford nor Fred MacMurray look quite bright enough to unravel the tangled skeins of this screen melodrama." Crawford would later call the picture "undiluted hokum."

* In 1942, MGM offered Warner Bros. $100,000 for the rights to Irwin Shaw's *The Hard Way,* planning to team Gable, Crawford, and Lana Turner. But Warner made the film itself in 1943 with Dennis Morgan, Ida Lupino, and Joan Leslie.

"If you think I made poor pictures after *A Woman's Face*, you should have seen the ones I went on suspension not to make!" Once more Joan asked to be allowed to leave the studio, refusing executives' requests to join in the all-star *Cry Havoc* (1943), a story of war nurses that featured Ann Sothern, Margaret Sullavan, and Joan Blondell. "Mr. Mayer didn't want me to leave," Joan has said, "but he knew how unhappy I was. I left by the back gate." Thus ended an eighteen-year professional liaison that witnessed Joan's rise from a bright-eyed bit player to one of the motion picture screen's most elegant, well-garbed actresses.

If bets had been taken in Hollywood at that time as to Crawford's future, the odds would have been greatly in her disfavor. Even she would later admit, "The consensus of opinion among the top brass was that I was washed up again." Two days after leaving Metro, Joan signed a two-film contract with Warner Bros. Meanwhile, she was having domestic problems. In 1942, she and Phillip Terry had adopted a towheaded boy who was initially called Phil Junior, but whose name was later changed to Christopher. The following year, Joan was forced by the boy's real mother to return him to her in New York. After a court hassle, Joan later regained custody of the boy.

The Warner Bros. hierarchy, who had acquired Joan's services for one-third of her old Metro fee, were indecisive over what to do with the famed star. They had on their VIP roster Bette Davis for high drama, Olivia de Havilland for sugar 'n' spice, Ann Sheridan for breezy toughness, Ida Lupino for suffering, Jane Wyman for comedy, and Barbara Stanwyck for both comedy and drama. With Alexis Smith, Joan Leslie, and Eleanor Parker each moving towards great popularity, the studio was top-heavy with female talent. Unwilling to take just any property (and Bette Davis is said to have made certain that few decent ones came Joan's way), Joan sat on the sidelines, gambling that one super-charged role would offset her lengthening absence from the screen. In 1944 Joan was used to decorate the studio's tribute to the *Hollywood Canteen* when she danced in one scene with a rehabilitating soldier (Dane Clark).

While playing the personal role of housewife, gardener, and mother, Joan was sent several scripts by the Burbank studio, all of which she rejected. None appealed to her. She even went so far as to ask to be taken off the Warner payroll, but, before this suggestion could be taken too seriously, producer Jerry Wald presented her with a story that had already been rejected by Bette Davis, Ann Sheridan, and Barbara Stanwyck. Joan was not too proud to read the script after such notable rejections, and told Wald that she would like to do the part. Michael Curtiz, who had been assigned to direct the film, was not excited about the prospect of handling an Adrian-draped Crawford, and only after being convinced by both Wald and Miss Crawford that she would alter willingly her old image, drop the broad-shouldered suit look, and play the housewife of the part, would he consent to work with the veteran star.

In this case, the move was a wise one because Joan *is Mildred Pierce* (1945). None of the other candidates for the part could have given the role the quiet tenderness of mother love or the air of sophistication while working herself tirelessly to make a proper home for herself and her two daughters. In Ranald MacDougall's scenario, adapted from James M. Cain's novel of 1941, Mildred evolves as a smarter woman than as depicted by Cain. The novelist had her slow-witted almost to the point of foolishness with regard to her feelings for her daughter.

In the 113-minute feature, Mildred's marriage to Bert Pierce (Bruce Bennett) has ended on a note of insolvency. It is now up to her to provide for her children—the younger Kay (Jo Ann Marlowe) later succumbs to illness. Mildred is determined that offspring Veda (Ann Blyth) will have all the luxuries of life that have evaded her. In a quirk of good luck, that only seems to happen in movies, Mildred finds herself in a restaurant sipping a cup of tea when one of the waitresses quits. Mildred rushes up to the hostess (Eve Arden) and begs for the job. On the job, Mildred intro-

With Dane Clark in
Hollywood Canteen ('44).

The star at home in 1945.

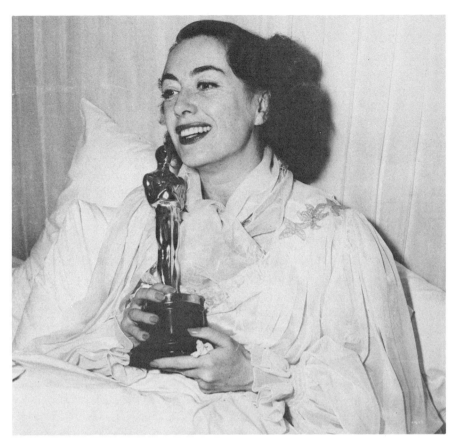

At home with her *Mildred Pierce* Oscar (March 1946).

With Jack Carson in *Mildred Pierce* ('45).

duces her home-made pies—made with the help of domestic Lottie (Butterfly McQueen) —to the trade and before long she wants to open her own restaurant.

Later, she meets suave Monte Beragon (Zachary Scott), a socially prominent man with financial difficulties who sells her one of his real-estate holdings for the establishment of her eatery. Ida (Arden) now goes to work for Mildred, and soon the dining spot is a success. Meanwhile, maturing Veda is becoming increasingly demanding and snobbish. She and Monte are seen everywhere together which upsets Mildred since she imagines herself to be in love with him. "I want you to do me a favor," she says to Monte. "Stay away from Veda." Monte seems indifferent to her request. She further explains, "I've worked long and hard trying to give Veda the things I've never had. I've done without a lot of things, including happiness sometimes, because I wanted her to have everything. Now I'm losing her. She's drifting away from me. She hardly speaks to me except to ask for money or poke fun at me in French because I work for a living."

Mildred blames her plight on Monte, insisting, "You're interfering with my life and my business and worst of all you're interfering with my plans for Veda and I won't stand for it." Monte's reaction is to tell Mildred that he is through with her. Mildred is satisfied and hands him a pay-off check to seal the break.

Soon thereafter comes a confrontation which certainly must have appealed to any feeling mother. Veda has concocted a story about being pregnant to wheedle money from the parents of a boy she has dated and considered marrying. The story is a lie. Veda is not pregnant and Mildred demands she return the money. Veda then lashes out, "Why do you think I want money so badly?. . . . With this money I can get away from you—from your chickens and your pies and your kitchen and everything that smells of grease. I can get away from this shack with its cheap furniture and this town and its dollar days and its women that wear uniforms and its men that wear overalls." She further insults her mother

by saying that money will not change her from "a common frump whose father lived over a grocery store and whose mother took in washing."

Mildred is horrified and tears up the ten-thousand-dollar check. "Get out, Veda!" she orders. "Get your things out of this house right now before I throw them into the street and you with them. Get out before I kill you." Torn between being a dutiful mother and, for a change, thinking of herself, Mildred then travels to forget. When she returns home, she asks Monte to marry her in order to provide a proper homelife for Veda. Monte agrees only on condition that she turn over to him one-third of the restaurant business, which is now a chain venture. Veda is gleeful because she can now be close to Monte, and the two have an affair without indulgent Mildred's knowledge. But on a surprise visit to Monte's beach house, Mildred finds the two of them in a compromising position and leaves. While getting into her car, she hears a pistol shot and runs back to find that Veda has killed Monte because he refused to take her seriously. Mildred gallantly covers for her daughter but the police detect the truth. Veda is left to face justice, while Mildred returns to Bert, the husband she had forsaken in favor of Veda.

Critic James Agee of *The Nation* rated *Mildred Pierce* as "one of the few anywhere near honest [performances]" by Joan and termed her performance "excellent." Other critics of the day were equally enthusiastic about the new Crawford and, in retrospect, the performance remains a substantially sound one. In *Joan Crawford,* author Harvey perceives, "Vital and ambitious but insecure and easily wounded, she was the summation of every role Crawford had ever played. All the essential facets of the various earlier Crawford personae were melted down into a new synthesis through the crucible of *Mildred Pierce.* . . . Every detail of her characterization is delicately underplayed, from her hushed line readings to the eloquently subtle control of those expressive eyes. . . . Even her penultimate confrontation with the ungrateful Veda is conducted with restraint all the more dramatic for its simmering understatement. Crawford reacts to her daughter's venomous assault with a slap like whiplash, and a grimace etched in sandstone. She has learned to use her angular face as a mask of stoic endurance. Her mercurial feelings ferment beneath this stolid facade, emanating from her eyes and, seemingly, even the pores of her skin. This constant battle for dominance between her proud self-control and emotional torment is the keynote to Crawford's interpretation of Mildred and all the best work she was to do thereafter."

While a realistic *Mildred Pierce* might have been better characterized by a Rosemary De Camp-type, Joan's built-in glamour (though disguised) was an understandable concession to box-office demands. One could hardly have asked for a better supporting cast: venal Ann Blyth, chummy but tart Eve Arden, gentle but loyal Bruce Bennett, crude but well-meaning Jack Carson (as Bennett's one-time business partner and would-be suitor of Mildred), and, of course, the Forties' most sophisticated scoundrel, Zachary Scott. Expert cinematographer Ernest Haller gave the production its proper tangible look and showed viewers a mature Crawford at her well-chiseled best. With her inexpensive garment rack wardrobe (at least in the opening sections of the film), it was a marvelously refreshing change from the swanky Crawford of her late MGM days.

Once it was clear to Warner Bros. that *Mildred Pierce* had a profitable future, the studio embarked on an extensive publicity campaign which cautioned moviegoers, "Don't tell what Mildred Pierce did!" Thousands of film patrons flocked to their local theatres to find out what new tricks Joan Crawford was up to now.

In January 1946, Joan received her first Oscar nomination. After twenty years of progressing from the movie jazz age to the suffering working girl to an over-indulgent mother, she was acknowledged by her peers to be worthy of an award. Her competition consisted of Ingrid Bergman (*The Bells of St. Mary's*), Greer Garson (*The Valley of Decision*), Jennifer Jones (*Love Letters*), and Gene Tierney (*Leave Her to Heaven*). As celebrities

entered Grauman's Chinese Theatre the evening of Thursday, March 7, 1946, for the award presentations, Joan lay in bed at home where her physician, Dr. William Branch, had confined her with the flu. Louella Parsons would later write, "few in Hollywood believed this. The feeling was that Joan could not bear to be present, win or lose, when the name of the actress who would receive the Oscar was announced. Defeat would be unbearable; winning would be overwhelming."

From the stage of Grauman's, Charles Boyer announced Joan the winner and the film's director, Michael Curtiz, accepted the statuette on her behalf. Later that evening, Curtiz and friends and the press photographers (of course!) drove to Joan's Brentwood home where champagne bubbled in celebration. The star who had been once dubbed "Box-Office Poison" was the lady of the hour. It was her moment of triumph.

Five days after winning her coveted Oscar, Joan filed suit in Los Angeles to divorce Phillip Terry, who had worked in a defense factory during most of the war. The charge was "cruel and inhuman treatment." On Thursday, April 25, 1946, the divorce was granted when Joan told the court that Terry had tried to pick her screen roles for her and that he had refused to allow her to go out at night. "Never again," she said with regard to marriage as she exited the courtroom. At the age of forty-two, Joan was single, the mother of two children, and Hollywood's actress of the year. She signed a seven-year pact with Warner Bros. at $200,000 per film. The trade papers signified this personal victory with a headlined article, "Crawford's back, and MGM hasn't got her!"

While her chief rival on the lot, Bette Davis, was emoting in *A Stolen Life* (1946), which she produced and took dual roles in, Joan's only film of the year was *Humoresque,* a remake of the Fannie Hurst story which had been filmed by Paramount in 1920 with Alma Rubens as the heroine. As Helen Wright, Joan was photographed at her most flattering and alluring by Ernest Haller. Her Helen is a neurotic, wealthy Manhattan socialite married to Victor (Paul Cavanagh). Theirs is a modern marriage in that Helen has *carte blanche* to adore and be adored by as many men as she chooses. Alcohol is also her friend and she says, "I like to drink. It's an escape." She meets Paul Boray (John Garfield), a dedicated violinist from the Lower East Side. She is unable to twist him around her finger as she can most men, and he becomes a challenge. In the course of a love-hate relationship, Helen tells her smart friends about Paul, "[You have] bad manners, Mr. Boray, the infallible sign of talent. Shall I make a prediction? Soon the world will divide itself into two camps, pro-Boray and anti-Boray."

Helen becomes very much pro-Boray as she falls deeply in love with him. A later confrontation with Paul's tenement-dwelling mother (Ruth Nelson) convinces her that it is hopeless, that his music must be the real love of his life. Realizing her destiny, Helen tells Paul, "You don't want me, not really. It's someone you made up. . . . You don't want me, Paul, I'm too wearing on the nerves. . . . You're married already. You're married to your work, you're married to your music. You'll never marry me. Don't forget your music, Paul, don't ever forget your music." Then she snarls, "I hate music. I detest it."

The night of Paul's important Symphony Hall concert finds Helen at her lush beach house. She has decided not to attend. She calls Paul before the concert begins to tell him she will not be there, and the character of Helen has a long scene in which the telephone conversation is depicted from her side. This scene surpasses even that of Anna Held's (Luise Rainer) in MGM's *The Great Ziegfeld* (1936). It is a *tour de force* as she tries to convince Paul that nothing is wrong. Although she has been drinking heavily, she tells him, "No, I'm not drinking, really I'm not. I swear it, darling. Oh, please believe me and don't scold. I don't want to be scolded anymore. Yes, I know . . . I know. I should have called you sooner but I meant to come right up to the very last minute. I was all dressed and ready as a matter of fact. What? Paul, it's so quiet here and it's such a long drive and there'll be so many people. Please try and understand. Don't make me explain."

[She has the radio on, over which can be heard the orchestra tuning up.] "The rest and quiet are doing me a world of good. It's so beautiful and peaceful. There isn't a soul on the beach. I can see the sky and the water. There's a smudge of smoke out there almost at the horizon. It must be a boat, far, far out. Paul, I wish we were on board that boat, so far out that we couldn't see anything but sky and water—nothing more. . . . What? Oh, right . . . go ahead. . . . Of course, I understand . . . and . . . good luck, darling. Paul, I . . . I love you." The phone conversation has lasted about two and one half minutes.

Helen continues to drink while the radio brings Paul's violin solo into her room. (The music heard is love music from Richard Wagner's *Tristan and Isolde.*) She empties the bottle, drinking the bourbon straight. She weaves her way through the room, fingers the cover of one of Paul's recordings, looks out the window, hears voices, and tosses her glass through the window. She wanders down the steps onto the beach, passes a man and his dog as the water laps at the shore. She is crying and puts her hands to her ears to blot out the music. She walks into the water, thus giving up her own life as an ending to a hopeless love affair. For many, it is a far superior aquatic suicide than either Fredric March's or James Mason's in the two best versions of *A Star Is Born.*

Joan, who caused quite a fashion stir when she wore rimless spectacles in the film, was honored with a Golden Globe Award for her *Humoresque* performance, her first such token by the Foreign Press of Hollywood.

There were plans to team Joan and rival Bette Davis in a version of Edith Wharton's *Ethan Frome,* but nothing materialized. It was later reactivated as a Jane Wyman vehicle, but that too was shelved. Instead Joan was handed *Possessed* (1947) by her guardian angel producer, Jerry Wald. Those who had thrived on Joan's Mildred Pierce or Helen Wright were bowled over by her Louise Howell in this grim melodrama directed by Curtis Bernhardt. Told in stark flashback form, she is the private nurse who slavishly pursues Van Heflin although he does not return her affections. Raymond Massey is the mature widower who wants to marry her. She agrees but becomes overwrought when Heflin intends to marry Geraldine Brooks, Massey's young adult daughter. Not only does an emotionally frazzled Joan hear the voice of Massey's late wife, but she envisions herself pushing Brooks down a flight of stairs. In desperation, she kills Heflin and then lapses into a state of catatonia, to be found by the police as she wanders the streets of Los Angeles.

For her very impressive acting in *Possessed,* Joan was again Oscar-nominated and she should have won the award. However, the prize went to Loretta Young for *The Farmer's Daughter.*

Trading on the box-office appeal of the new Crawford, Warner Bros. loaned her to Twentieth Century-Fox for the triangular sudsy drama *Daisy Kenyon* (1947), which was produced and directed by Otto Preminger. He has since claimed he does not remember a thing about the picture, while Henry Fonda points to it as one of the most odious projects shoved at him by the studio. In glossy, inconsequential terms, the regressive story focuses on New York artist Daisy Kenyon (Joan) who loves married man Dan O'Mara (Dana Andrews). While he stumbles and wonders whether he should divorce his capricious wife (Ruth Warrick)—there are the children to think of—Daisy weds returned war veteran Peter (Fonda). Then, when Dan does seek his divorce, he tries to persuade Daisy to leave her husband for him, but the lady wisely decides to remain with Peter. It was all so typical of the forgettable filmfare Joan made at Metro in the mid-Thirties.

In August 1947, Joan adopted two more babies, twin girls whom she named Cynthia and Cathy. Whereas her other two children were blonde, the twins had dark hair, much the same color of Joan's. Her favorite date was handsome lawyer Greg Bautzer, who was not the marrying kind. Wrote Sheilah Graham about this romance, "Joan would have been deliriously happy—for a while anyway. For she was in love with him and he with her." Miss Graham added, "I hope Joan

finds the man she seeks, because this is a great woman with much tenderness and loyalty to give—to the right man."

Joan was not able to find a suitable script at Warners until *Flamingo Road* (1949) came her way, once more uniting her with producer Jerry Wald and director Michael Curtiz. It was a felicitous rematching. In the early scenes of this tawdry tale, she was a bit overripe as the carnival dance girl Lane Bellamy, but she acquits herself excellently later as the girl from the wrong side of the tracks who loses blue-blood Fielding Carlisle (Zachary Scott) to another woman (Virginia Huston). After she is framed on a criminal charge by the southern town's political leader, Titus Semple (Sydney Greenstreet), she serves a prison term. When she is freed, she goes to work for Lute Mae Sanders (Gladys George) in a roadhouse which provides feminine companionship to men of means. One of these is Dan Reynolds (David Brian), a politician and enemy of Boss Semple. Lane and Reynolds later wed and move to the town's elite section on Flamingo Road. The ruthless Semple, out to ruin Reynolds, creates a scandal involving Lane and Carlisle after the latter kills himself. In a confrontation with Semple, Lane carries a pistol. Soon they struggle and Semple is killed. Lane is imprisoned, while her devoted husband works out a solution to the problem. Although audience reaction was milder to this than to *Mildred Pierce,* studio boss Jack L. Warner was sufficiently impressed by the box-office results to continue dynamic Joan in the same mold thereafter. In the meantime, she made a token guest appearance in the Technicolor *It's a Great Feeling* (1949), a spoof on the making of a movie star called Judy Adams (Doris Day).

In 1949, Joan received *Photoplay's* Gold Medal Award, but the acceptance had to be taken by son Christopher because she was recovering from a mild case of pneumonia. For the occasion, Christopher wore his uniform from the military academy he attended. Columnist Sidney Skolsky that year wrote with pride, "Joan Crawford is still the movie actresses' idea of a movie actress."

The Damned Don't Cry (1950) was the

Modeling her carnival outfit for *Flamingo Road* ('49).

Advertisement for *Possessed* ('47).

best that Warner Bros. could find for Crawford, even though Bette Davis and many others had left the lot in the post-World War II economy wave. This film was an amalgam of *Mildred Pierce* and *Flamingo Road.* She is the bored housewife who leaves her shabby surroundings after the death of her only child. From there, she finds excitement in the company of a master criminal (David Brian) and a petty crook (Steve Cochran), while an accountant (Kent Smith) sticks by her through the thickest moments. As the tough-as-nails dame, Joan is provided with some tart, if clichéd, dialogue. On one occasion she asks David Brian's character, "What am I, George . . . another wire service you've bought into . . . another race track you bought?" Later, she accepts the fact that she is nothing more than Brian's mistress. "I learned a long time ago, George, the customer is always right." Then there is the candid observation by Joan's "heroine" that summed up so well the type of role Joan was now playing so efficiently (and earnestly) onscreen. "If there is anything good about me, it's my credit." But the critics were not kind about Joan's performance in *The Damned Don't Cry.* "Miss Crawford runs through the whole routine of cheap motion-picture dramatics in her latter day hard-boiled, dead-pan style," noted Bosley Crowther of the *New York Times.*

She next went to Columbia Pictures for an updated remake of *Craig's Wife,* the title being changed to *Harriet Craig* (1950). The George Kelly play had been offered on Broadway in 1925 with Chrystal Herne starred. It was filmed by Pathé in 1928 with Irene Rich and by Columbia in 1936 with Rosalind Russell. Nasty Hollywood dwellers insisted that having Joan as the overfastidious mistress of a household with a disturbing passion for possessions was an example of type casting, but certainly there was nothing in Crawford's private personality to compare with the character's dislike of men.

That same year Joan made her first television appearance as a guest star on NBC-TV's "The Bob Hope Show" on Saturday, October 14. In 1951 she was blamed, in New York, for the break-up of the marriage of Yul Brynner (then star of Broadway's smash hit, *The King and I*) and actress Virginia Gilmore. Joan and Brynner had been seen together on several occasions, but she denied to Sheilah Graham that she had been responsible for the separation. Miss Graham rallied to Joan's defense by writing, "No one can break-up a marriage unless the crack is past repairing." That same year *Photoplay* chose Joan as one of "the twelve most beautiful women in Hollywood" because of her "beautiful bones," and because "she knows exactly what to do about herself—and, more important, does it." The magazine article went on to report, "It is inevitable Joan will remain an all-time symbol of Hollywood glamour. She should be an inspiration to every woman—to do something exciting about herself." The other eleven winners were Mona Freeman, Susan Hayward, Loretta Young, Arlene Dahl, Elizabeth Taylor, Rita Hayworth, Marlene Dietrich, Deborah Kerr, Ava Gardner, Ann Blyth, and Linda Darnell.

With her old friend, Robert Young, Joan took the lead in Warner Bros.' screening of Fay Kanin's play, *Goodbye, My Fancy,* adapted from the Broadway show that had starred Madeleine Carroll and Conrad Nagel. For many people, including Miss Crawford herself, this film failed to hit the mark. However, for this book's authors, it remains one of the more engaging of Joan's more recent pictures, revealing the allegedly tough superstar at her most feminine, liberated, and girlish. She is Congresswoman Agatha Reed who returns to the college from which she was expelled twenty years earlier. She is to receive an honorary degree. The college president is Dr. James Merrill (Young) who had been her romantic interest those many years ago. He had been a young professor and she a student. One night she had stayed out with him all evening, leading to her expulsion. She is now eager to renew their acquaintance, but he proves to be a rather spineless soul. Instead, she chooses as her romantic interest Matt Cole (Frank Lovejoy), a national news magazine photographer who has followed her throughout her career.

Perhaps what makes *Goodbye, My Fancy*

engaging on so many levels are the parallels between her character and the real-life Joan Crawford: each is a self-made woman, each has sacrificed romance for career, each is vulnerable to life, yet courageous for proper causes. After so many years of stardom, Crawford had come to expect a high degree of deference on the set from her co-workers. In *A Portrait of Joan,* she tells a tale on herself. " . . . this [*Goodbye, My Fancy*] cast included a young girl named Janice Rule whose personality definitely clashed with mine. I felt she was nonprofessional in her attitude, that she regarded movie work as something less than slumming and one day I told her so. 'Miss Rule,' I said, 'you'd better enjoy making films while you can, I doubt that you'll be with us long!'" Joan provides her own postscript to the anecdote, "I've since seen her on TV and I can only add superlatives. Miss Rule, my apologies. I think you're going to be with us a long, long time."

What vitiates the impact of the film is the dilution of the political aspects of the storyline, turning the feature into just another romantic venture despite the mature stars. As Crawford later said, "But *Goodbye, My Fancy* did nothing for any of us."

Warner Bros. seemed more intent upon turning out Doris Day musicals, and they assigned Joan to *This Woman Is Dangerous* (1952) which Joan says "could have been my swan song." It was a cheap melodrama which united her for a third and final time with David Brian. Here she is Beth Austin, the brains of a gang of hold-up men and the mistress to a ruthless killer (Brian). She is admitted to an out-of-state hospital when her eyesight begins to fail and genuinely falls in love with her doctor (Dennis Morgan). Her jealous lover follows her and the FBI trails him. The G-men get him before he gets her, and it is presumed that happiness lies ahead for Beth after serving a prison term. Bosley Crowther (*New York Times*) wrote a damning appraisal of the film and of Joan. "[This is a] pure contrivance for the display of Miss Crawford's stony charm. Those who admire the actress may be most tenderly moved by the evidence of the suffering she stolidly un-

dergoes. . . . And to these, the arrant posturing of Miss Crawford may appear the quintessence of acting art." Crowther's most lethal remark on the star was to describe Joan as "the incredibly durable star, whose theatrical personality has now reached the ossified stage. . . ."

Long before the late February 1952 release of *This Woman Is Dangerous,* Joan was aware of the rapid descent of her screen status. In search of fresh properties, she had come across the novel *Sudden Fear* by Edna Sherry and was determined that this should be her next vehicle. However, the screen rights were owned by independent producer Joseph Kaufman and it took a good deal of time to find him. When she did, Joan arranged through her agent Lew Wasserman to get out of her Warner Bros. pact, an agreement which she called "a good contract." Now a free-lance person, Joan learned the value of economy. She worked on a deferred salary–percentage deal, hired David Miller to direct the venture, and exhibited great patience while Lenore Coffee and Robert Smith reworked the scenario to her specifications. Exteriors for the movie were shot in San Francisco with Charles Lang, Jr., behind the camera. Since the lead character Myra Hudson (Joan) was a wealthy playwright, a house befitting her social level was rented at the corner of Green and Scott Streets in San Francisco, an imposing building in the city's high-priced Pacific Heights section.

The story of *Sudden Fear* (1952) is not unusual, but the camera work, music (by Elmer Bernstein), accelerating suspense, and acting by the three principals make it extraordinary. In New York, at the casting of her latest play, Myra rejects actor Lester Blaine (Jack Palance) for the lead because she feels he is not romantic enough in appearance. Later, on a train bound for San Francisco, she meets Blaine who charms her to the extent that she falls in love with the younger man. They are wed and seem idyllically happy until one day she turns on her dictating machine and overhears a recording of a telephone conversation between Blaine and Irene Neves (Gloria Grahame). With the help of Irene, to whom he is also married, Blaine plans to kill Myra within three days, before she can sign a new will she has had drawn up. Her death must appear accidental for insurance purposes.

Myra's initial, hysterical conclusion is to tell the police, but in her desperation she drops and breaks the recording, thus eliminating the evidence. She then devises her own plan to trap Blaine in Irene's apartment and kill him with Irene's gun. But at the final moment she loses her nerve. Then begins a telling chase through alleyways, dead-end streets, and over San Francisco hills. Myra is wearing a white scarf and fur coat during this chase (she on foot, he by auto), but so is Irene who is returning to her apartment. In the darkness, Blaine mistakes the figure of Irene for that of Myra and runs her down with his car, but also kills himself when his car goes out of control. With both pronounced dead, Myra is finally free of the fear that so suddenly engulfed her existence.

Redbook magazine, in selecting *Sudden Fear* as its Picture of the Month for September 1952, termed it "one of the best pictures she's [Joan] ever made." The *New York Times* labeled her work as "truly professional." Once again Joan was back on top of the box-office. When the Oscar nominations were announced in February 1952, the five nominees for Best Actress were Shirley Booth (*Come Back Little Sheba*), Joan Crawford (*Sudden Fear*), Bette Davis (*The Star*), Julie Harris (*The Member of the Wedding*), and Susan Hayward (*With a Song in My Heart*). At the Oscar ceremonies that year Miss Booth was announced the victor.

One of the major setbacks of Joan's career occurred when she left the cast of *From Here to Eternity* (1953)* over an alleged conflict concerning her wardrobe and character interpretation. In this Columbia picture under Fred Zinnemann's direction, she was to play Karen Holmes, the officer's wife who philanders on the beach with Burt Lancaster. On Joan's withdrawal from the project, younger Deborah Kerr was borrowed from MGM to

handle the part, and she won an Oscar nomination for her efforts.

Another 1953 project that did not materialize for Joan was *Lisbon,* based on an original story by Marty Rackins. Paramount bought the story for Joan, but the preliminary script displeased her because she was to lose the leading man to a bikini-clad younger girl. Director Irving Rapper would not alter the script and it was postponed indefinitely. Sheilah Graham's column observations included, "Irving should have realized this is *not* Miss Crawford's idea of fun in films!" Ray Milland would later buy the property and direct it for 1956 Republic release starring himself and Maureen O'Hara.

But Joan did make *Torch Song* (1953) at MGM. Not only was it her first full feature in Technicolor and the first film in fourteen years in which she danced, but it marked her temporary return, via the front gate, to the studio where she had started her career twenty-eight years earlier. Now Elizabeth Taylor, Deborah Kerr, and Eleanor Parker were the leading ladies on the lot. It was a one-picture agreement and her last MGM feature* to come. Shot on a taut twenty-four day schedule and on low budget, the story centers on Jenny Stewart (Joan), a dominating, selfish, neurotic Broadway musical-comedy star. She dances and sings (her voice was used for one song, "Tenderly," but the others were dubbed by India Adams) with a smile on her face, but offstage she alienates everyone around her. Then a blind pianist (Michael Wilding) comes into production rehearsals and the two disagree vehemently. Jenny finds herself attracted to him and learns that he had once worshipped her, but is unable to bring him to this admission. Beneath her hateful demeanor is the need to be loved, and she lets down all barriers to this man. The film ends with Jenny presumably a changed, loving female.

Joan had requested and gotten Charles Walters to direct the picture, having rightly admired his handling of such MGM musical

* Interestingly, within *Autumn Leaves* there is a beach love scene between Crawford and Cliff Robertson which duplicates almost exactly the famed wave-side embracing of Lancaster and Kerr in *From Here to Eternity.*

* Joan did guest star in "The Man from U.N.C.L.E." episode, *The Karate Killers* (NBC-TV, March 31, 1967), shot on the Metro lot and released abroad as a feature.

With Wendell Corey in
Harriet Craig ('50).

With Jack Palance in
Sudden Fear ('52).

With Michael Wilding in
Torch Song ('53).

With Ernest Borgnine, Ben
Cooper, Frank Marlowe,
Royal Dano, Scott Brady,
and John Carradine (rear)
in *Johnny Guitar* ('54).

145

successes as *Easter Parade* (1948) and *Lili* (1953). While chroniclers would sum up the film as "a rather trying effort about a Broadway actress who doesn't know what she does want and lives in solitary splendor stubbing out cigarettes all over the place" (David Shipman, *The Great Movie Stars, supra*), *Torch Song* is an excellent illustration of Crawford's supercharged determination to remain in the limelight. Almost fifty years old, she attempted and achieved the illusion of being a musical-comedy stage star who danced in and out of routines (including the rather tasteless "Two-Faced Woman" in which her skin changed to that of a mulatto) and romances at will. With a figure a woman half her age would have been proud to display, Joan drove herself with a vengeance to perform the dancing routines. Her pal William Haines (long retired from acting and then an interior decorator) was invited to the set to watch her dancing. That evening she phoned Haines to learn his reaction.

> *Haines:* Cranberry, you amaze me!
> *Joan:* God must have his hand on my shoulder, Willie.
> *Haines:* I don't know about the shoulder, Cranberry. But only God could get your legs up that high.

Aiding Crawford in adding an aura of credibility to the film was Marjorie Rambeau in a telling performance as Crawford's mother, Gig Young as her alcoholic escort, and, in a strangely inverse manner, Michael Wilding as the quiet-on-the-surface-but-seething-inside pianist. There is one moment in the scenario in which the musical-comedy star is comedic offstage. Crawford's Jenny Stewart sweeps into a plush restaurant where she joins the blind pianist for lunch. She then gives her order to the waiter, "Lobster newburg and *black* coffee . . . I am on a diet."

Because the Dore Schary regime at MGM chose to treat *Torch Song* as just another picture, it did not create the enduring career waves that Joan might have anticipated. Nevertheless, it proved to the industry and to the public (those members who were still attending movies and not glued to their TV sets) that she was still ready and most raring to go.

On Saturday, September 19, 1953, Joan made her video acting debut on CBS-TV's "Mirror Theatre," in an episode entitled *Because I Love Him.* Just as she had gravitated to radio in the Thirties and Forties as an outlet against typecasting, so in the Fifties and Sixties Joan would turn to television for acting exposure.

Joan went to Republic Pictures in 1954 (during the period when studio head Herbert J. Yates hoped to save his floundering concern with topflight name stars) for the oddball, gloomy Western, *Johnny Guitar.* The pre-release ads heralding the "Trucolor" film proclaimed, "Joan the glamorous! Joan the gunfighter! She's fire and steel in a story of passion and bitter hatred as big as the great Southwest!" Under Nicholas Ray's intriguing direction, Joan portrayed Vienna, the aggressive boss lady of a gambling saloon strategically located on Arizona land over where a railroad is planning to build its tracks. She has assorted local adversaries, including Emma Small (Mercedes McCambridge) and John McIvers (Ward Bond) who prefer the area be kept for cattle grazing. Emma's hatred of Vienna is two-fold: she also desires Vienna's lover, the Dancin' Kid (Scott Brady), to be hers, although she refuses to admit it.

The Kid is a bank robber whom McIvers wants to hang and he brings Emma and his men to Vienna's saloon on a windy night to find him. Vienna confronts her adversaries with, "You don't own the earth—not this part of it . . . I intend to be buried here, in the *twentieth* century." Vienna hires Johnny Guitar (Sterling Hayden) to perform in her saloon and falls in love with him. He later joins her in combating McIvers and his cronies.

In its day, *Johnny Guitar* was considered by most viewers as just another Western. In fact, *Variety* argued that Joan "should leave saddles and Levis to someone else and stick to big-city lights for a background." But in later years, this unique sagebrush tale was to gain a tremendous cult reputation, especially in France, and has remained one of the milestones in Joan's lengthy career.

Just as Joan had conflicted with Janice Rule in *Goodbye, My Fancy* and with Jack Palance in *Sudden Fear* (he thought her daily greeting to the soundstage crew was a nauseating, phony act), so in the course of making *Johnny Guitar* she and actress Mercedes McCambridge were at loggerheads. Years later, Joan would state she would prefer to forget this period of her filmmaking career and added that even her pet poodle got ill being at Republic Pictures.

Hollywood wags in the summer of 1954 were willing to bet that Joan would marry Jennings Lang, a representative for MCA, the agency handling Joan's career commitments. Lang was the third party in the famed Joan Bennett caper in December 1951 when her spouse, producer Walter Wanger, took pot shots at Lang in a parking lot, claiming the agent was romantically involved with the actress. Florabel Muir "whispered" in *Photoplay,* "Joan is frankly aglow when she appears, more and more frequently, on the arm of the tall MCA agent." Also in 1954 she was romantically paired with Milton Rackmil, the head of Universal-International, but columnist Erskine Johnson helped put an end to any marriage rumors by writing that the romance "adds up to zero." On Tuesday, May 10, 1955, in Las Vegas, she surprised everyone by marrying fifty-four-year-old Alfred Nu Steele in a civil ceremony. Steele, the president of Pepsi-Cola Company, was a graduate of Northwestern University (class of 1923) and had adopted the middle name of Nu from his college fraternity, Sigma Nu. He had formerly been a vice-president of the Coca-Cola Company. At fifty-one, Joan appeared to have found marital happiness although skeptics pronounced the union to be wrong for her. Louella Parsons finally discarded her doubts concerning the marriage and wrote, ". . . I could name a dozen women in Hollywood who have never known what it is to love a man truly and be loved truly in return." A month after Joan's wedding, the *Hollywood Reporter* disclosed, "The next part Joan Crawford wants to play is the mama of a Pepsi-Cola heir, or heiress."

Prior to her marriage, Joan had made *Female on the Beach* (1955) for Universal-International. Called an "old-fashioned mystery thriller" by the *New York Times,* it is a slow-paced yarn of a lonely widow (Joan) who rents a beach-house only to find that her handsome neighbor (Jeff Chandler) may have murdered its previous occupant (Judith Evelyn). It eventually develops that the real-estate agent (Jan Sterling) had done the crime in a pique of jealousy. As in *Johnny Guitar,* Joan sported a severe brush-cut hairdo, similar to the one made famous in the late Twenties by Kay Francis and Natalie Moorhead. The Robert Hill scenario for *Female* provided ample opportunity for Joan to look glamorous, wear a bathing suit, and display her still very comely figure (she still swam daily).

The one person, other than herself, who was most instrumental in prolonging her screen career at a time when most of her contemporaries had fallen into semi-retirement was producer Jerry Wald. Through his auspices, a six-picture deal was made for the star at Columbia Pictures. The first was *Queen Bee* (1955) in which director-scripter Ranald MacDougall craftily exploited every aspect of the Crawford legend. As Eva Phillips, she is a domineering woman of wealth, a modern-day bitch counterpart to Regina of Lillian Hellman's *The Little Foxes.* Gowned by Jean Louis, Eva taunts her husband (Barry Sullivan) who hates her, tempts her lover (John Ireland) who disrespects her, and causes the suicide of her sister-in-law (Betsy Palmer) by haughtily informing her that the man she loves (Ireland) is anything but pure. Ireland solves the dilemma by killing Eva and himself in an automobile crash. The *New York Herald-Tribune* observed coyly, "Miss Crawford plays her role with such silky villainy that we long to see her dispatched." When one considers the type of roles or lack of roles that Bette Davis, Marlene Dietrich, Claudette Colbert, and Rosalind Russell were resorting to at this time one has to marvel at

At home with husband Alfred Steele ('55).

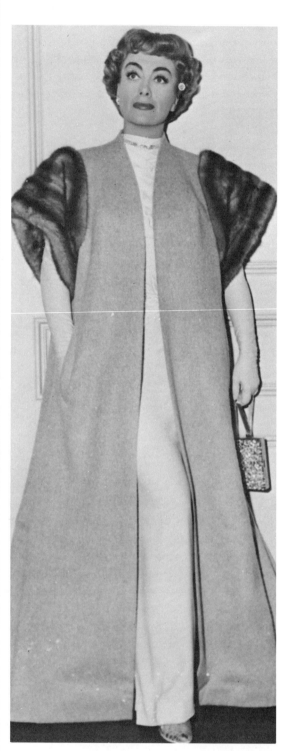
In a Jean Louis outfit for *Queen Bee* ('55).

With Jan Sterling in *Female on the Beach* ('55).

With Cliff Robertson in a pose
for *Autumn Leaves* ('56).

With Bette Davis in *What Ever
Happened to Baby Jane?* ('62).

Rehearsing with Bob Hope for
his TV variety show (October
1958).

Joan's persuasion in convincing film producers to star her in vehicles such as this.

In *Autumn Leaves* (1956), directed by Robert Aldrich for Columbia Pictures, Joan's Milly admits to being forty-two years old. As the title suggests, she is in the autumn of life, a middle-aged spinster-typist whose loneliness leads her to keep company with a younger man (Cliff Robertson). When he mentions marriage, Milly runs scared, but later weds him. Then she finds that he is mentally disturbed, leading to many moments (and screen minutes) of anguish. Eventually, he is cured and she discovers to her relief that the mentally healthy man still loves her. While the film's premise undoubtedly appealed to a certain segment of the public, it was the movie's theme song (by Joseph Kosma, Jacques Prevert, and Johnny Mercer) that emerged as the film's most popular element. With a cast that included Vera Miles, Lorne Greene, Ruth Donnelly, and Sheppard Strudwick, *Autumn Leaves* deserves a reassessment by film enthusiasts of the Seventies.

While other middle-aged actresses were seeking career rejuvenation by turning to the Broadway stage or summer stock, Joan, who was fearful of appearing professionally in front of live audiences, found a fresh field of combat in globe trotting with her husband on behalf of Pepsi-Cola. With her well-known liking for being efficiently organized and well prepared for any occasion and circumstance, Joan thrived on her new chores as Ambassadress of Good Will for the soft drink company.

She stopped long enough in her travels to star in the film *The Golden Virgin* which was more delicately retitled by Columbia as *The Story of Esther Costello* (1957). She hired David Miller to direct this black-and-white feature. The *New York Times* found Joan to be "tackling her most becoming assignment in several seasons." She is a wealthy American, recently separated from her womanizing husband (Rossano Brazzi), who discovers a new cause in life. She has adopted a young girl (Heather Sears) who is blind, deaf, and without speech due to an environmental and emotional shock. A fund is established on the girl's behalf and then Carlo (Brazzi) re-enters the scene, hoping to enrich himself through the charity enterprises. He ferociously rapes the girl which restores her senses, but Margaret (Joan) now wants to end his opportunistic ways forever. After depositing Esther in the care of a reporter (Lee Patterson) who loves her, Margaret at gun-point forces Carlo into her car and drives them both to their death. One scene in the melodrama should stick in the memory of every Joan Crawford fan. In the sequence which introduces Joan's character to the audience, a figure is seen descending a staircase. The camera moves upward, revealing Joan's trademark ankle-strapped shoes, then her shapely legs, and finally the star herself.

Her only professional work during 1958 was an appearance on CBS-TV's "G. E. Theatre" in an episode called *Strange Witness.* On Sunday, January 14, 1959, she starred as Ann Howard, a victim of traumatic aphasia induced when she is tied to a tropical tree trunk by a drunken husband while a crocodile fancies her as a delectable meal. The role was in *And One Was Loyal,* an episode of "G. E. Theatre." As would prove the case throughout the Sixties, every Crawford TV appearance was an occasion, no matter how slight the project, or how quickly it had been filmed. Also, in January 1959 it was announced that she had plans for a half-hour TV series to be called "The Joan Crawford Theatre," but this project did not materialize. She did appear in a pedestrian seventy-minute drama, *Della,* with Paul Burke, Charles Bickford, and Diane Baker, an unsold pilot for yet another series.

On April 19, 1959, four days before his fifty-eighth birthday, Alfred Nu Steele died in his sleep in Manhattan of a heart attack. Three weeks later, Joan was elected to the Board of Directors of the Pepsi-Cola Company, both as a tribute to her late husband and as a calculated business arrangement.

Once again producer Jerry Wald, now a production chief at Twentieth Century-Fox, came to Joan's professional rescue. He hired her as a special guest star ("and Joan Crawford as Amanda Farrow") in *The Best of Ev-*

erything (1959). She did not have a leading role (Hope Lange, Suzy Parker, and Diane Baker did), but Joan, the professional, managed to make the most of her assignment as editor of a book publishing house who has made herself into a remote but efficient editor through personal unhappiness. It is a long (122-minute) version of Rona Jaffe's best-seller about the lives and loves of young women who seek the best of everything in the supposedly glamorous Manhattan publishing world. Filmed in CinemaScope and color, it is a glossy, vapid account that focuses on a series of interweaving relationships. Joan shared several scenes with her *I Live My Life* co-star of twenty-four years earlier, Brian Aherne, and she displayed an authority with her lines that made one wonder whether she was speaking the words of orange-haired Amanda Farrow or of the real-life Joan Crawford. At one point in the melodrama, Amanda says to ambitious career-girl Caroline Bender (Hope Lange), a secretary who wants to become an editor, "You college graduates are all alike—you think you can breeze in and do everything so easily."

Amanda has a married lover (never seen onscreen) who frustrates her life and finally she tells him over the phone, "I won't be taken for granted. I will not be a convenience for you. I'm one small corner of your life. I've never asked for more, but I won't settle for less. Now you and your rabbit-faced wife can go to hell."

Still later the worldly-wise Amanda tries to give budding actress Gregg Adams (Suzy Parker) some cogent advice, "I've had more experience than you and for experience to be of value somehow someone must learn by it."

When a widower and former beau from Illinois with two kids asks Amanda to marry him, she agrees, because ". . . he treats me as if I am the gentlest, softest woman in the world . . . and maybe with enough time and tenderness and if it's not too late I can get to believe it myself."

Later, Amanda returns to the Fabian Publishing Company and confesses in a most genuinely touching manner, "It was too late for me . . . a lonely man, two children . . .

they needed too much . . . I found I had nothing to give . . . I had forgotten how. . . ." *Variety* reported of her performance, "Miss Crawford uses her own great authority to give vividness and meaning to a role that is sketchy at best."

After Steele's death and while Joan was filming promotionals at Fox concerning the company's upcoming products *(Blue Denim* and *The Blue Angel)* there appeared a headlined story stating, "Joan Crawford admits to being broke!" It has never been clear why or how this story appeared, but it was apparent to any levelheaded celebrity follower that Joan had reached a career crisis that far overshadowed her growing problems with her four children.

In 1959 and 1961, Joan was seen in episodes of the Zane Grey Theatre and displayed an affinity for Westerns that almost equalled that of her contemporary, Barbara Stanwyck. But, unlike the latter, Joan never fully learned to modulate her performances to the more intimate demands of the television medium.

Much of the next three years was devoted to making public appearances for Pepsi-Cola. Joan alerted the press, "I prepare for each appearance the way I do for a movie role. It's all part of acting. Acting is the greatest of all the arts. I wish I had five hundred years to study it." In 1961, when Fox was casting *Return to Peyton Place,* Joan Crawford and Bette Davis were touted for the two focal mother roles, but instead it was Eleanor Parker and Mary Astor who handled the assignments. Joan later claimed she had rejected the offer because it would have meant working on the Twentieth lot at the same time as Christina, then cast in Elvis Presley's *Wild in the Country* (1961), and she did not want to steal the limelight away from her actress daughter.

Then came the landmark offer from producer-director Robert Aldrich to co-star in a horror film with her old rival, Bette Davis. Allegedly, it was Crawford who brought the notion and the casting idea to Aldrich's attention. Movie audiences waited anxiously in lines to see Davis, wearing grotesque, clown-white makeup, and mistreating Joan, a helpless cripple. *What Ever Happened to Baby*

With Hope Lange in *The Best of Everything* ('59).

With Constance Ford (fourth from right) in *The Caretakers* ('63).

Jane? (1962) gave Miss Davis the best screen role she had had in six years (since MGM's *The Catered Affair,* 1956) and provided Joan with her first non-romantic part. Bette received top billing which was justifiable since she has more footage, but Joan's subdued underplaying all but steals the scenes she has with Miss Davis.

In 132 black-and-white minutes, *Baby Jane* chronicles the grand guignol story of two sisters, Jane (Davis) and Blanche Hudson (Joan), one-time show business figures who now live in seclusion in a decaying Los Angeles house. Jane had been a child vaudeville star and the apple of her daddy's eye while Blanche was a somber-faced child whose mother repeatedly predicted that her professional day would come. And it did—she became a famed movie star. Jane entered movies too, but was a failure. Blanche had been crippled in a mysterious auto accident some years before and is now confined to a wheelchair within her bedroom while plump, grotesque Jane grumblingly waits on her and torments her because she feels that Blanche is interfering with her dreamed-of comeback.

Blanche is first seen in the story watching one of her old movies *(Sadie McKee)* on television and her face becomes radiantly soft as she relives the moments. "I remember when it first came out," she says to Jane, "it got a tremendous reception. The critics described it as brilliant." Blanche's only contact with the outside world is Elvira Stitt (Maidie Norman), the black cleaning woman who hates Jane and is fearful for Blanche's safety because of Jane's heavy drinking and psychotic state of mind. When Jane suspects that Blanche intends selling their home and placing her in an institution, all hell breaks loose. Jane serves her sister a "din-din" of baked rat from the cellar and their dead, boiled canary. While Jane is out one afternoon, Blanche crawls down the stairs to telephone for help, but Jane returns before she can make the call and kicks Blanche into unconsciousness. She then drags her back to her room where she ties her to the bed.

Later, Jane murders Elvira when the domestic comes in to check on Blanche, and

when rotund Edwin Flagg (Victor Buono)—a mother-fixated pianist whom Jane has interested in helping her work out a comeback stage routine—also discovers Blanche, Jane fears he will return with the police. In desperation, she carts Blanche to the beach. There, near death, Blanche confesses that it was she who had engineered the accident that had crippled her, a confession that triggers Jane's complete mental breakdown. As the police find Jane's car at the beach, a crowd gathers around the sisters and Jane, believing them to be her fans, dances for the onlookers, while Blanche slowly dies.

Of the two co-stars, the *Saturday Review* stated, "Scenes that in lesser hands would verge on the ludicrous simply crackle with tension." The feature grossed $4.05 million in United States and Canadian rentals and made the two aging leading ladies marketable quantities once again.

The feud* that allegedly began between the two actresses in the mid-Forties reportedly flared up during the film's shooting, but both actresses were too professional to make public remarks about each other. They also embarked on a promotional tour for *Baby Jane* requiring a truce be made. In response to all the hullabaloo about a rivalry, Joan said simply, "It's ridiculous." Much later she would expand about her thoughts on the film. She found that director Aldrich had "many insecurities. . . . He loves evil, horrendous, vile things." As for Miss Davis, ". . . [she] is of a different temperament. She likes to scream and yell and I just sit and knit. She yelled and I knitted a scarf from Hollywood to Malibu." Ironically, when Miss Davis, who had been

---

* It was no accident that in 1962 both Joan *(A Portrait of Joan)* and Bette Davis *(The Lonely Life)* published their autobiographies. For different reasons each is an engaging study, although the Davis tome is far more honest. Of the Crawford tome, the *New York Herald-Tribune* reported, "Crawford fans . . . will have a field day with lavishly nostalgic photo layouts and the text, in which Jane Kesner Ardmore has contributed a literary style consistent with that of fan magazines in their heyday. Miss Crawford apparently hasn't a nasty thought in her head and her story is filled with righteousness and moral uplift which, after all, is a pretty durable formula in itself." One of the literary trade journals added, "All is here, including some that shouldn't be: [Joan Crawford's] self-righteous 'explanation' of the mother-daughter foul-up and her maddening paternalism vis-a-vis Franchot Tone; a thinly disguised attack upon Mercedes McCambridge."

153

Oscar-nominated for *Baby Jane,* failed to win the Award, it was Joan who accepted the Best Actress statuette on behalf of the winner, Anne Bancroft *(The Miracle Worker).* With silver-streaked hair and wearing what was described as "a ransom in diamonds," Joan wore a smile of triumph as she accepted for Miss Bancroft. Hollywood could only guess if her smile was one of genuine pleasure for Miss Bancroft or if it meant that she was happy that Miss Davis had not won.

In 1963, Joan was in an episode of CBS-TV's "Route 66" (she grew fearful of the crowds during the location shooting) and received third billing for *The Caretakers* (United Artists) as Lucretia Terry, the head psychiatric nurse of a mental hospital. Originally planned as a semi-documentary film, the story emerges as a thinly disguised and cheap copy of *The Snake Pit* (1948) with Polly Bergen as the main tormented soul. The film is relevant to the Joan Crawford canon in that she has a major physical therapy sequence in which she is dressed in tights, revealing her still very shapely figure. Clips from this scene as well as earlier Joan Crawford features were utilized for a segment of the tele-documentary series, "Hollywood and the Stars," in the fall of 1963.

On the domestic front, rumors abounded in 1963 that Joan would become New York state's next First Lady when she would marry divorced governor Nelson Rockefeller. From Philadelphia, where she picked up an award from the Philadelphia Club of Advertising Women, she denied the rumors by saying that she had met Rockefeller only once and "I don't need this publicity and I'm sure he doesn't. How can you be engaged to a man who's never asked you for a date?"

Joan campaigned with producer Joseph E. Levine to obtain the role of famed madam Polly Adler in Embassy's *A House Is Not a Home* (1964), but Shelley Winters was given the part. Instead, in a deal which left some of Hollywood baffled, Joan Blondell left Columbia's *Strait-Jacket* (1964) and Crawford was put in her stead. It was directed by William Castle and scripted by Robert (*Psycho*) Bloch. Two of Joan's co-stars from the ill-

fated *Della* project joined her for the class *B* project.

In this obvious, low-budget affair, Joan is Lucy Harbin who chops up her husband and his bed partner and then is admitted to a hospital for the criminally insane. Twenty years later she is released in the custody of her daughter Carol (Diane Baker). When a series of beheadings occur, Lucy is the number one suspect. In analyzing this Gothic horror film entry for her *New York Herald-Tribune* readers, Judith Crist editorialized, ". . . it's time to get Joan Crawford out of those housedress-horror *B* movies and back into haute couture. Miss Crawford, you see, is high class, too high class to withstand in mufti the banality of Robert Bloch's script, cheapjack production, inept and/or vacuous supporting players and direction better suited to the mist-and-cobweb idiocies of the Karloff school of suspense." What must have attracted Joan to this project, beyond the obvious job it offered her, was that the scenario provided her with some romantic scenes with thirty-five-year-old John Anthony Hayes.

Joan next went into production for Robert Aldrich in his film of gore *Hush . . . Hush, Sweet Charlotte* (Twentieth Century-Fox, 1965), again with Bette Davis. This was to provide Joan with an opportunity to get even with Miss Davis oncamera since the lady she was to portray would slap the weeping Davis character. After a few weeks of location work in Louisiana, Joan became ill with viral pneumonia (she had insisted the set be air-conditioned to a certain temperature), and Aldrich tried to work around her. Only later, from her hospital bed, did she learn that she had been replaced by Olivia de Havilland. This was the first time in her long career that Joan had held up any production.

Her health improved enough for her to guest star in a second William Castle horror entry, *I Saw What You Did* (Universal, 1965). She is killed off fairly soon in the proceedings by her neighbor-lover, John Ireland. The exploitation film did only average box-office business.

By 1966, Joan estimated that she had traveled some 875,000 miles for Pepsi-Cola, and

"I've enjoyed every minute of it." Each hotel at which she was scheduled to stop received advance instructions that her hotel suite was to be guarded on a twenty-four-hour basis by a uniformed security man and that such supplies as cracked ice, pens, pencils, paper pads, hair dryer, red and yellow roses, a maid, and liquor be available on her arrival. Still extremely kind to fans, Joan cordially autographed hundreds of photos and copies of her autobiography wherever she went. It still remained her policy to reply to all fan letters—either personally or with the help of her secretary—whenever possible, and her responses were generally warm and friendly.

She went to England for another macabre screen outing called *Berserk,* released by Columbia in 1968. She is Monica Rivers, the owner of a traveling circus whose sole desire is to make a success of the business. When a high-wire artist is killed, she exploits the accident as publicity for the circus. She later has an affair with the virile replacement, Frank Hawkins (Ty Hardin). He in turn becomes the object of sexual attraction to Monica's neglected daughter (Judy Geeson) whom it develops is the circus maniac, killing at random in her insane jealousy because her mother had continually neglected her in favor of the circus. Once again Joan had the occasion to wear the briefest of costumes (with flattering results) but her love scenes with Hardin were on the embarrassing side.

Always a charity devotee, Joan's philanthropic interests in the late Sixties included the Salvation Army, Muscular Dystrophy, Multiple Sclerosis, and the USO and she devoted many (well-publicized) hours in raising funds. While her guest-star episode on "The Lucy Show" (CBS-TV, February 26, 1968) attracted great publicity (Lucy thinks Joan is desperate for work and gets her an acting job in a charity benefit—allowing Joan to mimic Bette Davis' *Jezebel* performance), she pulled off a coup that few other stars could have done, let alone attempted. Her twenty-seven-year-old daughter Christina was appearing in CBS-TV's daytime soap opera "The Secret Storm," playing a twenty-four-year-old housewife in the midst of a divorce action. On October 16, 1968, she was rushed to the hospital where she underwent surgery for an ovarian tumor. Joan volunteered to fill in for her daughter* "because I didn't want them to give the part to someone else." She told her daughter,** "I'll never be as good as you, but I'll keep the spot warm for you." As for playing opposite Keith Charles, an actor in his late twenties, Joan said it did not bother her. "Isn't he beautiful, I thought to myself. So be twenty-four." Audience rating for the series went up noticeably during Joan's four-day stint. Said Christina of her mother's gesture, "It was fantastic that she would care that much." In 1969, Joan did the telefeature pilot for "Night Gallery" (NBC) playing in one of the three segments. In the Rod Serling-written episode, she is a wealthy woman who undergoes a painful operation which will permit her to see for just a few hours. She regains her sight on the night of the New York City blackout. The following year she played the leading guest role on the ninety-minute series "The Virginian" in an episode about a Easterner wed to a rich rancher.

She returned to England to star for producer Herman Cohen (also responsible for *Berserk)* in *Trog* (Warner Bros., 1970), a science-fiction mystery thriller. When in London for the shooting, Joan received a maximum of publicity and consented to several interviews.

She was asked a series of questions by *Today's Cinema,* including "What gives you a sense of excitement in movie-making today?" She replied, "Just making movies. I don't mean any movies. People ask me why I took this science-fiction role in *Trog.* . . . It's because I've never done any science fiction before, I've never played a lady scientist before, I've never played a doctor before. I'm going to play everything!" When asked "How would

* When Dorothy Malone had become ill during the filming of the nighttime soap opera series, *Peyton Place,* Joan had volunteered to replace her as Constance McKenzie. Lola Albright was utilized instead.
** Joan and Christina had appeared on TV talk shows and a telethon together, but had never acted publicly together. Joan claims she always encouraged Christina in her show business pursuits. "She was literally wheeled onto the set of my pictures as an infant. She grew up surrounded by lights. I've introduced her to every actor and director I've ever worked with. And then I started with the producers here [New York City]. She wants to do only theatre."

Advertisement for
Berserk! ('67).

in THE HERMAN COHEN PRODUCTION OF

"BERSERK!" x

Co-starring
TY HARDIN · DIANA DORS · MICHAEL GOUGH · JUDY GEESON · ROBERT HARDY
Screenplay by ABEN KANDEL and HERMAN COHEN Produced by HERMAN COHEN Directed by JIM O'CONNOLLY TECHNICOLOR®

In *Strait-Jacket* ('64).

As Monica Rivers in *Berserk!*

What becomes a Legend most?

Blackglama

BLACKGLAMA® IS THE WORLD'S FINEST NATURAL DARK RANCH MINK BRED ONLY IN AMERICA BY THE GREAT LAKES MINK MEN.

As a living legend, 1960s-style.

you most like to be remembered?" she shot back, "By living longer than anybody else."

Trog is a very silly, poorly executed exercise with a ludicrous monster, a troglodyte. The following year she turned out *My Way of Life* (Simon and Schuster), which was "written for every woman who wants to live beautifully and successfully, by a woman who triumphantly does both. . . . Miss Crawford shares with the reader her own recipes for entertaining, her decorating secrets, the preparations, big and small, that make it possible for her to appear anywhere, any time looking her best and perfectly dressed." Two of Crawford's less chic penchants are for plastic covers on her living room furniture and laminated pocket books.

In 1972, she was a guest star on the "Sixth Sense" series (ABC-TV, September 30, 1972). It proved to be her final acting assignment. There were rumors that she would join with Bette Davis and others in the film version of the musical *Follies* or that she would play in a female version of *Sleuth* on Broadway, but they remained rumors. On Sunday, April 8, 1973, she appeared at New York Town Hall as the guest of honor for one of the several retrospectives on Legendary Ladies where film clips were shown of twenty of her features. Alternately kittenish, frank, and coy, but always charming, she remarked, "I love playing bitches. There's a lot of bitch in every woman and a lot in every man." Regarding her famous platform shoe trademark, she admitted she knew the crude vernacular term given it by a segment of the public, then added, "They held me up a goddam long time." With the publicity the evening generated and the response of the audience, one could only wonder why she had queried host John Springer at the start of the tribute with, "What the hell am I doing here?"

After her March 1973 birthday, Pepsi-Cola* no longer kept Joan employed as their goodwill ambassadress. The reason given was that its corporate charter demanded compulsory retirement at the age of sixty-five, and, as many already knew, Crawford was

* In 1965, when Pepsi-Cola merged with Frito-Lay, Joan was no longer on the official top board of directors.

actually a few years past the official retirement mark. Unstated at the time, but known by those in financial circles, was that the new regime at Pepsi-Cola did not favor Miss Crawford's further participation in company matters. According to some accounts, when she left the firm, she lost the paid-for services of a secretary, her WATS line, and her yearly remuneration—status items often continued to other retired executives out of gratitude for their past loyalty. What would disturb the hard-working Joan even more than the forced, ungallant retirement coup, was a later interview with the Pepsico chairman in which it was reported that he said "he took an awful lot of crap from Joan Crawford."

Late in 1973, she moved from her large terrace apartment in the Imperial House on Fifth Avenue (with its white rug and white furniture in the living room) to a smaller abode on 150 East 69th Street. Her new apartment sported no rugs ("I gave up carpets years ago when I realized I couldn't keep them clean all the time"), plastic liners on the window sills, and yellow wax flowers and plastic plants (items that could be washed thoroughly and often). All of the furniture and the walls were treated with a vinylizing process to keep out the dirt. The parquet floors were washed and/ or waxed every other day and the draperies cleaned monthly. In short, Joan remained the efficient housekeeper to the end. (She once remarked, "There's a little bit of Harriet Craig in all of us.")

What proved to be Crawford's last performance was at the Rosalind Russell tribute-party at New York's Rainbow Room in 1974. Thereafter she remained mostly at home and went out only to see a few, close friends. She no longer colored her hair, but let it turn natural brown with streaks of gray. As she would inform columnist Shirley Eder when the latter asked her to dine out in the spring of 1977,

Shirley, I've been out! There's nothing out there I haven't seen or done. There's nothing more out there I want to see.

I don't have to go out anymore. I don't have to be on display. I've

With Michael Gough
and Bernard Kay in
Trog ('70).

In the telefeature
Night Gallery (NBC-
TV, '69).

Appealing to new
generations of fans.

159

served my time as the public Joan Crawford. Now for the first time in her life Joan Crawford is doing exactly as she pleases.

I watch television, including the soap operas. I read. I answer only the letters I want to. I don't have to make up or get dressed up. And, you know, I'd never go out in public looking like a lot of the kids in the business today.

I now do what pleases me and only me. I won't go out, . . .

Other things that Joan no longer did included drinking her accustomed 100-proof vodka, taking medications, and having a personal physician. She had become a Christian Scientist. As to her fading career, it bothered her greatly that she no longer received decent job offers. In 1976, she told writer Shirley Eder: "If I could buy back every print of all those terrible last movies I forced myself to make, I would gladly do it. . . . I'm not going to make another one of those as long as I live. I'm ashamed of having done them. If that's all they're offering women of my age—I said women, not men—then I'll rest on my laurels. . . . I took those movies not because I needed the money but because I'm a film actress who needed to act."

One aspect of Joan's life that did not change until the end was her standard of conduct. It applied to friends and family as well. Her four children had married, and she had been a grandmother four times. (She resented the term "grandmother" and preferred that it not be applied to her; "Aunt" Joan was fine.) Years before, she had stated when accused of imposing her sense of perfectionism* on her

* Writer Liz Smith would recall after Miss Crawford's death, "The things you've read about her are mostly all true. She had the personality of a true martinet with high expectations of herself and others. Once at a Christmas party in Hollywood, when her children were still young, I recall watching Miss Crawford greet more than forty guests. She had never seen many of them before but remembered every single name as well as what people were drinking. Through all this, she instructed her superpolite kids in the opening of their gifts. After each present was opened, the child receiving it had to pass around the room and show it, then sit down and record it in a book. This made for efficiency, but I remember thinking it was pretty tough on the kids."

adopted children that "I've tried to provide my children with what I didn't have: constructive discipline, a sense of security, a sense of sharing. . . . Sloppiness has never been tolerated in our home, nor has rudeness. . . . They're going into a world that isn't easy, a world where unless you are self-sufficient and strong, you can be destroyed."

As would be revealed in her will, Joan remained estranged from two of her children until the end. Son Christopher and the superstar had not been on good terms for more than twenty years. According to *Hollywood Reporter* writer Radie Harris, when Christopher, who had had long bouts of anti-establishment conduct over the years, had matured and wed, he brought his young wife to meet the movie actress. She allegedly refused them entrance inside her apartment. According to the same source, "Eventually, he found another 'Mom' in the maternal love of a former neighbor and it was to her that he wrote and sent gifts all during his embattled years in Vietnam." (Christopher, his wife, and their two children live on Long Island.) As for Christina, she sought a reconciliation with her mother when she remarried and became Mrs. David Koontz (of Tarzana, California). Crawford refused an invitation to her wedding.

Another aspect of dauntless Joan that remained the same was her penchant for writing and answering letters, an occupation that continued to the end. If an article appeared which intelligently recounted some aspect of the Crawford life and legend, the writer was sure to receive a note of appreciation from the star. After Joan's passing, Earl Wilson would report in his column, " 'Joan Crawford dead . . . why, I had a letter from her!' . . . Half a dozen people told me that. The last of the glamour queens wrote hundreds of thank-you and happy-birthday notes, and was still writing them last week. Sometimes she wrote them at 6 A.M. after reading the Bible and comics and having breakfast. She'd go back to bed for half an hour, then resume the pace of Miss Public Energy No. 1, getting by on four hours sleep."

What is reality and what is fantasy? Joan

Crawford's final years fall into this dualism. A controversial, much criticized *People* magazine article was written by show business correspondent Doris Lilly and published after Joan's death. The "close confidante and neighbor" reported,

> . . . She died from a lethal dose of loneliness and fear. Unbeknownst to even some of her closest friends, Joan had received an anonymous phone call in the winter of 1975. "I will kill you," the caller said. "You won't know where or when, but I will get you." Terrified, she called in the police and the FBI. For months her twenty-second-floor five-room apartment was under guard. A variety of exotic locks, latches, and alarms were installed. For the last eighteen months she had refused to set foot outside her apartment. To reach her, I was given a number to call, leave a message and wait for her to call back. When she slept, it was behind bolts in her bedroom, with a pale pink night-light burning.

Miss Lilly also commented,

> She stopped drinking completely six months ago and quit chain-smoking cold turkey. Her figure was slim and taut. . . . She didn't wear or need makeup. Thanks to expert plastic surgery and a superb bone structure, she could have passed for fifty-five. . . .

According to Miss Lilly, the star was desperately unhappy. She still missed her fourth and last husband, Alfred Steele (allegedly for years after his death in 1959 she still set a place for him at the dining table), regretted her estranged family situation, was devastated by her lack of film offers, and bemoaned her loss of the Pepsi post.

The events of Crawford's final months are a mixture of fact, fiction, and legend. It is known that she had injured her back while housecleaning (moving a dining room table) and that she suffered great pain from the episode. In February 1977, according to Miss Lilly, Joan began "'cleaning out,' sending me and a few other friends household items that she said she would no longer need." Around May 1st, Joan became quite ill and did require the services of a physician and a daily nurse (to aid Crawford's maid Frieda and Betty Barker, her personal secretary and close friend). Sunday, May 8th, Mother's Day,* she spent confined to bed. On Monday, she gave her dearly loved pet Shih Tzu dog, named Princess, to friends in the country to care for properly.

According to publicist Michael Sean O'Shea, a Crawford friend for over thirty-seven years, on the morning of Tuesday, May 10th, she had "arisen early" and had inquired if Frieda and the other helper had had breakfast. "She herself was about to have her morning tea," O'Shea mentioned. "She always started the day with tea and graham crackers. Just as the cup of tea was being put on her nightable, she slipped away." (According to another version, she had a premonition that the end was coming and asked that her lawyer, Edward S. Cowan, be informed. Then she died about 10 A.M.)

Those who suggest that perhaps Miss Crawford's death was not of natural causes (i.e. a heart attack) infer that the lack of an autopsy confirms the theory. However, Dr. Lawrence Greenman, an assistant medical examiner with the New York County office, later claimed no autopsy was performed because,

> I didn't think the circumstances called for one. There was nothing in my evaluation to lead me to suspect in any way. . . . I do know the location of the body, in her own

---

* Christina would continue to send Joan flowers on Mother's Day and other such holidays. Daughter Cynthia, a manager in a K-Mart store in Newton, Iowa, would say she had phoned Crawford on Mother's Day. "I just called to ask her how she was, and to say I love her. No, I did not see her. I wrote her letters and things like that."

bed, and she appeared to be well looked after. There was no disarray, no disorder. . . . The replies to all the questions I asked made me feel the cause of death was natural.

For generations of filmgoers and TV late show watchers, the name, vision, and voice of Joan Crawford had become a constant part of their lives. To accept that this superstar was no longer alive, was and is an emotional challenge.

As per Joan's will, her body was cremated (following the tradition of her husband, Alfred Steele). On Friday, May 13th, there was a very private memorial service held at Campbell's Funeral Parlor in New York City. Among those attending were Sydney Guilaroff, the famed Hollywood hairdresser (whom Crawford had brought to films), actress Geraldine Brooks, Betty Barker, Radie Harris, and three of Crawford's four children, Christina, Cathy, and Christopher. The very plain ceremony was in the Christian Science tradition, with Mrs. Marque Campbell (Joan's practioner) reading Bible selections.

On Tuesday, May 17th, there was a second memorial service at All Soul's Unitarian Church in Manhattan. Some 1,500 people attended and the service had Reverend Dr. Walter Donald Kring reading Joan's favorite essay, "Desiderata" by Max Ehrman. Geraldine Brooks and Cliff Robertson each delivered eulogies, and Anita Loos reminisced about the years she had spent at MGM with Miss Crawford. Pearl Bailey sang "He'll Understand." Daughter Christina was dressed in black; while daughter Cindy wore an emerald-green blouse. Christopher was *not* present.

Adding to the controversy over Joan's death was the rationale of her will, leading to further newspaper headlines. Both Christina and Christopher were excluded from bequests ("for reasons which are well known to them" wrote Miss Crawford in her last legal document), while Cathy (Lalonde) and Cynthia (Jordan) were each left $77,500. Publicist

O'Shea received $5,000 and secretaries Florence Walsh and Pettina Barker received $10,000 and $35,000 respectively.

Around the country there were special art house tributes to Crawford, with festivals of her films. Jack Valenti, president of the Motion Picture Association of America, requested that on Friday, May 20, 1977, all major studios in Hollywood halt activities briefly to pay silent tribute to Joan Crawford. "There will never be a bigger movie star than Joan Crawford," Valenti stated, "and, in our business, that is probably the largest legacy one can leave."

But some friends thought differently. "Christ, what Joan wanted was a job," said one West Coast confidante. Hairstylist Guilaroff would recount bitterly, "I've tried for two years to persuade the Motion Picture Academy to give her an honorary award. As early as last October, I pleaded again and then was told that it was too late—maybe next year—and now it is too late!" According to some sources, Joan was very disappointed that she had not been invited personally to attend the Bette Davis tribute given by the American Film Institute on March 1, 1977. According to Doris Lilly, ". . . it hurt. Nonetheless, Joan, an avid TV watcher, told me that she thought the [television] event was a glorious tribute to a great star."

"Joan to all of us, was not A star. She was THE star. Her likes will never come around again in our business." This was the tribute offered by friend Barbara Stanwyck. George Cukor,* who would organize a "Tribute to Joan Crawford" at the Academy of Motion Pictures Arts and Sciences on June 24, 1977, wrote a special praise of the late superstar for the Sunday *New York Times*:

> She was the perfect image of the movie star and, as such, largely the creation of her own indomitable will. She had, of course, very remarkable material to work with: a quick native intelligence, tremen-

* In Cukor's library there is a framed, signed picture of Crawford with the inscription, "For Dear George—and that offer of marriage holds good any time!"

dous animal vitality, a lovely figure, and, above all, her face, that
extraordinary sculptural construction of lines and planes, finely chis-
eled like the mask of some classical
divinity from fifth century Greece.
It caught the light superbly, so that
you could photograph her from any
angle, and the face moved beautifully. . . .

In the days before zoom lenses
and advanced electronics, cameras
often had to be mounted on great
cumbersome cranes, maneuvered
by as many as twelve men, and
close-ups might well require all this
to be pushed from extreme long
shots to within a few inches of an
actor's face. . . . The nearer the
camera, the more tender and yield-
ing she became—her eyes glisten-
ing, her lips avid in ecstatic acceptance. The camera saw, I suspect, a
side of her that no flesh-and-blood
lover ever saw.

Perhaps the best accolade came from the
enthusiastic fans themselves over the decades. Some years ago as she left the 21 Club
in Manhattan, Crawford was confronted by a
gang of construction workers. One yelled
"Hey, Joanie!" Ever the gracious movie star
in public, she shook hands cordially with
many of them. One of their number studied
her carefully and then remarked, "They don't
make them like you anymore, baby." They
certainly do not. . . .

FILMOGRAPHY

As Lucille Le Sueur:

LADY OF THE NIGHT *(Metro-Goldwyn, 1925)* 5,419 feet.

Presenter, Louis B. Mayer; director, Monta Bell; story, Adela Rogers St. John; screenplay, Alice D. G. Miller; art director, Cedric Gibbons; camera, Andre Barlatier; editor, Ralph Dawson.

Norma Shearer (Molly/Florence); Malcolm McGregor (David); George K. Arthur (Chunky); Fred Esmelton (Judge Banning); Dale Fuller (Miss Carr); Lew Harvey (Chris); Betty Morrisey (Gertie); uncredited: Lucille Le Sueur [Joan Crawford] (Double for Miss Shearer).

PROUD FLESH *(Metro-Goldwyn, 1925)* 5,770 feet.

Presenter, Louis B. Mayer; director, King Vidor; based on the novel by Lawrence Rising; screenplay, Harry Behn, Agnes Christine Johnston; assistant director, David Howard; camera, John Arnold.

Eleanor Boardman (Fernando); Pat O'Malley (Pat O'Malley); Harrison Ford (Don Jaime); Trixie Friganza (Mrs. McKee); William J. Kelly (Mr. McKee); Rosita Marstini (Vicente); Sojin (Wong); Evelyn Sherman (Spanish Aunt); George Nichols (Spanish Uncle); Margaret Seddon (Mrs. O'Malley); Lillian Elliott (Mrs. Casey); Priscilla Bonner (San Francisco Girl); Lucille Le Sueur [Joan Crawford] (Party Guest).

PRETTY LADIES *(Metro-Goldwyn, 1925)* 5,828 feet.

Director, Monta Bell; based on the story by Adela Rogers St. John; adaptor, Alice D. G. Miller; camera, Ira H. Morgan.

ZaSu Pitts (Maggie Keenan); Tom Moore (Al Cassidy); Ann Pennington (Herself); Lilyan Tashman (Selma Larson); Bernard Randall (Aaron Savage); Helena D'Algy (Adrienne); Conrad Nagel (Maggie's Dream Lover); Norma Shearer (Frances White); George K. Arthur (Roger Van Horn); Lucille Le Sueur [Joan Crawford] (Bobby); Paul Ellis (Warren Hadley); Roy D'Arcy (Paul Thompson); Gwen Lee (Fay); Dorothy Seastrom (Diamond Tights); Lew Harvey (Will Rogers); Chad Huber (Frisco); Walter Shumway (Mr. Gallagher); Dan Crimmins (Mr. Shean); Jimmie Quinn (Eddie Cantor).

As Joan Crawford:

THE CIRCLE *(MGM, 1925)* 5,511 feet.

Director, Frank Borzage; based on the play by W. Somerset Maugham; adaptor, Kenneth B. Clarke; wardrobe, Ethel Chaffin; art directors, Cedric Gibbons, James Basevi; camera, Chester A. Lyons.

Eleanor Boardman (Elizabeth); Malcolm McGregor (Edward Lutton); Alec B. Francis (Lord Clive Cheney); Eugenie Besserer (Lady Catherine); George Fawcett (Portenous); Creighton Hale (Arnold); Otto Hoffman (Dorker); Eulalie Jensen (Mrs. Shenstone); Joan Crawford (Young Lady Catherine); and Buddy Smith, Frank Braidewood, and Derek Glynne.

OLD CLOTHES *(Metro-Goldwyn, 1925)* 5,915 feet.

Supervisor, Jack Coogan, Sr.; director, Edward Cline; screenplay, Willard Mack; titles, Robert Hopkins; camera, Frank B. Good, Harry Davis.

Max Davidson (Max Ginsberg); Joan Crawford (Mary Riley); Allan Forrest (Nathan Burke); Lillian Elliott (Mrs. Burke); James Mason (Dapper Dan); Stanton Heck (The Adjuster); Dynamite (The Horse); Jackie Coogan (Tim Kelly).

SALLY, IRENE AND MARY *(MGM, 1925)* 5,564 feet.

Director, Edmund Goulding; based on the play by Edward Dowling, Cyrus Wood; screenplay, Goulding; art directors, Cedric Gibbons, Merrill Pye; camera, John Arnold; editors, Harold Young, Arthur Johns.

Constance Bennett (Sally); Joan Crawford (Irene); Sally O'Neal (Mary); William Haines (Jimmy Dugan); Henry Kolker (Marcus Morton); Douglas Gilmore (Nester); Ray Howard (College Kid); Kate Price (Mrs. Dugan); Aggie Herring (Mrs. O'Brien); Sam De Grasse (Officer O'Dare); Lillian Elliott (Mrs. O'Dare); Edna Mae Cooper (Maggie).

THE BOOB *(MGM, 1926)* 5,020 feet.

Director, William Wellman; story, George Scarborough, Annette Westbay; titles, Katherine Hilliker, H.

H. Caldwell; adaptor, Kenneth B. Clarke; art directors, Cedric Gibbons, Ben Carre; camera, William Daniels; editor, Ben Lewis.

Gertrude Olmstead (Amy); George K. Arthur (Peter Good); Joan Crawford (Jane); Charles Murray (Cactus Jim); Antonio D'Algy (Harry Benson); Hank Mann (Village Soda Clerk); Babe London (Fat Girl).

TRAMP, TRAMP, TRAMP *(First National, 1926)* 5,831 feet.

Director, Harry Edwards; story, Frank Capra, Tim Whelan, Hal Conklin, J. Frank Holliday, Gerald Duffy, Murray Roth; camera, Elgin Lessley.

Harry Langdon (Harry); Joan Crawford (Betty Burton); Edward Davis (John Burton); Carlton Griffin (Roger Caldwell); Alec B. Francis (Harry's Father); Brooks Benedict (Taxi Driver); Tom Murray (The Argentine).

PARIS *(MGM, 1926)* 5,580 feet.

Director/screenplay, Edmund Goulding; titles, Joe Farnham; wardrobe, Kathleen Kay, Maude Marsh, Andre-ani; art directors, Cedric Gibbons, Merrill Pye; camera, John Arnold; editor, Arthur Johns.

Charles Ray (Jerry); Joan Crawford (The Girl); Douglas Gilmore (The Cat); Michael Visaroff (Rocco); Rose Dione (Marcelle); Jean Galeron (Pianist).

WINNERS OF THE WILDERNESS *(MGM, 1927)* 6,343 feet.*

Director, W. S. Van Dyke II; continuity, Josephine Chippo; titles, Marian Ainslee; art director, David Townsend; wardrobe, Lucia Coulter; camera, Clyde De Vinna; editor, Conrad A. Nervig.

Tim McCoy (Colonel O'Hara); Joan Crawford (Renee Contrecoeur); Edward Connelly (General Contrecoeur); Roy D'Arcy (Captain Dumas); Louise Lorraine (Mimi); Edward Hearn (George Washington); Tom O'Brien (Timothy); Will Walling (General Braddock); Frank Cuttier (Governor de Vaudreuil); Lionel Belmore (Governor Dinwiddle); Chief Big Tree (Pontiac).

* Technicolor sequences.

THE TAXI DANCER *(MGM, 1927)* 6,289 feet.

Director, Harry Millarde; based on the novel by Robert Terry Shannon; screenplay, A. P. Younger; titles, Ralph Spence; wardrobe, Andre-ani; art directors, Cedric Gibbons, David Townsend; camera, Ira Morgan; editor, George Hively.

Joan Crawford (Joslyn Poe); Owen Moore (Lee Rogers); Marc MacDermott (Henry Brierhalter); Gertrude Astor (Kitty Lane); Rockliffe Fellowes (Stephen Bates); Douglas Gilmore (James Kelvin); William Orlamond (Doc Ganz); Claire McDowell (Aunt Mary); Bert Roach (Charlie Cook).

THE UNDERSTANDING HEART *(MGM, 1927)* 6,657 feet.

Director, Jack Conway; based on the novel by Peter Bernard Kyne; adaptor/screenplay, Edward T. Loewe, Jr.; titles, Joe Farnham; wardrobe, Andreani; art directors, Cedric Gibbons, B. H. Martin; camera, John Arnold; editor, John W. English.

Joan Crawford (Monica Dale); Rockliffe Fellowes (Bob Mason); Francis X. Bushman, Jr. (Tony Garland); Carmel Myers (Kelcey Dale); Richard Carle (Sheriff Bentley); Jerry Miley (Bardwell); Harvey Clark (Uncle Charley).

THE UNKNOWN *(MGM, 1927)* 5,517 feet.

Director/story, Tod Browning; screenplay, Waldemar Young; art directors, Cedric Gibbons, Richard Day; wardrobe, Lucia Coulter; camera, Merritt Gerstad; editor, Harry Reynolds, Errol Taggart.

Lon Chaney (Alonzo); Norman Kerry (Malabar); Joan Crawford (Estrellita); Nick De Ruiz (Zanzi); John George (Cojo); Frank Lanning (Costra).

SPRING FEVER *(MGM, 1927)* 6,705 feet.

Director, Edward Sedgwick; based on the play by Vincent Lawrence; screenplay, Albert Lewin, Frank Davis; titles, Ralph Spence; art directors, Cedric Gibbons, David Townsend; wardrobe, David Cox; camera, Ira Morgan; editor, Frank Sullivan.

William Haines (Jack Kelly); Joan Crawford (Allie Monte); George K. Arthur (Eustace Tewksbury); George Fawcett (Mr. Waters); Eileen Percy (Martha Lomsdom); Edward Earle (Johnson); Bert Woodruff (Pop Kelly); Lee Morgan (Oscar).

TWELVE MILES OUT *(MGM, 1927)* 7,899 feet.

Director, Jack Conway; based on the play by William Anthony McGuire; screenplay, A. P. Younger; titles, Joe Farnham; art directors, Cedric Gibbons, Eugene Hornbostel; wardrobe, Rene Hubert; camera, Ira Morgan; editor, Basil Wrangell.

John Gilbert (Jerry Fay); Ernest Torrence (Red McCue); Joan Crawford (Jane); Eileen Percy (Maizie); Paulette Duval (Trini); Dorothy Sebastian (Chiquita); Gwen Lee (Hulda); Edward Earle (John Burton); Bert Roach (Luke); Tom O'Brien (Irish).

WEST POINT *(MGM, 1928)* 8,134 feet.

Director, Edward Sedgwick; story/continuity, Raymond L. Schrock; titles, Joe Farnham; assistant director, Edward Brophy; wardrobe, Gilbert Clark; advisor, Major Raymond G. Moses; camera, Ira Morgan; editor, Frank Sullivan.

William Haines (Brice Wayne); Joan Crawford (Betty Channing); William Bakewell (Tex McNeil); Neil Neely (Bob Sperry); Ralph Emerson (Bob Chase); Leon Kellar (Captain Munson); Major Raymond G. Moses (Coach Towers).

ROSE-MARIE *(MGM, 1928)* 7,745 feet.

Director, Lucien Hubbard; based on the play by Otto Harbach, Oscar Hammerstein, II, Rudolf Friml, Herbert Stothart; screenplay, Hubbard; wardrobe, David Cox; music, Friml, Stothart; art directors, Cedric Gibbons, Richard Day; camera, John Arnold; editor, Carl L. Pierson.

Joan Crawford (Rose-Marie); James Murray (Jim Kenyon); House Peters (Sergeant Terence Malone); Creighton Hale (Etienne Duray); Gibson Gowland (Black Bastien); George Cooper (Fuzzy); Lionel Belmore (Henri Duray); William Orlamond (Emile la Flamme); Polly Moran (Lady Jane); Harry Gribbon (Trooper Gray); Gertrude Astor (Wanda); Ralph Yearsley (Jean); Sven Hugo Borg (Hudson).

ACROSS TO SINGAPORE *(MGM, 1928)* 6,598 feet.

Director, William Nigh; based on the novel *All the Brothers Were Valiant* by Ben Ames Williams; screenplay, Richard Schayer; titles, Joe Farnham; adaptor, Ted Shane; art director, Cedric Gibbons; wardrobe, David Cox; camera, John Seitz; editor, Ben Lewis.

Ramon Novarro (Joel Shore); Joan Crawford (Priscilla Crowninshield); Ernest Torrence (Captain Mark Shore); Frank Currier (Jeremiah Shore); Dan Wolheim (Noah Shore); Duke Martin (Matthew Shore); Edward Connelly (Joshua Crowninshield); James Mason (Finch).

THE LAW OF THE RANGE *(MGM, 1928)* 5,393 feet.

Director, William Nigh; story, Norman Houston; screenplay, Richard Schayer; titles, Robert Hopkins; wardrobe, Lucia Coulter; camera, Clyde De Vinna; editor, Dan Sharits.

Tim McCoy (Jim Lockheart); Joan Crawford (Betty Dallas); Rex Lease (The Solitaire Kid); Bodil Rosing (Mother Lockheart); Tenen Holtz (Cohen).

FOUR WALLS *(MGM, 1928)* 6,620 feet.

Director, William Nigh; based on the play by Dana Burnet, George Abbott; continuity, Alice D. G. Miller; titles, Joe Farnham; art director, Cedric Gibbons; wardrobe, David Cox; camera, James Wong Howe; editor, Harry Reynolds.

John Gilbert (Benny); Joan Crawford (Frieda); Vera Gordon (Mrs. Horowitz); Carmel Myers (Bertha); Robert Emmet O'Connor (Sullivan); Louis Natheaux (Monk); Jack Byron (Duke Roma).

OUR DANCING DAUGHTERS *(MGM, 1928)* 7,652 feet.

Director, Harry Beaumont; story/continuity, Josephine Lovett; titles, Marian Ainslee, Ruth Cummings; art director, Cedric Gibbons; assistant director, Harold S. Bucquet; wardrobe, David Cox; song, Ballard MacDonald, William Axt, and David Mendoza; camera, George Barnes; editor, William Hamilton.

Joan Crawford (Diana Medford); John Mack Brown (Ben Baline); Nils Asther (Norman); Dorothy Sebastian (Beatrice); Anita Page (Ann); Kathlyn Williams (Ann's Mother); Edward Nugent (Freddie); Dorothy Cumming (Diana's Mother); Huntley Gordon (Diana's Father); Evelyn Hall (Freddie's Mother); Sam De Grasse (Freddie's Father); Robert Livingston (One of the Crowd).

DREAM OF LOVE *(MGM, 1928)* 5,764 feet.

Director, Fred Niblo; based on the play *Adrienne Lecouvreur* by Augustin Eugene Scribe, Ernest Legouve; screenplay, Dorothy Farnum; titles, Marian Ainslee, John Howard Lawson, Ruth Cummings; art director, Cedric Gibbons; assistant director, Harold S. Bucquet; gowns, Adrian; camera, Oliver Marsh, William Daniels; editor, James McKay.

Nils Asther (Mauritz); Joan Crawford (Adrienne); Aileen Pringle (Duchess); Warner Oland (Duke); Carmel Myers (Countess); Harry Reinhardt (Count); Harry Myers (Baron); Alphonse Martell (Michonet); Fletcher Norton (Ivan).

THE DUKE STEPS OUT *(MGM, 1929)* 6,236 feet.

Director, James Cruze; story, Lucian Cary; adaptor/continuity, Raymond Schrock, Dale Van Every; titles, Joe Farnham; art director, Cedric Gibbons; song, William Axt and David Mendoza; wardrobe, David Cox; camera, Ira Morgan; editor, George Hively.

William Haines (Duke); Joan Crawford (Susie); Karl Dane (Barney); Tenen Holtz (Jake); Edward Nugent (Tommy Wells); Jack Roper (Poison Kerrigan); Delmer Daves (Bossy Edwards); Luke Cosgrave (Professor Widdicomb); Herbert Prior (Mr. Corbin).

HOLLYWOOD REVUE OF 1929 *(MGM, 1929)* 116 min.*

Producer, Harry Rapf; director, Charles Reisner; skits, Joe Farnham; dialogue, Al Boasberg, Robert E. Hopkins; art directors, Cedric Gibbons, Richard Day; songs, Arthur Freed and Nacio Herb Brown; Raymond Klages and Jesse Greer; Andy Rice and Martin Broones; Joe Trent and Louis Alter; Fred Fisher; Joe Goodwin and Gus Edwards; music arrangers, Arthur Lange, Ernest Klapholtz, Ray Heindorf; choreography, Sammy Lee, George Cunningham; assistant directors, Jack Cummings, Sandy Roth, Al Shenberg; costumes, David Cox, Henrietta Frazer, Joe Rapf; camera, John Arnold, Irving Ries, Maximilian Fabian, John M. Nicholaus; editors, William S. Gray, Cameron K. Wood.

Conrad Nagel, Jack Benny (Masters of Ceremonies); John Gilbert, Norma Shearer, Joan Crawford, Bessie Love, Lionel Barrymore, Cliff Edwards, Stan Laurel, Oliver Hardy, Anita Page, Nils Asther, The Brox Sisters, Natacha Natova and Co., Marion Davies, William Haines, Buster Keaton, Marie Dressler, Charles King, Polly Moran, Gus Edwards, Karl Dane, George K. Arthur, Ann Dvorak, Gwen Lee, Albertina Rasch Ballet, The Rounders, The Biltmore Quartet (Themselves).

* Technicolor sequences.

OUR MODERN MAIDENS *(MGM, 1929)* 6,976 feet.

Director, Jack Conway; story/continuity, Josephine Lovett; titles, Marian Ainslee, Ruth Cummings; art director, Cedric Gibbons; music, William Axt; choreography, George Cunningham; gowns, Adrian; camera, Oliver Marsh; editor, Sam Zimbalist.

Joan Crawford (Billie Brown); Rod La Rocque (Abbott); Douglas Fairbanks, Jr. (Gil); Anita Page (Kentucky); Edward Nugent (Reg); Josephine Dunn (Ginger); Albert Gran (B. Bickering Brown).

UNTAMED *(MGM, 1929)* 7,911 feet.

Director, Jack Conway; adaptor/continuity, Sylvia Thalberg, Frank Butler; dialogue, Willard Mack; titles, Lucille Newmark; art directors, Cedric Gibbons, Van Nest Polglase; songs, Joe Goodwin and Louis Alter; Nacio Herb Brown and Arthur Freed; gowns, Adrian; sound, Douglas Shearer; camera, Oliver Marsh; editors, William S. Gray, Charles Hockberg.

Joan Crawford (Bingo); Robert Montgomery (Andy); Ernest Torrence (Ben Murchison); Holmes Herbert (Howard Presley); John Miljan (Bennock); Gwen Lee (Marjory); Edward Nugent (Paul); Don Terry (Gregg); Gertrude Astor (Mrs. Mason); Milton Fahrney (Jollop); Lloyd Ingraham (Dowling); Grace Cunard (Billie); Wilson Benge (Bilcombe).

MONTANA MOON *(MGM, 1930)* 7,917 feet.

Director, Malcolm St. Clair; story/continuity, Sylvia Thalberg, Frank Butler; dialogue, Joe Farnham; art director, Cedric Gibbons; songs, Nacio Herb Brown and Arthur Freed; Herbert Stothart and Clifford Grey; gowns, Adrian; sound, Paul Neal, Douglas Shearer; camera, William Daniels; editors, Carl L. Pierson, Leslie F. Wilder.

Joan Crawford (Joan); John Mack Brown (Larry); Dorothy Sebastian (Elizabeth); Ricardo Cortez (Jeff); Benny Rubin (The Doctor); Cliff Edwards (Froggy); Karl Dane (Hank); Lloyd Ingraham (Mr. Prescott).

OUR BLUSHING BRIDES *(MGM, 1930)* 101 min.

Director, Harry Beaumont; story, Bess Meredyth; continuity/dialogue, Meredyth, John Howard Lawson; titles, Helen Mainardi; art director, Cedric Gibbons; ballet staged by Albertina Rasch; gowns, Adrian; sound, Russell Franks, Douglas Shearer; camera, Merritt B. Gerstad; editors, George Hively, Harold Palmer.

Joan Crawford (Jerry Marsh); Anita Page (Connie); Dorothy Sebastian (Franky); Robert Montgomery (Tony Jardine); Raymond Hackett (David Jardine); John Miljan (Martin W. Sanderson); Hedda Hopper (Mrs. Weaver); Albert Conti (Monsieur Pantoise); Edward Brophy (Joe Munsey); Robert Emmet O'Connor (The Detective); Martha Sleeper (Evelyn Woodforth); Mary Doran, Norma Drew, Gwen Lee, Claire Dodd, Catherine Moylan, Wilda Mansfield (Models); Louise Beavers (Amelia, the Maid).

PAID *(MGM, 1930)* 7,946 feet.

Director, Sam Wood; based on the play *Within the Law* by Bayard Veiller; adaptors, Lucien Hubbard, Charles MacArthur; dialogue, MacArthur; gowns, Adrian; art director, Cedric Gibbons; sound, Douglas Shearer; camera, Charles Rosher; editor, Hugh Wynn.

Joan Crawford (Mary Turner); Robert Armstrong (Joe Garson); Marie Prevost (Agnes Lynch); Kent Douglass [Douglass Montgomery] (Bob Gilder); John Miljan (Inspector Burke); Purnell Pratt (Edward Gilder); Hale Hamilton (District Attorney Demarest); Polly Moran (Polly); Robert Emmet O'Connor (Cassidy); Tyrrell Davis (Eddie Griggs); William Bakewell (Carney); George Cooper (Red); Gwen Lee (Bertha); Isabel Withers (Helen Morris).

DANCE, FOOLS, DANCE *(MGM, 1931)* 81 min.

Director, Harry Beaumont; story, Aurania Rouverol; continuity, Richard Schayer; dialogue, Rouverol; songs, Frank Crumit and Lou Klein; Dale Winbrow and L. Cornell; Roy Turk and Fred Ahlert; Dorothy Fields and Jimmy McHugh; camera, Charles Rosher; editor, George Hively.

Joan Crawford (Bonnie Jordan); Lester Vail (Bob Townsend); Cliff Edwards (Bert Scranton); William Bakewell (Rodney Jordan); William Holden (Stanley Jordan); Clark Gable (Jake Luva); Earle Foxe (Wally Baxter); Purnell B. Pratt (Parker); Hale Hamilton (Selby); Natalie Moorhead (Della); Joan Marsh (Sylvia); Russell Hopton (Whitey); James Donlan (Police Reporter); Mortimer Snow, Sherry Hall (Reporters); Robert Livingston (Jack, a Hood); Tommy Shugrue (Photographer); Harry Semels (Dance Extra).

LAUGHING SINNERS *(MGM, 1931)* 71 min.

Director, Harry Beaumont; based on the play *Torch Song* by Kenyon Nicholson; continuity, Bess Meredyth; dialogue, Martin Flavin; additional dialogue, Edith Fitzgerald; song, Martin Broones; sound, Charles E. Wallace; camera, Charles Rosher; editor, George Hively.

Joan Crawford (Ivy Stevens); Neil Hamilton (Howard Palmer); Clark Gable (Carl Loomis); Marjorie Rambeau (Ruby); Guy Kibbee (Cass Wheeler); Cliff Edwards (Mike); Roscoe Karns (Fred Geer); Gertrude Short (Edna); George Cooper (Joe); George F. Marion (Humpty); Bert Woodruff (Tink); Henry Armetta (Tony, the Chef); Lee Phelps (Salesman).

THIS MODERN AGE *(MGM, 1931)* 68 min.

Director, Nicholas Grinde; based on the story "Girls Together" by Mildred Cram; continuity/dialogue, Sylvia Thalberg, Frank Butler; camera, Charles Rosher; editor, William LeVanway.

Joan Crawford (Valentine Winters); Pauline Frederick (Diane Winters); Neil Hamilton (Bob Blake); Monroe Owsley (Tony); Hobart Bosworth (Mr. Blake); Emma Dunn (Mrs. Blake); Albert Conti (Andre de Graignon); Adrienne d'Ambricourt (Marie); Marcelle Corday (Alyce).

POSSESSED *(MGM, 1931)* 72 min.

Director, Clarence Brown; based on the play *The Mirage* by Edgar Selwyn; adaptor, Lenore Coffee; song, Max Leif, Joseph Meyer; camera, Oliver T. Marsh.

Joan Crawford (Marian Martin); Clark Gable (Mark Whitney); Wallace Ford (Al Mannings); Skeets Gallagher (Wally); Frank Conroy (Travers); Marjorie White (Vernice); John Miljan (John); Clara Blandick (Mother).

GRAND HOTEL *(MGM, 1932)* 115 min.

Director, Edmund Goulding; based on the play *Menschen in Hotel* by Vicki Baum; American stage version by William A. Drake; art director, Cedric Gibbons; gowns, Adrian; assistant director, Charles Dorian; sound, Douglas Shearer; camera, William Daniels; editor, Blanche Sewell.

Greta Garbo (Grusinskaya); John Barrymore (Baron Felix von Geigern); Joan Crawford (Flaemmchen); Wallace Beery (Preysing); Lionel Barrymore (Otto Kringelein); Lewis Stone (Dr. Ottenschlag); Jean Hersholt (Senf); Robert McWade (Meierheim); Purnell Pratt (Zinnowitz); Ferdinand Gottschalk (Pimenov); Rafaela Ottiano (Suzette); Morgan Wallace (Chauffeur); Tully Marshall (Gerstenkorn); Frank Conroy (Rohna); Murray Kinnell (Schweimann); Edwin Maxwell (Dr. Waitz); Mary Carlisle (Honeymooner); John Davidson (Hotel Manager); Sam McDaniel (Bartender); Rolfe Sedan, Herbert Evans (Clerks); Lee Phelps (Extra in Lobby).

LETTY LYNTON *(MGM, 1932)* 84 min.

Director, Clarence Brown; based on the novel by Marie Belloc Lowndes; adaptors, John Meehan, Wanda Tuchock; costumes, Adrian; camera, Oliver T. Marsh; editor, Conrad A. Nervig.

Joan Crawford (Letty Lynton); Robert Montgomery (Hale Darrow); Nils Asther (Emile Renaud); Lewis Stone (Mr. Haney); May Robson (Mrs. Lynton); Louise Closser Hale (Miranda); Emma Dunn (Mrs. Darrow); Walter Walker (Mr. Darrow); William Pawley (Hennessey).

RAIN *(United Artists, 1932)* 92 min.

Director, Lewis Milestone; based on the play *Rain* by John Colton, Clemence Randolph, and the story "Miss Thompson" by W. Somerset Maugham; screenplay, Maxwell Anderson; camera, Oliver T. Marsh; editor, W. Duncan Mansfield.

Joan Crawford (Sadie Thompson); Walter Huston (Reverend Alfred Davidson); William Gargan (Sergeant O'Hara); Guy Kibbee (Joe Horn); Walter Catlett (Quartermaster Bates); Beulah Bondi (Mrs. Davidson); Matt Moore (Dr. MacPhail); Kendall Lee (Mrs. MacPhail); Ben Hendricks (Griggs); Frederic Howard (Hodgson).

TODAY WE LIVE *(MGM, 1933)* 115 min.

Producer/director, Howard Hawks; based on the story "Turnabout" by William Faulkner; screenplay, Edith Fitzgerald, Dwight Taylor; costumes, Adrian; art director, Cedric Gibbons; sound, Douglas Shearer; camera, Oliver T. Marsh; editor, Edward Curtis.

Joan Crawford (Diana Boyce-Smith); Gary Cooper (Richard Bogard); Robert Young (Claude); Franchot Tone (Ronnie); Roscoe Karns (McGinnis); Louise Closser Hale (Applegate); Rollo Lloyd (Major); Hilda Vaughn (Eleanor).

DANCING LADY *(MGM, 1933)* 94 min.

Executive producer, David O. Selznick; associate producer, John W. Considine, Jr.; director, Robert Z. Leonard; based on the novel by James Warner Bellah; screenplay, Allen Rivkin, P. J. Wolfson; music, Lou Silvers; songs, Jimmy McHugh and Dorothy Fields; Burton Lane and Harold Adamson; Richard Rodgers and Lorenz Hart; choreography, Sammy Lee, Edward Prinz; costumes, Adrian; camera, Oliver T. Marsh; editor, Margaret Booth.

Joan Crawford (Janie Barlow); Clark Gable (Patch Gallegher); Franchot Tone (Tod Newton); Fred Astaire (Himself); Nelson Eddy (Himself); May Robson (Dolly Todhunter); Winnie Lightner (Rosette Henrietta La Rue); Robert Benchley (Ward King); Ted Healy (Steve); Moe Howard, Jerry Howard, Larry Fine (Three Stooges); Gloria Foy (Vivian Warner); Maynard Holmes (Jasper Bradley, Jr.); Sterling Holloway (Pinky, the Author); Florine McKinney (Grace Newton); Bonita Barker, Dale Dean, Shirley Aranson, Katharine Barnes, Lynn Bari (Chorus Girls); Jack Baxley (Barker); Frank Hagney (Cop); Pat Somerset (Tod's Friend); Charles Williams (Man Arrested in Burlesque House); Ferdinand Gottschalk (Judge); Eve Arden (Marcia, the "Southern" Actress); Matt McHugh (Marcia's Agent); Charlie Sullivan (Cabby); Harry Bradley, John Sheehan (Author's Pals); Stanley Blystone (Traffic Cop); Charles C. Wilson (Club Manager); Bill Elliott (Cafe Extra); Larry Steers, C. Montague Shaw (First Nighters); Art Jarrett (Art); Grant Mitchell (Bradley Sr.).

SADIE McKEE *(MGM, 1934)* 88 min.

Producer, Lawrence Weingarten; director, Clarence Brown; based on the story "Pretty Sadie McKee" by Vina Delmar; screenplay, John Meehan; costumes, Adrian; songs, Arthur Freed and Nacio Herb Brown; camera, Oliver T. Marsh; editor, Hugh Wynn.

Joan Crawford (Sadie McKee); Gene Raymond (Tommy Wallace); Franchot Tone (Michael Alderson); Esther Ralston (Dolly); Edward Arnold (Jack Brennon); Earl Oxford (Stooge); Jean Dixon (Opal); Leo Carroll (Phelps); Akim Tamiroff (Riccori); Zelda Sears (Mrs. Crawey); Helen Ware (Mrs. McKee); Gene Austin & Candy & Cocoa (Cafe Entertainers); Charles Williams (Cafe Pest); Lee Phelps (Chauffeur); Mary Forbes (Mrs. Alderson); Francis MacDonald (Another Chauffeur); Harry Bradley (Dr. Taylor); Wyndham Standing (Butler at Alderson House); Minerva Urecal

(Cook's Assistant at Brennon Home); Ethel Griffies (Woman in Subway).

CHAINED *(MGM, 1934)* 74 min.

Producer, Hunt Stromberg; director, Clarence Brown; story, Edgar Selwyn; screenplay, John Lee Mahin; costumes, Adrian; art directors, Cedric Gibbons, Alexander Toluboff, Edwin B. Willis; music, Herbert Stothart; camera, George Folsey; editor, Robert J. Kern.

Joan Crawford (Diane Lovering); Clark Gable (Mike Bradley); Otto Kruger (Richard Field); Stuart Erwin (Johnny); Una O'Connor (Amy); Marjorie Gateson (Mrs. Field); Hooper Atchley, Phillips Smalley, Edward Le Saint, Gordon De Main (S.S. Officials); Theresa Maxwell Conover (Secretary); Lee Phelps (Bartender); Ward Bond (Sailor); Grace Hayle, Nora Cecil (Spinsters); Paul Porcasi (Hotel Manager); Chris-Pin Martin (Peon); Sam Flint (Clerk); Keenan Wynn (Double for Joan Crawford in Speedboat Sequence).

FORSAKING ALL OTHERS *(MGM, 1934)* 82 min.

Producer, Bernard H. Hyman; director, W. S. Van Dyke, II; story, Edward Barry Roberts, Frank Morgan Cavett; costumes, Adrian; camera, Gregg Toland, George Folsey; editor, Tom Held.

Joan Crawford (Mary Clay); Clark Gable (Jeff Williams); Robert Montgomery (Dill Todd); Charles Butterworth (Shep); Billie Burke (Paula); Frances Drake (Connie); Rosalind Russell (Eleanor); Tom Ricketts (Wiffens); Arthur Treacher (Johnson); Greta Meyer (Bella).

NO MORE LADIES *(MGM, 1935)* 79 min.

Producer, Irving Thalberg; directors, Edward H. Griffith, George Cukor; based on the play by A. E. Thomas; screenplay, Donald Ogden Stewart, Horace Jackson; costumes, Adrian; art director, Cedric Gibbons; camera, Oliver T. Marsh; editor, Frank E. Hull.

Joan Crawford (Marcia Townsend); Robert Montgomery (Sherry Warren); Edna May Oliver (Fanny Townsend); Franchot Tone (James Salston); Charlie Ruggles (Edgar Holmes); Gail Patrick (Theresa Germaine); Vivienne Osborne (Lady Diana Moulton); Joan Burfield [Fontaine] (Caroline Rumsey); Arthur Treacher (Lord Moulton); David Horsley (James McIntyre Duffy); Jean Chatburn (Sally French); Charles Coleman (Stafford, the Butler); William Wagner (Butler); Walter Walker (Bit); Frank Mayo, Gertrude Astor, Jean Acker (Nightclub Extras); Donald Ogden Stewart (Drunk); Brooks Benedict (Joe Williams, the Bar Owner); Dave O'Brien (Party Guest); Lew Harvey, David Thursby (Bartenders).

I LIVE MY LIFE *(MGM, 1935)* 85 min.

Producer, Bernard H. Hyman; director, W. S. Van Dyke II; based on the story "Claustrophobia" by A. Carter Goodloe; adaptors, Gottfried Reinhardt, Ethel Borden; screenplay, Joseph L. Mankiewicz; costumes, Adrian; art director, Adrian; camera, George Folsey; editor, Tom Held.

Joan Crawford (Kay); Brian Aherne (Terry); Frank Morgan (Bentley); Aline MacMahon (Betty); Eric Blore (Grove); Fred Keating (Gene); Jessie Ralph (Grandma); Arthur Treacher (Gallup); Frank Conroy (Doctor); Etienne Girardot (Professor); Edward Brophy (Picture Hanger); Sterling Holloway (Mac); Hilda Vaughn (Miss Morrison); Vince Barnett (Clerk); Lionel Stander (Yaffitz); Hedda Hopper (Alvin's Mother); Esther Dale (Brumbaugh); Jan Duggan (Aunt Mathilde); Nella Walker (Ruth's Mother); Ronnie Cosbey (Alvin); Tom Dugan (Guard); George Baxter (Bishop); Howard Hickman (Teacher); Adrian Rosley, Blanche Craig, Howard Wilson, Arthur Stuart Hull (Bits); Armand "Curley" Wright (Greek Merchant); Freeman Wood (Waterbury, Jr.); Barbara Worth (Miss Waterbury); Harry Bradley (Curator); Agnes Anderson (Sheila); Harry Tyler (Photographer).

THE GORGEOUS HUSSY *(MGM, 1936)* 105 min.

Producer, Joseph L. Mankiewicz; director, Clarence Brown; based on the novel by Samuel Hopkins Adams; screenplay, Ainsworth Morgan, Stephen Morehouse Avery; art director, Cedric Gibbons; music, Herbert Stothart; costumes, Adrian; camera, George Folsey; editor, Blanche Sewell.

Joan Crawford (Peggy O'Neal Eaton); Robert Taylor (Bow Timberlake); Lionel Barrymore (Andrew Jackson); Melvyn Douglas (John Randolph); James Stewart (Roderick "Rowdy" Dow); Franchot Tone (John Eaton); Louis Calhern (Sunderland); Alison Skipworth (Mrs. Beall); Beulah Bondi (Rachel Jackson); Melville Cooper (Cuthbert); Edith Atwater (Lady Vaughn); Sidney Toler (Daniel Webster); Gene Lockhart (Major O'Neal); Phoebe Foster (Emily Donaldson); Clara Blandick (Louisa Abbott); Frank Conroy (John C. Calhoun); Nydia Westman (Maybelle); Louise Beavers (Aunt Sukey); Willard Robertson (Secretary Ingham); Charles Trowbridge (Martin Van Buren); Fred "Snowflake" Toones (Horatius); William Orlamond (Herr Oxrenrider); Ward Bond (Officer); Harry Strang (Navigator); Samuel S. Hinds (Commander); Sam McDaniel (Butler); Harry Holman (Auctioneer); Betty Blythe (Mrs. Wainwright); Else Janson (Dutch Minister's Wife); Oscar Apfel (Tompkins); Lee Phelps (Bartender).

LOVE ON THE RUN *(MGM, 1936)* 81 min.

Producer, Joseph L. Mankiewicz; director, W. S. Van Dyke II; based on the story "Beauty and the Beast" by Alan Green, Julian Brodie; screenplay, John Lee Mahin, Manuel Seff, Gladys Hurlbut; costumes, Adrian; art director, Cedric Gibbons; sound, Douglas Shearer; camera, Oliver T. Marsh; editor, Frank Sullivan.

Joan Crawford (Sally Parker); Clark Gable (Michael Anthony); Franchot Tone (Barnabas Pells); Reginald Owen (Baron Spandermann); Mona Maris (Baroness); Ivan Lebedeff (Prince Igor); Charles Judels (Lieutenant of Police); William Demarest (Editor); Dewey Robinson (Italian Father); Bobby "Bobs" Watson (Italian Boy); Betty Jane Graham (Italian Girl); Charles Trowbridge (Express Company Manager); George Davis (Sergeant of Police); Donald Meek (Caretaker); Harry Allen (Chauffeur); James Carson (French Waiter); Billy Gilbert (Cafe Manager); Egon Brecher (Dr. Corsay); Otto Fries (Mechanic); Norman Ainsley (Newspaper Reporter); Leonard Kinsky (Bit); Fred Cavens, Fred Malatesta (French Waiters); Frank Puglia (Waiter); Bobby Watson (Assistant Manager).

THE LAST OF MRS. CHEYNEY (MGM, 1937) 98 min.

Producer, Lawrence Weingarten; director, Richard Boleslawski; based on the play by Frederick Lonsdale; screenplay, Leon Gordon, Samson Raphaelson, Monckton Hoffe; art director, Cedric Gibbons; music, Dr. William Axt; costumes, Adrian; sound, Douglas Shearer; camera, George Folsey; editor, Frank Sullivan.

Joan Crawford (Fay Cheyney); Robert Montgomery (Lord Arthur); William Powell (Charles); Frank Morgan (Lord Kelton); Nigel Bruce (Sir William); Jessie Ralph (Duchess); Benita Hume (Kitty); Melville Cooper (William); Ralph Forbes (John); Colleen Clare (Joan); Leonard Carey (Ames); Sara Haden (Anna); Lumsden Hare (Inspector Witherspoon); Wallis Clark (George); Aileen Pringle (Marie); Bob Cory (Deck Steward); Vesey O'Daveren (Steward); Wilson Benge (Butler); Thomas Braidon (Head Steward).

THE BRIDE WORE RED (MGM, 1937) 103 min.

Producer, Joseph L. Mankiewicz; director, Dorothy Arzner; based on the play *The Girl from Trieste* by Ferenc Molnar; screenplay, Tess Slesinger, Bradbury Foote; art director, Cedric Gibbons; costumes, Adrian; music, Franz Waxman; sound, Douglas Shearer; camera, George Folsey; editor, Adrienne Fazan.

Joan Crawford (Annie Palowitz/Signorina Vivaldi); Franchot Tone (Guilio Conti); Robert Young (Rudi Pal); Reginald Owen (Admiral Ritter); Billie Burke (Contessa DeMilano); Lynne Carver (Magdalena Ritter); George Zucco (Count Armalia); Mary Philips (Maria); Paul Porcasi (Mobili); Dickie Moore (Pietro); Frank Puglia (Alberto); Charles Judels (Proprietor of Cordellera Bar); Ann Rutherford (Peasant Girl); Rafael Storm, Bob Coutiere (Hotel Clerks); Anna Demetrio (Signora Milani); Adrianna Cassellotti, Jean Lewis (Other Peasant Girls); Harry Wilson (Sailor at Bar).

MANNEQUIN (MGM, 1938) 95 min.

Producer, Joseph L. Mankiewicz; director, Frank Borzage; based on an unpublished story by Katharine Brush; screenplay, Lawrence Hazard; costumes, Adrian; art director, Cedric Gibbons; assistant director, Lew Borzage; music, Edward Ward; songs, Ward, Robert Wright, and Chet Forrest; set decorator, Edwin

B. Willis; sound, Douglas Shearer; camera, George Folsey; editor, Frederic Y. Smith.

Joan Crawford (Jessie Cassidy); Spencer Tracy (John L. Hennessey); Alan Curtis (Eddie Miller); Mary Philips (Beryl); Oscar O'Shea (Pa Cassidy); Elisabeth Risdon (Mrs. Cassidy); Leo Gorcey (Clifford); Ralph Morgan (Briggs); George Chandler (Swing Magoo); Bert Roach (Schwartz); Marie Blake (Mrs. Schwartz); Matt McHugh (Mike); Paul Fix (Smooch); Helen Troy (Rubbles Adair); Phillip Terry (Man at Stage Door); Gwen Lee (Girl Worker); Donald Kirke (Dave McIntyre); Gwen Lee, Virginia Blair, Jim Baker, Ruth Dwyer (Wedding Guests); Jimmy Conlin (Elevator Operator); Frank Jaquet (Stage Doorman).

THE SHINING HOUR (MGM, 1938) 76 min.

Producer, Joseph L. Mankiewicz; director, Frank Borzage; based on the play by Keith Winter; screenplay, Jane Murfin, Ogden Nash; music, Franz Waxman; choreography, Tony De Marco; costumes, Adrian; art director, Cedric Gibbons; sound, Douglas Shearer; camera, George Folsey; editor, Frank E. Hull.

Joan Crawford (Olivia Riley); Margaret Sullavan (Judy Linden); Melvyn Douglas (Henry Linden); Fay Bainter (Hannah Linden); Allyn Joslyn (Roger Franklin); Hattie McDaniel (Belvedere); Frank Albertson (Benny Collins); Oscar O'Shea (Charlie Collins); Harry Barris (Bertie); Tony De Marco (Olivia's Dance Partner); Claire Owen (Stewardess); Sarah Edwards (Woman); E. Allyn Warren (Leonard); Jack Raymond (Farmer); George Chandler (Press Agent); Granville Bates (Man); Frank Puglia (Headwaiter); Francis X. Bushman, Jr. (Doorman).

THE ICE FOLLIES OF 1939 (MGM, 1939) 82 min.

Producer, Harry Rapf; director, Reinhold Schunzel; story, Leonard Praskins; screenplay, Florence Ryerson, Edgar Allan Woolf; music, Roger Edens; songs, Cliff Friend and Dave Franklin; Arthur Freed and Nacio Herb Brown; Bernice Petkere and Marty Symes; Edens and Franz Waxman; costumes, Adrian; art director, Cedric Gibbons; sound, Douglas Shearer; camera, Oliver T. Marsh; editor, W. Donn Hayes.

Joan Crawford (Mary McKay); James Stewart (Larry Hall); Lew Ayres (Eddie Burgess); Lewis Stone (Douglas Tulliver); Lionel Stander (Mort Hodges); Truman Bradley (Paul Rodney); Marie Blake (Effie Lane); Bess Ehrhardt (Kitty Sherman); Charles Williams (Max Morton); Eddy Conrad (Hal Gibbs); Arthur Loft (Director); Mary Forbes (Lady Hilda); Charles D. Brown (Barney); Edward Earle (Man); Carl Switzer (Small Boy); Darla Hood (Sister); Adolphe Hebert, Larry Jackson (Skating Horse); James McNamara, Eddie Kane (Politicians); Libby Taylor (Black Maid).

THE WOMEN (MGM, 1939) 132 min.*

Producer, Hunt Stromberg; director, George Cukor; based on the play by Clare Boothe; screenplay, Anita

Loos, Jane Murfin; art director, Cedric Gibbons; music, Edward Ward, David Snell; costumes, Adrian; sound, Douglas Shearer; camera, Oliver T. Marsh, Joseph Ruttenberg; editor, Robert J. Kerns.

Norma Shearer (Mary Haines); Joan Crawford (Crystal Allen); Rosalind Russell (Sylvia Fowler); Mary Boland (Countess DeLave); Paulette Goddard (Miriam Aarons); Joan Fontaine (Peggy Day); Lucile Watson (Mrs. Moorehead); Phyllis Povah (Edith Potter); Florence Nash (Nancy Blake); Virginia Weidler (Little Mary); Ruth Hussey (Miss Watts); Muriel Hutchinson (Jane); Margaret Dumont (Mrs. Wagstaff); Dennie Moore (Olga); Mary Cecil (Maggie); Marjorie Main (Lucy); Esther Dale (Ingrid); Hedda Hopper (Dolly Dupuyster); Mildred Shay (Helene, the French Maid); Priscilla Lawson, Estelle Etterre (Hairdressers); Ann Morriss (Exercise Instructress); Mary Beth Hughes (Miss Trimmerback); Marjorie Wood (Sadie); Virginia Grey (Pat); Cora Witherspoon (Mrs. Van Adams); Veda Buckland (Woman); Charlotte Treadway (Her Companion); Theresa Harris (Olive); Vera Vague (Receptionist); May Beatty (Fat Woman); Hilda Plowright (Miss Fordyer); Judith Allen (Miss Archer, the Model); Dorothy Sebastian, Renie Riano (Saleswomen); Josephine Whittell (Mrs. Spencer); Rita Gould (Dietician); Lilian Bond (Mrs. Erskine); Gertrude Simpson (Stage Mother); Carole Lee Kilby (Theatrical Child); Lita Chevret, Dora Clemant, Ruth Alder (Women under Sunlamps); Natalie Moorhead (Woman in Modiste Salon); Marie Blake (Stock Room Girl); Dorothy Adams (Miss Atkinson); Carol Hughes (Salesgirl at Modiste Salon); Peggy Shannon (Mrs. Jones); Winifred Harris, May Beatty (Society Women).

* Technicolor sequences.

STRANGE CARGO (MGM, 1940) 113 min.

Producer, Joseph L. Mankiewicz; director, Frank Borzage; based on the novel Not Too Narrow, Not Too Deep by Richard Sale; screenplay, Lawrence Hazard; art director, Cedric Gibbons; music, Franz Waxman; sound, Douglas Shearer; camera, Robert Planck; editor, Robert J. Kern.

Clark Gable (Andre Verne); Joan Crawford (Julie); Ian Hunter (Cambreau); Peter Lorre (Cochon); Paul Lukas (Hessler); Albert Dekker (Moll); J. Edward Bromberg (Flaubert); Eduardo Ciannelli (Telez); Victor Varconi (Fisherman); John Arledge (Dufond); Frederic Worlock (Grideau); Paul Fix (Benet); Bernard Nedell (Marfeu); Francis McDonald (Moussenq); Betty Compson (Suzanne); Charles Judels (Renard); Jack Mulhall (Dunning); Dewey Robinson (Georges); Harry Cording, Richard Alexander, Bud Fine, James Pierce, Hal Wynants, Christian Frank, Mitchell Lewis, Stanley Andrews, Dick Cramer, Ray Teal, Jack Adair (Guards); Gene Coogan, Eddie Foster, Frank Lackteen, Harry Semels (Convicts); Art Dupuis (Orderly); Stanley Andrews (Constable); William Edmunds (Watchman).

SUSAN AND GOD (MGM, 1940) 117 min.

Producer, Hunt Stromberg; director, George Cukor; based on the play by Rachel Crothers; screenplay, Anita Loos; art director, Cedric Gibbons; costumes, Adrian; music, Herbert Stothart; sound, Douglas Shearer; camera, Robert Planck; editor, William H. Terhune.

Joan Crawford (Susan Trexel); Fredric March (Barry Trexel); Ruth Hussey (Charlotte); John Carroll (Clyde Rochester); Rita Hayworth (Leonora Stubbs); Nigel Bruce (Hutchins Stubbs); Bruce Cabot (Michael O'-Hara); Rose Hobart (Irene Burrows); Rita Quigley (Blossom Trexel); Norma Mitchell (Paige); Romaine Callender (Oliver Leeds); Marjorie Main (Mary); Aldrich Bowker (Patrick); Constance Collier (Lady Wiggam); Herbert Evans (Bronson); Cece Broadhurst (Cowboy Joe); Richard O. Crane (Bob); Don Castle (Attendant); Dan Dailey, Jr. (Homer); Louis Payne (Dave); Gloria DeHaven (Enid); Joan Leslie, Susan Peters, David Tillotach, William Lochner (Guests).

British release title: The Gay Mrs. Trexel.

A WOMAN'S FACE (MGM, 1941) 105 min.

Producer, Victor Saville; director, George Cukor; based on the play Il Etait Une Fois by Francis de Croisset; screenplay, Donald Ogden Stewart; art director, Cedric Gibbons; music, Bronislau Kaper; costumes, Adrian; sound, Douglas Shearer; camera, Robert Planck; editor, Frank Sullivan.

Joan Crawford (Anna Holm); Melvyn Douglas (Dr. Segert); Conrad Veidt (Torsten Barring); Reginald Owen (Bernard Dalvik); Albert Bassermann (Consul Barring); Marjorie Main (Emma); Donald Meek (Herman); Connie Gilchrist (Christina Dalvik); Richard Nichols (Lars Erik); Osa Massen (Vera Segert); Charles Quigley (Eric); Henry Kolker (Judge); George Zucco (Defense Attorney); Henry Daniell (Public Prosecutor); Robert Warwick, Gilbert Emery (Associate Judges); Sarah Padden (Police Matron); Rex Evans (Notary); Doris Day, Mary Ellen Popel (Girls at Party); Lionel Pape (Einer); Gwili Andre (Gusta); Cecil Stewart (Pianist); Veda Buckland (Nurse).

WHEN LADIES MEET (MGM, 1941) 105 min.

Producers, Robert Z. Leonard, Orville O. Dull; director, Leonard; based on the play by Rachel Crothers; screenplay, S. K. Lauren, Anita Loos; art director, Cedric Gibbons; music, Bronislau Kaper; costumes, Adrian; sound, Douglas Shearer; camera, Robert Planck; editor, Robert Kern.

Joan Crawford (Mary Howard); Robert Taylor (Jimmy Lee); Greer Garson (Claire Woodruff); Herbert Marshall (Rogers Woodruff); Spring Byington (Bridget Drake); Rafael Storm (Walter Del Canto); Max Willenz (Pierre); Florence Shirley (Janet Hopper); Leslie Francis (Homer Hopper); Olaf Hytten (Mathews, the Butler); Mona Barrie (Mabel Guiness); Mary Forbes

(Mother at Party); John Marlowe (Violinist); Harold Minjir (Clerk); Barbara Bedford (Anna, the Maid).

THEY ALL KISSED THE BRIDE (Columbia, 1942) 86 min.

Producer, Edward Kaufman; director, Alexander Hall; based on the story by Gina Kaus, Andrew P. Solt; screenplay, P. J. Wolfson; art directors, Lionel Banks, Cary Odell; music, Morris Stoloff; costumes, Irene; camera, Joseph Walker; editor, Viola Lawrence.

Joan Crawford (Margaret J. Drew); Melvyn Douglas (Michael Holmes); Roland Young (Marsh); Billie Burke (Mrs. Drew); Allen Jenkins (Johnny Johnson); Andrew Tombes (Crane); Helen Parrish (Vivian Drew); Emory Parnell (Mahony); Mary Treen (Susie Johnson); Nydia Westman (Secretary); Ivan Simpson (Dr. Cassell); Roger Clark (Stephen Pettingill); Gordon Jones (Taxi Driver); Edward Gargan (Private Policeman); Larry Parks (Joe Krim); George Pembroke, Charles Miller, Wyndham Standing (Department Store Heads); Douglas Wood (Hoover); Ann Doran (Maid); Dale Van Sickel (Marine); Charles Halton (Doctor).

REUNION IN FRANCE (MGM, 1942) 102 min.

Producer, Joseph L. Mankiewicz; director, Jules Dassin; story, Ladislas Bus-Fekete; screenplay, Jan Lustig, Marvin Borowsky, Marc Connelly; art director, Cedric Gibbons; music, Franz Waxman; costumes, Irene; camera, Robert Planck; editor, Elmo Vernon.

Joan Crawford (Michele de la Becque); Philip Dorn (Robert Croiset); John Wayne (Pat Talbot); John Carradine (Ulrich Windler); Albert Bassermann (General Schroeder); Reginald Owen (Schultz); Odette Myrtil (Mdme. Montanot); Ann Ayars (Juliette); Moroni Olsen (Grabeau); Henry Daniell (Fleoron); Arthur Space (Banker); Margaret Laurence (Clothilde); J. Edward Bromberg (Thibault); Peter Whitney (Soldier with Candy); Edith Evanson (Genevieve); Oliver Blake (Hypolite); Ann Codee (Rosalie); Morris Ankrum (Martin); Howard da Silva (Stregel); John Considine, Jr. (Boy); Barbara Bedford (Mdme. Vigouroux); William Edmunds (Driver); Greta Keller (Baroness Von Steinkamp); Walter Stahl (Baron Von Steinkamp); Major Farrell (Porter); Otto Reichow (Soldier); Ava Gardner (Girl); Martha Bamattre (Newsstand Woman).

ABOVE SUSPICION (MGM, 1943) 91 min.

Producer, Victor Saville; director, Richard Thorpe; based on the novel by Helen MacInnes; screenplay, Keith Winter, Melville Baker, Patricia Coleman; costumes, Irene, Gile Steele; music, Bronislau Kaper; assistant director, Bert Spurling; art directors, Cedric Gibbons, Randall Duell; set decorators, Edwin B. Willis, Hugh Hunt; sound, J. K. Burbridge; special effects, Warren Newcombe; camera, Robert Planck; editor, George Hively.

Joan Crawford (Frances Myles); Fred MacMurray (Richard Myles); Conrad Veidt (Hassert Seidel); Basil Rathbone (Sig von Aschenhausen); Reginald Owen (Dr. Mespelbrunn); Richard Ainley (Peter Galt); Ann Shoemaker (Aunt Ellen); Sara Haden (Aunt Hattie); Felix Bressart (Mr. A. Werner); Bruce Lester (Thornley); Johanna Hofer (Frau Kleist); Lotte Palfi (Ottillie); Cecil Cunningham (Countess); Alex Papana (Man in Paris); Rex Williams (Gestapo Leader); William Yetter (Hauptman); William "Wee Willie" Davis (Hans); Steven Geray (Anton); Lisa Golm (Frau Schultz); Ludwig Stossel (Herr Schultz); Henry Glynn (Chauffeur); Eily Malyon (Manageress); Marcelle Corday (Maid); Arthur Shields (Porter); Frank Lackteen (Arab Vendor); Peter Seal, Nicholas Vehr (Colonel Gerold's Aides); Egon Brecher (Gestapo Official); Peter Lawford (Student); Steven Muller (German Boy); Sven-Hugo Borg (German Guard); Ferdinand Schumann-Heink, Otto Reichow (Gestapo in Opera Box).

HOLLYWOOD CANTEEN (Warner Bros., 1944) 123 min.

Producer, Alex Gottlieb; director/screenplay, Delmer Daves; art director, Leo Kuter; set decorator, Casey Roberts; music adaptor, Ray Heindorf; music director, Leo F. Forbstein; choreography, LeRoy Prinz; wardrobe, Milo Anderson; camera, Bert Glennon; editor, Christian Nyby.

Joan Leslie (Herself); Robert Hutton (Slim); Dane Clark (Sergeant); Janis Paige (Angela); Andrews Sisters, Jack Benny, Joe E. Brown, Eddie Cantor, Kitty Carlisle, Jack Carson, Joan Crawford, Helmut Dantine, Bette Davis, Faye Emerson, Victor Francen, John Garfield, Sydney Greenstreet, Alan Hale, Paul Henreid, Andrea King, Peter Lorre, Ida Lupino, Irene Manning, Nora Martin, Joan McCracken, Dolores Moran, Dennis Morgan, Eleanor Parker, William Prince, Joyce Reynolds, John Ridgely, Roy Rogers & Trigger, S. Z. Sakall, Alexis Smith, Zachary Scott, Barbara Stanwyck, Craig Stevens, Joseph Szigeti, Donald Woods, Jane Wyman, Jimmy Dorsey & His Band, Carmen Cavallaro & His Orchestra, Golden Gate Quartet, Rosario & Antonio, Sons of the Pioneers (Themselves); Mark Stevens, Dick Erdman (Soldiers on Deck); Kem Dibbs (Soldier); Robin Raymond (Blonde on Street); George Turner (Sailor); Chef Joseph Milani, Mary Gordon (Themselves); Betty Bryson, Willard Van Simons, William Alcorn, Jack Mattis, Jack Coffey (Dance Specialties); Dorothy Malone, Julie Bishop, Robert Shayne, Colleen Townsend, Angela Greene, Paul Brinkman, Bill Kennedy (Themselves).

MILDRED PIERCE (Warner Bros., 1945) 113 min.

Producer, Jerry Wald; director, Michael Curtiz; based on the novel by James M. Cain; screenplay, Ranald MacDougall; assistant director, Frank Heath; art director, Anton Grot; set decorator, George James Hopkins; dialogue director, Herschel Daugherty; music, Max Steiner; music director, Leo F. Forbstein; orchestrator, Hugo Friedhofer; montages, James Leicester;

sound, Oliver S. Garretson; special effects, Willard Van Enger; camera, Ernest Haller; editor, David Weisbart.

Joan Crawford (Mildred Pierce); Jack Carson (Wally Fay); Zachary Scott (Monte Beragon); Eve Arden (Ida); Ann Blyth (Veda Pierce); Bruce Bennett (Bert Pierce); George Tobias (Mr. Chris); Lee Patrick (Maggie Binderhof); Moroni Olsen (Inespector Peterson); Jo Ann Marlowe (Kay Pierce); Barbara Brown (Mrs. Forrester); Butterfly McQueen (Lottie); Charles Trowbridge (Mr. Williams); John Compton (Ted Forrester); Joyce Compton, Marion Lessing, Lynne Baggett, Doria Caron, Marjorie Kane, Elyse Brown (Waitresses); Perk Lazelleo (Attorney's Clerk); Wallis Clark (Wally's Lawyer); Ramsay Ames, Helen Pender (Party Guests); Wheaton Chambers, William Ruhl (Personnel Men).

HUMORESQUE (Warner Bros., 1946) 125 min.

Producer, Jerry Wald; director, Jean Negulesco; based on the story by Fannie Hurst; screenplay, Clifford Odets, Zachary Gold; music, Franz Waxman; music director, Leo F. Forbstein; music advisor, Isaac Stern; art director, Hugh Reticker; set decorator, Clarence Steenson; assistant director, Phil Quinn; sound, David Forrest, Robert B. Lee; special effects, Roy Davidson; montage, James Leicester; camera, Ernest Haller; editor, Rudi Fehr.

Joan Crawford (Helen Wright); John Garfield (Paul Boray); Oscar Levant (Sid Jeffers); J. Carroll Naish (Rudy Boray); Joan Chandler (Gina); Tom D'Andrea (Phil Boray); Peggy Knudsen (Florence); Ruth Nelson (Esther Boray); Craig Stevens (Monte Loeffler); Paul Cavanagh (Victor Wright); Richard Gaines (Bauer); John Abbott (Rozner); Bobby Blake (Paul Boray as a Child); Tommy Cook (Phil Boray as a Child); Don McGuire (Eddie); Fritz Leiber (Haggerstrom); Peg LaCentra (Nightclub Singer); Richard Walsh (Teddy); Nestor Paiva (Orchestra Leader); Creighton Hale (Professor); Monte Blue (Furniture Moving Man); Patricia Barry (Fitzie, the Telephone Operator); Don Turner (Man with Dog); Ann Lawrence (Florence as a Girl); Sylvia Arslan (Gina as a Girl).

POSSESSED (Warner Bros., 1947) 108 min.

Producer, Jerry Wald; director, Curtis Bernhardt; based on the story "One Man's Secret!" by Rita Weiman; screenplay, Silvia Richards, Ranald MacDougall; music, Franx Waxman; orchestrator, Leonid Raab; music director, Leo F. Forbstein; assistant director, Sherry Shourds; art director, Anton Grot; set decorator, Fred MacLean; dialogue director, Herschel Daugherty; sound, Robert B. Lee; special effects, William McGann, Robert Burks; camera, Joseph Valentine; editor, Rudi Fehr.

Joan Crawford (Louise Howell); Van Heflin (David Sutton); Raymond Massey (Dean Graham); Geraldine Brooks (Carol Graham); Stanley Ridges (Dr. Harvey Williard); John Ridgely (Lieutenant Harker); Erskine Sanford (Dr. Max Sherman); Moroni Olsen (Dr.

Ames); Richard Miles (Wynn Graham); Erskine Sanford (Dr. Max Sherman); Isabel Withers (Nurse Rosen); Lisa Golm (Elsie, the Maid); Douglas Kennedy (Assistant District Attorney); Monte Blue (Norris, the Caretaker); Don McGuire (Dr. Craig, the Psychiatrist); Rory Mallinson (Coroner's Assistant); Clifton Young (Interne); Griff Barnett (Coroner); Ralph Dunn (Motorman on Trolley); Max Wagner, Dick Bartell (Men in Cafe); Rose Plummer (Woman in Cafe); Creighton Hale (Court Recorder); Jeffrey Sayre (Dance Extra); Philo McCullough (Edwards, the Butler); Sarah Padden (Mrs. Norris, the Caretaker's Wife); Wheaton Chambers (Waiter).

DAISY KENYON (Twentieth Century-Fox, 1947) 99 min.

Producer/director, Otto Preminger; based on the novel by Elizabeth Janeway; screenplay, David Hertz; art directors, Lyle Wheeler, George Davis; set decorators, Thomas Little, Walter W. Scott; music, David Raksin; music director, Alfred Newman; assistant director, Tom Dudley; sound, Eugene Grossman, Roger Heman; special effects, Fred Sersen; camera, Leon Shamroy; editor, Louis Loeffler.

Joan Crawford (Daisy Kenyon); Dana Andrews (Dan O'Mara); Henry Fonda (Peter); Ruth Warrick (Lucile O'Mara); Martha Stewart (Mary Angelus); Peggy Ann Garner (Rosamund); Connie Marshall (Marie); Nicholas Joy (Coverly); Art Baker (Lucile's Attorney); Robert Karnes (Attorney); John Davidson (Mervyn); Victoria Horne (Marsha); Charles Meredith (Judge); Roy Roberts (Dan's Attorney); Griff Barnett (Thompson); Tito Vuolo (Dino); Marion Marshall (Telephone Operator); George E. Stone (Waiter); John Butler, Jimmy Ames (Cab Drivers); John Garfield (Man in Restaurant); Monya Andre (Mrs. Ames); Mauritz Hugo (Mr. Ames).

FLAMINGO ROAD (Warner Bros., 1949) 96 min.

Executive producer, Michael Curtiz; producer, Jerry Wald; associate producer, George Amy; director, Curtiz; based on the play by Robert and Sally Wilder; screenplay, Robert Wilder; additional dialogue, Edmund H. North; art director, Leo K. Kuter; set decorator, Howard Winterbottom; music, Max Steiner; orchestrator, Murray Cutter; music director, Ray Heindorf; assistant director, Robert Vreeland; makeup, Perc Westmore, Eddie Allen; costumes, Travilla; sound, Robert B. Lee; second unit/montage director, David Curtiz; camera, Ted McCord; editor, Folmar Blangsted.

Joan Crawford (Lane Bellamy); Zachary Scott (Fielding Carlisle); David Brian (Dan Reynolds); Sydney Greenstreet (Titus Semple); Gladys George (Lute Mae Sanders); Virginia Huston (Annabelle Weldon); Fred Clark (Doc Waterson); Gertrude Michael (Millie); Alice White (Gracie); Sam McDaniel (Boatright); Tito Vuolo (Pete Ladas); Dick Ryan, Pat Gleason (Barkers); Tristram Coffin (Ed Parker); Dale Robertson (Tunis

Simms); Iris Adrian (Blanche); Carol Brewster, Sunny Knight (Waitresses); Lester Kimmel (Lawyer); Frank Scannell (Man); Sam McKim (Bellboy); Pierre Watkin (Senator).

IT'S A GREAT FEELING (Warner Bros., 1949) C-85 min.

Producer Alex Gottlieb; director, David Butler; story, I. A. L. Diamond; screenplay, Jack Rose, Mel Shavelson; Technicolor consultants, Natalie Kalmus, Mitchell Kovaleski; art director, Stanely Fleischer; set decorator, Lyle Reifsnider; music, Jule Styne; music director, Ray Heindorf; songs, Styne and Sammy Cahn; assistant director, Phil Quinn; makeup, Perc Westmore, Mickey Marcellino; costumes, Milo Anderson; choreography, LeRoy Prinz; sound, Dolf Thomas, David Forrest; special effects, William McGann, H. F. Koenekamp; camera, Wilifed M. Cline; editor, Irene Morra.

Dennis Morgan, Jack Carson (Themselves); Doris Day (Judy Adams); Bill Goodwin (Arthur Trent); Irving Bacon (Information Clerk); Claire Carleton (Grace); Harlan Warde (Publicity Man); Jacqueline de Wit (Trent's Secretary); The Famous Mazzone-Abbott Dancers (Specialty); Wilfred Lucas (Mr. Adams); Raoul Walsh, King Vidor, Michael Curtiz, David Butler, Gary Cooper, Ronald Reagan, Sydney Greenstreet, Jane Wyman, Danny Kaye, Joan Crawford, Edward G. Robinson, Eleanor Parker, Patricia Neal (Themselves); Pat Flaherty (Charlie, the Gate Guard); Ray Montgomery (Walsh's Assistant); Cosmo Sardo (Barber); Ralph Littlefield (Hayseed); Lois Austin (Saleslady); Forbes Murray (Distinguished Man); Rod Rogers, Peter Meersman, Olan Soule (Flacks); Sandra Gould (Train Passenger in Upper Berth); Errol Flynn (Jeffrey Bushdinkel, the Groom).

THE DAMNED DON'T CRY (Warner Bros., 1950) 103 min.

Producer, Jerry Wald; director, Vincent Sherman; story, Gertrude Walker; screenplay, Harold Medford, Jerome Weidman; art director, Robert Haas; music, Daniele Amfitheatrof; wardrobe, Sheila O'Brien; camera, Ted McCord; editor, Rudi Fehr.

Joan Crawford (Ethel Whitehead [Lorna Hansen Forbes]); David Brian (George Castleman); Steve Cochran (Nick Prenta); Kent Smith (Martin Blackford); Hugh Sanders (Grady); Selena Royle (Patricia Longworth); Jacqueline de Wit (Sandra); Morris Ankrum (Mr. Whitehead); Eddie Marr (Walter Talbot); Allan Smith (Surveyor); Tris Coffin (Maitre d'Hotel); Ned Glass (Taxi Driver); Dabbs Greer, Paul McGuire (Reporters); Rory Mallinson (Johnny Enders); John Maxwell (Doctor); Lyle Latell (Trooper).

HARRIET CRAIG (Columbia, 1950) 94 min.

Producer, William Dozier; director, Vincent Sherman; based on the play Craig's Wife by George Kelly; screenplay, Anne Froelick, James Gunn; art director, Walter Holscher; wardrobe, Sheila O'Brien; music,

Morris Stoloff; camera, Joseph Walker; editor, Viola Lawrence.

Joan Crawford (Harriet Craig); Wendell Corey (Walter Craig); Lucile Watson (Celia Fenwick); Allyn Joslyn (Billy Birkmire); William Bishop (Wes Miller); K. T. Stevens (Clare Raymond); Raymond Greenleaf (Henry Fenwick); Ellen Corby (Lottie); Fiona O'Shiel (Mrs. Frazier); Patric Mitchell (Danny Frazier); Virginia Brissac (Harriet's Mother); Douglas Wood (Mr. Norwood); Kathryn Card (Mrs. Norwood); Mira McKinney (Mrs. Winston); Al Murphy (Bartender); Susanne Rosser (Nurse).

GOODBYE, MY FANCY (Warner Bros. 1951) 107 min.

Producer, Henry Blanke; director, Vincent Sherman; based on the play by Fay Kanin; screenplay, Ivan Goff, Ben Roberts; art director, Stanley Fleischer; music, Ray Heindorf; wardrobe, Sheila O'Brien; camera, Ted McCord; editor, Rudi Fehr.

Joan Crawford (Agatha Reed); Robert Young (Dr. James Merrill); Frank Lovejoy (Matt Cole); Eve Arden (Woody); Janice Rule (Virginia Merrill); Lurene Tuttle (Ellen Griswold); Howard St. John (Claude Griswold); Viola Roache (Miss Shackleford); Ellen Corby (Miss Birdeshaw); Morgan Farley (Dr. Pitt); Virginia Gibson (Mary Nell Dodge); John Qualen (Professor Dingley); Ann Robin (Clarissa Carter); Mary Carver (Jon Wintner); Creighton Hale (Butler); Frank Hyer (Man); John Alvin (Jack White); John Hedloe (Telephone Man); Phil Tead (Reporter); Larry Williams, Fredrick Howard, Lucius Cook (Congressmen).

THIS WOMAN IS DANGEROUS (Warner Bros., 1952) 97 min.

Producer, Robert Sisk; director, Felix Feist; story, Bernard Girard; screenplay, Geoffrey Homes, George Worthing Yates; art director, Leo K. Kuter; music, David Buttolph; wardrobe, Sheila O'Brien; camera, Ted McCord; editor, James C. Moore.

Joan Crawford (Beth Austin); Dennis Morgan (Dr. Ben Halleck); David Brian (Matt Jackson); Richard Webb (Franklin); Mari Alden (Ann Jackson); Philip Carey (Will Jackson); Ian MacDonald (Joe Grossland); Katherine Warren (Admitting Nurse); George Chandler (Dr. Ryan); William Challee (Ned Shaw); Sherry Jackson (Susan Halleck); Douglas Fowley (Club Manager); Harry Lauter (Trooper); Karen Hale (Nurse); Charles Sullivan (Attendant); Cecil Weston (Matron); Jean Carry (Technician); Dick Bartell (Waiter); Mary Alan Hokanson (Prison Doctor); Eileen Stevens (Chambermaid); Dee Carroll (Telephone Operator).

SUDDEN FEAR (RKO, 1952) 110 min.

Producer, Joseph Kaufman; director, David Miller; based on the novel by Edna Sherry; screenplay, Lenore Coffee, Robert Smith; art director, Boris Leven; music/music director, Elmer Bernstein; wardrobe, Sheila O'-

Brien; assistant director, Ivan Volkman; camera, Charles Lang, Jr.; editor, Leon Barsha.

Joan Crawford (Myra Hudson); Jack Palance (Lester Blaine); Gloria Grahame (Irene Neves); Bruce Bennett (Steve Kearney); Virginia Huston (Ann Taylor); Michael "Touch" Connors (Junior Kearney).

TORCH SONG *(MGM, 1953)* C-90 min.

Producers, Henry Berman, Sidney Franklin, Jr.; director, Charles Walters; based on the story "Why Should I Cry?" by I. A. R. Wylie; screenplay, John Michael Hayes, Jan Lustig; wardrobe, Helen Rose; art director, Cedric Gibbons; music, Adolph Deutsch; songs, Deutsch, Kermit Goell, and Fred Spielman; Jack Lawrence and Walter Gross; Howard Dietz and Arthur Schwartz; choreography, Walters; camera, Robert Planck; editor, Albert Akst.

Joan Crawford (Jenny Stewart); Michael Wilding (Tye Graham); Gig Young (Cliff Willard); Marjorie Rambeau (Mrs. Stewart); Henry "Harry" Morgan (Joe Denner); Dorothy Patrick (Martha); James Todd (Philip Norton); Eugene Loring (Gene, the Dance Director); Paul Guilfoyle (Monty Rolfe); Benny Rubin (Charlie Maylor); Peter Chong (Peter); Maidie Norman (Anne); Nancy Gates (Celia Stewart); Chris Warfield (Chuck Peters); Rudy Render (Party Singer); Charles Walters (Ralph Ellis); John Rosser (Chauffeur); Norma Jean Salina (Margaret); Reginald Simpson (Cab Driver); Adolph Deutsch (Conductor); Mimi Gibson (Susie); Mitchell Lewis (Bill, the Doorman); Peggy King (Cora).

JOHNNY GUITAR *(Republic, 1954)* C-110 min.

Producer, Herbert J. Yates; director, Nicholas Ray; based on the novel by Roy Chanslor; screenplay, Philip Yordan; art director, James Sullivan; music, Victor Young; song, Peggy Lee and Young; wardrobe, Sheila O'Brien; assistant director, Herb Mendelson; camera, Harry Stradling; editor, Richard L. Van Enger.

Joan Crawford (Vienna); Sterling Hayden (Johnny Guitar); Mercedes McCambridge (Emma Small); Scott Brady (Dancin' Kid); Ward Bond (John McIvers); Ben Cooper (Turkey Ralston); Ernest Borgnine (Bart Lonergan); John Carradine (Old Tom); Royal Dano (Corey); Frank Ferguson (Marshal Williams); Paul Fix (Eddie); Rhys Williams (Mr. Andrews); Ian MacDonald (Pete); Will Wright (Ned); John Maxwell (Jake); Robert Osterloh (Sam); Trevor Bardette (Jenks); Sumner Williams, Sheb Wooley, Denver Pyle, Clem Harvey (Posse).

FEMALE ON THE BEACH *(Universal, 1955)* C-97 min.

Producer, Albert Zugsmith; director, Joseph Pevney; based on the play *The Besieged Heart* by Robert Hill; screenplay, Hill, Richard Alan Simmons; art director, Alexander Golitzen; music, Joseph Gershenson; wardrobe, Sheila O'Brien; assistant directors, John Sherwood, Phil Bowles; camera, Charles Lang; editor, Russell Schoengarth.

Joan Crawford (Lynn Markham); Jeff Chandler (Drummond Hall); Jan Sterling (Amy Rawlinson); Cecil Kellaway (Osbert Sorenson); Natalie Schafer (Queenie Sorenson); Charles Drake (Lieutenant Galley); Judith Evelyn (Eloise Crandall); Stuart Randall (Frankovitch); Marjorie Bennett (Mrs. Murchison); Romo Vincent (Pete Gomez); Nan Boardman (Mrs. Gomez); Jack Reitzen (Boat Attendant); Jim Ryland (Cop); Helene Heigh (Cleaning Woman); Judy Pine (Woman at Beach); Ed Fury (Roddy).

QUEEN BEE *(Columbia, 1955)* 95 min.

Producer, Jerry Wald; director, Ranald MacDougall; based on the novel by Edna Lee; screenplay, MacDougall; art director, Ross Bellah; music, Morris Stoloff; gowns, Jean Louis; assistant director, Irving Moore; camera, Charles Lang; editor, Viola Lawrence.

Joan Crawford (Eva Phillips); Barry Sullivan (John Avery Phillips); Betsy Palmer (Carol Lee Phillips); John Ireland (Judson Prentiss); Lucy Marlowe (Jennifer Stewart); William Leslie (Ty McKinnon); Fay Wray (Sue McKinnon); Katherine Anderson (Miss Breen); Tim Hovey (Ted); Linda Bennett (Trissa); Willa Pearl Curtis (Miss George); Bill Walker (Sam); Olan Soule (Dr. Pearson); Bob McCord (Man); Juanita Moore (Maid).

AUTUMN LEAVES *(Columbia, 1956)* 108 min.

Producer, William Goetz; director, Robert Aldrich; story/screenplay, Jack Jevne, Lewis Meltzer, Robert Blees; art director, Bill Glasgow; music, Hans Salter; music director, Morris Stoloff; song, Joseph Kosma, Jacques Prevert, and Johnny Mercer; gowns, Jean Louis; camera, Charles Lang; editor, Michael Luciano.

Joan Crawford (Milly); Cliff Robertson (Burt Hanson); Vera Miles (Virginia); Lorne Greene (Mr. Hanson); Ruth Donnelly (Liz); Sheppard Strudwick (Dr. Couzzens); Selmer Jackson (Mr. Wetherby); Maxine Cooper (Nurse Evans); Marjorie Bennett (Waitress); Frank Gerstle (Mr. Ramsey); Leonard Mudie (Colonel Hillyer); Maurice Manson (Dr. Masterson); Bob Hopkins (Desk Clerk); Frank Arnold (Butcher); Ralph Volkie (Doorman); Robert Sherman (Paul's Voice); Abdullah Abbas (Mexican Vendor); Mary Benoit, Paul Bradley, Bess Flowers (Bits).

THE STORY OF ESTHER COSTELLO *(Columbia, 1957)* 127 min.

Producer/director, David Miller; based on the novel by Nicholas Monsarrat; screenplay, Charles Kaufman; art directors, George Provis, Tony Masters; music, Lambert Williamson; assistant director, Peter Bolton, Roger Good; gowns, Jean Louis; camera, Robert Krasker; editor, Ralph Kemplen.

Joan Crawford (Margaret Landi); Rossano Brazzi (Carlo Landi); Heather Sears (Esther Costello); Lee Patterson (Harry Grant); Ron Randell (Wenzel); Fay

Compton (Mother Superior); John Loder (Paul Marchant); Denis O Dea (Father Devlin); Sidney James (Ryan); Bessie Love (Matron in Art Gallery); Robert Ayres (Mr. Wilson); Maureen Delaney (Jennie Costello); Estelle Brody (Tammy); June Clyde (Mrs. Forbes); Sally Smith (Susan North); Megs Jenkins (Nurse Evans); Andrew Cruickshank (Dr. Stein); and Diana Day, Victor Rietti, Sheila Manahan, Tony Quinn.

THE BEST OF EVERYTHING *(Twentieth Century-Fox, 1959)* C-122 min.

Producer, Jerry Wald; director, Jean Negulesco; based on the novel by Rona Jaffe; screenplay, Edith Sommer, Mann Rubin; art directors, Lyle Wheeler, Jack Martin Smith; set decorators, Walter M. Scott, Stuart A. Reiss; music, Alfred Newman; song, Sammy Cahn, Newman; orchestrators, Herbert Spencer, Earle Hagen; costumes, Adele Palmer; color consultant, Leonard Doss; makeup, Ben Nye; sound, Alfred Bruzlin, Harry Leonard; camera, William C. Mellor; editor, Robert Simpson.

Hope Lange (Caroline Bender); Stephen Boyd (Mike Rice); Suzy Parker (Gregg Adams); Diane Baker (April Morrison); Martha Hyer (Barbara Lemont); Brian Aherne (Mr. Shalimar); Robert Evans (Dexter Key); Brett Halsey (Eddie Davis); Louis Jourdan (David Savage); Joan Crawford (Amanda Farrow); Donald Harron (Sidney Carter); Sue Carson (Mary Agnes); Linda Hutchings (Jane); Lionel Kane (Paul Landis); June Blair (Brenda); Myrna Hansen (Judy Masson); Nora O'Mahoney (Scrubwoman); David Hoffman (Joe); Theodora Davitt (Margo Stewart); Julie Payne, Alena Murray, Rachel Stephens (Girls in Typing Pool); Wally Brown (Drunk).

WHAT EVER HAPPENED TO BABY JANE? *(Warner Bros., 1962)* 132 min.

Executive producer, Kenneth Hyman; producer/director, Robert Aldrich; based on the novel by Henry Farrell; screenplay, Lukas Heller; art director, William Glasgow; set decorator, George Sawley; assistant director, Tom Connors; makeup, Jack Obringer, Monty Westmore; choreography, Alex Romero; music, Frank De Vol; sound, Jack Solomon; special effects, Don Steward; camera, Ernest Haller; editor, Michael Luciano.

Bette Davis (Jane Hudson); Joan Crawford (Blanche Hudson); Victor Buono (Edwin Flagg); Anna Lee (Mrs. Bates); Maidie Norman (Elvira Stitt); Marjorie Bennett (Mrs. Flagg); Dave Willock (Ray Hudson); Ann Barton (Cora Hudson); Barbara Merrill (Liza Bates); Julie Allred (Young Jane); Gina Gillespie (Young Blanche); Bert Freed (Producer); Wesley Addy (Director).

THE CARETAKERS *(United Artists, 1963)* 97 min.

Producer, Hall Bartlett; associate producer, Jerry Paris; director, Bartlett; based on the book by Dariel Telfer; screen story, Bartlett, Paris; screenplay, Henry

F. Greenberg; art directors, Rolland M. Brooks, Claudio Guzman; set decorator, Frank Tuttle; title drawing, Irving Block; music, Elmer Bernstein; camera, Lucien Ballard; editor, William B. Murphy.

Robert Stack (Dr. Donovan MacLeod); Polly Bergen (Lorna Melford); Joan Crawford (Lucretia Terry); Janis Paige (Marion); Diane McBain (Alison Horne); Van Williams (Dr. Larry Denning); Constance Ford (Nurse Bracken); Sharon Hugueny (Connie); Herbert Marshall (Dr. Jubal Harrington); Ana St. Clair (Anna); Barbara Barrie (Edna); Robert Vaughn (Jim Melford); Susan Oliver (Cathy Clark); Ellen Corby (Irene).

STRAIT-JACKET *(Columbia, 1964)* 89 min.

Producer, William Castle; associate producer, Dona Holloway; director, Castle; screenplay, Robert Bloch; art director, Boris Leven; set decorator, Frank Tuttle; makeup, Ben Lane, Monty Westmore; assistant director, Herbert Greene; music, Van Alexander; sound, Charles J. Rice, Lambert Day; special effects, Richard Albain; camera, Arthur Arling; editor, Edwin Bryant.

Joan Crawford (Lucy Harbin); Diane Baker (Carol); Leif Erickson (Bill Cutler); Howard St. John (Raymond Fields); John Anthony Hayes (Michael Fields); Rochelle Hudson (Emily Cutler); George Kennedy (Leo Krause); Edith Atwater (Mrs. Fields); Mitchell Cox (Dr. Anderson); Lee Yeary (Frank Hardin); Patricia Krest (Stella Fulton); Robert Ward (Shoe Clerk); Lyn Lundgren (Beauty Operator); Laura Hess, Vickie Cos (Little Girls).

I SAW WHAT YOU DID *(Universal, 1965)* 82 min.

Producer/director, William Castle; based on the book *Out of the Dark* by Ursula Curtiss; screenplay, William McGivern; assistant directors, Terry Morse, Jr., Charles Scott, Jr.; art director, Walter Simonds; camera, Joe Biroc; editor, Eddie Bryant.

Joan Crawford (Amy); John Ireland (Steve Marak); Leif Erickson (David Mannering); Pat Breslin (Ellie Mannering); Andi Garrett (Libby); Sharyl Locke (Tess); Sarah Lane (Kit Austin); John Archer (John Austin); Joyce Meadows (Judith); Douglas Evans (Tom Ward); Barbara Wilkins (Mary Ward).

BERSERK! *(Columbia, 1968)* C-96 min.

Producer, Herman Cohen; associate producer, Robert Sterne; director, Jim O'Connolly; story/screenplay, Aben Kandel, Cohen; art director, Maurice Felling; set decorator, Helen Thomas; costumes, Jay Hutchinson; assistant director, Barry Langley; music/music director, John Scott; sound, Bert Ross, John Cox; camera, Desmond Dickinson; editor, Raymond Poulton.

Joan Crawford (Monica Rivers); Ty Hardin (Frank Hawkins); Diana Dors (Matilda); Michael Gough (Dorando); Judy Geeson (Angela Rivers); Robert Hardy (Detective Superintendent Brooks); Geoffrey Keen (Commissioner Dalby); Sydney Tafler (Harrison

Liston); George Claydon (Bruno); Philip Madoc (Lazlo); Ambrosine Phillpotts (Miss Burrows); Peter Burton (Gustavo); Golda Casimir (Bearded Lady); Ted Lune (Skeleton Man); Milton Reid (Strong Man); The Billy Smart Circus (Themselves); Byron Pringle (Detective Constable Bradford).

NIGHT GALLERY *(NBC, 1969)* C-100 min.

Producer, William Sackheim; associate producer, John Badham; teleplay, Rod Serling; music, William Goldenberg; camera, Richard Batcheller; editor, Edward M. Abroms.

Segment #1: Director, Boris Segal; with Ossie Davis, Roddy McDowall, George Macready, Barry Atwater, Tom Basham, Richard Hale.

Segment #2: Director, Steven Spielberg; with Joan Crawford (Miss Menlo); Barry Sullivan (Dr. Heatherton); Tom Bosley (Resnick); Byron Morrow (Pacher); Garry Goodrow (Louis).

Segment #3: Director, Barry Shear; with Richard Kiley, Sam Jaffe, Norma Crane, George Murdock.

TROG *(Warner Bros., 1970)* C-91 min.

Producer, Herman Cohen; associate producer, Harry Woolveridge; director, Freddie Francis; story, Peter Bryan, John Gilling; screenplay, Aben Kandel; assistant director, Douglas Hermes; art director, Geoffrey Tozer; set decorator, Helen Thomas; music/music director, John Scott; sound, Tony Dawe, Maurice Askew; Trog designed by Charles Parker; camera, Desmond Dickinson; editor, Oswald Hafenrichter.

Joan Crawford (Dr. Bruckton); Michael Gough (Sam Murdock); Bernard Kay (Inspector Greenham); David Griffin (Malcolm Travers); Kim Braden (Ann Brockton); Joe Cornelius (Trog); John Hamill (Cliff); Geoffrey Case (Bill); Thorley Walters (Magistrate); Jack May (Dr. Selbourne); Maurice Good, Rona Newton-John (Reporters); Paul Hansard (Dr. Kurtlimer); Robert Crewdson (Dr. Pierre Duval); Robert Hutton (Dr. Richard Warren); David Warbeck (Alan Davis); Brian Grellis (John Dennis); Simon Lack (Colonel Vickers); Chloe Franks (Little Girl); John Baker (Anaesthetist); Bartlett Mullins (Butcher); Shirley Conklin (Little Girl's Mother).

With Henry Fonda in *Jezebel* ('38).

178

CHAPTER 3

Bette Davis

5'3½"
122 pounds
Dark blonde hair
Blue eyes
Aries

"**I** was never sweet, even at an early age," Bette Davis observed recently. "I've played unattractive people all my life. As long as I caught the character, I didn't care." Some forty-seven years after her screen debut in *Bad Sister* (1931), Davis is still providing sharp-edged, if somewhat shriller, performances in today's entertainment marketplace. Whether appearing in feature films, made-for-television movies, TV talk shows, or on the lecture platform, she is undeniably a major attraction. As one of the most active and sterling of the still-working Queens of Hollywood's Golden Age, the electric Miss Davis amasses new press coverage and fans like a magnet drawing metal.

In every sense of the word, Bette Davis is a rugged individualist. From her earliest professional years onward, she dared to flaunt convention *if* she believed it would enhance her performance and her career. Impressionists have long had a field day exaggerating the trademark Davis stance, facial grimace, and oddly tempoed dialogue delivery. ("I disgust *you. You* disgust *me!*" "Give me the letter, Pe-e-tur.") But no mimic has ever been able to duplicate the inner drive of this plucky New Englander who has remained a potent personality for so many seasons.

179

Even the most ardent Davis endorser will grudgingly agree that at times the star's enthusiasm and unorthodox approach to her characterizations have led her into embarrassing outings (e.g. *Beyond the Forest*, 1949). But the two-time Oscar winner has always provided her viewers with entertainment, regardless of the calibre of the project or even the quality of her interpretation. She has that gift of intense magnetism that instills shades of meaning to the tritest of scripts. As a corollary, in her best parts she has managed generally to transfer herself into the part, rather than remain a personality playing herself.

When a professional such as Davis has been at her craft for as many years as she has, the trick is not to hone one's talents further, but to have the stamina to keep above the changing tide. Undoubtedly, it requires tremendous discipline and energy not to diminish one's presence in front of generation after generation of paying audiences. Davis, once tagged "The First Lady of the Screen," has proven herself continually capable of the demands of stardom.

As she admits, "I survived because I was tougher than everybody else. [Director-scripter] Joe Mankiewicz always told me, 'Bette when you die, they oughta put only one sentence on your tombstone—She did it the hard way!' And he was right. And you know something else? It's the only way."

Ruth Elizabeth Davis was born on Sunday, April 5, 1908, in Lowell, Massachusetts. She was the first daughter of Ruth Elizabeth Favor Davis and Harlow Morrell Davis, both of New England Pilgrim heritage. The Favors were descendants of a French Huguenot family, originally named Le Fievre, who migrated to this country in 1688. The Davis clan traced their ancestry back to James Davis, a Pilgrim who helped to found the city of Haverhill, Massachusetts, and who had once been accused of sorcery. Eighteen months after Ruth Elizabeth's arrival, a second daughter, Barbara, was born. The girls grew up calling their mother "Ruthie" while they addressed their stern father as "Daddy." To differentiate between the two Ruths in the Davis family, the younger earned the nickname of "Betty."

Harlow Davis was not only a rigid disciplinarian, but quite dedicated to his law profession. He had little time to devote to his family. In 1915, he left them in order to be free of encumbrances. He would later become a famed patent attorney. Ruthie moved herself and daughters to Newton, Massachusetts, where she supplemented her monthly alimony check by working as a governess and as a housemother at a girls' school. While neither Davis girl was snobbish, their mother's working chores made them the butt of many unpleasant remarks from fellow students. Years later, Bette would confess to a fan magazine how the slights of her contemporaries filled her with a desire to get even, but by the time she had achieved success, the revenge was empty. She no longer felt any need to prove herself to these once thoughtless girls.

When Ruthie Sr. decided to move to New York to become a photographer, her daughters were boarded out at a school called Crestalban, a 200-acre farm school in Berkshire Hills, Massachusetts. During the three years she spent at Crestalban, Betty was taught domestic arts and the customary academic subjects, and both were complemented with rigorous outdoor recreation. Although there were the usual school plays, Betty harbored no ambitions of becoming an actress. She once recalled, "The fact that I tried to run the productions, build the sets, and design the costumes had no professional significance. I directed because I wanted to order the other children about."

Wanting her family to be together, Ruthie took her girls out of Crestalban and moved them to Manhattan where they were enrolled in Public School 186. They moved into an apartment and jokingly called themselves "The Three Musketeers." During these trying years, the three Davis women moved from one address to another at a rapid pace while Ruthie endeavored to support them.

In New York, Ruthie's best friend was Myrtis Genthner, an avid reader who suggested to Betty that she alter the spelling of her name to Bette after the character in Balzac's *La Cousine Bette.* Miss Genthner also imparted to Bette the importance of reading and led her along this path from *The Bobbsey Twins* to *The Brothers Karamazov.*

Ruthie moved to East Orange, New Jersey, for a short spell, but then relocated to Newton, Massachusetts, where she opened a photography studio. Bette was now at the age when she would enter high school and had developed into a stubborn and headstrong young lady. She would later remember, "From that time on, I would brook no interference in anything I was determined to do."

A common factor among show business actresses who developed in the Twenties and Thirties was the driving ambition of the mothers (usually deserted by their husbands) who, if not always the most talented or versatile of businesswomen, had the pluck, imagination, and fortitude to gamble on a variety of jobs to aid the progress of their family's fortunes. Bette's Ruthie was no exception. One spring she noted an advertisement in a Boston paper for a housekeeper. The ad stated that the job provided free room and board for the family. Ruthie accepted this post with a minister in Provincetown, and so the summer of 1923 found the Davis trio at Cape Cod. As Bette would write in her autobiography, *The Lonely Life* (1962), composed in conjunction with Sandford Dody, "One would have thought we were the most carefree family in New England and we were. . . .How wonder-

ful that July was. And August. I stood on the edge of life and Bobby watched, with her earnest little face, her furrowed sunburned brow . . . .Bobby was always trying to catch up to me. I was a natural leader—she a follower. It is possible she grew up that summer in a way it took years for me to catch up with."

Bette later became a student at Newton High School where she discovered boys and love, but "I zealously guarded my chastity." She was popular with the fellows who took her on sleigh rides and to dances. In the classroom, she was quick to learn and maintained a high scholastic rating. Later, Ruthie advised both girls to enroll at Cushing Academy in Ashburnham, Massachusetts, a co-educational school which Ruthie had once attended herself. There, Bette became interested for the first time in dramatics, and there she met Harmon "Ham" Nelson, a student she fancied and who wanted to become a musician.

At Cushing, Bette played the role of Lola Pratt in a presentation of Booth Tarkington's *Seventeen*—the role that Ruth Gordon had made her own on Broadway—and thus the acting bug bit Miss Davis. Likewise, so did love. Bette and Nelson decided to go steady, but their relationship was loaded with quarrels, break-ups, and reconciliations. Aware of Ruthie's financial status, the principal of Cushing suggested to Bette that she help pay her tuition by waiting on tables in the school cafeteria. She was not inclined to take up this suggestion because of the fear that she would be ostracized by the other students. But Bette had to take the job in order to help out the family finances. To her relief, the other pupils generally understood and continued almost unanimously to accept her as one of them. She has called this experience "my primer in pride."

In the summer of 1925, Ruthie undertook a job of photographing vacationing theatre people at Peterborough, New Hampshire. She was also commissioned to photograph members of a stock company and students at the Mariarden School of Dancing. The dancing school was supervised by a Britisher named Roshanara who took a liking to Bette and undertook to instruct her, free of charge, in the rudiments of modern interpretive dancing. Also at Peterborough, gregarious, practical Ruthie became friends with stage actor Frank Conroy when he and Bette appeared together in an outdoor production of *A Midsummer Night's Dream.* He suggested that Bette ought to be allowed to pursue a career in acting. He reflected, "She has something you can't buy and something you can't imitate. Even if she doesn't open her mouth, she has the quality that draws the audience to her. I think that someday, if she works hard, she will be a fine actress." This was the inspiration that Bette required. When she returned to Cushing, she devoted most of her energies to the art of acting.

In 1927, Bette graduated from Cushing. After an unsuccessful attempt to get into summer stock (she was considered *too* young and *too* inexperienced), it was Frank Conroy's suggestion that she try out at Eva Le Gallienne's Fourteenth Street Repertory Theatre in Manhattan. To obtain funds for this move, Ruthie and Bette contacted Mr. Davis, hoping he would at this time provide the wherewithal. But he said, "Let her become a secretary! She'll earn money quicker." Nevertheless, Ruthie and Bette did go to New York, leaving Bobby with relatives.

Bette read the part of a seventy-year-old Dutch woman for the talented, austere Miss Le Gallienne. She was then asked questions regarding her attitudes towards the theatre in general. At the close of the interview, Miss Le Gallienne said coldly, "I can see that your attitude toward the theatre is not sincere enough to warrant taking you as a pupil. You are a frivolous little girl." This stern reproach did not bother Ruthie Davis who retreated—momentarily—to Norwalk, Connecticut, with Bette. But the Davis ladies were not to be rebuked so easily. They launched another assault on New York, this time at the Robert Milton-John Murray Anderson School of the Theatre. Ruthie talked to the manager while Bette waited in an outer office.

Although the tuition could not be paid in advance as was the institution's rule, Ruthie talked the man into accepting Bette as a student, and she herself went to work at a nearby girls' school as housemother. At the end of the first year at the school, Bette acted in *The Famous Mrs. Fair* which also represented her term examination. Bette won more than one scholarship at the school but she forfeited them when she left there in 1928 to accept an offer from director James Light of a good part in his intended production at the Provincetown Playhouse. The play, *The Earth Between,* was unexpectedly cancelled however, and Bette was left adrift.

Once again Frank Conroy came to the rescue by providing her with an appropriate letter of introduction to young George Cukor, then the director of a stock company in Rochester, New York. Bette was assigned a small part in Cukor's production of the rowdy, exuberant show *Broadway* which ran one week in Rochester. Bette learned to Charleston for the show and, thanks to the tutelage at the Milton-Anderson School where Agnes De Mille taught a class in body movement, Bette was able to take over for Rose Lerner in a larger, more demanding part when the latter tripped onstage during a matinee and sprained an ankle. Cukor was impressed enough with Bette's work to employ her for the following season.

Meanwhile, she joined the Cape Playhouse at Dennis, Massachusetts. She thought she had been hired as a resident ingenue but it developed there had been a misunderstanding. Fortunately, the well-regarded summer theatre required an usherette and Bette readily accepted the paying post. While thus employed, Laura Hope Crews, the star and director of A. A. Milne's *Mr. Pim Passes By,* needed a young actress who could deliver an English accent. Bette was accepted by Miss Crews, and was required to sing and play the piano. At one point during rehearsals, Miss Crews, a perfectionist, slapped Bette's wrist when she gestured too much in emphasis of her lines. It was a slap Bette would never forget.

After scoring a minor success as the English girl, Bette returned to Rochester for the winter season with Cukor's group. Among those working for Cukor were Miriam Hopkins, Frank McHugh, and Wallace Ford. Bette's big moment came with a production of *Yellow* with Louis Calhern as guest artist. She was to play his mistress, but when the adroit, mature Calhern complained that she was too youthful for the role, Cukor fired her. Neither director nor actress was to forget one another in the years ahead in Hollywood.

Fortunately, at this juncture, James Light was ready to proceed with his production of *The Earth Between* for the Provincetown Playhouse which operated at a MacDougall Street stable in Greenwich Village in New York City. Bette signed a run-of-the-play contract for thirty-five dollars weekly. The show opened on Tuesday, March 5, 1929, and Bette came to the attention of *New York Times* critic Brooks Atkinson who described her as "an interesting creature who plays in a soft, unassertive style." Noted reviewer Burns Mantle reported to his readers, "The performances are good, particularly that of Bette Davis, playing a wraith of a child with true emotional insight." Of her debut on a New York stage, Bette has said, "Nothing will equal the emotions I knew that night. I was a success in my first New York play!"

Candid, unceremonious Bette also reports in *The Lonely Life* that the night *The Earth Between* opened, her father arrived to witness his daughter's performance. He came backstage after the show, offering to take Bette out for supper. But by this point in the evening, a combination of opening night jitters and a developing case of measles (she had insisted upon going through with the show) had made her so ill, that she failed to respond in any way to her father's gesture. She has long regretted that occasion.

Ruthie nursed Bette through the measles and the young actress was able to accept the role of Hedvig in a road production of Ibsen's *The Wild Duck* which starred Blanche Yurka. One of Bette's cherished theatre memories had been seeing Miss Yurka perform in this drama in Boston years before. In Boston,

Miss Yurka gave Bette her deserved recognition by sharing a curtain call with her and then leaving her alone on the stage to receive an ovation. This successful tour, which also found Bette playing Boletta in *The Lady from the Sea,* was followed by a summer of stock (this time as a full-fledged actress) with the Cape Playhouse.

She then starred on Broadway at the Ritz Theatre as Donald Meek's daughter, Elaine, in the comedy, *Broken Dishes.* The play opened on Monday, November 5, 1929, and ran for 178 performances. "At last I was accepted as a bona-fide actress," Bette said of the role that paid her seventy-five dollars weekly and that brought her to the attention of Arthur Hornblow, Jr., who persuaded her to take a screen test for a Samuel Goldwyn movie (*The Devil to Pay,* 1930). The test, conducted at Paramount's facilities at Astoria, New York, was disastrous and Goldwyn, after viewing it, exclaimed, "Who wasted my time with that one?" The part was given to Myrna Loy.* Although Bette hated being photographed, she bowed to the inevitable that future screen tests would be offered, and had braces installed on her teeth as a probable straightening device. On stage, she was careful not to display the braces to audiences.

When *Broken Dishes* closed in the spring of 1930, Bette spent a third summer at the Cape Playhouse playing a variety of roles and then took to the road for a tour of *Broken Dishes.* In October 1930, while on tour, she received a call to report to the Lyceum Theatre in New York to take on the role of Alabama, a southern belle, in Richard Bennett's *Solid South.* Joan Bennett, Richard's youngest of three daughters, had originally been slated to play the part, but due to Hollywood commitments she dropped out ten days before the play's opening. The show opened on Tuesday, October 14, 1930, and received poor reviews, largely due to Richard Bennett's oversized temperament which flared up onstage whenever audiences did not respond the way he felt

* Miss Loy married producer Arthur Hornblow, Jr., in 1936; they were divorced in 1942.

they should. After only thirty-one performances, Bette was again jobless.

Nevertheless, *Solid South* did not go unnoticed. David Werner, a New York–based talent scout for Universal Studios, saw the play and thought Bette might work out as the lead in Universal's film version of *Strictly Dishonorable,* a 1929 Preston Sturges Broadway play which had starred Muriel Kirkland. Werner honestly alerted her (in case the perspicacious Bette had missed the truth) that she was not physically alluring in the Hollywood sense, but that she had a special stage quality that might shine through in films. On Werner's advice, Universal signed Bette to a six-month contract.

With Ruthie at her side, Bette took an expense-paid trip to California. They arrived in Los Angeles on Saturday, December 13, 1930, but no one met them at the train station. It later turned out there had been a studio representative there, but he could not see among the disembarking passengers anyone who resembled an actress. Bette had worn no makeup to cover her freckles and her mousy brown hair was pulled back into a practical knot.

At Universal, the publicity department sought to change her name to "Bettina Dawes," but Bette's New England stubbornness flared up and she refused to be called anything but Bette Davis. She claims that she did not want people to refer to her as "Between the Drawers." Upon meeting Bette, studio head Carl Laemmle, Jr., remarked "She has about as much sex appeal as Slim Summerville," and "I can't imagine anyone giving *her* a tumble." Consequently, she was cancelled out of *Strictly Dishonorable* and the role of Isabelle Parry went to Sidney Fox, another Universal contract player who was far more conventionally attractive.

Since Universal was obligated to pay Bette weekly for six months, she was put through the paces accorded all starlets, including the usual cheesecake photograph sessions. Even two-piece bathing suits and beach sandals failed to reveal her as a potential pin-up. Because of her plainness, she was nicknamed

"the little brown wren" by studio men and they tested her for a role in a Walter Huston film, *A House Divided* (1931), to be directed by William Wyler. However, she flunked this examination because she was forced to wear a low-cut dress which made her feel uncomfortable.* Helen Chandler was given the role.

Then she was finally put to work in the picture version of Booth Tarkington's story *The Flirt* which was released in April 1931 as *Bad Sister.* Bette was Laura Madison, the sweet girl who secretly loves the small-town doctor (Conrad Nagel) who, in turn, has been two-timed by Laura's impetuous, thrill-seeking sister (Sidney Fox). Also in the cast was a young Humphrey Bogart. For her role in the film, Bette had prepared her own makeup and used equal proportions to those she had applied onstage. Consequently, she photographed as a typical wallflower. One critic thought she was "like something that had been set out on the front porch for the Salvation Army." At least *Variety* assessed, "Bette Davis holds much promise in her handling of Laura, sweet, simple, and the very essence of repression."

On her $300 weekly salary, Bette and her mother moved to a small house on Alta Loma Terrace near the Hollywood Bowl and waited. Universal was not sure what to do with her. Studio cinematographer Karl Freund thought Bette had lovely eyes, but when director Robert Florey was casting *Murders in the Rue Morgue* (1932), it was Sidney Fox once again who claimed the role. Bette would later insist that it was Miss Fox's social relationship with Mr. Laemmle, Jr., that earned her such parts.

Allegedly, after screening *Bad Sister,* avuncular, European-born Carl Laemmle, Sr., joked about Bette, "Can you picture some poor guy goin' through hell and high water in a picture and endin' up with her at the fade out?" But when the studio needed an

---

* In *Mother Goddam* (Hawthorn Books Inc., 1974), in which author Whitney Stine's coverage of Bette Davis' career is published with the actresses' responses to his written remarks, Miss Davis recalls, "Mr. Wyler said in a loud voice, 'What do you think of these dames who show their chests and think they can get jobs?' It was truly one of the most heartbreaking moments of my career."

ingenue type to play Margaret Carter, John Boles' sweet daughter in *Seed* (1931), Bette was considered dispensable enough for the role. "If you blinked for a second, Margaret had disappeared," recalls Miss Davis.

Since the studio had mysteriously picked up Bette's option for an additional three-month term, she was available for a role in *Waterloo Bridge* (1931), directed by James Whale who was fast becoming a specialist in horror films. But *Waterloo Bridge*, which would be remade twice by MGM (1939, and in 1956 as *Gaby*), was a tender story of a soldier (Kent Douglas—later Douglass Montgomery) who falls in love with a London prostitute (Mae Clarke). As Janet, Douglas' sister, Bette was required to be sweet and in love with the idea of marriage. The production, based on Robert E. Sherwood's play, was inexpensively mounted and is the least remembered version of the once popular romantic drama.

Universal quickly ran out of material for its "little brown wren" and finished off her contract with loan-outs, the first of which was to RKO for *Way Back Home* (1932). Set "down Maine," she is the ingenue who is attacked by a drunken drifter (Stanley Fields) whose son (Frankie Darro) is her friend. She is saved by the sincere boy (Frank Albertson) who loves her, and the drunk is eventually killed by a train while escaping from the local parson (Phillips Lord—the radio actor who brought to movies his specialty of portraying cracker-barrel, philosophizing, old codgers). Bette had turned blonde for the improbably melodramatic, folksy *Way Back Home,* and thanks to cinematographer J. Roy Hunt, Bette photographed well. As Bette would admit in *Mother Goddam* (Hawthorn, 1974) to Whitney Stine, "This was the first encouragement I had had, as to my face on the screen. I was truly overjoyed." Bette would remain blonde for four years.

Meanwhile, she and Ruthie saw as many films as possible. Bette scrutinized the performances of all the screen stars (Joan Crawford, Greta Garbo, Jean Harlow, Kay Francis, Janet Gaynor, Irene Dunne, Ruth

Chatterton, et al.) hoping to discern their techniques for achieving cinema stardom. The starlet had little hope that Universal would renew her contract, but she wanted to be prepared for any eventuality.

Columbia borrowed her services for *The Menace* (1932) in which she played an English lass who faints and screams throughout. The picture was shot in eight days and Bette received second billing in this quickie mystery. But another blonde, Natalie Moorhead, was given the meatier part of the conniving stepmother of the lead, Walter Byron. Parsimonious Universal wanted to get its money's worth from Bette's services and loaned her to Capital Films Exchange for *Hell's House* (1932). Her co-stars were Junior Durkin and Pat O'Brien. Bette had little to do but to appear attractive. But "out of all bad comes some good. I have always believed this," says Bette, and it proved true with the embarrassing loan-outs from Universal.

When she returned to the home lot, she found that she was without a job. She, Ruthie, and Barbara, who had recently joined them, contemplated returning to New York. They had lived modestly in their rented Coldwater Canyon home and had saved as much of Bette's salary as they could toward that inevitable rainy day which was all too soon thrust upon them. Bette hesitated to return East as a failure, and there was one slight glimmer of hope. Murray Kinnell, a supporting player with whom she had worked in *The Menace,* was a long-standing friend of the distinguished "Mr." George Arliss, the class actor of the cinema. Kinnell had submitted Bette's name to Arliss as a possibility for the ingenue in a remake of *The Man Who Played God,* which the Britisher had done silently in 1922. Arliss preferred a stage-trained girl and Bette knew the prestigious advantage of working with the great man. Impatience runs high in Hollywood, though, especially when the pocketbook is running low, and the Davis musketeers prepared to leave for New York.

The day before they were due to depart, the telephone rang. It was George Arliss personally requesting Bette to meet him at Warner

Bros. that afternoon for a meeting. She lost no time in reaching the Burbank lot and, after a brief talk, Arliss told her that the role of Grace was hers.* As part of the standard practice in Hollywood at the time, she signed a contract** with the studio which provided them with options to continue using her services after the film, if they so chose. Studio head Jack L. Warner would keep Bette on the Warner Bros. payroll for eighteen years. According to Bette in her autobiography, "Mr. Arliss, through Murray Kinnell, had thrown me the lifeline, just as I was going down. Like Pearl White, I was snatched from the jaws of death."

While Universal had treated Bette shabbily, Warner Bros. was more astute in determining how to merchandize their latest contract commodity. Studio makeup genius Perc Westmore decided that Bette's ash-blonde hair should not only be bleached brighter than before, but coiffed into a sleek, chic hairdo that would highlight her profile. It worked wonders in transforming the rather mousy New York actress into a Thirties Hollywood version of feminine attractiveness. More importantly, with a part such as the fifth-billed role of Grace in *The Man Who Played God* (1932), Bette had some meaty material with which to work. She is the fiancée of the very mature concert pianist (Arliss —then in his mid-sixties) Montgomery Royale who loses his hearing in a bombing mishap. When the deaf performer later takes up

lip reading, he chances to discover that Bette's Grace actually loves a young man (Donald Cook) but refuses to leave Royale. The humane gentleman releases the girl from their engagement. Others in the stellar cast included Violet Heming, Louise Closser Hale, Hedda Hopper, and another relative newcomer, Ray Milland.

The Man Who Played God premiered at Warners' Western Theatre in Los Angeles on Sunday, February 14, 1932—the same date that *Hell's House* was released with much less fanfare. Most critics took notice of Bette, some for the first time. Although Mordaunt Hall *(New York Times)* criticized her for speaking "too rapidly for the microphone," *Variety* discovered her as "a vision of wide-eyed blonde beauty." Bette refers to this film —remade yet again, as *Sincerely Yours* (1955) with Liberace—as the turning point in her career.

Now Bette joined the roster of Warner Bros.-First National Players that included Arliss, Richard Barthelmess, Joan Blondell, Lilian Bond, Joe E. Brown, Anthony Bushell, Charles Butterworth, James Cagney, Ruth Chatterton, Donald Cook, Lil Dagover, Bebe Daniels, Douglas Fairbanks, Jr., Kay Francis, Ruth Hall, Ralf Harolde, David Manners, Marian Marsh, Marilyn Miller, Dorothy Peterson, William Powell, James Rennie, Edward G. Robinson, Polly Walters, Warren William, and Loretta Young.

Bette was rushed into two successive films. The first, *So Big* (1932), starred Barbara Stanwyck as Selina Peake, the long-suffering widow who strives to raise her fatherless son, Dirk (Hardie Albright), to live close to godliness and encourages him to become an architect. Bette is Dallas O'Mara, the wholesome girl Dirk brings home to meet his struggling mother and in whom Selina sees the hope that her son may yet amount to something in spite of his erring ways. Also in the cast, in second billing, was George Brent as Dirk's best friend and the kind of man Selina wishes Dirk had become.

The second apprenticeship was *The Rich Are Always with Us* (1932) starring Ruth Chatterton and George Brent (who would

* In *My Ten Years in the Studio* (Little, Brown & Co., 1940) Arliss would write, "I think that only two or three times in my experience have I ever got from an actor at rehearsal [a practice the lofty Mr. Arliss insisted upon] something beyond what I realized was in the part. Bette Davis proved to be one of these exceptions. I knew she had a 'nice little part' important to me— so I hoped for the best. I did not expect anything but a nice little performance. But when we rehearsed she startled me; the nice little part became a deep and vivid creation, and I felt rather humbled that this young girl had been able to discover and portray something that my imagination had failed to conceive. She startled me because quite unexpectedly I got from her a flash that illuminated mere words and inspired them with passion and emotion. That is the kind of light that cannot be hidden under a bushel, and I am not in the least surprised that Bette Davis is now the most important star on the screen.
** Jack L. Warner in his superficial autobiography, *My First Hundred Years in Hollywood* (Random House, 1964), insisted that his associate Rufus LeMaire told him of Bette Davis who had "a bit in *Bad Sister*" and she was brought over to join the Burbank lot.

wed one another in real life). Bette is a flashy Park Avenue blonde named Malbro who temporarily threatens the romantic bliss of Chatterton and Brent by falling in love with him. Not only does this film contain some archetypical early Davis dialogue ("Caroline, while we're all taking our hair down . . . what is a girl to do when she's terribly in love with a man and he won't take her seriously?"—imagine the darting Davis eyes punctuating her delivery), but it was in this sophisticated feature that Brent beat Paul Henreid to the punch by a decade: for it was first in *The Rich Are Always with Us*—and not in *Now, Voyager* (1942)—that the leading man lights two cigarettes simultaneously and hands one to Davis.

As the seventh of her nine 1932 releases, Bette had second billing (and the female lead) in the comedy *The Dark Horse,* a production line item from the Warner Bros. film factory. She is a determined young secretary with the Progressive Party who convinces her bosses that Hal Blake (Warren William) would make an ideal campaign manager for dark-horse gubenatorial candidate Zachary Hicks (Guy Kibbee). The only drawback is that Blake is in jail for nonpayment of alimony, but Kay dramatically points out that other great men (Bunyan of *Pilgrim's Progress,* Oscar Wilde of *The Ballad of Reading Gaol*) have spent time behind bars, and this should not interfere with the party's plans. Due to Kay's impassioned speech, Blake is hired.

Warners sent Bette and dapper Warren William on a personal appearance tour in the summer of 1932 to publicize *The Dark Horse.* At the Capitol Theatre in New York, they performed a sketch onstage called *The Burglar and the Lady* about two people who accidentally meet in an apartment they both intend to rob. On her return to Los Angeles, Bette found that Harmon Nelson was there, playing in a band. It was natural that they should gravitate toward each other once again, and when Nelson proposed marriage, Ruthie was all for it. She hinted that Bette's nervous disposition might come to an end through marriage. Realizing that Ruthie was most likely correct, Bette married Harmon O.

Nelson, Jr., on Thursday, August 18, 1932, at the Indian Mission in Yuma, Arizona. She was attended by her mother and sister, and immediately following the ceremony (officiated by Reverend Schalbaugh), they drove back to Los Angeles.

It was Darryl F. Zanuck, production manager at Warners, who insisted that Bette play Madge Norwood, the southern vixen of Peckerwood plantation, in *Cabin in the Cotton* (1932). Director Michael Curtiz did not want her because he felt she was sexless, but Zanuck had the last word on the matter. He could not help but agree that she was not beautiful, but he agreed wholeheartedly with George Arliss that she was on the verge of becoming "one of the great actresses" in Hollywood.

Sociologically, *Cabin in the Cotton* was atypical of the usual hard-hitting Warner Bros. action product ripped from the nation's headlines. For in this seventy-nine-minute entry about sharecroppers versus plantation owners, a special prologue states, "It is not the object of the producers to take sides. We are only concerned with presenting a picture of the conditions." But there was no ambivalence about Bette's role as the spoiled daughter of a dishonest planter (Berton Churchill), who flirts her way into the heart of an honest sharecropper (Richard Barthelmess). Although not a large role (Dorothy Jordan as the shantyville ingenue had the real female lead), Bette's character was colorful to say the very least. Bette had lines of dialogue that she delivered in such a flavorful way that they would become a permanent addition to camp culture. The fact that the hero was portrayed by still boyish ex-silent star Barthelmess, well remembered for his Americana interpretation of *Tol'able David,* did much to point up the oversized nature of Davis' performance.

Some of Bette's memorable verbal and visual interplay included:

Bette: You don't like me, do ya?
Barthelmess: (shuffling, embarrassed) I do.
Bette: Then come close. . . . Ay won't bite ya.

When not sashaying into a room and batting her eyelids as she drawls with her Georgia accent, "Sorry to interrupt ya little tet-a-tet," she performs her own inimitable version of "The Story of Willie the Weeper," which was guaranteed not to win her any recording contracts, but still would magnetize an audience immediately.

Perhaps the most memorable moment of Bette's early Warner films (and certainly one of the finest of the strident *Cabin in the Cotton*) occurs when Barthelmess, now residing in the Peckerwood mansion, is lured to Bette's bedroom. As the seductive bitch in heat, Bette tantalizes the hick Barthelmess with, "Turn ya back, while I get into somethin' restful." And before long, Bette is naked and Barthelmess is hers (at least until he regains his senses and rejoins the sharecroppers' cause and the still loyal Miss Jordan). And this is the film where Bette utters that oft-quoted line, "Ah'd love ta kiss ya, but ah jes washed mah hayuh."

In spite of her successful switch from ingenue to vixen, Warners continued to cast utilitarian Bette in supporting and often inconsequential roles. In *Three on a Match* (1932), she is true blue Ruth, one of the three girls who were pals at school and who meet years later to renew friendships. The other two are Mary (Joan Blondell) and Vivian (Ann Dvorak). The three light up cigarettes at their first get-together, with Vivian the third to light hers from the one match. The film was directed by Mervyn LeRoy who predicted stardom for vivacious Miss Blondell and dramatic Miss Dvorak but stated that Bette would not make it in pictures. "She has been cool to me ever since," he has admitted. Warner Bros. would remake the property in 1938 as *Broadway Musketeers* with Ann Sheridan, Margaret Lindsay, and Marie Wilson.

Warner Bros. borrowed Spencer Tracy from Fox for *20,000 Years in Sing Sing* (1933) when the intended star, James Cagney, proved to be too busy and rebellious. Tom Connors (Tracy) is a braggart mobster who is sent up the river on a felony charge, but is confident that his political connections will obtain his release. On the outside, his girlfriend Fay (Bette) strives to help him by bed-

ding down with an influential mobster (Harold Huber), but this liaison results in her being seriously injured in an automobile accident. Connors is permitted parole to visit her and when he encounters Joe Finn (Louis Calhern), the man responsible for his imprisonment, a fracas ensues. During the fight, Fay crawls out of her sick bed to retrieve Finn's gun which has fallen to the floor, and she shoots him in order to protect Connors. She tries to tell how the murder happened, but no one believes her, and Connors is returned to Sing Sing on a murder rap, now destined for the electric chair. If the plot sounds familiar to filmgoers, it should; it was reused by Warner Bros. for *Castle on the Hudson* (1940) with John Garfield and Ann Sheridan.

20,000 Years was the only time that Bette and Tracy would work together in films, although in 1940 they would be heard together in a version of *Dark Victory* on Cecil B. DeMille's "Lux Radio Theatre." And this was only the second of several times that Bette would work under the aegis of director Michael Curtiz,* and, unlike her pacifying role ("It must be a grand feeling to get everything you want") in *Three on a Match,* Bette here could pull out a few dramatic punches of her own as when she begs Tracy's Tom, "You promised you wouldn't leave me . . . you've gotta stay with me. . . . I won't let you go back up there. . . . Now you're free."

Bette was just another southern girl in *Parachute Jumper* (1933), an easily forgotten tale of an ex-Marine (Douglas Fairbanks, Jr.) who turns to flying liquor into the States from Canada for a mobster (Leo Carrillo). Then, in February 1933, Bette and "Ham" Nelson finally found time for a honeymoon, but it was an event that was shared with Bebe Daniels, George Brent, Warner Baxter, Loretta Young, Joan Blondell, Ginger Rogers, and about twelve other Warner Bros. contract players. The occasion was a thirty-two-day tour by

---

* Whitney Stine in *Mother Goddam* jocularly notes of *20,000 Years,* "Since this was essentially a man's picture, he [Curtiz] actually paid scant attention to Davis and in fact did not reshoot when her head lolled to one side in a key bed scene. For several moments the audience gazes up her nostrils, while Tracy is enjoying a flattering profile view. Cinematographer Barney McGill, however, lit a couple of marvelous close-ups framed artistically by the pillow."

train plugging the new Warner musical extravaganza, *42nd Street.* In thirty-two cities, the passengers disembarked onto the station platforms to tell the gathered populace about the new movie, and they even ventured into some metropolitan areas to demonstrate General Electric kitchens (a tie-in sponsor). The tour culminated in Washington, D.C., after a stopover in Manhattan where the stars strutted down Fifth Avenue in a special parade.

Bette received another lesson in art with the request from Mr. George Arliss that she be his co-star in *The Working Man* (1933). It was another career rescue for Bette after the slipshod *Parachute Jumper* and her refusal to star in the assembly-line *The Mind Reader* (1933) with Warren William. (Constance Cummings took over Bette's intended role.) In this Arliss prestige film, Bette's love interest was Theodore Newton, with the star playing their protector. Now the *New York Times'* Mordaunt Hall delighted in reporting to his readers, "Bette Davis, whose diction is music to the ears, does good work in the role of Jenny."

It was Darryl F. Zanuck, who was soon to leave Warner Bros. to form his Twentieth Century Pictures, who demanded that Bette be given billing* *over the title* for her next film, *Ex-Lady* (1933), a remake of 1931's *Illicit* which had starred Barbara Stanwyck. Although this was supposed to be a reward for hard-working Bette, she found the project "an ecstasy of poor taste." She was forced to play Helen Bauer, a commercial artist whose ideas of love and marriage are unconventional: she prefers to live with but not marry her lover who, in this case, is Gene Raymond. Eventually, after professional and domestic difficulties, she admits that marriage is the only proper way to live. *Film Daily's* analysis of this would-be tantalizer, in which Bette spent much time oncamera in flimsy negli-

gees and undergarments, stated that "some fairly hot scenes are sprinkled here and there but the story in general has no guts and the arguments for love without marriage are never very convincing or as shocking as intended."

In spite of the disappointment engendered by *Ex-Lady,* Bette was still considered by Warners to be a rising star, and she was top-billed in *Bureau of Missing Persons* (1933), originally titled *Headquarters.* George Brent was to have been her co-star, but, due to his heavy schedule, he was replaced by Pat O'Brien. Fast-paced, glib dialogue (including Bette's utterance as Norma Phillips, "Curiosity got the better of me. I wanted to see what I'd look like in a coffin") made this film entertaining as heroine Norma Phillips seeks the Bureau's help in searching for her husband. While intended by director Roy Del Ruth as a slap-the-knee type of parody, the film is confusing in that it meanders between fun and seriousness without settling on one or the other.

Star William Powell, earning $6,000 weekly, gave his okay to the script for *King of Fashion* and also approved the assignment of Bette as his co-star. The final product underwent a title change to *Fashions of 1934* (1934) and provided Bette with ample opportunity to wear some of Orry-Kelly's more spectacular costumes of the era. No longer was she the practically dressed, almost dowdy type. In fact, with the platinum blonde Garboesque wig and long false eyelashes, Bette seemed anything but Bette Davis as she moved through the story of a con artist (Powell) who illegally copies Parisian fashions which he bootlegs right off the ships as they land in New York from Europe. Bette would later retort about her transformation in this film,* "Never again did I allow anyone to go against my type with makeup, hair, etc. There was nothing left of Bette Davis in this film. I had hit the bottom of the barrel. . . . No makeup in the world was going to turn me into a glamour star such as Harlow."

---

* The lurid billboard ads read, "Introducing . . . filmdom's newest favorite in the stardom she earned in *Cabin in the Cotton* and *20,000 Years in Sing Sing.*" The film's promotional catchline was "WE DON'T DARE TELL YOU HOW DARING IT IS! . . . Never before has the screen had the courage to present a story so frank—so outspoken—yet so true! Get set for a surprise sensation!"

* *Fashions of 1934* proved popular thanks to urbane Powell, witty Verree Teasdale, and the production number "Spin a Little Web of Dreams" helmed by Busby Berkeley.

With Hardie Albright in *So Big* ('32).

With Doris Lloyd,
Douglass Montgomery,
Mae Clarke, and
Frederick Kerr in
Waterloo Bridge ('31).

Cheesecake, Warner Bros.-style (June 1933).

With George Arliss in *The Working Man* ('33).

191

In 1934, Bette became pregnant, an event that greatly delighted her but which Ham and Ruthie vetoed because a child at this point in her career would be a detriment. And, struggling on a musician's salary, Ham did not want Bette paying her own hospital bills. The pregnancy was terminated because, as Bette has sadly recalled, "I did as I was told."

For almost a year, Bette had been begging Warner Bros. to loan her to RKO for a projected screen version of W. Somerset Maugham's Of Human Bondage. But Jack L. Warner kept refusing. Instead, he cast her in program films. Warner did consider casting Bette as the Empress Josephine, along with Reginald Owen as Talleyrand, and Edward G. Robinson as Napoleon, in a film project, but "Little Caesar" vetoed the idea. Ironically, in her next film, The Big Shakedown (1934), the recently pregnant Bette played Norma Frank who nearly dies from childbirth. Of this "farfetched, overacted, and unbelievable" (Film Daily) picture, the only point of note is that Bette was assigned a new stand-in, Sally Sage, who would handle similar chores for the star in thirty-six other features.

While Bette refused to co-star with Warren William in The Case of the Howling Dog (1934)—a part which Mary Astor accepted—she did agree to join with James Cagney in Jimmy the Gent (1934). But this Michael Curtiz-directed venture was a comedy tailored to Cagney's special pugnacious talents, and Bette, as the faithful secretary Joan Martin, was left too often on the sidelines. As for Fog over Frisco (1934), it was much better served as a quickie double-bill item when remade in 1942 as Spy Ship with Craig Stevens, Irene Manning, and Maris Wrixon. However, as the shady San Franciscan who has induced her fiancé (Lyle Talbot) to sell stolen bonds, Bette showed much of the dramatic acting ability which would later make her famous. The film was a first for her in that her character was killed off in the plotline.

As she has often recounted in interviews, Bette's relentless pursuit of the Mildred Rogers' role paid off when Jack L. Warner finally agreed to allow her to be loaned out to RKO for the unsympathetic part in Of Human Bondage (1934). Maugham's novel is legend, but so is the screen's first interpretation* of the evil Mildred Rogers. Miss Rogers is a Cockney and Bette studied with a Britisher in order to speak with the proper accent. Leslie Howard was designated the star and he had wanted an English actress to portray Mildred. As a result, during much of the filming under John Cromwell's direction, he chose to ignore his co-lead. Only when he was notified that she was stealing the picture, did he sit up, take notice, and gradually become her friend.

With Howard's name above the title (Bette's credit was the first listed beneath the title), the film was released on June 27, 1934, and the world witnessed a Bette Davis different from those seen in previous cinema outings. She is bitchy ("For a gentleman with brains, you don't use them, do you?), opportunistic ("If you don't take me out, someone else will"), and haughty ("You're a bit too superior for me, my fine young friend"). At the age of twenty-four, Mildred Rogers is a waitress whom Philip Carey (Howard), an artist and medical intern born with a club foot, initially finds "anemic." However, he soon overcomes this feeling and falls hopelessly in love with the cruel, crude tea shop employee.

In the course of the eighty-three-minute scenario, she taunts Philip by dating a German named Emil Miller (Alan Hale) who dazzles her with his money to compensate for his bragging unrefined ways. She tells the aghast, sensitive Philip, "I'd rather wait for him than have you wait for me." She runs off with Miller, who refuses to marry her, and becomes pregnant with his child. She returns to Philip, explaining "you've always been so good to me, that is why I come to you." No sooner has she recovered from the birth of her child, than she runs off to Paris with Philip's colleague (Reginald Denny) who also deserts

* Two later versions were made, the first in 1946 with Eleanor Parker and Paul Henreid and the second in 1964 with Kim Novak and Laurence Harvey. Neither of these was equal to the 1934 film.

her. Once more she returns to Carey. By this time he is not anxious to renew his romantic interest in her, but again permits her to live with him. When he spurns her advances, she burns some securities left him by an uncle, smashes his art work, takes the baby and leaves. Some time later, Philip hears that she is in a hospital charity ward dying of locomotor ataxis, and she dies before he can see her. With her death, he is released from the attachment and finds consolation with the refined daughter (Frances Dee) of a friend (Reginald Owen).

There are three aspects to Bette's characterization of Mildred Rogers which even today make it an intriguing, if not always properly shaded, performance. In contrast to the two other females in the story (beauteous Frances Dee as the calm, good-natured Sally and Kay Johnson as the experienced, giving authoress Norah), Bette's tart goes strongly against the current of established cinema leading lady roles, just as Sadie Thompson of *Rain* had done previously. Little coincidence that this part was based on another character conceived by W. Somerset Maugham. Then, too, Bette was permitted to apply her own makeup for her scenes of degeneration, an accomplishment that had much to do with her deep portrayal of the wicked, tortured Mildred. Third, thanks to the scenario of Lester Cohen which satisfactorily (if in truncated form) adapted Maugham's text and the interpretation levied by director John Cromwell, Bette had ample occasion to unleash her dramatic prowess. Undoubtedly, her finest dramatic moment occurs when verbally she lashes out at Carey, a sequence made all the more effective by Leslie Howard's underplaying of the emotionally whipped young man, who flinches in embarrassment, disgust, and horror at her accusations.

Davis' sluttish Mildred spits out in her Cockney slang, "Yeew cad . . . yeew dirtee swine. I nev'ah cared for yeew . . . not once. I was always making a fool of yuh. Yuh bored me stiff. I hated yuh. It made me sick [eyes darting furiously, her slash of lipstick emphasizing her vicious mouth] when I had to let yuh kiss me. I only did it because yuh begged

me. . . . Yuh hounded, yuh drove me crazy, and, after yuh kissed me, I always used to wipe my mouth. [Her pacing, caged movements possess the telltale Davis swagger.] Wipe my mouth. But I made up for it . . . for every kiss I had to laugh. We laughed at yuh, Miller and me and Griffith and me. We laughed at yuh 'cause yuh were such a mug, a mug . . . a monster. You're a cripple, a cripple, a cripple!"

Rightly so, RKO, the home of patrician Ann Harding, Irene Dunne, and, at one time, Constance Bennett, counted on *Of Human Bondage* to be a prestigious picture. When the studio previewed the picture, audiences laughed in the wrong places. The horrified RKO executives reasoned—hopefully—that it was the music score which was at fault and had Max Steiner write a fresh accompaniment for it. Bette was too fearful to attend the next preview, but her mother and husband did. When they returned, an anxious Bette demanded their reaction. Ham insisted that she gave a sincere performance but he did not think it would help her career much [the reason other more famous actresses had rejected the role]. As Davis later admitted to *Modern Screen* magazine, ". . . I realized that he had spoken as he had for my own good, for my protection. He said, if the picture did go over with any enormous success, that would be my reward. But, if it didn't he didn't want me to feel too let down."

Of Human Bondage premiered at Radio City Music Hall in late June 1934. Mordaunt Hall (*New York Times*) reported, "At the first showing yesterday of this picture, the audience was so wrought up over the conduct of this vixen that when Carey finally expressed his contempt for Mildred's behavior, applause was heard from all sides. There was further outburst of applause when the film came to an end." As for Bette's stellar performance, he rated her portrayal "enormously effective."

Two Warner films, completed before *Of Human Bondage,* were next shoved into release. In *Housewife* (1934), which Bette has called "a horror," she is an advertising writer (earning $25,000 in Depression-weary Chi-

193

With Leslie Howard in *Of Human Bondage* ('34).

←

With Charles Farrell in *The Big Shakedown* ('34).

With Arthur Byron and Margaret Lindsay in *Fog over Frisco* ('34).

cago) thrown into daily contact with the man (George Brent) she once loved ("He was one of those mental men born to be glamorous"). But he chose to wed her classmate Ann Dvorak, and Bette decided to make something of her life professionally. "I tasted Illinois Central cinders till I escaped to New York. . . . I suddenly found I had some brains and decided to use them." Now back in Chicago, she vamps Brent, unmindful that he is both a husband and a father. The end result is that George and Ann weather the marital storm, while Bette eventually fades out of his life. The decisive divorce courtroom scene has Brent and Dvorak embracing, while Bette and John Halliday—he being Brent's wealthy client who loves Dvorak—settle for a liquid "celebration" to mark their respective defeats.

A point often ignored in cinema history studies of Miss Davis is that Ann Dvorak, who plays the film's title role, was established as a strong dramatic actress *long* before Bette, and it was she who set the standards for battling with a studio for better roles. In her quiet performance as Nan Wilson Reynolds, it is Miss Dvorak and *not* the already mannered Bette who woos the audience's attention and affection. It is Dvorak who provides the proper artistic control for the feature, while Bette, under Alfred E. Green's tutelage, runs rampant once again in her special interpretation of what a celluloid *femme fatale* should be like.

Shooting on *Bordertown* (1935), Bette's next picture, began September 17, 1934, on a rigid four-week schedule. Archie Mayo was the official director, but Paul Muni's omnipresent wife Bella was on the set counseling her husband in his every nuance of interpretation of the lead role. Muni's Johnny Ramirez is a Mexican-American lawyer who has studied for the bar in night school. When he is later disbarred, he heads south of the border where, at a gambling casino, he rises from bouncer to manager (remaining true to his image as *Scarface* [1932]). There he becomes infatuated with the wife, Marie (Bette), of the club owner (rotund Eugene Pallette). Marie takes an equal shine to the raven-haired Mexican but he eventually spurns her because of his friendship with her husband (his boss). Repulsed by her husband, Marie kills him by leaving his drunken body inside their car in the garage. The death is decreed to be a suicide, but she cracks up when Johnny still will not acknowledge her love. In a tirade of abuse, she screams, " . . . you're riffraff, and so am I. You belong to me, and you're goin' to stay with me because I'm holdin' on to you. I committed murder to get you!" Johnny is astounded. Later, she insists to the district attorney that he forced her to kill Charlie. On the witness stand, her mind snaps and she incoherently shouts that the electric-eye garage door made her do it. She is led out of the courtroom, and the story proceeds onward with Johnny's slumming society girlfriend (Margaret Lindsay) being killed in a car mishap. The disillusioned Johnny makes a bid for penance by selling the club and using the money to sponsor a school for deprived children. In 1941, Warner Bros. used the murder-insanity portion of this film in *They Drive by Night* in which Ida Lupino superbly played the spurned woman.

In the company of such a pyrotechnical player as Muni, Bette rose to new heights of (melo)drama, having a leading man whom she could bounce off with vigor. At one point in the proceedings, she tells Muni's Johnny Ramirez, "You must have an adding machine where your heart is," and the studio quickly calculated this film would be a box-office winner. It was! The advertisements noted that "A GREAT THRILL AWAITS YOU AS WARNER BROTHERS BRINGS THESE TWO SENSATIONAL PERSONALITIES TOGETHER IN *BORDERTOWN*. . . . THE BEAUTIFUL HELL-CAT OF *OF HUMAN BONDAGE* FLINGS A CHALLENGE TO THE DYNAMIC STAR OF *I AM A FUGITIVE!* HEAVEN HELP HER WHEN SHE FINDS OUT WHAT A MAN SHE'S TALKING TO! The studio promoted the production as a contest between snarling Muni and sultry Davis. According to *Film Weekly*, Bette won the battle hands down. It applauded her enactment of the mad woman as being "so cleverly done that one finds oneself being convinced in spite of one's better judgment."

When Bette had refused *The Case of the Howling Dog,* the studio had placed her on suspension and alerted other companies not to use her for any of their pictures. Paramount had wanted to borrow her for the lead in a Damon Runyon yarn, *Hold 'Em, Yale* (1935), to play opposite George Raft; the film would be made, but with Larry "Buster" Crabbe and Patricia Ellis. After two weeks of feuding, Bette and the studio came to terms and she returned to the lot.

In February 1935, to the very vocal amazement of Hollywood friends of Bette's when her name did not appear among those nominated as Best Actress of 1934, the Academy Award Committee opened the voting and permitted write-ins; it was to be a free-for-all contest. When the winners were announced on Tuesday, February 27, 1935, at the Biltmore Bowl, the Best Actress Oscar went to Claudette Colbert (*It Happened One Night*). Miss Colbert was so sure that Bette had won that she was about to board a New York-bound train when the announcement was made. The final tabulation of votes indicated that Bette had come in fourth, following Miss Colbert, Norma Shearer (*The Barretts of Wimpole Street*), and Grace Moore (*One Night of Love*). It was thereafter decreed by the Academy that, in the future, no write-in votes would be allowed, and the accounting firm of Price-Waterhouse was designated as vote counter.

If Hollywood could forget there was an outside world, so in turn could players on a film lot ignore state, national, or global events. The star system on the Warners' spread was as self-contained and caste-conscious as that of MGM or any other major company. By the mid-Thirties, with Hal B. Wallis replacing Darryl F. Zanuck as production chief under Jack L. Warner's direct supervision, star status at the Burbank facilities was rapidly altering. Ruth Chatterton had already departed, Kay Francis was the big money-making (and earning) actress at the studio, and other Warner Bros. regulars, such as Joan Blondell, Ruby Keeler, Ann Dvorak,

Aline MacMahon, Glenda Farrell, and Margaret Lindsay, had found themselves so pegged or overexposed in repetitious products that their years (or months) at the studio were already numbered. William Randolph Hearst had moved his Cosmopolitan Productions, Marion Davies, and her fourteen-room bungalow dressing room to the Burbank lot from MGM. Anita Louise, Josephine Hutchinson, and Olivia de Havilland were the most imposing ingenues, and somewhere stuck in the middle was Bette Davis.

Still unable or unwilling to express its faith in her box-office magnetism in superior products, the studio blithely cast her in a trio of stinkers: *The Girl from Tenth Avenue* (1935) opposite Ian Hunter, *Front Page Woman* (1935) as a sob-sister reporter rivaling her newspaperman fiancé (George Brent), and *Special Agent* (1935) as a crooked man's (Ricardo Cortez) girl Friday who agrees to help a U.S. government worker (George Brent).

There seemed to be no escape from the quagmire of mediocrity. Although Bette found her next script to be "maudlin and mawkish," she perceived it "had just enough material in it to build into something if I approached it properly." Originally bearing the less-than-earth-shattering title of *Hard Luck Dame,* the property was unveiled to the public as *Dangerous* on December 6, 1935.

As Joyce Heath, the fallen woman of the stage (purportedly the story of Jeanne Eagels), Bette undergoes a variety of emotions as the woman drinks her way into oblivion because she feels she is a jinx to everything, everyone, and especially to herself. A stagestruck architect (Franchot Tone) recognizes her in a sleazy section of town and follows her. She tells him her story, and he proposes to back her with $180,000 in a play that just may revitalize her career. The show is *But to Die* and according to its producer "only two women could have played it, Jeanne Eagels and Joyce Heath." He falls in love with her and asks his genteel fiancée (Margaret Lindsay) to release him from his promise to wed her, so he may marry Joyce. Little does he know—and herein lies the rub of the soap opera—that Joyce already has a spouse, bland Gordon Heath (John Eldredge), who refuses to give her a divorce.

She manages to delay answering her benefactor's proposal while she visits her clerk husband. When she fails to persuade him, she agrees to go away with him on a weekend to the country. In the speeding car, she informs him, "It's going to be your life or mine!. . . If you're killed [she spends more time emphasizing her speech with sidelong looks at Eldredge than at where she is driving], I'll be free. . . . If I'm killed, it won't matter any longer. . . . And, if we both die . . . good riddance." She rams the car into a tree. He is not killed but is crippled for life. In the tradition of *Of Human Bondage,* Bette has another denunciation speech. While recuperating at Tone's country cottage, she flirts with him but, knowing her own marital status and fearing his pity, she pretends that her prior seduction of him was only in jest. She laughs falsely and shouts, "Ah, I shouldn't laugh at you, should I, but I can't help it. You were so awkward that I almost laughed in your face at first and then it made me quite sick to think that anyone could be stupid enough to be taken in by a lot of old tricks. I thought you might at least be amusing but you turned out to be dull and stupid and so afraid. Well, you needn't be. I won't hurt your Sunday school romance or your oh-so-nice career. . . . Get out of here before you give me hysterics."

The play later opens on schedule, she is re-acclaimed, and then she realizes that her personal duty is to her husband—an ending required by the stringent Production Code. Tone returns to Lindsay and they wed (Bette witnesses it through a cab door window), leaving the anti-heroine to put a bright smile on her face and visit her husband at the hospital, carrying a bouquet of roses.

The making of *Dangerous* brought Bette both personal and professional frustrations. She fell in love with her leading man, MGM's Franchot Tone, but she was already wed, and he married Joan Crawford later that year, setting a course for their rivalry long before *What Ever Happened to Baby Jane?* (1962). And Bette was all too aware that Warner

Bros. had concocted her Joyce Heath role in *Dangerous* as a parallel to her Mildred Rogers in *Of Human Bondage.* Not only were there character similarities, but the lines sound as if some came from the identical typewriter. Joyce, in her rejection of Eldredge snarls, "Every time I think of your soft sticky hands touching me, . . . I get sick. . . . sick!" Then again, what real credibility can an actress bring to such dialogue as, "I owe you for bringing me back to life" or "I've been betrayed so often by tomorrows I don't dare promise them."

Reviewing the picture, the *New York Times* decided "that Bette Davis has been unable to match the grim standard she set as Mildred in *Of Human Bondage* is not to her discredit. In *Dangerous,* the new film at the Rivoli, she tries again. Except for a few sequences where the tension is convincing as well as deadly, she fails. . . . Best under taut restraint, Miss Davis is least satisfactory when lines lead her to be sputtery and even tearful."

Possibly to capitalize on the success of starring her with Leslie Howard in *Of Human Bondage,* Bette was chosen to portray the waitress in an Arizona desert way station in *The Petrified Forest* (1936). The role of a dreamy-eyed girl who wants to visit Bourges, France, and become an artist is a far cry from Joyce Heath. (And Davis rightly decided she must rid herself of the brassy blonde look and secretly stopped bleaching her hair—Hal B. Wallis did not notice for a year and a half!) Gaby is calm and not at all hysterical. Derived from Robert E. Sherwood's Broadway play (with Howard, Peggy Conklin, and Humphrey Bogart), the film tells of Alan Squier (Howard) who happens upon the desert service station-restaurant and falls in love with the proprietor's aesthetic-conscious daughter (Bette). He is impressed with her dreams and tries to figure a way for her to obtain the needed money to reach France. When escaped convict Duke Mantee (Bogart) and his cohorts arrive on the scene, Alan has a proper scheme: Duke is to shoot him and the life insurance money will go to Gaby.

Bette wisely played Gabrielle in a very re-

With Alison Skipworth
in *The Girl from 10th
Avenue* ('35).

With George Brent and
Craig Reynolds in *The
Golden Arrow* ('36).

strained manner, only occasionally lapsing into over-reaction. While hers was not the pivotal role, she had a key part. It is of her artist character that Squier says, "She is the future, the renewal of vitality and courage . . . . I don't know what she is but she is essential to me, to the whole God-forsaken country." Just as *Dangerous* would be remade into a C feature, *Singapore Woman* (1941) with Brenda Marshall, so the noteworthy, if stagy, *The Petrified Forest* would reemerge on the Warner Bros. production list in 1945 as a Nazi spy thriller entitled *Escape in the Desert* with Philip Dorn, Helmut Dantine, and Jean Sullivan.

In February 1936, Bette was nominated for an Academy Award for her performance in *Dangerous*. At the Thursday, March 5, 1936, banquet at the Biltmore Hotel in Los Angeles, Bette was the winner. Her competition had been Elisabeth Bergner (*Escape Me Never*), Claudette Colbert (*Private Worlds*), Katharine Hepburn (*Alice Adams*), Miriam Hopkins (*Becky Sharp*), and Merle Oberon (*The Dark Angel*). Bette later commented, "It's common knowledge that I got this first Oscar as a sort of delayed reward for *Of Human Bondage*." She has always maintained that Hepburn gave the better performance in *Alice Adams*. In fact, Bette recently stated, "I still spend my life wishing I looked like Katharine Hepburn!" At the banquet, attended by Hollywood luminaries in formal evening dress, Bette showed up wearing a navy blue and white print dinner dress which caused quite a stir. The following day, the Los Angeles press was not too kind to her.

And how did Warner Bros. reward their prize-winning star?* They rushed into a May 1936 release of *The Golden Arrow*, the latest screen teaming of Bette and her favorite leading man, George Brent. The silly venture sounds like a swashbuckler, but it is not. She poses as an heiress but in reality is a cafeteria cashier who pretends to be a girl of wealth at the behest of a publicity agent (Craig Reynolds). Brent is a journalist who is sent to interview newsworthy Bette and she talks him into marrying her. The action has them both sporting various black eyes and, at the fade-out, they face the camera to reveal that each has the same eye blackened. So much for Bette's first attempt at screwball comedy, a forte monopolized by Carole Lombard and later by Irene Dunne.

She begged Warner Bros. to loan her to RKO for John Ford's *Mary of Scotland* (1936), but they refused and Katharine Hepburn and Florence Eldredge starred in that historical drama. She then requested the female lead in Warners' *Anthony Adverse* (1936), but Jack L. Warner decided the younger and prettier Olivia de Havilland warranted that part (even though Bette had been the public's choice in a *Photoplay* magazine contest). Bette balked at her next assignment as a lady of mystery in *The Man in the Black Hat*, which was released as *Satan Met a Lady* (1936). Warner asked her to play the role, saying that he would find better things for her in the future. She agreed.

Satan Met a Lady is the second and weakest of the three screen versions of Dashiell Hammett's *The Maltese Falcon*. The 1931 edition starred Bebe Daniels and Ricardo Cortez; the 1941 version boasted Humphrey Bogart and Mary Astor. In the 1936 variation, directed by William Dieterle, the Falcon becomes a ram's horn encrusted with jewels. Bette, as Valerie Purvis, hires private detective Ted Shane (Warren William) to help her retrieve the object. There are a few dead bodies en route, and Valerie is the killer. The oddest transformation in the vitiated storyline is having the rotund Caspar Gutman portrayed by Alison Skipworth as Madame Barabbas. Bosley Crowther in the *New York Times* assessed Bette's case with, "After viewing *Satan Met a Lady* all thinking people must acknowledge that a 'Bette Davis Reclamation Project' (BDRP) to prevent the waste of this gifted lady's talents would not be a too-drastic addition to our various programs for the conservation of natural resources."

---

* To this day it still has never been decided just who supplied the nickname Oscar to the Academy Award trophy. Davis used to claim she did, explaining that the backside of the statuette reminded her of Harmon Oscar Nelson; Margaret Herrick, one-time executive director of the Academy, stated she titled the Award after her uncle, while columnist Sidney Skolsky insisted it was he who titled the prize.

Several possible Warner projects for Bette were considered, but did not see the light of day. Besides the aforementioned *Napoleon* with Edward G. Robinson, the studio thought of teaming Bette and Robinson in *Money Man* and *The Gamblers,* the latter to feature Errol Flynn and Basil Rathbone. On completion of *Satan Met a Lady,* Warner had delivered to Bette a script of what was to be a Technicolor feature of lumberjacking in the Washington state woods. It was Warner's wish that she be the woman of *God's Country and the Woman* (1936). She has called the part "stupid" and noted that "the heroine was an insufferable bore who scowled while everyone kept yelling 'Timber!' " She refused to accept the assignment. She stormed into Warner's office and told him to go ahead without her, that "if I never acted again in my life, I was not going to play in *God's Country.* It was now a matter of my own self-respect." Warner hit back with the revelation that he had taken an option on a new novel, *Gone with the Wind,* and if she were a good girl, he would star her as the heroine. "I bet it's a pip!" she is reported to have replied angrily and swept off the Warner lot. (She was replaced in *God's Country* by Beverly Roberts.) Bette was put on suspension by Warner Bros. for three months, minus salary, but she told pressmen, "If I continue to appear in mediocre pictures, I'll have no career worth fighting for."

As she sat out the first few weeks of suspension at the Nelson home at Laguna Beach, she was approached by Ludovico Toeplitz, a British filmmaker of Italian birth. He offered her two continental productions, the first to be made in Italy with Douglass Montgomery (entitled *I'll Take the Low Road*), the second to be made in France with Maurice Chevalier. After deciding that her Warner contract would not bind her abroad, she accepted. With Ham, she flew to Vancouver, Canada, then traveled across Canada to Montreal from where she sailed to England on board the *Duchess of Bedford.* They thought they were being quite clever traveling on a Sunday when court injunctions could not be served, which would prevent her from leaving the continent. But on their arrival in London, they were met by a process server. Bette was confident that the English courts would come to her defense, and hired brilliant barrister, Sir William Jowitt. Jack L. Warner had also arrived in England with his wife and, after preliminary discussions with Toeplitz which proved inconclusive, the matter went to court. The prosecution maintained that her stubbornness was born out of a desire for higher salary (she was making $1,700 per week), an accusation that was false. Her defense was that she wanted roles commensurate with her abilities. Her husband, at this point, was forced to return to the United States to look for work and she was alone on foreign lands to fight for her career. It was one of the most gallant moments of her illustrious life to date, a situation no less vital for the many retellings in the years since. She lost the initial case and intended to appeal when Mr. George Arliss visited her and suggested that she give it up and go back to Hollywood. "Go back gracefully and accept the decision," he urged. "You haven't lost as much as you think." In November 1936, she sailed for New York to "face the music" at Warners.

Back in Burbank, Jack L. Warner informed her that he would reimburse her for half her lawyer fees, would raise her salary, and handed her the script of *Marked Woman* (1937), which she considered to be worthy of her talents. Warner had not bought *Gone with the Wind;* it had been acquired by David O. Selznick. Warner did offer to release the film through their facilities if Selznick cast Errol Flynn as Rhett Butler and Bette as Scarlett O'Hara, but Bette refused to consider playing opposite Flynn at that later juncture. She would accept Clark Gable as the male lead, but by this time Selznick had decided to find a fresh face to star as the fiery O'Hara girl.

Davis was seen as Mary Dwight, a hostess in a clip joint, in *Marked Woman.* The business is owned by underworld King Johnny Vanning (Eduardo Ciannelli), who kills one of Mary's suckers (Damian O'Flynn) after he refuses to pay his exorbitant tab. In court, Mary's testimony helps to free Vanning. But

In the Place de la
Concorde, Paris, in
September 1936 with her
husband, Harmon
"Ham" Nelson.

With Humphrey Bogart
in *Marked Woman*
('37).

With fellow Oscar winner Victor McLaglen at the Los Angeles Biltmore Hotel (March 6, 1936).

With co-player and co-Oscar winner Fay Bainter and Jack L. Warner at the Oscars (March 3, 1939).

when her young sister (Jane Bryan) joins the club and is murdered by one of Vanning's men, Mary agrees to help the district attorney's special prosecutor David Graham (Humphrey Bogart) present a case against Vanning. Later, Mary is kidnapped and beaten by Vanning's men. They cut a scar across the right side of her face. She solicits the other girls who work for Vanning to testify against him. Together they all leave the courtroom. Graham follows them and tells Mary that he would like to do something more for her and suggests that they will meet again. She replies matter-of-factly, "What's the use of stalling? We both live in different worlds and that's the way we've got to leave it."

Variety responded to Bette's comeback feature with, "There is little doubt that, as an actress, Bette Davis has got it, and *Marked Woman* will help cement that fact. She is among the Hollywood few who can submerge themselves in a role to the point where they become the character they are playing." *Marked Woman* was based on the true story of racketeer Charles "Lucky" Luciano who had been prosecuted by New York District Attorney Thomas E. Dewey with the help of testimony from Luciano's team of prostitutes.

While Bette was busy on the soundstages of Warner Bros., Harmon Nelson chose to remain in New York where he had cut a record with Jimmy Dorsey's Orchestra and where he now concentrated on learning the business of music. It was hoped that he would return to California to open an office for a music firm.

Bette was also delighted with her next film, *Kid Galahad* (1937), in which she is cabaret singer Louise "Fluff" Phillips, mistress of pugnacious, cigar-smoking fight-promoter Nick Donati (Edward G. Robinson). The big discovery of the ring is Ward Guisenberry (Wayne Morris) who is dubbed "Kid Galahad" by Fluff because of his gallant manners. The Kid becomes champion but the promoter is gunned down by his crooked rival (Humphrey Bogart), and Fluff, who once had dreams of becoming a Broadway singing success, is left alone to disappear into the dark night. (It would be remade by Warner Bros.

in 1941 as *The Wagons Roll at Night,* switching the profession to the world of circuses, with Humphrey Bogart and Sylvia Sidney; and United Artists would remake it under its original title in 1962 with Elvis Presley and Lola Albright.

In the midst of a truce period, Warner Bros. and Bette agreed upon *That Certain Woman* (1937), a remake of Gloria Swanson's *The Trespasser* (1929), as Miss Davis' next vehicle. Edmund Goulding who had written and directed the earlier production—which had won Miss Swanson an Oscar nomination—repeated his duties on the updated version. The story was still unmitigated suds: a gangster's moll turns legitimate by getting a job as secretary to a married lawyer (Ian Hunter). They fall in love, but his marital status prevents any legalized union. She then meets rich boy (Henry Fonda) and marries the handsome man, but the marriage is annulled by his irate father (Donald Crisp). She is pregnant, however, and has a son. When the lawyer dies, he leaves a sizable bequest to her and her son, but she turns the boy over to Fonda and his new wife (Anita Louise) who has been crippled in a car accident. She then travels to Europe to forget the past, but Fonda finds her after his wife dies and the two rediscover each other under happier terms. It is all soap opera at its 1937 best (more kindly referred to as "a woman's picture"), and the final product demonstrated that Bette could not only handle her accustomed dramatics but could appear as sophisticated as Norma Shearer if given the opportunity.

One of the more overlooked screwball comedies of the Thirties is *It's Love I'm After,* Bette's fourth and final 1937 release. She continues to dismiss it as a poor attempt at comedy, but it reveals her at her chic best, capable at last of interplaying fully with the special charms of Leslie Howard. In roles which are take-offs on Alfred Lunt and Lynn Fontanne, Howard and Bette are stage actors who seemingly adore each other although they fight continuously. They have set a marriage date eleven times but have postponed the event each time. With Olivia de Havilland as a stagestruck heiress and Patric Knowles as her indulgent fiancé, there is an engaging quartet to interchange double takes and double entendres. At the finale, Bette's Joyce Arden decided she had best get Howard to a minister before he gets into further difficulties. The box-office results and Bette's performance proved that it was a wise decision to have allowed her to handle the role rather than Gertrude Lawrence or Ina Claire, both of whom had been originally suggested for the part.

Warners refused Bette one role which she now wanted, that of a street girl named Nana in the pending *The Life of Emile Zola* (1937) which was to star Paul Muni. Jack L. Warner thought the part too small and unflattering for a star of Bette's obvious magnitude and instead assigned Erin O'Brien-Moore to play the tart who inspires Zola's novel *Nana*. And of course there was still industry talk and public conjecture—thanks to crafty publicity-conscious David O. Selznick—that Bette still just might play Scarlett in *Gone with the Wind*. But when it was agreed that MGM would loan the services of Clark Gable for Rhett Butler in exchange for the financial privilege of releasing the epic, George Cukor was set as the (initial) director. Doubtlessly remembering the Bette Davis of the Rochester stock company days, he was in agreement with the Hollywood forces who thought she did not have sufficient sex appeal for the demanding part.

Perhaps to prove differently to the industry and to the public, Warner Bros. acquired the screen rights to *Jezebel** as the first of Bette's two 1938 releases. No longer would she be cranking out five or six program features per year; each of her motion pictures would now be an occasion heralded by the company and long anticipated by the public. The film was based on the short-lived 1933 Broadway play by Owen Davis, Sr., which had starred Miriam Hopkins (replacing an ailing Tallulah

Bankhead). Warners pulled out the stoppers on this production, budgeting the epic at $1.25 million. Although filmed in black-and-white, the Orry-Kelly designed gowns cost $30,000 alone, and all props and furniture used (if one is to have faith in the press releases) were antiques. Bette even loaned the studio the use of her heirloom candlesticks with hurricane chimneys.

Production began on October 21, 1937, and concluded on January 18, 1938, by which time her co-leading man, Henry Fonda, had left the production to go east to be with his wife who was expecting a baby. (The child was daughter Jane.) This situation would force Davis to handle several close-up shots without the offcamera services of Fonda to read his lines. Of more immediate concern to Bette was that producer Hal B. Wallis had selected William Wyler to direct the expansive film. She had never forgotten (or forgiven) his callous remark at Universal when she tested for *A House Divided*. As she would recollect in her autobiography, "Mr. Wyler, not remembering me or the incident, was, to put it mildly, taken back when I told him my grim little tale of woe. He was genuinely apologetic, saying he had come a long way since those days. I could not help believing he was sincere. With no revenge left in me, I started work on *Jezebel*." It was Davis who saved perfectionist Wyler from being fired from the project by promising Warner to work late each evening to help alleviate the slow production progress of the methodical director.

The lead character of Julie Marsden, in Bette's words, "was a blood sister of Scarlett's. Willful, perverse, and proud, she was every inch the Southern belle." Julie is a spirited, unconventional New Orleans beauty of the mid-1850s who loves Preston Dillard (Fonda), a hardworking, handsome young banker. He is not one to bend easily to her demands, and, to show her independence, she wears a (strapless, Orry-Kelly) red dress to the annual ball which is traditionally a white-gowned affair. In those days, a red dress indicated that the wearer was a scarlet woman and her blatant defiance of tradition alienates

---

* In *Mother Goddam*, Miss Davis relates that she urged the studio for over a year to purchase the screen rights to *Jezebel*. "J. L. asked me why? He insisted no one would want to see a film about a girl who wore a red dress to the New Orleans Comos Ball. The custom was to wear a white dress. I told Warner only ten million women would want to see this film. As it turned out, I was right."

her from her friends at the ball and causes Pres to sever their relationship. He leaves New Orleans while she pines away, confident that he will return to her, much as Scarlett O'Hara in *Gone with the Wind* has an almost enduring faith in her eventual capturing of Ashley Wilkes.

Pres does return, but it is with his Yankee wife (Margaret Lindsay). Before Julie is aware of Pres' wife, she puts on a white gown and sweeps into the living room, "Pres, I can't believe it's you heah. I've dreamed about it so long, a lifetime. No, longer than that. I put on this white dress to help me tell ya how humbly I ask ya to forgive me. Pres, I'm kneelin' t'ya to ask ya to forgive me and love me as I love you! When he then introduces his wife, Julie is dumbfounded. "Pres' wife!. . . You're funning. . . .Married. . . .My felicitations, Pres."

Later, wild with rage, Julie informs another admirer, Buck Cantrell (George Brent), that Pres has humiliated her and Buck challenges him to a duel. Before Pres can take part in such a duel, however, he is called away to the city where a mild yellow-fever epidemic has made his bank short-handed. His younger brother (Richard Cromwell) fights the duel for him and kills Buck. Thereafter, when Pres is stricken with the fever, Julie pleads with his stunned wife to permit her to accompany him to Lazarette Island for quarantine. Underlined by a sensitive Max Steiner score, this scene offered Davis what would become her typical moment of teary martyrdom. Audiences then (and now) could not help but be emotionally drawn to this self-sacrificing creature, no matter what her past actions. "Amy [Lindsay], of course it's your right to go. . . .You're his wife. But are you fit to go? Lovin' him isn't enough. If you gave him all your strength, would it be enough?. . .Do you know the Creole word for fever powder. . .for food and water?. . .His life and yours will hang on just things like that . . . and you'll both surely die."

Film Weekly called Bette's performance as Julie Marsden her "decisive victory," and noted that "she handles it as though, having brought her enemies to their knees, she has decided to be merciful. By the pure power of imaginative acting she gives a performance as vivid and inspiring as any star display of personality—and an infinitely deeper level of truth." *Time* magazine, which published a cover story on Bette Davis for its March 28, 1938, issue, was not flattering in its comparison of the film *Jezebel* and the best-selling novel *Gone with the Wind,* but the public thoroughly endorsed the film—causing David O. Selznick to seethe that Jack L. Warner had stolen the thunder from Metro's *Gone with the Wind.*

Although Bette had declined to star with Errol Flynn in *Gone with the Wind,* Bette was placed opposite him in *The Sisters* (1938), an early 1900s story involving the San Francisco earthquake and fire of 1906. She inherited the role of Louise Elliot from Kay Francis (in disfavor at the Warner lot) and Miriam Hopkins (newly signed to a Warner Bros. contract—many thought as back-up insurance in case Bette became temperamental again). Bette was given the role as another consolation offering after having been suspended by Warner Bros. for refusing both *Comet over Broadway* (1937) and *Garden of the Moon* (1938). Kay Francis was in the former, while Margaret Lindsay took the feminine lead in the latter.

Containing stock footage from *Old San Francisco* (1927) and *Frisco Jenny* (1933), *The Sisters* is definitely a "woman's picture" in that it tells of the struggles of Louise Elliot who marries for love while her other two sisters (Anita Louise and Jane Bryan) wed for money (Alan Hale) and adolescent worship (Dick Foran) respectively. Louise's husband, Frank Medlin (Flynn), is a proud newspaper reporter unable to settle down into domesticity. He turns to alcohol and then disappears. The earthquake occurs and she, with child, searches vainly for him. She retreats to safer Oakland, across the bay, where she suffers a miscarriage while boarding within a brothel. She returns to San Francisco never giving up hope that Frank will one day come home. She takes a job as secretary to a department store owner (Ian Hunter) who promptly falls in love with her. At a political ball honoring the inauguration of President William Taft, Frank appears at the event, on a balcony overlooking the ballroom. The three sisters stand together looking up at him, and Louise runs into his arms. Although he has been absent for three years, her love has not diminished and she heartily welcomes him back. Originally the film was to end without Frank's return, but the studio feared it would damage the box-office potential of the period offering, and the contrived new finale was devised.

Under the direction of Anatole Litvak (who had the previous year wed Miriam Hopkins), Bette offered herself in a new light as a rather docile, compliant creature who realizes that her man's needs and demands must come first. Offscreen she was aghast and hurt that Warner acceded to Flynn's insistence that he receive top billing in the production, proving that "the first lady of the screen" (*The Hollywood Reporter*) was not impervious to the whims of star status. Of her less than demanding acting chores in *The Sisters, Variety* kindly offered, "She turns in one of her most scintillating performances." Little has been written, except in Bette's autobiography, about the totalitarian attitude of director Litvak and how close to fatal mishap Bette came to during the staged earthquake scenes.

In October 1938, Bette separated from Harmon Nelson, now a Los Angeles advertising man. Unstated at that time, but suggested in *The Lonely Life,* is that another man was the cause of the final dissolution of the Nelson-Davis union. Unlike some recent celebrity biographies which have fabricated VIP love affairs to spice the narrative, one has faith that Miss Davis—as in other matters—does not lie. According to her, he was "the only man I ever met whom I could respect in every way. However, his strength, his brilliance, were such that I felt endangered. I was afraid his domination would affect my career. I genuinely fell in love with this titan who shattered every preconceived notion—every single dream. He was capable of taking complete charge and I was petrified. The relationship was tempestuous to the point of madness and I resisted the loss of my sovereignty to the

end. . . .The man of my life married another. Afterwards I was told, characteristically, that Tuesdays would be 'our day' (just like that, he said so)! Tuesdays! They weren't for me or Ruth Elizabeth!"

In November 1938, Bette made the statement, "There will be no reconciliation. Harmon will apply for a divorce." The following day he filed for divorce charging that she "neglected and failed to perform her duties as a wife" and that she "flew into a rage when asked to exhibit evidence of conjugal affection." He further said that she preferred to spend her time at home reading. The divorce was finalized on Friday, January 20, 1939. Now Bette's family consisted of mother Ruthie, sister Bobby, and faithful female Scottie dog, Tibby. Harmon Nelson, who later rewed, would die in October 1975. Interestingly enough, few of his obituaries even mentioned that he had once been married to Miss Davis.

That same month—January 1939—the Academy Award nominations were revealed for 1938. Bette was a nominee as Best Actress for *Jezebel.* There was no doubt that she would take Oscar home for a second time. She accepted the statuette at the Biltmore Hotel on Thursday, February 23, 1939. Her competition consisted of Fay Bainter (*White Banners*), Wendy Hiller (*Pygmalion*), Norma Shearer (*Marie Antoinette*), and Margaret Sullavan (*Three Comrades*). Miss Bainter was also nominated in the Best Supporting Actress category for *Jezebel* and won. This was the last time that a player was permitted nomination in both categories. Bette properly credits Fay Bainter's performance in *Jezebel* as providing the needed basis for her own characterization. It is Bainter's Aunt Belle who says of her niece, "I'm thinkin' about a woman called Jezebel, who did wrong in the sight of God." It is interesting to note that Miss Bainter's actress niece Dorothy Burgess had been Bette's co-worker and friend back in her Rochester, New York, days.

Prior to the Academy Award presentations, Bette had completed *Dark Victory* (1939), derived from the play by George Emerson Brewer, Jr., and Bertram Block which had been short-lived on Broadway in 1934 with Tallulah Bankhead. At one time Gloria Swanson had wanted to film the project; in 1935, David O. Selznick considered it for Greta Garbo and Fredric March; later in the Thirties, Samuel Goldwyn had purchased the screen rights for Merle Oberon or Marlene Dietrich, but in a fit of anger at Miss Oberon he had sold the rights to Warner Bros. where Irene Dunne had been the initial choice for the role of Judith Traherne.

During the filming, Bette was distraught from her divorce proceedings. She even asked director Edmund Goulding to release her because she was so upset. "Stay upset," he told her after viewing the rushes, and she was kept in the film. The role of Judith Traherne of the "station wagon set" is one of Bette's most famous and enduring. She is a spoiled rich girl accustomed to having her own way, but sudden blinding headaches curtail her activities. She is persuaded to visit Dr. Frederick Steele (George Brent) who agrees to operate, but later confides to their mutual friend Ann King (Geraldine Fitzgerald) that Judith's brain tumor will return. This time it will cause her death. Later, she learns the truth ("prognosis negative") but agrees to wed the doctor and to live for the present. They retire to a Vermont farm where, along with Ann and a housekeeper (Virginia Brissac), they enjoy a short but idyllic joint existence.

One afternoon, as Steele prepares to leave for a medical conference, Judith's eyesight begins to fail which indicates that the end is near. In the film's most touching sequence of events, she keeps the fact from him and in bidding him goodbye for what will be the final time, she says, "Nothing can hurt us now. What we have can't be destroyed. That's our victory. Our victory over the dark." With the help of Ann, she plants hyacinth bulbs in the garden. Then, calmly, bravely, she goes alone to her upstairs bedroom, lies down on the bed, and awaits death.*

* During the shooting of the telling death scene finale in *Dark Victory,* Bette's slow climb up the staircase was accompanied by a loud Max Steiner musical theme. Finding it quite distracting, she asked Hal B. Wallis, "Who's doing this scene . . . Max Steiner or me? It can't be both of us; so one of us has to go."

Having seen the completed film, Warner Bros. was forced to admit that their initial skepticism about the project was groundless. An extensive, impressive advertising campaign alerted the public, "Out of the blazing fires of her genius, the screen's most gifted actress has created a gallery of unforgettable women. Now Bette Davis, the winner of two Academy Awards, comes to you in the climax of all her dramatic triumphs. In the role she has waited eight [sic] years to play. In the greatest picture of a woman's love that the world has yet seen. See *Dark Victory,* a Warner Bros. picture, at your theatre Easter Week!"

Of the character she portrayed, Bette has said, "Judy Traherne is what I'm like. She was at least ninety percent me." Frank S. Nugent in the *New York Times* rated her "superb" while *Time* magazine printed that she "plucks every heartstring she can lay a finger on" and called the film "one of the best star vehicles Hollywood has produced this year." Bette, always an enthusiastic radio dramatic star, would recreate her role on "Lux Radio Theatre" on January 7, 1940, with Spencer Tracy and Lurene Tuttle her costars. The film would be remade in 1963 by United Artists as *Stolen Hours* with Susan Hayward and Michael Craig starring, and revamped as a 1976 telefeature with Elizabeth Montgomery and Anthony Hopkins.

Beginning with *Jezebel,* musical scores really played an integral part of the Bette Davis feature films. None was as impressive as Erich Wolfgang Korngold's score for *Juarez* (1939), adapted from the novel *The Phantom Crown* by Bertita Harding and the play *Juarez and Maximilian* by Franz Werfel. In her third costume picture, Bette (in black wig) is Carlota von Habsburg, wife to Maximilian (Brian Aherne), the French-designated Emperor of Mexico. She journeys to France to implore Napoleon III (Claude Rains) to help her husband in his fight in Mexico against the Mexican nationalist Benito Juarez (Paul Muni). When Napoleon declines to help, the high-strung Carlota, knowing that her husband is doomed, goes insane. "Help me. . . help me," she pleads, "they want to kill me."

She says, "The Evil One. He is trying to poison me. Help me to get to my husband." Maximilian's position is hopeless and he is stranded in Mexico where he is executed by Juarez's troops. The film was shot in two segments, ironically vitiating Bette's desire to work on the project so that she and Paul Muni could again act together before the cameras. Using posh sets and palaces, the Maximilian-Carlota portion of the narrative was lensed first. Then the sets were torn down and replaced with the shabbier ones used to depict the struggle of Juarez. The advertisements for the costly feature proclaimed, "A story so momentous that it required six Academy Award winners and a cast of 1186 players." Unfortunately, the film was not a success.

In the midst of her tremendously active 1939 screen year*—four major features—Bette finally bought a house. Whereas once she had rented a prior Garbo abode at $750 monthly, she now ensconced herself, her mother, sister, and three dogs in a compact, but still roomy, English farmhouse in Glendale named Riverbottom. It was only about five minutes away from the Burbank studio, which helped to alleviate the burden of arriving at the lot at 5:00 A.M. whenever she made a costume picture.

"This, above all, Bette's Best!" the advertisements informed eager fans regarding her next film, *The Old Maid* (1939). Originally a novel by Edith Wharton, it was dramatized by Zöe Akins and won a Pulitzer Prize as the best play of the 1934 Broadway season. The drama had starred Judith Anderson (as Delia) and Helen Menken (as Charlotte) and was known along Broadway as a "matinee show" because of its great appeal to feminine audiences. Producer Hal B. Wallis astutely bought the screen rights for Bette and starred her with Miriam Hopkins. George Brent was in support. Wallis' screen comedienne wife Louise Fazenda played a small but key role as Dora, the maid.

* During this period Davis was earning $4,000 per week, in comparison to James Cagney's $12,500, Edward G. Robinson's $8,500, Claude Rains' $6,000, George Raft's $5,500, Errol Flynn's $5,000, Pat O'Brien's $4,000, George Brent's $2,000, Frank McHugh's $1,600, John Garfield's $1,500, and Humphrey Bogart's $1,250.

Again in costumes of the mid-1800s, Bette is Charlotte Lovell, who comforts Clem Spender (Brent) after he is thrown aside by her willful cousin, Delia (Hopkins), who chooses to wed a man of means (Jerome Cowan). Clem departs for the Civil War and is killed at the battle of Vicksburg, leaving Charlotte alone and pregnant. To save her family the disgrace of unwed motherhood, she goes to the Far West to have a baby girl and returns to open a nursery school for war orphans, one of whom is her daughter, Tina. When Delia learns that Tina is Charlotte's daughter by Clem, she maliciously convinces her husband's brother (James Stephenson) not to marry Charlotte because of her ill health. When Delia's husband later dies she welcomes Charlotte and Tina into her home where the child grows up calling Delia "mother" and calling Charlotte "aunt." Now an adult, Tina (Jane Bryan) is about to marry Lanning Halsey (William Lundigan) and Charlotte, the night before the wedding, is determined to tell Tina the truth about her heritage. It was a scene guaranteed to draw tears from even the most stout-hearted viewer. She informs Delia, "Tonight she belongs to me! Tonight I want her to call me mother!" But she is unable to bare the truth. Now a frigid, stern-faced old maid, Charlotte receives a goodbye kiss from Tina as she embarks on her honeymoon.

As with the controversy over who really named Oscar *Oscar*, much conjecture, with little verification, has surrounded the notorious Davis-Hopkins feud that allegedly spewed forth on the set of *The Old Maid*. There is no doubt that the crafty, covetous Miss Hopkins was astutely aware of each and every bid she made for attention with her producers and the public, and that having passed through her Paramount and Samuel Goldwyn phases of Hollywood stardom, she was determined to become the Queen of the Warner Bros. lot. Miriam sometimes offered her best performances offcamera, flirtatiously and outrageously cajoling the sternest of filmmakers to her instant bidding. But she met her match in gusty Bette Davis who never had any use for vanity, pretense, or devious meth-

With Olivia de Havilland in *The Private Lives of Elizabeth and Essex* ('39).

→

In 1939.

With Miriam Hopkins in *The Old Maid* ('39).

210

ods. The late Miss Hopkins, sadly neglected in her declining professional years, can no longer defend herself, but Bette has stated that she was "her own worst enemy. I usually had better things to do than waste my energies on invective and cat fights."

But for the public during the fall of 1939 it was a different matter. Studio publicists heightened the supposed rivalry between the co-stars, and *Life* magazine reported, "The fact that Davis and Hopkins dislike each other intensely not only added to their pleasure in making the picture, but also proved so mutually stimulating that Hal Wallis, Warner Bros. production chief, plans to team them again in *Devotion*. [The story of the Bronte sisters was eventually made in 1943—released in 1946—and starred Ida Lupino and Olivia de Havilland.] Part of the jealousy between Misses Hopkins and Davis may be due to the fact that the stage version of *Jezebel,* starring Hopkins, lasted only four weeks, while the movie version got Bette Davis her second Academy Award." Not mentioned in the report was that on the set Miriam continually tried to upstage Bette, that in a highly dramatic segment deleted later from the release print, Miriam wore an exact copy of one of Bette's *Jezebel* costumes, and that despite the demand of the script that each co-star was to age, Miriam continued to look as young as an ingenue. At any rate, the public adored the film, adding yet another consolation to Bette's disappointment over Vivien Leigh having been hired to be Scarlett O'Hara in *Gone with the Wind.*

With three films in release during 1939, Bette was a tremendously valuable box-office commodity. She next was rushed into work on the story of England's Queen Elizabeth's love affair with the Earl of Essex adapted from Maxwell Anderson's play, *Elizabeth the Queen.* The play had been produced on Broadway in 1930 with Lynn Fontanne and Alfred Lunt in the leads, and would later be revived in 1966 with Judith Anderson and Donald Davis. Dame Judith and Charlton Heston played the leads in a 1968 TV special.

Bette would have much preferred that Laurence Olivier portray Essex, but Warner had other ideas and cast their swashbuckling box-office magnet, Errol Flynn, in the part. At his insistence, the title was changed to *The Knight and the Lady* but, in a counter bid, Bette persuaded the studio heads to reconsider. It emerged as *The Private Lives of Elizabeth and Essex* (1939), commonly abbreviated due to limited theatre marquee space as *Elizabeth and Essex.* Seeking authenticity in the role of the aging, powerful Queen Elizabeth,* Bette shaved the forward portion of her head, shaved away her eyebrows, and insisted that bags be drawn beneath her eyes. It was her first film in Technicolor, and she wore pasty-colored makeup and the heavy hooped gowns of the period.

In the proceedings, short on action but long on words (which bothered director Michael Curtiz), Essex has just returned from defeating the Spanish Fleet and been heralded as England's hero of the moment. He is received by his Queen who is in love with him and, after chiding him for the loss of her treasure ship, she states that "I don't know which I hate the most, you for making me love you or myself for needing it." And so progresses the narrative as the daring, vain Essex battles his love for glory and adventure with intermittent attempts to seduce the Queen into becoming his pawn. His enemies at court, chief among whom is Sir Walter Raleigh (Vincent Price), do their best to create enmity between the two lovers. Also sparking the flames of her regal doubts is Lady Penelope Gray (Olivia de Havilland), the young lady-in-waiting who openly loves the handsome Essex. In measured prose, the drama comes to a conclusion when Essex returns from Ireland, having been defeated by the rebel Tyrone, and seeks revenge on the Queen whom he thinks has betrayed him. His troops take over Whitehall. She disarms him with sweet talk; and he removes his troops, whereupon she has him hauled off to the Tower of London from whence he goes to his beheading. To protect the delicacy of Flynn fans, the climactic de-

* Charles Laughton, who had won an Oscar for *The Private Life of Henry VIII,* visited the set one day and Davis sang out, "Hello Daddy. I have a nerve trying to play Elizabeth at my age!" Laughton responded, "Never stop daring to hang yourself, Bette!"

capitation sequence was deleted from release prints.

Offcamera, Bette certainly did not fall prey to the charms of sex symbol Flynn, and on-screen, it was clear who had emerged the victor. "Bette Davis's Elizabeth is a strong, resolute, glamour-skimping characterization against which Mr. Flynn's Essex has about as much chance as a beanshooter against a tank."

For *Dark Victory,* Bette was nominated for a Best Actress Academy Award but lost, in February 1940, to Vivien Leigh for *Gone with the Wind.* Bette did, however, win the first annual *Redbook* magazine award for her "fine acting" during 1939 and, as she phrased it, "Awards were flowing in from everywhere."

Weighing less than one hundred pounds, Bette took a much needed six-month vacation. She headed east to New England where she stayed at Peckett's Inn at Franconia, a White Mountain (New Hampshire) lodge managed by Arthur Farnsworth. At nearby Sugar Hill, she bought a home which was called Butternut, situated on two hundred acres of rich, New England soil. In 1939, she was named the number six box-office draw in the nation by *Motion Picture Herald* (she was preceded by Mickey Rooney, Tyrone Power, Spencer Tracy, Clark Gable, and Shirley Temple), and was the top attraction of the Warner Bros. studio. She was called "the Fourth Warner Brother" by columnists and was squired about Hollywood by George Brent who was recently divorced from Constance Worth.

While Bette was on holiday, it was strongly rumored that Irene Dunne would play the lead in Warner Bros.' adaptation (140 minutes) of Rachel Field's period (1841) novel, *All This and Heaven Too.* In her effective way, Bette stormed the front office and the part she suddenly coveted was hers. With Anatole Litvak directing, she was Henriette Deluzy Desportes who becomes governess to the children of the Duke (Charles Boyer) and Duchess (Barbara O'Neil) De Praslin. The demonically jealous Duchess immediately thinks that her husband is having an affair with the attractive governess, although the relationship is strictly platonic. She later so enrages the Duke that he murders her and is imprisoned within his home by the authorities. Henriette is named an accomplice in the murder, but the Duke, after taking poison, vindicates her while on his death bed. She goes to America where she takes a teaching post in New York, arranged by her American friend (Jeffrey Lynn). Of Boyer, Bette has said, "[He] was so unbelievably attractive. You didn't want to say 'Good night, Monsieur le Duc,' but 'Here I am!' "

W. Somerset Maughan provided a basis for another Davis triumph with his play, *The Letter*—produced in England with Gladys Cooper, on Broadway in 1927 with Katharine Cornell, and as a film in 1929 with Jeanne Eagels. It would be produced yet again in an updated, uncredited remake entitled *The Unfaithful* (1947) with Ann Sheridan. Howard Koch astutely adapted the play for the film version. William Wyler, now a harmonious Davis enthusiast, directed it. Leslie Crosbie (Bette) kills Geoffrey Hammond (David Newell), a friend to both her and her rubber plantation—owner husband (Herbert Marshall), whom she claims attempted to rape her. Her attorney (James Stephenson) doubts her story which is proved to be a lie when Hammond's Eurasian widow (Gale Sondergaard) produces a letter written to the dead man by Leslie in which she had asked him to visit her the night of the murder. In a finale* demanded by the Hays Office that Leslie pay for her crime (even though she is acquitted by the jury), she is later stabbed to death in the garden by Hammond's widow. Wrote the *Hollywood Reporter,* "The star was never better in a role that called on every ounce of her great ability." Great credit for her haunting performance must go to cinematographer Tony Gaudio and music-composer Max Steiner. *The Letter* would earn Bette her fourth

* Even to this day, Davis believes that William Wyler was wrong in having her character say the climactic line ("With all my heart, I still love the man I killed!") looking directly at her screen husband (Marshall). As she stated on a recent "Dinah Shore Show," she feels it should have been said looking away, in a moment of emotional carelessness, as a revelation that seals the character's fate.

With Jack Carson in *The Bride Came C.O.D.* ('41).

With George Brent and Mary Astor in *The Great Lie* ('41).

With her maid, Edith
Kemp, at the Burbank
lot (August 1942).

With Teresa Wright in
The Little Foxes ('41).

Oscar bid, but she lost the Best Actress Award this time to Ginger Rogers for her change-of-pace role in *Kitty Foyle.*

On Wednesday, December 31, 1940, Bette was married to Arthur Farnsworth at Jane Bryan's ranch in Rimrock, Arizona. (Miss Bryan, a dear friend of Bette's, had married Justin Dart and retired from the screen.) Bette's second husband was thirty-three; she was thirty-two. At that time he was employed by the Minneapolis Honeywell Company as an aircraft technical expert in charge of Air Force training films made at the Walt Disney Studios. Although Butternut was their official home, they rented a house at Laguna Beach, California, which was their honeymoon cottage.

For *The Great Lie* (1941), Bette turned from vixen to sympathetic female in the role of Maggie Patterson, the former fiancée of playboy aviator Pete Van Allen (George Brent). As directed by Edmund Goulding, Bette is the martyr who agrees to adopt the baby that concert pianist Sandra Kovak (Mary Astor) has by Pete. For this very soapy melodrama, Mary Astor was accorded the Best Supporting Actress Academy Award for 1941. Through the years, Miss Astor has repeatedly acknowledged how much she owed to Bette for "giving" her the picture.

In July 1941, perhaps to show her fans that she was still capable of playing celluloid comedy, Bette was seen with James Cagney (he received top billing) in *The Bride Came C.O.D.* In this screwball comedy, Bette is oil-heiress Joan Winfield who finds herself trapped in an old desert ghost town with cocky pilot Cagney. *Time* magazine smartly summed up the project, "*The Bride Came C.O.D.* is a hot-weather hors d'oeuvre. It offers the curious spectacle of the screen's most talented tough guy roughhousing one of the screen's best dramatic actresses through ten reels of slapsticky summertime comedy. The result, seldom hilarious, is often funny."

Samuel Goldwyn "borrowed" Bette to the tune of more than $300,000 to star in his film version of Lillian Hellman's play, *The Little Foxes,* which was released by RKO in 1941. It was sweet revenge for Bette, since Gold-wyn had rejected her in 1929 after viewing her movie test. In 110-degree heat, the production went into full swing at Goldwyn's Los Angeles studio in May 1941. Again directed by William Wyler, a man she could now only greatly admire, Bette was asked to tone down her interpretation of Regina Giddens. She was insistent, however, and stated that she intended to play her part as envisioned by authoress Hellman and as played on Broadway in 1939 by Tallulah Bankhead. Bette walked off the set one day (the only time she had ever deserted a production), but was forced to return when Goldwyn pointed out that she was liable for a legal suit. Although Bette has always maintained that she gave a bad performance and that Miss Bankhead should have had the role, *The Little Foxes* became a major box-office triumph. *Newsweek* magazine applauded the production and its cast (including Herbert Marshall, Teresa Wright, Charles Dingle, Patricia Collinge, and Dan Duryea) and praised Bette with, "[she] jettisons her familiar mannerisms to give a vivid, caustic interpretation of the [southern-accented] conscienceless Regina."

Bette next wanted the supporting role of Cassandra Tower in Warner Bros.' pending *Kings Row* (1942), but Jack L. Warner would not permit her to undertake such a small, if telling, part and it went to ten-year-younger Betty Field. But the Board of Governors of the Academy of Motion Picture Arts and Sciences gave her a special vote of confidence when they elected Bette to the organization's highest post. She was voted the president, to succeed Walter Wanger. She was the first woman to hold that post in the Academy's fourteen-year history.

While vacationing in New York in 1939, Bette had seen the Broadway comedy *The Man Who Came to Dinner* starring Monty Woolley. She enjoyed the play so much that she suggested to Warners that they purchase it as a vehicle for herself and John Barrymore, with whom she was anxious to act. She jokingly said she wanted to play the part of the nurse, Miss Preen (created onstage by Mary Wickes), but, of course, it was again not a large enough part for her. Warners bought the screen rights for $250,000 and tested Barrymore, but found that he was impossible due to his inability to remember lines. Woolley was imported from New York to repeat his role, as was angular Miss Wickes. Bette took on the beefed-up role of Maggie Cutler, the smart aleck, and later in love, secretary to Sheridan Whiteside. Ann Sheridan, then reaching a crest of her popularity as "the oomph girl," had the decorative, breezy role of the flashy actress Lorraine Sheldon, who is commissioned by Whiteside to aid in putting a finish to Maggie's romance with the local newspaperman (Richard Travis). While the film was in production, the Hays Office had slapped a ban on women wearing "revealing" sweaters onscreen, and all of the knit tops which had been designed for Bette to model as Maggie Cutler were scrapped.

It became second nature for Bette's name to appear on the annual list of nominated actresses for the Academy Award, and she alphabetically headed the roll of those up for the Oscar for 1941 performances, this time for *The Little Foxes.* However, she lost to Joan Fontaine *(Suspicion).*

By 1942, Bette was often called "the First Lady of Cinema," eclipsing the once lofty Greta Garbo. As the undisputed Queen of the Warner lot, Bette had reached the status of top actress, a position she had long dreamed of attaining. A co-worker has stated, "Bette's never late. I've never seen her muff a line. She's a quick study, learns easily but always memorizes her scenes the night before." Bette blatantly told the world that she did not like Hollywood and preferred to live in New England. "I shiver each time I see an auction of a star's personal belongings advertised in the papers," she said. "I don't want that to happen to me. I don't want to own anything here I can't pack in a trunk."

If there had been some doubts in the past whether some vehicles had been suitable for the star, there was general agreement that *In This Our Life* (1942) was a bad mistake. Bette admits she was too old (thirty-four) for the role of young, hell-raising Stanley Timberlake, for which makeup artist Perc Westmore gave her Cupid lips, heavy and exaggerated

eyes, and a fluffy hair-do with bangs. It all made her look like a kewpie doll one wins at a county fair. Whether strutting around in a slip, puffing furiously on a cigarette, or rolling her eyes in heavy theatrics, Bette is badly miscast in this inferior version of Ellen Glasgow's novel. Co-workers such as Olivia de Havilland (as her sister Roy), Dennis Morgan (her lover, married to Roy), and George Brent (the man with whom Roy seeks consolation and whom Stanley covets) could not help to elevate this venture immodestly directed by John Huston. Bette has recently written, "As a finished product, *In This Our Life* was a mistake. It was a real box-office failure." What she did not care to add was that at the time of filming *In This Our Life,* John Huston was carrying on a romance with Olivia de Havilland, and Bette became more than miffed when too many flattering close-ups were given to de Havilland. Eventually, Huston left the project and Raoul Walsh completed the film. Before the picture was released, Davis had won her victory to have her share of close-ups be more in keeping with her star status. Despite everything, Bette and Olivia would become good friends.

An auspicious offspring of the film was the friendship that developed between Bette and Olivia de Havilland. Although they had worked together twice before on the soundstages, Miss de Havilland had been intimidated by the formidable Davis and was unable to strike up a friendship. During the filming of this later picture, however, they were able to reach a meeting of souls and became lifelong buddies.

After another run-in with the studio when she was ordered to leave the premises to begin a contractual twelve-week inactive period without pay (because she wanted to perform publicity duties for *In This Our Life),* Bette returned to a salary increase and a revised contract asking for three pictures yearly. The first was *Now, Voyager* (1942), for which she had to fight. The film was scripted by Casey Robinson from the novel by Olive Higgins Prouty. Although it was directed by Irving Rapper, Bette allegedly gave free advice to the director and also changed dialogue as the

With Olivia de Havilland in *In This Our Life* ('42).

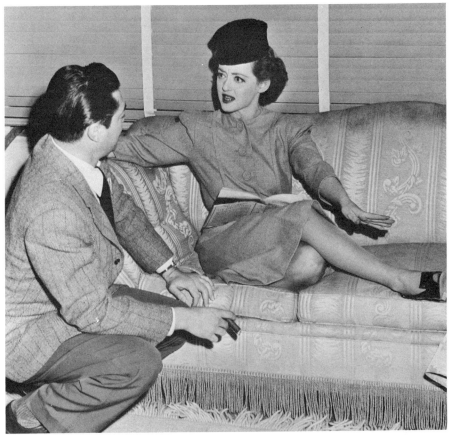

With director Vincent Sherman on the set of *Old Acquaintance* ('43).

With Ilka Chase and John Loder in *Now, Voyager* ('42).

filming progressed—both to the betterment of the finished product.

Next to *Dark Victory* and the later *All About Eve, Now, Voyager,* the telling tale of a Back Bay Boston frump who turns into a glamorous, worldly, independent woman, is Bette's best known feature. At the start, she is the spinsterish Charlotte Vale, with hair worn in a bun at the back of her head, large spectacles, sensible shoes with low heels, and plain, uninspiring dresses which do not camouflage her dumpy figure, and who is forced to retreat to her bedroom whenever her dominating blue-blood mother (Gladys Cooper) chooses to goad her. But thanks to the dramatic therapy of Dr. Jaquith (Claude Rains), a renowned psychiatrist, and to a South American ocean cruise where she meets and falls in love with Jerry Durrence (Paul Henreid), both of which aid the belated blossoming of her own character, she becomes a radiant, attractive woman. In the familiar storyline, her mother suffers a fatal heart attack, Charlotte breaks her engagement to wealthy Elliott Livingston (John Loder) because of her abiding attachment to married Jerry, and she becomes the unselfish den mother to Jerry's emotionally disturbed child, Tina (Janis Wilson). In an appropriately full swell of Max Steiner music, the 118-minute feature comes to a heady, satisfactory finale of self-denial. It is agreed that Tina will remain with Charlotte and that Jerry will make discreet visits to see "our child."

> *Jerry:* And will you be happy, Charlotte?
> *Charlotte:* Oh, Jerry, don't let's ask for the moon. . . . We have the stars. (The camera pans heavenward, fade-out, the end.)

For the fifth consecutive year, Bette was Oscar-nominated. In her sixth competition, she lost to Greer Garson for MGM's *Mrs. Miniver.* Max Steiner won an Oscar for his Tchaikovsky-like score for the box-office draw, *Now, Voyager.* The pop song "It Can't Be Wrong" was derived from "Charlotte's Theme" and there is an amazing similarity between the theme of *Now, Voyager* and that of Charles Chaplin's score for his *A Countess from Hong Kong* (1967).

In April 1943, Bette was once again feuding with her employers and reportedly lost to Ida Lupino the lead role in Warner Bros.' proposed film version of *Ethan Frome* which had been bought expressly for Bette. This project would later be slated for Jane Wyman, with some location filming done but then abandoned. It has not yet been realized on the screen. More worrisome to Bette than any of the younger competition on the Warner lot was the arrival from MGM of Miss Joan Crawford. Four years Bette's senior, she was the antithesis of the Burbank monarch in nearly every conceivable way except in their mutual devotion to survival at the top of stardom, and each would continue to have a fascinating hold on the public's spirit. While in later years Bette would gladly converse with talk show hosts and magazine interviewers about most every aspect of her career—both public and private—to date the public has not been made privy to the (sub)conscious campaign Bette waged to insure that she, and not newcomer Miss Crawford, was the champ at Warner Bros.

Hal B. Wallis purchased the screen rights to *Watch on the Rhine* (1943) following its Broadway success in 1941 with Paul Lukas, Mady Christians, and Lucile Watson. Lukas was signed to repeat his stage role of the Resistance leader and Bette was requested to play his wife, the studio counting on her name to give the production box-office impetus. Just as she felt that helping to organize the Hollywood Canteen for the diversion of servicemen was her patriotic duty, likewise she was convinced that participating in this message film would be useful in the Allied fight against the Axis powers in World War II. Plainly dressed, she is Sara Muller who returns to her suburban Washington, D.C., home with her husband, the leader of an European anti-Nazi underground movement, and their three youngsters. Once there Muller is forced to kill the devious Count de Brancovis (George Coulouris) who threatens to turn him over to the American Nazis. Muller then returns to Third Reich Germany alone where he hopes to free other members of the movement who have been imprisoned by the Gestapo. Sara bids him farewell (in a very well modulated scene), knowing that she will never see him again. Lukas won the Best Actor Academy Award for his performance.

From the beginning of the war, Bette had been active in selling bonds in her territory, designated by the U.S. government as Missouri and Oklahoma. In the latter state, she was made an honorary Indian chief and became known as "Princess Laughing Eyes." In Hollywood, she and John Garfield continued with preparations for founding the Hollywood Canteen which provided a home away from home for servicemen. A good deal of the funds needed for the continuation of the entertainment forum would be provided from the proceeds of the all-star Warner Bros. feature *Hollywood Canteen* (1944), a project urged on Jack L. Warner by the determined Garfield.

On Wednesday, August 25, 1943, Arthur Farnsworth died of a blood clot in his brain after having fallen on Hollywood Boulevard. He was in a coma for twenty-four hours and never regained consciousness. Earlier, in June, he had suffered a fall at the couple's New Hampshire home which doctors now claimed was responsible for his fatal condition. Bette has said, "I really didn't think I could continue at that point. In fact, I knew I couldn't." Prior to Farnsworth's death, Hollywood gossips predicted an end to the marriage when Bette showed what they considered to be an overly friendly attitude toward her ex-husband. With both feet on the Hollywood turf, columnist Cal York wrote there was "no truth to the report."

In 1943, Bette made a ten-minute short subject, *Stars on Horseback,* which also featured Olivia de Havilland, Priscilla Lane, Jerry Colonna, and Joel McCrea. Miss Davis' contribution to the personality-jammed *Thank Your Lucky Stars* (1943) was the uncharacteristic, amusing jitterbug number (in which she sang off-key) "They're Either Too Young or Too Old." However, she was back on familiar ground in *Old Acquaintance* (1943), based on the John Van Druten play of 1941 that had featured Jane Cowl and Peggy Wood. Contrived by producer Henry Blanke and director Vincent Sherman to pick up where *The Old Maid* had left off, it rematched Davis and Miriam Hopkins who was fast approaching the end of her major film days.

While many viewers found the plot too synthetic in its depiction of emotion, the film rang true for those filmgoers who have a strong respect for continuity of some (or any) sort in their lives. As Bette's Kitty Marlowe explains to Preston Drake (John Loder), the harassed husband of successful popular novelist and bitch Millie, ". . . she remembers the same things I do. That's important. For one thing, she's the only one I know who remembers when I used to be called Chunky." This is to rationalize why over the years serious writer Kit has tolerated the selfish relationship with Millie who has everything Kit ever wanted: professional success, a devoted husband, and a wonderful daughter. In the now *de rigueur* act of self-sacrifice, Bette's heroine graciously gives up the younger man (Gig Young) whom she has discovered is truly loved by Millie's grown-up daughter (Dolores Moran). Feeling noble but in need of understanding, Kit goes to see Millie who is now alone, and in typical, thoughtless, fantasy fashion, Millie announces that she intends to write a book based on their admirable friendship. Resigned that Millie will never change and that her own fate is sealed, she and her friend toast and drink champagne because "there comes a time in every woman's life when the only thing that helps is a glass of champagne." James Agee *(The Nation)* noted, "The odd thing is that the two ladies and Vincent Sherman, directing, make the whole business look fairly intelligent, detailed, and plausible; and that on the screen such trash can seem, even, mature and adventurous." One moment in the film which brought particular joy to the heart of every Davis fan was the screen moment when Hopkins' Millie becomes hysterical and Bette's

Kit has to slap her back to rationality. Unrestrained Bette admits that she enjoyed this bit of business as well.

In early 1944, Olivia de Havilland was waging a court battle against Warner Bros. Her eventual victory provided actors with a legal wedge against studio addition to contract periods whenever a player went on suspension. In the meantime, Bette was on the soundstages shooting her fifty-third motion picture, a soap opera to end them all: *Mr. Skeffington* (1944). *Time* magazine abbreviated the scenario and Bette's role by stating that "as a ruthless Gramercy Park beauty, vintage 1914, she has studied such archaic cinebelles as Anita Stewart to startling advantage. As a cloche-hatted bar-prowler of the 1920s, she is even more evocative. But, as the divorcée, she runs to caricature. Her makeup as an ex-beauty is a stentorian overstatement." Bette agrees that the abrupt change from the eternal young woman to the diphtheria-ravaged matron was too abrupt; but her greater sorrow about the film was the studio's final decision not to lense it in Technicolor.

In the course of this Vincent Sherman-directed exercise, Bette displayed all the acting traits that made her such easy prey for mimics and impressionists. The final scene again produced a marvelously effective renunciation. This time there was a fresh twist: Bette's character renounces her former, selfish life. Her cousin and long-time friend George Trellis (Walter Abel) insists that Fanny make an about-face.

> *George:* Ever since I've known you, you've thought only of yourself. You've spent your life in front of a mirror completely unaware of the people around you or the world you've lived in. Here's a chance for you to do something for someone else. . . . There are a lot worse things in this world than losing one's beauty.

She forces herself to go downstairs to see Job Skeffington (Claude Rains) not knowing that her Jewish ex-husband has been broken and blinded by his stay in a German concentration camp.

> *Fanny:* [to a frenzied crescendo of Max Steiner music] Oh, Job. Why dar-ling. . . . You can't be [pause, beat] . . . They didn't? [pause, beat]
> *Job:* Yes
> *Fanny:* The Naz . . .s
> *Job:* Sh-sh. . . .
> *Fanny:* Oh my poor dar-ling, Job. And all this time I've been thinking only of myself. Well, I never, never shall again. You're home safe with me.
> *Job:* [sobbing] Fanny, Fanny.

As she leads Job up the stairs, George witnesses the miraculous transformation in his relative.

> *George:* Fanny, I've never seen you look more beautiful.
> *Fanny:* A woman is beau-ti-ful, on-ly if she's loved. Isn't that right, Job?
> *George:* [to the maid (Dorothy Peterson)] It's all right Manby . . . no matter how old she becomes, he'll always see her as young and beautiful.

With such a well-mounted production and a heart-rending philosophy, how can one argue with the formula of *Mr. Skeffington*? During most of the film, Bette never looked more beautiful, thanks to Orry-Kelly's forty costumes and Perc Westmore's makeup.

During the winter of 1944-45, Hollywood speculated on the possible marriage of Bette to Lewis A. Riley, a corporal with the Second Army's 168th Signal Photo Company. She even rented a house in Phenix City, Alabama, to be near him for a while. In February 1945, Bette earned her seventh Academy Award nomination for her portrayal of Fanny Trellis Skeffington.* She failed to win, however, when the statuette went to Ingrid Bergman for MGM's *Gaslight*.

* There are many Davis aficionados who believe that Janie Clarkson, Fanny's unseen friend throughout the decades of the story of *Mr. Skeffington*, should have received a special Oscar prize.

In 1945, Bette turned down the offer to star as *Mildred Pierce* (1945) at Warner Bros.—a part also rejected by Barbara Stanwyck and Ann Sheridan—and the Oscar, the following year, went to Joan Crawford who played this martyr role.

Bette had only one film in release during 1945, but it was a tremendously taxing assignment, even for a performer of Miss Davis' calibre. It was *The Corn Is Green,* adapted from Emlyn Williams' play which had been produced on Broadway in 1940 with Ethel Barrymore—Sybil Thorndike did the role in London. As Miss L. C. Moffat, an English schoolteacher described as "fortyish," Bette had to wear thirty pounds of padding and period dresses throughout the sixty-nine days of shooting on the Warner lot. Simulated snowstorms were accomplished with the use of gypsum while a snowball fight was accomplished with chopped ice in 109-degree Burbank warmth.

Miss Moffat arrives at Glensarno, a Welsh mining town, to take deed to a recently inherited house. She finds the miners likable but ignorant and when she learns that children are sent to the mines at age twelve, she determines that, "I'm going to get those youngsters out of that mine if I have to black my face and go down and fetch them myself. . . . And when I walk in the dark I can touch with my hands where the corn is green." In the course of the drama, Miss Moffat takes special interest in Morgan Evans (John Dall) who is later seduced by Bessie (Joan Lorring), the daughter of Miss Moffat's cook (Rosalind Ivan). Miss Moffat's big moment comes when Morgan is to take an examination for entrance to Oxford University. The entire village awaits the outcome of the examination, even the Squire (Nigel Bruce). Morgan passes the entrance test, but then Bessie returns with a child fathered by Morgan. However, Miss Moffat adopts the baby and Morgan is free to go on to Oxford.

Advertisements for the film were geared toward making the public believe it was a love story with contemporary head shots of Bette and Dall (dressed in a business suit) looking up at her. The words "In her heart of hearts she knew she could never hold him. . . ." were emblazoned lengthwise down the ad and "A love that ripened too fast" appeared beneath the title. *Motion Picture* magazine recommended the movie with, "Only Bette Davis would dare do the screen translation of the schoolteacher." Oddly enough, for one of her more restrained acting jobs, Bette was overlooked by the Academy of Motion Picture Arts and Sciences. But she was not through with Miss Moffat, a role that would reappear later in her career.

On Thursday, November 29, 1945, Bette married William Grant Sherry, whom she had met at a Laguna Beach cocktail party. A former boxer and a licensed physiotherapist, Sherry's main interest was painting. The dimpled groom was thirty; Bette was thirty-seven. They were wed in Riverside, California, in the Mission Inn Chapel where Bette was escorted down the aisle by her stepfather of one week, Robert Woodbury Palmer. Bette wore a powder-blue wool suit and a feathered Breton sailor hat for the ceremony which she would have preferred to have been performed in an Episcopal church, but which was out of the question because she was a divorced woman. It was Sherry's first marriage. Sherry's temper came to the fore during their Mexican honeymoon when he tossed her out of the car. "I never seemed to bring out the best in men," she remembered in *The Lonely Life.*

Sensing the end was coming to studio domination of stars, Bette formed B.D., Inc., a production company which was to supervise six Davis projects. One possibility was the role of the British schoolmarm in Twentieth Century-Fox's *Anna and the King of Siam* (1946) which would have teamed Bette with Rex Harrison, an actor she much admired. But Warner Bros. would not loan her and Irene Dunne won the showcasing role. Instead, Bette agreed to make under her banner a new version of Elisabeth Bergner's British film of 1939, *A Stolen Life.* The 1946 edition cast Bette in dual roles and featured Glenn Ford, newly returned from the war. Davis' choice of

With Claude Rains and Richard Waring in *Mr. Skeffington* ('44).

With new husband William Grant Sherry at their wedding reception (November 30, 1945) in Riverside, California.

With Glenn Ford in *A Stolen Life* ('46).

In *The Corn Is Green* ('45).

leading man was unfortunate in that Ford looked more like her kid brother than a husband. The saving grace of this unsatisfactory melodrama was the gimmick of two Davises oncamera, often simultaneously; one as the extroverted, selfish Pat, the other as the quiet artist, Kate.

Curtis Bernhardt found directing Davis at this time a painful experience. He would later say, "Compared with Bette Davis, Joan Crawford, whom I subsequently directed in *Possessed* [1947], was as easy to work with as can be. She was naturally a little subdued because she was the studio's second-ranking star, Bette being number one. She threw her handbag at me several times when, having just done a picture with Bette, I called her Bette by mistake.

"The chief difference between Crawford and Davis is that, while Bette is an *actress* through and through, Joan is more a very talented *motion picture* star. That means that, while she is just as professional, she is also simpler.

"Granted, she's not as versatile as Bette. If Bette has an emotional scene, she tackles it completely consciously, and when you say 'Cut,' she might ask, 'Do you think that was a little too much this or a little too much that?

"But, when Crawford plays an emotional scene, you have to wait twenty minutes until she comes out of it after you have said, 'Cut,' because she is still crying or laughing or whatever; she's still going."

Bette's second 1946 feature was *Deception*, a remake of Jeanne Eagel's film *Jealousy* (1929) for which she was reunited with Paul Henreid and Claude Rains, both for the final time. In the Irving Rapper-directed drama, she weds Karel Novak (Henreid), a musician who has endured the miseries of a German concentration camp. He believes her virtuous and she tries to keep from him the truth regarding her one-time affair with Alexander Hollenius (Rains), a celebrated composer. She even kills Alexander who has threatened to expose her to her husband. Karel makes a successful concert appearance, after which she tells him the truth and confesses to having murdered the maestro. She is forgiven by her husband but must face the legal repercussions. Although sophisticated and slickly produced, the film was too contrived to satisfy audiences. It was post-World War II and times and tastes were changing fast.

In 1947, Bette was the highest paid female in the United States with a yearly salary of $328,000. That May 1st, she gave birth to a daughter christened Barbara Davis Sherry but whom she nicknamed BeeDee. Bette has written, "And for the first time in my life, I became a willing slave to another human being. I was thrilled that it was a girl. It seemed so right."

While *Deception* had been disappointing from a box-office standpoint, *Winter Meeting* was dismal. *Cue* magazine branded it "the talkiest piece of 1948." In this dialogue marathon, she is a middle-aged poet who hates her mother for having driven her father to suicide. She meets and falls in love with a young naval hero (James Davis—no relation!) who wants to become a priest but who feels unworthy of the pursuit. He eventually helps her to overcome her fears and hatred and then walks away from her to follow his own path. *Newsweek* called the movie "a thoroughly honest failure" and found that Bette's "talents are great enough to be sometimes apparent even in the midst of such unrewarding mediocrity." The film could hardly be labeled as an auspicious return to the screen for the star after an absence of more than a year.

If Hollywood observers were wondering why, with films like *Winter Meeting*, Bette was earning $364,000 in 1948 for her screen, radio, and related services, she gave some justification for her high income with the delightful comedy *June Bride* (1948). Her co-star, however, was as great an upstager as Miriam Hopkins, and some said more attractive. It was Robert Montgomery. Bretaigne Windust, who had handled *Winter Meeting*, did the same for *June Bride*, but here he insured that the pacing was rapid. Bette is Linda Gilman, editor of a top-grade woman's magazine who is ordered to go to Indiana to do a layout of a typical American wedding for the June issue. Her assistant turns out to be Carey Jackson (Montgomery), a former war

With Fay Bainter and
Mary Wickes in *June
Bride* ('48).

With Claude Rains in
Deception ('46).

correspondent who once was in love with her. She does not think very much of him, but she must take him. In Indiana, all manner of comic occurrences happen, with Linda and Carey renewing their love relationship in the end.

"If I don't get out . . . I'll just die! Living here is like waiting for the funeral to begin. No, it's like waiting in the coffin for them to carry you out!" While this may have been Bette's feelings about remaining at Warner Bros. in the late Forties, the dialogue quote is actually from *Beyond the Forest* (1949) which proved to be her final film at the studio. Anyone who has witnessed even a portion of this King Vidor-directed exercise must agree with Davis who has remarked, ". . . primarily it was terrible because I was too old for the part. I mean, I don't think you can believe for a moment that, if I, as Rosa Moline, was so determined to get to Chicago, I wouldn't just have upped and gone years ago. I told them they should have put Virginia Mayo in the part—she would have been great. It was all a great pity, because the book is very good and could have made a marvelous movie. The husband, for instance, is supposed to look like Eugene Pallette and be an absolute monster. So what do they do? They cast Joseph Cotten, who is so attractive and kind—why should any wife want to get away from him? The one interesting thing Vidor did in the film was to make the train into [a personification of] her lover; that bit was good. But all the rest was just crazy."

Garbed in a disfiguring black wig and unfortunately sleazy costumes and posturing in a caricature of herself, Bette was miserable throughout the filming of this project. When the film would later open, Dorothy Manners in the *Los Angeles Examiner* would report, "It is obvious that she took little direction from King Vidor, an artist well known for his restraint in directing. And the rest of the cast —all good actors—seem so dumbstruck by the antics of the star that they give the impression of merely watching from the sidelines." Mr. Vidor in his book *On Film Making* (David McKay, 1972) writes, "She

resented my directions and unbeknownst to me went to the head of the studio and told them that unless I was taken off the picture she would not appear for work the next day." When informed that Vidor would remain on the picture, Bette then counterattacked by saying that she would return to the project only if Warners would cancel the remainder of her contract.

On Monday, July 25, 1949, it was announced in the trade papers that through her agent, Lew Wasserman of MCA, Bette was terminating her Warner Bros. pact of eighteen years. She left undone such studio projects which had been planned for her as *The Two Worlds of Johnny Truro,* based on George Sklar's novel of a thirty-five-year-old woman in love with a twenty-year-old youth; *The African Queen* with Michael Redgrave as her co-star—it would be made in 1952 with Katharine Hepburn and Humphrey Bogart; and the oft-postponed *Ethan Frome* which at last report was to have co-starred David Farrar and Mildred Natwick. Ironically, Bette's greatest competitor at the studio, Joan Crawford, was to remain at the Burbank lot for more than two years after Davis, although her vehicles were roles Miss Davis might easily have played. In the post-Bette Davis period, it would be Doris Day and Virginia Mayo who would be the studio's leading female stars.

On Friday, October 21, 1949, Bette filed suit for divorce from Sherry, charging mental cruelty, an action which made 1949 quite a year of decisive change for her. She asked for custody of two-year-old BeeDee and at the same time obtained a temporary restraining court order to prevent her husband from doing her bodily harm. Sherry stated, "That part about my threatening her with bodily harm is just silly. I have an awful temper, it's true, but I can learn to control it." The suit was cancelled when Sherry promised to seek psychiatric help, but it was renewed the following April when Sherry created a scene in public. On Tuesday, July 4, 1950, when Bette obtained a divorce, she stated, "No one is very happy, really, about a divorce. It's the end of one era in your life and sometimes the beginning of another. Who knows?" She received custody of BeeDee. Sherry admitted that he intended to light "a great big firecracker" in honor of his July fourth independence and announced that he intended to marry Bette's nurse, Marion Richards (age twenty-three), the following month.

After leaving Warner Bros., Bette signed as a free-lance artist with producers Jack H. Shirball and Bruce Manning for *The Story of a Divorce*. As directed by Curtis Bernhardt, the project would be temporarily shelved for months by RKO. Meanwhile, she was contacted by Darryl F. Zanuck of Twentieth Century-Fox to do a rush take-over for ailing Claudette Colbert in *All about Eve* (1950) based on the story "The Wisdom of Eve" written by Mary Orr. Her leading man was Gary Merrill.

On Friday, July 28, 1950, following completion of *All about Eve*, Bette and Merrill were married in Juarez, Mexico. She was forty-two; he was thirty-four. It was his second marriage—her fourth. When asked to pose for photographers kissing her new groom, Bette responded, "I come from New England you know; there we don't do things like that in public."

By now, there can be hardly anyone who does not know the plotline of *All about Eve*, with its array of witticisms provided by director-scripter Joseph L. Mankiewicz. Within the confines of 138 minutes and through a cast including George Sanders, Anne Baxter, Celeste Holm, Hugh Marlowe, Thelma Ritter, and Marilyn Monroe, we learn all about Margo Channing (Bette), a famous stage actress afraid of growing old, who is in love with her director, Bill Samson (Merrill). ("Bill's thirty-two. He looks thirty-two. He looked it five years ago, he'll look it twenty years from now. I hate men.")

Bette has said, "It was pure heaven to play Margo!" and has admitted to thanking Claudette Colbert "all my life" for having had an injured back that prevented her from playing the role. Alton Cook *(New York World-Telegram)* assessed the "new" Bette: "Bette

Davis, for nearly two decades one of our greatest actresses and worst performers, finally is shaken out of her tear-jerking formula and demonstrates what a vivid, overwhelming force she possesses." The role and the film were tailored to revive Bette's career after a disaster like *Beyond the Forest*. She was honored with the *Look* Achievement Award and the New York Film Critics Award, and received her eighth Academy Award nomination as Best Actress. In the latter competition, she lost to Judy Holliday *(Born Yesterday)*.

On the heels of the success of *All about Eve,* RKO rushed the $1.8 million dollar *The Story of a Divorce* into release, under its new title, *Payment on Demand* (1951). In this quietly effective narrative, Bette is at her long-suffering best as the wife of an attorney (Barry Sullivan) who learns her spouse wants to end their twenty-year marriage. In flashback, she reconstructs the years to determine just what went wrong.

In 1951, when William Sherry ran ads in a Laguna Beach newspaper offering his services as a handyman at seventy-five cents an hour, Bette could not tolerate the embarrassment and flew off to Connecticut with her new husband. While there, the Merrills adopted a week-old baby girl whom they named Margot after the Channing character. (When Margot was three, the Merrills discovered that she was retarded.) The Merrills later returned to California where they took up residence in a Malibu beach house. Bette joined with George Brent at year's end on the radio series "Woman of the Year," based on the 1942 Katharine Hepburn-Spencer Tracy MGM movie.

Realizing the renewed box-office value in Davis, Douglas Fairbanks, Jr. (once wed to Joan Crawford) and his partner Daniel Angel summoned Bette and Gary to England to appear in *Another Man's Poison,* released in the States in 1952 by United Artists. She is a murdering spouse and Merrill is the convict who comes into her life. In the estimation of the *Hollywood Reporter,* "Bette Davis, queen of the vixens, combs her hair, lights cartons of cigarettes, snaps her fingers, and bites her

With Joseph Cotten in *Beyond the Forest* ('49).

With Hugh Marlowe and Gary Merrill in *All about Eve* ('50).

With Richard Anderson in *Payment on Demand* ('51).

In the stage show *Two's Company* ('52).

231

consonants, and it all adds up to a performance that you'd expect to find from a night club impersonation of the actress." The film did not do well financially and added nothing to Bette's professional stature.

Next, she took a cameo role (before they were called that) at her husband's home lot, Twentieth Century-Fox, where the distaff stars of the studio were, among others, Susan Hayward, Shelley Winters, and Jean Peters. As the bedridden paralytic, Bette made no pretense in *Phone Call from a Stranger* (1952) of being anything but her own age, and looking quite dowdy at that.

In an attempt to repeat the success of *All about Eve*, producer Bert E. Friedlob packaged Bette and Sterling Hayden as the leads of *The Star* (1952) at Twentieth Century-Fox. "Only the Star of Stars could accept the challenge of such a role," the ads proclaimed, "the greatest triumph of the twice winner of the Academy Award!" The role was originally slated for Joan Crawford. In this show business production, Bette played Margaret Elliot, a Hollywood has-been who has been reduced to auctioning her possessions after bankruptcy engulfs her. Through her one-time leading man Jim Johannson (Hayden), she decides to become a real woman and to forget about her fading career. "It is a marathon one-woman show and, all in all, proof that Bette Davis—with her strident voice, nervous stride, mobile hands, and popping eyes—is still her own best imitator." Bette received her ninth Oscar nomination for *The Star*, but lost to Shirley Booth for *Come Back, Little Sheba*.

Before *The Star* was in release, Bette accepted the challenge of Broadway after an absence of more than twenty years. *Two's Company* would be her first and last musical revue to date. During a solo on opening night tryout in Detroit, she fainted and was carried from the stage, but returned a few nights later when she adlibbed to wild applause and said, "You can't say I didn't fall for you." The hodgepodge revue show premiered on Thursday, December 4, 1952, at the Alvin Theatre. Bette's opening number was "Just Turn Me Loose on Broadway," and thereafter she ca-

vorted, sang, danced, and joked through assorted bits in which she posed as a hillbilly, a Tallulah Bankhead-type spoiling a Bette Davis opening night, Jeanne Eagels in *Rain*, and an Amanda-type from *Private Lives*. She also scraped through a rendition of "Just Like a Man." The revue closed after only eighty-nine performances.

Bette had been ill throughout the entire *Two's Company* ordeal (at one point Walter Winchell erroneously reported in his column that she had cancer of the jaw), and later had an impacted tooth extracted. Her doctor informed her that she was more ill than he had estimated. He diagnosed her condition as osteomyelitis of the jaw and a delicate operation was performed. The Merrills then purchased a home at Cape Elizabeth, Maine, where Bette recuperated and where they adopted a boy, Michael, a blond child born on January 5, 1954.

With so much time on her hands, Bette grew understandably bored and flare-ups were bound to occur with volatile Merrill. Then she was sent the script of an upcoming Twentieth Century-Fox film *Sir Walter Raleigh* for which she was asked to play Queen Elizabeth. She accepted the offer and was glad to have a constructive means of occupying her time. She arrived in Los Angeles with daughter BeeDee and their pet poodle and completed her stint in eleven days. Since the scenario had been restructured to give her a part equal to Sir Walter Raleigh's (Richard Todd), it was decided for both political and commercial reasons to retitle the Cinema-Scope and color vehicle *The Virgin Queen* (1955). For her repeat performance as the Queen, she again shaved her head in front and removed her eyebrows, as she had done in 1939. To rumors that Bette had been uncooperative at Fox during the filming of *The Virgin Queen*, Hedda Hopper came to her defense with, "The only difficulty the studio had was not with Bette, but with other players on the lot who wanted to spend their time watching her act. Finally, they had to be barred from the set as their visits were delaying the picture. The girl who was difficult in the cast was their new English import, Joan

Collins [as Beth Throgmorton]. They couldn't even find her one day."

At the Academy Award presentation on Wednesday, March 30, 1955, Bette literally stopped the telecast show by her entrance wearing a sequinned gold helmet to conceal her shaved head. She presented the Best Actor award to Marlon Brando for *On the Waterfront.* Like her rival Joan Crawford, Bette knew perfectly well the value of unique publicity.

In television-gutted Hollywood, decent cinema roles for even young actresses were difficult to come by; for someone of Bette's former rank, it was near impossible. To accept a supporting role would have meant the finish to her career; to agree to a film project at too little a salary was equally hazardous. Back in 1952, Columbia had planned to film *The Library* to be directed by its scripter Daniel Taradash. Mary Pickford and Irene Dunne were each tested for the film, but due to the still rampant Un-American Activities hearings uproar, production was continually postponed. Finally, it was reactivated under the title *Storm Center* (1956). Filming commenced in cost-saving black-and-white in August 1955 on location at Santa Rosa, California. As Jerry Vermilye in *Bette Davis* (Pyramid, 1973) weighed, "Davis gave a good performance as the dedicated librarian, but the story's melodramatic turns of plot detracted from the plausibility of so serious a theme." For many viewers, the sight of a mature, stocky Davis *slurping* clam chowder in a restaurant sequence was a shock of major proportion. The actress has always claimed she is proud to have done this anti-hypocrisy film.

The following year Bette was commissioned by producer Sam Zimbalist to assay for the motion picture screen the role of the mother in Paddy Chayefsky's television comedy of 1955 (NBC), *The Catered Affair* (1956). Thelma Ritter had done the TV role as a Jewish mother; the screen version was changed to encompass a poor Manhattan Irish family in the throes of their pretty daughter's (Debbie Reynolds) wedding plans. "You're going to have a wedding whether you like or not!" Bette's Aggie Hurley tells the girl, and informs her hard-working cabdriver husband (Ernest Borgnine) that he will have to find a way to pay for it. For the first time, Bette portrayed a dumpy, middle class hausfrau whose language consisted of dropping g's from her words, and it was generally decreed that Miss Ritter's television rendition of the role was much more agreeable.

Between 1956 and 1959, nearly fifty-year-old Bette performed solely on television where she appeared in episodes of "G. E. Theatre," "Schlitz Playhouse of Stars," "Ford Theatre," "Suspicion," "Studio 57," and others. The biggest mistake made about her transfer into the small screen medium was that she, her agent, and her press agent failed to generate the proper aura about her video performances, so that each would be a special occasion, not just another disguised bid by an anxious actress eager for exposure and work. Her comments at the time included, "The tragedy is we can't sit around and wait for good things. We have to take whatever comes along. . . . Any of us would be delighted to make movies again, if there were any to do. Unfortunately, this is the age of mediocrity in show business."

In 1959, Bette accepted cameo roles in two films. In the first, released by Warner Bros., she was a guest star, having the opportunity to play a role once interpreted oncamera by Elisabeth Bergner, Marlene Dietrich, and Tallulah Bankhead, that of Empress Catherine of Russia in *John Paul Jones.* To Robert Stack's title role hero, she represents the source of sea action to the man whose later years have been relegated to desk service. The Davis fans who witnessed this color feature were disappointed that there was not more of her; but undoubtedly she looked more attractive in her period wardrobe and wig than she had in years. In the second film, released by MGM, she is the dope-crazed dowager countess mother of Jacques de Gue (Alec Guinness) who plots to murder his wife (Irene Worth) and substitute a look-alike Britisher (also Guinness) in his place. The Daphne du Maurier novel *The Scapegoat* was

233

In *The Virgin Queen* ('55).

←
With Paul Kelly in *Storm Center* ('56).

In Hollywood with husband
Gary Merrill ('56).

With Alec Guinness in *The Scapegoat* ('59).

→

In *Pocketful of Miracles* ('61). The framed photo is of Ann-Margret.

With Alan Webb, Margaret Leighton, and Patrick O'Neal in the stage show *The Night of the Iguana* ('60).

237

much better than the resultant black-and-white film. Bette, in her near-white wig, disheveled makeup, and array of overly fussy bedjackets, was not a pretty sight to behold. The movie was co-produced in England by austere Guinness, who, according to Bette, ". . . cut my part into such shreds that my appearance in the final product made no sense at all. This is an actor who plays by himself, unto himself. In this particular picture he plays a dual role, so at least he was able to play with himself."

In June 1959, it was touted that Bette would co-star with Elizabeth Taylor and Montgomery Clift in the cinema version of Tennessee Williams' *Suddenly, Last Summer* for director Joseph L. Mankiewicz, but Katharine Hepburn was the final choice to play the egocentric Mrs. Venable. Instead, Bette made her first Western, appearing as the guest star on "Wagon Train" in the episode *The Ella Lindstrom Story* (NBC-TV, February 4, 1959), portraying a frontier woman who is dying of cancer and must prepare her seven fatherless children for pioneer life alone. Her next episode, the second of three on the Ward Bond-starring series, *The Elizabeth McQueeney Story* (October 28, 1959), would be yet another Davis pilot for a teleseries that did not sell. It provided Bette, as the mother hen of a brood of traveling "girls," with a chance to dance the can-can!

In October 1959, Bette and Gary Merrill embarked on a nationwide tour for Norman Corwin with one-night stands of dramatic readings from *The World of Carl Sandburg*. From Maine, they swung across the country to California where in San Francisco fans lined up at the stage door to catch a brief glimpse of their idol. The star disappointed them by leaving the Alcazar Theatre by another entrance. Little did they know that at the time Bette's personal problems involving a disintegrating marriage prevented her from standing in an alleyway to appease autograph seekers. The show garnered good reviews in California, but while in Los Angeles, in May 1960, Bette revealed that she had filed for divorce on the customary grounds of mental cruelty. In the suit, she asked for custody of the children. The divorce was granted on Wednesday, July 6, 1960. (One of Merrill's later romances would be with Rita Hayworth.)

When the Sandburg readings reached New York's Henry Miller Theatre on Wednesday, September 14, 1960, Merrill had been replaced with Leif Erickson (who had replaced Barry Sullivan). The show was not accepted by jaded New York theatre audiences and closed after only twenty-nine performances. While playing in Florida—prior to the New York engagement—Tennessee Williams had visited Bette and told her of his newest play *The Night of the Iguana* and asked her to read for a part, which she did. As a result, she was signed to play Maxine Faulk, the buxom, loose-moraled owner of the seedy Mexican hotel.

Before *Iguana* rehearsals were to start, she went to California to star with Glenn Ford in *Pocketful of Miracles* (1961), a remake of Columbia's *Lady for a Day* which had mustered an Oscar nomination for May Robson in 1933. The role of Apple Annie in the remake was originally assigned to Helen Hayes, but when prior commitments conflicted, Bette substituted. The Frank Capra-directed vehicle was loaded with veteran performers including Thomas Mitchell, Edward Everett Horton, John Litel, Jerome Cowan, Barton MacLane, and Snub Pollard. While Bette had the focal role of the proceedings, it was Glenn Ford, then riding the crest of his screen popularity, who was the big shot on the project, even to having his then steady girl, Hope Lange, as his nominal co-star. When Ford undiplomatically told the press that offering Bette this comeback chance was a return favor for her having chosen him to play opposite her in *A Stolen Life,* her wrath was volcanic. Nevertheless, the banal Damon Runyon story proved to be a moneywinner, demonstrating once again the fickleness of public tastes.

Beyond the *Pocketful* clash and the rejection of a mother role in *Return to Peyton Place* (1961)—eventually played by Mary Astor—the year was heightened in tragedy by the death of Bette's mother at age seventy-six after a long illness. (Bette's father had died in 1935.)

After a Chicago tryout of *The Night of the Iguana* in November 1961, where *Time* magazine judged it "a massive turkey," the overblown melodrama opened in New York on Thursday, December 28, 1961, where it received the New York Drama Critics Circle Award as the best American play of the season and where Margaret Leighton was honored with the Tony Award. Allegedly displeased with the male lead, Patrick O'Neal, Bette (flamboyant, red-wigged, and open-shirted) departed from the role of Maxine in April 1962 "to rest and walk in the country for about a hundred miles a day." She was replaced with Shelley Winters. The property was later sold to MGM for $400,000 by whom it was produced in 1964 with Ava Gardner as Maxine.

As she left Broadway, Bette had a letter in her pocket from producer-director Robert Aldrich asking her to go to Hollywood and co-star with Joan Crawford in his horror film *What Ever Happened to Baby Jane?* (1962). After selling the idea to Warner Bros., Aldrich launched into this low-budget black-and-white grand guignol tale. It proved to be the rejuvenation of two faltering screen careers. Perhaps no one except Bette Davis would have dared to expose herself oncamera in such garish paste-white makeup, and unkempt wardrobe, and with a vicious gutter personality that was so vividly oversized. Twelve years earlier Gloria Swanson had been Oscar-nominated for her role as the demented silent screen star Norma Desmond. Now Davis as (Baby) Jane Hudson offered a delineation equally as macabre, only more out of touch with reality. Just as in *All about Eve*, some of the *Baby Jane* lines were sharply autobiographic of Bette. At one point, she tells her would-be show act accompanist (Victor Buono), ". . . there's a lot of people who remember me . . . lots of 'em!" At the ghastly finale on the beach where Blanche (Crawford) has confessed that she had engineered her own crippling years before, Davis' Jane whimpers, "And all these years we might have been friends."

Everyone expected the two veteran stars to openly feud during the filming, but, according to Robert Aldrich, "I think it's proper to say that they really detested each other, but they behaved absolutely perfectly. There was never an abrasive word in public, and not once did they try to upstage each other." Bette has admitted, "Director Robert Aldrich was a genius in the way he handled Joan Crawford and me."

This film was a run-away sleeper of 1962. A new chapter in Davis' life had opened. Bette received her tenth Oscar nomination for her portrayal of hideous Jane Hudson, but was bypassed in favor of Anne Bancroft (*The Miracle Worker*). Joan Crawford, wearing an odd smile of triumph, picked up the statuette for the absent Miss Bancroft. As Bette would later reveal to columnist Joyce Haber of the *Los Angeles Times*, ". . . the fact that Miss Crawford got permission to accept for any of the other nominees was hysterical. Miss Crawford was being interviewed and photographed by the press, clutching Miss Bancroft's award. I was nominated, but she was receiving the acclaim. It would have meant a million more dollars to our film if I had won. Joan was thrilled I hadn't."

On September 21, 1962, a full-page ad appeared in the trade papers under "Situations Wanted, Women." Bette was seeking "Steady employment in Hollywood. (Has had Broadway.)" She has admitted in *Mother Goddam* that "the ad was tongue-in-cheek, but a deep dig as well." With *Baby Jane* a hit and her autobiography *The Lonely Life* on the bookstands, she was not fully unemployed, and claims that she could never have sponsored the ad without income from her media projects.

Bette had signed a contract with G. P. Putnam's Sons in the late Fifties when she was desperate for funds, and it was ironic that her tome should emerge at about the same time as two other books by confreres: Joan Crawford (*A Portrait of Joan*) and Olivia de Havilland (*Every Frenchman Has One*). Written with Sandford Dody, Bette's book was filled with "unflinching honesty," evidenced by such statements as "I know now that my mar-

As Margaret and Edith in *Dead Ringer* ('64).

With Joan Crawford in *What Ever Happened to Baby Jane?* ('62).

riages—all four of them—were a farce. Each was different . . . and yet all of them the same." Reviewing the book, the *Chicago Sunday Tribune* reported, "The volcanic, articulate Bette Davis has another winning performance in her provocative, highly readable autobiography." William K. Zinsser (*Saturday Review*) evaluated, "It has many of the ingredients of the films that Miss Davis played so indomitably on the screen—it is maudlin, intensely feminine, and often tedious in personal detail. It is also absolutely candid. Miss Davis blames herself more than anybody else. And her story comes to an ending that any scriptwriter for one of her movies, but nobody else, would envy: 'I have always said I would end up a lonely old woman on a hill.'"

Bette again turned to television in 1962 and 1963, but returned to the screen in 1964 with *Dead Ringer,* forcing her to cancel a cameo assignment in Frank Sinatra-Dean Martin's *Four for Texas* (1963). In this murder-horror film, she plays twins for the second time on film, Edith Philips and Margaret de Lorca. Edith is rather frumpy and murders Margaret. She then assumes her identity in the rich de Lorca estate only to discover that Margaret had been anything but a nice lady in that she had murdered her husband in order to pave the way for her marriage to a gigolo lover (Peter Lawford). The modest thriller also served to reunite Bette with Paul Henreid, the latter this time serving as her director.

On January 5, 1964, Bette's daughter Bee-Dee was married at age sixteen to wealthy Jeremy Hyman, a businessman (associated with Warner Bros.-Seven Arts) fifteen years her senior. Bette gave her consent, knowing that her daughter was mature enough to accept marriage and the responsibilities.

Crisscrossing the globe to wherever there was a film assignment, Bette went to Rome to portray the mother in Carlo Ponti's *The Empty Canvas* (1964). Bette found the experience exasperating since most of the filmmaking was conducted in Italian, a tongue alien to her. *The New Yorker* correctly pronounced the film "one of the worst pictures of this or any year."

For Joseph E. Levine, who had released *The Empty Canvas* through his Embassy Pictures, Bette accepted a secondary role to Susan Hayward in *Where Love Has Gone* (1964). The project derived from a Harold Robbins novel which in turn was a loosely based version of the Lana Turner-daughter Cheryl Crane-Johnny Stompanato murder case. Bette brought "all her old verve and intensity to the role" (*Saturday Review*) of the matriarch, but there had been much hassling in production when Miss Hayward and Bette did not see eye-to-eye as to who was the star of the proceedings. Susan won.

Also in 1964, Bette starred for Robert Aldrich in *Hush . . . Hush, Sweet Charlotte* (1964) with Olivia de Havilland and Joseph Cotten. Joan Crawford, originally signed to co-star, was forced to drop out due to prolonged illness. Another horror exercise, but of better quality than *Baby Jane,* Bette is Charlotte Hollis who refuses to give up her Louisiana homestead to make room for a super highway. Into this mess comes sophisticated Miriam (de Havilland), her cousin, who had gone north some years earlier. Miriam, it is expected, will clear away Charlotte's cobwebs, but, instead, she plots her death for money. Miss de Havilland had this to say of Bette, "She is the only true genius that we have had among the motion picture actresses. With Bette it is a genius for creating life. It could be beautiful life, or ugly life; to her it didn't matter. She would allow herself to look like a wreck or she could be utterly glamorous. The important thing was that crackling vitality that always came through."

"It's a problem between a nanny and a young boy," said Bette of her next release, the British-lensed *The Nanny* (1965). "I don't consider this a horror movie." She is the title character whose neglect has caused a child to drown in a bathtub while she visited her own daughter who had just had an abortion. The film came and went without much notice. Returning to the States, Bette sold her Bel Air home and moved to Westport, Connecticut,

With her married daughter
Barbara at JFK Airport (New
York) in May 1965.

→

With Ernest Borgnine in
Bunny O'Hare ('71).

With Elaine Taylor,
Christian Roberts, Jack
Hedley, and Sheila Hancock
in *The Anniversary* ('68).

her current domicile. Having fared so well in the past in television Westerns, she agreed to co-star in an episode of "Gunsmoke" (CBS-TV, October 1, 1966) and continued to pop up on TV talk and variety shows. She had truly become the indomitable Miss Davis.

The professional "almosts" of Bette's career in the Sixties included the Helen Lawson role in *Valley of the Dolls* (1967), a part later assigned to Judy Garland (who was replaced by Susan Hayward); the older lesbian actress in *The Killing of Sister George* (1967), which went to Beryl Reid; the title role in *The Greatest Mother of Them All,* a shelved project dealing with the Beverly Aadland-Errol Flynn affair; and the part of Hettie Green in *The Day the Plum Tree Shook,* an unrealized property also considered for Rosalind Russell. Perhaps the greatest defeat for Bette was losing the coveted role of Martha in Warner Bros.' *Who's Afraid of Virginia Woolf?* (1966). It went to Elizabeth Taylor who won an Oscar for her performance.

Once more returning to England, Bette made *The Anniversary* (1968), in which she played a one-eyed shrewish mother of three offspring who all have psychological problems. It is a horror movie, but *without* blood or mayhem. Instead, it is filled with perversion. Betty has referred to the film's director Roy Ward Baker as "a dilly."

Thereafter, there were no viable film offers until producers Harry Field and Arthur S. Cooper invited her to London to co-star with long-standing favorite Sir Michael Redgrave in *Connecting Rooms.* Bette was appreciative that it was not another macabre exercise, for she insisted she would not act in another. Based on the play *The Cellist* by Marion Hart, it was directed by scenarist Franklin Gollings and found Bette as Wanda Fleming residing in a rundown London boarding house. For her cello-playing scenes, Ian Fleming's sister, Amorlis, was hired to finger and bow the strings, while Bette, with her arms tied behind her, looked intense. The picture had only a modest release in England and was never officially distributed in the United States, although it had one test preview in an East Side New York theatre in 1971.

It was Robert Wagner who took a decisive interest in Bette's career. He invited her to guest star on his teleseries "It Takes a Thief" (ABC-TV, January 26, 1970), insuring that she was treated like the full star she was and is, and the two got along so well that they not only did a liquor commercial for magazines, but Wagner produced in England *Madame Sin* (1972), released in the United States as an ABC-TV network telefeature, in which an exquisitely gowned and coiffed Bette paraded about as a distaff Fu Manchu. There were thoughts that it might become a series, but no such luck.

Meanwhile, back in California, Bette had participated in the historic retirement tribute to Jack L. Warner. As she would later recall, "Sitting on the dais, looking around at all that was so familiar and dear to me, I thought, 'This is the end of it. This is the end of all of it as I knew it. It will never come back.' And I said my little private farewell."

There was considerable publicity about reuniting Bette with fellow Oscar-winner Ernest Borgnine in a generation-gap comedy-heist caper, *Bunny O'Hare* (1971), in which the mature couple portray motorcycle-riding, hippie robbers. But the project did not live up to expectations. In fact, Bette was so disgruntled with the final product (which had additional deletions and new scenes) that she launched a sizable lawsuit against the producers (American International Pictures), claiming a variety of professional grievances. Bette passed off the venture as "a broad, tastelessly, inartistically assembled production." The film had a very quiet and modest playoff engagement.

With her career running along unproductive tangents, Bette grasped at straws in the wind. She agreed to play a retired judge in *The Judge and Jake Wyler,* a Universal-produced teleseries pilot co-starring Doug McClure and James McEachin that was later expanded to a two-hour NBC telefeature when it was telecast on December 2, 1972. Much more satisfactory was the family Christmas (1971) spent at her Twin Bridges home in Westport with BeeDee, Jeremy Hyman, grandson Ashley, daughter Margot (on leave from the Lockland School), and son Michael (on college holiday).

Obviously not having profited from her *The Empty Canvas* experience, Bette agreed on almost overnight notice to fly to Rome to co-star with Alberto Sordi and Joseph Cotten in *Lo Scopone Scientifico (The Scientific Cardplayer/The Game)*. As directed by Luigi Comencini, Bette played her scene bedecked in a white wig and stylish clothes from a wheelchair. An on-the-set interpreter expedited communication between Bette and director Comencini, but the Hollywood star was outraged that bilingual Mr. Sordi "refused to speak English with me. . . . My name for Alberto Sordi was Alberto Sordid." When *Variety* reviewed the film in Rome, it noted, "Bette Davis dominates with a neat display of egomania and cruelty beneath a stance of gracious dignity." She is the aging American millionairess with a craving for card-playing who devotes her declining years to the pastime, with Joseph Cotten as her loyal but cowed partner. The picture has yet to have an American release.

Whereas most of her contemporaries have settled down to a life of retirement, Bette has refused to admit defeat. She bounced from a film fan student question-and-answer period at New York's New School (November 10, 1972) to MGM's Culver City lot to make yet another teleseries pilot, *Hello Mother, Goodbye* as the outrageously possessive mother of two very adult sons. The show found no sponsor for the 1973 video season.

Of the Sunday, February 11, 1973, engagement at New York's Town Hall where she was the first in a series of actresses to be saluted as "Legendary Ladies of the Screen" (others included Joan Crawford, Myrna Loy, Sylvia Sidney, and later Rosalind Russell and Lana Turner), Bette has admitted, "All the blood, sweat, and tears of forty-three years were suddenly worth it for a reception like this." Never one to stand on ceremony where another's joy is concerned, Bette agreed to stand next to Gary Merrill at the May 13, 1973, wedding of their son Michael to performer Chou-Chou Rains at a Westport, Connecticut, ceremony. Thereafter she sold the Twin Bridges home and leased a smaller Westport abode.

"Bette Davis as Miss Moffat"—this trade paper announcement in January 1974 was not an anachronism. She had been signed to star in the stage musical of *The Corn Is Green,** directed by Joshua Logan, with songs by Albert Hague and Emlyn Williams (the author of the original play) and a revised book by Williams and Logan which had the locale changed to the South of 1868 and transformed Morgan Evans into a black youth (Dorian Harlwood) who wants an education more than working in a cotton field. She was slated to sing six songs in her own inimitable manner. When asked how she expected to carry off the vocalizing, she shrugged, "I've sung thousands of times. I don't have any voice coaching. They're stuck with the way I sound." The show was scheduled to try-out in Baltimore for two weeks beginning September 9, but in late August Bette was hospitalized with a back injury. From her Harkness Pavilion Medical Center room in New York, she agonized over the expensive delay, "To lie here under these conditions, in traction, you really can think you'll go mad. . . . If you go about your life just the way I am and you don't hide, people respect you. When I'm not acting, I actually forget who I am. I shop around Westport, Connecticut, and I'm always surprised when people come up to me. Most of the time they tell me they think I'm wonderful. Their big beefs are about the new movies. . . . I'll tell you why I took the part of 'Moffat'—and if I had known how difficult this role was, I might have said, 'Thank you very much' and gone home. In the last script I was asked to read I ended up being hung in an attic. HUNG in an at-tic! I want to tell you. I've played a lot of funny parts in my career, but I said, 'Bette, you're NEVER-ah going to be seen hanging in an attic.'"

The show did get underway in Philadelphia in October 1974, but it met with negative reviews. By October 22, co-producer Eugene V. Wolsk announced that Bette had suffered a recurrence of her back injury and that the

* In the mid-Sixties the project had been considered as a vehicle for first Mary Martin and then Katharine Hepburn.

In the telefeature *Madame Sin* (ABC-TV, '72).

→

Playbill from the Philadelphia tryout of the musical *Miss Moffat* (October 1974).

On "The Dick Cavett Show" (ABC-TV, August 1974).

PLAYBILL

SHUBERT THEATRE

BETTE DAVIS

AS

MISS MOFFAT

production was finished. As for plans to replace the actress, they were discarded because "people wanted to see Miss Davis." (Anne Francine was Bette's standby in the musical.)

When she recovered from the $900,000 *Miss Moffat* debacle, Bette took to the road with her film clips–interview evening, traveling to universities and auditoriums throughout the United States and then to England and Australia. It proved to be an even greater hit attraction in London than anyone had anticipated.

When producer-director Dan Curtis was packaging his two-million-dollar thriller film, *Burnt Offerings* (United Artists, 1976), he contacted Bette Davis' agent to determine if she would consent to play Oliver Reed's aunt in the picture. When he received no response, he called her directly. She replied to his description of the role, "If I disappear in a sneeze, I'm not interested." He assured her that she did not. So, in August of 1975, she was on location near San Leandro, California, with the cast, including co-stars Reed, Karen Black, Eileen Heckart, and Burgess Meredith. The inestimable Bette earned a great deal of international publicity for openly rebuking Britisher Reed for his ungentlemanly behavior both on and off the set.

Burnt Offerings would open in November 1976 to very unfavorable reviews. *Newsweek* magazine's reviewer argued, "the movie merely piles on one special effect after another —none of them too special—and stalls for time. Even the title is a sham: nobody ever so much as lights a match. And nobody—not even the most gullible moviegoer—can expect to receive any present." Actually Davis' role as a very tame Auntie Mame-type was minimal; her performance was an exaggerated caricature of her image. As the *New York Post* noted of the storyline, ". . . Bette Davis died horribly in paroxysms worthy of that great actress. . . ." Despite the film's poor critical reception, *Burnt Offerings* grossed over $1,022,350 in its first six weeks of release. At many theatres, despite Davis' subordinate role, she was billed on marquees as the star of the thriller.

Demonstrating once again that she is a game lady, 1976 saw the release of a London-produced EMI Records Ltd. LP album entitled "Miss Bette Davis." The rather bizarre record* offers Davis in several talk-singing renditions of songs associated with her pictures, including: "They're Either Too Young or Too Old," "I've Written a Letter to Daddy," "Hush . . . Hush, Sweet Charlotte," a speech from *All about Eve* set to the background arrangement of "Liebestraume," and "It Can't Be Wrong" (from *Now, Voyager*). Perhaps the most satisfactory selection in this packaging is her dramatic rendition of "Mother of the Bride." It at least allows the veteran actress to utilize her vocal equipment for dramatic range rather than just nostalgic appeal.

Over the years there had been much talk about utilizing the life story of evangelist Aimee Semple McPherson for a Broadway show. At one point, in the late Fifties, Ann Sheridan was announced for the lead; in the Sixties, Rosalind Russell became interested in the subject matter. But nothing developed. Finally NBC-TV utilized the concept for an installment of "Hallmark Hall of Fame." The two-hour telecast, *The Disappearance of Aimee*, was shown on November 17, 1976, with Faye Dunaway (replacing Ann-Margret) in the title role. Bette was cast as Aimee's stern-willed mother and, like Miss Dunaway, was billed over the title in the credits. Because the dramatic rights to Aimee's amazing career were then unavailable, the producers of this special had to be content with focusing on the highlights of McPherson's alleged kidnapping in 1926 and the court case instituted by the Los Angeles district attorney who claimed it was a fraud designed to sidetrack attention from a romantic tryst. Little attention could be or was given to the background of the extraordinary Aimee, thus making the courtroom caper an isolated, inexplicable situation

* On a spring 1977 "Dinah Shore Show" TV outing Davis was scheduled to sing "I Wish You Love" from her British-recorded album; however, she had a terribly sore throat that day, and had to lip-synch the words to the song, a melody she labels her favorite. In fact, she added jocularly, she has requested that it be played at her funeral. That is one way, she explained, of insuring that people will cry for her lost presence.

to viewers too young to be aware of the subject's unique personality and fame.

The *New York Times* termed the show an "exercise in pointlessness with touches of class." But the paper's reviewer, John J. O'-Connor, was careful to note that "Bette Davis is fascinating as Minnie Kennedy, Aimee's dominating mother. Miss Davis, at this stage, can topple easily into self-parody, but she persists and finally pulls forth a remarkably strong and effective performance, cleverly stealing just about every scene in which she appears. Watch her remove her long gloves at the preliminary hearing. . . ." In the course of the proceedings, Bette's character had occasion to deliver several fund-raising sermons, sing "In the Sweet Bye and Bye," shake phlegmatic Miss Dunaway (a la the Davis-Miriam Hopkins skirmish of *Old Acquaintance*), and demonstrate anew what a tower of strength she is. As has been true in recent years, Bette's aging contours are more flatteringly presented when in period outfits and coiffures such as in *The Disappearance of Aimee.*

If Davis is still fighting that old battle for good roles (she had hoped to co-star in the musical film version of *A Little Night Music* with Elizabeth Taylor, but Hermione Gingold was signed to recreate her Broadway role of the grandmother), the actress need have no fear that she is or could be forgotten by the film industry or the public. The American Film Institute selected Miss Davis as the first woman subject to be honored by a Life Achievement Salute. The gala was presented to her by George Stevens, Jr., on March 1, 1977, at the Beverly Hilton Hotel. With more than one thousand persons in attendance at the award dinner, she was the first woman to be accorded the honor. Previous winners were John Ford, James Cagney, Orson Welles, and William Wyler. The award ceremonies were later telecast on March 21 to the delight of movie fans across the nation when hostess Jane introduced several of Bette's celebrity friends and co-workers, all of whom accoladed her with serio-witty remarks.

The CBS television network presentation started the proceedings with the line, "Fasten your seat belts, it's going to be a bumpy night," followed by well-selected clips from some of her feature films. Bette was then introduced by Stevens while the love theme from *Now, Voyager* filled the banquet room. With blonde to brown hair and looking better than she had in years, Bette was a far cry from cinematic Jane Hudson or Rosa Moline or Sweet Charlotte Hollis as she strode confidently to the speaker's table. The standing ovation lasted on television for one minute and seventeen seconds, obviously an edit job from the four and one-half minutes reported by Hank Grant in *The Hollywood Reporter* of March 3, 1977.

Hostess Jane Fonda explained her presence with "my connection with Bette Davis is a little oblique. . . . During the filming of *Jezebel,* my father's contract guaranteed that he would be through with his job and back in New York in time for my birth. . . . Bette Davis won her second Academy Award in spite of what I unintentionally put her through." Ms. Fonda introduced her father, Henry, who chirped, "Bette, I hope you appreciate that it takes two Fondas to salute one Davis." He went on to tell a charming story about an early date he had had with Bette "a hundred years ago" at Princeton University. When he gave her a tentative kiss while in the back seat of a car, she naively expected that they would be engaged to be married.

A generous showing of film clips (all for some strange reason in black-and-white) were interspersed between guest speaker appearances, and the viewer was reminded that *Of Human Bondage* was the film which firmly established the famous Davis speech mannerisms.

Her one-time director, William Wyler,* made it known that "she *was* difficult, but not in the usually accepted sense. She was diffi-

* In the well-executed book *Here's Looking at You, Kid* (Little Brown, & Company, 1976), author James R. Silke quotes filmmaker Henry Blanke as recollecting recently that during the making of *Jezebel,* "We had some snow scenes to shoot with fake snow and Bette was going to the mailbox to put a letter in and Wyler said, 'Bette, don't wiggle your ass so much; the big scenes are coming later.' And she was completely obedient. They were in love, of course, and how!" One can only wonder if Davis and/or Wyler were thinking of any of this as they performed for the audience on this special evening.

With Faye Dunaway in *The Disappearance of Aimee* (NBC-TV, '76).

With Karen Black in *Burnt Offerings* ('76).

Hollywood salutes
a real star.

BETTE DAVIS

The two-time Oscar-winner becomes the first woman to receive
the AFI Life Achievement Award for her memorable portrayals
of gutsy heroines and heroic villainesses. The all-star festivities include
film highlights from her long career.

**WITH HOST JANE FONDA AND SPECIAL GUESTS:
OLIVIA DeHAVILLAND, PETER FALK, GERALDINE FITZGERALD,
HENRY FONDA, LEE GRANT, PAUL HENREID, CELESTE HOLM,
JOE MANKIEWICZ, LIZA MINNELLI, CICELY TYSON,
ROBERT WAGNER, NATALIE WOOD.**

THE AMERICAN FILM INSTITUTE
SALUTE TO BETTE DAVIS
9:30-11PM, CBS●2

cult in the same way I was difficult. She wanted the best and to get it nothing was too much trouble. Sometimes she wanted more takes on a scene than even I did." Wyler went on to say, "No one I know brought more heart and devotion, more energy, honesty, integrity, ability, professionalism, more sheer damn hard work to a marvelous career than she did."

Natalie Wood, with husband Robert Wagner at her side, admitted, "I was absolutely thrilled to get the chance to work with her," while Wagner told Bette, "Lady, you're beautiful, just beautiful" (a line from *Madame Sin*).

Bette's co-star in *Dark Victory*, Geraldine Fitzgerald, with long, free-flowing hair (she was in Los Angeles for her singing appearance at Studio One) remembered nostalgic anecdotal warnings she had received prior to working with Bette. Miss Fitzgerald related that she had been told, "She [Davis] was only interested in getting her face in front of the camera. They said you must watch out all the time. If she smiled at you—if her character smiles at your Character—she's only trying to dazzle you so you won't notice that you're in the dark. If her character walks toward your character, it's because she's going to get in front of you with the camera. Above all, if her character extends a friendly hand to you or catches you by the shoulders, it isn't her character being friendly to your character —she is turning you away from the camera." Miss Fitzgerald admitted, "I was terrified." She was further warned, "The only thing to do is look for a piece of furniture in the scene, somehow get yourself wedged behind it so she can't move you around." In a more serious vein, Miss Fitzgerald concluded with, "Bette Davis was the most positive feature in my career. She really started me off—her kindness and her goodness and her generosity. This was a young girl who was that generous to everybody. She was celebrated for starting people's careers and, therefore, with great love and respect, I salute a great artist and am truly proud to be in this large congregation of her lovers and admirers."

Paul Henreid greeted the audience with,

"I'm here tonight as Bette Davis' friend and fellow smoker. Someone with whom she shared some very important cigarettes. He told of their working together to create the double lighting of cigarettes in *Now, Voyager,* although the director was against the script change. Henreid revealed that the final business of lighting the cigarettes had been approved by producer Hal B. Wallis. Henreid confided that the Warner brothers tried to make him look like George Brent and "I ended up looking like George Raft" but "Bette stood up for me. She had had to fight for the real Bette to come through and she fought just as hard for the real me."

Joseph L. Mankiewicz, Bette's director for *All about Eve,* admitted that he had never met her before the start of *Eve* but "Working with Bette, it goes without saying, from the first day to regrettably our last, was an experience as happy and rewarding as any I have known. . . . To this day, my greatest and deepest regret is that I hadn't worked with her before or since."

Celeste Holm's remarks about Bette's on-screen villainy led the way for clips of some of her more evil performances, about which Miss Holm pointed out ". . . Despite her villainy, or maybe because of it, she remains a heroine to every aspiring young actress in the world."

Wearing an unflattering hairdo and looking plumpish, Olivia de Havilland confessed, "Bette had the career I most admired. It was the career I wanted to have because she was a pioneer, a revolutionary in that she wanted to play real human beings, good and bad, lovely or ugly, whereas, I fear, most actresses wanted only to be beautiful and romantic. But, not Bette. She was the only young actress to combine character work with stardom. All actors and actresses want the Academy Award. Bette won two, and, later on, so did I. I must say this—if I owe mine to anyone I owe them to Bette. She was the inspiration of my career and I'm thrilled that she is the first woman to be honored in this way. It is *so* appropriate."

George Stevens, Jr., returned to the podium to explain that the Life Achievement

Award "is voted by the trustees to an individual who has advanced the art of film and whose work has stood the test of time." He added that seventy-five of Bette's films have been preserved for all time in the Library of Congress.

Following another long ovation, Bette accepted the award with "The American Film Institute Life Achievement Award is, to me, the frosting on the cake of my career." She acknowledged that she was grateful to everyone in the room but "there are four people I am eternally in debt to." She named Mr. George Arliss who gave her the chance to act in *The Man Who Played God;* Jack L. Warner who "gave me the opportunity to have a successful career" ("I think he finally did respect me—he said so once, anyway"); Hal B. Wallis "for the unbelievable opportunities he gave me as an actress by buying great novels and plays, having scripts written for me"; and William Wyler "because of his direction of me . . . I, for the first time, became a box office star." She noted that she was proud to be in the company of the previous four distinguished winners of the award, and "I will take second billing to any of them any time."

Bette wound up her speech with the line from *Cabin in the Cotton* which she claimed is one of her favorites, "Ah's love t' kiss ya, but ah jest washed mah hair."

During the proceedings, it was revealed that $128,000 was raised from the AFI dinner and that three Bette Davis Scholarships had been awarded at the Advanced Film Studios at Greystone in Los Angeles.

Following the hoopla of the AFI Award and the tremendous amount of publicity concerning Bette Davis, past, present, and future, there was a raft of rumors as to what her next film project might be. Davis still hoped somewhere and somehow she could participate—in any capacity— in a movie rendition of *Ethan Frome.* More likely was the suggestion by Hal B. Wallis to co-star Davis with Katharine Hepburn in *White Water,* in which Bette would be a banker's wife and hellion, and Hepburn a well-to-do, refined woman. Wallis admitted freely regarding his long-term relationship with Bette, "Of course, there were encounters from time to time, and we did have differences of opinion on scripts or whatever—but there was never any big 'locking of horns.' Sometimes I'd compromise, sometimes she would, but we'd always end up seeing eye to eye. And with Bette, I was always happy with the results of the efforts."

But instead, Davis signed up with Walt Disney Productions for *Return from Witch Mountain.* Her co-star was Christopher Lee. He was to play a nasty scientist who turns human beings into robots, while she would appear as his accomplice in kidnapping a youth with supernatural powers. On location, Bette was interviewed by Bob Thomas. "I'm having a great time," claimed the star. "I'm utterly fascinated by the miracles that the Disney technicians can accomplish. This is the first time I've encountered that side of the movie business and I am impressed. . . . The work is so easy. You're part of the whole [Disney organization], and there's no need to work up a characterization. When I think of how hard I've worked on films, trying to build characters! This picture may spoil me forever."

Following her work in the Disney Production, Bette decided to abandon her Connecticut home and moved to California once again. She leased a condominium in a block of new apartments owned on the West Coast by actor Roddy MacDowall. Her reason for the transference was that daughter "B.D." and her husband had moved to Pennsylvania with their son, and Davis' son Michael, a professor of law, lives in Germany. Bette's adopted daughter Margot is still at the Lockland School in Geneva, New York, where she has spent the last twenty-one years. Regarding retarded Margot, Bette has said, "She's learned to control herself. She does beautiful needlepoint and, although she can't cook, she can prepare the vegetables for dinner." She visits Bette on occasion, "But after a few weeks, we have both had it. Margot can't take the pressures of normal living, nor will she ever be able to. She's glad to get back to school and, frankly, since it can be a strain to have her around, I'm glad she's going because I know the environment there is better for her." But Davis insists, "I owe Margot the best life possible. And I will give it to her."

Concerning her famous temperament, she assesses, "I have a pretty healthy temper. I always have, and I don't see any improvement now that I'm getting older. I'm not naturally sharp-tongued, but if someone is sharp to me, rest assured I can reply. . . Most of the time I fight, it's with film people, and that's just self-preservation. Besides, if you become mellow, it just means you have given up the fight."

With her usual candor, she admits, "My biggest problem all my life was men. I never met one yet who could compete with the image the public made of Bette Davis. . . . I'm meant for a man. I get very lonely at night, and there's nothing glamorous about that. . . ."

FILMOGRAPHY

BAD SISTER *(Universal, 1931)* 68 min.
Producer, Carl Laemmle, Jr.; director, Hobart Henley; based on the novel *The Flirt* by Booth Tarkington; screenplay, Raymond L. Schrock, Tom Reed; additional dialogue, Edwin Knopf; camera, Karl Freund; editor, Ted J. Kent.
Conrad Nagel (Dr. Dick Lindley); Sidney Fox (Marianne Madison); Bette Davis (Laura Madison); ZaSu Pitts (Minnie); Slim Summerville (Sam); Charles Winninger (Mr. Madison); Emma Dunn (Mrs. Madison); Humphrey Bogart (Valentine Corliss); Bert Roach (Wade Trumbull); David Durand (Henrick Madison).

SEED *(Universal, 1931)* 96 min.
Producer/director, John M. Stahl; based on the novel by Charles G. Norris; screenplay, Gladys Lehman; camera, Jackson Rose; editor, Ted J. Kent.
John Boles (Bart Carter); Genevieve Tobin (Mildred); Lois Wilson (Peggy); Raymond Hackett (Junior Carter); Bette Davis (Margaret Carter); Frances Dade (Nancy); ZaSu Pitts (Jennie); Richard Tucker (Bliss); Jack Willis (Dicky Carter); Bill Willis (Danny Carter); Dick Winslow (Johnny Carter).

WATERLOO BRIDGE *(Universal, 1931)* 72 min.
Producer, Carl Laemmle, Jr.; director, James Whale; based on the play by Robert Sherwood; screenplay, Benn W. Levy; continuity/additional dialogue, Tom Reed; camera, Arthur Edeson; editor, Whale.

Mae Clarke (Myra); Kent Douglas [Douglass Montgomery] (Roy); Doris Lloyd (Kitty); Ethel Griffies (Mrs. Hoble); Enid Bennett (Mrs. Wetherby); Frederick Kerr (Mr. Wetherby); Bette Davis (Janet); Rita Carlisle (Old Woman).

WAY BACK HOME *(RKO, 1932)* 81 min.
Producer, Pandro S. Berman; director, William A. Seiter; based on radio characters created by Phillips H. Lord; screenplay, Jane Murfin; music, Max Steiner; art director, Max Ree; camera, J. Roy Hunt.
Phillips Lord (Seth Parker); Effie Palmer (Ma Parker); Mrs. Phillips Lord (Liz); Bennett Kilpack (Urphus); Raymond Hunter (Captain); Frank Albertson (David Clark); Bette Davis (Mary Lucy); Oscar Apfel (Wobblin); Stanley Fields (Rufe Turner); Dorothy Peterson (Runaway Rosie); Frankie Darro (Robbie).

THE MENACE *(Columbia, 1932)* 64 min.
Producer, Sam Nelson; director, Roy William Neil; based on the novel *The Feathered Serpent* by Edgar Wallace; screenplay, Dorothy Howell, Charles Logue; dialogue, Roy Chanslor; camera, L. William O'Connell.
H. B. Warner (Tracy); Bette Davis (Peggy); Walter Byron (Ronald); Natalie Moorhead (Caroline); William Davidson (Utterson); Crauford Kent (Lewis); Halliwell Hobbes (Phillips); Charles Gerrard (Bailiff); Murray Kinnell (Carr).

HELL'S HOUSE (*Capital Films Exchange, 1932*) 72 min.

Producer, Benjamin F. Zeidman; director/story, Howard Higgin; screenplay, Paul Gangelin and B. Harrison Orkow; camera, Allen S. Siegel; editor, Edward Schroeder.

Junior Durkin (Jimmy Mason); Pat O'Brien (Kelly); Bette Davis (Peggy Gardner); Junior Coghlan (Shorty); Charley Grapewin (Uncle Henry); Emma Dunn (Aunt Emma); Morgan Wallace (Frank Gebhardt); Hooper Atchley (Captain of the Guards); Wallis Clark (Judge Robinson); James Marcus (Superintendent Thompson); Mary Alden (Mrs. Mason).

THE MAN WHO PLAYED GOD (*Warner Bros., 1932*) 80 min.

Producer, Jack L. Warner; director, John Adolphi; based on a short story by Gouverneur Morris and the play *The Silent Voice* by Jules Eckert Goodman; screenplay, Julien Josephson, Maude Howell; camera, James Van Trees; editor, William Holmes.

George Arliss (Montgomery Royale); Violet Heming (Mildred); Ivan Simpson (Battle); Louise Closser Hale (Florence); Bette Davis (Grace); Andre Luguet (The King); Donald Cook (Harold); Charles Evans (The Doctor); Oscar Apfel (The Lip Reader); Paul Porcasi (The Concert Manager); Raymond Milland (Eddie); Dorothy Libaire (Jenny); William Janney (Boy); Grace Durkin (Girl); Russell Hopton (Reporter); Murray Kinnell (King's Aide); Harry Stubbs (Chitterdon); Hedda Hopper (His Wife); Wade Boteler (Detective); Alexander Ikonikoff, Michael Visaroff (Russian Officers).

British release title: *The Silent Voice.*

SO BIG (*Warner Bros., 1932*) 80 min.

Producer, Jack L. Warner; director, William A. Wellman; based on the novel by Edna Ferber; screenplay, J. Grubb Alexander; music, W. Franke Harling, Robert Lord; costumes, Orry-Kelly; art director, Jack Okey; camera, Sid Hickox; editor, William Holmes.

Barbara Stanwyck (Selina Peake); George Brent (Roelf); Dickie Moore (Dirk as a Boy); Guy Kibbee (August Hemple); Bette Davis (Dallas O'Mara); Mae Madison (Julie Hemple); Hardie Albright (Dirk Peake); Robert Warwick (Jan Steen); Earle Foxe (Pervus Dejong); Alan Hale (Klaus Pool); Dorothy Peterson (Maartje); Dawn O'Day [Anne Shirley] (Selina as a Little Girl); Dick Winslow (Roelf as a Boy); Harry Beresford (Adams Oems); Eulalie Jensen (Mrs. Hemple); Elizabeth Patterson (Mrs. Tebbits); Rita LaRoy (Paula); Blanche Frederici (Widow Parrienburg); Willard Robertson (The Doctor); Harry Holman (Country Doctor); Lionel Belmore (Reverend Dekker).

THE RICH ARE ALWAYS WITH US (*First National, 1932*) 73 min.

Producer, Samuel Bischoff; director, Alfred E. Green; based on the novel by E. Pettit; screenplay,

Austin Parker; gowns, Orry-Kelly; music, W. Franke Harling; camera, Ernest Haller; editor, George Marks.

Ruth Chatterton (Caroline Grannard); George Brent (Julian Tierney); Adrienne Dore (Allison Adair); Bette Davis (Malbro); John Miljan (Gregory Grannard); John Wray (Davis); Robert Warwick (The Doctor); Virginia Hammond (Flo); Walter Walker (Dante); Eula Guy (Mrs. Drake); Berton Churchill (The Judge).

THE DARK HORSE (*First National, 1932*) 75 min.

Associate producer, Samuel Bischoff; director, Alfred E. Green; story, Melville Crossman [Darryl Zanuck], Joseph Jackson, Courtney Terrett; screenplay, Joseph Jackson, Wilson Mizner; art director, Jack Okey; camera, Sol Polito; editor, George Marks.

Warren William (Hal S. Blake); Bette Davis (Kay Russell); Guy Kibbee (Zachary Hicks); Frank McHugh (Joe); Vivienne Osborne (Maybelle); Sam Hardy (Black); Robert Warwick (Clark); Harry Holman (Jones); Charles Sellon (Green); Robert Emmett O'-Connor (Sheriff); Berton Churchill (William A. Underwood).

CABIN IN THE COTTON (*First National, 1932*) 79 min.

Executive producer, Jack L. Warner; director, Michael Curtiz; based on the novel by Harry Harrison Kroll; screenplay, Paul Greene; camera, Barney McGill; editor, George Amy.

Richard Barthelmess (Marvin Blake); Dorothy Jordan (Betty Wright); Bette Davis (Madge Norwood); Henry B. Walthall (Old Eph); Berton Churchill (Lane Norwood); Walter Percival (Cleve Clinton); William Le Maire (Jake Fisher); Hardie Albright (Roland Neal); Tully Marshall (Old Slick Harness); Edmund Breese (Holmes Scott); John Marston (Russ Carter); Erville Alderson (Sock Fisher); Dorothy Peterson (Lilly Blake); Fred "Snowflake" Toones (Ezzy Daniels); Russell Simpson (Uncle Joe); Harry Cording (Ross Clinton); Virgina Hammond (Mrs. Norwood).

THREE ON A MATCH (*Warner Bros., 1932*) 63 min.

Associate producer, Samuel Bischoff; director, Mervyn LeRoy; story, Kubec Glasmon, John Bright; screenplay, Lucien Hubbard; art director, Robert Haas; camera, Sol Polito; editor, Ray Curtis.

Joan Blondell (Mary Keaton); Warren William (Robert Kirkwood); Ann Dvorak (Vivian Revere); Bette Davis (Ruth Westcott); Grant Mitchell (School Principal); Lyle Talbot (Michael Loftus); Sheila Terry (Naomi); Glenda Farrell (Mrs. Black); Clara Blandick (Mrs. Keaton); Buster Phelps (Junior); Humphrey Bogart (Harve); John Marston (Bilkerson); Patricia Ellis (Linda); Hale Hamilton (Defense Attorney); Edward Arnold (Ace); Allen Jenkins (Dick); Jack LaRue, Stanley Price (Mugs).

20,000 YEARS IN SING SING (*First National, 1933*) 77 min.

Associate producer, Robert Lord; director, Michael

Curtiz; based on the book by Warden Lewis E. Lawes; adaptors, Courtney Terrett, Lord; screenplay, Wilson Mizner, Brown Holmes; costumes, Orry-Kelly; music, Bernhard Kaum; camera, Barney McGill; editor, George Amy.

Spencer Tracy (Tom Connors); Bette Davis (Fay); Lyle Talbot (Bud); Sheila Terry (Billie); Edward McNamara (Chief of Guards); Warren Hymer (Hype); Spencer Charters (Daniels); Louis Calhern (Joe Finn); Arthur Byron (Warden Long); Grant Mitchell (Dr. Ames); Nella Walker (Mrs. Long); Harold Huber (Tony); William Le Maire (Black Jack); Arthur Hoyt (Dr. Meeker); George Pat Collins (Mike).

PARACHUTE JUMPER *(Warner Bros., 1933)* 65 min.

Executive producer, Jack L. Warner; director, Alfred E. Green; based on the story "Some Call It Love" by Rian James; screenplay, John Francis Larkin; art director, Jack Okey; camera, James Van Trees; editor, Ray Curtis.

Douglas Fairbanks, Jr. (Bill Keller); Leo Carrillo (Weber); Bette Davis (Alabama); Frank McHugh (Toodles); Claire Dood (Mrs. Newberry); Sheila Terry (Secretary); Harold Huber (Steve); Thomas E. Jackson (Coffey); George Pat Collins (Crowley); Harold Healy (Wilson); Ferdinand Munier (Hocheimer).

THE WORKING MAN *(Warner Bros., 1933)* 73 min.

Executive producer, Jack L. Warner; director, John Adolfi; based on the story "The Adopted Father" by Edgar Franklin; screenplay, Maude T. Howell, Charles Kenyon; art director, Jack Okey; gowns, Orry-Kelly; camera, Sol Polito; editor, Owen Marks.

George Arliss (John Reeves); Bette Davis (Jenny Hartland); Hardie Albright (Benjamin Burnett); Theodore Newton (Tommy Hartland); Gordon Westcott (Freddie Pettison); J. Farrell MacDonald (Hank Davidson); Charles Evans (Haslitt); Frederick Burton (Judge Larson); Pat Wing (Secretary); Edward Van Sloan (Briggs); Claire McDowell (Stenographer); Ruthelma Stevens (Mrs. Price); Edward Cooper (Butler); Harold Minjur (Tommy's Bridge Partner); Gertrude Sutton (Maid); Douglass Dumbrille (Lawyer Hammersmith); Richard Tucker (Board Member); James Bush (Bridge Player); Selmer Jackson, Clay Clement, James Donlan (Company Men).

EX-LADY *(Warner Bros., 1933)* 62 min.

Producing supervisor, Lucien Hubbard; director, Robert Florey; story, Edith Fitzgerald and Robert Riskin; screenplay, David Boehm; art director, Jack Okey; gowns, Orry-Kelly; camera, Tony Gaudio; editor, Harold McLernon.

Bette Davis (Helen Bauer); Gene Raymond (Don Peterson); Frank McHugh (Hugo Van Hugh); Monroe Owsley (Nick Mayvyn); Claire Dodd (Iris Van Hugh); Kay Strozzi (Peggy Smith); Ferdinand Gottschalk (Mr. Smith); Alphonse Ethier (Father); Bodil Rosing

(Mother); Gay Seabrook (Girl); Ynez (Rhumba Dancer).

BUREAU OF MISSING PERSONS *(First National, 1933)* 75 min.

Producer, Henry Blanke; director, Roy Del Ruth; based on the book *Missing Men* by John H. Ayers and Carol Bird; screenplay, Robert Presnell; art director, Robert Haas; camera, Barney McGill; editor, James Gibbon.

Bette Davis (Norma Phillips); Lewis Stone (Captain Webb); Pat O'Brien (Butch Saunders); Glenda Farrell (Belle); Allen Jenkins (Joe Musik); Ruth Donnelly (Pete); Hugh Herbert (Slade); Alan Dinehart (Therme Roberts); Marjorie Gateson (Mrs. Paul); Tad Alexander (Caesar Paul); Noel Francis (Alice); Wallis Clark (Mr. Paul); Adrian Morris (Irish Conlin); Clay Clement (Kingman); Henry Kolker (Mr. Arno).

FASHIONS OF 1934 *(First National, 1934)* 77 min.

Producer, Henry Blanke; director, William Dieterle; based on the story "The Fashion Plate" by Harry Collins, Warren Duff; screenplay, F. Hugh Herbert, Gene Markey, Kathryn Scola, Carl Erickson; songs, Sammy Fain and Irving Kahal; music director, Leo F. Forbstein; dances created and staged by Busby Berkeley; art directors, Jack Okey, Willy Pogany; gowns, Orry-Kelly; camera, William Rees; editor, Jack Killifer.

William Powell (Sherwood Nash); Bette Davis (Lynn Mason); Frank McHugh (Snap); Verree Teasdale (Grand Duchess Alix [Mabel McGuire]); Reginald Owen (Oscar Baroque); Hobart Cavanaugh (M. Gautier); Henry O'Neill (Duryea); Phillip Reed (Jimmy); Hugh Herbert (Joe Ward); Gordon Westcott (Harry Brent); Dorothy Burgess (Glenda); George Humbert (Glass Caponelli); Frank Darien (Jules); Harry Beresford (Book Seller); Helen Freeman (Mme. Margot); Tibby (Scotch Terrier); Sam McDaniel (Cleaning Man); Lee Phelps (Desk Clerk); Arthur Treacher (Butler); Martin Kosleck (Dance Director); Jane Darwell (Dowager); Georges Renavent (Fashion Salon Owner); Eric Wilton (Another Butler).

THE BIG SHAKEDOWN *(First National, 1934)* 64 min.

Producer, Samuel Bischoff; director, John Francis Dillon; story, Sam Engels; screenplay, Niven Busch, Rian James; camera, Sid Hickox; editor, James Gibbon.

Charles Farrell (Jimmy Morrell); Bette Davis (Norma Frank); Ricardo Cortez (Bernes); Glenda Farrell (Lil); Allen Jenkins (Lefty); Henry O'Neill (Sheffner); G. Pat Collins (Gyp); Adrian Morris (Trigger); Dewey Robinson (Slim); John Wray (Gardinella); Philip Faversham (John); Earle Foxe (Carey); Samuel S. Hinds (Kohlsadt); Sidney Miller (Jewish Boy); Elinor Jackson (Woman); Charles B. Williams (Timid Man); Robert Emmett O'Connor (Regan, the Bartender); Ben Taggert (Cop); Oscar Apfel (Doctor); John Hyams (Smith);

Edward LeSaint (Fillmore); Frank Layton (Dr. Boutellier).

JIMMY THE GENT *(Warner Bros., 1934)* 66 min.

Executive producer, Jack L. Warner; director, Michael Curtiz; based on the story "The Heir Chaser" by Laird Doyle, Ray Nazarro; screenplay, Bertram Milhauser; art director, Esdras Hartley; camera, Ira Morgan; editor, Tommy Richards.

James Cagney (Jimmy Corrigan); Bette Davis (Joan Martin); Alice White (Mabel); Allen Jenkins (Louie); Alan Dinehart (Charles Wallingham); Mayo Methot (Gladys Farrell); Hobart Cavanaugh (Worthington, the Southern Heir Imposter); Philip Faversham (Intern); Phillip Reed (Ronnie Gatson); Arthur Hohl (Joe Rector [Monty Varton]); Ralf Harolde (Hendrickson); Renee Whitney (Bessie, the Phone Girl); Merna Kennedy (Jitters, the Typist); Camile Rovelle (File Clerk); Joe Sawyer (Mike, the Heir Chaser); Stanley Mack (Pete); Tom Costello (Grant); Dennis O'Keefe (Chester Coots); Jane Darwell (Ettienne); Nora Lane (Posy Barton); Monica Bannister (Tea Assistant); Robert Warwick (Civil Judge).

FOG OVER FRISCO *(First National, 1934)* 67 min.

Production supervisor, Robert Lord; director, William Dieterle; story, George Dyer; screenplay, Robert N. Lee, Eugene Solow; camera, Tony Gaudio; editor, Hal McLernon.

Bette Davis (Arlene Bradford); Donald Woods (Tony Swirling); Margaret Lindsay (Val Bradford); Lyle Talbot (Spencer Carleton); Arthur Byron (Everett Bradford); Hugh Herbert (Izzy Wright); Robert Barrat (Thorne); Douglass Dumbrille (Joshua Maynard); Irving Pichel (Jake Bellow); Gordon Westcott (Joe Bellow); Henry O'Neill (Oren Porter); Charles Wilson (Sergeant O'Hagen); Alan Hale (Chief O'Malley); William B. Davidson (Joe Hague); Douglas Cosgrove (Lieutenant Davis); Harold Minjur (Archie Van Ness); William Demarest (Spike Smith); Harry Seymour (Bill, the Messenger); Dennis O'Keefe (Radio Announcer); Ed Peil (Police Sergeant); Robert Walker (Hood).

OF HUMAN BONDAGE *(RKO, 1934)* 83 min.

Producer, Pandro S. Berman; director, John Cromwell; based on the novel by W. Somerset Maugham; screenplay, Lester Cohen; music director, Max Steiner; art directors, Van Nest Polglase, Carroll Clark; costumes, Walter Plunkett; camera, Henry W. Gerrard; editor, William Morgan.

Leslie Howard (Philip Carey); Bette Davis (Mildred Rogers); Frances Dee (Sally Athelny); Reginald Owen (Thorpe Athelny); Reginald Denny (Harry Griffiths); Kay Johnson (Norah); Alan Hale (Emil Miller); Reginald Sheffield (Dunsford); Desmond Roberts (Dr. Jacobs); Tempe Pigott (Landlady).

HOUSEWIFE *(Warner Bros., 1934)* 69 min.

Executive producer, Jack L. Warner; director, Alfred E. Green; story, Robert Lord, Lillie Hayward; screenplay, Manuel Seff, Hayward; music director, Leo F. Forbstein; songs, Mort Dixon and Allie Wrubel; art director, Robert Haas; gowns, Orry-Kelly; camera, William Rees; editor, James Gibbon.

George Brent (William Reynolds); Ann Dvorak (Nan Wilson Reynolds); Bette Davis (Patricia Barclay [Ruth Smith]); John Halliday (Paul Duprey); Robert Barrat (Sam Blake); Hobart Cavanaugh (George Wilson); Ruth Donnelly (Dora Wilson); Joseph Cawthorn (Kruger); Harry Tyler (Plumber); Leila Bennett (Jennie); Ronald Cosbey (Buddy); Willard Robertson (Judge); John Murray (Salesman); Gordon "Bill" Elliott (Clerk); Leo White (Waiter); Eula Guy (Miss Finch); Phil Regan (Hathaway, the Crooner); John Hale (Doctor); Lee Phelps (Court Clerk); Charles Coleman (Bolton).

BORDERTOWN *(Warner Bros., 1935)* 80 min.

Executive producer, Jack L. Warner; director, Archie Mayo; based on the novel by Carroll Graham; screenplay, Laird Doyle, Wallace Smith; adaptor, Robert Lord; music, Bernhard Kaun; art director, Jack Okey; camera, Tony Gaudio; editor, Thomas Richards.

Paul Muni (Johnny Ramirez); Bette Davis (Marie Roark); Margaret Lindsay (Dale Elwell); Eugene Pallette (Charlie Roark); Soledad Jiminez (Mrs. Ramirez); Robert Barrat (Padre); Gavin Gordon (Brook Mandillo); Henry O'Neill (Chase); Arthur Stone (Manuel Diego); Hobart Cavanaugh (Drunk); William B. Davidson (Dr. Carter); Oscar Apfel (Judge at Law School); Samuel S. Hinds (Judge at Trial); Edward McWade (Dean); Wallis Clark (Friend); John Eberts (Alberto); Chris-Pin Martin (Jose); Eddie Shubert (Marketman); Carlos Villar (Headwaiter); Marjorie North (Janet); Addie McPhail (Carter's Girl); Frank Puglia (Commissioner); Alphonz Ethier (Banker); Eddie Lee (Sam); Vivian Tobin (Woman); Arthur Treacher (Butler); Ralph Navarro (Defense Attorney).

THE GIRL FROM TENTH AVENUE *(First National, 1935)* 69 min.

Production supervisor, Robert Lord; director, Alfred E. Green; based on the play by Hubert Henry Davies; screenplay, Charles Kenyon; gowns, Orry-Kelly; camera, James Van Trees; editor, Owen Marks.

Bette Davis (Miriam Brady); Ian Hunter (Geoffrey Sherwood); Colin Clive (John Marland); Alison Skipworth (Mrs. Martin); John Eldredge (Hugh Brown); Phillip Reed (Tony Hewlett); Katharine Alexander (Valentine French Marland); Helen Jerome Eddy (Miss Mansfield, the Secretary); Adrian Rosley (Marcel); Andre Cheron (Max); Edward McWade (Art Clerk); Brooks Benedict (Diner); Gordon "Bill" Elliott (Clerk at Club); Jack Norton (Man); Bess Flowers (Woman Guest); Mary Treen (Secretary).

FRONT PAGE WOMAN *(Warner Bros., 1935)* 80 min.

Producer, Samuel Bischoff; director, Michael Curtiz; based on the story "Women Are Bum Newspapermen" by Richard Macaulay; screenplay, Laird Doyle, Lillie Hayward, Roy Chanslor; music, Heinz Roemheld; art director, John Hughes; camera, Tony Gaudio; editor, Terry Morse.

Bette Davis (Ellen Garfield); George Brent (Curt Devlin); Roscoe Karns (Toots); Winifred Shaw (Inez Cordova); Joseph Crehan (Spike Kiley); Joseph King (Hartnett); J. Farrell MacDonald (Hallohan); Addison Richards (District Attorney); Dorothy Dare, June Martel (Show Girls); Gordon Westcott (Maitland Colter); J. Carrol Naish (Mr. Roberts); Walter Walker (Judge Rickard); DeWitt Jennings (Lieutenant); Huntley Gordon (Marvin Stone); Adrian Rosley (Tailor); Georges Renavent (Chinard); Miki Morita (Fuji); Jack Norton, Edward Keane (Reporters); Dick Winslow (Copy Boy); Charles Moore (Black Boy); Lester Dorr, Jerry Mandy (Waiters); Wade Boteler (Cop); Mary Treen (Nurse); Torben Meyer (Janitor); Frank DuFrane (Assistant District Attorney).

SPECIAL AGENT *(Warner Bros., 1935)* 76 min.

Producer, Martin Mooney; director, William Keighley; screen idea, Mooney; screenplay, Laird Doyle, Abem Finkel; music director, Leo F. Forbstein; art director, Esdras Hartley; camera, Sid Hickox; editor, Clarence Kolter.

Bette Davis (Julie Carston); George Brent (Bill Bradford); Ricardo Cortez (Carston); Joseph Sawyer (Rich); Joseph Crehan (Chief of Police); Henry O'Neill (District Attorney); Irving Pichel (U. S. District Attorney); Jack LaRue (Andrews); Robert Strange (Armitage); Joseph King (Wilson); J. Carrol Naish (Durrell); Paul Guilfoyle (Secretary to District Attorney); Robert Barrat (Head of Internal Revenue Department); Jack Mower, Eddy Chandler, Ed Hart, Charles Middleton, Thomas E. Jackson (Cops); Martha Tibbetts (Operator); John Alexander (Manager); Milton Kibbee (Player); Rob Montgomery, Huey White, Dutch Hendrian (Gangsters); Lee Phelps (Court Clerk).

DANGEROUS *(Warner Bros., 1935)* 78 min.

Producer, Harry Joe Brown; director, Alfred E. Green; story/screenplay, Laird Doyle; music director, Leo F. Forbstein; music contributor, Bernhard Kaun; gowns, Orry-Kelly; art director, Hugh Reticker; camera, Ernest Haller; editor, Tommy Richards.

Bette Davis (Joyce Heath); Franchot Tone (Don Bellows); Margaret Lindsay (Gail Armitage); Alison Skipworth (Mrs. Williams); John Eldredge (Gordon Heath); Dick Foran (Teddy); Pierre Watkin (George Sheffield); Walter Walker (Roger Farnsworth); George Irving (Charles Melton); William Davidson (Reed Walsh); Douglas Wood (Elmont); Richard Carle (Pitt Hanly); Milton Kibbee (Williams, Roger's Chauffeur); George Andre Beranger, Larry McGrath (Waiters);

Frank O'Connor (Bartender); Miki Morita (Cato); Gordon "Bill" Elliott (Male Lead in Play); Libby Taylor (Beulah); Craig Reynolds (Reporter); Eddie Foster (Passerby); Billy Wayne (Teddy's Chauffeur); Mary Treen (Nurse); Edward Keane (Doctor).

THE PETRIFIED FOREST *(Warner Bros., 1936)* 75 min.

Associate producer, Henry Blanke; director, Archie Mayo; based on the play by Robert Sherwood; screenplay, Charles Kenyon, Delmer Daves; music, Bernhard Kaun; music director, Leo F. Forbstein; assistant director, Dick Mayberry; art director, John Hughes; gowns, Orry-Kelly; sound, Charles Land; special effects, Warren E. Lynch, Fred Jackman, Willard Van Enger; camera, Sol Polito; editor, Owen Marks.

Leslie Howard (Alan Squier); Bette Davis (Gabrielle Maple); Genevieve Tobin (Mrs. Chisholm); Dick Foran (Buz Hertzlinger); Humphrey Bogart (Duke Mantee); Joe Sawyer (Jackie); Porter Hall (Jason Maple); Charley Grapewin (Gramp Maple); Paul Harvey (Mr. Chisholm); Eddie Acuff (Lineman); Adrian Morris (Ruby); Nina Campana (Paula); Slim Thompson (Slim); John Alexander (Joseph); Addison Richards (Radio Announcer).

THE GOLDEN ARROW *(First National, 1936)* 68 min.

Producer, Samuel Bischoff; director, Alfred E. Green; based on the play by Michael Arlen; screenplay, Charles Kenyon; music, W. Franke Harling, Heinz Roemheld; music director, Leo F. Forbstein; gowns, Orry-Kelly; camera, Arthur Edeson; editor, Thomas Pratt.

Bette Davis (Daisy Appleby); George Brent (Johnny Jones); Carol Hughes (Hortense Burke-Meyers); Eugene Pallette (Mr. Meyers); Dick Foran (Tommy Blake); Catharine Doucet (Mrs. Pommesby); Craig Reynolds (Jorgenson); Hobart Cavanaugh (De Wolfe); Henry O'Neill (Mr. Appleby); Ivan Lebedeff (Count Giggi Guilliano); G. P. Huntley, Jr. (Aubrey Rutherford); Rafael Storm (Prince Peter); E. E. Clive (Walker); Eddie Acuff (Davis); Earle A. Foxe (Parker); Carlyle Moore, Jr. (Mr. Rogers); Naomi Judge (Mrs. Clarke); Colleen Coleman (Miss Jones); Shirley Lloyd (Miss French); Larry Kent (Mr. Smith); Billy Arnold (Officer); Rudolf Anders (Max); Jose Rubic (Renaldo); George Sorrell (Marcel); Elsa Peterson (Woman); Bess Flowers (Miss Heckett); Cliff Saum (Guard); Edward Keane (Bixby); Gordon "Bill" Elliott, Frank Faylen, Eddie Fetherston (Reporters); Vesey O'Davoren (Butler); Viola Lowry (Woman); Major Nichols (Man); Alma Lloyd (Telephone Girl).

SATAN MET A LADY *(Warner Bros., 1936)* 66 min.

Producer, Henry Blanke; director, William Dieterle; based on the novel *The Maltese Falcon* by Dashiell Hammett; screenplay, Brown Holmes; music director,

Leo F. Forbstein; gowns, Orry-Kelly; camera, Arthur Edeson; editors, Max Parker, Warren Low.

Bette Davis (Valerie Purvis); Warren William (Ted Shane); Alison Skipworth (Madame Barabbas); Arthur Treacher (Anthony Travers); Winifred Shaw (Astrid Ames); Marie Wilson (Murgatroyd); Porter Hall (Mr. Ames); Maynard Holmes (Kenneth); Charles Wilson (Pollock); Olin Howland (Dunhill); Joseph King (Mc-Elroy); Barbara Blane (Babs); Eddie Shubert, Stuart Holmes, Francis Sayles, James Burtis (Detectives); Billy Bletcher, Alice La Mont (Parents of Sextuplets); Alphonse Martell (Headwaiter); John Elliott (City Father); Edward McWade (Richards).

MARKED WOMAN (Warner Bros., 1937) 96 min.

Executive producers, Jack L. Warner, Hal B. Wallis; producer, Lou Edelman; director, Lloyd Bacon; screenplay, Robert Rosson, Abem Finkel; additional dialogue, Seton I. Miller; music, Bernhard Kaun, Heinz Roemheld; music director, Leo F. Forbstein; art director, Max Parker; songs, Harry Warren and Al Dubin; camera, George Barnes; editor, Jack Killifer.

Bette Davis (Mary Dwight [Strauber]); Humphrey Bogart (David Graham); Jane Bryan (Betty Strauber); Eduardo Ciannelli (Johnny Vanning); Isabel Jewell (Emmy Lou Egan); Allen Jenkins (Louie); Mayo Methot (Estelle Porter); Lola Lane (Gabby Marvin); Ben Welden (Charley Delaney); Henry O'Neill (District Attorney Sheldon); Roselind Marquis (Florrie Liggett); John Litel (Gordon); Damian O'Flynn (Ralph Krawford); Robert Strange (George Beler); Archie Robbins (Bell Captain); William B. Davidson (Bob Crandall); John Sheehan (Vincent, a Sugar Daddy); Sam Wren (Mac); Kenneth Harlan (Eddie, a Sugar Daddy); Raymond Hatton (Lawyer at Jail); Frank Faylen (Taxi Driver); Harlan Briggs (Man in Phone Booth); Guy Usher (Ferguson, the Detective); Milton Kibbee (Male Secretary at D.A.'s Office); Jeffrey Sayre (Assistant to Graham); Herman Marks (Little Joe); Emmett Vogan (Court Clerk); Pierre Watkin (Judge); Mary Doyle (Nurse).

KID GALAHAD (Warner Bros., 1937) 100 min.

Executive producer, Hal B. Wallis; director, Michael Curtiz; based on the novel by Francis Wallace; screenplay, Seton I. Miller; music, Heinz Roemheld, Max Steiner; music director, Leo F. Forbstein; art director, Carl Jules Weyl; gowns, Orry-Kelly; songs, M. K. Jerome and Jack Scholl; camera, Tony Gaudio; editor, George Amy.

Edward G. Robinson (Nick Donati); Bette Davis (Louise "Fluff" Phillips); Humphrey Bogart (Turkey Morgan); Wayne Morris (Ward Guisenberry [Kid Galahad]); Jane Bryan (Marie Donati); Ben Welden (Buzz Stevens); Harry Carey (Silver Jackson); William Haade (Chuck McGraw); Joe Cunningham (Joe Taylor); Soledad Jimenez (Mrs. Donati); Harlan Tucker (Gunman); Veda Ann Borg (The Redhead); Frank Faylen (Barney); Bob Nestell (Tim O'Brian); George Blake

(Referee); Mary Doran (Operator); Joyce Compton (Drunken Girl on Phone); Horace McMahon, Max Hoffman, Edward Price, Billy Arnold, Harry Harvey, Philip Waldron, Milton Kibbee, Don Brodie (Reporters); Curtis Benton (Announcer); I. Stanford Jolley (Ringsider); Don De Fore (Another Ringsider); Lane Chandler (Timekeeper at Title Fight); John Shelton (Reporter at Press Conference); Mary Sunde (Blonde); John Ridgely (Photographer).

TV title: The Battling Bellhop.

THAT CERTAIN WOMAN (Warner Bros., 1937) 91 min.

Executive producer, Hal B. Wallis; director, Edmund Goulding; based on the screenplay The Trespasser by Goulding; screenplay, Goulding; music, Max Steiner; music director, Leo F. Forbstein; art director, Max Parker; gowns, Orry-Kelly; camera, Ernest Haller; editor, Jack Killifer.

Bette Davis (Mary Donnell); Henry Fonda (Jack Merrick); Ian Hunter (Lloyd Rogers); Anita Louise (Flip); Donald Crisp (Merrick Sr.); Hugh O'Connell (Virgil Whitaker); Katharine Alexander (Mrs. Rogers); Mary Phillips (Amy); Minor Watson (Tilden); Ben Welden (Harry Aqueilli); Sidney Toler (Neely); Charles Trowbridge (Dr. James); Norman Willis (Fred); Herbert Rawlinson (Dr. Hartman); Tim Henning (Kenyon); Dwane Day (Jackie); John Hamilton (American); Georges Renavent (Frenchman); Andre Rouseyrol (French Boy); Jack Mower, John Harron (Men); Frank Faylen, Granville Owen, Mike Lally, Charles Sherlock (Reporters); Etta McDaniel (Cook); Jack Ryan (Baggage Man).

IT'S LOVE I'M AFTER (First National, 1937) 90 min.

Executive producer, Hal B. Wallis; director, Archie Mayo; based on the story Gentleman after Midnight by Maurice Hanline; screenplay, Casey Robinson; art director, Carl Jules Weyl; music, Heinz Roemheld; music director, Leo F. Forbstein; gowns, Orry-Kelly; camera, James Van Trees; editor, Owen Marks.

Leslie Howard (Basil Underwood); Bette Davis (Joyce Arden); Olivia de Havilland (Marcia West); Eric Blore (Digges); Patric Knowles (Henry Grant); George Barbier (William West); Spring Byington (Aunt Ella Paisley); Bonita Granville (Gracie Kane); E. E. Clive (Butler); Veda Ann Borg (Elsie); Valerie Bergere (Joyce's Maid); Georgia Caine (Mrs. Kane); Sarah Edwards (Mrs. Hinkle); Grace Field (Mrs. Babson); Harvey Clark (Mr. Babson); Thomas Pogue (Mr. Hinkle); Ed Mortimer (Mr. Kane); Thomas R. Mills (Butler); Lionel Belmore (Friar Lawrence); Ellen Clancy [Janet Shaw], Patricia Walthall, Rosella Towne, Helen Valkis (Autograph Hunters); Herbert Ashley (Doorman); Paul Irving (House Manager); Jack Mower (Hotel Clerk); Irving Bacon (Elevator Man); Georgie Cooper (Woman Guest).

JEZEBEL *(Warner Bros., 1938)* 104 min.

Executive producer, Hal B. Wallis; associate producer, Henry Blanke; director, William Wyler; based on the play by Owen Davis, Sr.; screenplay, Clement Ripley, Abem Finkel, John Huston; screenplay contributor, Robert Bruckner; art director, Robert Haas; music, Max Steiner; music director, Leo F. Forbstein; songs, Harry Warren and Johnny Mercer; costumes, Orry-Kelly; camera, Ernest Haller; editor, Warren Low.

Bette Davis (Julie Marsden); Henry Fonda (Preston Dillard); George Brent (Buck Cantrell); Margaret Lindsay (Amy Bradford Dillard); Fay Bainter (Aunt Belle Massey); Richard Cromwell (Ted Dillard); Donald Crisp (Dr. Livingstone); Henry O'Neill (General Theopholus Bogardus); John Litel (Jean Le Cour); Gordon Oliver (Dick Allen); Janet Shaw (Molly Allen); Spring Byington (Mrs. Kendrick); Margaret Early (Stephanie Kendrick); Georgia Caine (Mrs. Petion); Irving Pichel (Huger); Georges Renavent (De Lautrec); Fred Lawrence (Bob); Ann Codee (Madame Poulard, the Dressmaker); Lew Payton (Uncle Cato); Eddie Anderson (Gros Bat); Stymie Beard (Ti Bat); Theresa Harris (Zetter); Sam McDaniel (Driver); Charles Wagenheim (Customer); Phillip Hurlic (Erronens); Davison Clark (Deputy Sheriff); Jack Norton (Drunk); Alan Bridge (New Orleans Sheriff); Louis Mercier (Bar Companion); Frederick Burton (Director).

THE SISTERS *(Warner Bros., 1938)* 95 min.

Producer, Hal B. Wallis in association with David Lewis; director, Anatole Litvak; based on the novel by Myron Brinig; screenplay, Milton Krims; music, Max Steiner; music director, Leo F. Forbstein; art director, Carl Jules Weyl; costumes, Orry-Kelly; camera, Tony Gaudio; editor, Warren Low.

Errol Flynn (Frank Medlin); Bette Davis (Louise Elliot); Anita Louise (Helen Elliot); Jane Bryan (Grace Elliot); Ian Hunter (William Benson); Henry Travers (Ned Elliot); Beulah Bondi (Rose Elliot); Donald Crisp (Tim Hazleton); Dick Foran (Tom Knivel); Patric Knowles (Norman French); Alan Hale (Sam Johnson); Janet Shaw (Stella Johnson); Lee Patrick (Flora Gibbon); Laura Hope Crewe (Flora's Mother); Harry Davenport (Doc Moore); Irving Bacon (Norman Forbes); Mayo Methot (Blonde); Paul Harvey (Caleb Ammon); Arthur Hoyt (Tom Selig); John Warburton (Lord Anthony Bittick); Stanley Fields (Ship's Captain); Ruth Garland (Lora Bennett); Larry Williams (Young Man); Vera Lewis (Woman); Susan Hayward, Paulette Evans, Frances Morris (Telephone Operators); Jack Mower (Ship's Officer); Peggy Moran (Girl); Georgia Cooper, Mira McKinney (Women).

DARK VICTORY *(Warner Bros., 1939)* 105 min.

Producer, Hal B. Wallis in association with David Lewis; director, Edmund Goulding; based on the play by George Emerson Brewer, Jr., Bertram Block; screenplay, Casey Robinson; music director, Leo F. Forbstein; music, Max Steiner; song, Goulding and Elsie Janis; costumes, Orry-Kelly; art director, Robert Haas; camera, Ernest Haller; editor, William Holmes.

Bette Davis (Judith Traherne); George Brent (Dr. Frederick Steele); Humphrey Bogart (Michael O'-Leary); Geraldine Fitzgerald (Ann King); Ronald Reagan (Alec Hamin); Henry Travers (Dr. Parsons); Cora Witherspoon (Carrie Spottswood); Virginia Brissac (Martha); Dorothy Peterson (Miss Wainwright); Charles Richman (Colonel Mantle); Herbert Rawlinson (Dr. Carter); Leonard Mudie (Dr. Driscoll); Fay Helm (Miss Dodd); Diane Bernard (Agatha); Jack Mower (Veterinarian); William Worthington, Alexander Leftwich (Specialists); Ila Rhodes (Secretary); Frank Darien (Anxious Little Man); Stuart Holmes (Doctor); John Harron, John Ridgely (Men); Rosella Towne (Girl in Box); Edgar Edwards (Trainer).

JUAREZ *(Warner Bros., 1939)* 125 min.

Producer, Hal B. Wallis in association with Henry Blanke; director, William Dieterle; based on the play *Juarez and Maximilian* by Franz Werfel and the book *The Phantom Crown* by Bertita Harding; screenplay, John Huston, Aeneas MacKenzie, Wolfgang Reinhardt; music, Erich Wolfgang Korngold; music director, Leo F. Forbstein; costumes, Orry-Kelly; art director, Anton Grot; camera, Tony Gaudio; editor, Warren Low.

Paul Muni (Benito Pablo Juarez); Bette Davis (Empress Carlota von Habsburg); Brian Aherne (Emperor Maximilian von Habsburg); Claude Rains (Louis Napoleon); John Garfield (Porfirio Diaz); Donald Crisp (Marechal Bazaine); Gale Sondergaard (Empress Eugenie); Joseph Calleia (Alejandro Uradi); Gilbert Roland (Colonel Miguel Lopez); Henry O'Neill (Miguel Miramon); Pedro De Cordoba (Riva Palacio); Montagu Love (Jose de Montares); Harry Davenport (Dr. Samuel Gasch); Walter Fenner (Achille Fould); Alex Leftwich (Drouyn de Lhuys); Georgia Caine (Countess Battenberg); Robert Warwick (Major DuPont); Bill Wilkerson (Tomas Mejia); Gennaro Curci (Senor de Leon); Hugh Sothern (John Bigelow); John Miljan (Escobedo); Irving Pichel (Carbajal); Frank Lackteen (Coachman); Walter Kingsford (Prince Metternich); Monte Blue (Lerdo de Tajada); Louis Calhern (LeMarc); Noble Johnson (Regules); Martin Garralaga (Negroni); Grant Mitchell (Mr. Harris).

THE OLD MAID *(Warner Bros., 1939)* 95 min.

Producer, Hal B. Wallis in association with Henry Blanke; director, Edmund Goulding; based on the play by Zöe Atkins and the novel by Edith Wharton; screenplay, Casey Robinson; music, Max Steiner; music director, Leo F. Forbstein; costumes, Orry-Kelly; art director, Robert Haas; camera, Tony Gaudio; editor, George Amy.

Bette Davis (Charlotte Lovell); Miriam Hopkins (Delia Lovell); George Brent (Clem Spender); Jane Bryan (Tina); Donald Crisp (Dr. Lanskell); Louise Fazenda (Dora); James Stephenson (Jim Ralston); Jerome Cowan (Joe Ralston); William Lundigan (Lanning Halsey); Cecilia Loftus (Grandmother); Rand Brooks (Jim); Janet Shaw (Dee); William Hopper (John); Marlene Burnett (Tina as a Child); Rod Cameron (Man); Doris Lloyd (Aristocratic Maid); Frederick Burton (Mr. Halsey).

THE PRIVATE LIVES OF ELIZABETH AND ESSEX
(Warner Bros., 1939) C-106 min.

Executive producer, Hal B. Wallis; associate producer, Robert Lord; director, Michael Curtiz; based on the play *Elizabeth the Queen* by Maxwell Anderson; screenplay, Norma Reilly Raine, Aeneas MacKenzie; music, Erich Wolfgang Korngold; orchestrators, Hugo Friedhofer, Milan Roder; assistant director, Sherry Shourds; dialogue director, Stanley Logan; art director, Anton Grot; costumes, Orry-Kelly; makeup, Perc Westmore; technical advisor, Ali Hubert; sound, C. A. Riggs; special effects, Byron Haskin, H. F. Koenekamp; camera, Sol Polito, W. Howard Greene; editor, Owen Marks.

Bette Davis (Queen Elizabeth); Errol Flynn (Robert Devereaux, the Earl of Essex); Olivia de Havilland (Lady Penelope Gray); Donald Crisp (Francis Bacon); Alan Hale (Earl of Tyrone); Vincent Price (Sir Walter Raleigh); Henry Stephenson (Lord Burghley); Henry Daniell (Sir Robert Cecil); James Stephenson (Sir Thomas Egerton); Nanette Fabray (Mistress Margaret Radcliffe); Ralph Forbes (Lord Knollys); Robert Warwick (Lord Mountjoy); Leo G. Carroll (Sir Edward Coke); and Forrester Harvey, Doris Lloyd, Maris Wrixon, Rosella Towne, John Sutton, Guy Bellis, I. Stanford Jolley.

A.k.a. *Elizabeth the Queen.*

ALL THIS AND HEAVEN TOO *(Warner Bros., 1940)* 140 min.

Producer, Hal. B. Wallis in association with David Lewis; director, Anatole Litvak; based on the novel by Rachel Lyman Field; screenplay, Casey Robinson; music, Max Steiner; music director, Leo F. Forbstein; costumes, Orry-Kelly; art director, Carl Jules Weyl; camera, Ernest Haller; editor, Warren Low.

Bette Davis (Henriette Deluzy Desportes); Charles Boyer (Duke De Praslin); Jeffrey Lynn (Reverend Henry Field); Barbara O'Neil (Duchesse De Praslin); Virginia Weidler (Louise); Walter Hampden (Pasquier); Harry Davenport (Pierre); Fritz Leiber (Albe); Helen Westley (Mme. Le Maire); Sibyl Harris (Mlle. Maillard); Janet Beecher (Miss Haines); Montagu Love (Marechal Sebastiani); George Coulouris (Charpentier); Henry Daniell (Broussels); Ian Keith (Delangle); June Lockhart (Isabelle); Ann Todd (Berthe); Richard Nichols (Raynald); Madge Terry (Madame Gauthier); Christian Rub (Loti); Frank Reicher (Police Official); Victor Kilian (Gendarme); Edward Fielding (Dr. Louis); Egon Brecher (Doctor); Ann Gillis (Emily Schuyler); Mary Anderson (Rebecca Jay); Peggy Stewart (Helen Lexington); Creighton Hale (Officer); Mary Forbes, Georgia Caine, Natalie Moorhead (La-

dies); Claire Du Brey, Virginia Brissac, Brenda Fowler (Nuns).

THE LETTER *(Warner Bros., 1940)* 95 min.

Producer, Hal B. Wallis in association with Robert Lord; director, William Wyler; based on the play by W. Somerset Maugham; screenplay, Howard Koch; music, Max Steiner; music director, Leo F. Forbstein; orchestrator, Hugo Friedhofer; gowns, Orry-Kelly; art director, Carl Jules Weyl; technical advisors, Louis Vincenot, John Vallasin; camera, Tony Gaudio; editor, George Amy.

Bette Davis (Leslie Crosbie); Herbert Marshall (Robert Crosbie); James Stephenson (Howard Joyce); Frieda Inescort (Dorothy Joyce); Gale Sondergaard (Mrs. Hammond); Bruce Lester (John Withers); Elizabeth Earl (Adele Ainsworth); Cecil Kellaway (Prescott); Victor Sen Yung (Ong Chi Seng); Willie Fung (Chung Hi); Doris Lloyd (Mrs. Cooper); Holmes Herbert, Charles Irwin (Bob's Friends); Leonard Mudie (Fred); Tetsu Komai (Head Boy); John Ridgely (Driver); Douglas Walton (Well-Wisher).

THE GREAT LIE *(Warner Bros., 1941)* 102 min.

Producer, Hal B. Wallis in association with Henry Blanke; director, Edmund Goulding; based on the novel *January Heights* by Polan Banks; screenplay, Lenore Coffee; music, Max Steiner; music director, Leo F. Forbstein; gowns, Orry-Kelly; art director, Carl Jules Weyl; camera, Tony Gaudio; editor, Ralph Dawson.

Bette Davis (Maggie Patterson); George Brent (Pete Van Allen); Mary Astor (Sandra Kovak); Lucile Watson (Aunt Ada); Hattie McDaniel (Violet); Grant Mitchell (Joshua Mason); Jerome Cowan (Jock Thompson); Sam McDaniel (Jefferson); Thurston Hall (Worthington James); Russell Hicks (Colonel Harrison); Olin Howland (Ed); J. Farrell MacDonald (Dr. Ferguson); Doris Lloyd (Bertha); Alphonse Martell (Waiter); Georgia Caine (Mrs. Pine); Charlotte Wynters (Mrs. Anderson); Cyril Ring (Harry Anderson); Georges Renavent (Maitre d'Hotel); Napoleon Simpson (Parker).

THE BRIDE CAME C.O.D. *(Warner Bros., 1941)* 90 min.

Producer, Hal B. Wallis in association with William Cagney; director, William Keighley; based on the story by Kenneth Earl, M. M. Musselman; screenplay, Julius J. Epstein, Philip G. Epstein; music, Max Steiner; music director, Leo F. Forbstein; gowns, Orry-Kelly; art director, Ted Smith; camera, Ernest Haller; editor, Thomas Richards.

James Cagney (Steve Collins); Bette Davis (Joan Winfield); Stuart Erwin (Tommy Keenan); Jack Carson (Allen Bryce); George Tobias (Peewee); Eugene Pallette (Lucius K. Winfield); Harry Davenport (Pop Tolliver); William Frawley (Deputy Sheriff McGee); Ed Brophy (Hinkle); Chick Chandler, Douglas Kennedy, Herbert Anderson, Creighton Hale, Frank Mayo, Jack Mower (Reporters); William Newell (McGee's Pilot);

William Hopper (Keenan's Pilot); Eddy Chandler, Tony Hughes, Lee Phelps (Policemen); Reid Kilpatrick (Announcer); Cliff Saum (Airport Mechanic); Richard Travis (Airline Dispatcher); The Rogers Dancers (Specialty); Alphonse Martell (Headwaiter); Sol Gorss (Reporters' Pilot).

THE LITTLE FOXES *(RKO, 1941)* 115 min.

Producer, Samuel Goldwyn; director, William Wyler; based on the play by Lillian Hellman; screenplay, Hellman; additional scenes/dialogue, Arthur Kober, Dorothy Parker, Alan Campbell; music/music director, Meredith Willson; assistant director, William Tummell; costumes, Orry-Kelly; art director, Stephen Goosson; set decorator, Howard Bristoll; sound, Frank Maher; camera, Gregg Toland; editor, Daniel Mandell.

Bette Davis (Regina Hubbard Giddens); Herbert Marshall (Horace Giddens); Teresa Wright (Alexandra Giddens); Richard Carlson (David Hewitt); Patricia Collinge (Birdie Hubbard); Dan Duryea (Leo Hubbard); Charles Dingle (Ben Hubbard); Carl Benton Reid (Oscar Hubbard); Jessica Grayson (Addie); John Marriott (Cal); Russell Hicks (William Marshall); Lucien Littlefield (Sam Naders); Virginia Brissac (Lucy Hewitt); Terry Nibert (Julia); Alan Bridge (Dawson, the Hotel Manager); Charles R. Moore (Simon); Kenny Washington (Servant); Lew Kelly (Train Companion); Henry Roquemore (Depositor); Hooper Atchley (Guest); Henry Thomas (Bit).

THE MAN WHO CAME TO DINNER *(Warner Bros., 1941)* 112 min.

Producer, Hal B. Wallis; associate producers, Jerry Wald, Jack Saper; director, William Keighley; based on the play by George S. Kaufman, Moss Hart; screenplay, Julius J. and Philip G. Epstein; music, Frederick Hollander; music director, Leo F. Forbstein; gowns, Orry-Kelly; art director, Robert Haas; camera, Tony Gaudio; editor, Jack Killifer.

Bette Davis (Maggie Cutler); Ann Sheridan (Lorraine Sheldon); Monty Woolley (Sheridan Whiteside); Dick Travis (Bert Jefferson); Jimmy Durante (Banjo); Reginald Gardiner (Beverly Carlton); Billie Burke (Mrs. Stanley); Elisabeth Fraser (June Stanley); Grant Mitchell (Ernest Stanley); George Barbier (Dr. Bradley); Mary Wickes (Miss Preen); Russell Arms (Richard Stanley); Ruth Vivian (Harriett Stanley); Edwin Stanley (John); Betty Roadman (Sarah); Charles Drake (Sandy); Nanette Vallon (Cosette); John Ridgely (Radio Man); Pat McVey (Harry); Laura Hope Crews (Mrs. Gibbons); Chester Clute (Mr. Gibbons); Frank Coghlan, Jr. (Telegram Boy); Vera Lewis (Woman); Frank Moran (Michaelson); Leslie Brooks (Girl); Creighton Hale (Radio Man).

IN THIS OUR LIFE *(Warner Bros., 1942)* 97 min.

Producer, Hal B. Wallis in association with David Lewis; director, John Huston, (uncredited) Raoul Walsh; based on the novel by Ellen Glasgow; screenplay, Howard Koch; music, Max Steiner; music director, Leo F. Forbstein; art director, Robert Haas; gowns, Orry-Kelly; camera, Ernest Haller; editor, William Holmes.

Bette Davis (Stanley Timberlake); Olivia de Havilland (Roy Timberlake); George Brent (Craig Fleming); Dennis Morgan (Peter Kingsmill); Charles Coburn (William Fitzroy); Frank Craven (Asa Timberlake); Billie Burke (Lavinia Timberlake); Hattie McDaniel (Minerva Clay); Lee Patrick (Betty Wilmoth); Mary Servoss (Charlotte Fitzroy); Ernest Anderson (Parry Clay); William Davidson (Jim Purdy); Edward Fielding (Dr. Buchanana); John Hamilton (Inspector); William Forrest (Ranger); Eddie Acuff, Elliott Sullivan, Walter Baldwin, Herbert Heywood, Alan Bridge (Workers); George Reed (Butler); Dudley Dickerson (Waiter); Ruth Ford (Young Mother); Walter Huston (Bartender); Humphrey Bogart, Mary Astor, Peter Lorre, Sydney Greenstreet, Ward Bond, Barton MacLane, Elisha Cook, Jr. (Roadhouse Customers); Ira Buck Woods, Sam McDaniel, Billy Mitchell, Napoleon Simpson, Sunshine Sammy Morrison, Jester Harrison, Freddie Jackson, Fred Kelsey (Blacks).

NOW, VOYAGER *(Warner Bros., 1942)* 118 min.

Producer, Hal B. Wallis; director, Irving Rapper; based on the novel by Olive Higgins Prouty; screenplay, Casey Robinson; music, Max Steiner; music director, Leo F. Forbstein; gowns, Orry-Kelly; art director, Robert Haas; camera, Sol Polito; editor, Warren Low.

Bette Davis (Charlotte Vale); Paul Henreid (Jerry D. Durrence); Claude Rains (Dr. Jaquith); Gladys Cooper (Mrs. Vale); Bonita Granville (June Vale); John Loder (Elliott Livingston); Ilka Chase (Lise Vale); Lee Patrick ("Deb" McIntyre); James Rennie (Frank McIntyre); Charles Drake (Leslie Trotter); Katharine Alexander (Miss Trask); Janis Wilson (Tina Durrence); Mary Wickes (Dora Pickford); Michael Ames [Tod Andrews] (Dr. Dan Regan); Franklyn Pangborn (Mr. Thompson); David Clyde (William); Claire du Brey (Hilda); Don Douglas (George Weston); Charlotte Wynters (Grace Weston); Frank Puglia (Manuel); Lester Matthews (Captain); Mary Field, Bill Edwards, Isabel Withers, Frank Dae (Passengers); Hilda Plowright (Justine); Tempe Pigott (Mrs. Smith); Ian Wolfe (Lloyd); Reed Hadley (Henry Montague); Elspeth Dudgeon (Aunt Hester).

WATCH ON THE RHINE *(Warner Bros., 1943)* 114 min.

Producer, Hal B. Wallis; director, Herman Shumlin; based on the play by Lillian Hellman; screenplay, Dashiell Hammett; additional scenes/dialogue, Hellman; music, Max Steiner; music director, Leo F. Forbstein; orchestrator, Hugo Friedhofer; gowns, Orry-Kelly; art director, Carl Jules Weyl; set decorator, Julia Heron; dialogue director, Edward Blatt; assistant director, Richard Mayberry; sound, Dolph Thomas; camera, Merritt Gerstad, Hal Mohr; editor, Rudi Fehr.

Bette Davis (Sara Muller); Paul Lukas (Kurt Muller); Geraldine Fitzgerald (Marthe de Brancovis); Lucile Watson (Fanny Farrelly); Beulah Bondi (Anise); George Coulouris (Teck de Brancovis); Donald Woods (David Farrelly); Henry Daniell (Phili Von Ramme); Donald Buka (Joshua Muller); Eric Roberts (Bodo Muller); Janis Wilson (Babette Muller); Helmut Dantine (Young Man); Mary Young (Mrs. Mellie Sewell); Kurt Katch (Herr Blecher); Erwin Kalser (Dr. Klauber); Robert O. Davis [Rudolph Anders] (Overdorff); Clyde Fillmore (Sam Chandler); Frank Wilson (Joseph); Clarence Muse (Horace); Violett McDowell (Belle); Joe Bernard (Trainman); Creighton Hale (Chauffeur); William Washington (Doc, the Black Boy); Elvira Curci, Anthony Caruso (Italian Couple); Alan Hale, Jr. (Boy); Hans von Morhart (German); Howard Hickman (Cyrus Penfield).

THANK YOUR LUCKY STARS (Warner Bros., 1943) 127 min.

Producer, Mark Hellinger; director, David Butler; story, Everett Freeman, Arthur Schwartz; screenplay, Norman Panama, Melvin Frank, James V. Kern; songs, Schwartz and Frank Loesser; vocal arranger, Dudley Chambers; orchestrators, Ray Heindorf, Maurice de Packh; music adaptor, Heinz Roemhold; gowns, Milo Anderson; art directors, Anton Grot, Leo K. Kuter; set decorator, Walter F. Tilford; dialogue director, Herbert Farjean; makeup, Perc Westmore; assistant director, Phil Quinn; choreography and dance stager, LeRoy Prinz; sound, Francis J. Scheid, Charles David Forrest; special effects, H. F. Koenekamp; camera, Arthur Edeson; editor, Irene Morra.

Eddie Cantor (Joe Sampson/Himself); Joan Leslie (Pat Dixon); Dennis Morgan (Tommy Randolph); Dinah Shore (Herself); S. Z. Sakall (Dr. Schlenna); Edward Everett Horton (Farnsworth); Ruth Donnelly (Nurse Hamilton); Joyce Reynolds (Girl with Book); Richard Lane (Barney Jackson); Don Wilson (Himself); Henry Armetta (Angelo); Willie Best (Soldier); Humphrey Bogart, Jack Carson, Bette Davis, Olivia de Havilland, Errol Flynn, John Garfield, Alan Hale, Ida Lupino, Ann Sheridan, Alexis Smith, George Tobias, Spike Jones & His City Slickers (Specialties); Frank Faylen (Sailor); Creighton Hale, Jack Mower (Engineers); Noble Johnson (Charlie, the Indian); Ed Gargan (Doorman); Billy Benedict (Bus Boy); *Ice Cold Katie Number:* Hattie McDaniel (Gossip); Rita Christiani (Ice Cold Katie); Jess Lee Brooks (Justice); Ford, Harris, and Jones (Trio); Mathew Jones (Gambler); *Errol Flynn Number:* Monte Blue, Art Foster, Fred Kelsey, Elmer Ballard, Buster Wiles, Howard Davies, Tudor Williams, Alan Cook, Fred McEvoy, Bobby Hale, Will Stanton, Charles Irwin, David Thursby, Henry Ibling, Earl Hunsaker, Hubert Hend, Dudley Kuzello, Ted Billings (Pub Characters); *Bette Davis Number:* Jack Norton (Drunk); Henri DeSoto (Maitre d'Hotel); Dick Elliott, Dick Earle (Customers); Harry Adams (Doorman); Sam Adams (Bartender); Conrad Wiedell (Jitterbugger); Charles Francis, Harry Bailey (Bald-Headed Men); Joan Winfield (Cigarette Girl); Nancy Worth, Sylvia Opert (Hatcheck Girls); *The Lucky Stars:* Harriette Haddon, Harriett Olsen, Nancy Worth, Joy Barlowe, Janet Barrett, Dorothy Schoemer, Dorothy Dayton, Lucille LaMarr, Sylvia Opert, Mary Landa; *Humphrey Bogart Sequence:* Matt McHugh (Fireman); *Ann Sheridan Number:* Georgia Lee Settle, Virginia Patton (Girls); *Good Neighbor Number:* Igor DeNavrotsky (Dancer); Brandon Hurst (Cab Driver); Angelita Mari (Duenna); Lynne Baggett (Miss Latin America); Mary Landa (Miss Spain).

OLD ACQUAINTANCE (Warner Bros., 1943) 110 min.

Producer, Henry Blanke; director, Vincent Sherman; based on the play by John Van Druten; screenplay, Van Druten, Lenore Coffee; art director, John Hughes; set decorator, Fred MacLean; music, Franz Waxman; orchestrator, Leonid Raab; music director, Leo F. Forbstein; assistant director, Art Lueker; sound, Robert B. Lee; camera, Sol Polito; editor, Terry Morse.

Bette Davis (Kitty Marlowe); Miriam Hopkins (Millie Drake); Gig Young (Rudd Kendall); John Loder (Preston Drake); Dolores Moran (Deirdre); Phillip Reed (Lucian Grant); Roscoe Karns (Charlie Archer); Anne Revere (Delle Carter); Leona Maricle (Julia Brondbank); Esther Dale (Harriett); George Lessey (Dean); Joseph Crehan (Editor); James Conlin (Photographer); Creighton Hale (Stage Manager); Francine Rufo (Deirdre as a Child); Ann Doran (Usher); Frank Mayo, Jack Mower, Major Sam Harris (Army Officers); Charles Sullivan (Taxi Driver).

MR. SKEFFINGTON (Warner Bros., 1944) 145 min.

Producers, Philip G. and Julius J. Epstein; director, Vincent Sherman; based on the novel by "Elizabeth"; screenplay, the Epsteins; music, Franz Waxman; music director, Leo F. Forbstein; orchestrator, Leonid Raab; art director, Robert Haas; set decorator, Fred MacLean; assistant director, William Kissel; sound, Robert B. Lee; montages, James Leicester; camera, Ernest Haller; editor, Ralph Dawson.

Bette Davis (Fanny Trellis Skeffington); Claude Rains (Job Skeffington); Walter Abel (George Trellis); Richard Waring (Trippy Trellis); George Coulouris (Dr. Byles); Marjorie Riordan (Young Fanny); Robert Shayne (MacMahon); John Alexander (Jim Conderley); Jerome Cowan (Edward Morrison); Johnny Mitchell (Himself); Peter Whitney (Chester Forbish); Dorothy Peterson (Manby); Bill Kennedy (Thatcher); Tom Stevenson (Reverend Hyslup); Walter Kingsford (Dr. Melton); Halliwell Hobbes (Seaman); Charles Drake (Bit); William Forrest (Clinton); Creighton Hale (Casey, the Employee); John Vosper (Artist); Vera Lewis, Janet Barrett (Witnesses); Ann Doran (Nursemaid); Gigi Perreau (Fanny at Age 2½); Bunny Sunshine (Fanny at Age Five); Dolores Gray (Singer); Molly Lamont (Miss Morris); Sylvia Arslan (Fanny at Age Ten); Mary Field (Mrs. Hyslup); Frances Sage (Skeffington's First Secretary); Helen Eby-Rock, Isabelle LaMal (Women in Cafe); Minerva Urecal (Woman in Beauty Shop).

HOLLYWOOD CANTEEN (*Warner Bros., 1944*) 123 min.

Producer, Alex Gottlieb; director/screenplay, Delmer Daves; art director, Leo Kuter; set decorator, Casey Roberts; music adaptor, Ray Heindorf; music director, Leo F. Forbstein; choreography, LeRoy Prinz; wardrobe, Milo Anderson; camera, Bert Glennon; editor, Christian Nyby.

Joan Leslie (Herself); Robert Hutton (Slim); Dane Clark (Sergeant); Janis Paige (Angela); Andrews Sisters, Jack Benny, Joe E. Brown, Eddie Cantor, Kitty Carlisle, Jack Carson, Joan Crawford, Helmut Dantine, Bette Davis, Faye Emerson, Victor Francen, John Garfield, Sydney Greenstreet, Alan Hale, Paul Henried, Andrea King, Peter Lorre, Ida Lupino, Irene Manning, Nora Martin, Joan McCracken, Dolores Moran, Dennis Morgan, Eleanor Parker, William Prince, Joyce Reynolds, John Ridgley, Roy Rogers & Trigger, S. Z. Sakall, Alexis Smith, Zachary Scott, Barbara Stanwyck, Craig Stevens, Joseph Szigeti, Donald Woods, Jane Wyman, Jimmy Dorsey & His Band, Carmen Cavallaro & His Orchestra, Golden Gate Quartet, Rosario & Antonio, Sons of the Pioneers (Themselves); Mark Stevens, Dick Erdman (Soldiers on Deck); Kem Dibbs (Soldier); Robin Raymond (Blonde on Street); George Turner (Sailor); Chef Joseph Milani, Mary Gordon (Themselves); Betty Bryson, Willard Van Simons, William Alcorn, Jack Mattis, Jack Coffey (Dance Specialties); Dorothy Malone, Julie Bishop, Robert Shayne, Colleen Townsend, Angela Greene, Paul Brinkman, Bill Kennedy (Themselves).

THE CORN IS GREEN (*Warner Bros., 1945*) 115 min.

Producer, Jack Chertok; director, Irving Rapper; based on the play by Emlyn Williams; screenplay, Casey Robinson; art director, Carl Jules Weyl; set decorator, Fred M. MacLean; technical advisor, Rhys Williams; music, Max Steiner; music director, Leo F. Forbstein; orchestrator, Hugo Friedhofer; assistant director, Robert Vreeland; sound, Robert B. Lee; montages, James Leicester; camera, Sol Polito; editor, Frederick Richards.

Bette Davis (Miss Lilly Moffat); John Dall (Morgan Evans); Joan Lorring (Bessie Watty); Nigel Bruce (The Squire); Rhys Williams (Mr. Jones); Rosalind Ivan (Mrs. Watty); Mildred Dunnock (Miss Ronberry); Gwyneth Hughes (Sarah Pugh); Billy Roy (Idwal Morris); Thomas Louden (Old Tom); Arthur Shields (William Davis); Leslie Vincent (John Owen); Robert Regent (Rhys Norman); Tony Ellis (Will Hughes); Elliott Dare (Glyn Thomas); Robert Cherry (Dai Evans); Gene Ross (Gwilym Jones); George Mathews (Trap

Driver); Brandon Hurst (Lewellyn Powell); Herbert Evans, Billy Evans, David Hughes, Robert Cory (Miners in Bar); Rhoda Williams (Wylodine); Stub Mussellman, Bert Speiser (Bits).

A STOLEN LIFE (*Warner Bros., 1946*) 109 min.

Producer, Bette Davis; director, Curtis Bernhardt; based on the novel by Karel J. Benes; screenplay, Catherine Turney; adaptor, Margaret Buell Wilder; art director, Robert Haas; set decorator, Fred M. MacLean; music, Max Steiner; music director, Leo F. Forbstein; orchestrator, Hugo Friedhofer; dialogue director, Jack Gage; assistant director, Jesse Hibbs; sound, Robert B. Lee; special effects, William McGann, E. Roy Davidson, Willard Van Enger, Russell Collings; camera, Sol Polito, Ernest Haller; editor, Rudi Fehr.

Bette Davis (Kate Bosworth/Pat Bosworth); Glenn Ford (Bill Emerson); Dane Clark (Karnock); Walter Brennan (Eben Folgor); Charles Ruggles (Freddie Lindley); Bruce Bennett (Jack Talbot); Peggy Knudsen (Diedra); Esther Dale (Mrs. Johnson); Clara Blandick (Martha); Joan Winfield (Lucy); Robert Dudley (Old Fisherman); Jack Mower, Harlan Briggs, Tom Fadden (Fishermen); Dale Van Sickel (Man in Launch); Creighton Hale (Attendant); James Flavin (Investigator); Monte Blue (Mr. Lippencott); Sherman Sanders (Patricia's Dancing Partner); Leo White, Paul Panzer (Waiters); Mary Forbes (Woman Art Patron); Rosalie Rey (Bridesmaid); Ruth Cherrington (Large Woman); Philo McCullough (Male Art Patron).

DECEPTION (*Warner Bros., 1946*) 110 min.

Producer, Henry Blanke; director, Irving Rapper; based on the play *Jealousy* by Louis Verneuil; screenplay, John Collier, Joseph Than; art director, Anton Grot; set decorator, George James Hopkins; music, Erich Wolfgang Korngold; assistant director, Jesse Hibbs; sound, Dolph Thomas; camera, Ernest Haller; editor, Alan Crosland, Jr.

Bette Davis (Christine Radcliffe); Paul Henreid (Karel Novak); Claude Rains (Alexander Hollenius); John Abbott (Bertram Gribble); Benson Fong (Manservant); Richard Walsh (Porter); Jane Harker, Suzi Crandall, Dick Erdman, Ross Ford, Russell Arms (Students); Lois Austin (Norma); Alex Pollard (Butler); Jean DeBriac (Andre); Einar Neilsen (Orchestra Conductor); Kenneth Hunter (Manager); Earl Dewey (Jovial Man); Marcelle Corday (Hatcheck Woman); Boyd Irwin (Elderly Gentleman); Cyril Delevanti (Beggar); Philo McCullough, Gertrude Carr, Bess Flowers, Richard Wang, Jean Wong, Ramon Ros (Wedding Guests).

WINTER MEETING (*Warner Bros., 1948*) 104 min.

Producer, Henry Blanke; director, Bretaigne Windust; based on the novel by Ethel Vance; screenplay, Catherine Turney; art director, Edward Carrere; set decorator, Fred MacLean; music, Max Steiner; music director, Leo F. Forbstein; orchestrator, Murray Cutter;

assistant director, Sherry Shourds; makeup, Perc Westmore; sound, Robert B. Lee; special effects, H. F. Koenekamp, Harry Barrdollar; camera, Ernest Haller; editor, Owen Marks.

Bette Davis (Susan Grieve); Janis Paige (Peggy Markham); James Davis (Slick Novak); John Hoyt (Stacey Grant); Florence Bates (Mrs. Castle); Walter Baldwin (Mr. Castle); Ransom Sherman (Mr. Moran); Hugh Charles (Headwaiter); George Taylor, Mike Lally, Doug Carter, Harry McKee, Joe Minitello (Waiters); Harry Lewis (Juvenile); Ezelle Poule, Russ Clarke (Cafe Couple); Laura Treadwell (Gray Lady); Lois Austin (Marcia); Robert Riordan (Marcia's Escort).

JUNE BRIDE *(Warner Bros., 1948)* 96 min.

Producer, Henry Blanke; director, Bretaigne Windust; based on the play *Feature for June* by Eileen Tighe, Graem Lorimer; screenplay, Ranald MacDougall; art director, Anton Grot; set decorator, William Wallace; music, David Buttolph; makeup, Perc Westmore; costumes, Edith Head; assistant director, Sherry Shourds; sound, Robert B. Lee; special effects, William McGann, H. F. Koenekamp; camera, Ted McCord; editor, Owen Marks.

Bette Davis (Linda Gilman); Robert Montgomery (Carey Jackson); Fay Bainter (Paula Winthrop); Betty Lynn (Boo Brinker); Tom Tully (Mr. Brinker); Barbara Bates (Jeanne Brinker); Jerome Cowan (Carleton Towne); Mary Wickes (Rosemary McNally); James Burke (Luke Potter); Raymond Roe (Bud Mitchell); Marjorie Bennett (Mrs. Brinker); Ray Montgomery (Jim Mitchell); George O'Hanlon (Scott Davis); Sandra Gould (Miss Rubens); Esther Howard (Mrs. Mitchell); Lottie Williams (Woody); Debbie Reynolds, Alice Kelley, Patricia Northrop (Boo's Girl Friends).

BEYOND THE FOREST *(Warner Bros., 1949)* 97 min.

Producer, Henry Blanke; director, King Vidor; based on the novel by Stuart Engstrand; screenplay, Lenore Coffee; music, Max Steiner; orchestrator, Murray Cutter; costumes, Edith Head; assistant director, Al Alleborn; makeup, Perc Westmore; sound, Charles Lang; special effects, William McGann, Edwin DuPar; camera, Robert Burks; editor, Rudi Fehr.

Bette Davis (Rosa Moline); Joseph Cotten (Dr. Lewis Moline); David Brian (Neil Latimer); Ruth Roman (Carol); Minor Watson (Moose); Dona Drake (Jenny); Regis Toomey (Sorren); Sarah Selby (Mildred Sorren); Mary Servoss (Mrs. Wetch); Frances Charles (Miss Elliott); Harry Tyler (Station Master); Creighton Hale (Old Man); Ann Doran (Edith Williams); Buddy Roosevelt (Man); Judith Wood (Waitress); Gail Bonney, Hallene Hill, June Ivans (Women); Charles Jordan (Jury Foreman); Frank Pharr (Coroner).

ALL ABOUT EVE *(Twentieth Century-Fox, 1950)* 138 min.

Producer, Darryl F. Zanuck; director, Joseph L. Mankiewicz; based on the story "The Wisdom of Eve" by Mary Orr; screenplay, Mankiewicz; music/music director, Alfred Newman; art directors, Lyle Wheeler, George W. Davis; costumes, Edith Head, Charles LeMaire; camera, Milton Krasner; editor, Barbara McLean.

Bette Davis (Margo Channing); Anne Baxter (Eve Harrington); George Sanders (Addison DeWitt/narrator); Celeste Holm (Karen Richards); Gary Merrill (Bill Sampson); Hugh Marlowe (Lloyd Richards); Thelma Ritter (Birdie); Marilyn Monroe (Miss Caswell); Gregory Ratoff (Max Fabian); Barbara Bates (Phoebe); Randy Stuart (Girl); Walter Hampden (Speaker at Dinner); Craig Hill (Leading Man); Leland Harris (Doorman); Barbara White (Autograph Seeker); Eddie Fisher (Stage Manager); William Pullen (Clerk); Claude Stroud (Pianist); Eugene Borden (Frenchman); Helen Mowery (Reporter); Steven Geray (Captain of Waiters); Bess Flowers (Well-Wisher).

PAYMENT ON DEMAND *(RKO, 1951)* 91 min.

Producers, Jack H. Skirball, Bruce Manning; director, Curtis Bernhardt; screenplay, Manning, Bernhardt; music, Victor Young; music director, C. Bakaleinikoff; art directors, Albert S. D'Agostino, Carroll Clark; Miss Davis' gowns, Edith Head; camera, Leo Tover; editor, Head; camera, Leo Tover; editor, Harry Marker.

Bette Davis (Joyce Ramsey); Barry Sullivan (David Ramsey); Jane Cowl (Mrs. Hedges); Kent Taylor (Robert Townsend); Betty Lynn (Martha Ramsey); John Sutton (Tunliffe); Frances Dee (Eileen Benson); Peggie Castle (Diana Ramsey); Otto Kruger (Prescott); Walter Sande (Swanson); Brett King (Phil Polanski); Richard Anderson (Jim); Natalie Schafer (Mrs. Blanton); Katherine Emery (Mrs. Gates); Lisa Golm (Molly); Kathleen Ellis (Receptionist); Mack Williams (Pinkins); Ilka Gruning (Mrs. Polanski); David Leonard (Mr. Polanski); Barbara Davis, Sherry Merrill (Diana as a Child); Ruth Lee (Aunt Edna); Jay Brooks (Butler); Lela Bliss (Mrs. Filson).

ANOTHER MAN'S POISON *(United Artists, 1952)* 88 min.

Producers, Douglas Fairbanks, Jr., Daniel M. Angel; director, Irving Rapper; based on the play *Deadlock* by Leslie Sands; screenplay, Val Guest; music, Paul Sawtell; art director, Cedric Dawe; camera, Robert Krasker; editor, Gordon Hales.

Bette Davis (Janet Frobisher); Gary Merrill (George Bates); Emlyn Williams (Dr. Henderson); Anthony Steel (Larry); Barbara Murray (Chris); Reginald Beckwith (Bigley); Edna Morris (Mrs. Bunting).

PHONE CALL FROM A STRANGER *(Twentieth Century-Fox, 1952)* 96 min.

Producer, Nunnally Johnson; director, Jean Negulesco; based on a story by I. A. R. Wylie; screenplay, Johnson; music, Franz Waxman; costumes, Eloise Jenssen; art directors, Lyle Wheeler, J. Russell Spencer; camera, Milton Krasner; editor, Hugh Fowler.

Shelley Winters (Binkey Gay); Gary Merrill (David Trask); Michael Rennie (Dr. Fortness); Keenan Wynn (Eddie Hoke); Evelyn Varden (Sally Carr); Warren Stevens (Marty Nelson); Beatrice Straight (Mrs. Fortness); Ted Donaldson (Jerry Fortness); Craig Stevens (Mike Carr); Helen Westcott (Jane Trask); Bette Davis (Marie Hoke); Hugh Beaumont (Dr. Brooks); Sidney Perkins (Stewardess); Harry Cheshire (Dr. Fletcher); Tom Powers (Dr. Fernwood); Nestor Paiva (Headwaiter); George Nader (Pilot); John Doucette (Bartender); William Neff (Co-Pilot); Ruth Robinson (Nurse).

THE STAR (Twentieth Century-Fox, 1952) 90 min.

Producer, Bert E. Friedlob; director, Stuart Heisler; screenplay, Katharine Albert, Dale Eunson; music, Victor Young; Miss Davis' costumes, Orry-Kelly; art director, Boris Levin; camera, Ernest Laszlo; editor, Otto Ludwig.

Bette Davis (Margaret Elliot); Sterling Hayden (Jim Johannson); Natalie Wood (Gretchen); Warner Anderson (Harry Stone); Minor Watson (Joe Morrison); June Travis (Phyllis Stone); Katherine Warren (Mrs. Morrison); Kay Riehl (Mrs. Adams); Barbara Woodell (Peggy Morgan); Fay Baker (Faith); Barbara Lawrence (Herself); David Alpert (Keith Barkley); Paul Frees (Richard Stanley).

THE VIRGIN QUEEN (Twentieth Century-Fox, 1955) C-92 min.

Producer, Charles Brackett; director, Henry Koster; screenplay, Harry Brown, Mindred Lord; color consultant, Leonard Doss; music, Franz Waxman; art directors, Lyle Wheeler, Leland Fuller; camera, Charles G. Clarke; editor, Robert Simpson.

Bette Davis (Queen Elizabeth); Richard Todd (Sir Walter Raleigh); Joan Collins (Beth Throgmorton); Jay Robinson (Chadwick); Herbert Marshall (Lord Leicester); Dan O'Herlihy (Lord Derry); Robert Douglas (Sir Christopher Hatton); Romney Brent (French Ambassador); Marjorie Hellen [Leslie Parrish] (Anne); Lisa Daniels (Mary); Lisa Davis (Jane); Barry Bernard (Patch Eye); Robert Adler (Postillion Rider); Noel Drayton (Tailor); Ian Murray (Gentleman of the Bedchamber); Margery Weston (Dame Bragg); Rod Taylor (Corporal Gwilym); David Thursby (Landlord); Arthur Gould-Porter (Randall, the Ship Builder); John Costello (Town Crier); Nelson Leigh, Frank Baker (Physicians); Ashley Cowan (Sailor).

STORM CENTER (Columbia, 1956) 86 min.

Producer, Julian Blaustein; director, Daniel Taradash; screenplay, Taradash, Elick Moll; music, George Duning; art director, Cary Odell; assistant director, Carter De Haven, Jr.; camera, Burnett Guffey; editor, William A. Lyon.

Bette Davis (Alicia Hull); Brian Keith (Paul Dun-

can); Kim Hunter (Martha Lockridge); Paul Kelly (Judge Robert Ellerbe); Kevin Coughlin (Freddie Slater); Joe Mantell (George Slater); Sallie Brophy (Laura Slater); Howard Wierum (Mayor Levering); Curtis Cooksey (Stacey Martin); Michael Raffetto (Edgar Greenbaum); Edward Platt (Reverend Wilson); Kathryn Grant (Hazel); Howard Wendell (Senator Bascomb); Burt Mustin (Carl); Edith Evanson (Mrs. Simmons); Joseph Kearns (Mr. Morrisey); Ted Marc (Bert); Rudy Lee (Charlie); Phillip Crompton (Joe); Dora Dee Stansauk, Lora Lee Stansauk (Paswolski Twins); Bucko Stafford (Jack); Malcolm Atterbury (Frank); Edwin Parker (Fireman); Paul Ryan (Mr. Fisher); George Selk (Bill); Mildred Hays (Mrs. Field); Emlen Davies (Miss Layton); Alexander Campbell (Jones).

THE CATERED AFFAIR (MGM, 1956) 92 min.

Producer, Sam Zimbalist; director, Richard Brooks; based on the teleplay by Paddy Chayefsky; screenplay, Gore Vidal; music, Andre Previn; art directors, Cedric Gibbons, Paul Groesse; assistant director, William Shanks; camera, John Alton; editors, Gene Ruggiero, Frank Santillo.

Bette Davis (Aggie Conlon Hurley); Ernest Borgnine (Tom Hurley); Debbie Reynolds (Jane Hurley); Barry Fitzgerald (Uncle Jack Conlon); Rod Taylor (Ralph Halloran); Robert Simon (Joe Halloran); Madge Kennedy (Mary Halloran); Dorothy Stickney (Mrs. Rafferty); Carol Veazie (Mrs. Casey); Joan Camden (Alice Scanlon); Ray Stricklyn (Eddie Hurley); Jay Adler (Sam Leiter); Dan Tobin (Hotel Caterer); Paul Denton (Bill Scanlon); Augusta Merighi (Mrs. Musso); Mae Clarke (Saleswoman); Jimmie Fox (Tailor); Don Devlin, Sammy Shack (Cabbies).

JOHN PAUL JONES (Warner Bros., 1959) C-126 min.

Producer, Samuel Bronston; director, John Farrow; based on the life of John Paul Jones; screenplay, Farrow, Jesse Lasky, Jr.; art director, Franz Bachelin; set decorator, Dario Simoni; costumes, Phyllis Dalton; music, Max Steiner; orchestrator, Murray Cutter; choreography, Hector Zaraspe; technical advisors, Rear Admiral J. L. Pratt, USN (Ret.), Captain Alan Villiers; makeup, Neville Smallwood; assistant director, Frank Losee; sound effects, Winston Ryder; special effects, Roscoe S. Cline; camera, Michael Kelber; editor, Eda Warren.

Robert Stack (John Paul Jones); Marisa Pavan (Aimee de Tellison); Charles Coburn (Benjamin Franklin); Erin O'Brien (Dorothea Danders); Bette Davis (Catherine the Great); Macdonald Carey (Patrick Henry); Jean-Pierre Aumont (King Louis XVI); David Farrar (John Wilkes); Peter Cushing (Captain Pearson); Susana Canales (Marie Antoinette); Jorge Riviere (Russian Chamberlain); Tom Brannum (Peter Wooley); Basil Sydney (Sir William Young); Bruce Cabot (Gunner Lowrie); Thomas Gomez (Esek Hopkins); John Charles Farrow (John Paul); Eric Pohlmann

(King George III); Frank Latimore (Lieutenant Richard Dale); Ford Rainey (Lieutenant Simpson); Macdonald Parke (Arthur Lee); Felix de Pomes (French Chamberlain).

THE SCAPEGOAT (MGM, 1959) 92 min.

Producer, Michael Balcon; associate producer, Dennis Van Thal; director, Robert Hamer; based on the novel by Daphne du Maurier; screenplay, Hamer; adaptor, Gore Vidal; makeup, Harry Frampton; music, Bronislau Kaper; camera, Paul Beeson; editor, Jack Harris.

Alec Guinness (John Barrett/Jacques de Gue); Bette Davis (The Countess); Nicole Maurey (Bela); Irene Worth (Francoise); Pamela Brown (Blanche); Annabel Bartlett (Marie-Noel); Geoffrey Keen (Gaston, the Chauffeur); Noel Howlett (Dr. Aloin); Peter Bull (Aristide); Leslie French (Lacoste); Alan Webb (Inspector); Maria Britneva (Maid); Eddie Byrne (Barman); Alexander Archdale (Gamekeeper); Peter Sallis (Customs' Official).

POCKETFUL OF MIRACLES (United Artists, 1961) C-136 min.

Producer, Frank Capra; associate producers, Glenn Ford, Joseph Sistrom; director, Capra; based on the story "Madame La Gimp" by Damon Runyon and the screenplay Lady for a Day by Robert Riskin; new screenplay, Hal Kantor, Harry Tugend; costumes, Edith Head, Walter Plunkett; music, Walter Scharf; song, James Van Heusen and Sammy Cahn; orchestrator, Gil Grau; choreography, Nick Castle; makeup, Wally Westmore; assistant director, Arthur J. Black, Jr.; sound, Hugo Grenzbach, Charles Grenzbach; art directors, Hal Pereira, Roland Anderson; set decorators, Sam Comer, Ray Moyer; process camera, Farciot Edouart; camera, Robert Bronner; editor, Frank P. Keller.

Glenn Ford (Dave, the Dude Conway); Bette Davis (Apple Annie [Mrs. E. Worthington Manville]); Hope Lange (Elizabeth "Queenie" Martin); Arthur O'Connell (Count Alfonso Romero); Peter Falk (Joy Boy/Narrator); Thomas Mitchell (Judge Henry G. Blake); Edward Everett Horton (Hutchins, the Butler); Mickey Shaughnessy (Junior); David Brian (Governor); Sheldon Leonard (Steve Darcey); Peter Mann (Carlos Romero); Ann-Margret (Louise); Barton MacLane (Police Commissioner); John Litel (Inspector McCrary); Jerome Cowan (Mayer); Jay Novello (Cortega, the Spanish Consul); Frank Ferguson, Willis Bouchey (Newspaper Editors); Fritz Feld (Pierre); Ellen Corby (Soho Sal); Gavin Gordon (Mr. Cole, the Hotel Manager); Benny Rubin (Fireaway); Hayden Rorke (Captain Moore); Mike Mazurki (Big Mike); Doodles Weaver (Pool Player); Snub Pollard (Knuckles); George E. Stone (Shimkey); Byron Foulger (Lloyd, the Assistant Hotel Manager); Betty Bronson (The Mayor's Wife); Romo Vincent (Kidnapped Reporter).

WHAT EVER HAPPENED TO BABY JANE? (Warner Bros., 1962) 132 min.

Executive producer, Kenneth Hyman; producer/director, Robert Aldrich; based on the novel by Henry Farrell; screenplay, Lukas Heller; art director, William Glasgow; set decorator, George Sawley; assistant director, Tom Connors; makeup, Jack Obringer, Monty Westmore; choreography, Alex Romero; music, Frank De Vol; sound, Jack Solomon; special effects, Don Steward; camera, Ernest Haller; editor, Michael Luciano.

Bette Davis (Jane Hudson); Joan Crawford (Blanche Hudson); Victor Buono (Edwin Flagg); Anna Lee (Mrs. Bates); Maidie Norman (Elvira Stitt); Marjorie Bennett (Mrs. Flagg); Dave Willock (Ray Hudson); Ann Barton (Cora Hudson); Barbara Merrill (Liza Bates); Julie Allred (Young Jane); Gina Gillespie (Young Blanche); Bert Freed (Producer); Wesley Addy (Director).

DEAD RINGER (Warner Bros., 1964) 115 min.

Producer, William H. Wright; director, Paul Henreid; based on the story by Rian James; screenplay, Albert Beich, Oscar Millard; art director, Perry Ferguson; set decorator, William Stevens; assistant directors, Charles L. Hansen, Lee White; Miss Davis' makeup, Gene Hibbs; music, Andre Previn; costumes, Don Feld; sound, Robert B. Lee; camera, Ernest Haller; editor, Folmar Blangsted.

Bette Davis (Margaret de Lorca/Edith Philips); Karl Malden (Sergeant Jim Hobbson); Peter Lawford (Tony Collins); Philip Carey (Sergeant Hoag); Jean Hagen (Dede Marshall); George Macready (Paul Harrison); Estelle Winwood (Matriarch); George Chandler (George); Mario Alcalde (Garcia); Cyril Delevanti (Henry); Monika Henreid (Janet); Bert Remsen (Dan); Charles Wyatt (Apartment Manager); Ken Lynch (Captain Johnson).

British release title: Dead Image.

THE EMPTY CANVAS (Embassy, 1964) 118 min.

Producer, Carlo Ponti; director, Damiano Damiani; based on the novel by Alberto Moravia; screenplay, Damiani, Tonino Guerra, Ugo Liberatore; art director, Carlo Egidi; set decorator, Dario Michell; music/music director, Luis Enriquez Bacalov; sound, Mario Messina; camera, Roberto Gerardi; editor, Renzo Lucidi.

Bette Davis (Dino's Mother); Horst Buchholz (Dino); Catherine Spaak (Cecilia); Isa Mirandi (Cecilia's Mother); Lea Padovani (Balestrieri's Widow); Daniela Rocca (Rita); Georges Wilson (Cecilia's Father); Leonida Repaci (Balestrieri); Luigi Giuliani (Luciani); Denny Parsi (A Nun); Mario Lanfranchi (Police Officer).

WHERE LOVE HAS GONE (Paramount, 1964) C-114 min.

Producer, Joseph E. Levine; director, Edward Dmytryk; based on the novel by Harold Robbins; screenplay, John Michael Hayes; art directors, Hal Pereira,

Walter Tyler; set decorators, Sam Comer, Arthur Krams; costumes, Edith Head; music, Walter Scharf; title song, Sammy Cahn and James Van Heusen; assistant director, D. Michael Moore; dialogue director, Frank London; sound, John Carter, Charles Grenzbach; special camera effects, Paul K. Lerpae; process camera, Farciot Edouart; camera, Joseph MacDonald; editor, Frank Bracht.

Susan Hayward (Valerie Hayden); Bette Davis (Mrs. Gerald Hayden); Michael Connors (Luke Miller); Joey Heatherton (Dani); Jane Greer (Marion Spicer); DeForest Kelley (Sam Corwin); George Macready (Gordon Harris); Anne Seymour (Dr. Sally Jennings); Willis Bouchey (Judge Murphy); Walter Reed (George Babson); Ann Doran (Mrs. Geraghty); Bartlett Robinson (Mr. Coleman); Whit Bissell (Professor Bell); Anthony Caruso (Rafael).

HUSH . . . HUSH, SWEET CHARLOTTE (Twentieth Century-Fox, 1964) 134 min.

Producer, Robert Aldrich; associate producer, Walter Blake; director, Aldrich; screenplay, Henry Farrell, Lukas Heller; music, Frank De Vol; song, De Vol and Mack David; art director, William Glasgow; choreography, Alex Ruiz; costumes, Norma Koch; assistant director, William McGarry, Sam Strangis; camera, Joseph Biroc; editor, Michael Luciano.

Bette Davis (Charlotte Hollis); Olivia de Havilland (Miriam Dearing); Joseph Cotten (Dr. Drew Bayliss); Agnes Moorehead (Velma Cruther); Cecil Kellaway (Harry Willis); Victor Buono (Big Sam Hollis); Mary Astor (Mrs. Jewel Mayhew); William Campbell (Paul Marchand); Wesley Addy (Sheriff Luke Standish); Bruce Dern (John Mayhew); George Kennedy (Foreman); Dave Willock (Taxi Driver); John Megna (Boy); Frank Ferguson (Newspaper Editor); Ellen Corby, Helen Kleeb, Marianne Stewart (Gossips).

THE NANNY (Twentieth Century-Fox, 1965) 93 min.

Producer, Jimmy Sangster; director, Seth Holt; based on the novel by Evelyn Piper; screenplay, Sangster; assistant director, Christopher Dryhurst; music, Richard Rodney Bennett; wardrobe consultant, Rosemary Burrows; camera, Harry Waxman; editor, James Needs.

Bette Davis (Nanny); Wendy Craig (Virgie); Jill Bennett (Pen); James Villiers (Bill); William Dix (Joey); Pamela Franklin (Bobby); Jack Watling (Dr. Medman); Maurice Denham (Dr. Beamaster); Alfred Burke (Dr. Wills); Nora Gordon (Mrs. Griggs); Sandra Power (Sarah); Harry Fowler (Milkman); Angharad Aubrey (Susay).

THE ANNIVERSARY (Twentieth Century-Fox, 1968) C-95 min.

Producer, Jimmy Sangster; director, Roy Ward Baker; based on the play by Bill MacIlwraith; screenplay, Sangster; art director, Reece Pemberton; music supervisor, Philip Martell; assistant director, Bert Batt;

wardrobe, Mary Gibson; makeup, George Partleton; sound, A. W. Lumkin, Les Hammond; camera, Harry Waxman; editor, Peter Weatherley.

Bette Davis (Mrs. Taggart); Sheila Hancock (Karen Taggart); Jack Hedley (Terry Taggart); James Cossins (Henry Taggart); Christian Roberts (Tom Taggart); Elaine Taylor (Shirley Blair); Timothy Bateson (Mr. Bird); Arnold Diamond (Headwaiter); and Albert Shepherd, Ralph Watson, Sally-Jane Spencer.

CONNECTING ROOMS (London Screen Distributors, 1971) C-103 min.

Producer, Harry Field; associate producer, Arthur S. Cooper; director, Franklin Gollings; based on the play The Cellist by Marion Hart; screenplay, Gollings; art directors, Herbert Smith, Morley Smith; set decorator, Jill Oxley; music/music director, Joan Shakespeare; songs, Joan Shakespeare and Derek Warne; sound, Bob Cox; camera, John Wilcox; editor, Jack Slade.

Bette Davis (Wanda Fleming); Michael Redgrave (James Wallraven); Alexis Kanner (Mickey Hollister); Kay Walsh (Mrs. Brent); Gabrielle Drake (Jean); Olga Georges-Picot (Claudia Fouchet); Leo Genn (Dr. Norman); Richard Wyler (Dick Grayson); Brian Wilde (Ellerman); John Woodnutt (Doctor); Tony Hughes (Lew); Mark Jones (Johnny); Eyes of Blue & The Ladybirds (Themselves); James Maxwell (Principal of Art College).

BUNNY O'HARE (American International, 1971) C-92 min.

Executive producers, James H. Nicholson, Samuel Z. Arkoff; co-producer, Norman T. Herman; producer/director, Gerd Oswald; story, Stanley Z. Cherry; screenplay, Cherry, Coslough Johnson; music, Billy Strange; assistant director, Rusty Meek; wardrobe, Phyllis Garr; makeup, Beau Wilson; sound, Howard Warren; camera, Loyal Griggs, John Stephens; second unit camera, Michael Dugan; editor, Fred Feitshans, Jr.

Bette Davis (Bunny O'Hare); Ernest Borgnine (Bill Green [Gruenwald]); Jack Cassidy (Lieutenant Horace Greeley); Joan Delaney (R. J. Hart); Jay Robinson (John C. Rupert); John Astin (Ad); Reva Rosa (Lulu); Robert Foulk (Commissioner Dingle); Brayden Linden (Frank); Karen Mae Johnson (Lola); Francis Cody (Rhett); J. Rob Jordan (Policeman Nerdman).

MADAME SIN (ABC-TV, 1972) C-76 min.

Executive producer, Robert Wagner; producers, Julian Wintle, Lou Morheim; director, David Greene; story, Lou Morheim, Barry Shear; screenplay, Barry Oringer, David Greene; assistant director, Dickie Bamber; production designer, Brian Eatwell; set decorator, Carolyn Scott; music, Michael Gibbs; sound, Hugh Davies; camera, Tony Richmond; editor, Peter Tanner.

Bette Davis (Madame Sin); Robert Wagner (Anthony Lawrence); Denholm Elliott (Malcolm De Vere); Gordon Jackson (Commander Cavendish); Dudley Sutton (Monk); Catherine Schell (Barbara); Pik-Sen Lim

(Nikko); Paul Maxwell (Connors); David Healy (Braden); Al Mancini (Fisherman); Alan Dobie (White); Roy Kinnear (Holidaymaker); Charles Lloyd Pack (Mr. Willoughby); Frank Middlemass (Dr. Henriques); Arnold Diamond (Lengett).

LO SCOPONE SCIENTIFICO (THE SCIENTIFIC CARDPLAYER) (C.I.C., 1972) C-113 min.

Producer, Dino De Laurentiis; director, Luigi Comencini; screenplay, Rodolfo Sonego; art director, Luigi Scaccianoce; music, Piero Piccioni; camera, Giuseppe Ruzzolini.

Alberto Sordi (Peppino); Silvana Mangano (Antonia); Joseph Cotten (George); Bette Davis (Millionairess); Domenica Modugno (Gighetto); Mario Carotenuto (Professor).

THE JUDGE AND JAKE WYLER (NBC-TV, 1972) C-100 min.

Producers, Richard Levinson, William Link; director, David Lowell Rich; teleplay, David Shaw, Levinson, Link; music, Gil Melle; camera, William Margulis.

Bette Davis (Judge Meredith); Doug McClure (Jake Wyler); Eric Braeden (Anton Granicek); Joan Van Ark (Alicia Dodd); Gary Conway (Frank Morrison); Lou Jacobi (Lieutenant Wolfson); James McEachin (Quint); Lisabeth Hush (Caroline Dodd); Kent Smith (Robert Dodd); Barbara Rhodes (Cloe Jones); John Randolph (James Rockmore); Milt Kamen (Mr. Gilbert); John Lupton (Senator Joseph Pritchard).

SCREAM PRETTY PEGGY (ABC-TV, 1973) C-76 min.

Producer, Lou Morheim; director, Gordon Hessler; teleplay, Jimmy Sangster, Arthur Hoffe; music, Bob Prince; camera, Leonard G. South; editor, Larry Strong.

Ted Bessell (Jeffrey Elliott); Sian Barbara Allen (Peggy Johns); Bette Davis (Mrs. Elliott); Charles Drake (George Thornton); Allan Arbus (Dr. Eugene Saks); Jessica Rains (Lloyd, the Office Girl); Johnnie Collins III (Student); Tovah Feldshuh (Agnes Thoroton); Christine Schmidtner (Jennifer Elliot).

BURNT OFFERINGS (United Artists, 1976) C-116 min.

Producer, Dan Curtis; associate producer, Robert Singer; director, Curtis; based on the novel by Robert Marasco; screenplay, William F. Nolan, Curtis; production designer, Eugene Lourie; set decorator, Solomon Brewer; costume designer, Ann Roth; costumes, Agnes Henry, Lucia De Martino, Carol Lunsford; makeup, Al Fleming; music/music box theme/music director, Robert Cobert; special effects, Cliff Wenger; camera, Jacques Marquette; editor, Dennis Virkler; assistant editor, Bernard Klotchman.

Karen Black (Marian Rolfe); Oliver Reed (Ben Rolfe); Burgess Meredith (Arnold Allardice); Eileen Heckart (Roz Allardice); Lee Montgomery (David Rolfe); Dub Taylor (Walker); Bette Davis (Aunt Elizabeth); Anthony James (Chauffeur); Orin Cannon (Minister); James T. Myers (Dr. Ross); Todd Turquand (Young Ben); Joseph Riley (Ben's Father).

RETURN FROM WITCH MOUNTAIN (Buena Vista, 1978) C

Producers, Ron Miller, Jerry Courtland; associate producer, Kevin Corcoran; director, John Hough; screenplay, Malcolm Marmorstein; assistant directors, Mike Dmytryk, Dorothy Kieffer, Randy Carter; art director, Jack Senter; set decorator, Frank McKelvy; ladies' wardrobe, Emily Sundby, Mary Dye; men's wardrobe, Rudy Nava-Luna, John George; stunt coordinator, Ted Duncan; special effects, Hal Bigger; camera, Frank Phillips; editor, Bob Bring.

With: Bette Davis, Christopher Lee, Kim Richards, Ike Eisenmann, Jack Soo, Dick Bakalyan, Ward Costello, Anthony James.

In *A Midsummer Night's Dream* ('35).

270

CHAPTER 4

Olivia de Havilland

5'3½"
107 pounds
Dark brown hair
Brown eyes
Cancer

Elsa Maxwell, international hostess and columnist, wrote in May 1949, "Great actresses are so rare, you can count all who have existed for many years on your fingers—actresses like Bernhardt, Duse, Helen Hayes, Bette Davis, Olivia de Havilland."

A decade earlier this telling statement would have confounded most readers. For like an iceberg, the essence of delicate Olivia de Havilland was long kept well beneath the surface. Throughout the Thirties, she was representative onscreen of the demure, pretty heroine who required a colorful actor to carry the storyline and to pull the weight at the box-office. For a long period, her home lot, Warner Bros., teamed her in a series of costume epics with swashbuckling Errol Flynn. Everyone—but perhaps Olivia—thought she had reached her professional pinnacle.

In that classic screen spectacle *Gone with the Wind* (1939), Olivia appeared as genteel Melanie Hamilton. It was an accurate piece of casting, for like that apparently docile, obliging young woman of fiction and film, Olivia had amazing reservoirs of strength. She too, like Melanie, eventually obtained nearly everything she wanted.

It was in 1943 that de Havilland, who had endured several well-publicized spats with her Oscar-winning sister Joan Fontaine, demonstrated that she was as forceful a lady offscreen as co-worker Bette Davis. Olivia launched a major law suit against Warner Bros. which revolutionized the actor-studio contractual pattern within the film industry. It also made her *persona non grata* with many major lots. For a time, it seemed her screen years were close to an end.

But, like the other tenacious leading ladies in this book, she possessed (and most assuredly still does) a resiliency that was remarkable. She gave an Oscar-winning performance of sacrificial mother love in Paramount's *To Each His Own* (1946). That same year, she was most engaging in contrasting dual roles in the thriller *The Dark Mirror*. Most thought she would win her second Oscar for etching the multi-faceted, emotionally disturbed heroine of *The Snake Pit* (1948). However, it was for the retiring Henry James heroine, Catherine Sloper of *The Heiress* (1949), that she received her second Academy Award.

In the mid-Fifties, Olivia departed the fragmenting Hollywood scene. Unlike many other veteran movie queens, she had legitimate reason for the geographical transfer. She had wed Pierre Galante, editor of *Paris-Match* magazine, and chosen to make France her new home base. There were occasional movie assignments in subsequent years (joining with Alan Ladd in the frontier yarn *The Proud Rebel,* 1958) and a fresh foray onto the Broadway stage (with Henry Fonda in *A Gift of Time,* 1962).

Then, in the Sixties, she participated in the grand guignol horror-film cycle. As a replacement for ailing Joan Crawford, she teamed again with Bette Davis, this time in the Gothic thriller, *Hush . . . Hush, Sweet Charlotte* (1965). The year before, she solo-starred in a massive tale of terror, *Lady in a Cage.* For assorted reasons, including a percentage-ownership deal, it has remained one of her favorite movie projects.

Today Olivia, unlike many of the big screen names of the Forties or Fifties, let alone the Thirties, remains a potent force in cinema circles. The constant revivals (and now TV showings) of *Gone with the Wind* have fortified her prestigious status a good deal. But it is the entrancing mixture of liberated womanhood, demure propriety, and gracious radiance that continues to spark a responsive chord with entertainment seekers.

Olivia de Havilland was born on Saturday, July 1, 1916, in Tokyo, Japan. Her mother was Lilian Augusta Ruse de Havilland of Berkshire, England, who, before her marriage, had studied acting at Sir Herbert Beerbohm Tree's Royal Academy of Dramatic Art. Lilian named her first-born daughter after the character Olivia in Shakespeare's *Twelfth Night.* The child's father, Walter Augustus de Havilland, a graduate of Cambridge University, headed a firm of British patent attorneys in Tokyo. He was descended from such distinguished forebears as Sir Peter de Havilland, an Oliver Cromwell supporter, and Sir George de Carteret who had figured prominently in the early settlement of

New Jersey. Moreover, Walter was cousin to the British aircraft designer-manufacturer, Sir Geoffrey de Havilland. About fifteen months after the birth of Olivia, a second daughter, Joan de Beauvoir de Havilland,* was born on October 22, 1917.

Both de Havilland girls were ill a good deal of the time. By 1919 Lilian decided to move her daughters to a more beneficial climate— perhaps Italy. This planned uprooting all but ended the de Havilland marriage. En route, Olivia developed a fever. When their ship docked in San Francisco, Mrs. de Havilland

* For a detailed study of the life and times of Joan de Havilland (better known as Joan Fontaine), the reader is referred to *The RKO Gals* (Arlington House, 1974).

272

took the ailing child to the child specialist, Dr. Langley Porter. He diagnosed that Olivia's tonsils needed to be removed and they were. Thereafter, Joan contracted pneumonia. During her convalescent period, Dr. Porter advised that Mrs. de Havilland take the girls to San Jose, where they were less likely to be adversely affected by the damp Bay fog climate. An even superior climate in Saratoga (about sixty miles south of San Francisco) caused Mrs. de Havilland to move herself and her children there.

Olivia developed into a rosy-cheeked girl. She was a timid young lady who loved animals. She was especially fond of dogs, so much so that, at the time, she considered it her major task to learn to imitate a dog's bark to perfection. So worried was Mrs. de Havilland about her daughters' health that she was overly protective about all their physical activity. Joan's anemic condition restricted her to the less strenuous pastime of reading, yet Olivia was frequently permitted to play assorted childhood games.

In retrospect, one can see easily the disastrous repercussions of Mrs. de Havilland's strict control of the girls' activities. "Livvie can, Joan can't." The family nickname of "Livvie" would follow Olivia through the years. She prefers that it be used only by intimate friends or family. Eventually, through rebellion against these enforced limitations, Olivia learned to swim, ride horses, and play field hockey. Both girls, whose upbringing more closely resembled that of the Brontes than of twentieth century youths, were given lessons in diction and elocution. These disciplines were administered by Lilian who hoped that one or both of her offspring might want to take up acting.

In 1924, Mrs. de Havilland returned to Tokyo to finalize her divorce. During this period she met George Fontaine, of French-Canadian descent, who had been born in Minnesota. Mr. Fontaine was general manager and part owner of Hale Brothers Department Store in San Jose. He was divorced and had a son, George, who resided with his maternal grandmother, Mrs. Cummings, in San Jose when he was not away at school. Mrs. de Havilland and the senior Fontaine were wed in 1925. (Some two years later, Walter de Havilland would marry his Japanese housekeeper.)

Olivia's introduction to formal education took place at Saratoga Grammar School. She proved to be a good student and a quick learner who required a minimum of studying. For one semester, in the sixth grade, Olivia attended Notre Dame Convent in Belmont, California, but returned to the Saratoga Grammar School where she graduated in June of 1930. It was at the Los Gatos Union High School where she realized that she was an actress. To hide her self-doubts and shyness, she assumed a countenance of poise, calm, and confidence. It was a facade which caused her to remark years later, "Every day I was sure the next day my classmates would begin to see through me."

In high school, she joined the dramatic club, earned trophies for oratory on the debating team and in a school public speaking contest, and played field hockey—winning a sweater emblem award. As a senior, she edited the yearbook, *The Wildcat.* During the summer vacation of 1932, she spent most of her time practicing typing to appease her stepfather, although her goal was to become a teacher of English and speech arts.

Unfortunately, everything was not running smoothly at home for Olivia. Her stepfather was a stickler for rules and regulations and insisted that his son and stepdaughters observe an 8:15 P.M. lights-out curfew. He also dictated that the girls could attend only a few parties but never wear lipstick. "My mother and stepfather probably weren't the only strict parents in our conservative little town," Olivia was to recollect many years later, "but they seemed the strictest to me then. And if I looked docile, inside I was seething. It just wasn't fair. . . and I knew it."

It was during the spring of her junior year at Union High School that the tension at home came to a climax. The English faculty had selected her to play the lead in the junior class play. George Fontaine reacted with stony-faced disapproval to this plum offering. He would not allow her to rehearse after

273

school hours or to perform at night. In desperation, she beseeched her mother to intercede on her behalf. However, Lilian was forced to abide by her husband's decision.

There remained but one course for Olivia to pursue. She packed her belongings into a suitcase and moved out of her parents' home. She went to a friend, the daughter of a Presbyterian minister, in whose home she was invited to live. Lilian Fontaine agreed that, under the particular circumstances, it was for the best. Mrs. de Havilland's bridge club contributed to a fund for the girl's support. As the lead in the junior class play, Olivia made her stage debut wearing a borrowed blue evening dress with a pink sash. It was the biggest thrill of her sixteen years.

To the inhabitants of Saratoga, she was known as a sweet, soft-spoken rebel because of her resistance to parental authority. Having sampled freedom, Olivia was determined never to return home. She supported herself by coaching other students in math, working as an assistant in the public library, and baby-sitting. That same year, 1933, she played the title role in *Alice in Wonderland* in the Saratoga Community Players' amateur production. She continued to maintain an A average in school and was honored with a scholarship to Mills College in Oakland, California, upon her graduation in 1934. While Olivia looked forward to college and possibly marriage to a young Yale University medical student she had met in Carmel the previous year, sister Joan's health had so deteriorated that out of desperation she had gone to live with her father and his new wife in Tokyo.

The path of Olivia's life took a major turn when, in the summer of 1934, she was picked to play the role of Puck in the Saratoga Community Players' presentation of Shakespeare's *A Midsummer Night's Dream.* Through the intervention of friends, she later met Felix Weisberger, the casting director for Max Reinhardt. The latter was preparing a production of *A Midsummer Night's Dream* for presentation at the Hollywood Bowl. At first, Olivia only requested permission to watch Reinhardt's rehearsals, but Weisberger asked her to audition. As a result, he offered Olivia the understudy role of Hermia, if she came to Hollywood a month hence.

Olivia accepted the job because she was eager, as always, to learn more about the theatre craft. She reasoned that although she would travel to Los Angeles, she could leave in plenty of time to report to Mills College in September. So convinced was she that she must take this opportunity that she even broke her engagement to her fiancé who insisted she must choose between the theatre and him.

While a trek down the coast to Los Angeles might not seem noteworthy to many, it was the first time that Olivia had been away from the Saratoga area since arriving from Tokyo in 1919. The teenager found the large city bewildering in many ways. Due to her timidity, she could not build up enough courage even to take a streetcar or bus because she had no idea how much a ride cost or where any given vehicle was bound, and she would not dream of asking the conductors.

When Olivia presented herself to the Reinhardt company, she discovered that Jean Rouverol had, in the meantime, been engaged as first understudy to Gloria Stuart in the role of Hermia. But days before the show's opening on September 17, 1934, at the Hollywood Bowl, Miss Rouverol left to take the part of W. C. Fields' daughter in Paramount's *It's a Gift.* Meanwhile, Miss Stuart had been working in First National's film *Maybe It's Love* and had only been able to attend three rehearsals to that date. It was clear that the conflict of schedules was too much, and she withdrew from the stage presentation. By attrition that left but one understudy to play Hermia on opening night—Olivia de Havilland. This circumstance was something she had not counted on. She would not leave Reinhardt without a Hermia, so she contacted Mills College to explain the situation. Its president informed her that the scholarship would be held for her until February, and so she signed for a four week on-tour engagement with Reinhardt.

On opening night, the great Max Reinhardt hugged her and spit over her left shoulder for luck. He told the petite miss, "There are 26,000 people here to see you." On hearing his German-accented words, her stomach went flighty, and her knees grew weak. She claims to have little recall of reaching the open air stage or of saying her lines. But after her first exit she remembers vividly, "There was all that wonderful applause and, just like that, I wasn't nervous any more and couldn't wait to get back on stage." After the opening, she was approached by agents who wished to represent her for movie jobs. She told them she was not interested—she considered her stage work only an enchanting episode before studying speech arts at Mills College. On tour, following the Hollywood Bowl premiere, she was singled out by the *San Francisco Examiner* with, "First I would name the Hermia of Olivia de Havilland. This girl is a wonder. I know nothing about her, her age, or what not, but when she acts Hermia she is everything."

The tour of *A Midsummer Night's Dream* concluded at the Faculty Glade and Greek Theatre of the University of California at Berkeley. The company then disbanded but a little later Reinhardt arranged to send the show on the road to Chicago, Milwaukee, and St. Louis. Olivia was asked to play Hermia in this company. (Mrs. Fontaine accompanied her daughter on this tour.)

It was while the group was in Milwaukee that Reinhardt asked her to forget about college in favor of joining him in the making of the screen version of *A Midsummer Night's Dream* to be filmed by Warner Bros. This would mean signing her name to a seven-year contract, at a starting salary of approximately $200 weekly. She finally agreed to the proposition and a would-be teacher was lost to the world of the lucrative cinema. At the same time, she turned down an offer to appear on Broadway in Zöe Akins' play, *The Old Maid.*

At the age of eighteen, the pretty-faced, brown-haired girl who stood five feet-three and one-quarter inches tall and weighed 107 pounds entered the compact world of the Warner Bros.-First National Studios. Her name was added to the contract roster that included James Cagney, Edward G. Robin-

son, Pat O'Brien, Paul Muni, Joe E. Brown, Kay Francis, Joan Blondell, Ann Dvorak, Barbara Stanwyck, Bette Davis, and Glenda Farrell.

After completing *A Midsummer Night's Dream* and before its release, she was seen for the first time oncamera as Joe E. Brown's girlfriend in his starring comedy, *Alibi Ike* (Warner Bros., 1935). He is Frank X. Farrell, a rookie baseball player with an effective pitch and a string of verbal alibis for just about every occasion. Olivia, as the sister of the club manager's wife (Ruth Donnelly), becomes his fiancée when he thrusts an engagement ring toward the surprised girl. Based on a Ring Lardner story, the premise is rather unlikely: why would a pretty young thing like Olivia permit herself to become entangled with such a wide-mouthed, unattractive nut? But at this point in cinema history, Brown was the marquee-bait and Olivia, to quote Frank S. Nugent of the *New York Times,* was merely a "charming newcomer."

Her second film, *The Irish in Us* (Warner Bros., 1935), was released in August, about two weeks after *Alibi Ike.* In this entry, she is Lucille Jackson, the pert daughter of police captain J. Farrell MacDonald and the person for whom patrolman Pat O'Brien sets his blue cap. Pat makes the tactical error of bringing her home to meet his family (ma, Mary Gordon; brothers, James Cagney and Frank McHugh) and soon Cagney decides to charm Olivia away from big brother. At this point, the predictable trouble begins. The brothers feud, with Cagney eventually claiming her heart while Olivia offers O'Brien a sisterly peck on the cheek to let him know that she still thinks he is tops. This was the third feature in which strong personalities Cagney and O'Brien, real-life pals, worked together. Olivia provided a comely balance of realism between the self-confident antics of Cagney and the often grim-faced displeasures of O'Brien. One critic of the time compared Olivia — "especially full face" — to actress Heather Angel, who was born in Britain in 1909 and had appeared in American-made films since 1933.

A Midsummer Night's Dream, co-directed

by Reinhardt and William Dieterle, was released by Warner Bros. in October 1935. Unfortunately, the public did not react kindly to ballet, woodland fairies, or Shakespeare. The fantasy, first staged in the late 1500s, was just too whimsical for Depression-saturated audiences who preferred action melodramas, wacky comedies, or high-toned love stories. If moviegoers were indifferent to the classy offering, the critics were appreciative of the brothers Warners' gallant effort to bring culture to the suspicious masses. The star-studded cast, headed by James Cagney as the tradesman Bottom, Mickey Rooney as Puck the wandering elf, and Joe E. Brown as Flute, received favorable mentions by the press. Richard Watts (*New York Herald-Tribune*) took time to note, " Miss Olivia de Havilland, she of the swanky name, is excellent" and *Newsweek* thought she "made a pleasing Hermia." The film was one of twelve nominated for an Academy Award as Best Picture of 1935 (MGM's *Mutiny on the Bounty* was the winner), and although none of the actors was mentioned at Oscar time, statuettes were bestowed upon Hal Mohr for his mystical camerawork, and Ralph Dawson for his film editing.

Meanwhile, Olivia's sister Joan had returned to California after a year of recuperation in the Orient. She had blossomed into a blonde beauty and had decided that she too would pursue a Hollywood career. Using the name Joan Burfield (after a Los Angeles street), she had a bit part in MGM's *No More Ladies* (1935) which starred Joan Crawford and Robert Montgomery. Then, for the next eighteen months, she was an idle and envious hopeful actress. She roomed with Olivia and her mother at the Chateau des Fleurs on Franklin Avenue in Hollywood until the three women moved into a house which Olivia rented in the Los Feliz district. Joan would later reveal: "We had to share the same bathroom too long," an indication that the sisters were not exactly bosom buddies.

Chance continued to play the major role in shaping Olivia's professional life. Had not a series of casting alterations occurred in a pending Warner Bros.-First National project,

it is unlikely that Olivia would have found herself in the enviable position of being an associate in a money-making studio film cycle.

Vitagraph (a studio incorporated in 1905) was purchased by Warner Bros. in 1925. Among the former's story properties was one called *Captain Blood.* The Rafael Sabatini adventure tale had been filmed in 1924 with J. Warren Kerrigan and Jean Paige. In 1935, executive producer Hal B. Wallis sought the services of British actor Robert Donat to star with Jean Muir in a talking version of the swashbuckling tale. But Donat, who had had such great success with *The Count of Monte Cristo* (United Artists, 1934), was physically unable to come to Hollywood at that time and production could be delayed no longer. In one of those enthusiastic spur-of-the-moment decisions it was decided to give the gymnastic title role to the Australian-born contract player, Errol Flynn, who had previously appeared in three inconsequential B films. Since it was thought that Olivia would better complement Flynn, she was assigned the feminine lead in place of Miss Muir.

The powers at the studio could not have been more correct. Not only were they physically well-matched, but their voices, each distinctive and elegant, blended easily. Soft-spoken in romantic scenes, their voices seemed to caress. Forceful in anger or defense, their voices melded into heaven-sent music which the viewer could believe was designed only for real lovers.

Within the context of Casey Robinson's scenario for *Captain Blood,* Peter Blood (Flynn) is a London physician during the rebellion against King James II. He is charged with treason when found administering to the wounds of a dissenter and is sentenced to a life of slavery. The innocent Blood, bearing the air of a true aristocrat, naturally is resentful at being put through the rigors of a chained prisoner. At the slave block, he openly fights Colonel Bishop (Lionel Atwill), the ruthless owner of West Indies mines whose slaves are known to work themselves to death. The colonel's beautiful niece Arabella (Olivia) is attracted to the manacled

Blood and buys him for the sum of ten pounds. She is then not sure what to do with her acquisition until,

Arabella: You're extremely foolish. It might have cost you your life. It was fortunate for you that I was here to save you.

Blood: I hardly consider it fortunate to be bought by anyone by the name of Bishop.

Arabella: You could learn a lesson in gratitude.

Blood: I can thank you for not interfering.

Arabella: As it happens, you are hardly in a position to have anything to say about it. You may join the others belonging to my uncle and henceforth you may take your orders from him.

At Port Royal, in Jamaica, Blood's medical expertise saves him from the grueling mine life. He becomes slave-physician to the island's governor (Henry Stephenson) and he is afforded the run of the island. Bishop suspects him of heading an escape plan, however, and has him whipped, an act which is interrupted by the invasion of the Spanish fleet. While the wild Spaniards pilfer the towns, Blood and his fellow slaves steal a ship and head into the Caribbean. They enter a pirate partnership with a wily and none-too-honest French pirate named Levasseur (Basil Rathbone) with whom they plunder the area —to the rousing background music supplied by Erich Wolfgang Korngold. The joint partnership results in the at-sea capture of Arabella. When Levasseur claims her as his, Blood decrees that they bid for her and he offers 20,000 pieces of eight. "I don't want to be bought by you," she states emphatically, to which he replies, "As a lady once said to a slave, 'you are hardly in a position to have anything to say about it.' "

Blood later kills his unscrupulous French pirate partner in a duel and becomes a British naval commander when Britain and France go to war after James II is overthrown. Blood is declared a hero after the defeat of a pair of French warships and is named governor of Jamaica. By this time, he and Arabella are in love and she becomes his wife.

Captain Blood cleverly used miniatures as well as stock footage to make the proceedings look even more luxurious than usual in such productions. Needless to say, the film was a huge box-office success. Andre Sennwald of the New York Times observed, "The photography recaptures the air of high romantic adventure," and noted, "Olivia de Havilland is a lady of rapturous loveliness and well worth fighting for." Olivia and Flynn would repeat their roles on "Lux Radio Theatre" on February 22, 1937.

Along with such entries as Lives of a Bengal Lancer (Paramount, 1935) and MGM's Mutiny on the Bounty, Captain Blood set the tone for the renewed cycle of swashbuckling epics that would grace Hollywood's output. Just as it was almost immediately decided that Errol Flynn was the successor to the sword-and-cloak king of the Twenties, Douglas Fairbanks, Sr., it seemed almost as obvious that Olivia was another example of the true heroine of cinema epic romances. She represented, or so it seemed to the public, all that was ladylike, docile, and gracious, yet beneath her lovely exterior beat an independent soul which could match the fire of any screen hero on any occasion. Not since Mary Astor's heroine to John Barrymore's Don Juan (Warner Bros., 1926) had such a radiant yet resourceful fair lady graced a period romantic adventure film.

Encouraged by the popularity of Captain Blood, Warner Bros. rushed into production Anthony Adverse (1936), based on the hot-selling novel of 1933. Sheridan Gibney adapted Hervey Allen's oversized book which was to be directed by Mervyn LeRoy. At a mammoth 139 minutes, the feature stuck fairly close (at least by Hollywood terms) to Allen's original plotline, telling of an Italian foundling named Adverse (Fredric March) who winds up in the care of a Scotch merchant (Edmund Gwenn) who is also his grandfather. Later young Adverse (March was actually a none-too-young thirty-eight) falls in love with Angela Guisseppi (Olivia), the daughter of the Scotsman's cook. Angela

With Warner Bros.
starlets Nan Grey, June
Travis, Maxine Doyle,
Dorothy Dare, and June
Martel in April 1935.

Publicity pose ('37).

With James Cagney in
The Irish in Us ('35).

With Fredric March in
Anthony Adverse ('36).

279

is a lovely thing upon whom Adverse bestows his affections before she is forced to move elsewhere when her father (Luis Alberni) and mother take better jobs and Adverse is sent to Cuba to protect his benefactor's investments.

In the course of this very episodic, sweeping yarn, the years pass and Adverse returns to Paris to find that Angela is now an opera singer and a mistress to Napoleon Bonaparte (Rollo Lloyd). Knowing that their lives have become too separated, Angela sends their child to him while the now-dead Scotsman's "friend," Faith (Gale Sondergaard), connives to take away from Adverse the inheritance awarded him by the dead man. Eventually, staunch Anthony succeeds in destroying her plans and, with his and Angela's son (Scotty Beckett), he sets sail for the new world to begin a new life.

The film was critically disclaimed as being too long, too tedious, and too improbable, with March and Olivia both mentioned as having been miscast. She was said to be too inexperienced to properly portray a mistress. However, the film did win four Academy Awards—for Cinematography, Musical Score, Film Editing, and the first-time-given Oscar for Best Supporting Actress to Gale Sondergaard. Director Mervyn LeRoy who had accepted Olivia over such other contenders as Bette Davis for the role of Angela lauded Miss de Havilland by admitting, "If there ever was a born actress, it is Olivia de Havilland. Her diction is superb. She can deliver a line with any inflection the director wants, as accurately as if it were played on a piano—and she has the greatest of arts—the ability to act as if she weren't acting at all."

Ironically, while Olivia was building a reputation as an enchanting ingenue of period ventures, she wanted to increase her scope of acting activities. The tenacity that would surface so fiercely in the mid-Forties was already at work within this ambitious miss. But the determined young actress was told by Warner studio chieftains, "We hired you because you photograph well. You don't have to act." While she did photograph admirably in costume pieces with the hair styles of bygone

eras, she must have felt that there had to be more to a screen career than that.

Offscreen, the stymied, baffled contract player was well-liked by technicians and fellow actors for her unspoiled manner which often bordered on the naive. Co-worker Claude Rains once said of Olivia, "If I may be permitted a touch of lyricism—the California smog may blot out the sun, but you never miss it in Olivia's presence. She is a shining, glowing idealist."

Warner Bros. was constantly on the lookout for new properties that could be fashioned into vehicles for the increasingly popular Errol Flynn. And of course, by this time, the public was already coming to expect that whenever Flynn would appear in a period adventure tale, sweet Olivia would be somewhere in the decorative background. Thus, at a cost of over one million dollars, the studio put before the cameras *The Charge of the Light Brigade* (1936), based on American journalist Michel Jacoby's account of the blunders behind the disastrous battle at Balaklava during the Crimean war (1854–56) in which 470 British cavalrymen lost their lives. True to moviemaking traditions, Jacoby, aided by co-scripter Rowland Leigh, was forced to glamorize the military affair, leaving out all mention of the British officers whose idiocy was responsible for the debacle. A truer version was offered in 1968 by British filmmakers, but that United Artists release proved a financial disappointment.

Hungarian-born Michael Curtiz who had directed *Captain Blood* with such sweeping style was assigned to *The Charge of the Light Brigade*. Errol Flynn starred as Major Geoffrey Vickers, a dedicated horse soldier. Olivia, despite the public's approval of the Flynn-de Havilland love team, was not the studio's first choice for the role of Elsa Campbell, Geoffrey's fiancée. Originally, blonde Anita Louise was intended for the part of the heroine who loves Geoffrey's younger brother Perry (Patric Knowles). But casting and production schedule changes required Miss Louise to be elsewhere on the lot and Olivia found herself in the co-starring role that could not have been better handled by any other actress.

The Charge of the Light Brigade has some of the most exciting on-horse battle scenes ever photographed (by Sol Polito), benefiting from the second unit direction of B. Reeves Eason and the Max Steiner music score. Within the story, Geoffrey Vickers is sent from his post in India to buy horses from the Arabs, and stops at Calcutta to renew his betrothal to Elsa. Later, he rescues her from the fort at Chukoti which is attacked by the hated Surat Khan (C. Henry Gordon) of Suristan, an Indian ruler who has signed a deadly pact with Russia. After Elsa has been placed safely out of the war zone—and unfortunately the focus of the storyline—Vickers heads the famous charge of 600 men against the Russian forces numbering some 25,000 in whose ranks Surat Khan rides. Vickers personally kills his adversary, but also dies (gallantly, of course) in the battle. Olivia, rustling through her scenes in appropriate silks, batting her luminous eyes on cue, and smiling that sweet look of hers which promises so much, was again considered "attractive," although "thematically unnecessary." In short, the film further established Errol Flynn as the romantic adventurer, while it displayed Olivia as merely the pretty, sweet, innocuous young supporting character.

As her seventh feature film, Warner cast Olivia in a contemporary comedy, *Call It a Day* (1937). The Dodie Smith play had enjoyed a 197 performance run on Broadway during 1936 and had already become a favorite of touring and amateur companies—Joan Fontaine would appear in a West Coast production of the show. Although much gentler and more romantic in its sexual slant, *Call It a Day* could almost be called the *Mary, Mary* of its day. And like that Jean Kerr sex romp, it received an unfair shake at the hands of moviemakers. What had seemed fresh and lighthearted onstage appeared leaden onscreen.

Even though Olivia was given top billing, the film's meaty assignments went to Ian Hunter and Frieda Inescort as her British par-

ents. Within the plotline, and thanks to spring fever, the entire Hilton family falls under the spell of romance: Olivia throws herself at a married artist (Walter Woolf King) whose wife (Peggy Wood) is flattered but yet a bit jealous. While Papa Hunter is pursued by an actress (Marcia Ralston), Mama Inescort is courted by Roland Young and the son (Peter Willes) falls in love with the pretty blonde (Anita Louise) next door. Director Archie Mayo handled the proceedings proficiently but without verve or enthusiasm, leading even the considerate *Variety* reporter to note, "An example of a fine cast rowing a very thin boat."

A shrewd interpreter of the Hollywood scene could have perhaps guessed that Warner Bros. was undergoing an uneasy period of adjustment in 1937. Kay Francis, once the highest-priced and most glamorous actress on the lot, was being phased out in a very ungenteel manner by the angered Warner Bros. Joan Blondell had played out her usefulness on the lot and would soon be joining husband Dick Powell at Columbia Pictures, while such former potential bright lights on the soundstages as Josephine Hutchinson, Aline MacMahon, and Jean Muir were gone from the lot. It would not be long before promising Lana Turner would depart from MGM along with her mentor, Mervyn LeRoy, and such zesty stalwarts of the lot as Glenda Farrell, Margaret Lindsay, and Anita Louise would fade from the Burbank scene.

While all the above were disappearing from the Warner roster, new faces were replacing them. In particular, there were disarming ingenue Jane Bryan, the protégée of rising studio queen Bette Davis (soon to be a second-time Oscar winner), Priscilla and Rosemary Lane, who in tandem with sisters Lola and Gale Page would make the super-successful *Four Daughters* (1938), *Daughters Courageous* (1938), *Four Wives* (1939), and *Four Mothers* (1941), and bouncy Jane Wyman who would inherit for a spell, the wisecracking mantle once worn by snappy Glenda "Torchy Blane" Farrell. And then there was ex-Paramount contractee Ann Sheridan who, in the late Thirties, would gain a new lease on her acting life at the studio when branded the "Oomph Girl."

Like other studios, Warner Bros. had the habit of promoting from without. It borrowed Paramount's Claudette Colbert for the plum role of *Tovarich* (1937), lured Carole Lombard to the lot for *Fools for Scandal* (1938), and hired Rosalind Russell from MGM to fill in a romantic lead in *Four's a Crowd* (1938). All of this left optimistic Olivia in a peculiar situation. The company had deliberately kept her in limbo so that she would not acquire delusions of grandeur such as those that inspired Bette Davis to sail off to England hoping to break her corporate contact.

If anything convinced Olivia, the public, and Warner Bros. that she was most useful in the Errol Flynn romantic adventure cycle, it was her appearance in *The Great Garrick* (1937). Dapper, polished Brian Aherne was given the lead role of the famed actor David Garrick who graced the eighteenth century, while Olivia was presented as Germaine De Le Corbe, the French actress who plots with fellow members of her stage troupe to poke fun at the visiting English player, Garrick. Naturally she does not plan on falling in love with the charming Britisher. The film was the first to be produced by Mervyn LeRoy who comments in his autobiography *Take One* (1974) that it was "not great but good enough to keep my nonflop record intact." The fact that James Whale, best known for helming *Frankenstein* (1931) and *The Invisible Man* (1933), directed the venture may have accounted for its unimpressive impact upon the public. Like the even more promising *Anthony Adverse,* these celluloid capers sorely required the flare that a dashing Errol Flynn would have added to the episodic approach. That these two historical entries were rather quickly forgotten by the public and industry alike was proof enough that they did not provide the zest expected by that time of a Flynn-de Havilland vehicle.

As further proof of her then-subordinate stature at the studio, Olivia was next assigned to the third-billed part of lovesick debutante Marcia West in *It's Love I'm After*

(First National, 1937). Olivia wore her Orry-Kelly wardrobe to good advantage, but it was Bette Davis and Leslie Howard as the Alfred Lunt–Lynn Fontanne type battling stage couple who commanded prime audience attention. Within this pungent screwball comedy, Basil Underwood (Howard) and Joyce Arden (Davis), a successful acting team, have postponed their marriage a dozen times when Henry Grant (Patric Knowles) asks Basil's help in discouraging his fiancé's (Olivia) infatuation with the actor.

At Marcia West's luxuriant home, Basil does everything to make himself appear ungentlemanly, insulting her family and making leering passes at her. She is undaunted, however, and likes him all the more for his seeming honesty. She breaks her betrothal to Grant in the moon-eyed belief that Basil really loves her. At this point, Joyce Arden, at Basil's plea, enters the scene to help him out of this sticky situation. Joyce pretends to be his estranged wife. When this ploy fails to dissuade Marcia, Joyce tells her that she is the mother of Basil's two offspring. This fib works, and Marcia willingly returns to the waiting Grant.

During the production-line filming of *It's Love I'm After,* decorous Olivia felt intimidated by regal Miss Davis. Olivia did her best to avoid the number-one dramatic star of the lot because she was under the impression that Bette did not care for her at all. What truth there may have been to this assumption *at the time* stemmed from Miss Davis' remembrance that she had lost out on the role of Angela in *Anthony Adverse* to newcomer Olivia.

For her first release of 1938, and her first in Technicolor, Olivia appeared as Serena Ferris, the feminine lead in *Gold Is Where You Find It,* an innocuous title for a somewhat interesting story directed with the usual verve and sweep by Michael Curtiz. George Brent, recently divorced from Constance Worth, was Olivia's leading man. Brent, who had acted opposite such Warner attractions as Kay Francis, Bette Davis, and Ruth Chatterton (whom he had married and divorced), liked Olivia who, he claims, "was a bit shy and not yet the actress she would later become, but she was beautiful to look at."

Taken from a Clements Ripley story, *Gold Is Where You Find It* was a tale of miners and ranchers of California's famous Placer County in the days following the Civil War. Brent is mine superintendent Jared Whitney whose diggings for gold are hampered by the area's ranchers, headed by crusty Colonel Ferris (Claude Rains). The Colonel's daughter (Olivia) turns the miner's head romantically, and the decision is made for the miners and ranchers to co-habit peacefully. To further point-up the peace that has befallen Placer County, the fade-out has Olivia and Brent, with arms intertwined, standing against a mountain with the sun setting behind its peak.

"Do you know you're very appealing?" Maid Marian (Olivia) asks of Robin (Errol Flynn) in Warners' two-million-dollar production of *The Adventures of Robin Hood* (1938). It is obvious that the renegade knight, formerly known as Sir Robin of Locksley, also considers this gentle woman a special person, especially after she saves him from death by hanging. He later steals into the castle to ask her to go with him to Sherwood Forest as his wife. It would mean her giving up the comforts of palace living. She tells him, "Even danger would mean nothing if you were with me," but she also alerts him that their love is secondary to the immediate cause of restoring King Richard the Lion-Hearted (Ian Hunter) to his throne, a post which has been usurped by the crafty Prince John (Claude Rains) and his blackguard associate Sir Guy Gisbourne (Basil Rathbone).

In this lyrical love story infused with gallantry and goodness, Maid Marian confesses to adoring Robin, "You remember that day in Sherwood Forest? I realized then, for the first time, that what you were doing was right and that we were wrong. You taught me, then, that England is bigger than just Normans and Saxons fighting and hating each other, that it belongs to all of us to live peacefully together, loyal only to Richard and to England." She adds quickly before he can interrupt, "I could help much more by watching for treachery here and leaving you free to protect Richard's people until he returns."

Although Maid Marian is a Norman, she is the ward of the beloved Saxon king who is being held captive in Austria following the third Crusade. She has gone along with the unfair doctrines of Prince John, a fellow Norman, until she recognizes the ideals of the heroic Saxon Robin Hood. For befriending Robin, she is imprisoned within the castle, but is later rescued by Robin, King Richard, and their followers, all disguised as Monks. It is interesting to note that Robin Hood, the hero of English ballads of the fourteenth or fifteenth century, has not been proved to be an actual historical figure. Scholars still disagree as to his authenticity.

The swordplay in *The Adventures of Robin Hood* is superb, and helped elevate Flynn into the position of the number-one swashbuckler of American films. The Technicolor is lush, the action and love scenes are enhanced by Erich Wolfgang Korngold's music, and Milo Anderson's costumes are authentically depicted. For the Sherwood Forest scenes, the company moved to the 2,400-acre Bidwell Park in Chico, California, a setting which would be used for such films as *The Great Waltz* (1938) and *Gone with the Wind* (1939). Many of the extra bit parts for the *Robin Hood* film were played by the willing inhabitants of Chico. For the record, a horse that served to carry Olivia through the Warner Bros. "Sherwood Forest" would later be purchased by Republic Studio's cowboy actor, Roy Rogers, who named the steed "Trigger."

This had been Olivia's third film with Flynn with whom, she was to admit some years later, she was deeply in love. "It lasted three years," she has said, "and I didn't tell him." She has called it a "crush," but also claims to have been "terrified" of him because of the realism he put into their love scenes. In Flynn's as-told-to autobiography, *My Wicked, Wicked Ways* (1959), published posthumously, he wrote that he loved her too and called her a "young lady of extraordinary charm." This was quite a compliment from such an experienced man of the world. Nothing came of the couple's unrequited love,

With Walter Woolf King in *Call It a Day* ('37).

With George Brent in *Gold Is Where You Find It* ('38).

With Errol Flynn in *The Adventures of Robin Hood* ('38).

With George Brent, John Payne, Pierre Watkin, and John Litel in *Wings of the Navy* ('39).

largely because of Flynn's various love-marriage episodes with others (Lili Damita, 1935–1943; Nora Eddington, 1943–1949).

Many years after making *Robin Hood*, Olivia would take her son to see the feature being revived at a Paris theatre. She has said, "Seeing *Robin Hood* after all those years made me realize how good all our adventure films were. . . ." One can only wonder what Olivia now thinks, or Errol Flynn would have thought, of the current "later adventures of Robin and Maid Marian" which was recently filmed in Spain with Sean Connery and Audrey Hepburn (Columbia, 1976).

Although *Robin Hood* was one of the movies nominated as the Best Picture of 1938, the Academy Award was bestowed upon the comedy *You Can't Take It with You. Robin Hood* did receive three so-called lesser awards, including one to Korngold for his original score. In January 1939, *Film Daily* newspaper in its annual poll of 536 newspaper, syndicate, and magazine critics selected the feature as one of 1938's ten best pictures. It was the only Warner Bros. film on the list. The movie's success did much to elevate Olivia's position on the studio lot.

Four's a Crowd (Warner Bros., 1938) is a situation comedy, before that title was applied to such screenplays. Again cast with Errol Flynn, Olivia received second billing but this time did not win him in the final scenes. In fact, up to the ending no one is quite sure who is to wed whom. As Lorri Dillingwell, she again sported an Orry-Kelly wardrobe and the hair stylist dressed her dark locks in a cascade of curls. In the Casey Robinson-Sid Herzig scenario, she is the granddaughter of millionaire John P. Dillingwell (Walter Connolly), a crochety old geezer who is fanatically devoted to miniature trains. Public relations man Robert Lansford (Flynn) wants the wealthy gentleman as a client and woos him through the pretense of an interest in the small trains as well as in Lorri, a girl who giggles a good deal too much.

Although "practically engaged to Buckley" (Patric Knowles), she is charmed by the quick-talking PR man and presumes herself to be in love with him. But it is difficult to imagine her character having a sensible thought inside her pretty head. In one scene between them, she says, "I don't want to love you." He replies, "Yes, you do." She asks, "Do I?" He answers, "Yes, you're sick," and takes her into his arms. She swoons when he kisses her.

To help his plan of obtaining Dillingwell as a client, Lansford resumes his former job with the newspaper owned by Buckley so he can maneuver an editorial campaign aimed at presenting the millionaire as the epitome of kindliness. The star lady reporter on the paper is clip-tongued Jean Christy (Rosalind Russell) with whom he makes love so she will not divulge his plans. Of course the inevitable triangle ensues with Flynn lying to both girls and with Christy, the brighter of the two, getting wise. In a mad climax, including a taxi ride to the home of the justice of the peace (Hugh Herbert), the four principals shift mates so often that it is not until the very end that befuddled Herbert pronounces Jean-Lansford and Lorri-Buckley as wives and husbands. It was all very bubbling and disarming, but equally inconsequential. And the film gave little hope that Olivia would ever usurp Carole Lombard's throne as the queen of screwball comedy.

Olivia's next offering was another contemporary comedy, one that is not particularly enjoyable or memorable. It took three writers (Jerry Wald, Maurice Lee, Richard Macaulay) to devise *Hard to Get* (Warner Bros., 1938), but it is best forgotten. It was yet another entry about a spoiled heiress, this time tamed by singing Dick Powell. The one plus factor of the film was the song "You Must Have Been a Beautiful Baby" which, within months of the film's release, was being sung by hipsters all over America.

At this juncture in Olivia's blossoming career, she was a well-known movie star to thousands of Americans, some of whom were not even able to pronounce her "foreign" name. She was not happy with many of her screen assignments, but audiences were not particularly aware of her displeasure. She has said of her personal life during this era, "Overnight success can be a dangerous thing. I didn't understand what was happening to me. I couldn't cope with the loss of privacy." She dated fun-loving James Stewart, Lew Ayres, and George Brent, and Louella Parsons spotted her jitterbugging with man-about-Hollywood Pat DeCicco at Victor Hugo's (a now-defunct Hollywood nightspot) to Benny Goodman's orchestra. When another gossip columnist announced her engagement to Howard Hughes, Hughes telephoned her with, "I understand we're engaged. Don't you think we should meet?" On New Year's Eve, 1938, they dined at Victor Hugo's. Of this first date, Olivia has commented, "He was very shy but very engaging. We danced and saw the new year in."

Olivia lived in an English sort of house covered with Virginia creepers on Los Feliz Boulevard in Los Angeles and drove a green Ford (later a green Buick). According to reporter Sidney Skolsky, the scribe who is famous for revealing the most intimate habits of stars, Olivia's favorite food was corn-on-the cob, but she claimed to be able to eat anything without fear of gaining weight. On the movie sets, she drew sketches of the other players on the backs of script pages and saved the scripts; she also saved all her love letters. She liked to read, but did not have time to read nearly everything that intrigued her. Her favorite author, she claimed, was Shakespeare. Her favorite color was blue. She loved to dance. Cigarettes were a "No-No" in her life and she was economical. Cooking was not one of her talents. And Skolsky offered her public this advice, "Boys, if you want to take her out some day, she prefers swimming and then horseback riding."

Meanwhile, onscreen she was the romantic interest of both George Brent and John Payne in *Wings of the Navy* (Warner Bros., 1939). The story, called "a little too pedestrian to fit the title" (*New York Times*), was the old plot ploy of two brothers (Brent, Payne) at a training base in Pensacola, Florida, and the girl (Olivia) who switches affections from Brent to Payne "with a feeling almost akin to pain." For the most part the feature served to bring the civilian population up to date on what could be expected of the United States naval airmen in the event of war. The three stars would repeat their roles in an abbreviated "Lux Radio Theatre" presentation on October 7, 1940.

"I got so bored, so *bored* that it just got me to a point where I nearly had a nervous breakdown," Olivia told Fellows of the American Film Institute's Center for Advanced Film Studies in Beverly Hills on October 23, 1974. "On *Dodge City* (Warner Bros., 1939), I was in such a depressed state that I could hardly remember the lines. I really mean it. It was an awful experience. I think of that film as a nadir emotionally." Co-starred for the fifth time with Errol Flynn (in his first Western), she is Abbie Irving, newspaper editor, who blames the newly appointed marshal (Flynn) of Dodge for the death of her brother (William Lundigan). She despises the marshal—she thinks—until she is aware that his intentions are good and he means to rid the town of its bad elements (chiefly Bruce Cabot). In Technicolor, the Michael Curtiz-directed film has everything to delight the Western fan: stampedes, saloon brawls, murders, street fights. Robert Buckner wrote the scenario and Max Steiner provided the musical score. The film's world premiere was held in Dodge City, Kansas, which was cause for a two-day celebration. Olivia, Flynn, and other notables of the picture were scheduled to attend, but the two stars did not make the trek. However, Alan Hale, Frank McHugh, and Ann Sheridan were at the festivities. The gala attracted some 150,000 persons (the town's population was about 10,000 in 1939) from across the state of Kansas.

Back in 1936, the Macmillan Company published some 60,000 copies of a 1,037-page novel called *Gone with the Wind,* written by an unknown Margaret Mitchell (Mrs. John R. Marsh) of Atlanta. Within a year, more than a million copies had been sold and in 1937 Miss Mitchell was honored with a Pulitzer Prize. By December 1939, the number of copies sold totaled 2,150,000 and by 1949 the book had gone into its sixty-fifth printing. Soon after its initial publication, producer David O. Selznick bought the screen rights for $50,000 as a project for his newly formed

With Laura Hope Crews in *Gone with the Wind* ('39).

←

With beau James Stewart at La Guardia Airport in New York ('39).

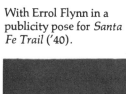

With Errol Flynn in a publicity pose for *Santa Fe Trail* ('40).

Selznick-International Pictures of Culver City, California—situated on the lot formerly owned by Pathé.

Selznick's first of many monumental tasks connected with the film was to adapt the novel for the screen. He hired playwright Sidney Howard (*The Silver Cord, Yellow Jack*) in the spring of 1937, but Howard's resultant 30,000-word script would have required five-and-one-half hours of movie time. During the next twenty-one months, no less than nine other writers were hired to work on the adaptation (including Jo Swerling, Ben Hecht, F. Scott Fitzgerald, John Van Druten), but the bulk of the final scripting, Selznick "had" to admit, was composed by him (much of it was written on the set).

Since the producer had no stable of contract players at this time, he was forced to negotiate for the loan of the actors who would portray the Mitchell characters. A deal was finally consummated with Selznick's father-in-law at MGM, Louis B. Mayer, for the screen services of Clark Gable, the public's choice as Rhett Butler. Selznick was forced to agree to MGM's handling of the film's distribution for which the studio would receive a sizable interest in the profits, and MGM was to finance one-half of the costs, estimated at $1,250,000.

Because Gable would not be available for soundstage work until late in 1938, Selznick wisely held the nation's interest by conducting a coast-to-coast search for an actress to play Scarlett O'Hara. The role of Ashley Wilkes was filled by Leslie Howard. While the search and screen tests continued for the girl who would be Scarlett, tests were also made to find the perfect Melanie Hamilton, described by authoress Mitchell as "a tiny, frailly built girl, who gave the appearance of a child masquerading in her mother's enormous hoop skirts—an illusion that was heightened by the shy, almost frightened look in her too large brown eyes. She had a cloud of curly dark hair which was so sternly repressed beneath its net that no vagrant tendrils escaped, and this dark mass, with its long widow peak, accentuated the heart shape of her face." Miss Mitchell further painted her word

portrait by writing, "Too wide across the cheek bones, too pointed at the chin, it was a sweet, timid face but a plain face, and she had no feminine tricks of allure to make observers forget its plainness. . . .But for all her plainness of feature and smallness of stature, there was a sedate dignity about her movements that was oddly touching and far older than her seventeen years."

Many actresses were considered for Melanie (among them were Geraldine Fitzgerald, Priscilla Lane, Jane Bryan, Ann Dvorak, Julie Hayden, Andrea Leeds, Anne Shirley, and Elizabeth Allen) while scores of others were interviewed, such as Olivia's sister, who was now under contract to RKO and was known as Joan Fontaine. When Joan was questioned by the film's director-designate, George Cukor, Joan flatly stated that she would be interested in playing Scarlett, but *not* Melanie. She added that perhaps Olivia might be a worthwhile candidate.

One Sunday afternoon in December 1938 Cukor accompanied the twenty-two-year-old Olivia to Selznick's home where she read a scene between Melanie and Scarlett, with Cukor enacting Scarlett. "You are *the* Melanie," Selznick informed her, an observance that coincided with hundreds of readers of fan magazines who had written letters suggesting her for the part. When Olivia confronted Jack L. Warner with her desire to play Melanie, he replied, "Oh, you don't want to play Melanie. Scarlett's the only part." Olivia responded with, "I don't give a darn about Scarlett. I want to play Melanie. I just love her enough to play her." Warner snorted, "You don't want to be in that picture. It's going to be the biggest bust in town." She begged to be loaned out but he refused with, "You'll go out there and you'll come back and you'll be difficult."

She promised that she would be a good girl, but still Warner refused his approval. A few days later, she called Warner's wife for tea and explained her plight. A short time later, an exchange was made. Selznick maintained a one-picture commitment for James Stewart of MGM and Warner Bros. wanted him for *No Time for Comedy* (1940) opposite Rosalind Russell. In January 1939, Selznick traded one Stewart screen appearance for one by de Havilland. Jack Warner backed down even further by offering to finance Selznick's epic 100 percent, if Warner Bros. stars Bette Davis and Errol Flynn were used as Scarlett and Rhett, but Miss Davis, although wanting desperately to play Scarlett, killed Warner's proposal by her refusal to star opposite Flynn.

On Sunday night, December 11, 1938, the first scenes of *Gone with the Wind* were shot when old sets on the forty-acre back lot of Selznick-International were set ablaze (at a cost of $26,000) to simulate the burning of Atlanta by the Yankees. Doubles were used for Rhett and Scarlett while seven Technicolor cameras captured the kerosene-soaked blaze from seven different strategic angles. As the flames died out, Selznick's actors' agent, brother Myron, appeared with British actor Laurence Olivier and the latter's love, actress Vivien Leigh. On January 16, 1939, the "discovery" of Miss Leigh ended the search for Scarlett when she was signed for the film, along with a seven-year contract. Meanwhile, on Monday evening, December 12, 1938, Olivia was heard on "Lux Radio Theatre" opposite Leslie Howard in *The Scarlet Pimpernel,* a casting assignment deemed timely to prepare fans for the secondary love team that would be so much a part of *Gone with the Wind.*

As the actual production of the historical melodrama got underway, Cukor was dismissed as director for working too slowly and for not giving enough attention to male star Clark Gable. Victor Fleming, with Gable's approval, was assigned to replace Cukor. But unknown to the production heads, or to each other, both Vivien Leigh and Olivia were soliciting help from Cukor on their roles during their free days offcamera. On July 1, 1939, with Sam Wood having taken over from an exhausted Fleming, *Gone with the Wind* wound-up production with some 475,000 feet of film exposed. Still to come was the enormous task of editing the tremendous amount of footage, as well as having a music score composed.

In the meantime, Selznick forged ahead with plans to put Daphne du Maurier's melodramatic novel *Rebecca* on the screen. He spoke to Olivia about playing the young wife, but she was unwilling to consider it since her sister was also under consideration. *Rebecca* (1940) would eventually star Joan Fontaine and mark the beginning of her celebrity period. A gentleman now residing in San Francisco was a member of the technical crew that worked on both *GWTW* and *Rebecca*. He recalls the starting day of the latter when Miss Fontaine addressed the crew with, "I hope you will like me as much as you liked my sister." The ex-crew man now states simply, "We didn't."

Possibly because Warner was still not convinced that *Gone with the Wind* would be a success, or, more probably, because he intended to demonstrate to increasingly self-willed Olivia that he was still very much her employer, he assigned her to the third-billed and superfluous role of Lady Penelope Gray in his filming of the Maxwell Anderson play, *Elizabeth the Queen.*

Changed to *The Private Lives of Elizabeth and Essex,* the Technicolor results were released on September 28, 1939, with Miss Bette Davis in one of her sturdiest screen characterizations as Queen Elizabeth I. Penelope Gray is a compliant lady-in-waiting at Whitehall who loves the handsome, dashing Earl of Essex (Errol Flynn). Alas, the queen is also involved with him which causes jealousy on Penelope's part. In the queen's chambers, Penelope introduces a song recently written by Sir Walter Raleigh (Vincent Price) of which she confidentially tells Mistress Margaret Radcliffe (Nanette Fabray), "The words will fit perfectly: a woman in love with a man much younger than herself." Mistress Margaret is aghast at her daring and suggests, "Are you mad, Pen? She'll beat you or send you to the Tower," but nevertheless, Pen begins the song. Elizabeth endures it until the words, "But when I'm young, and love so well, then I might hold you close forever more." She then goes into a rage and breaks her mirror. She orders Penelope out of the room after calling her such names as "brazen wench," "indecent hedgedrab," and "shameless baggage."

In a later scene, Olivia speaks the bulk of the limited dialogue allotted her when she asks Essex, "Do you love the queen?" He, "I do, my dear, deeply." She, "I wish you loved someone who loved you better." He, "Meaning?" She, "Oh, no one—myself perhaps—anyone who loves you better." He, "Why, doesn't the queen love me, sweets?" She, "She loves you, she loves you not." He, "Why do you tell me this?" She, "I'm afraid." He, "For me?" She, "I've heard her walking up and down her room at night, all night long, cursing you; cursing you because she must love you and can't help herself. It's wearing a terrible revenge for this love she scorns to bear you. Oh, Robert, be careful. You anger her too much." He, "Why? Isn't it the same with all lovers?" She, "Oh, no, I've never cursed you." He, "Aha, but if we were lovers you might. Thank your lucky stars [interestingly, a title of a later Flynn-de Havilland film venture] we're not." Still later, Penelope unwittingly takes part in a plot to keep Essex and Elizabeth apart, a scheme which results in his being sent to the dreaded Tower of London and ultimately to his beheading.

Of this costume venture, Olivia has assessed, "It was very hard for me to make *Elizabeth and Essex.* I was really miserable, but I did it because I had given him [Jack L. Warner] my word that I wouldn't be difficult."

Warner then loaned her to Samuel Goldwyn for a remake of *Raffles,* a project by which iconoclastic Goldwyn hoped to turn contract player David Niven into a screen sensation equal to Ronald Colman, Goldwyn's one-time pride and joy who starred in the original 1930 version. Olivia was against the loan-out but, again keeping to her bargain with her boss, she consented without visible argument. Now she can say, "I knew it was going to be a disaster. It had already been done by Ronald Colman wonderfully well. . . .I had nothing to do with that English scene [to be used in the film], I had nothing to do with that style of film and I was nothing to that part the way it was written. I knew that it would be a disaster for me, but I went ahead and did it. I never said one word, keeping my promise to him [Warner]. I kept it twice and he was penalizing me each time."

On December 15, 1939, *Gone with the Wind* had its glorious world premiere at Loew's Grand Theatre in Atlanta, following a twenty-four-hour celebration that included a parade down Peachtree Street and a grand costume ball attended by most of the film's stars. Jack L. Warner had forbidden Olivia to attend the festivities, but she took off on her own after having received suspensions for refusing to work in a third rendering of Maxwell Anderson's *Saturday's Children* (1940) (she was replaced by Anne Shirley) which she had done on "Lux Radio Theatre" with Robert Taylor on October 26, 1936, and for turning down the lead in an inconsequential programmer which was released in 1940 as *Flight Angels* (she was replaced by Virginia Bruce).

The evening of December 15, 1939, saw some 2,000 people (at ten dollars and up per seat) enter the Grand Theatre, the front of which had been restyled to represent the Wilkes plantation of Twelve Oaks. Thousands jammed the street outside the theatre while kleig lights focused on the facade. Olivia arrived wearing a dark evening gown with matching shoes and a white fur jacket. The Technicolor film, which ultimately cost $3.85 million, was a hit in Atlanta. At the end of the premiere, one gentleman, the president of Georgia Trust Company, said, "I've been crying and, by God, I'm not ashamed to say so." The following week, the motion picture debuted in New York at two theatres.

For those few readers who do not know Margaret Mitchell's story, it concerns the tragic, sorrowful end of a way of life and the people who survive the holocaust to bring new meaning to their lives through faith, strength, and determination. Scarlett O'Hara (Vivien Leigh) has strength but no faith and is incapable of real friendship except with one person, her competitor in love, Melanie Hamilton Wilkes (Olivia). Melanie marries her cousin Ashley, a weak man, while Scarlett imagines herself to be in love with the soulful gentleman. Scarlett's frigidity finishes her own marriage to Rhett Butler (Gable), the one man who understands her. Although she is free to openly pursue Ashley after Melanie's death, she realizes that Ashley is a fool and that she truly loves Rhett. Melanie's dying words to Scarlett, "Be kind to Captain Butler, he loves you so," possibly awaken her true feelings more than anything else. America's Civil War is the colorful, tumultuous backdrop for the love story of Scarlett O'Hara, the spoiled, strong-willed daughter of Gerald and Ellen (Thomas Mitchell, Barbara O'Neil), and of the assorted people who touch upon her life.

Everything about *GWTW* is majestic: the photography (Ernest Haller), the unforgettable musical score (Max Steiner), the interiors (Joseph B. Platt), costumes (Walter Plunkett), Scarlett's hats (John Fredericks), the color (Ray Rennahan, Wilfrid M. Cline Associates), and, of course, the stellar performances. *Liberty* magazine quite rightly called the picture, "a celluloid landmark—and tomorrow's screen tradition of today." The same publication also noted, "The two outstanding performances are Olivia de Havilland's gentle aristocrat, Melanie, and Hattie McDaniel's old colored mammy." *Time* noted that the film was a "U.S. legend" and "For almost four hours the drama keeps audiences on the edge of their seats with few letdowns." Frank S. Nugent (*New York Times*) did not find it to be the greatest film ever made, but he did write, ". . . it is the greatest motion mural we have seen and the most ambitious filmmaking venture in Hollywood's spectacular history."

The film, which by 1977 would have grossed $77 million, was nominated for thirteen Academy Awards. In the acting categories, Vivien Leigh was nominated as Best Actress, Clark Gable as Best Actor, and both Olivia and Hattie McDaniel as Best Supporting Actress. Since then Olivia has said, "In those days, regardless of billing or contract, the producer had the right to decide the cate-

gory; and Selznick, in order not to split the vote between Vivien and me, put me down as supporting. He never explained this to me and I wish he had, because it would have meant a great deal to me."

At Hollywood's Ambassador Hotel the night of Thursday, February 29, 1940, Miss Leigh won an Oscar as did Victor Fleming as Best Director, and the film was named Best of 1939. In close competition, Hattie McDaniel won over a very disappointed Olivia—the names of the winners had leaked out prior to the award ceremony, the last time this would happen. Olivia has said, "It was my very first nomination, and I knew I'd never get one at Warners. . . .But I tried to keep a stiff upper lip—and did, until I had some champagne at the banquet following the ceremonies." Then she cried and for the next two weeks. "I couldn't believe there was any good in the world." Olivia gradually overcame her defeat and eventually realized that Hattie's winning "was really so much more meaningful in a big way."

Raffles was released on January 16, 1940. David Niven was showcased as the slick jewel thief who deposits a note ("Sorry, but I have a better use for this") at the scene of each theft and calls himself "The Amateur Cracksman." A cricket player by reputation, he is invited to the palatial country house at Essex belonging to Lord and Lady Melrose (Lionel Pape, Dame May Whitty) where Gwen (Olivia) and her brother Bunny (Douglas Watson) are also guests. Police Inspector Mackenzie (Dudley Digges) shows up to protect Lady Melrose's priceless necklace from suspected burglary. Bunny confides to A. J. Raffles that he needs a thousand pounds to cover a gambling debt. Raffles promises to help, leading to the theft of the necklace, and the crook's eventual decision to give himself up to the police in order to collect the 1,000-pound reward for Bunny. Unfortunately, Olivia has little to do in *Raffles* except to look pretty in the Travis Banton costumes.

My Love Came Back (Warner Bros., 1940), albeit a cute comedy, did extremely little to exhibit Olivia's abilities. She is a prize-honored violinist sponsored financially by kindly

With Jack Carson,
James Cagney, Herbert
Heywood, and Rita
Hayworth in *Strawberry
Blonde* ('41).

→

The fashionable star in
1941.

With Dame May
Whitty, David Niven,
and Lionel Pape in
Raffles ('40).

old Mr. Malette (Charles Winninger) whose wife (Spring Byington) is baffled by her spouse's intentions.

On the other hand, she had a substantial part in her seventh film with Errol Flynn, *Santa Fe Trail* (Warner Bros., 1940), in which both stars' names were billed above the title. Historically, the Santa Fe Trail was followed by rail to Kansas and "by pure nerve from there on." However, the story in this big Michael Curtiz production does not take us beyond Kansas from where the maniacal John Brown (Raymond Massey) plans to free the slaves owned by the dastardly Southerners.

Within the 110-minute Western, Jeb Stuart (Flynn) and George Custer (Ronald Reagan), both West Point graduates, fall in love with Kit Carson Halliday (Olivia). How did the heroine obtain such a name? As she explains, "Mr. Carson and my dad were very good friends. They were so sure I was going to be a boy they named me before I was born." Never having been to Kansas, Jeb Stuart asks what the inhabitants there do on Saturday night for fun. Kit replies, "Well, as I remember, half of Leavenworth takes a bath and the other half gets drunk and since there are only two bathtubs in town things get kinda excitin' around midnight."

Since the railroad is not yet constructed beyond Leavenworth, it is the duty of Stuart and Custer to escort a wagon train of supplies to Santa Fe. En route, they are stopped by a "preacher" looking for his load of Bibles which happen to be rifles and the man of the cloth turns out to be the notorious John Brown. For much of the remaining screen time, Brown's raids keep the men busy from Kansas to Virginia until he is killed at Harper's Ferry. As the obligatory love interest of the two military men, Olivia is eventually paired off with Flynn. For the first time in a screen period outing with Flynn, Olivia had a really solid role, a tomboyish part that allowed her to show spunk and vigor.

It was at the start of the Forties that her romantic life altered. In 1940, Olivia met novelist Marcus Aurelius Goodrich at a dinner party. She was to relate a few years later, "He was not only a brilliant conversationalist, but extremely vibrant and interesting." It was the beginning of an intense courtship that would climax in marriage.

On the professional front, Olivia was obliged to adopt a bit of trickery with regard to roles she really coveted. On discovering that studio policy required that a script designated for production be first sent to makeup where the department head estimated the number of makeup people required for the project and the types of cosmetics, Miss de Havilland would casually enter the department and sneak out a script or two at a time. She would read them overnight and surreptitiously return them the next morning.

One of these ill-gotten scripts was *One Sunday Afternoon* which had been a Broadway play and also had been produced by Paramount in 1933 with Gary Cooper, Frances Fuller, and Fay Wray. Warners changed the title to *The Strawberry Blonde* and planned to star Ann Sheridan in the title role. After reading the scenario and being enchanted by it, Olivia went to see the studio's executive producer Hal B. Wallis and asked to play Amy Lind, the outspoken girl whom Biff Grimes weds. It was argued that it was not the plum role, but Olivia said, "Let anybody else play the title role, the point is that there's a woman I understand and I want to play her." Jack L. Warner also tried to argue her out of the idea, but when Sheridan adamantly refused to work in the film (she was on strike for better roles) and the relatively unknown Rita Hayworth was borrowed from Columbia as a replacement, the producers decided they needed a female star with a big enough draw to supply marquee insurance, and with James Cagney cast in the male lead, Olivia won the part she desired.

The Strawberry Blonde (Warner Bros., 1941) filmed in black and white, is set in New York of the Gay Nineties when two young hot shots, Biff Grimes (Cagney) and Hugo Barnstead (Jack Carson), vie for the love and affection of the neighborhood doll, Virginia Brush (Hayworth). As it develops, oafish Hugo, the go-getter, wins Virginia's hand in matrimony while Biff, studying to be a dentist, eventually marries Amy (Olivia), a nurse. When she first meets Biff on a blind date, she proves to be not only vocal concerning women's rights but gets right to the point, stating, "This is a pre-arranged date and we all know it. Let's get on with it. I've got to be back to work at eleven." It is she, not the flirtatious Virginia, who says, "Why'd we come here if we're not to be trifled with?"

The critics liked Olivia and *The Strawberry Blonde. Time* magazine alerted its readers, "[It] is a blithe, turn-of-the-century buggy ride. Cagney makes the hero a tough but obviously peachy fellow—Rita Hayworth takes the picture away from him, and dark-eyed Olivia de Havilland takes it away from both of them." There was a reported rift between Olivia and Cagney during the filming of this vehicle, when he accused her of upstaging the less-experienced Hayworth. However, the two Warner Bros. stars remained friends through the years. A third screen version of the property, a musical, would be produced by Warners in 1948, bearing its original title, with Dorothy Malone in the Lind role and Dennis Morgan as Biff Grimes.

Sometimes a quirk of medical bad luck can have an advantageous effect on one's professional career. Such was to happen with Olivia. In early 1941, she underwent an appendectomy and was confined to bed for twelve days after her hospital release. During her convalescence, Geraldine Fitzgerald and her husband, Edward Lindsey-Hogg, insisted that she stay with them, which she did. Olivia's sister, Joan, wed to Brian Aherne and anxiously working on *Suspicion* (1941), in hopes of winning the Oscar she lost for her *Rebecca* (1940), was not on hand to help Miss de Havilland. When the Lindsey-Hoggs were invited to Sunday lunch by Paramount scripter Charles Brackett, a very weakened Olivia accompanied them, but not on her own "steam"—she had to be carried into the Brackett home.

There, at the luncheon table, producer Arthur Hornblow, Jr., presented her with a script which had been written by Brackett and Billy Wilder from Ketti Frings' story, *Hold Back the Dawn,* which was to be filmed by Paramount. Olivia was asked to read the script, with the part of Emmy Brown in mind for herself, but she was cautioned not to mention it to anyone, not even to her agent. "I read it. I phoned them and told them I adored it and would love to do it."

Next came the chore of negotiating the loan-out. By coincidence, it was discovered that Jack L. Warner was so anxious to obtain the services of Paramount's Fred MacMurray for *Dive Bomber* (1941) that he would have traded any one of his contractees. Hornblow pretended disinterest in all that Warner had to offer. Finally, he said as casually as possible, "As a big favor to you, we'll take Olivia de Havilland." Warner was none the wiser, nor was Olivia's agent who telephoned her with, "You're going to be loaned to Paramount, but.it's all right, I've seen the script." Although still weak from her operation, she gladly went to work at Paramount in a role she knew she was going to enjoy, and for a director (Mitchell Leisen) whom she admired. She had gained weight from all the jello she was required to eat during her hospital stay, and in retrospect she has said, "I now think Emmy's plumpness is an advantage to the characterization."

Magazine ads heralded the arrival of *Hold Back the Dawn* (1941) with a full-face drawing of Charles Boyer captioned, "Master of Love. . . . His words of love set all women's hearts on fire." On either side of him stood full-length drawings of Olivia and Paulette Goddard. A comic-strip type of dialogue balloon has Olivia saying, "He made me afraid of myself . . . afraid to see the deep longing he had put in my heart."

Told in the then-popular flashback technique, Georges Iscovescu (Boyer) steals onto a Paramount soundstage where Mr. Saxon (Mitchell Leisen) is busily directing Veronica Lake in a scene from *I Wanted Wings* (1941). When Saxon breaks for lunch, an anxiety-ridden Georges relates his story. He is a dancer-gigolo of European extraction who has spent months waiting desperately at the Mexican-USA border for permission to enter the States. Upon the half-joking advice of his former dance partner (Goddard), Georges romances a naive school teacher (Olivia) from

Azusa, California, who is south of the border escorting a busload of little boys. He woos and weds her, but in a moment of conscience refuses to consummate the marriage. When she learns the truth of her situation, she crosses the border, attempting to drive while in a hysterical condition. Her car goes out of control and she is seriously injured. Georges then sneaks into the U.S. to see her in the hospital. From there, he goes to the Paramount Studios. Weeks later, back in Mexico, he is permitted to cross the border to join his wife who is waiting for him on the American side.

Newsweek called *Hold Back the Dawn* a "woman's picture but a superior variety of that lucrative screen species." The magazine rated Olivia's performance as "excellent." Bosley Crowther in the *New York Times* admitted, "Olivia de Havilland plays the school teacher as a woman with romantic fancies whose honesty and pride are her own—and the film's chief support. Incidentally, she is excellent."

With the success of this film, Olivia imagined that she would be handed more serious roles by Jack L. Warner. But while she may have been a strong dramatic star on loan-out, back on the home lot Bette Davis ruled the histrionic roost, with Ida Lupino and Mary Astor standing in the wings for Miss Davis' meaty leftovers. Warner chose to ignore the two chief successes of Olivia's career, both of which were gained at other studios, and cast her as Errol Flynn's adorable prop in *They Died with Their Boots On* (Warner Bros., 1941). This was the first of their co-starring vehicles to be directed by Raoul Walsh, the man destined to helm most of Flynn's productions in the Forties now that the studio, the swashbuckler, and temperamental Michael Curtiz had come to an irrevocable parting of the professional way. Flynn is seen as flamboyant General George Armstrong Custer, the U.S. Cavalry's second lieutenant who rises to the rank of brigadier general within two years and who, with his column of 264 men, is slaughtered in a last stand against the Sioux Indians at Little Big Horn in 1876.

Pretty and voluptuous Olivia is Beth Bacon, who becomes his wife. While he is pack- ing to leave her for the final time, his good-luck charm breaks and she says thoughtfully, "It will be the only time you have gone into a campaign without it." As they kiss goodbye, he tells her, "Waltzing through life with you has been a very gracious thing." In this production, very much a man's film, filled with gunfire, horses, battles, and death set to Max Steiner's rousing music, the feminine lead is merely a secondary consideration.

In January of 1941, the eighteen members of the New York Film Critics announced their selection of the top film actress of the year. After five ballots in which Olivia (for *Hold Back the Dawn*) and Joan Fontaine (for *Suspicion*) were neck-and-neck, Joan was announced the winner on the sixth ballot. In Hollywood, that same month, when the Oscar nominees were revealed, Olivia and Joan were again in competition as Best Actress, along with Bette Davis (for *The Little Foxes*), Greer Garson (for *Blossoms in the Dust*), and Barbara Stanwyck (for *Ball of Fire*). On Thursday, February 26, 1942, at the Biltmore Hotel, when Joan was declared the winner, Olivia clapped and shouted, "We've won." Later, however, she commented, "I've been runner-up so often it isn't funny any more. If it happens again I'm likely to break something." She also mentioned that she, as the older sister, wanted to win the Oscar in order that she not lose Joan's respect.

Back on the acting front, Olivia, who had become a naturalized citizen on November 28, 1941, was sandwiched into *The Male Animal* (Warner Bros., 1942) derived from the James Thurber and Elliott Nugent Broadway play of 1940. It developed into a highly amusing movie with Henry Fonda in the lead as a brainy college professor loaded with what are considered by all to be odd-ball ideas. While in a rare state of drunkenness, he declares himself to be "the male animal" who is protecting his rights. His wife is played by Olivia, described by the *New York Times* as "a delightfully pliant and saucy character." Despite her willingness to accept her husband's ideas, she is temporarily thrown off base by the appearance of her old beau (Jack Carson), the typical big, confident ex-football player. A decade later, the studio would revamp the property into a musical, *She's Working Her Way Through College,* with Ronald Reagan and Virginia Mayo in the leads.

Olivia was still pleading with Jack Warner to give her the opportunity of playing the types of roles assigned to Bette Davis (*The Letter,* 1940, *The Little Foxes,* 1941) but instead she was "rewarded" with the part of the good sister in *In This Our Life* (Warner Bros., 1942). The novel by Ellen Glasgow had won a Pulitzer Prize, but the film, directed by John Huston (the most wanted director in town after his work on *The Maltese Falcon* in 1941), is pure soap opera melodrama. Even Huston has called it "pretty heavy going."

Within the ninety-seven-minute Howard Koch screenplay, the Timberlake family of Virginia is no longer wealthy, due to the ineffectualness of the easy-going father (Frank Craven) who has lost his tobacco company to his brother-in-law (Charles Coburn). Timberlake and his wife (Billie Burke) apparently hoped for sons in that they bestowed boys' names on their two daughters—Stanley (Bette Davis) and Roy (Olivia). Only a veteran of radio drama listening could have untangled the intertwining threads of melodrama that follow. Stanley deserts her attorney fiancé Craig Fleming (George Brent) a few days before they are to wed in order to run off with Roy's husband (Dennis Morgan). Later, while driving in a pique of anger, Stanley becomes a hit-and-run driver. She blames the accident on the son (Ernest Anderson) of the Timberlake's cook (Hattie McDaniel). Roy knows Stanley is guilty because her alibi is faulty, and asks Craig to defend the cook's son. When Craig finds proof of Stanley's guilt, she goes to the uncle for help, but he, a dying man, hints instead at an incestuous affair which drives her from the house to her death when her car later runs off the road.

If *In This Our Life* proved anything, it demonstrated the tremendous difference in acting style between its two leading actresses: while Miss Davis overacted, Olivia was refreshingly natural. At the same time, this film marked the start of a lifelong friendship between Olivia and Bette. Twenty-three years later, when TV host Ralph Edwards

presented Miss Davis with "This Is Your Life," Olivia was one of those honoring the star. In a brief reminiscence of the Warner days, the husky-voiced Miss Davis remarked to Olivia, "You were always so damned pretty."

After turning down the lead opposite Jack Benny in Warners' 1942 *George Washington Slept Here* (she was replaced by Ann Sheridan), Olivia appeared in a seventeen-minute short at Twentieth Century-Fox entitled *Show Business at War* (1943). It was produced by *Time* magazine as one of *The March of Time* series. With a large retinue of stage and screen personalities (Bob Hope, Dorothy Lamour, Tyrone Power, Gertrude Lawrence, Lily Pons, to mention only a few), the short exploited the war efforts of the acting profession. Olivia, as well as Bette Davis, Joel McCrea, Priscilla Lane, and Jerry Colonna, was seen in a Warner Bros. ten-minute short, *Stars on Horseback* (1943). More importantly, for her home studio she was in the feature-length *Thank Your Lucky Stars* (1943) which contained cameo appearances by Warner Bros. contract players from Bette Davis to S. Z. Sakall.

In a flimsy plot dealing with a singer (Dennis Morgan) and a songwriter (Joan Leslie), the Warner Bros. studio is donated for the production of a show benefiting the war effort. With Ida Lupino and George Tobias, Olivia jitterbugged to a fast-tempo rendition* of the song "The Dreamer." In wearing the short-skirted outfit of a musical showgirl, Olivia revealed the shapeliness of her legs, but later confided that "It made me feel mean, mean." Errol Flynn was also in *Thank Your Lucky Stars,* and although he was not in the same sketch as Olivia, it marked the ninth and final film in which they would both appear.

By mid-1943, Olivia was the subject of articles in all the major fan magazines. Writers wondered about her husbandless life and John R. Franchey in *Screenland* observed that her beauty was unchanged "except that the eyes had grown up at last." She had been publicly chastised by columnist-commentator

---

* Her singing was dubbed by Lynn Martin.

299

With Charles Boyer in
Hold Back the Dawn
('41).

With Errol Flynn in
*They Died with Their
Boots On* ('41).

With Henry Fonda in
The Male Animal ('42).

With Bette Davis and
John Hamilton in *In
This Our Life* ('42).

Jimmy Fidler for damaging her Melanie Hamilton image by smoking cigarettes and dancing in nightclubs. She insisted that *no* problems existed with Warner Bros. stating, "I think my employers are wonderful. Sometimes they really pretend to think I'm a little clever, myself. And even talented. Why, nowadays they actually listen until I've finished talking."

Sara Hamilton of *Photoplay* described the actress as "looking like a cellophane Hedy Lamarr with candles lit inside. Glowing. Vibrant. Alive." Olivia openly admitted to being stubborn, "but I'm improving. I realize stubbornness is the strength of weak people and a poor substitute for a strong but flexible mind" and possessing a quick temper, "I've got one that, when aroused, leads me into saying hard, cruel things I regret, into being ruthless when ruthlessness is not really a part of my nature."

After dating Franchot Tone and Burgess Meredith, with whom she was thought to be in love, she entered into a romantic relationship with the young director of *In This Our Life*. Of him, she was to say later, "John [Huston] was a very great love of mine." In March 1944, she told an interviewer while in Alaska on a USO tour, "I am ready to marry John whenever he is free" (he was then married to Leslie Black). Some years later, she recalled their romance with, "John fell in love with me and pursued me relentlessly. I ran away from him on several occasions. Once he drove all night to find me in Carmel, abandoning a film to go after me."

Her best pal was Geraldine Fitzgerald (and her husband), while Jack Carson was a close male friend on the lot. Concerning the rumors that she and sister Joan were feuding (again), Olivia refuted them by referring to whatever misunderstandings existed as "healthy disagreements" between sisters. Writer-columnist Sidney Skolsky revealed that the sisters "do quarrel occasionally, but it is never over professional jealousy."

Olivia had moved to a small house near Coldwater Canyon with "Shadrack," an Airedale dog given her by Huston before he went off to war. She personally answered fan letters, blushed easily, loved to eat, but had to watch her diet. She liked going to movies to see Ronald Colman, Katharine Hepburn, Bette Davis, Charles Laughton, and Frank Morgan. She reportedly slept alone in a large antique bed in white or pink nightgowns and with the windows open. It was generally agreed that she was very popular, but had few "true friends."

When questioned about the type of man she would marry, she replied, "lean and hard and dark. He mustn't be 'arty' or wear bow ties. He can't wear grease of any kind on his hair, and he must be intelligent." When not working, she devoted most of her time to talking with servicemen at the Hollywood Canteen.

In April 1943, Olivia began production of the much-plagued *Devotion*, a film about the Bronte Sisters which Warners would not release for nearly three years. She was also placed on contract suspension for refusing a loan-out to Columbia to work in an untitled, unfinished script.

Princess O'Rourke (Warner Bros., 1943), supposedly an original screenplay by Norman Krasna (for which he won an Oscar), is obviously derived from the story of Cinderella, a fairy tale believed to have come from China in the ninth century A.D. Heralded by many critics as "one of the best comedies of the year," the feature has Olivia in top billing as Princess Maria, a royal refugee from a European nation. She is in New York with her guardian uncle (Charles Coburn) who recommends that she take a trip west to a ranch. She boards a plane piloted by Eddie O'Rourke (Robert Cummings) and resorts to an overdose of sleeping pills to calm her nerves. When O'Rourke is forced to land the plane ahead of schedule due to fog, he becomes the drugged girl's benefactor by taking her to his apartment. She, of course, falls in love with him. Later, she renounces her throne to marry the man she loves and they are wed in the White House by a Supreme Court justice (Harry Davenport).

The *New York Times'* Bosley Crowther found Olivia "charming" in this confection and *Variety* opined that she "shines brightly." Although many Hollywood psychics predicted an Oscar for her comedic contributions, Olivia's name was not among those nominated in the winter of 1944. Sister Joan was nominated for *The Constant Nymph,* but lost to Jennifer Jones of *The Song of Bernadette.*

Within days of the August 1943 completion of *Princess O'Rourke,* Olivia was put to work on another comedy, *Government Girl* (1943), made on loan to RKO. In the title role, she was a wartime Washington secretary with the War Construction Board. When an industrial boy wonder (Sonny Tufts) appears on the scene to speed up the production of bomber planes, she is assigned to show him the ins-and-outs of government bureacracy. He surpasses his factory-line quota but, in so doing, steps on a few toes and eliminates certain red tape. When he is forced to appear before a Senate investigating committee, the secretary, who now loves him, testifies on his behalf. The *Nation's* James Agee declared, "some of it is awful, especially some of the [slapstick] things gentle little Olivia de Havilland has to do for the laughs of the canaille." *Screenland* magazine recorded, "although she overplays it a bit, we enjoyed Olivia de Havilland's performance."

In 1943, Olivia's contract with Warner Bros. had reached the end of its seven-year course. However, because of six suspensions, the period of contract was extended for aggregates of the layoff time. "It appeared that I should be shackled to Warners ad infinitum." In mid-August 1943, she met with attorney Martin Gang who informed her of the old "anti-peonage" law in California that limited to seven years the time for which an employer can enforce a contract against an employee. The two-paragraph law, as Olivia and Gang interpreted it, meant calendar years.

So lawyer and client filed for "declaratory relief" in California Superior Court on November 5, 1943. Bette Davis had sued earlier, but had gone to England for the court hearings. This had been a mistake inasmuch as the British barristers were not familiar with the situation and she lost her case against Warner Bros. Other studio stars, such as George Brent and Ann Sheridan, had threatened court action but considered the Warner empire too mighty to tackle.

Because of the courtroom action, Olivia re-ceived headline attention by Los Angeles newspapers. But since the reporters, also un-ionized, were employed by newspapers who depended on the large studios for advertising money, the reports were not sympathetic to Miss de Havilland. It was not until March 1944 that a decision was handed down by Judge Charles S. Burnell. Olivia had won her case. Jack L. Warner appealed the decision immediately and enjoined some 150 film companies (some of which were defunct) from hiring her. The next hearing, with the Appellate Court, was scheduled for September 10, 1944.

With so much free time to spare, Olivia entertained servicemen in hospitals on USO tours to the Aleutians and South Pacific. War correspondent Ernie Pyle wrote of Olivia's countenance, "It was so beautiful I couldn't do anything but stand and stare at her." She contracted pneumonia in the Southwest Pacific where she was hospitalized at Suva in the Fiji Islands for three weeks.

Once back in the U.S., she actively campaigned for the re-election of President Franklin D. Roosevelt and, although her contract forbade outside acting services, she performed on "Lux Radio Theatre" on May 1, 1944, with Paul Lukas in *Appointment for Love* (in the Margaret Sullavan role), and on September 18, 1944, with William Powell in *Suspicion* (in sister Joan's role).

When the three judge Appellate Court did convene on this landmark case, it decided unanimously in Olivia's favor. But again Jack L. Warner appealed, this time to the Supreme Court of California, and thus there was yet another delay for Olivia in pursuing her acting career.

On January 22, 1945, she was heard on "Lux Radio Theatre" with Dennis O'Keefe and June Duprez in *Tender Comrade* (in the role created onscreen by Ginger Rogers). On February 3, 1945, her lawyer, Martin Gang, telephoned her with the jubilant news that the Supreme Court had decreed that no further review of the case was necessary because the Appellate decision had been unanimous.

As a result of Olivia's daring court suit, she had freed the slaves of Hollywood studios. There were many screen performers thankful for her courage, including the men under contract who had gone to war and could have had their contracts extended for the length of time they spent in uniform. The judgment became universally known as "The de Havilland Decision" and can be found in the law books under *D.*

Immediately upon winning her freedom from Warner Bros., Olivia's agent negotiated a two-picture pact with Paramount. She went to work on *The Well-Groomed Bride,* completed in early April 1945 but not released until February 1946. On Sunday, August 21, 1945, on CBS radio, Olivia assisted Orson Welles as soliloquist for *God and Uranium,* written and directed by Norman Corwin. It was a radio "special" which pre-empted the regularly scheduled broadcasts. As a result of the two features which she made in 1945 for 1946 release, Olivia's income for 1945 was $206,994.

The Well-Groomed Bride was an inauspicious, disappointing return to the screen. At the time Olivia had agreed to replace the originally cast Paulette Goddard who withdrew due to a pregnancy. Her agent, Bert Allenberg, convinced her that if Paramount was willing to risk a lawsuit by Warner Bros. for using her it would be a good chance to establish a precedent so other studios would thereafter hire her. On the first day of filming on *The Well-Groomed Bride,* de Havilland was advised by her lawyer Martin Gang that the Supreme Court had decided *two days earlier* not to review her case with Warner Bros. Had she been advised of the fact earlier, she would have withdrawn from the inane Paramount property.

In the Sidney Lanfield-directed fluff, she is Margie Dawson who possesses a magnum of champagne with which she plans to celebrate the return of her fiancé (Sonny Tufts), an Army officer, who has been away for two years. Trouble emerges in the person of U.S. Navy Lieutenant Dudley Briggs (Ray Milland) who covets that champagne so he can launch a newly built aircraft carrier. They argue, they bill and coo, and finally they fall in love. The *New York Times'* critic found, and justly so, that the film "strains mightily to soar into the realm of absurdity, but it just doesn't get up enough momentum to take flight."

At the start of Olivia's second film at Paramount on June 25, 1945, she weighted a scant ninety-seven pounds. This condition proved workable within the film, since the story was shot in sequence and Josephine "Jody" Norris in the opening scenes of *To Each His Own* (1946) is a young girl. Olivia and her character gained weight as the character she portrays went from youthfulness to pregnancy to being a hardened businesswoman and then to becoming a middle-aged spinster.

The scenario by Charles Brackett and Jacques Thery was aimed at female audiences, but male moviegoers were able to appreciate the tearjerking situation of a mother's unrequited love for her son. Told in flashback, we find that Jody Norris, whose father (Griff Barnett) runs the town's drug store, is a sweet innocent girl who turns down the marriage proposal of Alex Piersen (Phillip Terry). It is 1918 and an American soldier-flyer named Captain Cosgrove (John Lund in his screen debut) is brought to town as the main attraction of a war-benefit celebration. In landing his plane, the ace suffers minor injuries and is taken to the Norris drug store for medication. He is placed on a cot in a back room where he is later found by Jody as she leaves to attend the celebration dance. They talk and she is attracted by the dashing hero. At the dance, she congratulates Alex who has proposed to and been accepted by another girl (Mary Anderson).

After the ball, Cosgrove invites Jody to take a spin with him in the plane, believing that he will be able to seduce her. But then he changes his mind since she is too nice a girl. He confesses his intentions, but she asks him to spend the last few hours with her before he must leave. "I've only got until dawn, too," she says, and it is obvious that she is in love with the flyer. Sometime later, Jody reveals that she is pregnant. When she later goes to New York to see a doctor (Willard Robertson) about her condition, she is informed that she must have immediate surgery (an abortion) "either that or living in constant danger of peritonitis." She whispers, "You think I'll die," and the doctor answers gravely, "Yes."

She has not quite made up her mind just what to do when she learns that Cosgrove has been shot down in France. She tells her father, "They talk about him as if he's dead. Just dead. But he's not dead, not while his baby's alive—and it's going to be. I don't care what the doctor said. I don't care if I do die. That baby's going to get its chance for life." Jody has the child anonymously out of town, and plots with the hospital nurse (Victoria Horne) to have the infant deposited at the doorstep of Belle Ingham (Alma Macrorie—who is also the film's editor) who already has too many children to raise. As the story gets around town, Judy will then offer to take care of the infant herself.

It is a logical plan, but Corinna Piersen (Mary Anderson), Alex's wife, has just lost her baby and Belle takes the foundling to her. Jody is furious but can do nothing after witnessing the joy of Corinna and Alex. As the boy grows, Jody visits the Piersen home often and bestows upon him the nickname of "Griggsy." Later, Jody has a row with Corinna over the child, but loses the battle when Corinna points out selfishly that the child will forever be labeled illegitimate if the truth is revealed.

Jody leaves town after the death of her father and sets up a cosmetic business with Mac Tilton (Bill Goodwin). The business is a huge success and Jody develops into an efficient, frosty-toned, cigarette-puffing executive. She blackmails Alex and Corinna into allowing Griggsy to live with her (she has been paying their bills since their pianola factory went broke), but the boy (Bill Ward) merely acknowledges her as Aunt Jody and is homesick. In a heartbreaking, dramatically effective scene, she tries to explain to Griggsy who she really is, "It isn't easy and I want you to help me. Have you ever wondered why Corinna—your mother—let you come and live with me?" The boys replies, "I guess you asked her." She continues, "Yes, Griggsy, but why did I want you?" He answers, "You're lonely." She, "Yes, Griggsy, but why you especially?" He stammers, "I don't know." She says, "Well, that's what I'm trying to explain. You see, Corinna and Alex loved you very much but you were their adopted child. Do you know what adopted means?" The boy exclaims that he comprehends the meaning of the word and that is why his mother loves him so much, and "You haven't any right to talk to me about it." He runs from the room and she is forced to return him to Corinna and Alex. She later tells her partner that she has not the right to call herself the boy's mother because "Just bringing a child into the world doesn't make you that. It's being there always. It's nursing him through whooping cough and measles and knowing what to say when he's hurt. It's all the things I've missed." She tells Mac that she will go to London to get away. There she will take charge of their overseas interests.

The scene shifts to 1944 London where she is a stout, middle-aged woman (costumer Edith Head designed a one-piece foundation for her, under which she wore padding) on nighttime lookout for German U-Bombs with Lord Desham (Roland Culver). They do not get along well, but he rather likes her. When she learns that an American soldier named Gregory Piersen is arriving in London by train, she rushes to the station to meet him but he is also met by his English fiancée (Virginia Welles) in uniform. Gregory (John Lund—with dark hair) vaguely remembers Josephine as a friend from back home, but he is more interested in marrying his girlfriend, an accomplishment they find difficult until Lord Desham moves in to pull a few strings. Desham is especially anxious to help after insinuating to Josephine that, "The way you carry on one would think that he is your own son." She replies, "He *is* my son. Oh, he doesn't know it and he never will. . . . I'd like to give him the sun and the moon and the stars. All his life I've wanted to . . . all he wants is his girl. I can't help him there." Desham arranges the marriage at a hotel and after the ceremony they go to the dance floor where he asks Gregory to think about the reasons Miss Norris has taken such a keen interest in him. "It's odd, isn't it? You're both Americans—not enough. Both from the same little town—not enough. . . . Well, if you ever figure it out let me know." While Desham is leading a pensive Miss Norris to the dance floor, Gregory *has* figured it out and cuts in

On the set of *Princess O'Rourke* ('43).

With Sonny Tufts in *Government Girl* ('43).

306

With John Lund in *To Each His Own* ('46).

With Roland Culver in *To Each His Own.*

307

on them with, "I think this is our dance, Mother."

Directed by Mitchell Leisen, Olivia's choice for supervising her in this important freelance role, the film "spins dangerously on the brink of bathos but it seldom spills over into that treacherous chasm" (New York Times). The Times writer also stated that Olivia "may now take her exalted place alongside Helen Hayes, Ruth Chatterton, and Bette Davis as a tragic heroine. . . ." Leisen has said of his star in this production, "Olivia is a very flexible actress. She listens to what you have to say, and she will do her best to do it as you want it."

A month after To Each His Own began packing in theatre audiences (Variety reported that by the end of 1946 the feature had grossed $3,500,000 against Paramount's cost of $1,600,000), Warner Bros. released Devotion. The production history of that period melodrama could make a story of its own, with the studio over the years planning it as a vehicle for first this actress, then that one, including at one point a production for those feuding co-stars Bette Davis and Miriam Hopkins. The completed, shelved, and finally released product was ill-received by critics ("An insult to plain intelligence," carped the New York Times). Nevertheless, the Curtis Bernhardt-directed Bronte biography attracted certain moviegoers merely because of its cast.

Olivia plays Charlotte, ambitious and arrogant, the authoress of Jane Eyre; Ida Lupino is Emily, quiet, brooding, and doomed, the authoress of Wuthering Heights. Paul Henreid is a family friend who forms the apex of a love triangle; Arthur Kennedy is the drunken Bronte brother; Sydney Greenstreet has a cameo appearance as the burly William Thackeray. Filmmakers have often deviated from truth, but in glamorizing the existence of the Yorkshire Brontes, screenwriter Keith Winters made the subjects appear too unnatural to be at all believable to post-World War II moviegoers. The highlights of this wooden venture are Ernest Haller's cinematography, Erich Wolfgang Korngold's music, and the impressive sets designed under wartime strictures by Casey Roberts. All in all, Devotion

(a title ironically applicable to Olivia's tenure at the studio) was a sad finale to her Warner Bros. years. For observers of the Hollywood scene, it was difficult to associate the shy, optimistic young actress who arrived on the Burbank lot for Alibi Ike with the experienced acting tyro who in 1946 could hold an audience's interest so rapturously with her performance in the demanding To Each His Own.

In June 1946, Olivia proved once again what an organizer she was. Like many other players in the late Thirties and early Forties she had been duped into joining the Independent Citizens Committee of the Arts, Sciences, and Professions. When she and a dozen other members, including Ronald Reagan, began to suspect the organization's true motives, she organized a movement demanding that the Committee issue a resolution declaring its opposition to Communism in the United States. At an executive board meeting of the Committee, Olivia proposed a declaration. Chaos reigned and de Havilland resigned from the group in July 1946. Some other members quit before it was disbanded in the fall of 1946.

Sensing that a movie star's activities must be diversified in the new Hollywood, Olivia took to summer stock stages at Westport, Connecticut, in August 1946 as the lead in What Every Woman Knows. While there, she became re-acquainted with Marcus Goodrich, eighteen years her senior, and a man of many careers including seaman, journalist, advertising man, stage manager, naval officer, and novelist (his Delilah of 1941 had been a best seller). "We saw each other three times that first week," she remembers, and during the second week, on Monday, August 26, 1946, they were married. "I waited a long time before I found the man I wanted," she said later. "I got so lonely that I thought what I was looking for wasn't possible. . . . He is a man who has the courage to be serious. He's a fighter for what he believes. He is an educated, literate man. Everything that interests me."

They returned to Los Angeles where the groom's sister-in-law, Joan Fontaine, publicly scorned him and where he berated the

Hollywood natives for being pretentious. Hollywoodites struck back by inferring that he would ruin Olivia's screen career. They simply could not see what she saw in him. "I've got a high unpopularity rating," he admitted with a grin while Olivia said, "Mark's the first man I could ever trust."

Her cinematic year concluded with a "good psychiatric melodrama" (Life magazine), The Dark Mirror, made at Universal-International before the summer stock trip. She plays twins, Terry and Ruth Collins, one of whom has murdered a dinner companion. Since they are identical in looks (to permit the audience and screenplay characters to tell the sisters apart, they wear monograms on their jewelry and bathrobes) and have often substituted for one another on jobs and dates, the witnesses are unable to point to the guilty one at a police line-up. Both are released. The chief of detectives (Thomas Mitchell) is baffled, so he calls in a psychiatrist (Lew Ayres) who has made a study of twins. He persuades the women to undergo a series of scientific tests (ink-blots, word associations).

When both sisters fall in love with the doctor, Terry tries to force Ruth into committing suicide by encouraging her to take drugs and by making her believe she said or did things which she cannot recall. The psychiatrist concludes that only one sister is capable of murder and sets a plot into motion to reveal Terry's homicidal tendencies. With the detective's help, he sets the scene for Ruth's faked demise at which point Terry, no longer supported by the good, stronger sister, loses her mind. Ruth watches her sister's hard, distorted features with disbelief.

Motion Picture magazine declared, "Olivia de Havilland follows up her terrific performance in To Each His Own with an equally fine one [sic] in this." The Nation's James Agee wrote, "I very much like Olivia de Havilland's performance. She has for a long time been one of the prettiest women in movies; lately she has not only become prettier than ever, but has started to act." At a time when other twins, Bette Davis and Bette Davis in A Stolen Life (Warner Bros.), were clawing it out for 107 minutes over Glenn Ford, the Robert Siodmak-directed The Dark Mirror was

held to be "a brisk, supercharged eighty-five minutes" (Life magazine). Some years later (1971), in a London lecture, Olivia was to remark about The Dark Mirror, "That was a tremendously hard film to do. The technical problems involved in playing a dual role were extremely difficult to solve, and that horrible Terry I had to play in that picture haunts me to this day."

Olivia garnered her third Oscar nomination for To Each His Own. Up until the final second before the Best Actress was proclaimed at the Shrine Auditorium the evening of Thursday, March 13, 1947, it was even betting between Olivia and Rosalind Russell (for Sister Kenny). When Ray Milland, the Best Actor of 1945 for The Lost Weekend, announced the winner, a jubilant Olivia de Havilland accepted the statuette with a wide grin. As she walked offstage, Joan Fontaine, standing in the wings, stretched out her hand to congratulate her. But Olivia quickly dropped her smile and strode off in another direction. She was heard to say, "I don't know why she does that when she knows how I feel." The sister feud was played to the hilt the next morning in all the nation's newspapers. Some years later, Olivia would remember the incident with, "My public relations man asked me about a photograph of us together but my answer was NO—not unless she apologized. But Joan doesn't apologize easily. I told the P.R. man it was his business to make sure we weren't exposed to each other—but he let me down."

The day after Olivia received the Oscar it was announced by Twentieth Century-Fox that her next picture would be for them—an adaptation of Mary Jane Ward's best-selling novel The Snake Pit. In 1945, while making movies for the U.S. War Department, director Anatole Litvak bought the film rights to the novel for $75,000. For a year after he returned to Hollywood, he was unable to interest any studio in producing the book, the story of an adult woman in a mental hospital. His original choice for the project was Ingrid Bergman, but she was not interested in it.

Finally, Darryl F. Zanuck, embarking on a series of message pictures, summoned the courage to make it and paid Litvak $175,000

310

With husband Marcus A. Goodrich at their wedding in Wilton, Connecticut (August 26, 1946).

←

At the Stork Club in Manhattan with Dorothy Lamour and Joan Fontaine (May 1946).

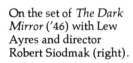

On the set of *The Dark Mirror* ('46) with Lew Ayres and director Robert Siodmak (right).

for the property rights and assigned him to direct and co-produce with Robert Bassler. Litvak's first move was to visit several mental institutions along with the cast and technical crew where he had secreted microphones in the wards to capture the nocturnal mutterings of the patients. Olivia dieted to lose some fourteen pounds for the role of Virginia Cunningham because she felt that the character must appear gaunt.

The Snake Pit (1948) opens wih Virginia seated on a bench in the sunshine. A voice asks if she knows where she is; she does not. As she enters a large, gloomy building and sees the locked doors, the bars, the writhing, giggling women, she realizes she is in a mental hospital. She has been committed by her husband (Mark Stevens) out of love, not malice, because she has withdrawn from reality. Whereas Miss Ward's novel does not define Virginia's illness, the movie writers, Millen Brand and Frank Partos, decided to make her a victim of schizophrenia.

Throughout flashbacks, the viewer witnesses the incidents of her life that brought her to this terrible place: inadequate parents (Natalie Schafer, Damian O'Flynn) who made her feel rejected and unloved, a suitor (Leif Erickson) who reminded her of her father, and a husband (Stevens) with whom she felt guilty. She is lucid until one of the institution's doctors (Howard Freeman) prods her to answer his questions by pointing a threatening finger at her. When she bites the finger and has a violent relapse, she is confined to a tepid bath intended to calm her down. Her piercing screams of anguish fill the motion picture screen.

Under the guidance of psychiatrist Dr. Mark Kirk (Leo Genn), she gradually emerges from insanity to a state of reason. As an indication of this improvement, she is graduated from one ward to another, each one containing women patients with equal measures of sanity. During her progress, she is permitted to have a picnic on the asylum grounds with her husband. When unable to remember what day it is, she says, "Then I've lost another day. I don't suppose I'll ever find it."

Olivia's well-modulated performance as the confused, tormented Virginia Cunningham was declared a triumph by all critics. *Life* magazine rated her as "giving the best performance by an American movie actress this year." *Time* credited the film with establishing Olivia "not so much as a star, a dubious title she already held, but as an actress." *Redbook* magazine accoladed her dramatics as "a notable acting achievement," and further said, "It is seldom one finds on the screen—or the stage, for that matter—a performance so carefully wrought, so beautifully sustained and so artfully executed." Soon after the film's release, Olivia remarked that "this picture is going to do so much good. When I visited the institutions for the mentally ill, I felt a great surge of compassion for the people. We are all victims of life, you see, and these people are the ones who have been hardest pressed."

The Snake Pit (so-named because of the ancient practice of tossing an insane person into a pit of snakes on the theory that the shock would return the afflicted human to normalcy) was released on November 3, 1948, in New York and Chicago and was a fast box-office success. (By 1977, the film had taken in $4,100,000 in domestic and Canadian rentals.) Olivia was honored by the New York Film Critics as Best Actress of 1948, and she received her fourth Academy Award nomination but lost to Jane Wyman for *Johnny Belinda.*

By her own admission, veteran actress Olivia de Havilland in 1949 was able to command a salary of $200,000 per film, "but I am allowed actually, after taxes, only about $28,000 of it." To rumors that she was also interested in film producing, she responded, "that would not work. I could not be concerned about my investment and my performance at the same time. So, either I would not make the money I would hope to make, or my work would suffer."

Elsa Maxwell, in an interview, found Olivia to possess "new quiet happiness" and referred to her as "the greatest actress we have today, on the stage or in Hollywood."

In the spring of 1949, the Goodriches moved into yet another abode, this time a house on Oakmont Drive in Brentwood.

(They had first lived in the Shoreham Apartments, owned and run by director Mitchell Leisen; in 1947 the couple had a house in Benedict Canyon; in 1948 they were residing in a house on Rockingham Road in Brentwood.) They spent most of their leisure time outdoors. One of his favorite pastimes was playing croquet with such mallet masters as Darryl Zanuck and Olivia's agent, Kurt Frings. *Photoplay* noted, "No longer the restless girl of yesterday, Olivia has found happiness in marriage and her career." Celeste Holm, with whom she worked in *The Snake Pit,* called her "a truly wonderful person," while scriptwriter Millen Brand confessed with adulation, "I feel there is nothing [I] could do that would be too good for her." Olivia stated shyly in early 1949, without actually revealing her pregnancy, "I think it would be perfectly wonderful to have a son. That is our hope."

While *The Snake Pit* was receiving nationwide attention, Olivia had completed *The Heiress* at Paramount, slated for September 1949 release. Taken from Henry James' well-regarded novel, *Washington Square, The Heiress* had been a Ruth and Augustus Goetz Broadway presentation in 1947 with Wendy Hiller, Basil Rathbone, and Peter Cookson. Olivia was producer-director William Wyler's instant choice to portray the shy, naive, homely, awkward Catherine Sloper in his screen version.

Set in the New York City of the mid-1800s (when Washington Square was green and neat), Dr. Austin Sloper (Ralph Richardson) lives in the stately manor at Number Sixteen Washington Square with daughter Catherine whom he resents for lacking the beauty and charm of his dead wife. She yearns to please him, but regardless of what she does she receives only criticism from him. She is an heiress in that she receives $10,000 a year from her mother's estate and will receive an additional $20,000 upon the death of her father. Even with this fact generally known throughout the civilized portions of the city, the suitors who deign to call upon the awkward, plain Miss Sloper are soon disenchanted.

Then along comes Morris Townsend (Montgomery Clift). He pursues her aggressively and convinces her that he is in love with her. Dr. Sloper judges him to be a fortune hunter and refuses to permit her to continue seeing him. He takes Catherine on an European trip which only serves to make her heart grow fonder. On their return to New York, Catherine reveals her plan to marry Morris. The father objects, but Catherine renounces the inheritance that will come to her and plans an elopement. On the designated night she is packed and waiting, but Morris does not appear. The next day, she battles with her sick father who threatens to change his will and she bitterly gives him writing material with which to fulfill his threat. He hesitates because he does not wish to disinherit his only child, but indicates that he does not know what she may do next. Coldly, she replies, "That's right, father. You'll *never* know—will you?"

For the seven years following Dr. Sloper's death, Catherine lives alone in the house left to her. Then one day her finicky Aunt Lavinia (Miriam Hopkins) informs her that Morris has returned and wishes to see her. Catherine thoughtfully agrees, and is cordial to Morris who confesses his love for her and renders the excuse that he did not show up for their elopement seven years before because he did not wish her to sacrifice her rightful inheritance. Now he proposes a second elopement. She agrees. This time however she bars the door and, while he frantically pounds on it and calls her name, she slowly ascends the staircase to her bedroom. Her revenge is complete. "I can be very cruel," she said of her intentions to jilt him, "for I have been taught by masters."

Olivia's transformation from the bewildered, beleaguered girl of the film's opening to the hard-faced, bitter spinster at the fadeout is a masterpiece of celluloid acting. Eileen Creelman of the *New York Sun* called it "one of those vital performances which illuminates every facet of a far from simple character." Hedda Hopper reported, "Right here let me predict that Olivia will cop an Oscar for her performance."

At the conclusion of her work on *The Heiress,* Olivia took to her bed for seven weeks when informed by the physicians that her

Receiving her Oscar for *To Each His Own* from Ray Milland (March 13, 1947).

With Leo Genn in *The Snake Pit* ('48).

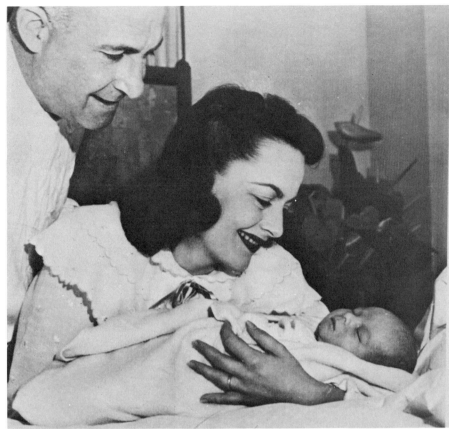

With husband Marcus Goodrich and their child Benjamin (October 22, 1949).

With Montgomery Clift in *The Heiress* ('49).

pregnancy was in danger of miscarrying. During those months of confinement, she realized that if she was ever going to fulfill her promise to Max Reinhardt to one day play Juliet, she must do it soon. On September 27, 1949, a boy who was named Benjamin was born to Olivia and Marcus Goodrich.

For her performance in *The Heiress,* Olivia received her second New York Film Critics Award, as well as the Women's National Press Club Distinguished Achievement Award presented to her by President Harry S. Truman. At the RKO Pantages Theatre in Hollywood on the evening of Thursday, March 23, 1950, she was awarded her second Oscar. Her acceptance speech, composed by Goodrich, engendered critical press comment and no one who heard or read it knew for certain whether she was truly thankful for the honor or merely gloating over a second Oscar. The unpopular speech, regarded by *Life* magazine as having been given in a "grand-lady manner," was "Your award for *To Each His Own* I took as an incentive. I have always tried to venture forward. Thank you for this very generous assurance that I have not failed."

Nevertheless, Olivia of the Warner Bros. "graduate school of dramatic arts" had proven to her former employers what she had tried to tell them for years: that she was certainly capable of playing more demanding parts than the demure, hoopskirted damsels of the Errol Flynn adventure epics. To her many awards was added a special one in October 1950 from the Independent Theatre Owners' Association "as the top money-making actress of 1949-1950, and for elevating the prestige of the Motion Picture Industry." She was also rated Best Actress at the International Film Festival at Venice, Italy. At the end of 1950, *Variety* reported that *The Dark Mirror, The Snake Pit,* and *The Heiress* in combination had grossed over $15 million.

Olivia was the first choice of Marlon Brando as his co-star in the film version of *A Streetcar Named Desire* (1951), but the role of Blanche du Bois went to Vivien Leigh for which she won her second Oscar. It is doubtful that Olivia would have proved available,

anyway, since the determined actress had already made other plans.

In September 1950, the Goodriches moved to a New York City apartment (reportedly with some three tons of homey necessities) and Olivia went into rehearsals for *Romeo and Juliet.* Douglas Watson co-starred as Romeo in this Dwight Deere Wiman production. In January 1951, the vehicle went on tryout tour. On Saturday, March 11, 1951, it opened at the Broadhurst Theatre. While some critics greeted the revival with warm praise, John Chapman *(New York Daily News)* represented the public view when he reported, ". . . [It] is a thing of almost Oriental splendor in its trappings—and an astonishingly colorless affair in its acting. I admire the brave determination of movie queen Olivia de Havilland to play Shakespeare's fated lass, but feel impelled to report that Juliet seems quite far beyond her range as an actress."

Soon after the disappointing New York opening, Olivia debuted on live television (with Watson) in a five-minute scene from the play for an Actors Equity program. The Broadway venture closed after only forty-five performances. Prophetically, Olivia had commented before the opening, "Of course it can flop, I know that. If it does—I'll just have to lick my wounds and try again."

She did just that. She tried again with Shaw's *Candida,* first on tour and, when it was favorably received, then on Broadway commencing on Tuesday, April 22, 1952, at the National Theatre. Critics were bound to compare Olivia's performance with that of Katharine Cornell who played the role four times (1924, 1937, 1942, 1946), and they concluded that they preferred Miss Cornell. Richard Watts, Jr. *(New York Post)* informed his readers, "Miss de Havilland's Candida was earnest, industrious, and extremely well-meaning, but it was also curiously dull, colorless, and lacking in the necessary humor, graciousness, and beauty of the part. I thought, too, that she made Shaw's compassionate and understanding heroine arch and rather patronizing, in addition to endowing her with a kind of disconcerting sharpness." The play closed after its planned thirty-two performances. Olivia took solace by stating, "Eighty percent of the reviews all over the country were raves. We broke records in nine houses and played it for 323 performances."

In June 1952, Olivia announced that she was returning to movies for Twentieth Century-Fox's adaptation of the Daphne du Maurier novel *My Cousin Rachel.* What part the fact that her sister Joan had enjoyed a great success in a version of Miss du Maurier's *Rebecca* played in Olivia's choice of this screen vehicle will be left to the reader's judgment. As regal Olivia bade farewell to Broadway, she mentioned that she hoped to be back in a year for *Portrait of a Lady.* (The play would be staged in 1954, but Jennifer Jones would be the star of this Henry James property.) Olivia arrived back in Los Angeles after an absence of almost two years with son Benjamin but without husband Marcus. The couple had decided upon a divorce which would be filed on August 26, 1952. An acquaintance was quoted as saying "She tried to run Marcus and Marcus tried to run her career."

George Cukor originally wished to make *My Cousin Rachel* with Greta Garbo, but the Swedish legend was reticent about making a screen return. Mr. Cukor graciously accepted Olivia as a substitute and persuaded Darryl F. Zanuck to hire British actor Richard Burton as the male lead. Cukor then quit the project because of his displeasure over the sets and script, and the film was directed by Henry Koster. The popular du Maurier thriller, adapted for the screen by Nunnally Johnson, is situated in a gloomy setting in Cornwall and provides an inconclusive ending to the mystery of whether Rachel (Olivia) is a murderess or the most noble of women.

Young Englishman Philip Ashley (Burton) falls in love with Rachel, the beautiful widow of his guardian, but he has the nagging suspicion that she was responsible for her husband's demise. Nevertheless, Philip succumbs to her charms and deeds his earthly gains to her name. His doubts about her overcome his love and he arranges for her death by tampering with a footbridge over which she must cross on her daily walk. After she is dead, he has reason to believe that she was

after all innocent of all accusations. Bosley Crowther informed his *New York Times* readers, "In this agreeable creation, Olivia de Havilland does a dandy job of playing the soft and gracious Rachel with just a faint suggestion of the viper's tongue." As a result of *My Cousin Rachel,* Olivia, unlike many of her screen contemporaries, was able to retain her standing as a top-ranking major female star, not just a box-office shadow of her former self.

When the French government invited her to attend the Cannes Film Festival, she accepted. Accompanied by her son, she arrived in Paris in April 1953 for her first visit to France and for her first film festival. There she met and was quietly courted and pursued by Pierre Paul Galante, the Secrétaire Général of the French publication *Paris Match.* In the summer of 1953, dauntless Olivia ventured on the stage again in *The Dazzling Hour,* presented in La Jolla, California. Columnist Cal York observed, "[Her] lukewarm success in a mediocre play . . . should convince her that her heart and talents belong in Hollywood, not the theatre." (Nevertheless the show was a big local success and was held over for a second week.) Her divorce from Goodrich became final on August 26, 1953, with the court granting her the custody of her son Benjamin. And it was also in 1953 that she made the Hollywood gossip column written by Edith Gwynn when she entertained guests "wearing a dramatic coachman coat of midnight blue satin, the full skirt sweeping along from a tiny, fitted waistline."

George Cukor, in 1953, considered transforming the Thomas Hardy novel *Far from the Madding Crowd* to the screen with Olivia as the star, but these ideas were soon abandoned. (The novel would be filmed in 1967 by MGM with Julie Christie and directed by John Schlesinger.) In January 1954, newsman Mike Connolly informed his readers that Olivia had inherited "the sexy role" that Rita Hayworth had been lined up to do in *The Human Beast* at Columbia. But when the project, based on the Emile Zola story, emerged as *Human Desire* (1954), it was Gloria Grahame who played the sultry wife of

With co-Oscar winner
Broderick Crawford
(March 25, 1950).

→
With husband-to-be
Pierre Galante in London
(March 1955).

With Richard Burton in
My Cousin Rachel ('52).

319

Broderick Crawford who wants lover Glenn Ford to knock off her lummox of a spouse. It seemed that Olivia had other involvements at the time. Pierre Galante had traveled to California to visit Olivia and he suggested that she vacation in Paris. "For a while, I resisted," she has said. "I felt that if I went back, I'd never leave." The couple became engaged in Paris, but the French government would not permit her, a divorced woman, to immediately marry a Catholic French citizen. She would be required to sustain a nine-month's surveillance period by the government. They were married finally on Saturday, April 2, 1955, in Paris. "It was the same day as Napoleon's wedding," commented Olivia. The Galantes took up official residence in Paris.

That Lady (Twentieth Century-Fox, 1955), directed by Terence Young, was filmed in Spain for Atlanta Productions. It derived from a 1949 Broadway play that had starred Katharine Cornell. Olivia took the role of the title character of whom exploitation advertisements noted, "England had its Amber . . . America had its Scarlett . . . But you'll never forget the woman of Spain marked for all time as *That Lady*." As Ana de Mendoza, the one-eyed princess of Spain (Olivia wore a black patch over her right eye), she is loved by the seventeenth-century ruler of the Spaniards, Philip II (Paul Scofield), but is too love-starved to remain faithful to him. By romantically consorting with Antonio Perez (Gilbert Roland), one of Philip's entrusted ministers, she creates one of Spain's infamous at-court scandals. Obviously produced at relatively high costs, the film was unsuccessful largely due to an over-abundance of dialogue (scripted by Anthony Veiller and Sy Bartlett from a novel by Kate O'Brien) and too little fiery action.

Olivia had returned to Hollywood before her wedding to Galante to co-star in Stanley Kramer's highly touted production of the best-selling novel *Not as a Stranger* (United Artists, 1955). Claiming a readership of over three million, the 948-page novel was adapted for the screen by Edna and Edward Anhalt. Every member of the cast was hand-picked by Kramer who remarked before the film's

opening, "I had a group of gifted actors, the best I could." Since the adult melodrama is an inside look at hospital and medical people, Kramer herded his players into four Los Angeles hospitals for basic training. After initially viewing an operation, Olivia remarked, "I read the script, studied books on nursing, learned operating techniques and terminology. But if I'd stopped there and assumed I then knew something about hospital life, it would have been like looking at the surface of the sea without being aware of the life that goes on underneath." The star reportedly spent six hours a day at the hospitals understudying nurses and then rushed to the studio soundstage for evening rehearsal. One nurse told Kramer, "If that's a sample of the glamorous life of a movie star, she can have it."

Olivia went blonde for the part of Kristina Hedvigson, a frugal, Swedish-accented nurse. Virginia Christine, also in the movie as Kristina's friend Bruni, was given the task of teaching Olivia to speak with an accent. Miss Christine remembers, "She welcomed me with open arms and we literally lived together until the accent became easy for her." Miss Christine rates Olivia as "gracious and charming as can be."

The movie-going public was pre-conditioned for the film's June 1955 release with full-page magazine advertisements proclaiming, "Stands alone. First as a book. . . . Now as a Motion Picture." The total advertising, publicity, and exploitation budget amounted to nearly one million dollars, the biggest in the history of United Artists Studio.

Not as a Stranger concerned Lucas Marsh (Robert Mitchum), a medical student without funds. In order to garner tuition he charms and marries a mature nurse, Kristina (Olivia), who has saved much of her salary. Upon Lucas' graduation, the couple travel to a small midwestern town where he becomes a perfectionist in the company of aging Dr. Runkleman (Charles Bickford). While one of the easiest women to get along with, Kristina comprehends that her gifted husband does not truly love her but bravely tolerates his ungentlemanly behavior, even when he makes love to the town siren (Gloria Grahame). Little by little, she realizes that he no longer needs her and Kristina asks for a divorce, although she is three months pregnant. When Dr. Runkleman suffers a serious heart attack, Lucas performs emergency surgery on his friend, but makes a blunder during the operation and Runkleman dies. Lucas then understands that he, too, is human and capable of error. He returns to Kristina for love and comfort.

On opening day at Manhattan's Capitol Theatre, the film grossed $15,000. Total U.S.-Canadian rental receipts to date are an impressive $7.1 million. If the critics were impressed by the blossoming talents of taciturn, iconoclastic Robert Mitchum as the idealistic healer, reviewers were less enthused by the contrived story structure around the lead players—"but her beaming adoration of the young doctor is something that is not plausibly explained" (New York Times), and by the gimmicky casting of crooner-Academy Award winner Frank Sinatra as the breezy, money-oriented physician pal of Mitchum. In the midst of condemning this popularly accepted production as being too slick, Olivia's well-turned performance was almost taken for granted—a compliment in one sense, but one that precluded her nomination for an Academy Award.

Hoping to work more often in France, her adopted homeland, Olivia starred in the title role of The Ambassador's Daughter (United Artists, 1956), her first screen comedy in a decade. With the city of Paris providing attractive backdrops, the film is the would-be merry romp of a soldier named Danny (John Forsythe) who picks up a girl named Joan (Olivia). Thinking she is a Dior model, he frolics with her about the city until he learns that she has been playing a game. It develops that she had bet a U.S. Senator (Adolphe Menjou) that GIs were well enough behaved to be allowed carte blanche throughout Paris. She points out to Danny that the Senator had advocated closing the city to soldiers on leave, and that she merely wanted to prove him wrong. She further confesses that she is the daughter of the U.S. Ambassador (Edward Arnold) and that she is engaged to marry a prince (Francis Lederer), but none of these admissions seem to matter since the soldier

and girl are now in love with one another. In truth, as Bosley Crowther in the New York Times wrote, "Miss de Havilland, for all her grace and sweetness, is not exactly a girl." (Olivia was then thirty-nine.) The entire project, even with a first rate screen appearance by former MGM star Myrna Loy as the Senator's chic wife, would have been much better received as an hour teleplay. (But the Belgian Film Critics awarded Olivia their Prix Femina for the best comedy performance by an actress that year.)

On July 18, 1956, Olivia became a mother for the second time when a daughter was born in Neuilly-sur-Seine, France. The baby was christened Gisele.

In the summer of 1957, Olivia once again returned to Hollywood "looking ten years younger than she should" (Newsweek) for a role that she chose to do for producer Samuel Goldwyn, Jr. She bunked-in at the Beverly Hills Hotel and gave interviews which expressed her opinions on subjects ranging from bosoms ("With the aggressive bosom, American women risk losing their femininity") to her feud with Joan Fontaine ("It's all over. . . . I took a very English view of this. The English keep it inside you know. But living in France has helped me this way") to her children ("I wanted to bring the children but it seemed unwise to upset their routines"— Ben was at school in Switzerland and fifteen-month-old Gisele was at home in Paris). Of the French she observed, "They lack organization, but they understand the art of living." She referred to life in Hollywood as "monastic" in that "I'm up at six-thirty and in bed before nine. Here, I'm not very French. I see food only as fuel and I eat the best fuel— steaks and celery."

The film for which Olivia returned to Hollywood was The Proud Rebel (Buena Vista, 1958), directed by her long-time associate, Michael Curtiz. It is not a Western in the true definition of the word, but rather a tale of human compassion, set in the post-Civil War wilderness of Illinois. As Linnett Moore, a lonely frontier woman, Olivia's costumes consisted of floppy straw hats and shapeless, colorless dresses. Shot partially on location in Utah, it is the chronicle of a rebel, John

As Kristina Hedvigson in *Not as a Stranger* ('55).

With John Forsythe in *The Ambassador's Daughter* ('56).

With Alan Ladd in *The Proud Rebel* ('58).

With Dirk Bogarde in *Libel* ('59).

323

Chandler (Alan Ladd), who heads north in search of a doctor to cure his son David (David Ladd) who had turned mute at the sight of the killing of his mother in Atlanta during the war. With them is David's dog, Lance, who is coveted by the Burleigh sons (Dean Stanton, Thomas Pittman) as father and son plod into Illinois.

A fight ensues when John is jailed, but Miss Moore pays his fine and he is released to work on her farm. The senior Burleigh (Dean Jagger) wants her land for sheep grazing, but Linnett and John successfully hold it. John locates a physician (Cecil Kellaway) to perform an operation on his son and sells the dog to raise money. The operation is not a success and the boy now yearns for his dog. When John learns that the Burleighs have the animal, he tries to reacquire it, but a gunfight breaks out. As John is about to be done-in from behind by one of the Burleighs, David finds his voice and warns him in time. John then settles with the Burleighs and returns to Linnett's farm with his son and dog.

Variety credited the product with being "a truly heartwarming film" and Olivia with having "gained new depth and stature as a dramatic actress." Paul V. Beckley of the *New York Herald-Tribune* found "Olivia de Havilland seems a bit out of place in early sequences . . . but she hitches up her dialect and manner as the picture continues and gives a generally creditable performance." What veteran moviegoer who had seen the young Olivia in *Call It a Day* or *Hard to Get* could have possibly imagined that Miss de Havilland would ripen into such a solid professional?

Before leaving Hollywood for Paris, Olivia was chastened by irrepressible British-born columnist Sheilah Graham for missing "a good chance to reconcile with her mother, when Mrs. Fontaine came here to stay with Joan Fontaine for a few days while doing a role in *The Bigamist*. The quarrel dates from Livvie's marriage with Marcus Goodrich," Ms. Graham continued, "and it's too bad she doesn't kiss and make up with her mother. One of these days it may be too late." (In the spring of 1960, Olivia brought both her chil-

dren to Saratoga, California, so they could visit daily with their grandmother.)

Olivia stopped off in New York long enough to appear on television as the mystery guest on the popular panel show "What's My Line?" Wearing a blindfold, as were the other panelists, Arlene Francis, in endeavoring to identify the guest, asked, "Are you legitimate?" (meaning an actress), at which Olivia's eyes widened and she replied in her disguised voice, "I certainly am."

Unlike her contemporaries—and even younger actresses—who were glad to settle for an occasional guest-cameo role now and then in films, Olivia continued to turn up only in substantial screen assignments, proving once again she was not simply a demure, maturing woman, but rather a solid professional who attracted viable projects even in a vastly changing show business world. In 1959, she worked at MGM's London studio as Lady Maggie Loddon in the filming of a play written by Edward Wooll, *Libel* (staged on Broadway in 1935 with Colin Clive and Joan Marion). Although hers is a secondary role to that of the male lead (Dirk Bogarde), it is important in that it is she who urges her husband to sue for libel when he is accused in the tabloids of being an imposter. The accuser is Jeffrey Buckenham (Paul Massie) who had been a war prisoner of the Germans with Sir Mark (Bogarde) and Frank Welney (also Bogarde), the latter a bit part actor who greatly resembles Loddon. It is Buckenham's contention that Welney murdered Loddon during their escape from prison and thereafter assumed his identity.

Much of the onscreen action takes place in the courtroom, with an interspersing of flashbacks to hold back the tedium, but the results were "A rubbery old turkey stuffed with chestnuts" *(Time)*. Olivia, like the other co-stars, received her share of jibes for appearing in this misfire, " . . . [she] plays the wife as if she were balancing Big Ben on her hat" *(New York Times)*. It was to be the actress' last film part for three years.

In 1960, at the Galantes' well-appointed white town house on the Right Bank of Paris, Olivia composed a book in which she humorously recounted her experiences as an American in Paris. Tentatively bearing the title *Parlez-Vous,* and then *My War with the French,* the memoir was published by Random House in 1961 under the provocative title, *Every Frenchman Has One* (a liver, that is). The tongue-in-cheek account proved to be jocularly philosophical. "Not every comment is the most original ever made on the subject," reported the *Chicago Sunday Tribune,* "and the style, which can only be classified as chattily unpretentious, becomes a trifle monotonous after a while. But the chapters are brief, the stories entertaining, and Miss de Havilland sounds like a delightful person." The *New York Times'* reviewer suggested, "Should the author, perish forbid, ever leave stage and screen, she can launch a commentator's career at the drop of a corsage bouquet." The book would enjoy five printings and later be issued in paperback. It had two printings in an English edition.

In March 1961, Olivia attended, at MGM's expense, a three-day gala celebration in Atlanta for the latest revival of *Gone with the Wind.* Vivien Leigh, the other surviving lead from the 1939 classic, also attended.

"Making *Light in the Piazza* [MGM, 1962] was quite an extraordinary experience," the often cryptic Olivia commented about her next picture. Filmed in Florence, Rome, and London, it is the bittersweet story of Margaret Johnson (Olivia) and her efforts to do what is right for her twenty-six-year-old daughter Clara (Yvette Mimieux) who has the mind of a ten-year-old due to a childhood accident. While vacationing in Italy with her mother, the beautiful young woman falls in love with a dashing Italian (George Hamilton). When the romance blossoms toward marriage, Margaret sends for her ex-husband (Barry Sullivan) who journeys from Connecticut with the stoic advice that Clara should be placed in a posh institution. When he returns to America, Margaret refuses to accept his advice and plunges ahead with wedding plans because she has the notion that Clara will survive with the surroundings to be provided by the wealthy boy and his aristocratic parents (Rossano Brazzi and Nancy Nevinson).

She is less than forthright in concealing the truth about Clara, but bestows a dowry on her amounting to $15,000. As she watches the marriage ceremony, she feels that she has done the right thing. *Variety* noted of Olivia's presence in this well turned out, color, widescreen soap opera, "Miss de Havilland's performance is one of great consistency and subtle projection." *Time* thought she "plays the mother with dignity and restraint." Olivia's co-star, the charming continental Rossano Brazzi, had this to say of her, "Olivia is a rare combination—beauty and brains. I see so many perfectly beautiful young actresses in Hollywood but they are just so much meat." The film which had cost a mere $553,280.75 grossed $2,345,000. Only those closely involved in the production knew that in order to tighten up the 101-minute drama, last-minute editing had deleted some of the football game and several of Olivia's close-ups.

On January 2, 1962, game Olivia arrived in New York to begin rehearsal for her third attempt on the Broadway boards. In Garson Kanin's *A Gift of Time,* she performed the gripping part of the wife whose husband (Henry Fonda) is dying of incurable stomach cancer. After a trial run in Philadelphia, the grim drama opened at New York's Ethel Barrymore Theatre on Thursday, February 22, 1962, to mixed reactions from the audience (one man vomited into the aisle). *Newsweek* printed that Olivia "grows with her part and rises magnificently to the play's climax." That finale is the request by the dying man for his wife to fetch his razor. She finds it, strops it, and holds him as he slices his wrist. Her final words are, "I love you, I love you, please die." The *New York Daily Mirror's* drama critic, like so many others, complimented the actors on their compelling performances, but suggested that the play "will have a limited appeal, for valiant death and physical dissolution are matters likely to frighten escapists [but not Olivia]." Before the death of the play (after only ninety-one performances), Olivia was seen on "The Ed Sullivan Show" on CBS-TV in a scene from the play with Fonda. In April 1962, she, George C. Scott, and director Otto Preminger

Playbill for the Broadway
play *A Gift of Time*
(February 1962).

→
With James Caan in *Lady in a
Cage* ('64).

With Rossano Brazzi in *Light in
the Piazza* ('62).

327

offered their appraisals of the Academy Awards on CBS-TV's "Calendar." Ever-industrious Olivia was also a guest on CBS-TV's word-skill game, "Password." All these appearances were geared to help promote her Broadway venture.

At the Santa Monica Civic Auditorium on Tuesday, April 9, 1963, she presented an Oscar to Sam Spiegel for his production of *Lawrence of Arabia.* Olivia had flown to California to star in *Lady in a Cage* (Paramount, 1964), described by Louella Parsons as "an unusual psychological thriller." Olivia indicated to the ubiquitous Miss Parsons that she might write another book—fictional—but that she hoped to make more movies, too. "I love to work. It's something I need very much," she confided to Louella. Questioned by another interviewer (Joseph Finnigan) about making a French film, Olivia responded, "I've been offered them but I want a role that is for a foreigner because I have an accent." She also stated her objection to doing television plays, "I won't do television because they would interrupt me every fifteen minutes for a commercial. Can you imagine what would happen if somebody disturbed a movie every fifteen minutes in a theatre?"

With *Lady in a Cage,* Olivia entered the horror movie sweepstakes that had previously lured Bette Davis and Joan Crawford (*What Ever Happened to Baby Jane?,* 1962, and others). Olivia is Mrs. Hilyard, a doting mother to her twenty-nine-year-old son Malcolm (William Swan) who has left her alone in their three-story mansion in Los Angeles over the Fourth of July weekend. Upstairs, he has left her a note, but hours will pass before she learns of its existence or contents. Wealthy, intelligent, and pretty, Mrs. Hilyard is recuperating from a broken hip and the only way she can maneuver upstairs is via her specially installed "Safe-T" elevator. She enters the elevator a composed, cultured woman. The thing slowly ascends and then stops between floors, about ten feet above the main level. Eventually, a bewhiskered wino (Jeff Corey) hears her and investigates. Within the house, he finds several treasures, including a well-stocked wine cellar. He takes a toaster to a second-hand dealer (Charles Seel) and solicits his fat friend Sade (Ann Sothern) to re-enter the house for more loot. They are followed by three young hoodlums (James Caan, Jennifer Billingsley, Rafael Campos) who take over the place. "Take anything you want," Mrs. Hilyard pleads, "but in the name of humanity help me get out of this horrible cage." Later, the wino is killed by the marauding trio and then Sade is locked inside the wine closet, never to be seen again. Still later, Mrs. Hilyard stabs the ringleader (Caan), and his two cohorts rush out to their freedom.

Time magazine called the black drama "a routine withdrawal from Hollywood's bottomless blood bank, but it does give Olivia a chance to go ape." *Variety* managed to credit Olivia with doing "about as well as possible under the dire circumstances." To help sell the film, Olivia made personal appearances in many U.S. cities. When asked by Sheilah Graham why she was knocking herself out that way, Olivia succinctly replied, "Because I have a [ten] percentage of the picture. It's as simple as that." *Lady in a Cage* attracted far better reviews abroad than at home. The British *Films and Filming* magazine selected Olivia as Best Actress of the Year for her performance in this grand guignol tale.

By mid-1964, rumors were rampant concerning trouble in the Galante marriage, but Olivia's only response was "That is one subject I do not discuss." Later that year, she came back to America to replace the ill (with recurring virus pneumonia) Joan Crawford in Robert Aldrich's *Hush . . . Hush, Sweet Charlotte* (Twentieth Century-Fox, 1964).

Described by the *New York Herald-Tribune* as "Grandest Grand Guignol," *Hush . . . Hush* is the narrative of Charlotte Hollis (Bette Davis), a recluse within her Louisiana mansion which is threatened with destruction by the highway commission in order to make way for a new road. Charlotte has been withdrawn for so long that she often confuses reality and lives with the memory of the unsolved ax murder of her married lover, John Mayhew (Bruce Dern). She is alone in the rusty old house except for Velma Cruther (Agnes Moorehead), the unkempt housekeeper who lives elsewhere. Charlotte is determined that her home will not be torn down and sends for her sophisticated cousin Miriam (Olivia) who once lived with Charlotte and her father (Victor Buono) when she was a poor relative, but who now lives up north. The grisly denouement to the hoary tale finds Miriam and her secret lover, Dr. Drew Bayliss (Joseph Cotten), meeting an unsavory end. The next day, as Charlotte is taken away by the police, a Lloyds of London insurance investigator (Cecil Kellaway) hands her a letter through the car window. In the note is a confession by John Mayhew's widow (Mary Astor) revealing who the true murderer of John was.

Almost to the same degree as *What Ever Happened to Baby Jane?*, Bette Davis' devotees delighted in this celluloid mayhem, even approving the oversized scene-chewing by Agnes Moorehead. Mary Astor in a small role is excellent, but the acting honors—far and away—belong to Olivia. *Time* magazine claimed her as "the tidy one . . . who flings away her composure but retains her chic even in low company." Released in Los Angeles in December 1964 in order to qualify for the 1964 Oscars, the film was nominated in seven categories but failed to win any of them. The theme song, written by Frank De Vol and Mack David, is still played on radio.

Olivia and Bette embarked on a joint personal appearance tour on behalf of the film, and Olivia revealed, "We call ourselves Maxine and Laverne [Andrews]." The film's production had been held up for eight weeks waiting for Joan Crawford, when Bette suggested Olivia as a replacement. "She arrived in Hollywood within the week," Bette said. "She was given only one week for rehearsals and the tiring costume fittings (by Norma Koch) and she was ready, went in there and performed as if she had had as much time as the rest of us." Olivia and Bette also appeared together on ABC-TV's "Hollywood Palace" and on April 13, 1965, Olivia was hostess on the "Bell Telephone Hour Easter Show" on NBC-TV. That summer, she headed the ten-member jury at the Cannes Film Festival that chose the best motion picture represented. Also in 1965, Olivia revealed that she and Pierre Galante, although legally separated, continued to live apart in their home. The separation took place years before (reportedly in 1961) when even Joan Fontaine knew about it but did not tell reporters. "She is absolutely no worse than any other sister," said Olivia. At the revelation of Olivia's unusual marital status, Sheilah Graham speculated that Pierre might even be best man "if and when Olivia marries Luther Davis whom she met during their *Lady in a Cage* romp." Davis was producer/writer of the feature.

On November 23, 1966, Olivia was seen for the first time in a television drama, as part of the "Stage 67" series on ABV-TV. Entitled *Noon Wine* and from the story by Katherine Anne Porter, the segment was directed by Sam Peckinpah and had Olivia as a worried Texas ranch wife. Jason Robards, Jr., and Theodore Bikel were her co-stars. The following year, she did another drama, this time for the "Danny Thomas Show" on NBC-TV. "When I left to live in Paris in 1953," she explained to reporters, "TV made no sense to me. I'd just made *My Cousin Rachel,* so why should I contribute to the downfall of the movies? . . . Now TV has destroyed itself by showing old movies." Her second outing in the video medium was entitled *The Last Hunters,* shown on January 29, 1968, on NBC-TV. In the story of the pursuit of a Nazi war criminal, her co-star was Richard Todd. "The second one I didn't like very much," she has cryptically stated.

After completing *The Last Hunters,* but before its TV airing, she journeyed to Atlanta, Georgia, on October 3, 1967, for the seventy-millimeter widescreen premiere of *Gone with the Wind* and the film's sixth national release. This time, with Vivien Leigh dead, the affair was attended by Olivia, Ann Rutherford, Evelyn Keyes, and Victor Jory. Olivia has said of the occasion, "It troubled me very much because I suddenly realized that all these great actors had died before their time. I felt so much alive and saw them, and felt that they were still somehow with me. I felt a

With Jason Robards, Jr., in *Noon Wine* episode (ABC-TV, November 23, 1966) of "ABC Stage 67."

→

At the October 1967 national re-issue showing of *Gone with the Wind* in Atlanta, Georgia.

With Joseph Cotten in *Hush . . . Hush, Sweet Charlotte* ('64).

presence, and somehow, because of the film, I suppose they will all live on."

Olivia did a cameo role in the Joseph E. Levine exploitation version of Harold Robbins' best-selling *The Adventurers* (Paramount, 1970). The film was shot in Italy, Colombia, and the U.S., and Olivia played a wealthy American tourist married to John Ireland. She has a European affair with much younger Bekum Fehmiu, he being the searching son of a South American ruler. Too long a film (at 171 minutes), it is rambling, difficult to follow, obvious in its sexual titillation, and frequently dull. Of Olivia, *Variety* noted, "Observing her in this film is an embarrassment," while Howard Thompson in the *New York Times* insisted that she "maintains a fixed, intelligent expression."

While in England in the summer of 1971, Olivia had dinner with Britain's Prime Minister Edward Heath whom she had met some ten years earlier. Immediately, press people from around the globe exaggerated the meeting into a romance. Olivia made a simple statement to all inquiries, "I do not intend to marry him and he does not intend to marry me." While in London, she lectured at the National Film Theatre where she said after a review of her film clips, "I am so pleased at this gracious reception, and so relieved too, because when they told me they were going to show those clips made when I was eighteen and twenty-one-years old, I was afraid I would come out here, thirty-six years older and twenty pounds heavier, and nobody would recognize me."

In 1971, Olivia's son was a twenty-two-year-old University of Paris student while Gisele, at fourteen, was in high school. Pierre Galante had, by then, moved out of their home into an apartment nearby. In the autumn of 1971, a full-page ad appeared in *The Hollywood Reporter* headlined with "A tribute to Olivia de Havilland," placed there by one Mr. Joseph Yohanna, an auditor with the Los Angeles Board of Education and a lifelong, devoted fan of Olivia's. At the suggestion of her sister Joan, Olivia embarked on a lecture tour of the U.S. which took her to Philadelphia, Richmond, Minneapolis, Dal-

las, and other cities. She reminisced about her experiences in Hollywood during the Golden Years and thereafter. She stopped off in California to make an ABC telefeature entitled *The Screaming Woman* which was premiered on January 29, 1972. Filmed in Santa Barbara on an empty forty-five-acre estate, it relates the account of Laura Wynant (Olivia), a lady of some fifty summers who returns home after a nervous breakdown to find a woman buried alive beneath an old smoke house. No one believes her until she uncovers the poor soul who had been buried there by Ed Nelson. *The Hollywood Reporter* lauded Olivia for giving "an excellent, well-textured performance."

The film for which Olivia was in London in 1971 was *Pope Joan* (Columbia, 1972) in which she had the role of a Mother Superior. Boasting a top-notch cast (Liv Ullmann, Trevor Howard, Maximilian Schell), the feature nonetheless proved to be forgettable to the few Americans who saw it during its very brief release in this country. Joan (Ullmann) is a present-day evangelist who envisions herself to be the reincarnation of Pope Joan, the ninth-century visionary who almost became the Papal leader. In the early portion of the vision, the Mother Superior (Olivia) befriends the girl and places her in charge of the convent's library. After the death of Emperor Charlemagne, the pagans run amuck, defiling the convent and crucifying the Mother Superior. Joan later progresses to becoming secretary to Pope Leo (Howard) and lover to an artistic monk (Schell). She is ultimately killed by the populace when she is revealed to be pregnant. Rex Reed in the *New York Daily News* terms the proceedings "a demented exercise in religious hysteria that could turn off movies forever."

Olivia attended the preview reception in November 1973 at the Los Angeles County Museum of "The Great American Films" series. Both before and after this event she visited with her mother in Santa Barbara who was living at a residence for retired teachers. Joan was in attendance which made the reunion complete. Olivia stated that she planned to write her autobiography, and informed a reporter that she was an avid "man watcher." She shocked the reporter by saying, "I want to find a juicy, fifty-eight-year-old. . . ."

In 1974, she was offered the role of Lisolette Mueller in the Irwin Allen production of *The Towering Inferno* for Twentieth Century-Fox/Warner Bros. release. She declined for two main reasons: 1) she wished to be with daughter Gisele during the girl's difficult school examination period and 2) Olivia planned to begin her autobiography. Thus Jennifer Jones was substituted and came close to garnering an Oscar nomination for her work on the disaster story epic. Ironically, Olivia had once said of her Warner Bros. conflicts, "I do not feel that I shall really have had the last word until I one day make a picture at Warners, play in it the sort of role I wanted to play those many years ago, and receive an Academy nomination."

On February 20, 1975, Lilian Fontaine died of cancer in Santa Barbara at the age of eighty-seven (her husband George had died in 1956). Both Olivia and Joan were at their mother's bedside. It was Olivia who arranged for the memorial service held in Saratoga, California, on March 27, 1975.

After this recent period of performing inactivity, Olivia suddenly became a busy show business worker again. Along with Kirk Douglas, John Wayne, and Gregory Peck, she co-narrated *The Father of Liberty,* a film gift from the French government to the American bi-centennial. The historical salute was shipped to Mt. Vernon, where it was shown throughout 1976.

When United Artists promoted a Warner Bros. retrospective salute in mid-1976, Olivia agreed to come to New York to publicize the series. She repeated the sentiment, "I always wanted to end up with Errol [Flynn]. . . . Errol and I arrived at Warner Bros. within four weeks of each other. We didn't meet till June [1935] when we made *Captain Blood.* I used to listen for his voice in the makeup department. He didn't know I had a crush on him. I kept it hidden in the best costume tradition. Things didn't work out, anyway. We were always misunderstanding each other."

Of her former employer, Jack Warner, Olivia mused, ". . . I was fond of him. He ran an awfully good lot, but he distrusted actors and thought they were children and delinquents. . . . We wanted him to be an understanding parent and I guess the role we cast him in panicked him."

Of her domestic life, Olivia noted that her son, a statistician, is in Texas, where his father's family came from, and that her daughter is a law student in Paris. As for the star's relationship with sister Joan Fontaine, "We have periods when we communicate, and those when we don't. . . . And right now we don't."

In the fall of 1976, she joined Jimmy Stewart, Jack Lemmon, Joseph Cotten, George Kennedy, and Brenda Vaccaro for Universal's *Airport '77.* She plays a romantic soul who meets a former love on the doomed flight. In the course of the filming, one scene called for 4,000 gallons of water to cascade on the set. Co-worker Brenda Vaccaro reported, "I almost lost a lung and nearly died of pneumonia." Olivia, the pro, commented, "All that got swept away was an eyelash." After completing her role in this disaster epic, Olivia flew to Vienna to join the cast of *Behind the Iron Mask* (1977), an international co-production featuring such performers as Beau Bridges, Ursula Andress, Rex Harrison, Cornel Wilde, Jose Ferrer, and Olivia.

Meanwhile, when NBC-TV was preparing to telecast (November 7-8, 1976) *Gone with the Wind* as a two-part special, Olivia was approached to hostess the event. But when she learned that classic film was to be broken up at arbitrary spots to allow for commercials, she adamantly refused the lucrative offer. "For this film to be shown in such a crude manner in this Bicentennial year is, I think, most insensitive and very foolish. . . . I'm quite sure that Clark Gable, Vivien Leigh, and Leslie Howard are up there somewhere right now incensed over the proceedings."

When *Airport '77* was released in the spring of 1977, it received no plaudits from the critics. ". . . [It] looks less like the work of a director and writers than like a corporate decision," insisted Vincent Canby (*New York*

With Liv Ullmann in
Pope Joan ('72).

With Bekum Fehmiu,
Candice Bergen, and
Rossano Brazzi in *The
Adventurers* ('70).

334

Olivia of the Seventies.

As the subject of TV's "This Is Your Life" ('71) with surprise guest Bette Davis.

Times). Although acting a bit grand as art patroness Emily Livingston, Olivia's scenes, especially with Joseph Cotten, offered the film's few moments of semi-enjoyment. But one wonders if Olivia might not have been wiser to have accepted the role she was offered in an Italian picture (to be shot at the same time as *Airport '77*) in which she would have had the challenging assignment of playing an aging prostitute in an Italian whorehouse. "I would have loved doing the Italian picture," de Havilland says. "But I couldn't because of my twenty-year-old daughter Gisele. She's so sensitive—a beautifully brought up child. I didn't want her or her friends to see me in such a sordid environment as a bordello. I wanted to play a respectable role."

As for the future, Olivia claims she wants to make more films. "If something marvelous would come along, I'd certainly . . . do it. I'd also consider doing a television series if it were really exceptional. A mini-series would appeal to me. I'd like to be seen in a television classic such as *Upstairs, Downstairs,* for example."

Obviously, meticulous, energetic, determined Olivia will continue to be a recurring force on the show business scene. No longer the demure, innocent ingenue, she is a self-sufficient matron who fosters a variety of drives and interests. When recently asked how her friends would characterize her, she replied, "Why, I don't know. Well-meaning, I suppose they'd say. Yes, well-meaning—but watch out!"

FILMOGRAPHY

ALIBI IKE *(Warner Bros., 1935)* 73 min.

Producer, Edward Chodorov; director, Ray Enright; story, Ring Lardner; screenplay, William Wister Haines; camera, Arthur Todd.

Joe E. Brown (Frank X. Farrell); Olivia de Havilland (Dolly); Roscoe Karns (Cary); William Frawley (Cap); Joseph King (Owner); Ruth Donnelly (Bess); Paul Harvey (Crawford); Eddie Shubert (Jack Mack); G. Pat Collins (Lieutenant); Spencer Charters (Minister); Gene Morgan (Smitty); Jack Norton (Reporter); George Riley (Ball Player); Cliff Saum (Kelly); Joseph Crehan (Conductor); Jed Prouty (Jewelry Merchant); Jack Cheatham (Operator); Eddy Chandler, Bruce Mitchell (Detectives); Fred "Snowflake" Toones (Elevator Operator); Gordon "Bill" Elliott, Milton Kibbee (Fans); Selmer Jackson (Announcer); Frank Sully (Player).

THE IRISH IN US *(Warner Bros., 1935)* 84 min.

Producer, Sam Bischoff; director, Lloyd Bacon; story, Frank Orsatti; screenplay, Earl Baldwin; art director, Esdras Hartley; music director, Leo F. Forbstein; makeup, Perc Westmore; assistant director, Jack Sullivan; camera, George Barnes; editor, James Gibbon.

James Cagney (Danny O'Hara); Pat O'Brien (Pat O'Hara); Olivia de Havilland (Lucille Jackson); Frank McHugh (Mike O'Hara); Allen Jenkins (Car-Barn McCarthy); Mary Gordon (Mrs. O'Hara); J. Farrell MacDonald (Captain Jackson); Thomas Jackson (Doc Mullins); Harvey Perry (Joe Delaney); Mabel Colcord (Neighbor); Edward Keane (Doctor); Herb Heywood (Cook); Lucille Collins (Girl); Bess Flowers (Lady in Ring); Jack McHugh (Messenger Boy); Mushy Callahan (Messenger Boy); Emmett Vogan, Edward Gargan (Men).

A MIDSUMMER NIGHT'S DREAM *(Warner Bros., 1935)* 132 min.

Producer, Jack L. Warner; directors, Max Reinhardt,

William Dieterle; based on the play by William Shakespeare; screenplay, Charles Kenyon, Mary McCall, Jr.; art director, Anton Grot; dialogue director, Stanley Logan; music director, Leo F. Forbstein; music arranger, Erich Wolfgang Korngold; costumes, Max Ree; choreography, Bronislava Nijinska, Nini Theilade; makeup, Perc Westmore; assistant director, Sherry Shourds; camera, Hal Mohr; editor, Ralph Dawson.

James Cagney (Bottom); Dick Powell (Lysander); Joe E. Brown (Flute); Jean Muir (Helena); Hugh Herbert (Snout); Ian Hunter (Theseus); Frank McHugh (Quince); Victor Jory (Oberon); Olivia de Havilland (Hermia); Ross Alexander (Demetrius); Grant Mitchell (Egeus); Nini Theilade (Prima Ballerina Fairy); Verree Teasdale (Hippolyta, Queen of the Amazons); Anita Louise (Titania); Mickey Rooney (Puck); Dewey Robinson (Snug); Hobart Cavanaugh (Philostrate); Otis Harlan (Starveling); Arthur Treacher (Ninny's Tomb); Katherine Frey (Pease-Blossom); Helen Westcott (Cobweb); Fred Sale (Moth); Billy Barty (Mustard Seed).

CAPTAIN BLOOD *(First National, 1935)* 119 min.

Executive producer, Hal B. Wallis; associate producers, Harry Joe Brown, Gordon Hollingshead; director, Michael Curtiz; based on the novel by Rafael Sabatini; screenplay, Casey Robinson; assistant director, Sherry Shourds; fencing master, Fred Cavens; dialogue director, Stanley Logan; art director, Anton Grot; gowns, Milo Anderson; music, Erich Wolfgang Korngold; orchestrators, Hugo Friedhofer, Ray Heindorf; sound, C. A. Riggs; camera, Hal Mohr; additional camera, Ernest Haller; editor, George Amy.

Errol Flynn (Peter Blood); Olivia de Havilland (Arabella Bishop); Lionel Atwill (Colonel Bishop); Basil Rathbone (Captain Levasseur); Ross Alexander (Jeremy Pitt); Guy Kibbee (Hagthorpe); Henry Stephenson (Lord Willoughby); Robert Barrat (Wolverstone); Hobart Cavanaugh (Dr. Bronson); Donald Meek (Dr. Whacker); Jessie Ralph (Mrs. Barlowe); Forrester Harvey (Honesty Nuttall); Frank McGlynn, Sr. (Reverend Ogle); Holmes Herbert (Captain Gardner); David Torrence (Andrew Baynes); J. Carroll Naish (Cahusac); Pedro De Cordoba (Don Diego); George Hassell (Governor Steed); Harry Cording (Kent); Leonard Mudie (Baron Jeffreys); Ivan Simpson (Prosecutor); Stuart Casey (Captain Hobart); Denis d'Auburn (Lord Gildoy); Mary Forbes (Mrs. Steed); E. E. Clive (Court Clerk); Colin Kenny (Lord Chester Dyke); Maude Leslie (Mrs. Baynes); Gardner James (Branded Slave); Vernon Steele (King James II); Georges Renavent (French Captain); Murray Kinnell (Clerk in Governor Steed's Court); Harry Cording (Kent); Maude Leslie (Baynes' Wife); Stymie Beard (Governor's Attendant); Ivan Simpson (Judge Advocate); Yola D'Avril, Tina Menard (Girls in Tavern); Sam Appel (Gunner); Chris-Pin Martin (Sentry); Frank Puglia (French Officer); Artie Ortego, Gene Al-

sace, Kansas Moehring, Tom Steele, Blackie Whiteford, Jim Thorpe, William Yetter, Buddy Roosevelt, Jimmy Mason (Pirates).

ANTHONY ADVERSE *(Warner Bros., 1936)* 139 min.

Producer, Henry Blanke; director, Mervyn LeRoy; based on the novel by Hervey Allen; screenplay, Sheridan Gibney; music, Erich Wolfgang Korngold; music director, Leo F. Forbstein; technical advisor, Dwight Franklin; camera, Tony Gaudio; editor, Ralph Dawson.

Fredric March (Anthony Adverse); Olivia de Havilland (Angela Guisseppi); Anita Louise (Maria); Edmund Gwenn (John Bonnyfeather); Claude Rains (Don Luis); Donald Woods (Vincente Nolte); Louis Hayward (Dennis Moore); Gale Sondergaard (Faith); Akim Tamiroff (Carlo Cibo); Steffi Duna (Neleta); Billy Mauch (Anthony at Age Ten); Henry O'Neill (Father Xavier); Ralph Morgan (De Bruille); Fritz Leiber (Ouvrard); Luis Alberni (Tony Guisseppi); Marilyn Knowlden (Florence Udney at Age Ten); Ann Howard (Angela as a Child); Rollo Lloyd (Napoleon Bonaparte); George E. Stone (Sancho); Joseph Crehan (Captain Elisha Jorham); Clara Blandick (Mrs. Jorham); Scotty Beckett (Little Boy Anthony); Addison Richards (Captain Matanza); J. Carrol Naish (Major Doumet); Pedro De Cordoba (Brother Francois); Grace Stafford (Lucia); Joseph King (Captain on Boat to America); Eily Malyon (Mother Superior); Leonard Mudie (De Bourrienne); Rafaela Ottiano (Senora Rovina); Mathilde Comont (Guisseppi, the Cook); William Ricciardi (Driver to Leghorn); Frank Reicher (Driver of Coach to Paris); Paul Sotoff (Ferdinando); Bess Flowers, Myra Marsh (Nuns); Barlowe Borland (Clerk); Fred Malatesta (Stranger); Edward Keane (Officer).

THE CHARGE OF THE LIGHT BRIGADE *(Warner Bros., 1936)* 115 min.

Executive producer, Hal B. Wallis; associate producer, Samuel Bischoff; based on a story by Michel Jacoby; screenplay, Jacoby, Rowland Leigh; dialogue director, Stanley Logan; music, Max Steiner; orchestrator, Hugo Friedhofer; technical advisor, Captain E. Rochfort-John; technical advisor of drills and tactics, Major Sam Harris; director of horse action, B. Reeves Eason; assistant director, Jack Sullivan; art director, John Hughes; gowns, Milo Anderson; sound, C. A. Riggs; special effects, Fred Jackman, H. F. Koenekamp; camera, Sol Polito; editor, George Amy.

Errol Flynn (Captain Geoffrey Vickers); Olivia de Havilland (Elsa Campbell); Patric Knowles (Captain Perry Vickers); Donald Crisp (Colonel Campbell); Henry Stephenson (Sir Charles Macefield); Nigel Bruce (Sir Benjamin Warrenton); David Niven (Captain James Randall); G. P. Huntley, Jr. (Major Jowett); Spring Byington (Lady Octavia Warrenton); C. Henry Gordon (Surat Khan); E. E. Clive (Sir Humphrey Harcourt); Lumsden Hare (Colonel Woodward); Robert

Barrat (Count Igor Volonoff); Walter Holbrook (Cornet Barclay); Charles Sedgwick (Cornet Pearson); J. Carrol Naish (Subahdar Major Puran Singh); Scotty Beckett (Prema Singh); Princess Baigum (Prema's Mother); George Regas (Wazir); Helen Sanborn (Mrs. Jowett); George Sorel (Surwan); George Davis (Suristani); Carlos San Martin (Court Interpreter); Dick Botiller (Native); Herbert Evans (Major Domo); Jon Kristen (Panjari); Phyllis Coghlan (Woman at Ball); Stephen Moritz, Arthur Thalasso, Jack Curtis, Lal Chand Mehra (Sepoys); R. Singh, Jimmy Aubrey, David Thursby, Denis d'Auburn (Orderlies); Martin Garralaga, Frank Lackteen (Panjaris); Reginald Sheffield (Bentham); Georges Renavent (General Canrobert); Wilfred Lucas (Captain); Yakima Canutt (Double for Errol Flynn).

CALL IT A DAY (Warner Bros., 1937) 89 min.

Producer, Hal B. Wallis; associate producer, Henry Blanke; director, Archie Mayo; based on the play by Dodie Smith; screenplay, Casey Robinson; camera, Ernest Haller; editor, James Gibbon.

Olivia de Havilland (Catherine Hilton); Ian Hunter (Roger Hilton); Frieda Inescort (Dorothy Hilton); Anita Louise (Joan Collette); Alice Brady (Muriel Weston); Roland Young (Frank Haines); Bonita Granville (Ann Hilton); Marcia Ralston (Beatrice Gwynn); Peggy Wood (Ethel); Walter Woolf King (Paul); Peter Willes (Martin Hilton); Una O'Connor (Char Woman); Beryl Mercer (Cook); Elsa Buchanan (Vera); Mary Field (Elsie Lester); Robert Adair (Butler); Jack Richardson (Grocery Store Owner); Sidney Bracy (Flower Shop Owner); Louise Stanley (Girl on Bus); May Beatty (Landlady); Cecil Weston (Beatrice's Maid); Leyland Hodgson (Sir Harold).

THE GREAT GARRICK (Warner Bros., 1937) 89 min.

Producer/supervisor, Mervyn LeRoy; director, James Whale; based on the story "Ladies and Gentlemen" by Ernst Vadja; screenplay, Vadja; music director, Leo F. Forbstein; music, Adolph Deutsch; art director, Anton Grot; assistant director, Sherry Shourds; costumes, Milo Anderson; music director, Leo F. Forbstein; sound, C. A. Riggs; camera, Ernest Haller; editor, Warren Low.

Brian Aherne (David Garrick); Olivia de Havilland (Germaine De Le Corbe); Edward Everett Horton (Tubby); Melville Cooper (M. Picard); Luis Alberni (Basset); Lionel Atwill (Beaumarchais); Marie Wilson (Nicolle); Lana Turner (Auber); Linda Perry (Molle); Craig Reynolds (Janin); Dorothy Tree (Madame Moreau); Chester Clute (Moreau); Etienne Girardot (Jean Cabot); Albert Dekker (Le Brun); Milton Owen (Captain Thierre); Trevor Bardette (Noverre, the Blacksmith); E. E. Clive (Vendor); Harry Davenport (Innkeeper of Turk's Head); Paul Everton (Innkeeper of the Adam and Eve); Jack Norton (Drunken Gentleman); *Hamlet Sequence:* Leyland Hodgson (Man in Box);

Fritz Leiber (Horatio); Fritz Leiber, Jr. (Fortinbras); Corbet Morris (Osric); Olaf Hytten (Ambassador); Constance Tellissier (Woman in Box); Connie Leon (Woman in Audience); Elspeth Dudgeon (Old Witch); Ben Welden (Blacksmith).

ITS LOVE I'M AFTER (First National, 1937) 90 min.

Executive producer, Hal B. Wallis; director, Archie Mayo; based on the story "Gentleman After Midnight" by Maurice Hanline; screenplay, Casey Robinson; art director, Carl Jules Weyl; music, Heinz Roemheld; music director, Leo F. Forbstein; gowns, Orry-Kelly; camera, James Van Trees; editor, Owen Marks.

Leslie Howard (Basil Underwood); Bette Davis (Joyce Arden); Olivia de Havilland (Marcia West); Eric Blore (Digges); Patric Knowles (Henry Grant); George Barbier (William West); Spring Byington (Aunt Ella Paisley); Bonita Granville (Gracie Kane); E. E. Clive (Butler); Veda Ann Borg (Elsie); Valerie Bergere (Joyce's Maid); Georgia Caine (Mrs. Kane); Sarah Edwards (Mrs. Hinkle); Grace Field (Mrs. Babson); Harvey Clark (Mr. Babson); Thomas Pogue (Mr. Hinkle); Ed Mortimer (Mr. Kane); Thomas R. Mills (Butler); Lionel Belmore (Friar Lawrence); Ellen Clancy [Janet Shaw], Patricia Walthall, Rosella Towne, Helen Valkis (Autograph Hunters); Herbert Ashley (Doorman); Paul Irving (House Manager); Jack Mower (Hotel Clerk); Irving Bacon (Elevator Man); Georgie Cooper (Woman Guest).

GOLD IS WHERE YOU FIND IT (Warner Bros., 1938) C-90 min.

Producer, Hal B. Wallis; associate producer, Sam Bischoff; director, Michael Curtiz; story, Clements Ripley; screenplay, Warren Duff, Robert Buckner; music director, Leo F. Forbstein; music, Max Steiner; special camera effects, Byron Haskin; camera, Sol Polito; editor, Clarence Kolster.

George Brent (Jared Whitney); Olivia de Havilland (Serena Ferris); Claude Rains (Colonel Ferris); Margaret Lindsay (Rosanne Ferris); John Litel (Ralph Ferris); Tim Holt (Lanceford Ferris); Barton MacLane (Slag Minton); Henry O'Neill (Judge); Marcia Ralston (Molly Featherstone); George F. Hayes (Enoch Howitt); Sidney Toler (Harrison McCoy); Robert McWade (Crouch); Clarence Kolb (Senator Walsh); Russell Simpson (McKenzie); Harry Davenport (Dr. Parsons); Willie Best (Helper); Moroni Olsen (Senator Hearst); Granville Bates (Nixon); Charles Halton (Turner); Erville Alderson (Cryder); Cy Kendall (Kingan); Robert Homans (Grogan); Eddy Chandler (Deputy); Richard Botiller (Ramon); Cliff Saum (Medicine Man); Arthur Aylesworth, Raymond Brown, Guy Wilkerson, Jack Rutherford, Frank Pharr (Ranchers); Walter Rogers (General Grant); Edmund Cobb, James Farley (Miners); Milton Kibbee, Sarah Edwards, Sue Moore (Guests); Alan Davis (Clerk).

THE ADVENTURES OF ROBIN HOOD (*First National, 1938*) C-102 min.

Executive producer, Hal B. Wallis; associate producer, Henry Blanke; directors, Michael Curtiz, William Keighley; based upon the legends of Robin Hood; contributor to screenplay treatment, Rowland Leigh; screenplay, Norman Reilly Raine, Seton I. Miller; dialogue director, Irving Rapper; art director, Carl Jules Weyl; music, Erich Wolfgang Korngold; orchestrators, Hugo Friedhofer, Milan Roder; assistant directors, Lee Katz, Jack Sullivan; costumes, Milo Anderson; makeup, Perc Westmore; technical advisor, Louis Van Den Ecker; fencing master, Fred Cavens; archery supervisor, Howard Hill; jousting scenes directed by B. Reeves Eason; sound, C. A. Riggs; camera, Sol Polito, Tony Gaudio; editor, Ralph Dawson.

Errol Flynn (Robin Hood); Olivia de Havilland (Maid Marian); Claude Rains (Prince John); Basil Rathbone (Sir Guy of Gisbourne); Ian Hunter (King Richard); Eugene Pallette (Friar Tuck); Alan Hale (Little John); Melville Cooper (High Sheriff of Nottingham); Patric Knowles (Will Scarlett); Herbert Mundin (Much, the Miller's Son); Montagu Love (Bishop of Black Canon); Harry Cording (Dicken Malbott); Robert Warwick (Sir Geoffrey); Robert Noble (Sir Ralfe); Kenneth Hunter (Sir Mortimer); Leonard Willey (Sir Essex); Lester Mathews (Sir Ivor); Colin Kenny (Sir Baldwin); Howard Hill (Captain of Archers); Ivan F. Simpson (Proprietor of Kent Road Tavern); Charles McNaughton (Crippen); Lionel Belmore (Humility Prin, the Tavern Keeper); Janet Shaw (Humility's Daughter); Austin Fairman (Sir Nigel); Crauford Kent (Sir Norbett); Val Stanton, Ernie Stanton, Olaf Hytten, Alec Hartford, Peter Hobbes, Edward Dew, Sidney Baron (Robin's Outlaws); John Sutton, Paul Power, Ivo Henderson, Jack Deery (Richard's Knights); Marten Lamont (Sir Guy's Squire); Hal Brazeale (High Sheriff's Squire); Leonard Mudie (Town Crier); Denis d'Auburn, Cyril Thornton, Gerald Rogers, Charles Irwin (Saxon Men); Connie Leon, Phyllis Coghlan (Saxon Women); Herbert Evans (Senechal); Frank Hagney, James Baker (Men-at-Arms); Thomas R. Mills (Priest); George Bunny (Butcher); Dave Thursby (Archer); Joe North (Friar); Jack Richardson (Serf); Claude Wisberg (Blacksmith); Bob St. Angelo (Pierre de Caan); Lowden Adams (Old Crusader); Holmes Herbert (Referee); Reginald Sheffield (Herald); D'Arcy Corrigan (Villager).

FOUR'S A CROWD (*Warner Bros., 1938*) 91 min.

Executive producer, Hal B. Wallis; associate producer, David Lewis; director, Michael Curtiz; story, Wallace Sullivan; screenplay, Casey Robinson, Sig Herzig; music, Heinz Roemheld, Ray Heindorf; dialogue director, Irving Rapper; assistant director, Sherry Shourds; art director, Max Parker; gowns, Orry-Kelly; sound, Robert B. Lee; camera, Ernest Haller; editor, Clarence Kolster.

Errol Flynn (Robert Kensington Lansford); Olivia de Havilland (Lorri Dillingwell); Rosalind Russell (Jean Christy); Patric Knowles (Patterson Buckley); Walter Connolly (John P. Dillingwell); Hugh Herbert (Silas Jenkins); Melville Cooper (Bingham); Franklin Pangborn (Preston); Herman Bing (Herman, the Barber); Margaret Hamilton (Amy); Joseph Crehan (Pierce, the Butler); Joe Cunningham (Young); Dennie Moore (Buckley's Secretary); Gloria Blondell, Carole Landis (Lansford's Secretaries); Renie Riano (Mrs. Jenkins); Spencer Charters (Charlie); Charles Trowbridge (Dr. Ives).

HARD TO GET (*Warner Bros., 1938*) 80 min.

Producer, Hal B. Wallis; associate producer, Sam Bischhoff; director, Ray Enright; based on the story "Classified" by Stephen Morehouse Avery; screen story, Wally Klein, Joseph Schrank; screenplay, Jerry Wald, Maurice Lee, Richard Macaulay; art director, Anton Grot; songs, Harry Warren and Johnny Mercer; music director, Leo F. Forbstein; camera, Charles Rosher; editor, Thomas Richards.

Dick Powell (Bill Davis); Olivia de Havilland (Margaret Richards); Charles Winninger ("Big Ben" Richards); Allen Jenkins (Roscoe); Bonita Granville (Connie Richards); Melville Cooper (Case); Isabel Jeans (Henrietta Richards); Thurston Hall (John Atwater); Penny Singleton (Hattie); Grady Sutton (Stanley Potter); John Ridgely (Schaff); Jack Mower (Burke); Granville Bates (Judge Harkness); Nella Walker (Mrs. Atwater); Sidney Bracy (Carl, the Butler); Lottie Williams (Ellen, the Maid); Herbert Evans (Williams, the Chauffeur); Dick Rich (Truck Driver); Edgar Dearing (Eddie, the Motorcycle Cop); Arthur Housman (Drunk); Arthur Hoyt (Man at Flower Convention); Vera Lewis (Mrs. Petewyle); Jimmy Conlin (Dour Diner); Herbert Ashley (Waiter); Irving Bacon (Attendant at Gas Station); Cliff Saum, Ben Hendricks (Rivet Throwers); Herbert Rawlinson (Mr. Jones); George Kirby (Servant).

WINGS OF THE NAVY (*Warner Bros., 1939*) 89 min.

Producers, Jack L. Warner, Hal B. Wallis; associate producer, Lou Edelman; director, Lloyd Bacon; story-screenplay, Michael Fessier; camera, Arthur Edeson, Elmer Dyer; editor, William Holmes.

George Brent (Cass Harrington); Olivia de Havilland (Irene Dale); John Payne (Jerry Harrington); Frank McHugh (Scat Allen); John Litel (Commander Clark); Victor Jory (Lieutenant Parsons); Henry O'Neill (Prologue Speaker); John Ridgely (Dan Morrison); John Gallaudet (Lieutenant Harry White); Don Briggs, Regis Toomey (Instructors); Edgar Edwards (Ted Parsons); Albert Morin (Armando Costa); Jonathan Hale (Commandant); Pierre Watkin (Captain March); Don Douglas (Officer of the Day); Max Hoffman (Officer); Alan Davis (Check Pilot); Renie Riano (Woman); Lee Phelps (Conductor); Selmer Jackson (Doctor); Ed Keane (Psychology Examiner); Fred Hamilton (Cadet);

Walter Miller (Henry); Morgan Conway (Duty Officer); Ed Parker, Larry Williams, Carlyle Moore, Jr. (Navy Men); Mary Gordon (Housekeeper); Emmett Vogan (Flight Commander); Max Wagner (Boss Mechanic).

DODGE CITY *(Warner Bros., 1939)* C-104 min.

Executive producer, Hal B. Wallis; associate producer, Robert Lord; director, Michael Curtiz; screenplay, Robert Buckner; music, Max Steiner; orchestrator, Hugo Friedhofer; assistant director, Sherry Shourds; dialogue director, Jo Graham; costumes, Milo Anderson; makeup, Perc Westmore; art director, Ted Smith; sound, Oliver S. Garretson; special effects, Byron Haskin, Rex Wimpy; camera, Sol Polito; associate Technicolor camera, Ray Rennahan; editor, George Amy.

Errol Flynn (Wade Hatton); Olivia de Havilland (Abbie Irving); Ann Sheridan (Ruby Gilman); Bruce Cabot (Jeff Surrett); Frank McHugh (Joe Clemens); Alan Hale (Rusty Hart); John Litel (Matt Cole); Victor Jory (Yancy); Henry Travers (Dr. Irving); Henry O'Neill (Colonel Dodge); Guinn "Big Boy" Williams (Tex Baird); Gloria Holden (Mrs. Cole); Douglas Fowley (Munger); William Lundigan (Lee Irving); Georgia Caine (Mrs. Irving); Charles Halton (Surrett's Lawyer); Ward Bond (Bud Taylor); Bobs Watson (Harry Cole); Nat Carr (Crocker); Russell Simpson (Orth); Clem Bevans (Charlie, the Barber); Cora Witherspoon (Mrs. McCoy); Joe Crehan (Hammond); Thurston Hall (Twitchell); Chester Clute (Coggins); Monte Blue (Barlow, the Indian Agent); James Burke (Cattle Auctioneer); Robert Homans (Mail Clerk); George Guhl (Jason, the Marshall); Spencer Charters (Clergyman); Bud Osborne (Stagecoach Driver/Waiter); Pat O'Malley (Conductor); Earle Hodgins (Spieler).

THE PRIVATE LIVES OF ELIZABETH AND ESSEX *(Warner Bros., 1939)* C-106 min.

Executive producer, Hal B. Wallis; associate producer, Robert Lord; director, Michael Curtiz; based on the play *Elizabeth the Queen* by Maxwell Anderson; screenplay, Norman Reilly Raine, Aeneas MacKenzie; music, Erich Wolfgang Korngold; orchestrators, Hugo Friedhofer, Milan Roder; assistant director, Sherry Shourds; dialogue director, Stanley Logan; art director, Anton Grot; costumes, Orry-Kelly; makeup, Perc Westmore; technical advisor, Ali Hubert; sound, C. A. Riggs; special effects, Byron Haskin, H. F. Koenekamp; camera, Sol Polito; associate Technicolor camera, W. Howard Greene; editor, Owen Marks.

Bette Davis (Queen Elizabeth); Errol Flynn (Robert Devereaux, the Earl of Essex); Olivia de Havilland (Lady Penelope Gray); Donald Crisp (Francis Bacon); Alan Hale (Earl of Tyrone); Vincent Price (Sir Walter Raleigh); Henry Stephenson (Lord Burghley); Henry Daniell (Sir Robert Cecil); James Stephenson (Sir Thomas Egerton); Nanette Fabray (Mistress Margaret Radcliffe); Ralph Forbes (Lord Knollys); Robert Warwick (Lord Mountjoy); Leo G. Carroll (Sir Edward Coke); and Forrester Harvey, Doris Lloyd, Maris Wrixon, Rosella Towne, John Sutton, Guy Bellis, Stanford I. Jolley.

A.k.a. *Elizabeth the Queen.*

GONE WITH THE WIND *(MGM, 1939)* C-229 min.

Producer, David O. Selznick; directors, Victor Fleming, (uncredited) George Cukor and Sam Wood; based on the novel by Margaret Mitchell; screenplay, Sidney Howard; production designer, William Cameron Menzies; art director, Lyle Wheeler; set decorator, Joseph B. Platt; Technicolor consultant, Natalie Kalmus; costumes, Walter Plunkett; makeup, Monty Westmore; Miss Leigh's hats, John Fredericks; music, Max Steiner; choreography, Frank Floyd, Eddie Prinz; second unit director, B. Reeves Eason; assistant director, Eric Stacey; sound, Frank Maher; fire effects, Lee Zavitz; special camera effects, Jack Cosgrove; camera, Ernest Haller; Technicolor camera, Ray Rennahan, Wilfrid M. Cline; editors, Hal C. Kern, James E. Newcom.

Clark Gable (Rhett Butler); Vivien Leigh (Scarlett O'Hara); Leslie Howard (Ashley Wilkes); Olivia de Havilland (Melanie Hamilton); Hattie McDaniel (Mammy); Thomas Mitchell (Gerald O'Hara); Barbara O'Neil (Mrs. O'Hara); Laura Hope Crews (Aunt Pittypat Hamilton); Harry Davenport (Dr. Meade); Ona Munson (Belle Watling); Evelyn Keyes (Suellen O'Hara); Ann Rutherford (Careen O'Hara); Butterfly McQueen (Prissy); Alicia Rhett (India Wilkes); Everett Brown (Big Sam); Eddie Anderson (Uncle Peter); Rand Brooks (Charles Hamilton); Carroll Nye (Frank Kennedy); Jane Darwell (Mrs. Merriwether); Mary Anderson (Maybelle Merriwether); Isabel Jewell (Emmy Slattery); Victor Jory (Jonas Wilkerson); Cammie King (Bonnie Blue Butler); Lillian Kemble Cooper (Bonnie's Nurse); Ward Bond (Tom, a Yankee Captain); Paul Hurst (The Yankee Deserter); George Reeves (Brent Tarleton); Fred Crane (Stuart Tarleton); James Bush (Gentleman); Eric Linden (An Amputation Case); Guy Wilkerson (Wounded Card Player); Frank Faylen (Soldier Aiding Dr. Meade); Adrian Morris (Carpetbagger Orator); J. M. Kerrigan (Johnny Gallegher); Olin Howland (Yankee Businessman); Yakima Canutt, Blue Washington (Renegades); Si Jenks (Yankee on Street); Harry Strang (Tom's Aide).

RAFFLES *(United Artists, 1940)* 71 min.

Producer, Samuel Goldwyn; director, Sam Wood; based on the novel *The Amateur Cracksman* by E. W. Hornung; screenplay, John Van Druten, Sidney Howard; music, Victor Young; camera, Gregg Toland; editor, Sherman Todd.

David Niven (Raffles); Olivia de Havilland (Gwen); Dame May Whitty (Lady Melrose); Dudley Digges (Mackenzie); Douglas Walton (Bunny); Lionel Pape (Lord Melrose); E. E. Clive (Barraclough); Peter Godfrey (Crawshay); Margaret Sedden (Maud Holden);

Gilbert Emery (Bingham); Hilda Plowright (Wilson); Vesey O'Daveren (The Butler); George Cathrey (The Footman); Keith Hitchcock (Morton); Forrester Harvey (Umpire); James Finlayson (Cabby); George Atkinson, Eric Wilton, Frank Baker (Attendants); Herbert Clifton, George Kirby, Gibson Gowland (Villagers); Wilfred Lucas, Larry Dodds, John Power, Colin Kenny (Cops); David Clyde, Charles Irwin, Leyland Hodgson (Plainclothesmen); David Thursby (Passenger).

MY LOVE CAME BACK (Warner Bros., 1940) 81 min.

Producers, Jack L. Warner, Hal B. Wallis; associate producer, Wolfgang Reinhardt; director, Curtis Bernhardt; story, Walter Reisch; screenplay, Ivan Goff, Robert Buckner, Earl Baldwin; art director, Max Parker; music, Heinz Roemheld; orchestrator, Ray Heindorf; music director, Leo F. Forbstein; camera, Charles Rosher; editor, Rudi Fehr.

Olivia de Havilland (Amelia Cullen); Jeffrey Lynn (Tony Baldwin); Eddie Albert (Dusty Rhodes); Jane Wyman (Joe O'Keefe); Charles Winninger (Julius Malette); Spring Byington (Mrs. Malette); William Orr (Paul Malette); Ann Gillis (Valerie Malette); S. Z. Sakall (Ludwig); Grant Mitchell (Dr. Kobbe); Charles Trowbridge (Dr. Downey); Mabel Taliaferro (Dowager); Sidney Bracy (Butler); Nanette Vallon (Sophie); William Davidson (Agent); Tommy Baker (Boy); Creighton Hale (Clerk); William Roberts (Office Boy); Wedgwood Newell (Treasurer); Jack Mower, Richard Kipling (Executives); Richard Clayton (Valerie's Escort).

SANTA FE TRAIL (Warner Bros., 1940) 110 min.

Executive producer, Hal B. Wallis; associate producer, Robert Fellows; director, Michael Curtiz; screenplay, Robert Buckner; music, Max Steiner; orchestrator, Hugo Friedhofer; assistant director, Jack Sullivan; art director, John Hughes; dialogue director, Jo Graham; makeup, Perc Westmore; costumes, Milo Anderson; sound, Robert B. Lee; special effects, Byron Haskin, H. D. Koenekamp; camera, Sol Polito; editor, George Amy.

Errol Flynn (Jeb Stuart); Olivia de Havilland (Kit Carson Halliday); Raymond Massey (John Brown); Ronald Reagan (George Custer); Alan Hale (Barefoot Brody); Guinn "Big Boy" Williams (Tex Bell); Van Heflin (Rader); Henry O'Neill (Cyrus Halliday); William Lundigan (Bob Halliday); John Litel (Harlan); Gene Reynolds (Jason Brown); Alan Baxter (Oliver Brown); Moroni Olsen (Robert E. Lee); Erville Alderson (Jefferson Davis); Susan Peters (Charlotte Davis); Charles D. Brown (Major Sumner); David Bruce (Phil Sheridan); Frank Wilcox (James Longstreet); William Marshall (George Pickett); George Haywood (John Hood); Russell Simpson (Shoubel Morgan); Joseph Sawyer (Kitzmiller); Hobart Cavanaugh (Barber Doyle); Spencer Charters (Conductor); Ward Bond (Townley); Wilfred Lucas (Weiner); Charles Middleton

(Gentry); Russell Hicks (J. Boyce Russell); Napoleon Simpson (Samson); Cliff Clark (Instructor); Emmett Vogan (Lieutenant); Selmer Jackson, Joseph Crehan, William Hopper (Officers); Clinton Rosemond, Bernice Pilot, Libby Taylor, Mildred Gover (Blacks); Roy Barcroft, Frank Mayo (Engineers); Grace Stafford (Farmer's Wife); Louis Jean Heydt (Farmer); Lane Chandler (Adjutant); Addison Richards (Sheriff); Edmund Cobb, Ed Peil, Ed Hearn, Eddy Chandler (Guards); Victor Kilian (Dispatch Rider).

THE STRAWBERRY BLONDE (Warner Bros., 1941) 97 min.

Producers, Jack L. Warner, Hal B. Wallis; associate producer, William Cagney; director, Raoul Walsh; based on the play One Sunday Afternoon by James Hagan; screenplay, Julius J. Epstein, Philip G. Epstein; dialogue director, Hugh Cummings; art director, Robert Haas; music, Heinz Roemheld; orchestrator, Ray Heindorf; makeup, Perc Westmore; costumes, Orry-Kelly; assistant director, Russ Saunders; sound, Robert B. Lee; camera, James Wong Howe; editor, William Holmes.

James Cagney (Biff Grimes); Olivia de Havilland (Amy Lind); Rita Hayworth (Virginia Brush); Alan Hale (Old Man Grimes); George Tobias (Nick Pappalas); Jack Carson (Hugo Barnstead); Una O'Connor (Mrs. Mulcahey); George Reeves (Harold); Lucile Fairbanks (Harold's Girl); Edward McNamara (Big Joe); Herbert Heywood (Toby); Helen Lynd (Josephine); Roy Gordon (Bank President); Tim Ryan (Street Cleaner Foreman); Addison Richards (Official); Frank Mayo (Policeman); Susan Peters (Girl); Frank Orth (Baxter); Herbert Anderson (Boy); George Campeau (Sailor); Abe Dinovitch (Singer); Creighton Hale (Secretary); Russell Hicks (Treadway); Ann Edmonds (Girl); Dorothy Vaughan (Woman).

HOLD BACK THE DAWN (Paramount, 1941) 115 min.

Producer, Arthur Hornblow; director, Mitchel Leisen; based on the story by Ketti Frings; screenplay, Charles Brackett, Billy Wilder; art directors, Hans Dreier, Robert Usher; camera, Leo Tover; editor, Doane Harrison.

Charles Boyer (Georges Iscovescu); Olivia de Havilland (Emmy Brown); Paulette Goddard (Anita Dixon); Victor Francen (Van Den Luecken); Walter Abel (Inspector Hammock); Curt Bois (Bonbois); Rosemary De Camp (Berta Kurz); Eric Feldary (Josef Kurz); Nestor Paiva (Flores); Eva Puig (Lupita); Micheline Cheirel (Christine); Madeleine LeBeau (Anni); Billy Lee (Tony); Mikhail Rasumny (Mechanic); Mitchell Leisen (Mr. Saxon); Brian Donlevy, Richard Webb, Veronica Lake (On the Set Film Actors); Sonny Boy Williams (Sam); Don Douglas (Joe); Gertrude Astor (Young Woman at Climax Bar); Jesus Topete, Tony Roux (Mechanics); June Pickrell (Mrs. Brown); Buddy Messinger (Elevator Boy); Ray Mala (Husky Young Mexican Bridegroom); Soledad Jiminez (Old Peon's Wife); Placido Sigueiros (Old Peon).

THEY DIED WITH THEIR BOOTS ON *(Warner Bros., 1941)* 140 min.

Executive producer, Hal B. Wallis; associate producer, Robert Fellows; director, Raoul Walsh; screenplay, Wally Kine, Aeneas MacKenzie; music, Max Steiner; art director, John Hughes; assistant director, Russell Saunders; dialogue director, Edward A. Blatt; technical advisor, Lieutenant Colonel J. G. Taylor, U.S. Army, Retired; gowns, Milo Anderson; makeup, Perc Westmore; sound, Dolph Thomas; camera, Bert Glennon; editor, William Holmes.

Errol Flynn (George Armstrong Custer); Olivia de Havilland (Elizabeth Bacon Custer); Arthur Kennedy (Ned Sharp, Jr.); Charley Grapewin (California Joe); Gene Lockhart (Samuel Bacon); Anthony Quinn (Crazy Horse); Stanley Ridges (Major Romulus Taipe); John Litel (General Philip Sheridan); Walter Hampden (Senator Sharop); Sydney Greenstreet (General Winfield Scott); Regis Toomey (Fitzhugh Lee); Hattie McDaniel (Callie); G. P. Huntley, Jr. (Lieutenant Butler); Frank Wilcox (Captain Webb); Joe Sawyer (Sergeant Doolittle); Minor Watson (Senator Smith); Gig Young (Lieutenant Roberts); John Ridgley (Second Lieutenant Davis); Joseph Crehan (President Grant); Aileen Pringle (Mrs. Sharp); Anna Q. Nilsson (Mrs. Taipe); Harry Lewis (Youth); Tod Andrews (Cadet Brown); Walter Brooke (Rosser); Selmer Jackson (Captain McCook); William Hopper (Frazier); Eddie Acuff (Corporal Smith); Sam McDaniel (Waiter); George Reed (Charles); Pat McVey (Jones); George Eldredge (Captain Riley); Harry Strang, Max Hoffman, Jr., Frank Mayo (Orderlies); Irving Bacon (Salesman); Virginia Brissac (Woman); Walter Baldwin (Settler); Francis Ford (Veteran); Frank Ferguson (Grant's Secretary).

THE MALE ANIMAL *(Warner Bros., 1942)* 101 min.

Producer, Hal B. Wallis; associate producer, Wolfgang Reinhardt; director, Elliott Nugent; based on the play by James Thurber and Nugent; screenplay, Julius and Philip Epstein, Stephen Morehouse Avery; camera, Arthur Edeson; editor, Thomas Richards.

Henry Fonda (Tommy Turner); Olivia de Havilland (Ellen Turner); Joan Leslie (Patricia Stanley); Jack Carson (Joe Ferguson); Eugene Pallette (Ed Keller); Herbert Anderson (Michael Barnes); Hattie McDaniel (Cleota); Ivan Simpson (Dr. Damon); Don DeFore (Wally); Jean Ames (Hot Garters Garner); Minna Phillips (Mrs. Blanche Lamon); Regina Wallace (Mrs. Myrtle Keller); Frank Mayo (Coach Sprague); William Davidson (Alumnus); Bobby Barnes (Nutsy Miller); Albert Faulkner (Boy); Jane Randolph (Secretary); Spec O'Donnell, Don Phillips, Juanita Stark, Audrey Long, Marijo James, Charles Drake, Audra Lindley, Joan Winfield, Gig Young, Ann Edmonds (Students);

Walter Brooke, Hank Mann, William Hopper, Al Lloyd, Ed Graham, Cliff Saum, Glen Cavender, Creighton Hale (Reporters).

IN THIS OUR LIFE *(Warner Bros., 1942)* 97 min.

Producer, Hal B. Wallis, in association with David Lewis; director, John Huston, (uncredited) Raoul Walsh; based on the novel by Ellen Glasgow; screenplay, Howard Koch; music, Max Steiner; music director, Leo F. Forbstein; art director, Robert Haas; gowns, Orry-Kelly; camera, Ernest Haller; editor, William Holmes.

Bette Davis (Stanley Timberlake); Olivia de Havilland (Roy Timberlake); George Brent (Craig Fleming); Dennis Morgan (Peter Kingsmill); Charles Coburn (William Fitzroy); Frank Craven (Asa Timberlake); Billie Burke (Lavinia Timberlake); Hattie McDaniel (Minerva Clay); Lee Patrick (Betty Wilmoth); Mary Servoss (Charlotte Fitzroy); Ernest Anderson (Parry Clay); William Davidson (Jim Purdy); Edward Fielding (Dr. Buchanan); John Hamilton (Inspector); William Forrest (Ranger); Eddie Acuff, Elliott Sullivan, Walter Baldwin, Herbert Heywood, Alan Bridge (Workers); George Reed (Butler); Dudley Dickerson (Waiter); Ruth Ford (Young Mother); Walter Huston (Bartender); Humphrey Bogart, Mary Astor, Peter Lorre, Sydney Greenstreet, Ward Bond, Barton MacLane, Elisha Cook, Jr. (Roadhouse Customers); Ira Buck Wood, Sam McDaniel, Billy Mitchell, Napoleon Simpson, Sunshine Sammy Morrison, Jester Harrison, Freddie Jackson, Fred Kelsey (Blacks).

THANK YOUR LUCKY STARS *(Warner Bros., 1943)* 127 min.

Producer, Mark Hellinger; director, David Butler; story, Everett Freeman, Arthur Schwartz; screenplay, Norman Panama, Melvin Frank, James V. Kern; songs, Schwartz and Frank Loesser; vocal arranger, Dudley Chambers; orchestrator, Ray Heindorf, Maurice de Packh; music adaptor, Heinz Roemheld; gowns, Milo Anderson; art directors, Anton Grot, Leo K. Kuter; set decorator, Walter F. Tilford; dialogue director, Herbert Farjean; makeup, Perc Westmore; assistant director, Phil Quinn; choreography/dance stager, LeRoy Prinz; sound, Francis J. Scheid, Charles David Forrest; special effects, H. F. Koenekamp; camera, Arthur Edeson; editor, Irene Morra.

Eddie Cantor (Joe Sampson/Himself); Joan Leslie (Pat Dixon); Dennis Morgan (Tommy Randolph); Dinah Shore (Herself); S. Z. Sakall (Dr. Schlenna); Edward Everett Horton (Farnsworth); Ruth Donnelly (Nurse Hamilton); Joyce Reynolds (Girl with Book); Richard Lane (Barney Jackson); Don Wilson (Himself); Henry Armetta (Angelo); Willie Best (Soldier); Humphrey Bogart, Jack Carson, Bette Davis, Olivia de Havilland, Errol Flynn, John Garfield, Alan Hale, Ida Lupino, Ann Sheridan, Alexis Smith, George Tobias, Spike Jones & His City Slickers (Specialties); Frank

Faylen (Sailor); Creighton Hale, Jack Mower (Engineers); Noble Johnson (Charlie, the Indian); Ed Gargan (Doorman); Billy Benedict (Bus Boy); *Ice Cold Katie Number:* Hattie McDaniel (Gossip); Rita Christiani (Ice Cold Katie); Jess Lee Brooks (Justice); Ford, Harris, and Jones (Trio); Mathew Jones (Gambler); *Errol Flynn Number:* Monte Blue (Bartender); Art Foster, Fred Kelsey, Elmer Ballard, Buster Wiles, Howard Davies, Tudor Williams, Alan Cook, Fred McEvoy, Bobby Hale, Will Stanton, Charles Irwin, David Thursby, Henry Ibling, Earl Hunsaker, Hubert Hend, Dudley Kuzello, Ted Billings (Pub Characters); *Bette Davis Number:* Jack Norton (Drunk); Henri DeSoto (Maitre d'Hotel); Dick Elliott, Dick Earle (Customers); Harry Adams (Doorman); Sam Adams (Bartender); Conrad Wiedell (Jitterbug); Charles Francis, Harry Bailey (Bald-Headed Men); Joan Winfield (Cigarette Girl); Nancy Worth, Sylvia Opert (Hatcheck Girls); *The Lucky Stars:* Harriette Haddon, Harriett Olsen, Nancy Worth, Joy Barlowe, Janet Barrett, Dorothy Schoemer, Dorothy Dayton, Lucille LaMarr, Sylvia Opert, Mary Landa; *Humphrey Bogart Sequence:* Matt McHugh (Fireman); *Ann Sheridan Number:* Georgia Lee Settle, Virginia Patton (Girls); *Good Neighbor Number:* Igor DeNavrotsky (Dancer); Brandon Hurst (Cab Driver); Angelita Mari (Duenna); Lynne Baggett (Miss Latin America); Mary Landa (Miss Spain).

PRINCESS O'ROURKE *(Warner Bros., 1943)* 94 min.

Producer, Hal B. Wallis; director/screenplay, Norman Krasna; art director, Max Parker; set decorator, George James Hopkins; music, Frederick Hollander; music director, Leo F. Forbstein; songs, Ira Gershwin and E. Y. Harburg; Arthur Schwartz; assistant director, Frank Heath; sound, Stanley Jones; camera, Ernest Haller; editor, Warren Low.

Olivia de Havilland (Maria); Robert Cummings (Eddie O'Rourke); Jack Carson (Dave); Jane Wyman (Jean); Charles Coburn (Uncle); Gladys Cooper (Miss Haskell); Harry Davenport (Supreme Court Justice); Minor Watson (Washburn); Ray Walker ("G" Man); Nana Bryant (Mrs. Mulvaney); Nydia Westman (Mrs. Bowers); Curt Bois (Count Peter De Chandome); Dave Willock (Delivery Boy); John Dilson (Elevator Man); David Clyde (Butler); Julie Bishop (Stewardess); Frank Mayo (Business Man); Vera Lewis, Harry Bradley (Couple); Mary Field (Clara Stilwell); Ferike Boros (Mrs. Pulaski); Nan Wynn (Girl Singer); Katherine Price (Housekeeper); Bill Kennedy, Jack Mower, Roland Drew (Dispatchers).

GOVERNMENT GIRL *(RKO, 1943)* 94 min.

Producer, Dudley Nichols; associate producer, Edward Donahue; director, Nichols; story, Adela Rogers St. John; screenplay, Nichols; adaptor, Budd Schulberg; art director, Albert S. D'Agostino; set decorators, Darrell Silvera, Al Fields; music, Leigh Harline; music director, C. Bakaleinikoff; assistant director, J. D. Star-

key; sound, Roy Meadows, James G. Stewart; special effects, Vernon L. Walker; camera, Frank Redman; editor, Roland Gross.

Olivia de Havilland (Smokey); Sonny Tufts (Browne); Anne Shirley (May); Jess Barker (Dana); James Dunn (Sergeant Joe); Paul Stewart (Branch); Agnes Moorehead (Mrs. Wright); Harry Davenport (Senator MacVickers); Una O'Connor (Mrs. Harris); Sig Ruman (Ambassador); Jane Darwell (Miss Trask); George Givot (Count Bodinsky); Paul Stanton (Mr. Harvester); Art Smith (Marqueenie); Joan Valerie (Miss MacVickers); Harry Shannon (Mr. Gibson); Ray Walker (Tom Holliday); Emory Parnell (The Chief); Larry Steers, Russell Huestes, James Carlisle, Bert Moorhouse, Fred Norton (Business Men); Warren Hymer, Harry Tenbrook (MPs); Karl Miller (Janitor); Charles Meakin (Business Man); Bruce Edwards, Lawrence Tierney (FBI Men); Barbara Hale (Bit); Ian Wolfe (Hotel Clerk); Babe Green, Wally Dean, Louis Payne, Donald Hall, Harry Bailey (Senators).

THE WELL-GROOMED BRIDE *(Paramount, 1946)* 75 min.

Producer, Fred Kohlmar; director, Sidney Lanfield; story, Robert Russell; screenplay, Claude Binyon, Russell; art directors, Hans Dreier, Earl Hedrick; set decorator, Kenneth Swartz; music, Roy Webb; assistant director, Oscar Rudolph; sound, Wallace Nogle, Joel Moss; special effects, Gordon Jennings; process camera, Farciot Edouart; camera, John F. Seitz; editor, William Shea.

Olivia de Havilland (Margie); Ray Milland (Lieutenant Briggs); Sonny Tufts (Torchy); James Gleason (Captain Hornby); Constance Dowling (Rita Sloane); Percy Kilbride (Mr. Dawson); Jean Heather (Wickley); Jay Norris (Mitch); Jack Reilly (Buck); George Turner (Goose); Tom Fadden (Justice); Donald Beddoe (Hotel Clerk); William Forrest (Major James Smith); James Millican, Dale Van Sickel (SPs); Frank Faylen (Taxi Driver); Noel Neill (Wave); Minerva Urecal (Woman); Charles Mayon, Roger Creed, William Haade (MPs).

TO EACH HIS OWN *(Paramount, 1946)* 122 min.

Producer, Charles Brackett; director, Mitchell Leisen; story, Brackett; screenplay, Brackett, Jacques Thery; art directors, Hans Dreier, Roland Anderson; set decorators, Sam Comer, James M. Walters; assistant director, John Coonan; sound, John Cope, Don McKay; special camera effects, Gordon Jennings; process camera, Farciot Edouart; camera, Daniel L. Fapp; editor, Alma Macrorie.

Olivia de Havilland (Miss Josephine Norris); John Lund (Captain Cosgrove/Gregory); Mary Anderson (Corinna Piersen); Roland Culver (Lord Desham); Phillip Terry (Alex Piersen); Bill Goodwin (Mac Tilton); Virginia Welles (Liz Lorimer); Victoria Horne (Daisy Gingres); Griff Barnett (Mr. Norris); Alma Macrorie (Belle Ingham); Bill Ward (Griggsy at Age

Five-and-a-Half); Frank Faylen (Babe); Arthur Loft (Mr. Clinton); Willard Robertson (Dr. Hunt); Virginia Farmer (Mrs. Clinton); Doris Lloyd (Miss Pringle); Clyde Cook (Mr. Harkett); Ida Moore (Miss Claflin); Mary Young (Mrs. Nix); Chester Clute (Clarence Ingham); Crane Whitley (Police Captain); Leyland Hodgson (Porter at Reindeer Club); Reginald Sheffield (Headwaiter); Will Stanton (Funny Little Waiter); Gladys Blake (Lorena); William Hunter, Jack Clifford (Policemen); Clara Reid (Ida); Jack Rogers (Cockney Taxi Driver); James Millican (Lieutenant Flyer); Almeda Fowler (Sara); Anthony Ellis (Messenger Boy); Gloria Williams (Woman); Beverly Thompson, Lucy Knoch (WACs).

DEVOTION (Warner Bros., 1946) 107 min.

Producer, Robert Buckner; director, Curtis Bernhardt; story, Theodore Reeves; screenplay, Keith Winter; assistant director, Jesse Hibbs; art director, Robert M. Haas; set decorator, Casey Roberts; dialogue director, James Vincent; music, Erich Wolfgang Korngold; music director, Leo Forbstein; sound, Stanley Jones; special effects, Jack Holden, Jack Oakie, Rex Wimpy; camera, Ernest Haller; editor, Rudi Fehr.

Olivia de Havilland (Charlotte Bronte); Ida Lupino (Emily Bronte); Nancy Coleman (Ann Bronte); Paul Henreid (Nichols); Sydney Greenstreet (Thackeray); Arthur Kennedy (Branwell Bronte); Dame May Whitty (Lady Thornton); Victor Francen (Monsieur Heger); Montagu Love (Reverend Bronte); Ethel Griffies (Aunt Branwell); Odette Myrtil (Madame Heger); Edmond Breon (Sir John Thornton); Marie deBecker (Tabby); Donald Stuart (Butcher); Forrester Harvey (Hoggs); Yorke Sherwood (Man); Billy Bevan (Draper); John Meredith (Draper's Assistant); David Thursby (Farmer); David Clyde (Land Agent); P. J. Kelly (Shepherd); Doris Lloyd (Mrs. Ingham); Violet Seton (Mrs. Crump); Sylvia Opert, Elyane Lima, Anne Goldthwaite, Irina Semochenko (French Girl Students); Howard Davies (Englishman); Hartney Arthur (Man); Reginald Sheffield (Dickens); Brandon Hurst (Duke of Wellington); Elspeth Dudgeon (Elderly Woman).

THE DARK MIRROR (Universal, 1946) 85 min.

Producer, Nunnally Johnson; director, Robert Siodmak; based on the novel by Vladimir Pozner; screenplay, Johnson; production designer, Duncan Cramer; set decorator, Hugh Hunt; music, Dimitri Tiomkin; assistant director, Jack Voglin; sound, Fred Lau; special effects, J. Devereaux Jennings, Paul Lerpae; camera, Milton Krasner; editor, Ernest Nims.

Olivia de Havilland (Terry Collins/Ruth Collins); Lew Ayres (Dr. Scott Elliott); Thomas Mitchell (Lieutenant of Detectives Stevenson); Richard Long (Rusty); Charles Evans (District Attorney Girard); Garry Owen (Franklin); Lester Allen (George Benson); Lela Bliss (Mrs. Didriksen); Marta Mitrovich (Miss Beade); Amelita Ward (Photo-Double); William Halligan

(Sergeant Temple); Ida Moore (Mrs. O'Brien, the Cleaning Lady); Charles McAvoy (Janitor O'Brien); Jack Cheatham (Policeman); Lane Chandler (Intern); Jack Gargan (Waiter); Ralph Peters (Dumb Cop) Lane Watson (Mike, the Assistant).

THE SNAKE PIT (Twentieth Century-Fox, 1948) 108 min.

Executive producer, Darryl F. Zanuck; producers, Robert Bassler, Anatole Litvak; director, Litvak; based on the novel by Mary Jane Ward; screenplay, Frank Partos, Millen Brand; art directors, Lyle Wheeler, Joseph C. Wright; set decorators, Thomas Little, Ernest Lansing; music/music director, Alfred Newman; orchestrator, Edward Powell; assistant directors, Henry Weinberger, Dave Silver; makeup, Ben Nye; costumes, Bonnie Cashin; sound, Arthur L. Kirbach, Harry M. Leonard; camera, Leo Tover; editor, Dorothy Spencer.

Olivia de Havilland (Virginia Cunningham); Mark Stevens (Robert Cunningham); Leo Genn (Dr. Mark Kirk); Celeste Holm (Grace); Glenn Langan (Dr. Terry); Helen Craig (Miss Davis); Leif Erickson (Gordon); Beulah Bondi (Mrs. Greer); Lee Patrick, Isabel Jewell, Victoria Horne, Tamara Shayne, Grace Poggi (Inmates); Howard Freeman (Dr. Curtis); Natalie Schafer (Mrs. Stuart); Ruth Donnelly (Ruth); Katherine Locke (Margaret); Frank Conroy (Dr. Jonathan Gifford); Minna Gombell (Miss Hart); June Storey (Miss Bixby, the Ward Nurse); Ann Doran (Valerie); Damian O'Flynn (Mr. Stuart); Lora Lee Michel (Virginia at Age Six); Esther Somers (Miss Vance); Jacqueline de Wit (Miss Sommerville); Betsy Blair (Hester); Lela Bliss (Miss Greene); Virginia Brissac (Miss Seiffert); Queenie Smith (Lola); Mae Marsh (Tommy's Mother); Ashley Cowan (Young Man); Sally Shepherd (Nurse); Geraldine Garrick, Theresa Lyon, Sylvia Andrew, Jeri Jordan, Geraldine Garrick, Marie Blake, Ellen Lowe (Patients).

THE HEIRESS (Paramount, 1949) 115 min.

Producer, William Wyler; associate producers, Lester Koenig, Robert Wyler; director, Wyler; based on the novel Washington Square by Henry James; screenplay, Ruth and Augustus Goetz; art director, John Meehan; set decorator, Emile Kuri; music, Aaron Copland; assistant director, C. C. Coleman, Jr.; makeup, Wally Westmore, Hal Lierly, Bill Woods; sound, Hugo Grenzbach, John Cope; special effects, Gordon Jennings; camera, Leo Tover; editor, William Hornbeck.

Olivia de Havilland (Catherine Sloper); Montgomery Clift (Morris Townsend); Ralph Richardson (Dr. Austin Sloper); Miriam Hopkins (Lavinia Penniman); Vanessa Brown (Maria); Mona Freeman (Marian Almond); Ray Collins (Jefferson Almond); Betty Linley (Mrs. Montgomery); Selena Royle (Elizabeth Almond); Paul Lees (Arthur Townsend); Harry Antrim (Mr. Abeel); Russ Conway (Quintus); David Thursby (Geier).

MY COUSIN RACHEL *(Twentieth Century-Fox, 1953)* 98 min.

Producer, Nunnally Johnson; director, Henry Koster; based on the novel by Daphne du Maurier; screenplay, Johnson; music, Franz Waxman; art directors, Lyle Wheeler, John De Cuir; set decorators, Walter M. Scott; orchestrator, Edward Powell; sound, Alfred Bruzlin, Roger Heman; camera, Joseph La Shelle; editor, Louis Loeffler.

Olivia de Havilland (Rachel); Richard Burton (Philip Ashley); Audrey Dalton (Louise); Ronald Squire (Nick Kendall); George Dolenz (Rainaldi); John Sutton (Ambrose Ashley); Tudor Owen (Seecombe); J. M. Kerrigan (Reverend Pascoe); Margaret Brewster (Mrs. Pascoe); Alma Lawton (Mary Pascoe); Ola Lorraine, Kathleen Mason (Pascoe Children); Earl Robie (Philip at Age Five); Nicholas Koster (Philip at Age Ten); Robin Camp (Philip at Age Fifteen); Argentina Brunetti (Signora); Mario Siletti (Caretaker); Lumsden Hare (Tamblyn); Trevor Ward (Lewin); Victor Wood (Foreman); George Plues (Coachman); Bruce Payne (Groom); James Fairfax, Oreste Seragnoli (Servants).

THAT LADY *(Twentieth Century-Fox, 1955)* C-100 min.

Producer, Sy Bartlett; associate producer, Ronald Kinnoch; director, Terence Young; screenplay, Anthony Veiller, Bartlett; art director, Frank White; music director, John Addison; camera, Robert Krasker.

Olivia de Havilland (Ana de Mendoza); Gilbert Roland (Antonio Perez); Paul Scofield (Philip of Spain); Françoise Rosay (Bernadina); Dennis Price (Mateo Vasquez); Christopher Lee (Bit).

NOT AS A STRANGER *(United Artists, 1955)* 135 min.

Producer/director, Stanley Kramer; based on the novel by Morton Thompson; screenplay, Edna and Edward Anhalt; music/music director, George Antheil; orchestrator, Ernest Gold; production designer, Rudolph Sternad; art director, Howard Richmond; set decorator, Victor Gangelin; costumes, Joe King; gowns, Don Loper; makeup, Bill Wood; assistant director, Carter De Haven, Jr.; dialogue director, Anne Kramer; technical advisors, Morton Maxwell, M.D., Josh Fields, M.D., Marjorie Lefevre, R.N.; sound, Earl Snyder; camera, Franz Planer; editor, Fred Knudtson.

Olivia de Havilland (Kristina Hedvigson); Robert Mitchum (Lucas Marsh); Frank Sinatra (Alfred Boone); Gloria Grahame (Harriet Lang); Broderick Crawford (Dr. Aarons); Charles Bickford (Dr. Runkleman); Myron McCormick (Dr. Snider); Lon Chaney, Jr. (Job Marsh); Jesse White (Ben Cosgrove); Henry "Harry" Morgan (Oley); Lee Marvin (Brundage); Virginia Christine (Bruni); Whit Bissell (Dr. Dietrich); Jack Raine (Dr. Lettering); Mae Clarke (Miss O'Dell).

THE AMBASSADOR'S DAUGHTER *(United Artists, 1956)* C-102 min.

Producer, Norman Krasna; associate producer, Denise Tual; director/screenplay, Krasna; art director, Leon Barsacqu; music director, Jacques Metchen; clothes, Christian Dior; camera, Michael Kelber; editor, Roger Dwyre.

Olivia de Havilland (Joan); John Forsythe (Danny); Myrna Loy (Mrs. Cartwright); Adolphe Menjou (Senator Cartwright); Francis Lederer (Prince Nicholas Obelski); Edward Arnold (Ambassador Fiske); Minor Watson (General Harvey); Tommy Noonan (Al).

THE PROUD REBEL *(Buena Vista, 1958)* C-103 min.

Producer, Samuel Goldwyn, Jr.; director, Michael Curtiz; story, James Edward Grant; screenplay, Joseph Petracca, Lillie Hayward; art director, McClure Capps; set decorator, Victor Gangelin; music, Jerome Moross; orchestrator, Bernard Mayers; assistant director, Paul Helmick; Miss de Havilland's costumes, Mary Wills; makeup, Don Cash, George Bau; sound, Don Hall, Jr.; camera, Ted McCord; editor, Aaron Stell.

Alan Ladd (John Chandler); Olivia de Havilland (Linnett Moore); Dean Jagger (Harry Burleigh); David Ladd (David Chandler); Cecil Kellaway (Dr. Enos Davis); Dean Stanton (Jeb Burleigh); Thomas Pittman (Tom Burleigh); Henry Hull (Judge Morley); Eli Mintz (Gorman); James Westerfield (Birm Bates); John Carradine (Traveling Salesman); King (Lance, the Dog).

LIBEL *(MGM, 1959)* 100 min.

Producer, Anatole de Grunwald; director, Anthony Asquith; based on the play by Edward Wooll; screenplay, de Grunwald, Karl Tunberg; art director, Paul Sheriff; music, Benjamin Frankel; assistant director, David Middlemas; Miss de Havilland's gowns, Christian Dior; special effects, Tom Howard; camera, Robert Krasker; editor, Frank Clark.

Dirk Bogarde (Sir Mark Loddon/Frank Welney/Number Fifteen); Olivia de Havilland (Lady Maggie Loddon); Paul Massie (Jeffrey Buckenham); Robert Morley (Sir Wilfred); Wilfrid Hyde-White (Hubert Foxley); Anthony Dawson (Gerald Loddon); Richard Wattis (Judge); Richard Dimbleby (Himself); Martin Miller (Dr. Schrott); Millicent Martin (Maisie); Bill Shine (Guide); Ivan Samson (Admiral Loddon); Sebastian Saville (Michael Loddon); Gordon Stern (Maddox); Josephine Middleton (Mrs. Squires); Kenneth Griffith (Fitch); Joyce Carey (Miss Sykes).

LIGHT IN THE PIAZZA *(MGM, 1962)* C-101 min.

Producer, Arthur Freed; director, Guy Green; based on the novel by Elizabeth Spencer; screenplay, Julius J. Epstein; art director, Frank White; music, Mario Nascimbene; music director, Dock Mathieson; Miss de Havilland's gowns, Christian Dior; assistant director, Basil Rayburn; makeup, Tom Smith; sound, Cyril

Swern, Robert Carrick; special effects, Tom Howard; camera, Otto Heller; editor, Frank Clarke.

Olivia de Havilland (Margaret Johnson); Rossano Brazzi (Signor Naccarelli); Yvette Mimieux (Clara Johnson); George Hamilton (Farizio Naccarelli); Barry Sullivan (Noel Johnson); Isabel Dean (Miss Hawtree); Moultrie Kelsall (The Minister); Nancy Nevinson (Signora Naccarelli).

LADY IN A CAGE (Paramount, 1964) 100 min.

Producer, Luther Davis; director, Walter Grauman; screenplay, Davis; art director, Rudolph Sternad; set decorator, Joseph Kish; makeup, Wally Westmore, Gene Hibbs; assistant director, Howard Alston; sound, Frank McWhorter; camera, Lee Garmes; editor, Leon Barsha.

Olivia de Havilland (Mrs. Hilyard); Ann Sothern (Sade); Jeff Corey (The Wino); James Caan (Randall); Jennifer Billingsley (Elaine); Rafael Campos (Essie); William Swan (Malcolm Hilyard); Charles Seel (Junkyard Proprietor); Scatman Crothers (His Assistant).

HUSH . . . HUSH, SWEET CHARLOTTE (Twentieth Century-Fox, 1964) C-133 min.

Producer, Robert Aldrich; associate producer, Walter Blake; director, Aldrich; story, Henry Farrell; screenplay, Farrell, Lukas Heller; music, Frank De Vol; title song, De Vol and Mack David; choreography, Alex Ruiz; assistant directors, William McGarry, Sam Strangis; costumes, Norma Koch; art director, William Glasgow; sound, Bernard Fredricks; camera, Joseph Biroc; editor, Michael Luciano.

Bette Davis (Charlotte Hollis); Olivia de Havilland (Miriam Deering); Joseph Cotten (Dr. Drew Bayliss); Agnes Moorehead (Velma Cruther); Cecil Kellaway (Harry Willis); Victor Buono (Big Sam Hollis); Mary Astor (Mrs. Jewel Mayhew); William Campbell (Paul Marchand); Wesley Addy (Sheriff Luke Standish); Bruce Dern (John Mayhew); Dave Willock (Taxi Driver); George Kennedy (Foreman); John Megna (Boy); Ellen Corby, Helen Kleeb, Marianne Stewart (Gossips); Frank Ferguson (News Editor).

THE ADVENTURERS (Paramount, 1970) C-171 min.

Producer/director, Lewis Gilbert; based on the novel by Harold Robbins; screenplay, Michael Hastings, Gilbert; second unit director, Ernest Day; director of action sequences, Bob Simmons; assistant director, Bill Cartlidge; production designer, Tony Masters; art directors, John Hoesli, Aurelio Crugnola, Jack Maxted, Harry Pottle; set decorators, Vernon Dixon, Franco Fumagalli; music, Antonio Carlos Jobim; music director/additional music, Eumir Deodato; costumes, Ronald Paterson; sound, Vernon Harris; camera, Claude Renoir; second unit camera, Skeets Kelly; editor, Anne V. Coates.

Bekim Fehmiu (Dax Xenos); Alan Badel (Rojo);

Candice Bergen (Sue Ann Daley); Ernest Borgnine (Fat Cat); Leigh Taylor-Young (Amparo); Fernando Rey (Jaime Xenos); Thommy Berggren (Sergei Nikovitch); Charles Aznavour (Marcel Campion); Olivia de Havilland (Deborah Hadley); John Ireland (Mr. Hadley); Delia Boccardo (Caroline de Coyne); Sydney Tafler (Colonel Gutierrez); Rossano Brazzi (Baron de Coyne); Anna Moffo (Dania Leonardi); Christian Roberts (Robert); Yorgo Voyagis (El Lobo); Jorge Martinez de Hoyos (El Condor); Angela Scoular (Denisonde); Lois Maxwell (Smart Woman at Fashion Show); Helena Ronee (Lexie); Randi Lind (Blonde at Polo Game); David Canon (Hadley's Secretary); Anthony Hickox (Robert as a Child); Carl Eklund (Sergei as a Child).

THE SCREAMING WOMAN (ABC-TV, 1972) C-76 min.

Producer, William Frye; director, Jack Smight; based on the story by Ray Bradbury; teleplay, Merwin Gerard; costumes, Edith Head; music, John Williams; art director, John E. Chilberg II; set decorator, Don Sullivan; camera, Sam Leavitt; editor, Robert F. Shugrue.

Olivia de Havilland (Laura Wynant); Joseph Cotten (George Tresvant); Walter Pidgeon (Dr. Amos Larkin); Ed Nelson (Carl Nesbitt); Laraine Stephens (Caroline Wynant); Charles Robinson (Howard Wynant); Alexandra Hay (Evie Carson); Charles Drake (Ken Bronson); Joyce Cunning (Bernice Wilson); Ray Montgomery (Ted Wilson); Gene Andrusco (David); Jan Arvan (Martin); Russell C. Wiggins (Harry Sands); John Alderman (Slater).

POPE JOAN (Columbia, 1972) C-132 min.

Executive producer, Leonard C. Lane; producer, Kurt Unger; associate producer, John Briley; director, Michael Anderson; screenplay, John Briley; assistant directors, Peter Bolton, David Tringham, Jake Wright; music, Maurice Jarre; costumes, Elizabeth Haffenden, Joan Bridge; production designer, Elliott Scott; art director, Norman Dorme; sound, Cyril Swern, Ken Scrivenor; sound editor, Alfred Cox; camera, Billy Williams; editor, Bill Lenny.

Liv Ullmann (Joan); Keir Dullea (Dr. Stevens); Robert Beatty (Dr. Corwin); Jeremy Kemp (Joan's Father); Natasa Nicolescu (Joan's Mother); Sharon Winter (Young Joan); Margareta Pogonat (Village Woman); Richard Bebb (Lord of the Manor); Peter Arne (Richard); Patrick Magee (Elder Monk); George Innes, Nigel Havers (Young Monk); Lesley-Anne Down (Cecilia); Susan Macready (Sister Nunciata); Sheelah Wilcocks (Sister Louise); Olivia de Havilland (Mother Superior); Andre Morell (Emperor Louis); Martin Benson (Lothair); Franco Nero (Louis); Kurt Christian (Prince Charles); Maximilian Schell (Adrian); Trevor Howard (Pope Leo); John Byron (Cardinal Jerome); Derek Farr (Cardinal Brisni); Katharine Schofield (Alma); John Shrapnel (Father James); Terrence Hardiman (Cardinal Anastasius).

AIRPORT '77 (*Universal, 1977*) C

Executive producer, Jennings Lang; producer, William Frye; director, Jerry Jameson; screenplay, David Spector, Michael Scheff; art director, George Webb; set decorator, Mickey Michaels; costume designer, Edith Head; technical advisor, Fred Zendar; stunt coordinator, Stan Barrett; assistant directors, Wilbur Mosier, Bob Graner, Jim Nasella; second unit director, Michael Moore; sound, Darin Knight; special visual effects, Albert Whitlock; special effects, Whitey McMahan, Frank Brendel; camera, Philip Lathrop; editor, Terry Williams.

Jack Lemmon (Don Gallagher); Lee Grant (Karen Wallace); Brenda Vaccaro (Eve Clayton); Joseph Cotten (Nicholas St. Downs III); Olivia de Havilland (Emily Livinston); Darren McGavin (Buchek); Christopher Lee (Martin Wallace); Robert Foxworth (Chambers); Robert Hooks (Eddie); George Kennedy (Patrone); James Stewart (Stevens); Monte Markham (Banker); Kathleen Quinlan (Julie); Gil Gerard (Frank Powers); James Booth (Ralph Crawford); Monica Lewis (Anne); Maidie Norman (Dorothy); Pamela Bellwood (Lisa); Arlene Golonka (Mrs. Tern); George Furth (Lucas); Richard Vanture (Commander Guay).

BEHIND THE IRON MASK (*Sascha Wien Films, 1977*) C

Executive producer, Heinz Lazek; producer, Ted Richmond; director, Zen Annakin; based upon the novel *The Man in the Iron Mask* by Alexandre Dumas and a screenplay by George Bruce; new screenplay, David Ambrose; art director, Theo Harisch; costumes, Tony Pueo; music, Riz Ortolani; camera, Jack Cardiff.

With: Beau Bridges, Sylvia Kristel, Ursula Andress, Cornel Wilde, Ian McShane, Lloyd Bridges, Alan Hale, Helmut Dantine, Olivia de Havilland (Queen Anne), Jose Ferrer (Athos), Rex Harrison (Colbert).

A promotional shot for *The Guilt of Janet Ames* ('46).   348

CHAPTER 5

Rosalind Russell

5'5"
120 pounds
Black hair
Dark brown eyes
Gemini

"**I**t's important to make news," the late Rosalind Russell once said about maintaining her show business standing. Throughout her five-decade career, the stylish star displayed boundless energy in pushing herself to the top and remaining there. Quite appropriately, she would portray on stage and in films vivid *Auntie Mame* whose creed might well have been coined especially for Rosalind: "*Life is a banquet and most of you poor fools are starving to death!*"

Over the many years, Russell's Hollywood career underwent remarkable alterations. Each was engineered by Rosalind's determination never to remain *too* long in any given performing stereotype. (She did not always succeed in this goal.) In the Thirties, she was often onscreen as the "other woman" of major films or the attractive, resilient leading lady of minor ones. This was in keeping with her MGM contractee status as the actress oft-assigned Joan Crawford or Myrna Loy discard roles. Occasionally, this newcomer smashed out of the mold as when on loan to Columbia where she portrayed the shrewish spouse of *Craig's Wife* (1936) with insight and imagination.

It was the role of tart-mouthed, hypocritical, brawling Sylvia Fowler in MGM's all-star *The Women* (1939) which provided Rosalind with the proper transition to the

Forties. In the new decade, she became the celluloid progenitor of the hyperactive career worker who discovers in the final reel that she is a very feminine creature. *His Girl Friday* (1940), *My Sister Eileen* (1942), and (too) many entries thereafter demonstrated repeatedly how apt a successor to Carole Lombard, the screwball comedy queen, she was. But Rosalind craved to express her creative juices in other molds. It led to such (over)dramatic interpretations as *Sister Kenny* (1946), *Mourning Becomes Electra* (1947) both Oscar-nominated parts—and the much-ignored thriller, *The Velvet Touch* (1948). (Less kindly observers suggested Rosalind should have stuck to her forte, broad comedy.)

By the Fifties, frightened, changing Hollywood had little need for mature cinema queens like Rosalind. Thus, she returned to Broadway as the singing, dancing, joking star of *Wonderful Town* (1953). This musical rendition of *My Sister Eileen* delighted a mass of ticket buyers and made the actress a viable force in show business' new era. Her unglamorous film role of the spinster school teacher in *Picnic* (1955) should have paved the path for Rosalind's new screen future. But too many considered it a novelty performance and it remained for the ambitious actress to return to Broadway again, this time as the volatile *Auntie Mame* (1956). It was a shrewd move, winning her a new cluster of stage awards and additional boosters. Two years later, she recreated the role of chic Mame Dennis for Warner Bros. and won her fourth Oscar bid. It remained the role with which she was most associated.

Undoubtedly, Rosalind might have coasted along in her Auntie Mame guise for years to come. (She rejected the Broadway musical version, *Mame,* but did play a Mame-like offshoot in the unsuccessful film *Rosie!* in 1968.) However, as a reproven box-office name, she chose to star in a series of major features, each based on a Broadway hit. They offered the desired variety of character studies, but they were demanding artistic challenges that she could not and did not always meet. Among them were: the loving Brooklyn Jewish matron of *A Majority of One* (1961), the emotionally starved wife and mother of *Five Finger Exercise* (1962), and the limelight-bent mama of a stripper named *Gypsy* (1962). Later, Rosalind turned cinematically benevolent, playing a mother superior in *The Trouble with Angels* (1966). It was a saccharine entry bolstered more by impish Hayley Mills than by the mugging of Russell and company. Russell donned nun's garb again for the far less popular sequel, *Where Angels Go . . . Trouble Follows* (1968).

In her last decade, Rosalind's time was devoted largely to charitable works and to battling ill health. She showed remarkable fortitude in coping with her ailments. "Rosalind came to terms with her life and she gave of herself in every way," said director George Cukor. "She met death with the same gallantry."

Rosalind McKnight Russell was born a Catholic in Waterbury, Connecticut, on Sunday, June 4, 1908, to James Edward and Clara Agnes McKnight Russell. She was the fourth of seven children, preceded by Clara, John, and James, and followed by Mary Jane, Josephine, and George. Rosalind often commented, "I'm the ham in the middle." She was named, not for a character from Shakespeare as one might suspect, but for a ship— the S. S. *Rosalind* on which her parents had once taken a vacation to Nova Scotia.

Before her marriage, Clara McKnight Russell had been a fashion editor for a national magazine. James Edward, a well-to-do trial lawyer who had worked his way through Yale Law School, was of the old-fashioned but effective persuasion that if a parent spares the rod he will wind up with a spoiled child. Another of his doctrines was that children should have "all the freedom that is compatible with good manners, ethical conduct, and family honor." Edward also passed on his tallness to his children: he stood 6'2", compared to his wife's 5'3".

Rosalind was a chubby-faced youngster until she reached the age of five or six. Then she shot upward, lost her baby face, and became mostly arms and legs. She was a prankster like most energetic kids, and one of her special tricks was locking her younger sister Mary Jane in dark closets. In an effort to escape the expected parental retribution, she ran to the skirts of the family's Irish cook, a two hundred pounder, who sometimes managed to stave off a threatened spanking.

Rosalind was a lively little girl, whose father attributed her vivacity to being "in tune with life." She was also loud. When her mother would complain about this trait, her father would reply, "She's the only one I can understand at the dinner table."

At the top of the Russells' thirteen-room Victorian house, complete with stained glass windows, carved doors, and gargoyles, was an attic which housed the family billiard table, a miniature bowling alley, and a card table! There, Rosalind, who was already known as Roz, was introduced to indoor sports. She delighted in beating her brothers at billiards and learned to play poker like a true Mississippi River gambler. Out back of the house stood a stable containing two horses. There, she became acquainted with the outdoor sport of riding. Her father, moreover, insisted that the older children take turns riding each day after school, no matter how inclement the weather might be. Often, for a fee, Rosalind would ride her horse as she led the others behind her, while her brothers and sisters dawdled elsewhere. Mr. Russell, who always inspected the horses when he returned from work, therefore believed that his offspring were obeying his instructions to ride each day. "Don't think I did this because I loved horses," Rosalind was to write in *The Saturday Evening Post* in 1962, "I loved money, and I charged each brother and sister what I thought the traffic would bear."

It was not long before she was known as the neighborhood tomboy because of her competitive antics with the boys. During such exhibits of feminine prowess, she fractured, in turn, her left leg, her left wrist, her left collarbone, and her left arm (twice). Although the family physician stated that her bones were brittle, she was blessed with rapid recuperative powers and always bounced back for more. She was also inclined toward music, and learned to beat her brother's tap drums as well as play a kazoo, ukulele, and banjo. At summer camp she won a cup for being the best all-around athlete, and at the age of twelve considered herself eligible as a contestant in a regatta diving contest held at Laurel Beach, Connecticut. "I could dive noiselessly," she remembered. "I was built like a pipe cleaner, so there was nothing about me to splash when I hit the water."

Although her chief competitor in this event was a well-developed lass of eighteen, "I told myself confidently that diving form, not maiden form would pay off." Everything went well for Rosalind, and her self-confidence was high until she stood on tip-toe on the springboard for the big dive. At that moment, the single button on her bathing suit—the one that held it in place—popped off, and her suit fell to her knees, "exposing practically nothing." She blushed from mortification and jumped, feet first, into the water. Weeping, she swam for the shore where the first objects she could spot through her tears were the brown and white sport shoes she knew to be filled by her father's feet. He looked down, but she could not look up at him. His words of the moment, "Rosalind, a winner never quits and a quitter never wins," would forever remain with the scrawny, naked girl in the water.

At an early age, Rosalind derived much-wanted attention from making faces (crossed eyes, screwed-up nose and mouth), and she practiced with new grimaces in front of the various mirrors in the house. To appease her mother, not because of personal pleasure, she studied toe dancing. At the conclusion of one laborious session, just to gain attention she screamed, "Look! My toes are bleeding!"

Her sister, Mary Jane, once reported that Rosalind "always wanted to be the boss of everything." She was a naturally bright student in school and found that she could pass the required subjects with a minimum of effort. It was during her later years at Notre Dame Academy, a convent school which her mother had also attended, that Rosalind became an admirer of Rudolph Valentino. One day to alleviate her academic boredom she ran off to the local movie house which was showing one of the Sheik's features. When she was fourteen, she wrote a Christmas play which she staged for family and friends. She took on the roles of the Spirit of Christmas, Santa Claus, and Baby Jesus, deftly changing from one costume to another.

With high school behind her, in 1926 Rosalind was enrolled at the all-woman Marymount College in Tarrytown, New York. During her first year, she was given the lead in the freshman class play, based on the life of St. Francis Xavier. She wore a beard, wig, and flowing toga. "I was so filled with bubbles of excitement that I felt like a carbonated drink." Her performance as the sainted man, required to flagellate himself onstage, reportedly produced tears throughout the audience and Rosalind fell victim to acting fever. Later that year she acted in the college's Christmas play and the following year she was selected by the senior class to join their annual presentation.

James Edward Russell died of a heart attack while Rosalind—age nineteen—was at Marymount. His estate, which he left to his wife and children, was valued at $500,000. However, his last will and testament, considered unique at the time, provided for his offspring to have as much education as they wished, but none of them was to receive any inheritance until each had worked for three years. "He didn't want us to sit around, drink cocktails, play bridge, and wait for husbands. We had to get going."

Rosalind got going by not returning to Marymount. Instead, she enrolled at the American Academy of Dramatic Arts in New York City. To her mother, who thrived on attending the theatre but whose opinion of stage actors was far from high, Rosalind fibbed a little by saying that her ultimate career goal was to teach drama. "Teaching will be nice, Rosalind," her mother confided, "because you'll have long vacations. Moreover, it will be a broadening experience."

In the spring of 1929, as she neared the completion of her one-year Academy course, Rosalind fulfilled the requirement that each student play the lead in one school play. She was Fay Cheyney, the not-so-honest lady who mends her ways, in *The Last of Mrs. Cheyney,* written by Frederick Lonsdale. In the audience for her starring performance, along with her mother and sister Mary Jane, were talent scouts and a gentleman who owned a summer stock company in Greenwich, Connecticut. The latter went backstage and offered Rosalind a spot in his repertory group at a salary of $150 a week (a good sum in 1929) but she, who had been told that actors were always expected to haggle over salary figures, replied boldly, "not enough." The gentleman made a speedy exit.

Although Rosalind did not get that job, the offer itself was sufficient to convince Mrs. Russell that her daughter was good enough to pursue a career on the stage. For four days after leaving the Academy, Rosalind walked the sidewalks from agents' offices to casting offices. On the fifth day, she learned that Ed Casey whose summer theatre was located at Saranac Lake, New York, was in need of actresses. The determined fledgling cornered Casey and his wife in the lobby of the Astor Hotel, where she asked for a weekly salary of $150 based on her non-existent experience of having worked onstage in Pittsburgh.

Casey was hesitant to pay that much, but Mrs. Casey liked Rosalind and she was hired. The Casey Company performed in a tent at Saranac Lake and during the thirteen-week engagement Rosalind acted in twenty-six plays. "We rehearsed all morning, played golf every afternoon, and stayed up all night.

We lived on youth, energy, and no sleep. It was a wonderful summer."

From there, she became the leading lady to E. E. Clive's Copley Theatre in Boston, a repertory company composed largely of British actors. She assimilated an English accent so well that most of the company believed she was London-born. The summer of 1930 found her doing stock work at Lake Placid, New York, and at Stockbridge, Massachusetts.

On October 16, 1930, she opened with the fourth edition of *The Garrick Gaieties* at the Guild Theatre in Manhattan. In this revue, which consisted of sketches that spoofed theatre and The Theatre Guild, Rosalind played Nina Guild in a burlesque of Eugene O'Neill's *Strange Interlude* and, in another sequence, she portrayed the Queen to Albert Carroll's King George. She toured with *The Garrick Gaieties* at $300 a week and after that toured briefly in *Roar China!* and in *As Husbands Go*. On April 20, 1931, she was back on Broadway at the Lyceum Theatre as a southern belle named Miss Mallory in *Company's Coming*. This show closed after eight performances and Rosalind returned to summer stock at Worcester and Boston, working for William Brady. This engagement was followed with a job on the Wee and Leventhal-owned Subway Circuit. ". . . as all actors know, [they] paid the least money of any organization that ever existed. . . . I refused to work for minimum [$40]. I had gotten quite a fancy sum of money from the Theatre Guild and was very impressed by that. So I said, 'No. I just can't do it.' They gave me five dollars more, and I said all right!"

To supplement her income, Rosalind played pinochle with producer Leventhal who was a born card-loser. "I managed to hit him for about seventy dollars at least once a week," she was to recall. "He was even worse as a pinochle player than he was as a producer." She also modeled dresses at Saks Fifth Avenue for a brief period. "I sold everything I wore and I spent everything I earned for lunch at 21."

Talent, a play starring popular Mady Christians, was considered by many as a sure-fire hit for Broadway. Roz took a fea-

tured role, but soon found herself out of a job when the play closed in out-of-town tryouts in the fall of 1933. While playing in Baltimore in a road company revival of *The Second Man* with Bert Lytell, she received a notice in the mail suggesting that she call at the New York offices of Universal Studios.

Although "I had always said that I wanted no part of films—at least not this early in my career," she trooped to the Radio City building which then housed the Universal offices. A company man told her the studio was interested in her and offered Rosalind $300 a week. When "I shook my head and said I'd have to have $750," the man counter-offered with $400. That is when Rosalind's burgeoning dictatorial nature demonstrated itself in full force. "I'm either worth $750 a week or I'm not worth a dime," she proclaimed. "I'll go to the coast . . . you'll pay all my expenses out and back. You can test me every day for two weeks, and I'll be paid $100 a test. If you like me after looking at my tests, you will pay me $750 a week. Otherwise I'll return to New York." To her mild astonishment, she was hired on that optional type of agreement.

After arriving in Hollywood, she deposited her luggage at a hotel and immediately checked in at Universal. She was forced to wait for an hour before the casting director found time to meet with her. His quick solution to the problem of what to do with her was to send her to the makeup department. The cosmetic artists passed her over to the hair stylists who were also too busy to pay her much heed. So a frustrated Rosalind returned to her hotel.

From there, she contacted Charlotte Wynters (later to become Mrs. Barton MacLane), an actress whom she had known in Eastern stock and who had become a featured player in movies. At Charlotte's invitation, she moved into her apartment where she sat for three days before Universal contacted her to appear for screen test number one. She was sent a script and was alerted to report to the studio makeup department at 6:00 the following morning.

In return for her punctuality, she was once more given the run-around by both makeup

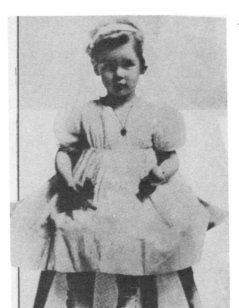

At the age of six.

MGM glamour pose in →
'35.

With Billie Burke and Joan Crawford
in *Forsaking All Others* ('34).

artists and hair stylists who were too busy to be concerned with the newcomer. After a fruitless wait, she walked over to the appointed stage nine for the test and waited in the dark. Finally, director John Stahl, who was to handle the audition, came into the building and asked the obvious (to him) question, "Why aren't you made up?" In attempting a reply, she lost her temper and said, "I couldn't care what I look like. I know the cues. I know the lines. I'm paid to act. So twirl the film in your Kodak or whatever you do." She made the test, collected her $100, and went home.

In the weeks that followed, she was to make eight more such tests, most of them showing the side or back of her head as she fed lines to handsome, male potentials. During this time, she also made a test at MGM for Gregory LaCava who was casting *What Every Woman Knows* (1934). The professionalism at MGM impressed her so much—compared to Universal's state of confusion—that she wanted to work for them instead.

But as luck would have it, Carl Laemmle, Jr., who ran Universal, returned from a European trip and announced that he intended to pick up Rosalind's option with a seven-year contract. This, she did not want—not after having experienced the superior quality of the Metro lot.

She pondered the predicament when roommate Charlotte happened to mention that Junior Laemmle was particularly fond of beautiful women. This small fact provided Rosalind's quick mind with an outrageous plan of escape. For her meeting with the young executive, where she expected to receive the good news, she wore a red and white dress with a wide boatneck "that showed all my collarbones." She painted her mouth into a red blotch, greased her hair with vaseline, plopped a sad-looking hat atop all that greased hair, stepped into a pair of dirty white shoes with rundown heels, and carefully twisted her stockings so that the seams ran crookedly down her legs.

Once inside Laemmle's office, she sat on a couch with her eyes glued to the carpet. As Miss Russell related to Mike Steen for the

book of interviews *Hollywood Speaks* (1974), "The outfit wasn't comical, but it was really pretty sexless. And I wore a very tight bra which I didn't need, being sunken-chested. Mr. Laemmle was very polite, but I couldn't look at him. He said, 'You're the young actress from New York.' I said in a nasal voice, 'I'm very unhappy here.' He said, 'Pardon me?' I said, 'I'm very unhappy here.' He said, 'I hope no one has mistreated you.' I said, 'No. No. I'm just very unhappy here, and I want to go back to New York.' This went on for about ten minutes, and he said, 'Well I think we can arrange for you to go back.' I said, 'I want to go back, and I need a piece of paper to tell me I can go.' There was an agent named Al Melnick sitting outside who knew me from New York. He couldn't get over the way I looked and was acting. He kept saying, 'How are you, Roz?' I would only reply a quick, 'I'm fine.' It was a riot. So within about ten minutes I got a release. . . ."

Roz happily dashed home to clean up and then rushed to MGM where she signed a standard term contract at $750 a week. This was in August 1934 and "that was the start of my marathon in pictures."

The role for which she was tested in *What Every Woman Knows* was given to another contractee (Madge Evans), but Roz's initial onscreen efforts were impressive in *Evelyn Prentice* (MGM, 1934). In the role of the divorced Nancy Harrison, she puts the storyline into action by having a quick out-of-town affair with criminal lawyer John Prentice (William Powell). When John's wife Evelyn (Myrna Loy) learns of her husband's infidelity, she has an affair with a youngish poet (Harvey Stephens) to whom she writes revealing letters of love. Released in November 1934, *Evelyn Prentice* was aimed at cashing in on the growing popularity of the Powell-Loy (Nick and Nora Charles) witty combination of *The Thin Man* (June 1934) but fans were largely disappointed with the seriousness with which lawyer Prentice and wife Evelyn viewed this particular murder and domestic conflict.

In rapid succession, Rosalind had a small parts on loan to Paramount for *The President*

Vanishes (November 1934) as the wife of an American lobbyist (Sidney Blackmer), in *Forsaking All Others* (December 1934) as the sophisticated, well-gowned (by Adrian) sister to Joan Crawford who periodically switches from one romantic partner to another (from Robert Montgomery to Clark Gable), and in *The Night Is Young* (January 1935) as the Austrian Countess Rafay who adores musical theatre and Archduke Franz Otto (Ramon Novarro) while he pines for songstress Lisl Gluck (Evelyn Laye). Roz was again a loser at love in MGM's *West Point of the Air* (February 1935), in which she played an actress who would like to ensnare Robert Young for herself rather than have him become the ace of the Army's air corps, the goal his gruff father (Wallace Beery) set for him. Young prefers flying and the general's daughter (Maureen O'Sullivan) to a backseat life with the flighty stage performer.

The S. S. Van Dine mystery stories provided many anxious moments for movie fans, beginning in 1929 when the first Philo Vance (William Powell) solved his first onscreen murder. Powell portrayed Vance five times: *The Canary Murder Case* (Paramount, 1929), *The Greene Murder Case* (Paramount, 1929), *The Benson Murder Case* (Paramount, 1930), *Paramount on Parade* (1930), and *The Kennel Murder Case* (Warner Bros., 1933). Basil Rathbone and Warren William tackled the Vance characterization once each, *The Bishop Murder Case* (MGM, 1930) and *The Dragon Murder Case* (Warner Bros., 1934) respectively. In 1935 MGM offered the least effective Vance in the acting personage of foreign-accented Paul Luckas in *The Casino Murder Case*. In second billing, Rosalind is Doris Llewellyn who blunderingly offers aid to detective Vance while members of her family are being killed by poison. While the *New York Times'* Andre Sennwald related, "Rosalind Russell works very hard at being agreeable in the Myrna Loy style, but with no vast success," Rosalind referred to the film as "a real bomb" and "the worst picture I ever made."

Besides Charlotte Wynters, Rosalind's other good friend was actress Nedda Harrigan, the wife of portly character actor Walter Connolly (and still later she would wed Joshua Logan). While Charlotte and Nedda shared popularity with men, Rosalind rarely found herself having a second date with the same man. In puzzling why this was so, her friends bluntly told her, "You just talk too much." She wore clothes well and when she failed to convince anyone that she could be the sexy man-luring type (as in *West Point of the Air*), MGM focused on presenting her as a clotheshorse, both onscreen and in fan magazine layouts.

In April 1935, Roz was seen in *Reckless* (MGM) as society girl Jo Mercer, garbed in the high fashion of the day. She is a stout fellow who displays good breeding by fine sportsmanship when she loses her fiancé (Franchot Tone) to showgirl Mona Leslie (Jean Harlow). To Mona she says, "Now that I've seen you I can understand my defeat," while to her ex-beau she confides, "I won't say she is any better than I am, but she's just as good." At Jo's wedding, later, to Ralph (Leon Ames), her ex-suitor apologizes to her and drunkenly states that he had been coerced by Mona into marrying her.

China Seas (MGM, 1935), another Jean Harlow vehicle (this time with Clark Gable), has Rosalind as the very aristocratic and very British* Sybil Barclay. Roz is a passenger on the *Kin Lung*, a ship captained by Alan Gaskell (Gable) en route from Hong Kong to Singapore. Gaskell and Sybil are past sweethearts who still have a yen for one another. Also on board is Gaskell's mistress, China Doll (Harlow), who has an instant jealous fit when she sees how close Gaskell and Sybil are. After much adventure, involving Chinese pirates eager to capture the ship's cargo of

---

* Miss Russell related to Mike Steen in his oral history, *Hollywood Speaks* "I played the second woman from about nine months to a year. I played the love competition to Myrna Loy or Jean Harlow, which was always a laugh. Clark Gable would go for me for ten minutes, then run right back to Jean Harlow. I wasn't very convincing in those parts because I was always very lofty, very 'Lady Mary.' I had lines like: 'What can you see in that girl? Dear me. She seems so vulgar. . . . Again [in *China Seas*], I was very British. I came from jolly old London and went out to the wilds of China. Clark asks Jean, 'Why don't you like her?' whatever my name was, and Jean says, 'I don't know. She's just so 'refeened.' It's a pronunciation I've used ever since. I'll say, 'She's one of the 'refeened' types.' I don't even know anymore that I'm saying it."

gold, Sybil reappears in the plot. She tells Gaskell that he really loves China Doll. Rosalind, in fifth billing, was still losing the man!

Of this period in her career, Rosalind would later reveal to *Time* magazine (March 30, 1953), "I never had the big publicity build-up. In the eyes of the studio, my work was limited . . . when I asked for better publicity, they would say 'There just isn't any story in you. Now, if you were born on the wrong side of the tracks, we could start out with the old torn wallpaper and then pan over to your mink-lined swimming pool.'"

In the spring of 1935, Myrna Loy, who had ascended the Hollywood ladder from bit parts to playing Oriental ladies of mystery to the exalted level of one of MGM's brightest stars, went on a strike for more money. While she bided her time with a boat trip to Europe, she was first replaced by Luise Rainer in *Escapade* (1935) with William Powell. In June 1935, it was announced that Rosalind would be substituted for the errant Miss Loy in the studio's film version of Major Herbert O. Yardley's book of World War I espionage, *American Black Chamber*. The *Hollywood Reporter* of June 6 pointed out, "This is the biggest break to date for Miss Russell, who has been steadily climbing since being brought out here from the New York stage."

Paired with William Powell, the film emerged as *Rendezvous* in October 1935, and Andre Sennwald (*New York Times*) referred to Rosalind as "Metro-Goldwyn-Mayer's second-string Myrna Loy," whose part "might have seemed considerably less kittenish if Miss Loy had been in [it]." At one point in this account of espionage-laden Washington, D.C., Powell's character has to slug heroine Roz to keep her from bouncing into the path of bullets. Powell did the same thing to Myrna Loy in the famous *The Thin Man*.

By January 1936, Rosalind had taken what was described by *Time* magazine as "the smallest house in Beverly Hills." The house consisted of kitchen, bedroom, living room, and bath. As a hobby she collected first editions of children's books. It was reported that she suffered from chronic insomnia, and sometimes could not fall asleep until dawn.

She entertained often and used "every decorous reason she [could] invent to detain guests." (In the course of the year, sister Mary Jane would be a house guest when she tested at MGM for a screen contract that did not materialize.)

Despite the views of critics such as Andre Sennwald, Louis B. Mayer was pleased with Rosalind's performance in *Rendezvous*, and although Miss Loy returned to her slot at the studio, Rosalind would continue to be Mayer's ace-in-the-stable whenever Loy threatened to depart from the lot. Rosalind later said that she and Miss Loy became good friends through it all and "Myrna and I still roar with laughter when we talk about it." As Roz confessed to *The Saturday Evening Post* in 1962, "Once I was in the wardrobe department being fitted, ready to replace her in a part when Myrna walked in, 'Take it off, Roz, darling. They just gave me the raise.'"

Critic Richard Watts of the *New York Herald-Tribune* placed himself squarely in Rosalind's corner after viewing *Rendezvous* by writing that he wished "Miss Russell, who is one of the most interesting and beautiful of the cinema's new lady sophisticates, hadn't been forced to appear as a complete nitwit, but anyway she is one of the greatest pleasures of the film, even if miscast as one of the dumbest women of all time."

With Miss Loy back to work, MGM was at a loss as to their immediate plans for Rosalind. Obviously, she couldn't return to the type of roles previous to *Rendezvous* in which she lost the man to Jean Harlow, Joan Crawford, or Maureen O'Sullivan, so she was temporarily loaned to Twentieth Century-Fox for two successive films. During the shooting of the first one, *It Had to Happen* (1936), she was stricken with a recurring thyroid problem. Although she was ill throughout much of the filming, it does not show in her performance. Once again she is a sophisticate (named Beatrice) who initially encounters Italian immigrant, Enrico Scaffa (George Raft) aboard a trans-Atlantic ship; she travels first class while he rides in steerage. When they meet again, it is four years later and she is wed to corporation banker Rodman Drake (Alan

Dinehart) while Enrico, having won the favor of the city's mayor, is now a high politico on the city payroll. Drake's corporation is shy four million dollars and Enrico offers to protect him from prosecution if the funds are returned. In the interim, he makes a hearty play for Beatrice who actually pretends to swoon over Enrico's advances but later tells him that she finds him bearable only after several hearty drinks of champagne. When he asks why he's not good enough for her, she replies, "Because I'm really a snob and have had tradition and prejudices drilled into me ever since I can remember." At the finale, she is left holding her traditions when her husband takes off for parts unknown with the four-million-dollar kitty.

Although she received fourth billing in *Under Two Flags* (Twentieth Century-Fox, 1936), she did not lose the man. In fact, he (Ronald Colman) was hers from the start. It is just that Claudette Colbert,* as Cigarette, who has a passion for Colman, gets in the way of their romance from time to time. Colman's commandant, Major Doyle (Victor McLaglen), who has a yen for the fiery Cigarette, incorrectly believes that Corporal Victor (Colman) is courting her and eases him out of the scene with a transfer to a desert outpost which is habitually surrounded by hostile Arabs. Cigarette follows, but only to tell Corporal Victor that she has decided to marry the major. That is when the Arabs attack and Cigarette is killed by the fiendish Sidi Ben Youssiff (Onslow Stevens). The corporal lives to return to the waiting arms of his true love.

Roz was back at the MGM lot for the filming of Robert Louis Stevenson's macabre tale, "Suicide Club," which for some well-intentioned reason reached the screen with the innocuous title, *Trouble for Two* (1936). The two of the title are Prince Florizel (Robert Montgomery with a moustache) and Colonel Geraldine (Frank Morgan) who seek a touch of excitement before Florizel must leave to marry Princess Brenda of Irania. These marriage plans were not made in heaven, but by the ruling factions of both mythical nations some twenty years before, and the prince has no idea what his betrothed is like. In London, on their quest for a good time, the two gentlemen meet a young man (Louis Hayward) with tarts who introduces them to the Suicide Club which is comprised of persons who are bored with life and play a game of cards to see which of them is to die that day. In the club is the cynical, snobbish Miss Vandeleur (Rosalind) who, it develops, is actually Princess Brenda. The club abounds with intrigue as well as a plot to overthrow a government. But through the prince, Miss Vandeleur finds a reason for continuing her life on a level less dedicated to death. The potentially engaging project failed to arouse much interest among filmgoers. It was just another picture.

There was but one woman making a striking success at directing Hollywood movies in the mid-Thirties, Dorothy Arzner. When Miss Arzner undertook the translation of the George Kelly play *Craig's Wife,* to the talking screen for Columbia (it had been silently filmed in 1928 by Pathé with Irene Rich and Warner Baxter, and had been a 1925 Broadway presentation with Chrystal Herne), she insisted that Harry Cohn borrow Rosalind from MGM for the title role. At a cost of $280,000 and after a four-week shooting schedule, *Craig's Wife* reached the country's cinema screens October 2, 1936, with Rosalind in her first top billed performance.

At age twenty-eight, she portrayed Harriet Craig, a complex woman of "maturity," and did it well. The wife of Walter Craig (John Boles) has the security of a well-organized house with every piece of furniture and accessory positioned just as she wants it. She is obsessed with her demands that no one should disrupt even the smallest ash tray. She dominates her husband and servants (Jane Darwell and Nydia Westman) who become no more than fixtures within this house that is not a home. Eventually, all of Mrs. Craig's family, including a niece (Dorothy Wilson) and Walter Craig's aunt (Alma Kruger), servants, and friends leave her. Now alone,

* The part had originally been set for studio head Darryl F. Zanuck's French import, Simone Simon. When that actress was deemed insufficient for the demands of the part, the role was considered for Clara Bow but given to Miss Colbert.

With Alan Marshal in
Night Must Fall ('37).

→

With George Raft in a pose
for *It Had to Happen* ('36).

With Cesar Romero in
Rendezvous ('35).

she discovers that her self-built shrine is an awesome, empty place. Her performance was judged by Frank S. Nugent (*New York Times*) as "viciously eloquent." While *Rendezvous* of the previous year had raised her from the second fiddle status, *Craig's Wife* established her as an actress and a star. Rosalind would re-create the role, with Herbert Marshall as Craig, on the "Lux Radio Theatre" on May 12, 1941. The property would be remade by Columbia in 1950 as *Harriet Craig*, with Joan Crawford as the fussy woman and Wendall Corey as her hen-pecked spouse.

Rosalind returned to MGM for the screen version of Emlyn Williams' play *Night Must Fall* (1937), a shocker that had enjoyed a two-year London run but saw only two months of presentation on Broadway in late 1936. The film catapulted Robert Montgomery from his celluloid playboy category into stardom by showing him as Danny, a hotel pageboy whose insane conceit causes him to commit two murders and to plan a third. The brash young Cockney has brutally murdered a woman at his place of employment and buried her body, minus the head, in a woods. Mrs. Bransom (Dame May Whitty) a wheelchair-confined hypochondriac, sends for Danny to give him a tongue-lashing for playing around with her maid (Merle Tottenham). But she becomes so enchanted by him that she hires the lad as her nurse-companion.

He moves into the Bransom cottage, bag and baggage, which includes a mysterious leather hat box. Also living in the cottage is Mrs. Bransom's niece Olivia (Rosalind) who has little sympathy for Aunty's complaints of ill health. Olivia takes an immediate dislike to Danny, a feeling which soon develops into fascination. She suspects that he is the murderer of the woman at the hotel and even protects him and his hat box when the police inspector (Matthew Boulton) calls. When the headless body is found, Olivia is certain that the hat box contains the head, but she continues to silently watch the man as he charms the old lady. Twice Olivia attempts to leave, but she returns each time. The second return is the night Danny murders Mrs. Bransom by

smothering her with a pillow. As he plots to kill Olivia too, the police investigator returns and Danny, now that his deeds are known, is reduced to a blithering idiot. *Time* magazine considered the movie as "easily the most interesting item in the year's cinema file on criminology." Although both Montgomery and Dame May received Oscar nominations, neither won.

Rosalind abandoned drama for the MGM comedy *Live, Love and Learn* (1937), again opposite debonair Robert Montgomery. She is Julie Stoddard, a social register heiress who meets artist Bob Graham (Montgomery) when her horse jumps a countryside wall and collides with his painting of a portion of the landscape. The demure, self-effacing society gal takes a shine to the dedicated artist and soon has him altar-bound. They set up house-keeping within a Greenwich Village garret (which seems too posh for a struggling artist). Their neighbor is a booze-consuming wit (Robert Benchley). Lily Chalmers (Helen Vinson) appears on the scene to threaten the matrimonial bliss of the Grahams but only temporarily. The *New York Sun* found that the movie "makes the usual point of Metro's recent comedies, that all the moral people are stuffed shirts, that only the irresponsible lunatics know how to live."

Man-Proof (MGM, 1938) was next on Rosalind's agenda, in while she has the second-billed role, following Myrna Loy and Franchot Tone. Again as a rich gal, she marries unemployed Walter Pidgeon who has jilted Loy but who returns from his honeymoon still entranced with chic Miss Loy. On the sidelines, waiting for Myrna to come to her senses is Tone. The *New York Times* criticized the affair for having taken place in "the glamorous, opulent, unreal world of Metro-Goldwyn-Mayer."

Roz was loaned to Warner Bros. in 1938 for the third-slot role of Jean Christy, an aggressive newspaper woman, in *Four's a Crowd*. The remainder of the "crowd" is made up of Errol Flynn in a rare comedy role, Olivia de Havilland, and Patric Knowles. The piece, as directed by Michael Curtiz, is concerned with Flynn as public relations hotshot R. K. Lansford who wants wealthy, cantankerous John P. Dillingwell (Walter Connolly) as a client. In pursuit of his goal, he courts the rich man's pretty but giggly granddaughter Lorri (de Havilland). To feel the pulse of the situation, he returns to his old job of managing editor of a newspaper owned by Patterson Buckley (Knowles), where he likewise pursues Jean (Roz) in order to keep her from revealing his plans. Jean is more worldly than the naive granddaughter and perceives that Lansford is up to no good. Hoping to divert Jean's suspicions, he proposes marriage. He smoothly shifts gears to extricate himself from both situations, but winds up in a taxi cab with the two girls and Knowles, bound for a Justice of the Peace (Hugh Herbert). A marriage is scheduled to take place, but no one is too sure who will marry whom. Jean states matter of factly, "Oh, what a mess this is," and it is, but she winds up as Lansford's bride, while Lorri marries Buckley.

For Roz's oncamera wedding outfit, Orry-Kelly designed a dark, two piece pin-striped dress to match the dark, pin-striped suit worn by Flynn. Under Curtiz' breezy direction. Roz displayed the fast-tongued dialogue for which she was to soon become noted. She would later rate Flynn as "the most handsome actor I've worked with. . . .He was also the most courteous, mannerly, and chivalrous star I ever knew. Just by kissing your hand, that man could make the old heart throb."

As the second film to be made at its British headquarters, MGM chose the A. J. Cronin book, *The Citadel* (1938). Rosalind, the only American in the cast, was in the solid company of English actors Robert Donat, Ralph Richardson, Rex Harrison, Emlyn Williams, Francis Sullivan, and Cecil Parker. Filmed at on-the-spot locales in Wales and London, the film recounted the story of Andrew Manson (Donat), a dedicated man of medicine who sets up a practice in a small Welsh town. He loves his work and is awed by the wonders of medical knowledge. He woos and weds Christine (Rosalind), the local school marm who is the ideal wife for such a man. Later, when Andrew becomes discouraged at his inability to control the spread of tuberculosis,

they go to London where they meet the Harley Street Doctor Lawford (Rex Harrison) through whom Andrew becomes intrigued with the financial remunerations offered by society folk with imaginary or minor ills. Against Christine's advice, Manson enters the world of profiteering. Eventually, because of her standards, he learns that his London practice is unfulfilling for him and they return to small-town doctoring. As directed by King Vidor, *The Citadel* was named by *Film Daily* as one of the ten best movies of 1938 and was selected as the number one motion picture of the year by the New York Film Critics. It was also honored with the *Look* magazine Achievement Award and was nominated for several Academy Awards (but won none). Rosalind was honored by *Boxoffice* magazine as recipient of its Blue Ribbon award.

Since MGM had not had the opportunity to appraise Rosalind's serious acting in *The Citadel*, they consequently placed her opposite Robert Montgomery in *Fast and Loose* (1939), their fifth and last film together. The programmer (the studio was still trying to punish Montgomery for wanting to break out of his established screen mold) was the second of three whodunit movies adapted from a Marco Page detective novel, concerning the hectic adventures of Joel Sloane and his wife, Garda, a rare-book dealer. Because *The Thin Man* series (also a MGM product) of films was doing so well at the box-office, the studio obviously sought to ring up additional dollars with the Sloane duo. Inexplicably, however, the lead characters were played by different actors in each film. In the initial entry, *Fast Company* (1938), Joel and Garda were played by Melvyn Douglas and Florence Rice; in the second, *Fast and Loose*, it was Montgomery and Rosalind; while the third and final outing, *Fast and Furious* (1939), had Franchot Tone and Ann Sothern enacting the roles. *Fast and Loose* has been described as "jauntily paced" and as a "deft light comedy" which fits the bill of detective Joel who gets dragged into the middle of a pair of murders, committed in the hope of acquiring a rare Shakespearian manuscript valued at $500,000. Of course, since Garda is quite

With director Dorothy
Arzner on the set of *Craig's
Wife* ('36).

With Myrna Loy, Franchot Tone,
and Walter Pidgeon in a publicity
shot for *Man-Proof* ('38).

In a pose from *The Citadel* ('38) with Robert Donat.

With Walter Connolly, Errol Flynn, and Olivia de Havilland in *Four's a Crowd* ('38).

At Santa Anita race track with her mother (February 1938).

A promotional shot with Robert Montgomery for *Fast and Loose* ('39).

knowledgeable in the area of rare documents, she is brought into the case by a wide-eyed husband. She all but solves the mystery for him.

On February 20, 1939, a constantly busy Roz was heard over the Cecil B. DeMille-hosted "Lux Radio Theatre" in an hour-long version of *Stage Door.* She took on the role of Terry Randall, played by Katharine Hepburn in the 1937 RKO film. Also in the radio cast, from the original movie were Ginger Rogers and Adolphe Menjou. During 1939, Rosalind was also a guest on the inaugural program of "Silver Theatre" hosted by Conrad Nagel, and made a special appearance on the "Edgar Bergen and Charlie McCarthy Show."

According to legend, Rosalind auditioned five times before producer Hunt Stromberg and director George Cukor finally accepted her as Sylvia Fowler in their screen presentation of *The Women* (MGM, 1939). When Roz burlesqued the character in her fifth test, director Cukor hired her—thus leaving behind forever the pretty-faced Russell of *The Citadel.* Her cinema fate was unknowingly sealed. In her lengthy interview with Mike Steen, *supra,* Miss Russell recalls, "I had just [sic] finished a drama, *Night Must Fall.* . . . Hunt Stromberg produced that, and he was going to produce *The Women.* So I went to Elizabeth Arden one day and I came out in a rather red hat. Dolled up, you know. I drove to the studio. It was about five in the afternoon. I knew Hunt, and I went up to his office and said, 'Hunt, tell me. Why haven't you tested me for the part of Sylvia? Why haven't you considered me at all for it?. . .He said, 'We considered you, but you are too beautiful.' . . . I said, 'Now, Hunt, that is ridiculous. Just ridiculous.' He said, 'What we want is somebody to look funny.' So I crossed my eyes and said, 'Will this do? If not, I'll go down to the makeup people and come back with a wart!' He said, 'We would like to get a laugh every time she pokes her head around a door. You are very fine dramatic actress, but you are not a comedienne.' I said, 'Ah, ah, ah, ah, ah, you cannot say that. No decisions can be made like that until I've played comedy. Then you might say,

'you don't make me laugh.' That is your privilege. . . .We laughed and had a friendly chat, and I went home. As I came into my house, the phone was ringing. It was Hunt and he said, 'Roz, I want you to come and make the test.' I must say, my first words were, "What about Miss [Ilka] Chase [who had done the role on Broadway and had been hired to repeat it in the film version]? He sharply replied, 'You haven't got the part yet.' But he said, 'Her contract isn't exclusive for this part alone. She'll get something else, if and when, but. . . .' So they sent a Red Arrow delivery boy with the script."

Clare Boothe wrote *The Women* as a play, and it became a Broadway hit of the 1936-1937 season. When MGM acquired the screen rights, there was but one director who knew women almost as well as women themselves—George Cukor. Three big names filled the starring spots: Norma Shearer, Joan Crawford, and Rosalind—with Paulette Goddard, Mary Boland, and Joan Fontaine in support. Adapted for the screen by Anita Loos* and Jane Murfin, it is a story of virulent women who, when miserable, get a big kick out of seeing their friends miserable too.

Norma Shearer as Mary Haines appears to be the most normal of the story's ladies but she exudes too much sweetness to be credible. It is the news of Mary's husband's affair with shopgirl Crystal Allen (Crawford) that provides the impetus for the whole plot. Sylvia Fowler (Roz) learns of the affair while at the beauty parlor and is unable to contain herself until she can pass on the information to the girls. She enthusiastically advises Mary to try the same beauty shop and the same manicurist, knowing that this way her friend will certainly hear the gossip about herself. Mary is horrified at learning of her husband's indiscretion and files for divorce. She travels to Reno to spend the requisite residency time, choosing the famous Double Bar T Ranch for her home base. There the Countess (Boland),

* In 1938, Anita Loos had scripted a film project, *The Canadians,* which was penciled in to star Clark Gable with Mae West. Upon reading the script, the screen comedienne refused the project, but did suggest that Rosalind Russell would be ideal for the part. The MGM authorities dropped the vehicle.

Peggy (Fontaine), and Miriam (Goddard) are also waiting for their freedom. Sylvia makes her appearance soon after and all goes well until she discovers that Miriam is the other woman in her husband's love life. She yanks Miriam off her horse, and that is when the film's hilarious fight scene begins. It is a long sequence in which Sylvia gets her hat pulled down around her ears, and is pushed into a large cactus. It concludes with Sylvia crawling in the dust on her belly toward Miriam, who thinks the brawl has concluded. But Sylvia opens wide her big mouth and bites the back of one of Miriam's shapely legs. Rosalind later admitted, "The yelp she emitted could be heard south of the border, and I do mean Mexico."

Later, with everyone's divorce final and after Crystal has married Mary's ex, it is learned that Crystal is two-timing him with Buck, the Countess' new husband. "Crystal and Sylvia are as thick as thieves," Mary is informed. The two-faced Sylvia is literally on the edge of her seat waiting to see Crystal do herself in. Mary finally gets up enough courage to retrieve her lonely, beloved man from the unfaithful Crystal. She succeeds and Crystal gets her expected come-uppance by discovering that Buck, whom she thought was rich, has not a penny to his name. Sylvia remains her irrepressible self, and goes off in search of other, fresh gossip.

Rosalind would say, "It was *The Women* that gave my career its greatest impetus," and this is certainly true. Miss Russell told Mike Steen, "George [Cukor] was an enormous help. He changed my career. No question that I owe it to George. He has wonderful insight into women. He had me doing things that frightened me at times. For instance, there was a powder room scene, sort of an El Morocco powder room. There were many women in the powder room. George said to me, 'Now, when all those other women leave, I want you to examine your teeth.' I said, 'What?' He said, 'Yeah, I want you to look at your teeth in the mirror, then put your lipstick on and take your finger and spread it all over your mouth.' I said, 'George! You have been peeping!' He said, 'I know when women make up in front of other women, they do it

rather daintily, but when you are alone, you do do those things.' He gave you wonderful pieces of business."

Moviegoers who had not thought of her as anything more than a competent actress now considered her fantastic, because she did not seem to take herself very seriously. In the fight scene and a reducing salon sequence in *The Women*, she is ungainly and almost sympathetic until she opens her mouth to hurl an insult. There were no men in the cast; the gentler sex was referred to but never seen (the original ending was filmed with Mary dashing toward the arms of her ex-husband and his shadow fell within the camera's range, but this scene was later reshot, omitting the man's shadow). *The Women* would be done for NBC-TV's "Producers Showcase" on February 7, 1955, with Paulette Goddard as Sylvia and re-made as a movie with songs by MGM in 1956 as *The Opposite Sex,* with men in the cast and Dolores Gray as Sylvia. Then, in 1974, an attempt to revive the play flopped on Broadway. In this misadventure, Alexis Smith was Sylvia.

The Front Page, a play written by Charles MacArthur and Ben Hecht, had been a Broadway hit in 1928-1929 with Osgood Perkins and Lee Tracy as stars. The hilarious newspaper tale of a managing editor and his star reporter had been transferred to film by United Artists in 1931 with Adolphe Menjou and Pat O'Brien in the leads. Then, in 1939, Howard Hawks concocted the idea of a remake, suggesting to Columbia Pictures' head Harry Cohn that the reporter be transformed into a woman and with her as the divorced wife of the editor, but now in love with another man.

Cohn accepted the idea, along with Hawks' choice of Cary Grant as the editor. The revamped Hildy Johnson role was first offered to Columbia contract star Jean Arthur, who rejected it. Likewise, it was passed over by Irene Dunne, Claudette Colbert, and Ginger Rogers. In going over his list of possibilities, Cohn came across the name Rosalind Russell and telephoned MGM. The rest of the story surrounding *His Girl Friday* (1940) is cinematic history.

Rosalind played Hildy Johnson in the

Charles Lederer-rewritten script to Grant's Walter Burns. Hildy claims to despise Burns and claims to love her fiancé (Ralph Bellamy), but when the steam has cleared from the rapid-fire story, she decides that being Bellamy's wife would be too dull. She belongs to the newspaper world inhabited by her ex-spouse. Lederer's dialogue is crisp, quick, caustic, and funny. Because of audience laughter, many lines went unheard which prompted many a movie fan to see the picture a second or third time.

Hildy is aggressive, independent, determined, and tenacious, and is dressed in pinstriped suits with matching hats. Rosalind, in playing the role, was the epitome of the 1940 liberated woman—professionally—who continued to need the love of a man to make her complete. This film and The Women, released only five months apart, fully established Rosalind as one of the cinema's top comediennes, in the same league (almost) with reigning screwball funster Carole Lombard. Rosalind should have been at least nominated for an Oscar for His Girl Friday, but was not. The original play, The Front Page, was revived in 1946 on Broadway and then again in 1969 with Bert Convy as Hildy, and was remade, tastelessly, as a movie in 1974 by Billy Wilder for Universal, starring Jack Lemmon as Hildy Johnson.

It was because of The Women that a twenty-three-year-old man bound for America on a trans-Atlantic voyage vowed that he would like to either kill Rosalind Russell or marry her. Danish-born Frederick Brisson, son of actor Carl Brisson, had little to do during the ocean crossing and his deck chair happened to be placed just outside the main salon. Inside, three times a day, The Women was projected for the edification of the ship's passengers. Brisson was unable to escape the soundtrack voices and even ventured into the salon one time to see what all the loud women's voices were about. He made up his mind that he had to meet the Russell woman.

In the spring of 1940, when Brisson arrived in Hollywood to become an actor's manager, he stayed with Cary Grant. During the filming of His Girl Friday, Cary and Rosalind often took dinner together and for one such date, Cary brought Brisson along. Rosalind has recorded her initial opinion of Brisson with "H'mm, not bad. Not bad at all." She has also remembered, "Freddie started calling me, and after playing hard to get for a time, I went out with him one night. We had a hilarious time, and presently were dating regularly." Up to meeting Brisson, she had enjoyed certain dates, but it had seemed to her that "men are naturally shy. It's up to the women to get in there and tell them what they want—what they have to have." A great deal of her time in 1939-1940 was spent playing tennis and golf at Beverly Hills country clubs where she invariably beat her male opponents.

She was loaned to Warner Bros. a second time (along with James Stewart of MGM) for the Epstein brothers' screen adaptation of the S. N. Behrman play, No Time for Comedy (1940). The play had enjoyed a 1939 Broadway run with Katharine Cornell and Laurence Olivier. As a stage actress who weds the writer (Stewart) of a successful comedy in which she stars, Rosalind's screen person is toned down considerably from the raucous-voiced Sylvia of The Women and the ubiquitous, self-sufficient Hildy of His Girl Friday. It is a pleasing, conventional comedy with the writer, Gaylord Esterbrook (Stewart), making the decision that he will renounce comedy playwriting in favor of creating a serious piece for his wife. She is against his plan, but Gaylord is inspired by Amanda Swift (Genevieve Tobin), a beguiling patroness of the arts, whose husband Philo (Charles Ruggles) matter-of-factly accepts his wife's little enthusiasms. In a meeting with Amanda, Linda (Rosalind) suggests, "Love Gay if you must, but please don't ruin his style." He writes a serious play which is a bombastic failure, and returns to his understanding, loving wife, a humbled, but much more caring husband. Bosley Crowther found that Rosalind ". . . is excellent . . . in a cool, collected way."

In release simultaneously with No Time for Comedy was another comedy, Hired Wife (1940), this time on a Russell loan arrangement to Universal. Here she is back to being "Miss Efficient" as Kendal Browning, secretary to Stephen Dexter (Brian Aherne), a ce-

With co-stars Joan
Crawford and Norma
Shearer in *The Women*
('39).

With James Stewart in *No
Time for Comedy* ('40).

With John Carroll in
Hired Wife ('40).

With Ralph Bellamy and
Cary Grant in an on-the-
set publicity shot for *His
Girl Friday* ('40).

371

ment company executive. She jokingly refers to herself as "Little Miss Cement," but is persuaded to marry Dexter as a matter of convenience in order to preserve the company from bankruptcy. Of course, she is in love with the boss-husband, while he is dashing off to hold hands with a blonde golddigger named Phyllis Walden (Virginia Bruce). Kendal contrives a number of ways to convince the man that they are made for one another, but the ploy that finally works is when she gets poor buddy Jose (John Carroll) to pretend to be a rich South American and to sweep the unsuspecting Phyllis off her high heels. Of Rosalind, one critic suggested, "Maybe the lady patrons will find her a bit too glib, too sleekly formidable. But we don't; we think she's perfect."

In a fourth successive loan-out, Rosalind went to star (with top billing) opposite Melvyn Douglas in the comedy *This Thing Called Love* (1941), a film considered risqué for its day. Its daring theme is the trial marriage of explorer Tice Collins (Douglas) to Ann Winters (Rosalind), an executive with an insurance company. Miss Russell told Mike Steen in his August 1971 interview with her, "I had the same office set in I don't know how many pictures! Ten or fifteen! The same cameraman, Joe Walker, and the same propman named Blackie. The opening shot was always an air shot over New York. Then it would bleed into my suite of offices on the fortieth floor of Radio City. I would have the same desk and the same side chairs and bookcase. Out the window behind me was always a view of the Empire State Building, in order to identify the setting. I used to say to Joe Walker, 'Joe, where was the Empire State Building in the last picture?' which had only been a couple of months before. He would say, 'I had it a little to the left.' I'd say, 'Well, this time throw it over on the right.' Then I would say, 'Blackie, how many telephones did we have the last time?' He'd say, "You had about nine.' So I'd say, 'Well, throw in thirteen. This will be a big double A picture!' I would always open with about the same dialogue, give a lot of cheap orders."

Ann calls the shots in stating that it is to be marriage without sex during a three-month period of compatibility testing. Nevertheless, she parades before the sensitive soul wearing diaphanous nightgowns and drinking champagne as if the bottlers might withhold the next week's supply. He procures a Mexican statue of the frowning god of fertility that he places in his living room. But to no avail. After a number of humorous misunderstandings, Ann is ready to share her bed with her not-so-patient husband. She opens his bedroom door wide enough to pass the fertility god through the opening. The statue is now smiling, and winks at the fade-out camera. The movie was adapted by George Seaton, Ken Englund, and P. J. Wolfson from the Edwin Burke play presented on Broadway in 1928 with Violet Heming and Minor Watson; in 1930 it was turned into a film from Pathé starring Constance Bennett and Edmund Lowe.

MGM reclaimed Rosalind as Clark Gable's top co-star (their first film together in six years) in the rather pedestrian *They Met in Bombay* (1941). As Anya Von Duren, she is a super clever jewel thief who focuses her plans on the capture of the diamond pendant owned by the Duchess of Beltravers (Jessie Ralph). At the same time, confidence man Gerald Meldrick (Gable) poses as a Lloyds of London detective in order to obtain the same pendant. Anya makes the snatch, but is tricked out of it by Meldrick. They form a partnership when the police get wise to their scheme and they leave India via a tramp freighter operated by the slimy Captain Chang (Peter Lorre) who turns them over to the authorities. They again escape and Meldrick dons the uniform of a British officer.

Before Gerald can say "Jolly Roger," he is sent into battle against the Japanese where he wins a Victoria Cross for his brave efforts. Now stalwart and honest, he agrees to go to prison for his thievery and Anya tearfully agrees to wait for him. Many critics clamped down on the absurdities of the film: "Preposterous" stated the *Hollywood Reporter*; "Nothing more than a B-picture with delusions of grandeur," claimed the *New York Times*. However, everyone agreed that Gable and Russell, with their "light, breezy and sure" styles (Film Daily), were worth seeing. Everyone at MGM, including its co-stars, foresaw a flop in They Met in Bombay, but because of the popularity of the leads, the film became a hit with audiences. Rosalind was to admit some years later, "Clark Gable was a great kisser," but she claimed that he was "also a great scene stealer."

With The Feminine Touch (MGM, 1941), Rosalind was right back into the marital fracas. This time she is wed to Don Ameche (on loan from Twentieth Century-Fox) who is a professor with a theory. The theory is that jealousy is evil and unnecessary. It is also his bland contention that any problem in matrimony can be solved with honey-toned words rather than with argument. However, when his wife is beset upon by a publisher-on-the-make (Van Heflin), the professor tosses his fancy theory out a window by planting a "haymaker" on the usurper's jaw.

Rosalind's MGM contract expired with Design for Scandal, filmed in the summer of 1941 (released on November 11th). She is a judge in this comedy, who dishes out a fine to wealthy Judson Blair (Edward Arnold) at the rate of $4,000 a week for toying with the affections (among other things) of a pretty blonde plaintiff (Mary Beth Hughes). Angry at the stiff judicial decision, Blair hires Jeff Sherman (Walter Pidgeon) to get friendly with the hardnosed judge in an attempt to find a juicy skeleton possibly hanging in her personal closet. Blair figures to appeal the judgment by proving that the judge has made a mistake or two in her lifetime. But the only thing that Sherman can deduce is that she is impossibly virtuous and he falls in love with her. They find supposed happiness with one another, while old Blair is stuck paying the weekly penalty.

In September 1941, Hollywood tossed a benefit at the Hollywood Bowl to raise funds to build entertainment centers for the United Service Organization (USO). Many big-name movie stars pitched in to help. Nelson Eddy sang; Norma Shearer, Loretta Young, and Hattie McDaniel made appeal speeches; Orson Welles read a Walt Whitman poem;

Jane Withers sang the "Hut Sut" song; and Rosalind, Cary Grant, Irene Dunne, and Charles Boyer staged what was called a "wholesale love scene." The event was climaxed with a buffet of U.S. Army cooked beans.

Since Frederick Brisson had become Rosalind's steady date, along with becoming her agent, Los Angeles newspaper columnists were convinced the duo would wed. Rosalind nixed the elopement rumors by telling Ruth Waterbury of Photoplay magazine, "You know the kind of family I come from, a rather old-fashioned family. When I get married, when I fall in love, I'll do it in an old-fashioned way." A few weeks after insisting that Brisson was "my good friend," she announced their engagement.

The first to hear the news was Rosalind's mother, who placed the notice in the Waterbury, Connecticut, newspaper. It was not long before the word reached California via the wire services. Louis B. Mayer and his producers sent Rosalind a large crate containing silver flatware "right down to the lemonade spoons." Rosalind and Frederick were wed in an old-fashioned ceremony on Saturday, October 25, 1941, at the Santa Ynez Mission in the Danish settlement of Solvang, near Santa Barbara, California. Cary Grant* was Brisson's best man, with Charlotte Wynters as Rosalind's matron of honor. The bride wore a white wedding gown of Danish design. To most people, since Roz was the star in the family, Brisson became known as "Rosalind Russell's husband," a tag he soon learned to accept if not like.

MGM had offered Rosalind a contract renewal at a salary of $7,500 a week for fifty-two weeks for a seven-year period, but Rosalind rejected it. As she would later say to researcher Mike Steen, "I wanted to free-lance

* Years later Grant would recall, "Freddie [Brisson] and I were to wait outside a side door and make our entry just as Roz and the bridesmaids started the long procession from the back of the church. Being an actor, I always tried out my props and, the night before in the rehearsal, the door worked properly. But now, as I heard our cue, I tried to open the door—but someone had left the catch on the inside! I started to rattle the door—but no one heard us because the music had started! Luckily, one man heard the noise—Arthur Hornblow—and we walked in just in time."

With Melvyn Douglas in
a pose for *This Thing
Called Love* ('41).

With Don Ameche in
The Feminine Touch
('41).

because I wanted to have a family . . . a large family was our intention. When a professional woman such as myself marries, you have to make the decision whether your marriage and family is first or second. My decision was that my family would come first regardless."

Her initial free-lance job was for Paramount at $100,000. She was signed to replace Claudette Colbert in *Take a Letter, Darling* (1942). Miss Colbert was shifted to *The Palm Beach Story* (Paramount, 1942), originally assigned to Carole Lombard who died in an airplane crash on January 16, 1942. *Take a Letter, Darling,* scripted by Claude Binyon, offers no plot surprises, nor is it more than a cute little tale of advertising executive A. M. MacGregor (Rosalind) who hires handsome Tom Varney (Fred MacMurray) to act as her man Friday. The idea is to have Tom pose as her intended so that the wives of her clients will not be jealous of her. When one of the clients is pretty Ethel Caldwell (Constance Moore) who wants Tom to handle her account, the lady chief finds that the jealousy

she feels is due to her love for the hired man. It goes almost without stating that the final scene has her in his arms, very much the adoring, humble miss.

Rosalind had averaged four movies a year from the time she had signed her MGM contract. While most of them were above average, there were a few that could be labeled mistakes. "I'll match my flops with anybody," she once said. "There are only two ways to get ahead in Hollywood. You either have to get one great picture a year—these propel you forward—or your impact has to be made with a lot of pictures." Her record spoke for itself; she chose the latter.

Obviously, what was needed in Roz's career was a bonanza of a hit and just such an event presented itself to her in the film production of the 1940 Broadway hit play, *My Sister Eileen,* which had starred Shirley Booth and Jo Ann Sayers. Joseph Fields and Jerome Chodorov adapted their play for the screen, and Alexander Hall directed. Ruth Sherwood (Rosalind) and her blonde, curvaceous baby sister Eileen (Janet Blair) arrive in

With husband Frederick Brisson on their wedding day (October 25, 1941).

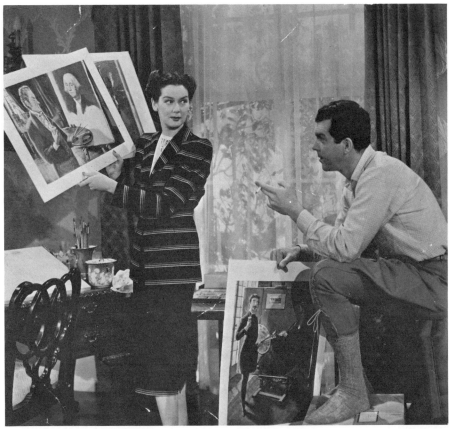

With Fred MacMurray
in *Take a Letter, Darling*
('42).

With Janet Blair in *My
Sister Eileen* ('42).

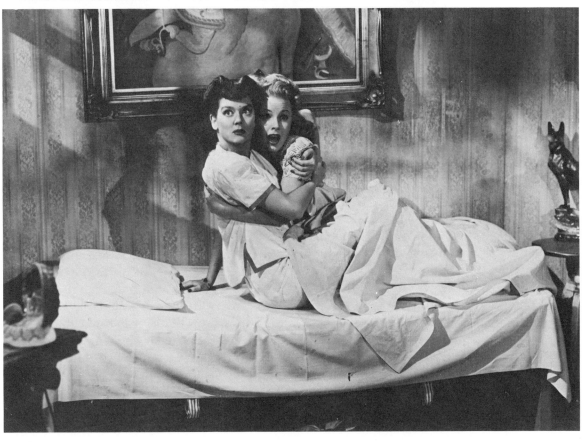

Manhattan where they hope to find careers as, respectively, a writer and an actress. They have left Papa (Grant Mitchell) and Grandma (Elizabeth Patterson) back in Columbus, Ohio, and they now rent a Greenwich Village apartment, the windows of which are at sidewalk level. Privacy is a non-existent commodity for the Sherwood girls. They encounter numerous characters in their quest for careers: their landlord (George Tobias); a mad Greek; the "Wreck" (Gordon Jones) from Georgia Tech and his scared secret wife (Jeff Donnell), the apartment's former and very sexy tenant (June Havoc) whose boyfriends still assume she lives there, and Bob Baker (Brian Aherne), a magazine editor. Baker likes Ruth's writing, but advises her to concentrate on facts in her own life rather than attempt fiction.

Later, Bob loses his job over her, but she receives an assignment to cover the arrival of the Portuguese navy at a Brooklyn shipyard. She is on the spot, but the non-English-speaking Portuguese chase her back to Greenwich Village and, when they sight Eileen, all hell breaks loose. The girls eventually draw the enamored sailors out of their apartment by leading them in a Conga line out to the street. Still later, Eileen is arrested for disturbing the peace, but the police force has never had a prettier prisoner and she is quickly released. At intervals, the film's action is halted by blasts which shake bodies and the apartment; it seems a new subway is being built nearby. The blasting has finally stopped when Bob Baker dashes in to tell Ruth that he has sold her stories to a magazine, and then he proposes to her. Just then the subway drilling replaces the blasting and The Three Stooges troop into the apartment. "We must have made a wrong turn," they say bewilderedly.

The New York Times' Bosley Crowther called the film "gay and bouncing" while he judged Rosalind as playing "the smart sister with a delightfully dour and cynical air." In 1953, the property would become a Broadway musical; in 1955, it was to be remade by Columbia with Technicolor and music and Betty Garrett as Ruth; and in 1960, it would become a one-season CBS-TV series with Elaine

Stritch. Rosalind received her first Oscar nomination as Best Actress for her dazzling, effervescent, supercharged characterization of Ruth. But in a tight race, the winner was Greer Garson for MGM's *Mrs. Miniver.*

In December 1942, Frederick Brisson became a U.S. citizen, and the following day he was commissioned a lieutenant in the U.S. Army. He served, first, at Santa Ana, California, where a group of soldiers and ex-actors recorded war propaganda radio programs. Also in Brisson's contingent was Major Donald Crisp, a former client. From there, Brisson was sent to Santa Fe, New Mexico. Rosalind added to the war effort by touring within the auspices of the USO in gowns she had finagled out of Harry Cohn of Columbia. Her patriotism took her to Washington, D.C. (among other cities) where she and Mamie Eisenhower became friends.

Her next film, a drama and her first at RKO, *Flight for Freedom* (1943), was originally slated for Katharine Hepburn. It is the traumatic account of "the world's greatest woman flyer" who sacrifices everything to aid the United States Navy in detecting pre-Pearl Harbor Japanese military installations in the Pacific. These bases are first seen, by accident, by another flyer, handsome and happy-go-lucky Randy Britton (Fred MacMurray) while flying above the Japanese Mandated Islands. He takes the news back to the Navy and Tonie Carter (Rosalind) is asked to make a flight in which she and her navigator (Britton is later chosen for the task) will fake getting lost so the Navy can conduct a "search" and thereby reconnoiter the area.

During the film's duller moments, Tonie insists that she loves Paul Turner (Herbert Marshall) but we, the audience, know that her true feelings are for Britton. In a goodbye speech to Paul, which translates as more of a mother's words to her little boy, Tonie says, "Suppose you don't hear from me for some time; no matter what happens I want you to know that I'm coming back. Now, you believe that every minute I'm away, won't you?" With chin held high, she flies to New Guinea for a secret rendezvous with Britton. There, after a mean-looking Japanese proprietor (Richard Loo) shows her to her hotel accommodations, she encounters Britton, also known as Harry Johnson. The plans are for him to stow away on her plane, but while blinking stars are reflected in her eyes, Britton proposes to her and she says, "Why didn't you let me know—before? Before it was too late?"

She tells him that she loves Paul, but we know she is just being gallant. Her ploy is to make him believe she does not care, with such words, as "You're so sure, aren't you? So sure that all you have to do is take me in your arms and I'll follow and leave Paul behind. I won't because I've had it happen to me. I've been walked out on and left to break inside and pick up the pieces alone. I know what it means. I'll never do that to anyone. Never. I've got plans of my own and, believe it or not, they don't include you. They're plans for a lifetime of peace and security and a whole lot of happiness." She flies away the next morning, without Britton, and instead of pretending to get lost, guides her plane into the clouds above the oxygen zone where she passes out. Closely resembling the last flight of Amelia Earhart, the film was sanctioned by Earhart's widower, publisher George Palmer Putnam. This movie, directed by Lothar Mendes, is heavy with heroics and, for some less indulgent viewers, proved to be hard-going.

With the completion of her work on *Flight for Freedom*, Rosalind went to Palm Springs to rest before the birth of her baby. Columnist Cal York gossiped, "A friend told us Roz frankly admitted as soon as she'd gotten married she intended to have a child. But at that she'll be a wonderful mother." On Friday, May 7, 1943, a son, whom the Brissons named Carl Lance, was born. The proud father was provided a furlough to be present for the boy's arrival. Rosalind's first post-motherhood acting job was on "Lux Radio Theatre" on September 20, 1943, when she repeated her Tonie Carter of *Flight for Freedom*. Her co-star was George Brent.

Seven months after she had become a mother, Rosalind was seen as yet another aggressive businesswoman in *What a Woman!* (Columbia, 1943). She is a noted author's agent who figures college professor Michael Cobb (Willard Parker) ought to be in movies and she propels him in that direction. Meanwhile, Henry Pepper (Brian Aherne), a writer for *Knickerbocker* magazine, gets in the way as he attempts to get to know the real Carol Kingsley (Roz) for a forthcoming biographical profile. He informs her that she is utilizing about ten percent of her womanly charms and that the remaining ninety percent are aching to be released. That is the start, of course, of something big between agent and writer, and the sappy professor is left in the lurch. The comedy offered little new in the tried and true vein of Roz Russell filmfare.

One morning in 1944, Rosalind collapsed on her bedroom floor. She was immediately hospitalized and doctors diagnosed her trouble as emanating from the old thyroid condition. Some sources at the time insisted upon implying that she had suffered a nervous collapse. It was agreed medically that due to the birth of her son her thyroid, which had theretofore been overactive, had now reversed itself and become underactive. After two weeks of rest, she was mobile again, but did not make any motion pictures for 1944 release. She actively participated on the Hollywood Committee to elect Thomas E. Dewey President of the United States. Her co-workers included—among others—Ginger Rogers, Cecil B. DeMille, Anne Baxter, Hedda Hopper, and Adolphe Menjou. Their gallant efforts proved to be in vain when Franklin D. Roosevelt was the popular choice for a fourth term.

Thirteen months were to pass before a new Rosalind Russell feature film was to be in release. She returned to the screen in the Warner Bros.' version of Louise Randall Pierson's rollicking autobiography *Roughly Speaking* (1945). Under the direction of Michael Curtiz, Rosalind was asked to enact the authoress' life during a forty-year span. The aging process consisted of white streaks in her dark hair, and little more. Through no fault of Roz's or Curtiz's, the film, touted as a comedy-drama, was too long (117 minutes) and did not capture fully the novel's fun. It begins with Rosalind as teenage Louise in her par-

379

With Cary Grant receiving their "Golden Apple Awards" from the Women's Press Club of Hollywood (December 1942).

With John Alvin, Craig Stevens, Donald Woods, and Ann Doran in *Roughly Speaking* ('45).

ents' proper Bostonian home. Louise then plunges into a mismatched marriage to an overly-stuffy Yale man (Donald Woods) whom she later divorces, and from there the plot has her marry good-natured Harold Pierson (Jack Carson). From these two marriages spring a great many children and several comedic-sad experiences. The overall effort is pleasant enough, but it did not create any terrific box-office rush. Once again, Jack Carson proved that he could handle a sensitive role with a great deal of subtlety.

Roz went back to Columbia to portray yet another kind of professional (a psychiatrist) in *She Wouldn't Say Yes* (1945). Virginia Van Upp's scenario leaves a good deal to be desired, especially comedy, as the good lady doctor is analyzed by a comic-strip creator (Lee Bowman) who tells her to leave her inhibitions behind and fall in love. After what seems an endless period of film time, she comprehends his message and the cartoonist wins her—but who really cares?

For many years, Rosalind had been a member of the League for Crippled Children, an organization founded by wives of doctors and those interested in helping crippled children. In 1940 she had met Sister Elizabeth Kenny, a nurse from the Australian back country (in England and Australia, experienced graduate nurses earn the title of Sister), whose new and successful treatment of infantile paralysis had caused controversy in U.S. medical circles, but whose treatment was endorsed by the National Foundation for Infantile Paralysis. Rosalind passionately wanted to portray Sister Kenny onscreen and began a campaign of selling the idea to Hollywood producers.

No one was interested—understandably—but Rosalind was not one to give in easily. She was solidly behind the woman whom she once described as looking like "an M4 tank, but her eyes were the loneliest and loveliest I've ever looked into," and wanted desperately to aid the woman's cause. Rosalind owed a picture to RKO (she had contracted to do three films for them), and informed the studio's production head, Charles Koerner, that she would approve no other script unless he gave serious consideration to a Kenny story. Koerner, pushed into a corner, finally relented and sent scripter Dudley Nichols to Minneapolis where Sister Kenny worked. Nichols came up with a script which, although biased heavily in favor of Sister Kenny and her methods, is interesting and provided Rosalind with her best dramatic acting job to date wherein she "plays the title character with tremendous vitality and warmth" (New York Times).

The movie life of Sister Kenny (1946) commences with the young Australian country nurse healing a child of polio by administering applications of hot compresses and by exercising the victim's limbs. Her ideas are opposed by Dr. Brack (Philip Merivale), and she rejects a suitor (Dean Jagger) so that she may dedicate her entire existence to proving that her therapy theories are correct. She keeps on fighting and the years pass her by as she turns from a slim, dark-haired girl into a portly, white-haired practitioner. Along the way, she is befriended by a sympathetic doctor (Alexander Knox), an alliance which is close to being a love affair of the minds. Bosley Crowther of the New York Times unkindly remarked that Rosalind's makeup, toward the film's end, made her look like "something between George Washington and Ethel Barrymore."

Released in July 1946, the motion picture did not do well in the United States, but fared better in foreign distribution. Rosalind later said, "In the end, that picture did pull out of the red and made a profit for the studio. So I didn't feel too badly about my stubborn attitude." Her acting in Sister Kenny earned her an Academy Award nomination, her second, but she lost out in the final vote to Olivia de Havilland (To Each His Own). As something of a consolation prize, Roz received the Golden Globe Award from the Hollywood Foreign Press Association, the Blue Ribbon Award from Boxoffice magazine, a medal from Parents magazine, and the New York Foreign Press Circle Award.

Continuing in the dramatic vein, a dubious professional decision, Roz next appeared in The Guilt of Janet Ames (Columbia, 1947).

Of this film she admitted later, "I rarely mention [it] except in an unaudible whisper." Three writers (Louella MacFarlane, Allen Rivkin, Devery Freeman) threw together an adaptation of a Lenore Coffee story and came up with a faulty script. Janet Ames (Rosalind) must know why her Army husband sacrificed his life so that five of his battlefront buddies might survive. One of those who was saved through Janet's G.I. husband's heroics is Smithfield Cobb (Melvyn Douglas), a newspaperman whose chief hobby is liquor. Janet envies him his life, but also hates him for having been partially responsible for her husband's death. What she does not know is that Cobb is something of a pseudo-psychiatrist and through him she finds that her marriage to Mr. Ames had become a dull thing, from which he might have sought relief willingly in the form of death. The neurotic woman thus finds reason for her guilt. Those relatively few filmgoers who suffered through this pretentious entry had an opportunity to see Sid Caesar in his pre-television starring days.

Because he had done her a favor with Sister Kenny, director-producer-writer Dudley Nichols begged Rosalind to star in his screen adaptation of Eugene O'Neill's play Mourning Becomes Electra for RKO (1947). After toying with the idea of playing the mother Christina (Greta Garbo had been a serious choice for the role of Christina, but at age forty-two she thought herself too young to play Roz's mother oncamera; the part was given to Katina Paxinou), Roz agreed to portray Lavinia Mannon. After a few days of soundstage work, she confided to her friend Loretta Young, "I can't imagine what I'm doing in this picture—it's all hate!"

The six-hour play was sliced to a three-hour film, but that too was shortened for general distribution. Regardless, the project resulted in a dull, talkative, overly melodramatic movie. Nichols, in awe of the great playwright, refused to vary from O'Neill's basic script and dialogue.

Derived from the Greek tragedy series by Sophocles, the Oresteia, Sophocles' heroine Electra becomes Lavinia Mannon who hates her mother (Paxinou). The mother kills her husband (Raymond Massey) and takes a lover (Leo Genn) who is also coveted by Lavinia. When Lavinia later learns that her mother is having an affair with the man she covets, she reveals the news to her brother (Michael Redgrave) and, together, they murder the lover. The mother is then forced into suicide and the son shoots himself. At the story's end, Lavinia is left in the Mannon home to brood to her heart's content. It is her decision to "live alone with the dead, and keep their secrets, and let them hound me, until the curse is paid out and the last Mannon is let die." Critic James Agee (*Time* magazine) credited the film with "some fine performances, notably Rosalind Russell as the cold-blooded daughter and Katina Paxinou as the hot-blooded mother." The $2,250,000 production, as many in Hollywood could have predicted, and did, was a financial failure, mainly due to the gloomy theme which the average moviegoer cheerfully chose to avoid.

For her single film performance of 1947, Rosalind was nominated a third time for an Academy Award. Bookmakers gave her four-to-one odds as the favorite to win over the four other contenders: Joan Crawford (*Possessed*), Susan Hayward (*Smash-Up—The Story of a Woman*), Dorothy McGuire (*Gentleman's Agreement*), and Loretta Young (*The Farmer's Daughter*). A confident Rosalind dressed in a white chiffon gown, arrived at the Los Angeles Shrine Auditorium with her husband on the evening of Saturday, March 20, 1948. Nearly everyone in Hollywood predicted that she would receive an Oscar. She was almost halfway out of her seat when presenter Fredric March tore open the Price-Waterhouse-sealed envelope containing the name of the Best Actress. It was Loretta Young. Rosalind quickly regained her composure, but was the first star to exit the Auditorium. Two hours later, she rushed into the Mocambo nightclub where she cheerfully hugged Miss Young. Asked how she felt about losing, Rosalind stated, "I feel worse for Travis Banton who designed this dress for the occasion." It was the biggest upset in the

history of the Academy Awards, but Rosalind proved to the world of Hollywood that she was an indestructible professional.

Earlier in the year, however, she had been awarded her second Golden Globe, the Laurel Award, and the Film Critics Circle Award from the New York Foreign Language Press for her work in *Mourning Becomes Electra*. *Look* magazine also honored her with its Gold Plaque for 1947.

In 1947, Frederick Brisson began his career as a producer with the formation of Independent Artists Corporation. The initial corporate venture was *The Velvet Touch* (RKO, 1948) with Rosalind starring as stage actress Valerie Stanton. Fan magazine ads proclaimed, "Rosalind Russell tells the private life of a public idol with never an idle moment!" An advertisement in *Redbook* magazine of July 1948 stated, "Rosalind has her eye on three men . . . three men have their eye on Rosalind . . . *one* of them is up to no good!" Both ads tend to mislead the reader into believing that the film is a comedy. It is anything but a comedy!

It was Rosalind's fourth successive drama, and one that had a predictable plot *and* a predictable ending. Valerie's producer (Leon Ames) insists that she keep to comedy roles despite her wishes to turn dramatic with *Hedda Gabler*. When he threatens to blackmail her in order to make her see the light, she clobbers him with a heavy statuette. She suffers for the remainder of the story coping with her crime-ridden conscience. Portly Sydney Greenstreet shines as the admiring but suspicious detective captain assigned to the case, and Leo Genn is man number three who loves her and does not suspect a thing until she very nearly commits suicide while onstage in the Ibsen play. Hair-stylist Fred Phillips and costume designer Travis Banton helped Rosalind to assume the look of the self-assured, prominent legitimate actress and the filmmakers involved must be credited with having created one of the most successful backstage looks at theatre yet put on film. Unfortunately, filmgoers were not impressed enough by the ambiance of the story to accept the motion picture as a viable drama.

With Leo Genn in *The Velvet Touch* ('48).

←

As Lavinia Mannon in *Mourning Becomes Electra* ('47).

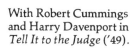

With Robert Cummings and Harry Davenport in *Tell It to the Judge* ('49).

Rosalind's father-in-law, Carl Brisson, was a renowned musical star of whom she once said, "Now there was a man. I loved him." In the spring of 1949, he opened a singing engagement at the Cocoanut Grove Club in Los Angeles where he referred to son Frederick as his brother in a futile effort to conceal his true age (he was born December 24, 1893). The three Brissons were good friends and often attended Hollywood parties together. Not all of these shindigs were lively and when Carl failed to put a spark into them with his singing act, Rosalind invariably jumped in with ideas for saving the night.

Evie Johnson (Van's wife) once said, "I don't think I've ever seen her out of sorts. She's buoyant, like champagne." Rosalind's good friend Loretta Young offered, "Rosalind is always Roz. She has a natural instinct for ridiculing herself and not anyone else." The Brissons lived in a Beverly Hills French Provincial home (formerly owned by Mary Boland) with a living room painted chartreuse (later beige) from where Rosalind embarked on fund-raising sojourns on behalf of the many charities she sponsored. The Roman Catholic religion continued to be a source of comfort to her, but she jokingly referred to her parish church as "Our Lady of the Cadillacs."

In 1949, after four relatively disappointing dramatic films, Rosalind bounced backed in a comedy at Columbia, *Tell It to the Judge,* directed by Loretta Young's brother-in-law, former actor Norman Foster. She was cast as a big-league lawyer with aspirations toward a federal appointment as judge. When her personal life becomes somewhat flawed by her husband's (Robert Cummings) attention to a blonde (Marie McDonald), she divorces him, but he pursues her up and down the eastern seaboard until she relents. A portion of Cummings' pursuit consists of their avoiding arrest during the raid of a gambling joint by opening the establishment's back door and falling into the "ocean," which was a 75,000 gallon tank of water on the soundstage. It took an entire day to properly film this scene, and both stars were pretty much water-

logged by the time the sequence was finalized.

A Woman of Distinction (Columbia, 1950) came next, with Roz filming on the same lot where Joan Crawford was performing Miss Russell's old role in *Craig's Wife* in the remake entitled *Harriet Craig. A Woman of Distinction* provided Roz with a new leading man, Ray Milland. In this slapstick comedy, with Joseph Walker again her cinematographer, Rosalind is Susan Middlecott, dean of women at a New England girls' school who becomes involved with a visiting British astronomer (Milland). Along the way, the duo become smeared with mud, fall out of chairs, and get their heads stuck in venetian blinds. It seemed embarrassing to more than a few fans that two such mature, high-powered stars should be engaged in such child's play.

In January 1951, Rosalind emceed a dinner dance and fashion show held at the Embassy Room of the Ambassador Hotel in Los Angeles which netted $6,000 for the Damon Runyon Cancer Fund. Some of the models who displayed the Don Loper creations were Virginia Mayo, Audrey Totter, June Havoc, Claire Trevor, Joan Evans, Ann Blyth, and Corinne Calvet.

Rosalind's screen career was definitely on the decline in the early Fifties. At age forty-three, she no longer could play convincingly the youthful businesswoman who does not realize until some one hundred celluloid minutes have passed that she requires a man. The type of story that *A Woman of Distinction* represented was old hat and not in demand. Her career, if it was to survive, required a distinct change of pace. A friend, Joshua Logan, told her, "Get the feel of audience again. Listen to it. Practice on the road and see what comes of it." Enthused about attempting Broadway again, Roz singed to play Gillian, the lovable witch, in the national touring production of *Bell, Book and Candle* (played in New York by Lilli Palmer and in the 1958 Columbia film by Kim Novak).

Starting on December 21, 1951, at the Playhouse in Wilmington, Delaware, the tour extended for eighteen weeks, concluding in

Chicago. After the first few weeks, the star admitted, "I'd become sluggish working with the camera. The stage demands that you use forty-two new muscles and you can't let down for one minute." The cost of the national production was estimated at $140,000, but during Rosalind's tour it grossed $600,000.

Back in Hollywood, the Brissons attended a party at the home of William Powell where Joseph Fields, writer and director, asked Rosalind to sing. She sang with what she calls "the vocal cords of a frog" and Fields tempted her with the proposition of starring on Broadway in *Wonderful Town,* a musical version of *My Sister Eileen.* She was positive that she could not carry off such a demanding vocal assignment, but when Fields indicated that George Abbott might direct, she agreed to go to New York to talk about it.

The first meeting was inconclusive and Rosalind returned to Hollywood to star in her husband's movie *Never Wave at a WAC* (RKO, 1952) which she had tried-out on CBS-TV's "Schlitz Playhouse of Stars" on October 19, 1951, to favorable reviews. The mild movie version was released on December 18, 1952. Rosalind is Jo McBain, a Perle Mesta type of Washington matron who is divorced from Andrew McBain (Paul Douglas) and in love with Lieutenant Colonel Schuyler Fairchild (William Ching). While her ex-husband is doing research work for the U.S. Army, her paramour is to be transferred to Paris. Thinking that she will be stationed near him, she joins the WACs, but her pre-Army connections in Washington, including her father the Senator (Charles Dingle) can do no better than station her stateside as one of her ex-husband's research guinea pigs. She regains love and affection for McBain, after many slapstick, far-fetched comedic sequences involving Marie Wilson. The *New York Times'* critic observed, "Although *Never Wave at a Wac* is never hilarious, it does put a comic slant on the regimented ladies." Unfortunately, the film had a penny-pinching aura about it. Unknown to many, with the issuance of this modestly budgeted

feature, another segment in the history of Hollywood came to a close since this was the last of the typical Roz Russell comedies. And a good portion of the declining filmgoing public did not even know the film existed.

During the early Fifties, Roz had been one of the originators, along with Charles Boyer, Dick Powell, and Joel McCrea, of the "Four Star Playhouse" repertoire for CBS-TV. The format called for at least one of the four to appear in each week's anthology-style episodes. Rosalind dropped out of the line-up, convinced she would rather do something creative on the stage. Soon thereafter, McCrea also changed his mind. The remaining two stars picked up David Niven as a partner, and later Ida Lupino joined them on a part-time basis.

Rosalind returned to New York "to tell them I'm not doing their musical," but, after days of persistent pleading by Fields and producer Robert Fryer, she agreed to do it. The show was to open in the autumn of 1952. Rosalind first gave a speech at Madison Square Garden on behalf of Republican Presidential candidate Dwight D. Eisenhower, and the next day she began rehearsals for *Wonderful Town.* In spite of her father-in-law's incredulous query, "Are you going to bring *that* voice to Broadway?" she plunged into singing the Adolph Green-Betty Comden songs set to Leonard Bernstein's music.

The show tried out in New Haven where the second-act ballet was deleted. After the Boston stay, the first act was revamped to provide more laughs. By the time the musical played Philadelphia, Russell had won her battle to delete an unworkable opening number and the "Christopher Street" song and dance had been inserted. Beyond the creative and emotional chaos of the break-in, Roz suffered a back injury in Boston when a chorus boy dropped her during a dance routine. *Wonderful Town* opened at New York's Winter Garden Theatre on Wednesday, February 25, 1953. The critics kidded her singing of such duets as "Ohio" (with Edie Adams) and her raucous renditions of "One Hundred Easy Ways [to Lose a Man]" and "Conga!"

With Marie Wilson in
Never Wave at a WAC
('52).

In *Wonderful Town* on
Broadway ('52).

insisting that the star sang like "a raven with a throat condition" or "like the Ambrose Lightship calling to its mate." But, generally, they loved her and the show. Richard Watts, Jr. (*New York Post*), enthused, "There is no getting away from the fact that Hollywood names make news in the theater, sometimes deservedly. Miss Russell is decidely among the deserving ones. As the older sister, she plays with such humor, gusto, skill, and relish, and throws herself into the spirit of the occasion with such engaging abandon, that she registers a definite and entirely deserved triumph." William Hawkins (*New York World-Telegram and Sun*) championed, "Miss Russell scales about eight gamuts in the course of the evening. She sings harmony like a Duncan Sister, puts away a delightful gagged-up lyric about losing her men, pantomimes some wildly bad fiction and practices a conga that would ground the Flying Codonas. . . . As if that were not enough, she adds a fantastic parody of swing, performed in a shrewd daze, and sings a wildly paced ragtime affair. This gal is a star and a half in

one." Summing up the fourth estate's reaction was Brooks Atkinson (*New York Times*), ". . . Miss Russell gives a memorably versatile comic performance. She is tall, willowy and gawky; she is droll, sardonic and incredulous. Her comedy can be broad and also subtle. For she radiates the genuine comic spirit." By March, the show was sold out and Decca Records, the producer of the original cast album, was avalanched with 100,000 orders.

In April 1953, Rosalind was presented by Faye Emerson with an Antoinette Perry Award as Best Actress in a musical; the show's musical director, Lehman Engle, was likewise honored, along with set designer Raoul Péne du Bois, and choreographer Donald Saddler. Roz also won the Donaldson Award, the New York Critics' Circle Award, and the Barter Theatre Award. In *Variety*'s Drama Critics Annual Poll, she was singled out for "the best feminine performance in a musical" and the *Los Angeles Times* picked her as "The Woman of the Year." *Time* magazine added the frosting to Rosalind's jubilant cake by saying, "Anyone of the thirteen chorus girls can dance better than she does. But, like such great performers as Ethel Merman and Bea Lillie, [she] represents the triumph of personality over technique: she communicates to her audience all the rewarding warmth and humor of shared experience." She played Broadway for a year and a half and from there went on a very successful tour.

On returning to California in spring 1955, Brisson, who had masterminded with two partners, Harold Prince and Robert Griffith, the Broadway hit musicals *Pajama Game* and *Damn Yankees,* placed Roz into his movie production of *The Girl Rush* (Paramount, 1955). It was Brisson's contention that moviegoers who had enjoyed *Wonderful Town* would gallop to their theaters to see Rosalind in a screen musical. In her first Technicolor and VistaVision widescreen production and playing opposite lead Fernando Lamas, she is the daughter of a dead gambler who goes to Las Vegas to collect her inheritance—a boarded-up building. She endeavors to make it into a glittering casino with girlie shows, and finds love in the process. To juice up the minimal, carefully budgeted proceedings, there were Eddie Albert and Gloria De Haven as the supporting love team, and Marion Lorne (the bumbling delight of TV's "Mr. Peepers") and James Gleason for comedy relief. Despite the bouyant presence of Roz (on mule-back or in tights or singing "An Occasional Man") and a coast-to-coast promotion tour, the film sunk from its own badly misjudged overweight. In New York, the film opened on the bottom half of double-bills in Brooklyn!

In September 1955, Rosalind gave a quickie interview to Harrison Kinney of *McCall's* magazine when she promoted *The Girl Rush* and also told readers, "I haven't any logical answer to why I've been happily married to one man for twenty years [at the time it was actually fourteen years]. I do know that a woman should learn early that everything in her marriage is not going to be her way." She went on to explain that a wife ought to be a source of pride for a husband, not only in running the household but in

dressing well. "Simply put, a joy of living is invariably a woman's beauty secret, and don't forget it."

While on the New York City portion of her tour, she appeared on Ed Sullivan's "Toast of the Town" on August 21, 1955, over CBS-TV. Sullivan devoted his hour-long show to Rosalind Russell, the living legend.

Before she had unpacked her traveling cases, back in Hollywood, Rosalind went into the Joshua Logan-directed production of William Inge's *Picnic* (Columbia, 1955) in the part of Rosemary (played on Broadway by angular Eileen Heckart). Roz told chronicler Mike Steen, *supra,* "Josh Logan came to see me and he didn't get . . . *nic* out. He said, 'Roz, would you like to play Rosemary in *Pic'* I said, 'Yesss!' He said, 'Wait a minute. Maybe you wouldn't. You know it isn't the lead.' I said, 'I'm going to do it!' I was very flattered that he would see me as an old-maid schoolteacher in Kansas." "At last, here was the opportunity I was looking for to create a new image," Rosalind wrote in *The Saturday Evening Post* in 1962. "Rosemary was a lonely old maid who, with horrible shamelessness, wanted a man. I knew that to do the part, to reveal a desperate woman with her guard completely down, would take a certain amount of courage."

Picnic starred over-aged William Holden as the youngish drifter Hal Carter who lands in Salinson, Kansas (actually filmed in 1955's humid summer weather at Hutchinson, Kansas), and sends the pulses of several women soaring. Kim Novak is the object of his local prowling while Susan Strasberg, as the younger sister, awakens to the wonder of the male figure. Rosemary, the old-maid schoolteacher, gets drunk and throws herself at Hal at the picnic and rips his shirt from his muscular body. She then practically attacks her constant, patient escort (Arthur O'Connell). It was a different Rosalind Russell that fans saw and liked. She was believable without makeup and convincingly appeared as a middle-aged virgin who is afraid of sex but at the same time realizes it must be now or never.

Miss Russell insists that a good portion of her Rosemary role was cut from the release print of *Picnic.* "I had two or three scenes in my room, none of which were in it. One of these scenes I particularly regretted being cut. She was waiting for her boyfriend, . . . and she went to the mirror. She looked at herself and took her hands and tried to pull her face up. Then she picked up the mascara and spit into it and put it on her eyes. You knew by the way she pulled her face up that she wished she were younger, and she did the typical thing of somebody who tries to cover it with makeup. It didn't run seven seconds, but it said so much. When you lose a scene like that, it hurts."

Roz might well have had an elusive Oscar had her pride not been so important. The studio promoted her as a probable candidate as Best Supporting Actress, but she objected vehemently, stating that her performance (by special billing) entitled her to Best Actress consideration. Consequently, she was *not* nominated at all. Had she allowed her name to be entered as Best Supporting, chances are that she would have overshadowed 1955's winner, Jo Van Fleet of *East of Eden.*

Sandwiched between her scenes for *Picnic,* Rosalind managed to be seen twice (August 28, 1955, and September 4, 1955) on "The Loretta Young Show" over NBC-TV, and on March 18, 1956, she portrayed a spinster on "GE Theatre" in *The Night Goes On* (CBS-TV).

Always anxious to try her skill at writing, Rosalind, with the help of Larry Marcus, wrote a story called *The Unguarded Moment* from which Marcus and Herb Meadows fashioned a screenplay for Universal. The movie emerged in August 1956 with Esther Williams (minus bathing-suit scenes) as a high school teacher who is accused of sexually attacking a student (John Saxon). It is debatable whether Rosalind co-authored the story with herself in mind to portray the teacher, but it did serve as a means of journalistic expression, something she had always wanted to do.

In Rosalind's own words, "During *Picnic,* I read the galleys of Patrick Dennis's new book, *Auntie Mame.* I immediately got in touch with Bobby Fryer, *Auntie Mame's*

producer, and Morton Da Costa, the director, and told them I would do it on Broadway." The novel, which had been on the best-seller lists for eighty-seven weeks, was adapted for the stage by Jerome Lawrence and Robert E. Lee.

With twenty-five percent of the show owned by her, Rosalind opened as *Auntie Mame* on Wednesday, October 31, 1956, at the Broadhurst Theatre. Here was the opportunity to regain her top-paid film-star status, a position she had ironically relinquished by accepting the demanding, but supporting role in *Picnic.* In the twenty-five scene changes of the comedy, she had fourteen separate costumes and five different wigs requiring her to switch from one to another in times ranging from ten seconds to two minutes. Her most elaborate change of costumes (to a yellow chiffon peignoir with ostrich feathers, for example) had six assistants helping. When asked in an interview how she got her tremendous energy, she responded, "People are always asking if I get my energy from yogurt or some secret formula. Ha! I admit to vitamins when I don't forget them, but my energy is *au naturel,* thank the good Lord. Add lots of food and the fact that I came of sturdy Irish stock." Her weight during *Auntie Mame* was a slim 120 pounds.

The critics were wild about her exuberant performance ("Absolutely perfect," *Life* magazine) which was the crux of the show. Without a dynamic personality such as Roz's, the stage production, very episodic in format, could have easily fallen apart. On May 14, 1957, the Frederick Brisson-Robert Griffith-Harold Prince musical version of *Anna Christie,* called *New Girl in Town* (with Gwen Verdon), opened on Broadway, which brought the Brissons together in New York (fourteen-year-old Lance had been living with his mother at the Hotel Pierre before Frederick joined them). In July 1957, Roz took a well-earned month's vacation from *Auntie Mame,* but returned in August and played the role until January 18, 1958, when she left to make the movie version in Hollywood at Warner Bros. She was replaced on Broadway by Greer Garson while three touring companies

As *Auntie Mame* on Broadway in 1957.

←

On the set of *The Girl Rush* ('55).

With Arthur O'Connell in *Picnic* ('55).

took to the road (Constance Bennett, Sylvia Sidney, and Eve Arden each interpreted the madcap woman).

Morton Da Costa also directed the 1958 film, adapted by Betty Comden and Adolph Green, while Orry-Kelly had a creator's dream designing the flamboyant array of costumes. The set decoration was accomplished by George James Hopkins, and Bronislau Kaper composed the music. But it is Rosalind Russell's movie: her wild yet kind-hearted, goofy yet wise, unconscionable yet caring, characterization of the most unique person ever to radiate sunshine on Beekman Place.

The story revolves around the central character of Auntie Mame, an obviously well-to-do (at the start) perennial partygiver. It is during one of these prohibition-era shindigs, attended by every type of person imaginable, that maid Norah Muldoon (Connie Gilchrist) delivers Mame's orphaned nephew Patrick (Jan Handzlik) to his aunt with whom he and Norah will reside. Although she hadn't expected the youth till the following day, she greets him hurriedly and tells him to circulate among the guests. In order for the boy to make a game of it, she tells him to take pad and pencil and write down any words he hears but does not understand. After the last free-loading guest has departed and the very drunk, English-accented Vera Charles (Coral Browne), "the first lady of the American stage," has been carted off, Mame greets her nephew with, "Oh, there you are, my little love. Well, now you come right over here with your Auntie Mame and sit down for one minute and we'll really get to know each other." She obviously looks forward to raising the boy and tells him, "Your Auntie Mame's going to open doors for you, Patrick, doors you never even dreamed existed. Oh, what times we're going to have."

When the 1929 stockmarket crash occurs, Mame's fortune is gone. She tries her hand at several salary-providing jobs—acting, sales, and switchboard operator—but fails miserably on each count. She then meets Beauregard Burnside (Forrest Tucker) who has money, charm, and a southern estate. They are wed, but during their extended European honeymoon, Beauregard falls off an Alpine mountain and Mame is a bereft but rich widow. She decides to write her memoirs, assisted by Brian O'Bannion (Robin Hughes) and her mousy secretary, Agnes Gooch (Peggy Cass). As Mame dresses up meek Agnes for a date with O'Bannion, she instructs the frightened woman, "Live, live, live. Life is a banquet and most poor suckers are starving to death."

Meanwhile, Patrick is now grown up and handsome (Roger Smith) and wants to marry snooty Gloria Upson (Joanna Barnes) who belongs to society's "top drawer" and whose parents (Lee Patrick and Willard Waterman) are very square, bigoted folk—the type Mame finds intolerable. She puts an end to the romance by revealing their true traits to Patrick and he takes a shine to Pegeen Ryan (Pippa Scott), the domestic of whom Mame fully approves. They marry and have a son who is taken under the ageless Mame's wing. Mame proposes a trip to India to the boy with the promise of opening new doors to him, "Doors you never even dreamed existed. Oh, what times we're going to have." Patrick and Pegeen resign themselves to the boy's joyous fate.

While more bland and slapstick than the play, the film does sparkle nearly every second. And, like the play, it belongs to Rosalind Russell. Perhaps she was playing herself (she claims *Mame* is almost a carbon copy of one of her sisters), but it is the greatest portrayal of her professional career. She *is* the character. No other actress could have done as well (although Eve Arden almost came close on stage). *Variety* called it a "faithfully funny recording of the hit play" and stated, "Miss Russell scores because her native intelligence augments her sharp comedy sense," and *Life* magazine credited her performance as "superb." The film would gross $9.3 million in U. S. and Canadian distributors' domestic rentals.

On November 30, 1958, four days after the official release of *Auntie Mame*, Rosalind starred on television in the CBS network two-hour, color, prime-time (nine to eleven) Ford Spectacular Special of *Wonderful Town*.

With both events occurring simultaneously, *Life* observed that Roz would "make the U.S. a livelier, brighter, noisier, happier land."

The Academy Award nominations in February 1959 gave Rosalind her fourth bid as Best Actress. Beforehand, she had been presented with her third Golden Globe Award from the Hollywood Foreign Press. The competition for the Oscar was stiff: Deborah Kerr (*Separate Tables*), Shirley MacLaine (*Some Came Running*), Elizabeth Taylor (*Cat on a Hot Tin Roof*), and Susan Hayward (*I Want to Live!*). All except Miss MacLaine were previous nominees and had never won. During the Monday, April 6, 1959, ceremonies at the Pantages Theatres, with an estimated video audience of 67,851,000, Angela Lansbury, Joan Collins, and Dana Wynter sang that year's comedy song, in which they revealed "Any of our grandmothers could have done as well." The NBC camera swung over the theatre audience for a close-up of Rosalind who was *not* smiling. The winner of the Best Actress trophy that night was Susan Hayward, a five-time nominee. The saga of *Auntie Mame* was not over, for it would be translated into a 1966 Broadway musical (*Mame*) with Angela Lansbury in the lead, and still later into a musical movie in 1974 with Lucille Ball struggling through the lead.

In June 1959, Noël Coward informed friends and columnists that he wanted "boxoffice blockbuster" Rosalind Russell to star in his next play, but this wish did not reach fruition. (She would have been excellent in Coward's musical *Sail Away*, 1961) which floundered on Broadway with Elaine Stritch in the lead.) In fact, Rosalind, except for charity and committee work, did nothing professionally until three years after the release of *Auntie Mame.*

It is nearly impossible for any major public figure not to endure periods of public or peer disapproval. Rosalind entered into such a period during the early Sixties when in quick succession she plucked three meaty lead roles in movies which were based on Broadway successes and had been performed on the stage by actresses wrongly overlooked for the film versions. It did nothing to endear Rosal-ind to a good many in the industry. But she was determined to have her way, whether she was suitable or not for any of the three demanding parts!

A Majority of One (Warner Bros., 1961) had starred plump Gertrude Berg as the Jewish Mrs. Jacoby through 556 performances on Broadway in 1959. Miss Berg had been "promised" the movie role, but, to her and others' surprise, she was to read in the *New York Times* that Rosalind had been signed to do it. This obvious box-office baiting maneuver by producer-director Mervyn LeRoy (evidently fearful of casting a Jewish lady to play a Jewish role) caused Hedda Hopper to write, "So, in Hollywood only Christians are allowed to portray Jews." Rosalind would admit, "I doubt that I ever worked so hard before in preparing myself for a part." Disguised in a gray wig and wearing "Mrs. Jacoby-type clothes," she walked and shopped in the Bronx and Brooklyn Yiddish sections and rode the subways to obtain the feeling of being a native New Yorker. She also questioned her Jewish friends about speech and customs.

Within the scenario, Mrs. Jacoby is a widow with memories; since her only son had been killed in the Pacific during World War II, she is not anxious to think kindly of the Japanese. When her daughter's (Madlyn Rhue) husband (Ray Danton) is sent to Tokyo on a trade mission, the daughter asks Mama to go along. The idea is none too appealing, but she agrees to accompany them. Aboard ship she encounters a Japanese industrialist, Mr. Asano (Alec Guinness), with whom she gets along very well until the son-in-law insinuates that Asano is playing up to her to get on the good side of him for business reasons. Later, the trade meetings are halted when Mr. Asano is insulted by the outspoken son-in-law, but Mrs. Jacoby patches things up and the talks are successfully resumed. During a series of get-acquainted sequences, during which Mr. Asano teaches Mrs. Jacoby something of Japanese culture, he proposes marriage to her. She reluctantly rejects him because of her feeling that they each have too many memories and prejudices to overcome.

Implanting her prints at
Grauman's Chinese Theatre
in 1959.

In *Auntie Mame* ('58).

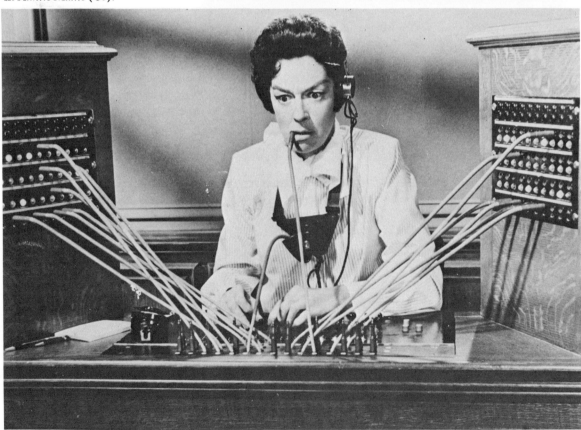

With son Lance ('60).

With Alec Guinness in *A Majority of One* ('61).

Some months later, back in New York, Mr. Asano is a U.N. delegate and renews his friendship with Mrs. Jacoby which the audience assumes will lead to much more.

Employing a Semitic accent that slipped occasionally from Brooklyn to Beekman Place, Rosalind looked matronly enough, but one could not get beyond the impression that it was actually Auntie Mame dressed in a kimono and a gray wig.

Frederick Brisson had co-produced (with The Playwrights' Company) a "new" play by Peter Shaffer in London and New York in 1959 with Jessica Tandy and Roland Culver. Directed by John Gielgud, both stage runs of *Five Finger Exercise* were considered successful. But when it was announced that Columbia would produce a film version of the play with Brisson again producing, it was little surprise to anyone that Rosalind garnered the lead role in the 1962 black-and-white film.

Originally, Alec Guinness was to play opposite Rosalind again, but he bowed out and Jack Hawkins was substituted. The scene of the drama of family tensions and frustrations was switched from England to Carmel-by-the-Sea and suffered in the translation. In the Harrington family beach house, Louise (Rosalind), the mother, has scorned her husband Stanley (Hawkins) for many years because of his coarseness and lack of what she considers culture. The children, Philip (Richard Beymer) and Pamela (Annette Gorman), are pampered and restless. Into this unhappy environment comes Walter (Maximilian Schell), a German refugee whom Louise has hired to tutor Pamela and who has bitter memories of his family.

Walter makes several mistakes by attempting to solve the family's problems, but the error Louise commits is to assume that Walter will be charmed enough by her to want her as a lover. All he desires is to be part of an atmosphere of family love. When he confesses to Louise that he thinks of her as a mother, she orders him to leave. With his departure, the family members are left to solve their own problems (one of which is the son's too strong, dependent feeling for Walter). Paul V. Beckley's observation in the *New York Herald-Tribune* was, "Rosalind Russell plays the mother like a subdued Auntie Mame," while Hollis Alpert denounced her in *The Saturday Review* with, "Was it Daniel Mann who was responsible for Rosalind Russell's at times ludicrous performance, or was it the eminent lady herself?"

As a result of *Five Finger Exercise,* Roz was the butt of some very unkind Hollywood "in" jokes. Some insisted "Roz wanted to play *Five Finger Exercise* badly. . .and she did." Others suggested that in a year when former cinema greats Bette Davis and Joan Crawford were staging comebacks in grand guignol horror films like *What Ever Happened To Baby Jane?* Roz had unwittingly offered her own entry in the cycle.

In turn, no one could mistake Rosalind for her Auntie Mame self in *Gypsy* (Warner Bros., 1962). In fact, she emerges as a loud Rosalind Russell who is trying very, very hard to be "socko" like Ethel Merman. Miss Merman, who created the important lead role of Gypsy Rose Lee's mother, Rose, on Broadway in 1959, was not considered by Warner Bros. as box-office insurance. Hence, the switch in actresses was made. In all fairness to Rosalind, Warners was wrong and so was Roz to have undertaken such a strong musical role. Natalie Wood, in the title role, displays pretty legs and caressable shoulders, but a stripper she is not. Mervyn LeRoy directed and produced these two ladies, and he too should have known better.

The story, familiar to most theater and filmgoers by now, is about the domineering, stagestruck mother who propels her two daughters into show business, guided by a obsession for their stardom. Her total being is motivated to making a success of their lives. Time passes her by and she has nothing left to do but get old. Rosalind "sings" most of the five songs assigned to her character with Lisa Kirk's belting voice dubbed in for the stronger notes. Despite its many flaws, the film attracted box-office grosses to the tune of $6 million in U.S. and Canadian distributors' rentals.

Time magazine noncommittedly found, "Roz is a Roz is a Roz is a Roz," but Bosley

Crowther of the *New York Times* was not ambiguous when he wrote, "That tornado of a stage mother that Ethel Merman portrayed on Broadway in the musical comedy *Gypsy* comes out little more than a big wind in the portrayal that Rosalind Russell gives her in the transfer of the comedy to the screen." The film's finale is unsatisfactory and quite disappointing. At the time in Gypsy's life when she finally gets the nerve and confidence to tell her mother to leave her alone, she later relents and takes Mama to a party with her. Once again the blandness of the Hollywood syndrome had taken its toll on a property. In 1974, *Gypsy* would be revived on Broadway, after a successful London and American tour, with Angela Lansbury as Mama Rose.

Having exhausted her array of stage properties to turn into screen vehicles, Roz settled back into private life for four years.

Not that the very well-known actress was not asked to grace assorted vehicles. David Merrick, who had wanted Ethel Merman and had considered Betty Hutton for the role, asked Roz to star in *Hello, Dolly!* Why did she refuse this blockbuster role? As she later informed Mike Steen for *Hollywood Speaks*, " . . . I wasn't excited over it when I read it. I thought it just another musical, and frankly, I didn't think the script very good. It only has one good number, the title song, and that wasn't even in it at that time. . . .What can be layered onto a show like that is the difference between a hit and a semihit or a failure. It also needs a popular star."

Roz did return to the screen in a winsome comedy, *The Trouble with Angels* (1966), directed by Ida Lupino. The film is based on the novel *Life with Mother Superior* by Jane Trahey and was filmed in a Philadelphia suburb and in Hollywood. Interestingly, Gypsy Rose Lee has a supporting role as a civilian recruited by the nuns of St. Francis Academy to give tips to the young novices on the art of physical balance (i.e. walking with poise). Rosalind received top billing, but it is Hayley Mills, as a naughty future nun Mary Clancy, whose exploits provide the story framework and who gains the most attention. The world-wise Mother Superior (Rosalind) calmly meets Mary's challenge head-on and manages to make a responsible lass of her. Bosley Crowther (*New York Times*) erased the Patrick Dennis stigma attached to Roz by crediting the star as playing the lofty Mother Superior "with such an air of serene composure that you'd never think she once went wild as Auntie Mame." On the other hand, Rex Reed thought the film "harmless, but as indigestible as cold tea at a wedding breakfast."

In a interview with *Life* magazine's David Zeitlin, which resulted in the September 10, 1965 article entitled "The Indestructible Roz," Roz stated, "It's okay to have talent, but talent is the least of it. In a performance or a career, you've got to have vitality. I've worked with actors and actresses far better than I'll ever be—as far as talent goes. But what they have just doesn't register because they don't have a resilience, and they don't have the drive underneath to project. . . . Sometimes what you have to do is almost claw your work onto film."

Between her scenes on *The Trouble with Angels,* Rosalind worked in Jamaica as the horribly outlandish Madame Rosepettle in the film version of Arthur L. Kopit's play, *Oh Dad, Poor Dad, Mamma's Hung You in the Closet and I'm Feeling So Sad* (Paramount, 1967). Hermione Gingold had the role at New York's Phoenix Theatre in 1962, in the national touring company, and was among the most bizarrely impressive actresses who starred in the vehicle in summer stock. The film had been completed in 1965, but underwent mammoth editing, revisions, new musical score additions, and alterations before its eventual 1967 distribution. Its release prompted *Time* magazine to pen, "They should have stuffed it." To *Life*'s David Zeitlind in 1965, Roz confided, "It takes a lot of concentration going from Mother Superior to Madame Rosepettle, that awful woman . . .that fiend, the mom to end all moms, the most frightful creature I've ever played. But I think so hard about one character that the other lady is automatically dismissed. It's just like erasing a blackboard."

Within this weird cinema exercise known as *Oh Dad,* "Dad" (Jonathan Winters),

On the set of *Gypsy* with director Mervyn LeRoy in March 1962.

With Annette Gorman, Maximilian Schell, and Jack Hawkins in *Five Finger Exercise* ('62).

With Bette Davis arriving
in New York in November
1962.

With Karl Malden,
Natalie Wood, and Ann
Jilliann in *Gypsy*.

At a Hollywood costume ball in
December 1966.

←

With Hayley Mills and June Harding in
The Trouble with Angels ('66).

whose earthly remains are carted around by his deranged wife in a coffin, sits upon a cloud in heaven trying to beguile his down-below son (Robert Morse) toward a stable manhood. The widow (Rosalind) unwittingly foils his carefully conceived plans. She first marries Commodore Roseabove (Hugh Griffith) whose early demise via drowning throws her into mourning. But she is not too grief-stricken to "rescue" her son from an over-sexed gal (Barbara Harris) whose presence was engineered by Dad. With two coffins containing as many dead husbands, Madame Rosepettle Roseabove leaves her Jamaican vacation spot with Sonny, who is unfortunate enough to be forever Mama's boy. Of this stylized back comedy which became inane, arch slapstick oncamera, *Variety* rated Rosalind with showing "more professional guts than good judgment in accepting weird-for-her film roles, as this particular film again exemplifies." (Some of the blame for the picture's failure had to rest with director Richard Quine.)

Still another play and another actress' stage vehicle was the basis for Rosalind's 1968 release, *Rosie!* (Universal). The comedy, adapted from the French by and starring Ruth Gordon, had run for only twenty-eight performances on Broadway in 1965. Since this is a Ross Hunter production, which is synonymous with well-mounted if vapid filmfare, the focus is on the look rather than the content. But the storyline is so weak and outdated that not many Americans saw it during its rather limited run. Rosie Lord (Rosalind) is a lady of means whose daughters (Audrey Meadows and Vanessa Brown) wish to have her committed to a mental hospital so they can gain control of her wealth before she might squander it. They are thwarted in their efforts by an attorney (Brian Aherne), Rosie's granddaughter (Sandra Dee), and the latter's love interest (James Farentino). At the end of the ninety-eight minutes, Rosie wins the attorney's affection and the unfeeling daughters are relegated to domestic exile. *Variety's* snappy critique included, "Essentially a drama with comedy overtones, *Rosie!* could be called 'Whatever Happened to Auntie Mame?'"

Whereas *The Trouble with Angels* had provided box-office interest (it grossed $4.2 million in distributors' domestic rentals) with its sure-fire display of long-legged (Mary Wickes) and hard-nosed but soft-hearted (Binnie Barnes) nuns, the sequel *Where Angels Go—Trouble Follows* (Columbia, 1968) is a rehash of the predecessor, with comely Stella Stevens supplanting Hayley Mills as the thorn in Mother Superior's (Rosalind) side. As young Sister George, Miss Stevens feels she must be close to the young people in their search for reason but learns through several close calls that she must maintain a degree of aloofness. In the opinion of *Variety,* the film is "mildly amusing and innocuous." Not even the guest appearances of Milton Berle, Arthur Godfrey, Van Johnson, Robert Taylor, and William Lundigan served to bolster the box-office receipts of this weak effort.

Even before Dorothy Gilman's suspense novel, *The Unexpected Mrs. Pollifax,* was published in 1970, her agent sent the galleys to Charles Forsythe, staff associate of Frederick Brisson. It was hoped that the property might be of interest to Rosalind. Forsythe was enthused about the prospects and phoned Russell, "I have found your next picture and you must use all of your best *Mame* instincts to create the role."

But as it turned out, Rosalind was fearful that the critics might say she was repeating herself if she made the character too much like *Mame.* Using the name C. A. McKnight (her mother's) Rosalind penned—and repenned—and repenned—the screen version which was filmed in Mexico and Wyoming in late 1970 but not released until March 1971 by United Artists.

Produced by Frederick Brisson, *Mrs. Pollifax—Spy* is the tale of a New Jersey widow who winds up in the employ of the C.I.A. She is a bit absent-minded, but is assigned to smuggle microfilm out of Albania (who would ever suspect a dizzy woman of this nefarious assignment?). If it was physical exercise the star wanted, she got plenty of it in this project. She and younger co-star Darren

McGavin slid down hillsides, waded rivers, crawled on hands and knees through mud, and rode burros. In *Show* magazine's estimation, the film was "reminiscent of those 'fifties' patriotic comedies that in 1971 seem more than a trifle cavalier."

It was after completing *Mrs. Pollifax* that veteran star Rosalind Russell was struck down by rheumatoid arthritis.* The painful disease settled in her hands, knees, and ankles, but she fought the crippling ailment with "fierce willpower, exercise, and injections of gold." The gold, in liquid form and $100 per dose, was injected into her hips and she swam every day that she was able to move.

The year 1969 also provided Rosalind with another major upset. For some twelve years prior, Rosalind and Brisson had been packaging a stage musical to be based on the life of Coco Chanel, the famed Parisian couturier. By 1968 announcements were publicly made that the Alan Jay Lerner book and song show would soon go into actual production. It was assumed that Rosalind would have the title role in the expensive venture. But it was not to be. Granted, Miss Russell was never happy with the book, yet she was ready to star in the show. However at a later date the aged Miss Chanel, who had final say over the casting of her stage counterpart, was approached with the suggestion that Katharine Hepburn, and not Rosalind, be given the part. Some observers on the scene insist that the infirm Miss Chanel thought the negotiators meant Audrey Hepburn, and she gave her consent. For whatever assortment of reasons, Katharine Hepburn was given the plum assignment in the Frederick Brisson production and opened in the show on Broadway on December 18, 1969. Rosalind was deeply hurt by the out-

---

* When Dr. Richard Freyberg informed Roz that she had been one of the severest cases of rheumatoid arthritis he had ever seen, he added, "You will have to learn to live with this because we have found no cure for it yet. You may have a remission on your own, which would be God-given but would make you believe I am a miracle worker. Or you may get worse, at which point you will consider me a flop."

Russell would later react with, "If I beat this rap, I promise myself, my God, Dr. Freyberg, and anybody else who may be listening, that I will do everything in my power to wipe out this disease that I would not wish on Hitler . . . well, *maybe* on Hitler."

come, but managed to put on a brave face and was among the first to congratulate Miss Hepburn on opening night at the Mark Hellinger Theatre. (Years later, Brisson would reveal that on the night of the opening Roz was in great pain with the on-setting rheumatoid arthritis. "But she somehow managed to laugh her way through the lavish party Earl Blackwell gave for the cast afterwards and to shake hands with over a hundred friends. . . . The next morning her hands were swollen to twice their size.")

Also during 1968-1969, it was mentioned in the trade press that Miss Russell would be Hetty Green, the rich eccentric in the Joseph E. Levine-proposed film version of the novel *The Day They Shook the Plum Tree.* (Another rumored star for this project was Bette Davis.) The venture never came to be. Then, it was touted that Rosalind would portray Aimee Semple McPherson in a Brisson-produced stage musical, but this did not come to pass either.*

In 1971, Rosalind made appearances on several of the major talk shows, her aim being to promote the crusade against arthritis. Audiences were shocked to see Roz with her bloated face, a victim of the reaction of cortisone drugs in her own battle against arthritis. As Roz told writer Mike Steen, "I never in my life have had so much mail! You are seen by millions and millions of people, and I think that is as good an ad as you can get. I wasn't used to that. I am still staggered, . . ." (Despite her health problems, Roz could joke about her physical looks, calling herself "Miss Chipmunk" with the big cheeks.) In September 1972 Rosalind and Clint Eastwood were named by President Richard M. Nixon to six-year terms as members of the National Council on the Arts. They replaced Helen Hayes and Charlton Heston.

On November 8, 1972, Rosalind appeared in what was to be her last film role. On ABC-TV she starred with Douglas Fairbanks, Jr., and Maureen O'Sullivan in the telefeature *The Crooked Hearts.* Roz had worked with Miss O'Sullivan in *West Point of the Air* in 1935 and lost the man to her, but she had never before worked with the still very suave Mr. Fairbanks. Shot at the Twentieth Century-Fox studios and on location in Santa Barbara, it is the story of a con man (Fairbanks) and his unsuccessful attempts to bilk a widow (Rosalind) of her fortune. Miss O'Sullivan is his shady lady friend. On the Fox set, Roz told Leslie Raddatz of *TV Guide,* "A lot of people give up. Not me," and she did a little dance step to show her determination at fighting arthritis which had left its tell-tale traces in her hands.

At the Oscar ceremonies on Tuesday, March 27, 1973, Rosalind was honored with the Jean Hersholt Humanitarian Award, presented to her by her very good friend Frank Sinatra,* and in November 1973 she was cochairperson with Anita May of a benefit premiere of Columbia's *The Way We Were* which raised $150,000 for Cedars-Sinai Hospital. She was said to have signed a deal to film a TV pilot called *Phyllis in Philadelphia* but this did not see the light of day. In February 1974 she was an oncamera narrator for the ABC-TV two-part special, *The Movies,* a trip into nostalgia. At the Los Angeles International Film Exposition on Sunday, March 31, 1974, at the Paramount Theatre, she was honored by a special tribute, during which scenes were shown of twelve of her feature films. She also attended the five-hour-long celebration honoring James Cagney at the Los Angeles Century Plaza Hotel.

In April 1974, she was credited with saying that if she had been in charge of casting *Mame,* the movie version of the hit musical, she would have chosen Cher Bono rather than Lucille Ball to portray the lead. However, a month later she paid tribute to Miss Ball, who

* The project at one time had been announced as a vehicle for Ann Sheridan. At first, when Miss Russell was suggested for the project, she was to play the lead role. Later, it was announced that if the show did happen, she would portray the evangelist's mother. As it developed, in the November 1976 TV movie Bette Davis portrayed the mama of Aimee Semple McPherson (Faye Dunaway).

* Sinatra said in presenting Roz with the Award, ". . . [she] has been nominated for an Oscar four times. But knowing her as I do, she would rather have this one than the other four." Russell's teary response was, "This is for me the Impossible Dream. I accept it with a sense of guilt, knowing that it belongs to all those who ease the pain, bind the wounds and fill the emptiness of others."

With Robert Morse in
*Oh Dad, Poor Dad,
Mamma's Hung You in
the Closet and I'm
Feeling So Sad* ('67).

With James Farentino in
Rosie! ('68).

Kicking up a storm in England in February 1971.

With Darren McGavin in *Mrs. Pollifax—Spy* ('71).

had been named Humanitarian of the Year by the Sunair Foundation, at the Foundation's festivities held at the Beverly Hilton Hotel. In July 1974, Rosalind was named "The Ideal Woman of Any Era" at the twenty-seventh reunion of General Patton's Sixth Armored Division, held in Anaheim, California.

On Sunday, September 22, 1974, Roz was toasted in a retrospective at New York's Town Hall. (Previous honorees of John Springer's series of salutes to ladies of the screen were Bette Davis, Myrna Loy, Sylvia Sidney, and Joan Crawford, with the later-saluted Lana Turner receiving the biggest turnout.) Frederick Brisson described it as "an evening in which the audience wouldn't sit down. It wasn't just a standing ovation. It was continuous standing. Then, afterwards they threw flowers at Roz like she was an opera star." She told the audience that she was considering a return to the stage in a musical version of Thomas Wolfe's *Look Homeward Angel.* Clips of her films were shown and she answered a few questions submitted to her by audience members. She was gracious, imposing, but hardly revealing in her brief remarks, generally repeating anecdotes and statements that she had made to the press before. A few days later, Addison Verrill in *Variety* commented, "The lobby at intermission resembled a gay bar. Understandably, then, the biggest ovation went to clips from *The Women.*" The following evening at the Rainbow Room, "New York's most glamorous restaurant," Rosalind was guest of honor at a dinner hosted by Joan Crawford. The formal event was attended by, among others, Henry Fonda, Joan Bennett, Peggy Lee, Butterfly McQueen, and Tammy Grimes.

In a period of Russell tributes, she was asked by the San Francisco Opera Company to appear as the Duchess of Krakenthorp in their November 1974 production of Donizetti's *The Daughter of the Regiment.* She rejected the offer and Hermione Gingold replaced her. Previously, on Sunday, October 6, 1974, she was honored by the American National Theatre at a dinner-dance held in Bel Air. The event was sponsored by ANTA

West, for which John Forsythe served as emcee while guests such as Natalie Wood, Janet Blair, and Edie Adams contributed to the program. Rosalind and Miss Adams sang the "Ohio" duet from *Wonderful Town.* In the thirty-nine years since the inception of ANTA, this was only the third occasion that a celebrity was so honored. In 1972 Alfred Lunt and Lynn Fontanne, and in 1973 Katharine Cornell, were subjects of tributes.

In November 1974, the Brissons' son Lance became a deputy of Los Angeles Supervisor Baxter Ward's staff. Earlier he had been employed by *Look* magazine and was partially responsible for the expose of San Francisco mayor Joseph Alioto's alleged affiliations with unsavory organizations.

In December 1974, Rosalind appeared at the Ford Theatre in Washington, D.C. for yet another retrospective, "A Tribute to Rosalind Russell—The Career of an American Woman." Again, film clips were shown and John Daly, former host of TV's "What's My Line?," moderated a question-and-answer period. In the front row of the audience were President and Mrs. Gerald Ford.

Lance Brisson was wed to Patricia Morrow (of "Peyton Place" TV fame) on Saturday, March 15, 1975, in a private church ceremony. Enclosed with the wedding invitation was a card stating, "Patricia and Lance will not be accepting any gifts except donations to the Franciscan Center for the Poor . . . in Los Angeles."

A week later, on March 22, 1975, Rosalind appeared on a TV telethon on behalf of the Arthritis Foundation in an appeal for funds, and thereafter was in a film clip for the Tony Awards, but the following month she was admitted to Cedars-Sinai Hospital for treatment of viral pneumonia. "I thought I just had a cold," she said later. "Then I fell unconscious —for three days. If Freddie hadn't been home, I wouldn't have lived through the night. Cedars saved my life—nine doctors, and I don't know how many nurses." She was given a clean bill of health and released from the hospital on Wednesday, May 14, 1975.

In June 1975, she received the Straw Hat

Special Achievement Award from Cary Grant. The honor is bestowed annually to a graduate of a stock acting company who has advanced to further distinction in the arts.

When Rosalind returned to Cedars-Sinai Hospital in October 1975 for a kidney infection, the public at large was unaware how near to death she was. As the seemingly indefatigable actress later reported, "My kidneys stopped working. My body was quickly poisoning itself to death. I was writhing in an agony of death." The assorted specialists brought in as consultants had only a negative prognosis. "They said I should just be allowed to die with a minimum of pain," Russell later told *The National Enquirer*. "But I refused to be cheated out of my life." As Brisson remembers the traumatic time, "I held her hand and prayed, waiting through what the doctors thought would be her last night. But in the morning, to everyone's surprise, Roz started on the slow road to recovery. The miracle had happened." When Rosalind was finally released from the hospital, she remained at home for a lengthy recuperation. It was during this period, on November 28, 1975, that Brisson's eighty-one-year-old mother, Cleo, died.

When Rosalind was forced to cancel all her Arthritis Foundation charity work, her pal Jane Wyman agreed to substitute for her. It was another indication to the industry and to the now-aware public that Rosalind might never be able to return to public appearances again. But then Rosalind surprised everyone by turning out at the World of Entertainment tribute at the Beverly Hilton Hotel (on February 3, 1976) for Israel's Prime Minister Yitzhak Rabin.

More remarkable was the showmanship she displayed in April when she accompanied her husband to New York for the opening of *So Long, 174th Street*. (It was a musical version of *Enter Laughing* and starred her one-time movie co-star, Robert Morse. The show closed very quickly.) Looking much fitter than she had in a long time, Rosalind gave interviews to the press, recorded radio commercials for her husband's show, and announced that she had been working with

Chris Chase on her autobiography. A few months after the Brissons returned to the coast, Rosalind entered UCLA Medical Center for surgery to have her right hip joint replaced, hoping it would ease her arthritic condition.

By the time Russell was hospitalized for her hip operation, it had become common knowledge to her close friends and associates that her recent bouts of dire ill health had been complicated by a cancerous condition. When she was discharged from the hospital in the autumn of 1976, it was recognized that she was going home to await death.* Although her physical condition was extremely poor, her mental state in general remained amazingly upbeat and practical. In fact, some weeks before the end, the brave but realistic lady hostessed a dinner party. Many attendees considered it a "farewell appearance." Some guests would later comment how vivacious the actress had been at the occasion.

Then on Sunday, November 28, 1976, at 10:10 A.M., Rosalind died at her Beverly Hills home. With her at the time of death was her husband, her son Lance and his wife Patricia, and Father Curtis. It was a major news item that had to be heard or read at least twice to be believed. Rosalind had always seemed so indestructible that it was difficult to accept that she had passed away.

Only after her demise did Dr. Martin J. Cline reveal to the public at large that she had been suffering from a combination of cancer and rheumatoid arthritis for over fifteen years. He noted that she had undergone a radical mastectomy fifteen years prior, and another more recently. Until approximately a year before, she had had no further problem with the cancer. "It didn't bother her particularly and didn't bother her career. I don't think she believed she had it any more," Cline observed. When the symptoms reappeared, she began receiving chemotherapy and responded to the treatment for the next eight months or so. Thereafter, coping with the disease became extremely painful.

* As Brisson would reveal later, she had begged, "Please, Freddie, let me come home. You promised that when the time came I could be in my own house, in my own bed."

409

With director George
Cukor preparing for
the ABC-TV special
The Movies
(March 31, 1973).

The Living Legend,
1970s-style.

TOWN HALL PRESENTS

A TRIBUTE TO ROSALIND RUSSELL

Produced by John Springer

In Person
and
on Screen

Village Voice,
8/23-30/74

SUNDAY SEPT. 22 7:30 P.M.
ORCHESTRA $10 $8 BALCONY $8 $6
Mail Orders accepted. Send self-addressed stamped envelope to
Town Hall 113 West 43rd St. NY 10036 JU 2-4536

Town Hall

Funeral services were held on December 1, 1976, at 11:00 A.M. at the Church of the Good Shepherd in Beverly Hills. Among those mourners attending the low requiem Mass were Cary Grant, Gregory Peck, Frank Sinatra, Kirk Douglas, James Stewart, and Jack Lemmon. In his eulogy, Peck stated, "She represented everything good about Hollywood." Sinatra said, "I have a feeling God woke up Sunday and said 'You better send for Roz; she's suffered enough.'" Burial took place thereafter at Holy Cross Cemetery. The actress had specified that, instead of flowers, donations could be made to the Rosalind Russell Memorial Fund to help establish a medical research center in her name. Sadly, on December 22nd, Rosalind was to have received the St. Louise De Marillac Humanitarian Award from the Association of Ladies of Charity of St. Vincent de Paul Archdiocese of Los Angeles at a luncheon at the Beverly Hilton Hotel. It was among a number of salutes planned to let the dying star know how beloved she was in the community.

Among those others eulogizing the late star was Robert Young who told the press, "She epitomized elegance, charm, humor, and a lovely sense of the joy of living." "She added great dignity to the world," stated Red Skelton.

Perhaps the best analysis of the distinctive star came from Rosalind herself. She once assessed, "It's okay to have talent. But talent is the least of it. In a performance or a career, you've got to have vitality." And Miss Rosalind Russell certainly did!

FILMOGRAPHY

EVELYN PRENTICE *(MGM, 1934)* 80 min.

Producer, John W. Considine, Jr.; director, William K. Howard; based on the novel by W. E. Woodward; screenplay, Lenore Coffee; music, Oscar Raclin; art directors, Cedric Gibbons, Arnold Gillespie, Edwin B. Willis; wardrobe, Dolly Tree; camera, Charles G. Clarke; editor, Frank Hull.

Myrna Loy (Evelyn Prentice); William Powell (John Prentice); Una Merkel (Amy Drexel); Harvey Stephens (Lawrence Kennard); Isabel Jewell (Judith Wilson); Rosalind Russell (Nancy Harrison); Henry Wadsworth (Chester Wylie); Edward Brophy (Eddie Delaney); Cora Sue Collins (Dorothy Prentice); Jessie Ralph (Mrs. Blake); Perry Ivins (Dr. Gillette); Sam Flint (Dr. Lyons); Pat O'Malley (Detective Pat Thompson); J. P. McGowan (Detective Mack Clark); Jack Mulhall (Gregory); Wilbur Mack, Garry Owen, Phil Tead (Reporters); Herman Bing (Klein, the Antique Dealer); Samuel S. Hinds (Newton); Georgia Caine (Mrs. Newton); John Hyams (Mr. Humphreys); Howard Hickman (Mr. Whitlock); Sam McDaniel (Porter); Billy Gilbert (Barney, the Cafe Owner); Crauford Kent (Guest).

THE PRESIDENT VANISHES *(Paramount, 1934)* 86 min.

Director, William Wellman; screenplay, Lynn Starling, Carey Wilson, Cedric Worth; camera, Barney McGill; editor, Hanson Fritch.

Arthur Byron (President Stanley Craig); Janet Beecher (Mrs. Craig); Paul Kelly (Chick Moffat); Peggy Conklin (Alma Cronin); Rosalind Russell (Sally Voorman); Sidney Blackmer (D. L. Voorman); Douglas Wood (Roger Grant); Walter Kingsford (Drew); DeWitt Jennings (Cullen); Charles Grapewin (Richard Norton); Charles Richman (Corcoran); Jason Robards (Kilbourne); Paul Harvey (Skinner); Robert McWade (Vice-President Molleson); Edward Arnold (Secretary of War Wardell); Osgood Perkins (Harris Brownell); Edward Ellis (Lincoln Lee); Andy Devine (Val Orcott); Harry Woods (Kramer); Irene Franklin (Mrs. Orcott); Clara Blandick (Mrs. Delling); Charles K. French, William Worthington, William S. Holmes, Charles Meakin, Art Howard, Ed Lewis, Ed Mortimer, Emmett King, Edgar Sherrod, Henry Herbert (Senators and Congressmen).

British release title: *The Strange Conspiracy.*

FORSAKING ALL OTHERS *(MGM, 1934)* 84 min.

Producer, Bernard H. Hyman; director, W. S. Van Dyke II; based on the play by Edward Barry Roberts, Frank Morgan Cavett; screenplay, Joseph L. Mankiewicz; music, Dr. William Axt; art directors, Cedric Gibbons, Edwin B. Willis; gowns, Adrian; song, Gus Kahn and Walter Donaldson; camera, Gregg Toland, George Folsey; editor, Tom Held.

Joan Crawford (Mary Clay); Clark Gable (Jeff Williams); Robert Montgomery (Dill Todd); Charles Butterworth (Shep); Billie Burke (Paula); Frances Drake (Connie); Rosalind Russell (Eleanor); Tom Ricketts (Wiffens); Arthur Treacher (Johnson); Greta Meyer (Bella).

THE NIGHT IS YOUNG *(MGM, 1935)* 78 min.

Producer, Harry Rapf; director, Dudley Murphy; based on the story by Vicki Baum; screenplay, Edgar Allan Woolf, Franz Shulz; songs, Sigmund Romberg and Oscar Hammerstein, II; camera, James Wong Howe; editor, Conrad A. Nervig.

Ramon Novarro (Franz Otto); Evelyn Laye (Lisl Gluck); Charles Butterworth (Willy); Una Merkel (Fanni); Henry Stephenson (Emperor); Edward Everett Horton (Szereny); Rosalind Russell (Countess Rafay); Donald Cook (Toni); Charles Judels (Riccordi); Herman Bing (Nepomuk); Christian Rub (Cafe Proprietor); Alberti Conti (Moehler); Elspeth Dudgeon (Duchess); Gustav von Seyffertitz (Ambassador); Carlos J. de Valdez (Adjutant); Snub Pollard (Drummer).

WEST POINT OF THE AIR *(MGM, 1935)* 100 min.

Producer, Monta Bell; director, Richard Rosson; story, James K. McGuinness, John Monk Saunders; screenplay, Frank Wead, Arthur J. Beckhard; camera, Clyde DeVinna, Elmer Dyer; editor, Frank Sullivan.

Wallace Beery (Big Mike); Robert Young (Little Mike); Maureen O'Sullivan (Skip Carter); Russell Hardie (Phil Carter); Lewis Stone (Captain Carter); James Gleason (Joe Bags); Rosalind Russell (Dare); Henry Wadsworth (Pettis); Robert Livingston (Pippinger); Robert Taylor (Jaskarelli); Frank Conroy (Captain Cannon); G. Pat Collins (Lieutenant Kelly); Ronnie Cosby (Mike as a Boy); Bobbie Caldwell (Phil as a Boy); Marilyn Spinner (Skip as a Girl).

THE CASINO MURDER CASE *(MGM, 1935)* 85 min.

Producer, Lucien Hubbard; director, Edwin L. Marin; based on the novel by S. S. Van Dine; screenplay, Florence Ryerson, Edgar Allan Woolf; camera, Charles Clarke; editor, Conrad A. Nervig.

Paul Lukas (Philo Vance); Rosalind Russell (Doris); Alison Skipworth (Mrs. Llewellyn); Donald Cook (Lynn); Arthur Byron (Kincaid); Ted Healy (Sergeant Heath); Eric Blore (Currie); Isabel Jewell (Amelia); Louise Fazenda (Becky); Leslie Fenton (Dr. Kane); Louise Henry (Virginia); Purnell Pratt (Inspector Markham); Leo G. Carroll (Smith); Charles Sellon (Dr. Doremus); William Demarest (Auctioneer); Grace Hayle (Fat Lady); Ernie Adams (Husband of Fat Lady); Milton Kibbee, Tom Herbert (Reporters); Keye Luke (Taki); Edna Bennett (Nurse).

RECKLESS (MGM, 1935) 96 min.

Producer, David O. Selznick; director, Victor Fleming; story, Oliver Jeffries; screenplay, P. J. Wolfson; songs, Gus Kahn and Walter Donaldson; Oscar Hammerstein II and Jerome Kern; Herbert Magidson and Con Conrad; Harold Adamson and Burton Lane; Adamson, Ed H. Knopf, and Jack King; camera, George Folsey; editor, Margaret Booth.

Jean Harlow (Mona); William Powell (Ned Riley); Franchot Tone (Bob Harrison); May Robson (Granny); Ted Healy (Smiley); Nat Pendleton (Blossom); Robert Light (Paul Mercer); Rosalind Russell (Jo); Henry Stephenson (Harrison); Louise Henry (Louise); James Ellison (Dale Every); Leon Ames (Ralph Watson); Man Mountain Dean (Himself); Farina (Gold Dust); Allan Jones (Allan); Carl Randall, Nina Mae McKinney (Themselves).

CHINA SEAS (MGM, 1935) 89 min.

Producer, Albert Lewis; director, Tay Garnett; based on the novel by Crosbie Garstin; screenplay, Jules Furthman, James Kevin McGuinness; song, Arthur Freed and Nacio Herb Brown; costumes, Adrian; art director, Cedric Gibbons; camera, Ray June; editor, William Levanway.

Clark Gable (Captain Alan Gaskell); Jean Harlow (China Doll [Dolly Portland]); Wallace Beery (Jamesy MacArdle); Lewis Stone (Tom Davids); Rosalind Russell (Sybil Barclay); Dudley Digges (Dawson); C. Aubrey Smith (Sir Guy Wilmerding); Robert Benchley (Charlie McCaleb); William Henry (Rockwell); Live Demaigret (Mrs. Volberg); Lilian Bond (Mrs. Timmons); Edward Brophy (Wilbur Timmons); Soo Yong (Yu-Lan); Carol Ann Beery (Carol Ann); Akim Tamiroff (Romanoff); Ivan Lebedeff (Ngah); Hattie McDaniel (Isabel McCarthy); Donald Meek (Chess Player); Emily Ritzroy (Lady); Pat Flaherty (Second Officer Kingston); Forrester Harvey (Steward); Tom Gubbins (Ship's Officer); Charles Irwin (Bertie, the Purser); Willie Fung (Cabin Boy); Chester Gan (Rickshaw Boy).

RENDEZVOUS (MGM, 1935) 96 min.

Producer, Lawrence Weingarten; director, William K. Howard; based on the book *American Black Chamber* by Herbert O. Yardley; screenplay, Bella Spewack, Samuel Spewack, P. J. Wolfson, George Oppenheimer;

music, Dr. William Axt; camera, William Daniels; editor, Hugh Wynn.

William Powell (Lieutenant Bill Gordon [Anson Meridan]); Rosalind Russell (Joel Carter); Binnie Barnes (Olivia Karloff); Lionel Atwill (Major Charles Brennan); Cesar Romero (Captain Nikki Nikolajeff); Samuel S. Hinds (John Carter, Assistant Secretary of War); Henry Stephenson (Gregory, the Russian Ambassador); Charles Grapewin (Professor Martin); Frank Reicher (Dr. Jackson); Leonard Mudie (Roberts); Howard Hickman (G-Man); Charles Trowbridge (Secretary of War Baker); Margaret Dumont (Mrs. Hendricks); Sid Silvers (Recruiter); Eileen O'Malley (Red Cross Nurse); Murray Kinnell (de Segroff); Bert Morehouse (Second Lieutenant); Blair Davies (Sentry); Cyril Ring, Rollo Dix (Orderlies); Lowden Adams (Butler); Leonid Snegoff (Kaieneff); John Arthur (Code Room Clerk); Bob Perry (Another G-Man); Al Bridge (Sergeant); Lee Phelps (Cop); Edward Earle (Man in Code Room); Frank O'Connor (Officer); Milburn Stone (Carter's Aide); Rudolph Anders (Radio Operator); Edgar Dearing (M.P.); Theodor Von Eltz (Desk Clerk Assistant).

IT HAD TO HAPPEN (Twentieth Century-Fox, 1936) 79 min.

Producer, Darryl F. Zanuck; director, Roy Del Ruth; story, Rupert Hughes; screenplay, Howard Ellis Smith, Kathryn Scola; camera, Peverell Marley.

George Raft (Enrico Scaffa); Leo Carrillo (Giuseppe); Rosalind Russell (Beatrice); Alan Dinehart (Rodman Drake); Arthur Hohl (Honest John Pelkey); Arline Judge (Miss Sullivan); Andrew Tombes (Dooley); Pierre Watkin (District Attorney); Paul Stanton (Mayor of New York); James Burke (Foreman); John Sheehan (Pelkey's Secretary); Torben Meyer (Sign Painter); Thomas Jackson (Mayor's Secretary); Robert Emmett O'Connor (Policeman); Selmer Jackson (Immigration Officer); Frank Moran, John Kelly (Moving Men); Harry Stubbs (Bailiff); John Dilson (Juror); Gladden James, Bud Geary, Lew Kelly (Chauffeurs); Herbert Heywood (Trainer); Leo Loy (Chinese); Frank Meredith (Motor Cop); James C. Morton (Bartender); Jack Curtis, James Dundee, Harry Woods, G. Pat Collins, Ben Hendricks (Workmen).

UNDER TWO FLAGS (Twentieth Century-Fox, 1936) 105 min.

Producer, Darryl F. Zanuck; associate producer, Raymond Griffith; director, Frank Lloyd; based on the novel by Ouida; screenplay, W. P. Lipscomb, Walter Ferris; music director, Louis Silvers; camera, Ernest Palmer, Sidney Wagner; editor, Ralph Dietrich.

Ronald Colman (Corporal Victor); Claudette Colbert (Cigarette); Victor McLaglen (Major Doyle); Rosalind Russell (Lady Venetia); J. Edward Bromberg (Colonel Ferol); Nigel Bruce (Captain Menzies); Herbert Mundin (Rake); Gregory Ratoff (Lynn); C. Henry Gordon (Lieutenant Petaine); John Carradine (Cafard); William

Ricciardi (Cigarette's Father); Lumsden Hare (Lord Seraph); Fritz Leiber (French Governor); Onslow Stevens (Sidi Ben Youssiff); Louis Mercier (Barron); Francis McDonald (Hussan); Thomas Beck (Pierre); Harry Semels (Sergeant Malines); Frank Lackteen (Ben Hamidon); Jamiel Hasson (Arab Liaison Officer); Frank Reicher (French General); Gwendolyn Logan (Lady Cairn); Hans Von Morhart (Hans); Tor Johnson (Bidou); Marc Lawrence (Grivon); Ronald "Jack" Pennick (Corporal Vaux); Rolfe Sedan (Mouche); Eugene Borden (Villon); Nicholas Soussanin (Levine); George Jackson (Sentry); George Decount (Soldier); Rosita Harlan (Ivan's Girl).

TROUBLE FOR TWO *(MGM, 1936)* 75 min.

Producer, Louis D. Lighton; director, J. Walter Ruben; suggested by the story "Suicide Club" by Robert Louis Stevenson; screenplay, Manuel Seff, Edward E. Paramore, Jr.; music, Franz Waxman; art director, Cedric Gibbons; camera, Charles Clarke; editor, Robert J. Kern.

Robert Montgomery (Prince Florizel); Rosalind Russell (Miss Vandeleur [Princess Brenda]); Frank Morgan (Colonel Geraldine); Reginald Owen (Dr. Franz Noel, President of the Club); Louis Hayward (Young Man with Cream Tarts); E. E. Clive (The King); Walter Kingsford (Malthus); Ivan Simpson (Collins); Tom Moore (Mayor O'Rork); Robert Greig (Fat Man); Guy Bates Post (Ambassador); Pedro De Cordoba (Sergei); Leyland Hodgson (Captain Rich); Pat Flaherty (Ship Captain); Frank Darien (King's Aide); Tom Ricketts (Excited Club Member); Pat O'Malley (Purser); Leonard Carey (Valet); Bill O'Brien (Club Waiter); Paul Porcasi (Cafe Proprietor); Sidney Bracy (Henchman); Frank McGlynn, Jr. (Club Member); Larry Steers (Officer); Olaf Hytten (Butler); Edgar Norton (Herald); Fred Graham (Club Guard).

CRAIG'S WIFE *(Columbia, 1936)* 75 min.

Director, Dorothy Arzner; based on the play by George Kelly; screenplay, Mary C. McCall, Jr.; camera, Lucien Ballard; editor, Viola Lawrence.

Rosalind Russell (Harriet Craig); John Boles (Walter Craig); Billie Burke (Mrs. Frazier); Jane Darwell (Mrs. Harold); Dorothy Wilson (Ethel Handreth); Alma Kruger (Miss Austen); Thomas Mitchell (Fergus Passmore); Raymond Walburn (Billy Birkmire); Robert Allen (Gene Fredericks); Elisabeth Risdon (Mrs. Landreth); Nydia Westman (Mazie); Kathleen Burke (Adelaide Passmore).

NIGHT MUST FALL *(MGM, 1937)* 117 min.

Producer, Hunt Stromberg; director, Richard Thorpe; based on the play by Emlyn Williams; screenplay, John Van Druten; art director, Cedric Gibbons; music, Edward Ward; camera, Ray June; editor, Robert J. Kern.

Robert Montgomery (Danny); Rosalind Russell (Olivia); Dame May Whitty (Mrs. Bransom); Alan

Marshal (Justin); Merle Tottenham (Dora); Kathleen Harrison (Mrs. Terrence); Matthew Boulton (Belsize); Eily Malyon (Nurse); E. E. Clive (Guide); Beryl Mercer (Saleslady); Winifred Harris (Mrs. Laurie).

LIVE, LOVE AND LEARN *(MGM, 1937)* 78 min.

Producer, Harry Rapf; director, George Fitzmaurice; story, Marion Parsonnet; suggested by a story by Helen Grace Carlisle; screenplay, Charles Brackett, Cyril Hume, Richard Maibaum; camera, Ray June; editor, Conrad A. Nervig.

Robert Montgomery (Bob Graham); Rosalind Russell (Julie Stoddard); Robert Benchley (Oscar); Helen Vinson (Lily Chalmers); Mickey Rooney (Jerry Crum); Monty Woolley (Mr. Bawltitude); E. E. Clive (Mr. Palmiston); Charles Judels (Pedro Filipe); Maude Eburne (Mrs. Crump); Harlan Briggs (Justice of the Peace); June Clayworth (Post); Al Shean (Fraum); George Cooper (Bus Driver); Billy Gilbert (Newsboy); Dorothy Appleby (Lou); Ena Gregory (Bessie); Kate Price (Wilma); Heinie Conklin (Elmer); Billy Dooley (Fritz); John Kelly, Joe Caits, Philip Tully, John Quillan, Frank Marlowe (Sailors); James Flavin, Jack Perrin, Frank Sully, Jerry Miley, Russ Clark (Marines); June Clayworth (Annabelle Post); Ann Rutherford (Class President); Minerva Urecal, Virginia Sale, Maxine Elliott Hicks (Sisters); Rollo Lloyd (Agent); Soledad Jimenez (Spanish Woman).

MAN-PROOF *(MGM, 1938)* 74 min.

Producer, Louis D. Lighton; director, Richard Thorpe; story, Fanny Heaslip Lea; screenplay, Vincent Lawrence, Waldemar Young, George Oppenheimer; camera, Karl Freund; editor, George Boemler.

Myrna Loy (Mimi Swift); Rosalind Russell (Elizabeth); Franchot Tone (Jimmy Kilmartin); Walter Pidgeon (Alan Wythe); Nana Bryant (Meg Swift); John Miljan (Tommy Gaunt); Ruth Hussey (Jane); Rita Johnson (Florence); William Stack (Minister); Leonard Penn (Bob); Oscar O'Shea (Gus, the Bartender); Marie Blake (Telephone Girl); Dan Toby (Fight Announcer); Aileen Pringle, Grace Hayle, Laura Treadwell (Women); Mary Howard, Frances Reid (Girls); Betty Blythe (Country Club Woman); Dorothy Vaughan (Matron); Claude King (Man at Party); Joyce Compton (Guest); Francis X. Bushman, Jr. (Young Man at Fight).

FOUR'S A CROWD *(Warner Bros., 1938)* 91 min.

Executive producer, Hal B. Wallis; associate producer, David Lewis; director, Michael Curtiz; story, Wallace Sullivan; screenplay, Casey Robinson, Sig Herzig; music, Heinz Roemheld, Ray Heindorf; dialogue director, Irving Rapper; assistant director, Sherry Shourds; art director, Max Parker; gowns, Orry-Kelly; sound, Robert B. Lee; camera, Ernest Haller; editor, Clarence Kilster.

Errol Flynn (Robert Kensington Lansford); Olivia de Havilland (Lorri Dillingwell); Rosalind Russell (Jean

Christy); Patric Knowles (Patterson Buckley); Walter Connolly (John P. Dillingwell); Hugh Herbert (Silas Jenkins); Melville Cooper (Bingham); Franklin Pangborn (Preston); Herman Bing (Herman, the Barber); Margaret Hamilton (Amy); Joseph Crehan (Pierce, the Butler); Joe Cunningham (Young); Dennie Moore (Buckley's Secretary); Gloria Blondell, Carole Landis (Lansford's Secretaries); Renie Riano (Mrs. Jenkins); Charles Trowbridge (Dr. Ives), Spencer Charters (Charlie).

THE CITADEL (MGM, 1938) 110 min.

Producer, Victor Saville; director, King Vidor; based on the novel by A. J. Cronin; screenplay, Ian Dalrymple, Frank Wead, Elizabeth Hill, Emlyn Williams; music, Louis Levy; camera, Harry Stradling; editor, Charles Frend.

Robert Donat (Andrew Manson); Rosalind Russell (Christine Manson); Ralph Richardson (Denny); Rex Harrison (Dr. Lawford); Emlyn Williams (Owen); Penelope Dudley Ward (Toppy Leroy); Francis L. Sullivan (Ben Chenkin); Mary Clare (Mrs. Orlando); Cecil Parker (Charles Every); Nora Swinburne (Mrs. Thornton); Edward Chapman (Joe Morgan); Athene Seyler (Lady Raebank); Felix Aylmer (Mr. Boon); Joyce Bland (Nurse Sharp); Percy Parsons (Mr. Stillman); Dilys Davis (Mrs. Page); Basil Gill (Dr. Page); Joss Ambler (Dr. A. H. Llewellyn).

FAST AND LOOSE (MGM, 1939) 80 min.

Producer, Frederick Stephani; director, Edwin L. Marin; story-screenplay, Harry Kurnitz; camera, George Folsey; editor, Elmo Vernon.

Robert Montgomery (Joel Sloane); Rosalind Russell (Garda Sloane); Reginald Owen (Vincent Charlton); Ralph Morgan (Nicholas Torrent); Etienne Girardot (Christopher Gates); Alan Dinehart (Dave Hillard); Jo Ann Sayers (Christina Torrent); Joan Marsh (Bobby Neville); Anthony Allan [John Hubbard] (Phil Sergeant); Tom Collins (Gerald Torrent); Sidney Blackmer (Lucky Nolan); Ian Wolfe (Wilkes).

THE WOMEN (MGM, 1939) 132 min.*

Producer, Hunt Stromberg; director, George Cukor; based on the play by Clare Boothe; screenplay, Anita Loos, Jane Murfin; art director, Cedric Gibbons; music, Edward Ward, David Snell; costumes, Adrian; sound, Douglas Shearer; camera, Oliver T. Marsh, Joseph Ruttenberg; editor, Robert J. Kerns.

Norma Shearer (Mary Haines); Joan Crawford (Crystal Allen); Rosalind Russell (Sylvia Fowler); Mary Boland (Countess DeLave); Paulette Goddard (Miriam Aarons); Joan Fontaine (Peggy Day); Lucile Watson (Mrs. Moorehead); Phyllis Povah (Edith Potter); Florence Nash (Nancy Blake); Virginia Weidler (Little Mary); Ruth Hussey (Miss Watts); Muriel Hutchinson (Jane); Margaret Dumont (Mrs. Wagstaff); Dennie Moore (Olga); Mary Cecil (Maggie); Marjorie Main (Lucy); Esther Dale (Ingrid); Hedda

Hopper (Dolly Dupuyster); Mildred Shay (Helene, the French Maid); Priscilla Lawson, Estelle Etterre (Hairdressers); Ann Morriss (Exercise Instructress); Mary Beth Hughes (Miss Trimmerback); Marjorie Wood (Sadie); Virginia Grey (Pat); Cora Witherspoon (Mrs. Van Adams); Veda Buckland (Woman); Charlotte Treadway (Her Companion); Theresa Harris (Olive); Vera Vague (Receptionist); May Beatty (Fat Woman); Hilda Plowright (Miss Fordyer); Judith Allen (Miss Archer, the Model); Dorothy Sebastian, Renie Riano (Saleswomen); Josephine Whittell (Mrs. Spencer); Rita Gould (Dietician); Lilian Bond (Mrs. Erskine); Gertrude Simpson (Stage Mother); Carole Lee Kilby (Theatrical Child); Lita Chevret, Dora Clemant, Ruth Alder (Women under Sunlamps); Natalie Moorhead (Woman in Modiste Salon); Marie Blake (Stock Room Girl); Dorothy Adams (Miss Atkinson); Carol Hughes (Salesgirl at Modiste Salon); Peggy Shannon (Mrs. Jones); Winifred Harris, May Beatty (Society Women).

* Technicolor sequences.

HIS GIRL FRIDAY (Columbia, 1940) 92 min.

Producer/director, Howard Hawks; based on the play The Front Page by Ben Hecht, Charles MacArthur; screenplay, Charles Lederer; music director, Morris W. Stoloff; camera, Joseph Walker; editor, Gene Havlick.

Cary Grant (Walter Burns); Rosalind Russell (Hildy Johnson); Ralph Bellamy (Bruce Baldwin); Gene Lockhart (Sheriff Hartwell); Helen Mack (Mollie Malloy); Porter Hall (Murphy); Ernest Truex (Roy Bensinger); Cliff Edwards (Endicott); Clarence Kolb (Mayor); Roscoe Karns (McCue); Frank Jenks (Wilson); Regis Toomey (Sanders); Abner Biberman (Diamond Louie); Frank Orth (Duffy); John Qualen (Earl Williams); Alma Kruger (Mrs. Baldwin); Billy Gilbert (Joe Pettibone); Pat West (Warden Conley); Edwin Maxwell (Dr. Egelhoffer); Irving Bacon (Gus); Earl Dwire (Mr. Davis); Ralph Dunn (Guard); Pat Flaherty, Edmund Cobb (Cops).

NO TIME FOR COMEDY (Warner Bros., 1940) 93 min.

Producers, Jack L. Warner, Hal B. Wallis; associate producer, Robert Lord; director, William Keighley; based on the play by S. N. Behrman; screenplay, Julius J. and Philip G. Epstein; camera, Ernest Haller; editor, Owen Marks.

James Stewart (Gaylord Esterbrook); Rosalind Russell (Linda Esterbrook); Charles Ruggles (Philo Swift); Genevieve Tobin (Amanda Swift); Louise Beavers (Clementine); Allyn Joslyn (Morgan Carrel); Clarence Kolb (Richard Benson); Robert Greig (Robert); J. M. Kerrigan (Jim); Lawrence Grosmith (Frank); Robert Emmet O'Connor (Desk Sergeant); Herbert Haywood (Doorman); Frank Faylen (Cab Driver); James Burke (Sergeant); Edgar Dearing (Sweeny); Herbert Anderson (Actor).

HIRED WIFE (*Universal, 1940*) 93 min.

Associate producer, Glenn Tryon; director, William Seiter; story, George Beck; screenplay, Richard Connell, Gladys Lehman; art director, Jack Otterson; camera, Milton Krasner; editor, Milton Brown.

Rosalind Russell (Kendal Browning); Brian Aherne (Stephen Dexter); Virginia Bruce (Phyllis Walden); Robert Benchley (Van Horn); John Carroll (Jose); Hobart Cavanaugh (William); Richard Lane (McNab); Leonard Carey (Peterson); William Davidson (Munford); Selmer Jackson (Hudson); William Halligan (Latimer); George Humbert (Chef); Virginia Brissac (Miss Collins); Chester Clute (Peabody).

THIS THING CALLED LOVE (*Columbia, 1941*) 98 min.

Producer, William Perlberg; director, Alexander Hall; based on the play by Edwin Burke; screenplay, George Seaton, Ken Englund, P. J. Wolfson; camera, Joseph Walker.

Rosalind Russell (Ann Winters); Melvyn Douglas (Tice Collins); Binnie Barnes (Charlotte Campbell); Allyn Joslyn (Harry Bertrand); Gloria Dickson (Florence Bertrand); Lee J. Cobb (Julie Diestro); Gloria Holden (Genevieve Hooper); Paul McGrath (Gordon Daniels); Leona Maricle (Ruth Howland); Don Beddoe (Tom Howland); Rosina Galli (Mrs. Diestro); Sig Arno (Arno).

British release title: *Married But Single.*

THEY MET IN BOMBAY (*MGM, 1941*) 86 min.

Producer, Hunt Stromberg; director, Clarence Brown; story, John Kafka; screenplay, Edwin Justus Mayer, Anita Loos, Leon Gordon; art director, Cedric Gibbons; music, Herbert Stothart; special effects, Warren Newcombe; camera, William Daniels; editor, Blanche Sewell.

Clark Gable (Gerald Meldrick); Rosalind Russell (Anya Von Duren); Peter Lorre (Captain Chang); Jessie Ralph (Duchess of Beltravers); Reginald Owen (General); Matthew Boulton (Inspector Cressney); Leslie Vincent (Lieutenant Ashley); Eduardo Ciannelli (Hotel Manager); Jay Novello (Bolo); Rosina Galli (Carmencita); Luis Alberni (Maitre d'Hotel); Adelaide Whytal (Old Lady); Harry North (Clerk); Nanette Vallon (Beauty Operator); Lilyan Irene (Duchess' Maid); James B. Leong (Third Mate); Duke Chan (Radio Operator); Eric Lonsdale (Sergeant); Chester Gan (Woo Ling Woo); David Clyde, David Thursby (Sergeants); Stephen Chase, Cornelius Keefe (Officers); Key Luke (Mr. Toy); Roland Got (Young Foo Sing); Lee Tung-Foo (Elder Foo Sing); Harry Cording (Corporal); Judith Wood (Nurse); Philip Ahn, Richard Loo (Japanese Officers).

THE FEMININE TOUCH (*MGM, 1941*) 97 min.

Producer, Joseph L. Mankiewicz; director, W. S. Van Dyke II; screenplay, George Oppenheimer, Edmund L. Hartmann, and Ogden Nash; music, Franz Waxman; art director, Cedric Gibbons; special effects, Warren Newcombe; camera, Ray June; editor, Albert Akst.

Rosalind Russell (Julie Hathaway); Don Ameche (John Hathaway); Kay Francis (Nellie Woods); Van Heflin (Elliott Morgan); Donald Meek (Captain Makepeace Liveright); Gordon Jones (Rubber-Legs Ryan); Henry Daniell (Shelley Mason); Sidney Blackmer (Freddie Bond); Grant Mitchell (Dean Hutchinson); David Clyde (Brighton).

DESIGN FOR SCANDAL (*MGM, 1941*) 85 min.

Producer, John W. Considine, Jr.; director, Norman Taurog; screenplay, Lionel Houser; art director, Cedric Gibbons; set decorator, Edwin B. Willis; music, Franz Waxman; camera, Leonard Smith, William Daniels; editor, Elmo Vernon.

Rosalind Russell (Cornelia Porter); Walter Pidgeon (Jeff Sherman); Edward Arnold (Judson M. Blair); Vera Vague (Jane Porter); Lee Bowman (Walter Caldwell); Jean Rogers (Dotty); Donald Meek (Mr. Wade); Guy Kibbee (Judge Graham); Mary Beth Hughes (Adele Blair); Bobby Larson (Freddie); Leon Belasco (Alexander Raoul); Charles Coleman (Wilton); Thurston Hall (Northcott); Edgar Dearing (Joe, the Foreman); Eddie Dunn (Eddie Smith, a Miner); George Magrill, John Butler (Miners); John Dilson (Court Clerk); Dick Bartell, Robert Emmett Keane (Aides); Josephine Whittell (Woman); Anne Revere (Nettie, the Maid); Mitchell Ingraham (Storekeeper); Ed Thomas (Steward); Anne O'Neal (Travel Bureau Woman); Dorothy Morris, Marjorie "Babe" Kane (Telephone Operators); Milton Kibbee (Court Clerk); Syd Saylor (Taxi Driver).

TAKE A LETTER, DARLING (*Paramount, 1942*) 93 min.

Associate producer, Fred Kohlmar; director, Mitchell Leisen; story, George Beck; screenplay, Claude Binyon; art directors, Hans Dreier, Roland Anderson; camera, John Mescal; editors, Doane Harrison, Thomas Scott.

Rosalind Russell (A. M. MacGregor); Fred MacMurry (Tom Varney); Macdonald Carey (Jonathan Caldwell); Constance Moore (Ethel Caldwell); Robert Benchley (G. B. Atwater); Charles Arnt (Bud Newton); Cecil Kellaway (Uncle George); Kathleen Howard (Aunt Minnie); Margaret Seddon (Aunt Judy); Dooley Wilson (Moses); George H. Reed (Sam); Margaret Hayes (Sally); Sonny Boy Williams (Mickey Dowling); John Holland (Secretary); Florine McKinney (Young Mother); Amo Ingraham (Tall Willowy Brunette); Dorothy Granger (Switchboard Operator); Jean Del Val (Headwaiter), Stanley Mack (Border); Virginia Brissac (Mrs. Dowling, the Landlady); Eddie Acuff (Man Who Picks Teeth); David James (Baby); Nell Craig (Assistant Saleslady).

MY SISTER EILEEN (*Columbia, 1942*) 96 min.

Producer, Max Gordon; director, Alexander Hall; based on the play by Joseph Fields and Jerome Chodorov; screenplay, Fields, Chodorov; art director, Lionel Banks; music director, Morris Stoloff; camera, Joseph Walker; editor, Viola Lawrence.

Rosalind Russell (Ruth Sherwood); Brian Aherne (Robert Baker); Janet Blair (Eileen Sherwood); George Tobias (Appopolous); Allyn Joslyn (Ohio Clark); Elizabeth Patterson (Grandma Sherwood); Grant Mitchell (Walter Sherwood); Richard Quine (Frank Lippincott); June Havoc (Effie Shelton); Donald MacBride (Officer Lonigan); Gordon Jones ("The Wreck"); Jeff Donnell (Helen Loomis); Clyde Fillmore (Ralph Craven); Minna Phillips (Mrs. Wade); Frank Sully (Jansen); Charles La Torre (Captain Anadato); Danny Mummert (Boy); Almira Sessions (Prospective Tenant); Kirk Alyn, George Adrian, Tom Lincir (Cadets); Ann Doran (Receptionist); Bob Kellard (Bus Driver); Forrest Tucker (Sand Hog); The Three Stooges (Bus Passengers); Walter Sande, Pat Lane, Ralph Dunn (Policemen); Arnold Stang (Jimmy).

FLIGHT FOR FREEDOM (RKO, 1943) 101 min.

Producer, David Hempstead; director, Lothar Mendes; story, Horace McCoy; screenplay, Oliver H. P. Garrett, S. K. Lauren; adaptor, Jane Murfin; music, Roy Webb; music director, C. Bakaleinikoff; art directors, Albert S. D'Agostino, Carroll Clark; set decorators, Darrell Silvera, Harley Miller; assistant directors, J. D. Starkey, Ruby Rosenberg; sound, Terry Kellum, James Stewart; special camera effects, Vernon L. Walker; camera, Lee Garmes; editor, Roland Gross.

Rosalind Russell (Tonie Carter); Fred MacMurray (Randy Britton); Herbert Marshall (Paul Turner); Eduardo Ciannelli (Johnny Salvini); Walter Kingsford (Admiral Graves); Damian O'Flynn (Pete); Jack Carr (Bill); Matt McHugh (Mac); Richard Loo (Mr. Yokahato); Charles Lung (Flyer); Jack Cheatham (Doorman); Bud McTaggart, Bruce Edwards (Flyers); Byron Shores (George Lake); James Eagles (Charlie); Theodore Von Eltz (Commander George); Mary Treen (Newspaper Woman); William Forrest (Vice-Consul); Kathleen Ellis (Telephone Operator).

WHAT A WOMAN! (Columbia, 1943) 94 min.

Producer/director, Irving Cummings; story, Erik Charell; screenplay, Therese Lewis, Barry Trivers; art directors, Lionel Banks, Van Nest Polglase; set decorator, William Kiernan; assistant director, Abby Berlin; music, John Leipold; music director, Morris Stoloff; sound, Ed Bernds; camera, Joseph Walker; editor, Al Clark.

Rosalind Russell (Carol Kingsley); Brian Aherne (Henry Pepper); Willard Parker (Michael Cobb); Alan Dinehart (Pat O'Shea); Edward Fielding (Senator Minsley); Ann Savage (Jane Hughes); Norma Varden (Miss Timmons); Douglas Wood (Dean Shaeffer); Grady Sutton (Clerk); Lilyan Irene (Ninna); Frank Dawson (Ben); Irving Bacon (Newsman); Shelley Winters (Girl Actress); Isabel Withers (Telephone Operator); Hobart Cavanaugh (Mailman); Edward Earle (Livingstone Lawyer); Shimen Ruskin (Gadajalski); Bess Flowers (Dawson); Hal K. Dawson (Foster); Barbara Brown (Receptionist); Byron Foulger (Desk Clerk); Doris Lloyd (Dramatic Coach); Pierre Watkin (Senator); Mary Forbes (Senator's Wife); Gertrude Hoffman (Night Maid); Selmer Jackson (Bruce); Ken Carpenter (Radio Announcer).

British release title: *The Beautiful Cheat.*

ROUGHLY SPEAKING (Warner Bros., 1945) 117 min.

Producer, Henry Blanke; director, Michael Curtiz; based on the book by Louise Randall Pierson; screenplay, Pierson; art director, Robert Haas; set decorator, George James Hopkins; music, Max Steiner; orchestrator, Hugo Friedhofer; music director, Leo F. Forbstein; assistant director, Frank Heath; sound, Dolph Thomas; montages, James Leicester; special effects, Roy Davidson, Hans Koenekamp; camera, Joseph Walker; editor, David Weisbart.

Prologue in 1902: Ray Collins (Mr. Randall); Kathleen Lockhart (Mrs. Randall); Cora Sue Collins (Elinor Randall); Ann Todd (Louise Randall); Andy Clyde (Matt); Arthur Shields (Minister); Helene Thimig (Olga, the Maid); Greta Grandstedt (Anna, the Maid); *Beginning 1905:* Rosalind Russell (Louise Randall); Ann Doran (Alice Abbott); Hobart Cavanaugh (The Teacher); Eily Malyon (The Dean); Alan Hale (Mr. Norton); Donald Woods (Rodney Crane); Craig Stevens (Jack Leslie); John Alvin (Lawton Meckall); Mary Servoss (Rose); Francis Pierlot (Dr. Lewis); Manart Kippen (Dr. Bowditch); George Carleton (The Judge); Jack Carson (Harold Pierson); Frank Puglia (Tony); John Qualen (Ole Olsen); Chester Clute (The Proprietor); Irving Bacon (Customer in Music Shop); Barbara Brown (Relief Worker); Sig Arno (George); Ann Lawrence (Barbara, Age 9-11); Mona Freeman (Barbara, Age 15-20); Andrea King (Barbara, Age 21-29); Mickey Kuhn (John, Age 7-10); Johnny Treul (John, Age 14-19); Robert Hutton (John, Age 20-28); John Calkins (Rodney, Age 6-9); Richard Winer (Rodney, Age 13-18); John Sheridan (Rodney, Age 19-27); Jo Ann Marlowe (Louise Jr., Age 5-6); Patsy Lee Parsons (Louise Jr., Age 12-17); Jean Sullivan (Louise Jr., Age 18-26); Gregory Muradien (Frankie, Age 3-4); John Sheffield (Frankie, Age 9); Robert Arthur (Frankie, Age 17); Joyce Compton (Prissy Girl); Marie Blake, Claire Meade (Nurses); Harry Harvey, Jr. (Billy Winters); Emmett Vogan (Auctioneer); Pierre Watkin, Charles Anthony Hughes (Financiers); Jody Gilbert (Woman in Store); Bill Moss (Sergeant).

SHE WOULDN'T SAY YES (Columbia, 1945) 86 min.

Producer, Virginia Van Upp; director, Alexander Hall; story, Laslo Gorog, William Thiele; screenplay, Van Upp, John Jacoby, Sarett Tobias; art directors, Stephen Goosson, Van Nest Polglase; set decorator, Wilbur Menefee; assistant director, Rex Bailey; music, Marlin Skiles; music director, Morris Stoloff; sound,

Jack Goodrich; camera, Joseph Walker; editor, Viola Lawrence.

Rosalind Russell (Susan Lane); Lee Bowman (Michael Kent); Adele Jergens (Allura); Charles Winninger (Dr. Lane); Harry Davenport (Albert); Sara Haden (Laura Pitts); Percy Kilbride (Judge Whittaker); Lewis Russell (Colonel Brady); Mary Green (Passenger); Mabel Paige (Mrs. Whittaker); George Cleveland (Ticket Seller); Charles Arnt (Train Conductor); Almira Sessions (Miss Downer); Mantan Moreland, Willie Best (Porters); Ida Moore, Eily Malyon (Spinsters); Arthur Q. Bryan (Little Man); John Tyrrell (Traveling Salesman); Ernest Whitman (Bartender); Dudley Dickerson (Waiter); Cora Witherspoon (Patient); Marilyn Johnson, Doris Houck (Girls); Darren McGavin (The Kid); Sam McDaniel (Steward); Clarence Muse, Jesse Graves, Nick Stewart (Other Porters); Carl Switzer (Delivery Boy); Ed Gargan, Tom Dugan (Cab Drivers).

SISTER KENNY *(RKO, 1946)* 116 min.

Producer, Dudley Nichols; associate producer, Edward Donahue; director, Nichols; based on the book *And They Shall Walk* by Elizabeth Kenny in collaboration with Martha Ostenso; screenplay, Nichols, Alexander Knox, Mary McCarthy; art directors, Albert S. D'Agostino, William E. Flannery; set decorators, Darrell Silvera, Harley Miller; music, Alexander Tansman; music director, C. Bakaleinikoff; assistant director, Harry D'Arcy; dialogue director, Jack Gage; sound, Earl A. Wolcott, Clem Portman; special effects, Vernon L. Walker; camera, George Barnes; editor, Roland Bross.

Rosalind Russell (Elizabeth Kenny); Alexander Knox (Dr. McDonnell); Dean Jagger (Kevin Connors); Philip Merivale (Dr. Brack); Beulah Bondi (Mary Kenny); Charles Dingle (Michael Kenny); John Litel (Medical Director); Doreen McCann (Dorrie); Fay Helm (Mrs. McIntyre); Charles Kemper (Mr. McIntyre); Dorothy Peterson (Agnes); Gloria Holden (Mrs. McDonnell); Virginia Brissac (Mrs. Johnson); Frank Reicher (Chuter); Paul Stanton (Dr. Gideon); Charles Halton (Mr. Smith); Alan Lee (Farm Hand); David Martinson (Cobbler); Lloyd Ingraham (Farmer); Ellen Corby, Nan Leslie (Nurses); Doris Lloyd (Matron); Egon Brecher (Frenchman); Lumsden Hare (Dr. Shadrack); Regis Toomey, Leo Bonnell (Reporters); Daphne Moore (Waitress); Franklyn Farnum (Doctor); Gertrude Astor (Bit).

THE GUILT OF JANET AMES *(Columbia, 1947)* 83 min.

Director, Henry Levin; story, Lenore Coffee; screenplay, Louella MacFarlane, Allen Rivkin, Devery Freeman; art directors, Stephen Goosson, Walter Holscher; set decorators, George Montgomery, Frank Tuttle; music, George Duning; music director, Morris Stoloff; songs, Allan Roberts and Doris Fisher; assistant director, Milton Feldman; sound, Frank Goodwin; camera, Joseph Walker; editor, Charles Nelson.

Rosalind Russell (Janet Ames); Melvyn Douglas (Smithfield Cobb); Sid Caesar (Sammy Weaver); Betsy Blair (Katie); Nina Foch (Susie Pierson); Charles Cane (Walker); Harry Von Zell (Carter); Bruce Harper (Junior); Arthur Space (Nelson); Richard Benedict (Joe Burton); Frank Orth (Danny); Ray Walker (Sidney); Doreen McCann (Emmy Merino); Hugh Beaumont (Frank Merino); Thomas Jackson (Police Sergeant); Edwin Cooper (Surgeon); Emory Parnell (Susie's Father); Victoria Horne, Wanda Perry, Eve Marsh, Kathleen O'Malley (Nurses); Pat Lane, Fred Howard (Doctors); William Forrest (Dr. Morton); Steve Benton (Ambulance Attendant).

MOURNING BECOMES ELECTRA (RKO, 1947) 175 min.

Producer, Dudley Nichols in association with the Theatre Guild; director, Nichols; based on the play by Eugene O'Neill; screenplay, Nichols; art director, Albert S. D'Agostino; set decorators, Darrell Silvera, Maurice Yates; music, Richard Hageman; orchestrator, Lucien Cailliet; music director, C. Bakaleinikoff; dialogue director, Jack Gage; assistant director, Harry Mancke; sound, Earl Wolcott, Clem Portman; special effects, Vernon L. Walker, Russell Cully; camera, George Barnes; editors, Roland Gross, Chandler House.

Rosalind Russell (Lavinia Mannon); Michael Redgrave (Orin Mannon); Raymond Massey (Ezra Mannon); Katina Paxinou (Christina Mannon); Leon Genn (Adam Brent); Kirk Douglas (Peter Niles); Nancy Coleman (Hazel Niles); Henry Hull (Seth Beckwith); Thurston Hall (Dr. Blake); Sara Allgood (Landlady); Walter Baldwin (Amos Ames); Elisabeth Risdon (Mrs. Hills); Erskine Sanford (Josiah Borden); Jimmy Conlin (Abner Small); Tito Vuolo (Joe Silva); Lee Baker (Reverend Hills); Nora Cecil (Louise Ames); Marie Blake (Minnie Ames); Clem Bevans (Ira Mackel); Jean Clarendon (Eben Nobel); Colin Kenny (Policeman).

THE VELVET TOUCH *(RKO, 1948)* 97 min.

Producer, Frederick Brisson; associate producer, Edward Donahue; director, John Gage; story, William Mercer, Annabel Ross; screenplay, Leo Rosten; adaptor, Walter Reilly; production designer, William Flannery; set decorators, Darrell Silvera, Maurice Yates; music, Leigh Harline; music director, C. Bakaleinikoff; songs, Mort Greene and Harline; assistant director, Maxwell O. Henry; makeup, Fred Phillips; costumes, Travis Banton; sound, Richard Van Hessen, Clem Portman; special effects, Russell A. Cully; camera, Joseph Walker; editor, Chandler House.

Rosalind Russell (Valerie Stanton); Leo Genn (Michael Morrell); Claire Trevor (Marian Webster); Sydney Greenstreet (Captain Danbury); Leon Ames (Gordon Dunning); Frank McHugh (Ernie Boyle); Walter Kingsford (Peter Gunther); Dan Tobin (Jeff Trent); Lex Barker (Paul Banton); Nydia Westman (Susan Crane); Theresa Harris (Nancy); Irving Bacon (Albert); Esther Howard (Pansy Dupont); Harry Hayden (Mr. Crouch); Martha Hyer (Helen Adams); Louis Mason (Terry); James Flavin (Sergeant Oliphant); Bessie Wade (Bertha in *Hedda Gabler* Scene); Bess Flowers (Woman at Party); Jim Drum, Allen Ray, Gill Wallace (Reporters).

TELL IT TO THE JUDGE *(Columbia, 1949)* 87 min.

Producer, Buddy Adler; director, Norman Foster; story, Devery Freeman; screenplay, Nat Perrin; additional dialogue, Roland Kibbee; art director, Carl Anderson; set decorator, William Kiernan; music, Werner R. Heymann; music director, Morris Stoloff; assistant director, Sam Nelson; makeup, Fred Phillips; costumes, Jean Louis; sound, George Cooper; camera, Joseph Walker; editor, Charles Nelson.

Rosalind Russell (Marsha Meredith); Robert Cummings (Pete Webb); Gig Young (Alexander Darvac); Marie McDonald (Ginger Simmons); Harry Davenport (Judge MacKenzie Meredith); Fay Baker (Valerie Hobson); Katharine Warren (Kitty Lawton); Douglass Dumbrille (George Ellerby); Clem Bevans (Roogle); Grandon Rhodes (Ken Craig); Louise Beavers (Cleo); Thurston Hall (Senator Caswell); Jay Novello (Gancellos); William Bevan (Winston); Steven Geray (François); William Newell (Bartender); Polly Bailey (Dumpy Woman); Bill Lechner (Elevator Boy); Harlan Warde (Pete's Associate); Herbert Vigran (Reporter); Lee Phelps (Police Sergeant); Lester Dorr (Incoming Reporter); Dorothy Vaughn (Another Dumpy Woman).

A WOMAN OF DISTINCTION *(Columbia, 1950)* 85 min.

Producer, Buddy Adler; director, Edward Buzzell; story, Hugo Butler, Ian McLellan Hunter; screenplay, Charles Hoffman; additional dialogue, Frank Tashlin; art director, Robert Peterson; music director, Morris Stoloff; camera, Joseph Walker; editor, Charles Nelson.

Rosalind Russell (Susan Middlecott); Ray Milland (Alec Stevenson); Edmund Gwenn (Mark Middlecott); Janis Carter (Teddy Evans); Mary Jane Saunders (Louisa); Francis Lederer (Paul Simons); Jerome Courtland (Jerome); Alex Gerry (Herman Pomeroy); Charles Evans (Dr. McFall); Charlotte Wynters (Miss Withers); Clifton Young (Chet); Gale Gordon (Station Clerk); Jean Willes (Pearl); Wanda McKay (Merle); Elizabeth Flourney (Laura); Harry Tyler (Bit); Harry Cheshire (Steward); John Smith (Boy); Myron Healey (Cameraman); Pat O'Malley (Conductor); Harry Harvey, Jr. (Joe); Lucille Ball (Guest Star).

NEVER WAVE AT A WAC *(RKO, 1952)* 87 min.

Producer, Frederick Brisson; director, Norman Z. McLeod; story, Frederick Kohner, Fred Brady; screenplay, Ken Englund; music/music director, Elmer Bernstein; art director, William E. Flannery; set decorator, Howard Bristol; sound, Bob Cook; camera, William Daniels; editor, Stanley Johnson.

Rosalind Russell (Jo McBain); Paul Douglas (Andrew McBain); Marie Wilson (Clara Schneiderman); William Ching (Lieutenant Colonel Schuyler Fairchild); Arleen Whelan (Sergeant Toni Wayne); Leif Erickson (Sergeant Noisy Jackson); Charles Dingle (Senator Tom Reynolds); Lurene Tuttle (Captain Murchinson); Hillary Brooke (Phyllis Turnbull); Frieda Inescort (Lily Mae Gorham); Regis Toomey (General Prager); Louise Beavers (Artamesa); and Virginia Christine, Olan Soule, Jane Seymour, Louise Lorimer, Jeanne Dean.

British release title: *The Private Wore Skirts.*

THE GIRL RUSH *(Paramount, 1955)* C-85 min.

Producer, Frederick Brisson; associate producer, Robert Alton; director, Robert Pirosh; story, Phoebe and Henry Ephron; screenplay, Pirosh, Jerome Davis; art directors, Hal Pereira, Malcolm Bert; songs, Hugh Martin and Ralph Blane; choreography, Alton; assistant director, Daniel McCauley; music director, M. S. I. Spence-Hagen; camera, William Daniels.

Rosalind Russell (Kim Halliday); Fernando Lamas (Victor Monte); Eddie Albert (Elliot Atterbury); Gloria De Haven (Taffy Tremaine); Marion Lorne (Aunt Clara); James Gleason (Ether Ferguson); Robert Fortier (Pete Tremaine); Matt Mattox, Don Chrichton, George Chakiris (Specialty Dancers); Douglas Fowley (Charlie); Jesse White (Pit Boss); Larry Gates (Hap Halliday); and George Chandler, Lester Dorr, Shelly Fabares.

PICNIC *(Columbia, 1956)* C-115 min.

Producer, Fred Kohlmar; director, Joshua Logan; based on the play by William Inge; screenplay, Daniel Taradash; art director, William Flannery; music director, Morris Stoloff; music, George Duning; orchestrator, Arthur Morton; gowns, Jean Louis; assistant director, Carter De Haven, Jr.; camera, James Wong Howe; editors, Charles Nelson, William A. Lyon.

William Holden (Hal Carter); Rosalind Russell (Rosemary Sydney); Kim Novak (Madge Owens); Betty Field (Flo Owens); Susan Strasberg (Millie Owens); Cliff Robertson (Alan); Arthur O'Connell (Howard Bevans); Verna Felton (Mrs. Helen Potts); Reta Shaw (Linda Sue Breckenridge); Nick Adams (Bomber); Raymond Bailey (Mr. Benson); Elizabeth W. Wilson (Christine Schoenwalder); Phyllis Newman (Juanita Badger); Don C. Harvey, Steven Benton (Policemen); Henry P. Watson (President of Chamber of Commerce); Henry Pegueo (Mayor); George Bemis (Neighbor).

AUNTIE MAME *(Warner Bros., 1958)* C-143 min.

Director, Morton Da Costa; based on the novel by Patrick Dennis and the play by Jerome Lawrence and Robert E. Lee; screenplay, Betty Comden, Adolph Green; art director, Malcolm Bert; set decorator, George James Hopkins; consultant for interior decor, Robert Hanley; Miss Russell's makeup, Gene Hibbs; music, Bronislau Kaper; music supervisor, Ray Heindorf; costumes, Orry-Kelly; assistant director, Don

Page; sound, M. A. Merrick; camera, Harry Stradling, Jr.; editor, William Ziegler.

Rosalind Russell (Mame Dennis); Forrest Tucker (Beauregard Burnside); Coral Browne (Vera Charles); Fred Clark (Mr. Babcock); Roger Smith (Patrick Dennis); Patric Knowles (Lindsay Woolsey); Peggy Cass (Agnes Gooch); Jan Handzlik (Patrick Dennis as a Child); Joanna Barnes (Gloria Upson); Pippa Scott (Pegeen Ryan); Lee Patrick (Mrs. Upson); Willard Waterman (Mr. Upson); Robin Hughes (Brian 'O'-Bannion); Connie Gilchrist (Norah Muldoon); Yuki Shimoda (Ito); Brook Byron (Sally Cato); Carol Veazie (Mrs. Burnside); Henry Brandon (Acacius Page).

A MAJORITY OF ONE (Warner Bros., 1961) C-153 min.

Producer/director, Mervyn LeRoy; based on the play by Leonard Spigelgass; screenplay, Spigelgass; art director, John Beckman; set decorator, Ralph S. Hurst; costumes, Orry-Kelly; music, Max Steiner; orchestrator, Murray Cutter; makeup, Jean Burt Reilly; assistant director, Gil Kissel; sound, Stanley Jones; camera, Harry Stradling, Jr.; editor, Philip W. Anderson.

Rosalind Russell (Mrs. Jacoby); Alec Guinness (Koichi Asano); Ray Danton (Jerome Black); Madlyn Rhue (Alice Black); Mae Questel (Mrs. Rubin); Marc Marno (Eddie); Gary Vinson (Mr. McMillan); Sharon Hugheny (Bride); Frank Wilcox (Noah Putnam); Francis De Sales (American Embassy Representative); Yuki Shimoda (Mr. Asano's Secretary); Harriet MacGibbon (Mrs. Putnam); Alan Mowbray (Captain Norcross); Tsuruko Kobayashi (Mr. Asano's Daughter-in-Law); Lillian Adams (Mrs. Stein); Shirley Cytron, Arlen Stuart, Belle Mitchell (Neighbors); Bob Shield (Announcer); Dale Ishimoto (Taxi Driver).

FIVE FINGER EXERCISE (Columbia, 1962) 109 min.

Producer, Frederick Brisson; director, Daniel Mann; based on the play by Peter Shaffer; screenplay, Frances Goodrich, Albert Hackett; art director, Ross Bellah; set decorator, William Kiernan; Miss Russell's gowns, Orry-Kelly; makeup, Ben Lane, Gene Hibbs; assistant director, R. Robert Rosenbaum; music, Jerome Moross; sound, James Z. Flaster, Charles J. Rice; camera, Harry Stradling; editor, William A. Lyon.

Rosalind Russell (Louise Harrington); Jack Hawkins (Stanley Harrington); Maximilian Schell (Walter); Annette Gorman (Pamela Harrington); Richard Beymer (Philip Harrington); Lana Wood (Mary); Terry Huntingdon (Helen Hunting); William Quinn (Salesman); Kathy West (Alice); Valora Noland (Girl); Mary Benoit (Woman); Jeannine Riley, Karen Parker (Girls); Bart Conrad (Announcer).

GYPSY (Warner Bros., 1962) C-142 min.

Producer/director, Mervyn LeRoy; based on the musical play by Arthur Laurents, Jule Styne, and Stephen Sondheim, and the memoirs of Gypsy Rose Lee; screenplay, Leonard Spigelgass; art director, John Beckman;

set decorator, Ralph S. Hurst; makeup, Gordon Bau; Miss Russell's makeup, Gene Hibbs; assistant director, Gil Kissel; music supervisor/conductor, Frank Perkins; orchestrators, Perkins and Carl Brandt; choreography, Robert Tucker; sound, M. A. Merric, Dolph Thomas; camera, Harry Stradling; editor, Philip W. Anderson.

Rosalind Russell (Rose); Natalie Wood (Louise); Karl Malden (Herbie Sommers); Paul Wallace (Tulsa); Betty Bruce (Tessie Tura); Parley Baer (Mr. Kringelein); Harry Shannon (Grandpa); Suzanne Cupito (Baby June); Ann Jilliann (Dainty June); Diane Pace (Baby Louise); Faith Dane (Mazeppa); Roxanne Arlen (Electra); Jean Willes (Betty Cratchitt); George Petrie (George); Ben Lessy (Mervyn Goldstone); Jack Benny (Himself); Bert Michaels, Dick Foster, Jim Hubbard, Jeff Parker, Mike Cody, Bo Wagner (Farmboys); Terry Hope, Shirley Chandler, Francie Karath, Paula Martin, Dee Ann Johnston, Renee Aubry (Hollywood Blondes); Trudi Ames (Hawaiian Girl); Harvey Korman (Phil).

THE TROUBLE WITH ANGELS (Columbia, 1966) C-112 min.

Producer, William Frye; director, Ida Lupino; based on the novel by Jane Trahey; screenplay, Blanche Hanalis; music, Jerry Goldsmith; orchestrator, Arthur Morton; assistant director, Terry Nelson; costume coordinator, Helen Colvig; art director, John Beckman; set decorator, Victor Gangelin; makeup, Ben Lane; sound, Charles Rice, Josh Westmoreland; camera, Lionel Lindon; editor, Robert C. Jones.

Rosalind Russell (Mother Superior); Hayley Mills (Mary Clancy); Jim Hutton (Mr. Petrie); Binnie Barnes (Sister Celestine); June Harding (Rachel Devery); Gypsy Rose Lee (Mrs. Phipps); Mary Wickes (Sister Clarissa); Camilla Sparv (Sister Constance); Kent Smith (Uncle George); Margalo Gillmore (Sister Barbara); Portia Nelson (Sister Elizabeth); Barbara Hunter (Marvel-Ann); Pat McCaffrie (Mr. Devery); Jim Boles (Mr. Gottschalk); Marge Redmond (Sister Liguori); Marjorie Eaton (Sister Ursula); Bernadette Withers (Valerie); Judith Lowry (Sister Prudence); Harry Harvey, Sr. (Mr. Grissom).

OH, DAD, POOR DAD (Mamma's Hung You in the Closet and I'm Feelin' So Sad) (Paramount, 1967) C-86 min.

Producers, Ray Stark, Stanley Rubin; directors, Richard Quine, (uncredited) Alexander Mackendricks; based on the play by Arthur L. Kopit; screenplay, Ian Bernard; narration written by Pat McCormick, Herbert Baker; music, Neal Hefti; art director, Phil Jeffries; set decorator, William Kiernan; makeup, Robert Schiffer; costumes, Galanos, Howard Shoup; assistant director, Mickey McCardle; sound, Josh Westmoreland, John Wilkinson; special effects, Charles Spurgeon; process camera, Farciot Edouart; camera, Geoffrey Unsworth; second unit camera, Skeets Kelley; editors, Warren Low, David Wages.

Rosalind Russell (Madame Rosepettle); Robert

Morse (Jonathan); Barbara Harris (Rosalie); Hugh Griffith (Commodore Roseabove); Jonathan Winters (Dad/Narrator); Lionel Jeffries (Airport Commander); Cyril Delavanti (Hawkins); Hiram Sherman (Breckenduff); George Kirby (Moses); Janis Hansen (The Other Woman).

ROSIE! (Universal, 1968) C-98 min.

Executive producer, Ross Hunter; producer, Jacque Mapes; director, David Lowell Rich; based on the play *A Very Rich Woman* by Ruth Gordon, adapted from *Les Joies De Famille* by Philippe Heriat; screenplay, Samuel Taylor; music, Lyn Murray; music supervisor, Joseph Gershenson; song, Johnny Mercer and Harry Warren; art directors, Alexander Golitzen, George C. Webb; set decorator, Howard Bristol; makeup, Bud Westmore; assistant director, Joseph Kenny; sound, Waldon O. Watson, Melvin M. Metcalfe; camera, Clifford Stine; editor, Stuart Gilmore.

Rosalind Russell (Rosie Lord); Sandra Dee (Daphne Shaw); Brian Aherne (Oliver Stevenson); Audrey Meadows (Mildred Deever); James Farentino (David Wheelwright); Vanessa Brown (Edith Shaw); Leslie Nielsen (Cabot Shaw); Margaret Hamilton (Mae); Reginald Owen (Patrick); Juanita Moore (Nurse); Virginia Grey (Mrs. Peters); Dean Harens (Willetts); Richard Derr (Lawyer); Walter Woolf King (Judge); Ron Stokes (Taxi Driver); Doodles Weaver (Florist); Hal Lynch (Man).

WHERE ANGELS GO—TROUBLE FOLLOWS! (Columbia, 1968) C-95 min.

Producer, William Frye; director, James Neilson; based on characters created by Jane Trahey; screenplay, Blanche Hanalis; music, Lalo Schifrin; title song, Schifrin, Tommy Boyce, and Bobby Hart; production designer, Lyle Wheeler; set decorator, Frank Tuttle; assistant director, Carl Beringer; costumes, Moss Mabry; makeup, Ben Lane; sound, Charles J. Rice, William Ford, Jack Haynes; camera, Sam Leavitt; editor, Adrienne Fazan.

Rosalind Russell (Mother Simplicis); Stella Stevens (Sister George); Binnie Barnes (Sister Celestine); Mary Wickes (Sister Clarissa); Dolores Sutton (Sister Rose Marie); Susan Saint James (Rosabelle); Barbara Hunter (Marvel Ann Clancy); Alice Rawlings (Patty); Hilaire Thompson (Hilarie); Devon Douglas (Devon); Ellen Moss (Tanya); Cherrie Lamour (Cherie); June Fairchild (June); Michael Christian (Motorcycle Leader); Jon Hill (Cyclist); John Findletter (Jud Ferriday); Tom Logan (Tom); Milton Berle (Film Director); Arthur Godfrey (Bishop); Van Johnson (Father Chase); William Lundigan (Mr. Clancy); Robert Taylor (Mr. Farriday).

MRS. POLLIFAX—SPY (United Artists, 1971) C-110 min.

Producer, Frederick Brisson; associate producer, Charles Forsythe; director, Leslie Martinson; based on the novel *The Unexpected Mrs. Pollifax* by Dorothy Gilman; screenplay, C. A. McKnight [Rosalind Russell]; music/music director, Lalo Schifrin; dance music and "Merdita" theme, Andre Previn; assistant directors, Fred Gammon, Fred Giles, Clifford Coleman; art director, Jack Poplin; set decorator, William Kuehl; costumes, Noel Taylor; makeup, Fred Williams; sound, Everett A. Hughes; camera, Joseph Biroc; second unit camera, Mark H. Davis; editors, Stefan Arnsten, Philip W. Anderson.

Rosalind Russell (Mrs. Emily Pollifax); Darren McGavin (Johnny Farrell); Nehemiah Persoff (General Berisha); Harold Gould (Colonel Nexdhet); Albert Paulsen (General Perdido); John Beck (Sergeant Lulash); Dana Elcar (Carstairs); James Wellman (Mason); Dennis Cross (Bishop); Nick Katurich (Stefan); Don Diamond (Bookshop Proprietor); Robert Donner (Larrabee); Tom Hallick (Roger); Vassily Sulich (Albanian Private); Patrick Dennis (Tourist).

THE CROOKED HEARTS (ABC-TV, 1972) C-76 min.

Executive producer, Lee Rich; producer, Allen S. Epstein; director, Jay Sandrich; based on the novel *Lonelyheart 4122* by Colin Watson; teleplay, A. J. Russell; music, Billy Goldenberg; art director, Jan Scott; set decorator, James G. Cane; camera, Joseph Biroc; editor, Gene Fowler, Jr.

Rosalind Russell (Laurita Dorsey); Douglas Fairbanks, Jr. (Rex Willoughby); Ross Martin (Daniel Shane); Michael Murphy (Frank Adamic); Maureen O'Sullivan (Lillian Stanton); Kent Smith (James Simpson); Liam Dunne (Writer); Dick Van Patten (Edward, the Hotel Clerk); Penny Marshall (Waitress); Patrick Campbell (Cab Driver); William Zuckert (Security Guard); Kenneth Tobey (Fisherman).

As Martha Wilkison in *The Violent Men* ('55).

CHAPTER 6

Barbara Stanwyck

5'5"
115 pounds
Auburn hair
Blue-violet eyes
Cancer

Barbara Stanwyck remains a one-of-a-kind breed. Unlike most major stars, she has never been subject to temperament on the soundstage and has remained throughout the years one of the most liked players on film sets. It is a tribute that movie technicians and fellow performers accord few superstars. And unlike most of her contemporaries who also became cinema legends, Barbara Stanwyck has rarely sunk to self-caricature. As a matter of fact, her professional posture is too tough, honest, and self-styled to be carbon-copied easily or successfully. (Her one professional vulnerability is her cultivated diction which wavers incongruously back into Brooklynese enunciation on occasion.)

As did superstar Joan Crawford, Barbara learned that successful show business survival required adapting with the times. During her decades on the screen, she altered her image to suit changing public tastes. But bursting through it all has been her engrossing individuality. Reliable Stanwyck made her movie reputation in the Thirties as the self-sufficient miss who by hook or crook came out ahead in the game of life. Perhaps the penultimate Stanwyck performance of her earlier cinema years was the much-censored *Baby Face* (1933), in which she utilized every wile conceivable to conquer life but eventually found herself vulnerable to true love.

If anything supercharged Barbara's screen career in the late Thirties, it was her romance and marriage to MGM's handsome screen idol Robert Taylor. It demonstrated to moviegoers that the offscreen actress had a definite sexuality and desirability about her, qualities which frequently eluded the camera in her movie roles.

Most veteran moviegoers (or now younger generations of late-show TV watchers) think of Stanwyck in terms of the ultimate screen neurotics. *Double Indemnity* (1944) and *The Strange Love of Martha Ivers* (1946) are excellent examples of this stereotyping. Devotees of this type of Stanwyck performance relish her machine-gun delivery of vituperative dialogue, which her insolent character would deliver with relish and extreme credibility. *But* there was also Stanwyck the facile comedienne, who could shine in Preston Sturges' witty *The Lady Eve* (1941) or radiate as an amusing broad in *Ball of Fire* (1941) and *Lady of Burlesque* (1943). And what of the romantic Stanwyck, the heroine of *Remember the Night* (1940), *Christmas in Connecticut* (1945), and *My Reputation* (1946)?

In the Fifties, when movie roles became fewer (or non-existent) for mature stars of Barbara's magnitude, she readily accepted assignments in lesser films. In this period, she capered through a series of Westerns, a genre she always preferred since the days of *Annie Oakley* (1936) and *Union Pacific* (1939). Once again she demonstrated how integrity of performance, uniqueness of manner (her lionesslike, prowling walk; her snarling delivery of dialogue), and expert stunting ability could make even the least plausible quickie Western film interesting to the viewer.

Although she had tried her luck in TV with an anthology series in 1960, it was the hour-long Western program, "The Big Valley" (1965-1969), which brought her renewed popularity, a good many awards, and a chance to demonstrate her mettle against the new breed of generally marshmallow performers.

Truly, Barbara Stanwyck is in every way exemplary of the term "living legend."

She was a "change-of-life" baby, born in Brooklyn, New York, on Tuesday, July 16, 1907. Named Ruby, she was the fifth and last child of Byron and Catherine (McGee) Stevens of 246 Classon Avenue. Ruby had been preceded in birth by a brother, Byron Malcolm, two years earlier, but there were three sisters (Mildred, Maude, and Mabel) who were several years older. When Ruby was two years old, her mother was accidentally killed when she was shoved by a drunken man from an open-sided trolley car. Mrs. Stevens died after hitting her head against the curb. Unable to overcome his grief, Byron Sr. quit his job as a laborer, deserted his five children, and took to the sea on a merchant steamer. He later died aboard ship and was buried at sea.

When their father left home, Mildred, the only unmarried older sister, undertook to support Ruby and Byron, but she was a vaudeville dancer and was often required to be away from home. Since neither Maude nor Mabel could provide homes for the youngsters, Mildred was forced to place them in a series of foster homes. "My memories of Brooklyn are not very pleasant ones," Ruby was to recall in 1932. "I was boarded out and always being changed from one boarding place to another. I never knew what it was to have any one cuddle me or fuss over me or mother me, except when my sisters came to see me."

For the next traumatic eleven years, Ruby was shifted around which meant that a succession of schools provided her basic education. But there were periods when she did not attend school at all. She was a fast study, though, and had few difficulties learning the three R's. Mildred taught her dancing and introduced her to the world of the cinema. Reading, street fighting, street dancing, street language, and Pearl White serials became her life, but she also had an inclination toward religion. Since she found needed solace when she attended church services, she thought she might like to become a missionary when she grew up—either that or an actress. She could not quite make up her mind at this point. However, there was not much time for this child to daydream because her days, which passed quickly, were too filled with disturbing changes.

At the age of thirteen, on completion of the sixth grade at Brooklyn's P.S. 121, she decided that she must get a job. By adding three years to her age and with the help of cosmetics to make her look older, she qualified, so the story goes,* for a job with the Brooklyn telephone company as a file clerk in their billing department at a salary of thirteen dollars a week. This post did not last long and from there she allegedly became a bundle wrapper in the basement of the Abraham & Straus Department Store in Brooklyn. This was followed by a short-lived job with the Conde Nast Company as a pattern cutter. "I needed a job badly," she once remembered, "so when I applied, I told the man I knew how to sew." It was not long before her lie was discovered and "I was asked for my resignation before I even found my way to the ladies' room."

Next, she held jobs, supposedly, as a receptionist and a file clerk, but then she read that the Remick Music Company was in need of dancers for a new revue at the Strand Roof in Times Square. She auditioned and listed sister Mildred's experience background as her own. She got the job as a chorus girl at thirty-five dollars per week. At this same time, she was befriended by a suitor of Mildred's named James "Buck" McCarthy, who was one-half of the vaudeville team

known as Miller and Mack. Buck taught her various dance steps and added to her self-confidence. He liked her so well that he appointed himself as her godfather, and would be her friend and confidante for life.

Ruby did not prove to be the city's best hoofer at first, but Earl Lindsay, the dance director at the Strand Roof, gave her an ultimatum: straighten up or get lost. After his endearing speech, she concentrated on her dancing and was soon moved up front from the back row of the chorus. But the revue did not last very long and soon she was out of a job until Lindsay was able to place her in another line-up.

Meanwhile, she had made friends with two other show dancers, Mae Clarke and Wanda Mansfield, with whom she shared rooms. (Miss Clarke would later enter movies where she gained fame by having a juicy grapefruit squished into her face by James Cagney in *Public Enemy*, 1931. Miss Mansfield was destined to forego a show business career in favor of becoming helpmate to songwriter Walter Donaldson.) "We weren't dreaming of becoming great actresses," Ruby was to later admit. "I was going to be a great dancer. It didn't work out because I simply *wasn't* a great dancer. If I'd made a guess, then, as to which of us would make it big, I'd have guessed Mae because she was the better dancer and the most vivacious."

Through the aegis of Earl Lindsay, Ruby obtained dancing jobs at some of Manhattan's swankier night spots such as The Everglades, The Club Anatole, and The Silver Slipper. During the periods of inactivity when none of the three roommates had incomes, they frequented The Tavern near Times Square owned by Billy La Hiff, Nancy Carroll's uncle. It was La Hiff's generous habit to provide free lunches to unemployed chorus girls.

In 1924, Ruby won a job with the show *Keep Kool*, intended to divert New Yorkers' minds from the summer heat. The revue opened on May 22nd and closed on August 30th. A portion of the show was incorporated into the touring company of *The Ziegfeld Follies of 1924* and Ruby was included. She was

* Ella Smith in her fine book *Starring Barbara Stanwyck* (Crown, 1974) states "A number of early jobs have been erroneously listed for Stanwyck. . . ."

seen in a sketch spoofing George M. Cohan, Eugene O'Neill, and Avery Hopwood and in a modified strip number behind a see-through screen.

In August 1925, ambitious Ruby was in a Shubert Brothers revue, *Gay Paree,* which had her as a member of a human chandelier of scantily clad cuties, to be followed by another few months of professional inactivity. While paying a visit to Billy La Hiff's free lunch counter, she met Willard Mack, a director, writer, and producer in search of a girl to play a nightclub dancer with a small speaking part in his forthcoming dramatic presentation of *The Noose.* Ruby was hired. Before the out-of-town tryouts, however, Mack reasoned that the name of Ruby Stevens was not dramatic enough to entice the customers, so he sought a new name for his titian-haired find. While glancing through some old theatre posters, he came upon one heralding the Belasco Theatre's 1900 production of *Barbara Frietchie* which featured an English actress known as Jane Stanwyck. By juxtaposing the four names, he quickly arrived at Barbara Stanwyck and Ruby Stevens was rechristened.

The Noose flopped in its pre-Broadway showing and Mack hastily rewrote it. He expanded the role of the showgirl who loves a convicted bootlegger. He provided her with a third-act scene in which she tearfully requests his body for proper burial after the hanging. She then learns that his sentence has been commuted. The drama opened on Wednesday, October 20, 1926, at the Hudson Theatre where the critics acclaimed Barbara Stanwyck as a "real discovery" (*Theatre* magazine).

During the nine-month run of the hit play, she was screen-tested by MGM and by Cosmopolitan Pictures. Both tests were unflatteringly photographed but she accepted an offer from William Randolph Hearst's Cosmopolitan company to play the heroine hoofer's (Lois Wilson) chum in the silent feature *Broadway Nights* (First National, 1927), lensed in New York. Sam Hardy is the male lead as the heroine's husband, and in special cameo appearances are Sylvia Sidney and June Collyer. Barbara disclaims this as her film debut because it is such a bad film.

The Noose went on tour after its New York closing. During this time, she fell in love with the show's leading man, Rex Cherryman, of whom she was to say, "I adored him. Everything about him was so vivid, or perhaps it was because he was an actor and knew how to project." With the play's finish, Cherryman embarked on an ocean voyage to Europe from which he did not return. "He had died aboard ship. I suppose he died of a heart attack. I never really knew. But I nearly died, too, getting over the loss of him."

Back in New York, she occupied her time with a featured dancing part in the revue *A Night in Spain* in May 1927 and was then chosen by Arthur Hopkins, producer-director-writer, as the lead in his pending production of *Burlesque.* Hopkins thought she possessed the quality he wanted, "a sort of rough poignancy," for the part of Bonny, the vaudeville dancer whose comedian husband (Hal Skelly) takes to alcohol after she walks out on him. (They are re-united in the final act).

The engrossing drama opened at the Plymouth Theatre on Thursday, September 1, 1927, and was an immediate success. The fourth estate lauded Barbara as having given a "quietly sincere interpretation of the music hall wife" (*New York Times*) and said "[her] performance was touching and true" (*New York World*). The play was to occupy two years of her career, on Broadway and on an East Coast tour.

The poor orphan girl from Brooklyn who once said her childhood was "completely awful" was making a name for herself in theatre marquee lights, and virtual stage stardom seemed within easy grasp. "It is very satisfying to have attained one's dreams," she said. "If only one could feel that it is permanent. Personally, I'm always afraid that it won't last—that something will take it away."

Early in the run of *Burlesque,* the talented and witty Oscar Levant escorted variety-vaudeville headliner Frank Fay (real name Francis Donner) backstage to meet Barbara. Their initial introduction was not the friendliest, but after a few dates they began to like one another and by the end of 1927 they decided that they were in love. Fay was well known on the Orpheum Circuit for his wise-cracking and hard drinking habits, but the couple became inseparable during the months they were in New York together. One of his earlier romances had been stage comedienne Patsy Kelly who said her relationship with Fay ended the day she stopped calling him Mr. Fay in favor of Frank.

Fay was busy with *Harry Delmar's Revels* and vaudevillian appearances at the Palace Theatre, but in the summer of 1928 he went to St. Louis, Missouri, as master of ceremonies at the Missouri Theatre. When Barbara's play began its Broadway vacation period, she boarded a train to St. Louis where she arrived at 1:00 P.M. on Sunday, August 26, 1928. An hour and a quarter later, the couple stood in ceremony before justice of the peace Harry Pfeifer who pronounced them husband and wife. Barbara was twenty; Fay was thirty-one. It was his third marriage—he had been married previously to singer Frances White and to actress Lee Buchanan. At 5:00 that same afternoon, Barbara left St. Louis by train for Newark, New Jersey, where she opened the following evening in *Burlesque*. She told newsmen that she planned to retire from the stage when the play closed in Chicago that winter. Her retirement plans did not materialize, however, and she performed in February and March of 1929 with Fay in vaudeville routines at the Palace Theatre.

Out in Hollywood, Paramount Pictures wanted her for the screen version of *Burlesque,* but she refused to leave her husband, and Nancy Carroll enacted the role that Barbara had created onstage. The film's title was *The Dance of Life* (1929). Ironically, a few months later, Fay accepted a Warner Bros.' two-year contract offer and they moved to California.

The couple set up housekeeping in a rented house at Malibu and Frank went to work as the emcee in Warner Bros.' Technicolor musical, *The Show of Shows* (1929). Barbara had also accepted one of the many screen offers that came her way and signed an optional deal with United Artists producer, Joseph

Schenck. This action later prompted producer Arthur Hopkins to observe, "One of the theatre's great potential actresses was embalmed in celluloid."

Motion pictures had just entered the talking era and actors with pleasing voices were much in demand. Stage actor William Boyd (not to be confused with William "Hopalong" Boyd) was one of Barbara's co-workers in *The Locked Door* (1929), while Rod La Rocque received star billing as the villain. Directed by George Fitzmaurice, the film was adapted from Channing Pollock's play *The Sign on the Door,* which played on Broadway in 1919 with Mary Ryan. The melodrama has Barbara as secretary Ann Carter who falls victim to the charms of the evil Frank Devereaux (La Rocque). He escorts her to a gambling ship which is raided by the police and a photographer snaps their pictures. Devereaux, however, manages to buy the snapshot negative. A year later, after Ann has wed respectable Lawrence Reagan (Boyd), Devereaux covets Reagan's pretty sister (Betty Bronson). When Ann begs him to leave the girl alone, Devereaux produces the telltale photo. While they are conferring in a room with a "Do Not Disturb" sign hung on the doorknob, Devereaux is shot. Of course Ann is the chief suspect. But Devereaux survives long enough to reveal that he had been shot by Reagan but that the shooting episode was accidental. The critics blasted the antiquated vehicle, but were quite kind to Barbara in her official screen debut. "Miss Barbara Stanwyck gives an honest and moving picture as the distraught wife" (*New York Herald-Tribune*). The *New York Times* credited Barbara with acquitting "herself favorably."

Fortunately Columbia Pictures picked up her option to star her as *Mexicali Rose* (1929), in which she was instructed by director Erle C. Kenton to slink about the uninspired setting and be a mantrap. Within the flimsy tale, she is wed to Sam Hardy (her real-life actor friend from the Broadway days) but is hard-put to remain faithful. She ensnares her husband's handsome ward (William Janney) into her bed and sets out to make his life miserable. Ultimately, she is murdered by Hardy. The film proved to be another potboiler, but through no fault of Barbara's who tried hard but was given little, if any, concrete direction.

After two such undistinguished films, Barbara was considered as practically dispensable on the Hollywood scene. For six months, her career consisted of keeping house for Fay, interspersed with periodic screen tests. One of the tests made at Warner Bros. captured her dramatic scene from *The Noose* in which she begged for the remains of her to-be-hanged love, but still nothing came her way.

Recounting the drama of this unknowingly career-turning test, Barbara once said, "It was a night test and I guess they figured they'd get the kid in and out in a hurry. There was no director, no makeup man and no script. . . . A man came in and said 'I've been asked to do a test—can you suggest something?'. . . I told him I could do a scene from *The Noose* without a script. He set the light and gave me some pointers. I knew it was wasted motion but I thought, what the hell, and gave it my best.

"When it was over, I was amazed to find tears in his eyes. He seemed to be searching for words. At last he said, 'I want to apologize for the way this studio has treated you tonight. It doesn't mean anything coming from me. I'm leaving Hollywood a failure. But I want you to know it's been a privilege to make this test with a real actress—a privilege I won't forget'. . . . And he kissed my hand as if I'd been Sarah Bernhardt. I will always be grateful to that man for those words and that gesture because they sent belief in myself back to me. Incidentally, that 'failure' was the man who was to win a knighthood for his great screen achievements—Sir Alexander Korda."

Her husband had always been famous for his escapades, and as his drinking and carousing increased, she grew bitter and unhappy. Fay's further success at Warners in *Under the Texas Moon* (1930) and *Matrimonial Bed* (1930) earned him, he thought, a permanency in the film colony and he bought a $250,000 mansion in Brentwood Heights. Then one night while assisting Fay in a *Los Angeles Examiner*-sponsored benefit show,

Barbara was spotted by Harry Cohn of Columbia. Cohn sent Frank Capra, one of his new directors, to her with the request to make a test for the upcoming Columbia picture entitled *Ladies of Leisure.* She refused the test with several choice words, and succeeded in talking Capra out of even considering her. He figured she was not interested and terminated their interview. A few hours later, Fay was on the telephone bawling out Capra for mistreating his wife and insisting that he view her *The Noose* screen test. Capra viewed the scene and knew then that he had found the girl for the part of Kay Arnold in *Ladies of Leisure* (1930).

Adapted by Jo Swerling from Milton Herbert Gropper's 1924 play *Ladies of the Evening* (with Beth Merrill on Broadway), it is the snappy tale of a pair of hard-crusted "party girls" (Barbara and Marie Prevost). The former is hired by an artist (Ralph Graves) to pose for a portrait he calls "Hope." He not only brings out the true woman on canvas, but has her purring to his words of love, until his father (Lowell Sherman) tries to break them up. When this happens, she sets out to commit suicide, but is saved in time for a happy reunion with the artist. Capra worked closely with Barbara, unlike her prior two film directors, and evoked naturalness from her and helped her forget that there was a camera watching her every moment. It was due to his help and her innate abilities that critics such as the one at *Photoplay* magazine credited her with an "astonishing performance."

Columbia quickly inked her name to a non-exclusive contract, and she was suddenly the most sought-after young actress in Hollywood. Warner Bros. acquired her screen services for *Illicit* (1931) in top billing as Anne Vincent, and listed her as "Miss Barbara Stanwyck." The story of *Illicit* is more in tune with the mid-Seventies than 1931 in that the heroine enjoys a relationship with a man (James Rennie) on a live-in basis, but when they finally marry, the romance falls apart. The property would be remade two years later by Warner Bros. under the title *Ex-Lady* and star Bette Davis.

On February 27, 1931 the press announced

that Barbara had been signed to an exclusive long-term contract with Warner Bros., an announcement which proved to be partially erroneous. It was true that she had signed a pact with the Jack L. Warner-headed corporation, but on a non-exclusive arrangement; thus, the rising actress was pledged to both Columbia and Warner Bros.

In the Columbia-released *Ten Cents a Dance* (1931), only recently revived for film scholar viewing, Barbara was directed by Lionel Barrymore in her role as a bored taxi-dancer named Barbara O'Neil.

In his book *Barbara Stanwyck* (Pyramid, 1975), Jerry Vermilye recalls a scene from the film in which a crude customer inquires at the dance hall, "What's a guy gotta do to dance with you gals?" "All ya need is a ticket and some courage," replies Stanwyck's Barbara O'Neil. "This type of rejoinder," assesses Vermilye, "delivered with cool assurance, is characteristic of the Stanwyck of those Depression years—a girl whose veneer of sophistication never completely masks the fact that she knows how to handle men—and how to put them in their place, when necessary."

In the Jo Swerling script, she escapes by marrying a weak-willed clerk (Monroe Owsley) who succeeds in complicating her life by embezzling money from his firm. At the dance hall, she meets a rich man (Ricardo Cortez) who loans her the money to clear the husband, but intimates that, in return, he would like her to get a divorce and marry him. Because of the two box-office attractions (Barbara and Cortez), the eighty-minute feature made money in spite of its poor construction (director Barrymore, then in the early throes of arthritis, was often literally asleep on the job due to the medications he took). Cortez went on record by accolading Barbara with the statement, "I admired her for her dignity and professionalism."

Her initial contract film for Warner Bros. was *Night Nurse* (1931) in the title role of Lora Hart, whose first after-training assignment is to play nursemaid to the two little girls of Mrs. Richey (Charlotte Merriam). The wealthy widow Richey show little interest in her daughters. She prefers booze and her burly chauffeur (Clark Gable), and nurse

Hart soon discovers a plot devised by the chauffeur to starve the children to death, marry the tipsy widow, and obtain the trust fund set aside for them. Lora's vivacious roommate (Joan Blondell) advises her to tell the police, but instead, Lora determines to stop the skullduggery with the help of bootlegger boyfriend Mortie (Ben Lyon). The chauffeur threatens her life and then knocks her cold with a sock to the jaw. But she is undaunted and is able with Mortie's help to squash the dastardly plan. This soapy melodrama, directed by William Wellman, was summed up by the *Hollywood Reporter* with, "The best things about *Night Nurse* are its title and cast names plus the Misses Stanwyck and Blondell stripping two or three times during the picture."

Less than a month after *Night Nurse* was in release, Columbia distributed its big-budgeted feature, *The Miracle Woman* (1931). Rated by *Silver Screen* magazine as "splendid" and "a brilliantly directed [by Frank Capra] study of modern evangelism that is bound to cause a lot of discussion," the film casts Barbara as Florence Fallon, a minister's daughter. With bitterness in her heart after her dad's death, the girl under the money-hungry guidance of a promoter (Sam Hardy) turns to commercial preaching. In the tradition of Aimee Semple McPherson with a dash of Elmer Gantry, the story relates how the quick-buck artist builds a tabernacle for her and surrounds Florence with lions inside a cage from which she delivers her sermons. During one such session, she is joined by a volunteer (David Manners), a handsome blind ex-war aviator who has given up thoughts of suicide through his faith in her. The promoter realizes that the two of them are falling in love and tries to break up the costly liaison, even to the extent of burning the tabernacle. Florence then finds true religion with the Salvation Army and confesses genuine love for the blind young man.

The Miracle Woman proved to be the film which firmly established Barbara as a movie star. Her price per picture had climbed to $50,000 at Warner Bros. and she fully expected Columbia to follow suit. But parsimonious, shrewd, crude Harry Cohn was not

With Louis Natheaux in
Mexicali Rose ('29).

←

With Rod LaRocque and
William "Stage" Boyd in
The Locked Door ('29).

With Monroe Owsley in
Ten Cents a Dance ('31).

431

so quick to agree, and she rejected the next Columbia film assignment. This led to a court decision which Barbara lost, but Cohn then turned around and matched the Warner salary on his own.

Thus, Barbara was next seen in the role of Lulu Smith in *Forbidden* (Columbia, 1932), a melodramatic soap-opera theme that has her in love with married, debonair Adolphe Menjou. They have fun, laughs, and a boy that Menjou, a top-ranking politician who must guard his public image, adopts as his own. In the *Back Street* tradition, Barbara's Lulu Smith lives in the shadow of his life, accepting his favors and existing for the few chances she has of seeing her baby. Later, she weds a reporter (Ralph Bellamy) hoping to discourage the newsman from prying too much into Menjou's past. When he does learn the truth and threatens to reveal the scandalous relationship, Barbara kills him. The long (eighty-five-minute) film was Barbara's third production under the increasingly capable direction of Frank Capra. A film like *Forbidden* could only have been made in the freer morality period of the pre-Production Code days.

While her career zoomed, Frank Fay's Hollywood popularity was fading. His last two films, *Bright Lights* and *God's Gift to Women,* both 1931 releases, were anything but personal hits. He assumed this professional slump was temporary. Meanwhile, Barbara maintained the offscreen role of the faithful helpmate and told columnist Sidney Skolsky in February 1932 that she was very content to make his coffee and get his slippers.

The Barbara of this period wore little makeup offscreen, was afraid of horses, played tennis, and swam daily in the Fay pool. She was said to be a fancier of plain foods, with meat and potatoes her favorite dish. She smoked cigarettes, and according to Clara Beranger of *Liberty* magazine "not with the dainty affection of some women smokers, but with the unaffected enjoyment of a man." Writer Beranger further found her to be "lusty" and a "square shooter." In 1932, Barbara stood five-feet, five-inches, and weighed 115 pounds. The color of her eyes was between blue and violet and, although she liked to wear wide-brimmed hats, Fay insisted that she wear small, turned-up chapeaus.

In March 1932 she traveled to Manhattan with Fay where they appeared in a vaudeville revue at the Palace Theatre. During the two weeks of her stage appearances which began on Sunday, March 6, she was interviewed by Marion Carter of the *New York Journal* who leaped onto the Stanwyck bandwagon by writing, "Miss Stanwyck is a very fine, sincere young person. The adulation of hundreds of thousands of fans throughout the world has not turned her head. Although she is one of America's finest actresses, there is nothing temperamental, affected or artificial about her."

Shopworn (Columbia, 1932) was one of those contemporary, topical plots where the poor girl (Barbara) meets the rich boy (Regis Toomey) and is ostracized by his mother (Clara Blandick). The theme would be used over and over again in films, although this Nicholas Grinde-directed example is not one of the better renditions of this format.

Barbara fared much better at Warner Bros. as Selina Peake in the 1932 version of Edna Ferber's *So Big*. The famed property had been previously filmed in 1925 by First National with Colleen Moore and would be made a third time in 1953 by Warners with Jane Wyman. Through the proceedings, directed by William Wellman, the character of Selina ages from a child (played by actress Dawn O'Day—later Anne Shirley) to an elderly, white-haired woman. Barbara's onscreen character is a widow, left with a farm and a little boy (Dickie Moore) to raise. The boy is nicknamed "So Big" and she sacrifices her personal happiness to educate him and to instill in him the goodness harvested through hard work. The grown-up son (Hardie Albright) is a disappointment, however, because of his inclination toward easy living. The youth's friend, Roelf (George Brent), turns out to be the one most influenced by Selina's teachings.

It is easy today to pass over *So Big* as just another vehicle (one of four, actually) made by Stanwyck during 1932. But this chronicle type of drama elevated her to the league of major women stars such as Ann Harding, Irene Dunne, and Warner Bros.' own Ruth Chatterton who specialized in this type of decade-stretching narrative in which the heroine ages over years of trauma. William Boehnel (*New York World Telegram*) would laud, "By her performance in *So Big,* Barbara Stanwyck definitely establishes herself with this writer as being a brilliant emotional actress. . . . No matter what one may think about the picture, the final conviction of anyone who sees Miss Stanwyck's Selina Peake will be that she herself contributes a fine and stirring performance, making of it a characterization which is direct and eloquent all the way."

In *The Purchase Price,* also directed by Wellman for Warner Bros. in 1932, Barbara is again teamed with George Brent. Here, she is Joan Gordon, a world-weary nightclub girl who answers his advertisement for a cook and wife. On his farm in North Dakota, she is repelled at first by both the surroundings and by his manners, and relegates him to the barn on their wedding night when he forces himself on her. They ultimately find joint harmony after a few horrendous storms and a brawl between Brent and a New York gambler (Lyle Talbot) who had hoped to take Barbara home with him to Manhattan. *Time* magazine observed, "Rare until recently has been the cinema heroine who preferred the stupid poor man to the bright city fellow. The viewpoint of *The Purchase Price* is simple and masculine. It advertises the virtue of hard work and loyalty."

On Monday, December 5, 1932, Barbara and Frank adopted a ten-month-old boy whom they named Dion Anthony. The blue-eyed, blond-haired child was expected to bring the couple closer together and hopefully help to curtail Fay's recurring craving for alcohol. Called both Dion and Tony, the little boy became the center of attention within the Fay household—for a while. This event also demonstrated that Miss Stanwyck, known as a "tough babe," could have a most domestic orientation.

Due to her busy schedule, Barbara was un-able to fulfill a Warners assignment in *Jewel Robbery* (1932) opposite William Powell and was replaced with Kay Francis. Barbara did find time for a few days' work in a two-reeler, called *The Slippery Pearls,* also dealing with jewels and their robbery, for the Hollywood Masquers Club. The short subject boasted a complement of filmdom's great, including Frank Fay, all of whom donated their modest salaries to various charities.

In January 1933, Barbara was seen in what was to be her last Columbia feature film for five years. As directed by Frank Capra for the fourth time, she is Megan Davis, an American in trouble in China of the 1920s, in *The Bitter Tea of General Yen.* She is a missionary in Shanghai bent on rescuing war-ravaged orphans, but she is taken prisoner by an imperious warlord, General Yen (Nils Asther). At first, she hates the man because of his unscrupulous methods, but when she discovers that it is a means of survival on his part, she learns to sympathize with him. His mistress (Toshia Mori) brings about the ruler's downfall by confiding secrets to Yen's enemies, and as Megan admits her love for him, the General, determined to have an honorable death, drinks a cup of tea which he has poisoned.

Said to be too arty for movie audiences of 1933, *The Bitter Tea of General Yen* was chosen to transform New York's Radio City Music Hall from a planned showcase for stage extravaganzas into a movie house. The date was January 11, 1933. Although many critics chose to dislike the feature, one defender, Otis Ferguson (*The New Republic*), called it the "Number one story about China." Years later, in a retrospective review of the film, the British *Monthly Film Bulletin* would analyze, "*The Bitter Tea of General Yen* bows to no one: audience, moralists, or Art with a Capital A. With a brilliantly lucid and literate script by Edward Paramore, Capra is able to demonstrate time and time and time again the gap yawning between East and West, a *philosophical* distance which has little to do with racial prejudice but which still keeps the lovers inexorably apart." As this English journal points out, there are more than a few parallels

With Betty Jane Graham and
Marcia Mae Jones in a pose for
Night Nurse ('31).

With Richard Cromwell in *The
Miracle Woman* ('31).

434

With Ralph Bellamy in
Forbidden ('32).

With Hal Price in
Shopworn ('32).

435

With Nils Asther in *The Bitter Tea of General Yen* ('33).

With Hardie Albright, George Brent, and Bette Davis in *So Big* ('32).

With husband Frank Fay at the Los Angeles Biltmore Hotel (February 1934).

With Robert Young in *Red Salute* ('35).

437

between this Capra film and Joseph von Sternberg's *Shanghai Express* (1932) with Marlene Dietrich and Rouben Mamoulian's *Queen Christina* (1933) with Greta Garbo. Yet Stanwyck's portrayal, which sets this film's heroine apart from the leading ladies of the other two features, depicts Megan as a victim more of ignorance and sentiment than of fate. As Nils Asther's General tells Megan, "To do good works you must have wisdom; you depend too much on your beauty." Later, he observes, "You are afraid of death, as you are of living." Thus, here again, Barbara was portraying a character far removed from what many had already termed her stereotype, the self-sufficient broad. It was just another illustration of the versatility of roles that gained her the respect of the film industry, even if her associates were not always aware of the reasons for their adoration.

After *The Bitter Tea,* which ended her Columbia contractual agreement, Barbara concentrated on working exclusively for Warner Bros., the studio where Ruth Chatterton and Kay Francis were ruling the roost and such diverse other leading ladies as Bette Davis, Joan Blondell, and Ruby Keeler were fast becoming major bread-winners for the lot. The first film for Barbara was *Ladies They Talk About* (1933) in which she is a convict at San Quentin's wing for women. The daughter of a church deacon, she obviously has trod a less than righteous path to have wound up in prison for bank robbery. She sneers at, hates, and shoots the man (Preston Foster) responsible for having designated San Quentin as her mailing address, but the snappy tale concludes with the two of them professing love for each other. In the very racy *Baby Face* (1933), she is a blonde (the fair-haired wigs did little for her appearance) who uses men for what they can do for her monetary status. She moves along quickly—ever upward—until she encounters Mr. Trenholm (George Brent), a banker whom she weds. His financial ruin is accomplished, but she steps forward just in time with enough money to save him from imprisonment. It is presumed that they live happily ever after. Because of its sexy and immoral proclivities, the feature was scorned by the office of the industry censor, Will Hays, until certain scenes were modified. The film's denunciation was a prime factor in the resignation of Darryl F. Zanuck from the Warner Bros. studio production staff.

With Barbara's financial assistance (said to amount to $125,000), Frank Fay assembled in Los Angeles a vaudeville type of revue which he brought to New York after previewing at larger cities along the way. The show, called *Tattle Tales,* opened at the Broadhurst Theatre on Thursday, June 1, 1933, at the height of the hottest New York summer on record. Also in the cast, Barbara offered scenes from her movies, *Ladies of Leisure* and *The Miracle Woman.* Critic Burns Mantle (*New York Daily News*) classified the show as "Class B quality," but rated the Fays as "still a little bit of Class A." He judged Barbara with having been "blessed with that certain subtle something that distinguishes the real from the imitation, a sort of unconscious self-consciousness that we classify frequently as poise."

Before embarking on *Tattle Tales,* Barbara had completed her fourth and final 1933 release, *Ever in My Heart* (Warner Bros.), which was released in mid-October. In this tragic tale, directed in a crisp way by Archie Mayo, she is an American who weds a German (Otto Kruger) and later finds that he is a spy. The period is about 1910, when the Germans loomed large in the business of pre-World War I espionage. After the death of their son, Barbara slips poison into the wine of her unsuspecting spouse and into her own as well, which concludes the account.

Tattle Tales survived twenty-eight Broadhurst performances and the Fays, with deflated pocketbooks, returned to Hollywood. A discouraged Frank settled down to romancing liquor, while Barbara went back to making one film after another at Warner Bros. *Gambling Lady* (1934) presents her as a card sharp named Lady Lee who marries socialite Carry Madison (Joel McCrea). Their former respective loves (Pat O'Brien and Claire Dodd) present problems but a happy ending is realized. *A Lost Lady* (1934), derived from the award-winning Willa Cather novel and a 1924 silent film with Irene Rich, has the star as the wife of Frank Morgan whom she shuns in favor of younger, more virile Ricardo Cortez. She returns ultimately to Morgan after he has a heart attack, deciding she prefers his company after all. In *The Secret Bride* (1935), she is Ruth Vincent who weds secretly the attorney general (Warren William) who then attempts to clear her father (Grant Mitchell), the governor, of bribery charges. William Dieterle directed this programmer about which he said, "Of all the films I directed [this] is the picture I don't like to think about any more." *The Woman in Red* (1935) proved to be her last film in the line-up of Warner Bros. soap-opera assignments. This time, Barbara is an earthy girl named Shelby Barrett who weds a man (Gene Raymond) of high society and is ostracized by the "in crowd" as having been faithless with John Eldredge.

There were contract negotiations between Barbara and Universal Pictures, but nothing materialized. She thus chose to free-lance, which her agent, Zeppo Marx, felt was a better move for her career. Her initial vehicle was *Red Salute* (United Artists, 1935) for producer Edward Small. It was her first comedy, albeit one of a controversial political nature. She is Drue Van Allen, a rebellious college girl influenced by Communist infiltrators. One in particular is Hardie Albright from whom she is separated by her father (Purnell Pratt) who sends her to Mexico. There, she encounters a U.S. Army private (Robert Young) who goes AWOL and accompanies her on a madcap journey in a stolen trailer. As United Artists discovered to its chagrin, America was not ready to accept Communist ideology oncamera or to see it on motion picture screens no matter how disguised. The film was ignored or not shown at all in many cities. Later, revivals were attempted under the title *Her Enlisted Man*.

In August 1935, to the surprise of few in the know, the Fays separated. In recent months, Frank's behavior had become strange, at best. He leaned heavily toward religion, yet he would swear a blue streak over the slightest affront. Once, in a rage, he threw little Dion into the swimming pool. The fading star's alcoholic binges were becoming more and more frequent. Some of his public antics created newspaper attention. The combination of events caused Barbara to take Dion and depart from the Fay home. She announced her intention to file for divorce, but meanwhile permitted Frank to see their son once a week. She soon ended this arrangement when she discovered that Fay was using the boy as an instrument to woo her back. With the help of agent Marx, Barbara bought a 140-acre ranch in the San Fernando Valley which became known as Marwyck. There, Dion had his own pony and every day an ex-Russian cavalry officer named Boris gave him riding lessons. The one-time horse-shy Barbara Stanwyck now learned to love the four-legged animals. Her old pal, Buck Mack, took up residence with Barbara and Dion and became her all-around assistant.

In the midst of her uprooted personal life, Barbara was offered the role that would place her at the top of the movie star ladder. RKO signed her for a one-film deal as *Annie Oakley* (1935), to be directed by George Stevens. The character of the rugged markswoman from Ohio's backwoods who establishes a name for herself in the 1880s was molded to fit Barbara. Clearly a liberated woman, Annie Oakley faced the all-male competition in rifle shooting and surpassed them all. One man (Preston Foster) in particular was the star of Buffalo Bill's (Moroni Olsen) Wild West Show and Stanwyck's heroine falls in love with him. When his luck later runs out, she finds him at a street shooting gallery where they are reunited while youngsters stare in disbelief at seeing the real, live Annie Oakley. Of Annie Oakley, Barbara once said, "Modern women could learn a great deal from her. She was a woman of all ages, deeply feminine in spite of all her shooting ability—which she developed to support her family." It is an ironic fact of show business history that Barbara's very engaging performance as this historical character would be overshadowed by Ethel Merman's show-stopping performance on Broadway in *Annie*

Get Your Gun and by the more publicized characterization by Betty Hutton in the 1950 movie version of the musical.

On Tuesday, December 31, 1935, Barbara won her divorce from Fay, obtaining legal custody of Dion. The final decree was accomplished after a bitter court trial over the boy. As a compromise, Frank was granted "reasonable" visitation rights. Further court appearances would occur throughout the next three years, however, and the matter would not be resolved until Judge Goodwin Knight of the California Superior Court would specifically designate defined visitation days and hours when Fay could see Dion.

After *Annie Oakley,* Barbara signed a non-exclusive contract with RKO which called for one picture a year. Then, on the heels of *Annie*'s success, Barbara was offered and accepted the feminine lead (although in third billing to Wallace Beery and John Boles) in Twentieth Century-Fox's *A Message to Garcia* (1936). It was an unfortunate casting in that, as a Cuban senorita, she speaks English without a Spanish accent and appears more like a girl from America's eastern seaboard than a Caribbean native. While John Boles as an American soldier conducts an espionage mission during the Spanish-American war and burly Beery as a soldier of fortune hams his way through the George Marshall-directed proceedings, Barbara has little to do but to stare moon-eyed at Boles. As the *New York Post* observed, ". . . she has been photographed attractively [by Rudolph Mate] and she's a good enough trouper to keep in the background when the spotlight doesn't focus on her."

Her 1936 stint at RKO was her second comedy, *The Bride Walks Out,* opposite Gene Raymond as the husband. Their plight, dictated by the husband, is survival on his thirty-dollar-a-week salary. He prevents her from adding dollars to the family coffers by relying on her pre-marital profession as a model because of pride. But they manage, and the dialogue by Philip G. Epstein and P. J. Wolfson is nicely sharp. Once again, Barbara displays her capability for comedy.

But MGM next chose to use her services in

a melodrama called *His Brother's Wife* (1936). She was co-starred with Robert Taylor. Barbara had met Taylor a few weeks before production began and the couple, seen everywhere together, became filmland's most talked-about candidates for matrimony. The plot of their initial screen teaming is far from distinguished but the film earned box-office profits because of its stars. Barbara is Rita Wilson, a model who becomes infatuated with a playboy scientist (Taylor). However, he is too busy searching out a cure for spotted fever. When he plunges into a jungle for research, she spitefully weds his brother (John Eldredge), a man whom she does not love. Soon after, she too heads for the jungle where she inoculates herself with the fever virus and the scientist quickly discovers a cure. Naturally, Rita is saved.

On Monday, August 3, 1936, Barbara was heard for the first time on the Cecil B. De-Mille-hosted "Lux Radio Theatre" which had debuted on the airwaves two months prior. Barbara and Fred MacMurray were heard as the young lovers in a condensation of *Main Street*. This marked the start of a long friendship between Barbara and DeMille, during which time he was to use her more often on his radio show than any other actress—she starred on the program sixteen times.

By now she had signed a new non-exclusive pact with Twentieth Century-Fox and was starred for the second time with Joel McCrea. In *Banjo on My Knee* (1936) she danced and sang onscreen for the first time in the role of Pearl, a folksy gal who marries McCrea only to have him dash off because the police are on his trail. During his lengthy absence, she takes a job as an entertainer where she dances with Buddy Ebsen and sings with Tony Martin. *Variety* acknowledged that she had a "deep and throaty" singing voice.

In RKO's *The Plough and the Stars* (1936), shot prior to *Banjo on My Knee* but released after, John Ford offered an artful rendition of the Sean O'Casey play. Barbara is Nora Clitheroe caught in the onslaught of the 1916 Irish rebellion. The role was played on Broadway in 1927 by Sara Allgood. Two film versions were photographed in 1936: in that di-

440

rected by Ford Nora is wed to Jack (Preston Foster) whose appointment as head of the Citizens Army causes their lives to be filled with danger; in the second version, thought by the RKO hierarchy to be more interesting, they are lovers. For the role of Nora, Barbara cultivated an Irish brogue and her wardrobe, for the most part, was drab. The *New York Daily News* rated her as being "in the class of the screen's great tragediennes."

Her first film at Paramount was also the first movie to employ the character of Dr. James Kildare, later the subject of a film series at MGM. Joel McCrea is Kildare in *Internes Can't Take Money* (1937), a crime drama in which he administers first-aid to Janet Haley (Barbara). He falls in love with her, but her only mission is to find her missing daughter. With the help of a gangster (Lloyd Nolan), they find the kidnapped little girl and discover love with one another. Back at Twentieth Century-Fox, she was re-teamed with Robert Taylor in *This Is My Affair* (1937), a costume piece in which she plays Lil Duryea, a music hall entertainer. She is attracted to a U.S. naval officer (Taylor) who is posing as a member of a bank-robbing mob headed by gruff Victor McLaglen. Taylor has been appointed secretly by President McKinley (Frank Conroy), and when the President is assassinated, there is no one to vouch for his innocence. Lil pleads with the new President, Theodore Roosevelt (Sidney Blackmer), who agrees to release the officer from prison. In costumes designed by Royer, who would dress Alice Faye in some of her best (*In Old Chicago*, 1938), Barbara is stunning to behold.

Stella Dallas, written by Olive Higgins Prouty, had been a successful novel of 1922 after magazine serialization, and had been filmed in 1925 with Belle Bennett, the year after it had been a Broadway play. Early in 1937, Samuel Goldwyn decided to remake the property for United Artists distribution and the title role became one coveted by several actresses. Goldwyn's top preference was Ruth Chatterton, the co-star of his popular *Dodsworth* (1936), but she rejected it. Goldwyn contractee Joel McCrea, knowing that

Barbara wanted it, interceded on her behalf with a sales pitch to the film's director, King Vidor. Vidor suggested a screen test. Thinking back to her early bad experience with soundstage auditions, Barbara was initially adamant about not doing another test. But she was finally persuaded to relent and the footage was shown to Goldwyn who gave her the plum role of *Stella Dallas.*

Within the 195-minute melodrama, she is an ill-educated poor girl who marries a sophisticate named Stephen Dallas (John Boles). The couple have nothing in common but their daughter Laurel, who soon becomes Stella's reason for living. When the household breaks up, Stella happily assumes responsibility for Laurel, nicknamed Lolly, who grows to be a pretty young woman (Anne Shirley) with the quiet good taste inherited from her dad.

Later, after agreeing to free Stephen so he may wed Helen Morrison, Stella finds that Laurel admires and would like to emulate the good Mrs. Morrison. Stella persuades her daughter to make her home with the newlyweds who can offer her much more. The heart-rending scene of the film is of Laurel's wedding with Stella peering into the window from behind an iron fence. Plainly dressed and devoid of makeup, she refuses to move at the request of a cop. Tugging at a handkerchief held to her mouth, she smiles at her daughter's good fortune and walks off jauntily, realizing that Laurel's future is in good hands.

Barbara has often confessed that she regards *Stella Dallas* the best of her many films. As the flamboyant, crude floozy with a fineness underneath, she acted the role to perfection by revealing the character's inner goodness to audiences with a tear or a quiver of the upper lip. "There was unusual stimulation in the dual nature of the part," the star explained. "It was like playing two different women simultaneously." Director Vidor has called her "a professional's professional, a superb technician with a voice quality that immediately hooked you with its humaneness. She was a big favorite with all her co-workers on the set as well as the public, and

With Melvyn Douglas
and Andy Clyde in
Annie Oakley ('35).

With Buddy Ebsen and
Walter Brennan in *Banjo
on My Knee* ('36).

442

With Robert Taylor in a
promotional pose for *This Is
My Affair* ('37).

On the set of *Internes Can't
Take Money* ('37) with May
Carlson, Frances Jean
Petersen, Chloe Pat Church,
Yvonne Dunkerley, and
Joel McCrea.

rightly so. From a director's viewpoint, she was a joy to work with—no problems." Young co-star Anne Shirley once said, "The whole word is pro. Miss Stanwyck was hired and paid to perform a service. She presented herself for work before time. She was prepared to the very top of her ability. Dialogue learned perfectly."

The critics heartily endorsed Barbara's performance as *Stella Dallas*. "Miss Stanwyck's performance is as courageous as it is fine" (*New York Times*). "[She] turns in a sensitive, beautifully shaded characterization" (*New York World-Telegram*). In October 1937, three months after the film's release, "Stella Dallas" became a serial drama on radio, depicting episodes in the character's later life; Anne Elstner was heard as Stella in this soap opera which enjoyed many years of popularity.

Barbara's obligatory film for RKO in 1937 was a comedy, *Breakfast for Two,* in which she was cast opposite suave Herbert Marshall. "I couldn't possibly have followed Stella with another emotional role," she said. It is a movie filled with gags and wild, Keystone Kops-type action. She is a Texas heiress who first battles wealthy playboy Marshall and then loves him—very typical plotting of the decade.

In the early months of 1938, Barbara was one of five nominees for an Academy Award as Best Actress for her performance in *Stella Dallas.* Her competitors for the Oscar were Irene Dunne (*The Awful Truth*), Greta Garbo (*Camille*), Janet Gaynor (*A Star Is Born*), and Luise Rainer (*The Good Earth*). On Oscar night, Thursday, March 10, 1938, at the Biltmore Hotel, the Best Actress Award was given to Luise Rainer, the first person to ever win in two successive years—her performance as Anna Held in MGM's *The Great Ziegfeld* had netted her the 1936 honor. A disappointed Barbara said, "My heart's blood was in that film. I should have won."

She now considered herself above the programmer type of films and began rejecting scripts presented by both Twentieth and RKO. Her contract swan song with the former studio was *Always Goodbye* (1938) in

which she played Margot Weston, another celluloid sacrificing mother. In a lighter vein than *Stella Dallas,* Margot Weston is an unwed mother who gives her child up for adoption but later wants him (John Russell) back after she has made a successful modeling career for herself. On hand to lend support are Herbert Marshall, Ian Hunter, and Lynn Bari. It is a remake of 1933's *Gallant Lady* from Twentieth Century-United Artists which had starred Ann Harding. *Photoplay* gingerly observed of the less-than-spectacular *Always Goodbye,* "Most women will go for this sentimental picture."

In 1938, Barbara demanded in court that ex-husband Frank Fay be given a psychiatric examination to decide the outcome of yet another custodial hassle over Dion. Meanwhile, Robert Taylor acquired a ranch next to Marwyck. Her relationship with Taylor appeared serious to the point where she even froze homemade ice cream for him from a recipe given her by his doting mother. Dion's pet name for Taylor was "Gentleman Bob" and the two became friends, much to the consternation of Mr. Fay.

Columnist Sidney Skolsky told the world on March 17, 1938, that Barbara's best friends were Joan Crawford, Franchot Tone, and the Zeppo Marxes, and that she spent every Saturday night with Crawford and Tone who were then wed. It was revealed that Miss Stanwyck preferred tailored clothes, chain-smoked cigarettes from a jeweled case given her by Miss Crawford, and permitted her close friends to call her "Stany." She was allergic to dogs, had a marble bathtub, and slept in silk nightgowns. While she was suspended by both Twentieth and RKO from November 1937 to April 1938, one of her two race horses won at Santa Anita Race Track and she commented, "I'm glad someone in the family is working."

She had made it known in the winter of 1937 that she wanted the role of *Jezebel* at Warner Bros., but Bette Davis won that meaty role. Although Barbara was cooperative with the members of the press, she made it a house rule that none of them should set foot inside her home; this was an ordinance which she has kept throughout her lengthy career to date.

At RKO, she made what would prove to be her last film for the studio for three years. In *The Mad Miss Manton* (1938), described as a screwball comedy, she is heiress Melsa Manton, who is abetted by six girlfriends in solving a double murder that has the police baffled. Her attempts are put down in print by newsman Peter Ames (Henry Fonda) who later learns to love her madcap ways. Due to his hatred of his insipid role, Fonda ignored Barbara offscreen, but would later remember her as "one of the dear people of the world—a perfect delight to work with."

Cecil B. DeMille, long a fan of Barbara's ("I have never worked with an actress who was more cooperative, less temperamental and a better workman . . ."), handed her the top role of Mollie Monahan in his marathon rebuilding of the *Union Pacific* (Paramount, 1939). Her co-star was again Joel McCrea, with screen newcomer Robert Preston as McCrea's competition for her love. Blessed with a large budget and filmed on location in Utah and California's San Fernando Valley, the epic-proportioned feature relates the story of the construction of the rail line that was to connect the nation. Mollie Monahan is postmistress of the portable town that follows the rail-building crew. In the course of her job, she takes a shine to muscular gambler Dick Allen (Preston) until a Congressional troubleshooter (McCrea) arrives on the scene.

Affecting an Irish brogue, Barbara did her own stunt work in the film ("I've always been a frustrated stuntman at heart") and survives with McCrea, in tandem, Indian attacks, rail breakdowns, and the villainy of Sid Campeau (Brian Donlevy). The expansive film premiered at Omaha, Nebraska, on Friday, April 29, 1939, where "some 400,000 persons dug up grandfather's plug hat and Sharpe's rifle and tooled to town for the big doings," reported Lucius Beebe in the *New York Herald-Tribune.*

Columbia presented her with another non-comedy role in *Golden Boy* (1939), the picture that made a star of dimple-cheeked William Holden. The property, written by Clifford Odets and done on Broadway in 1937 with Stella Adler in the female lead, provided Holden with many hours of soundstage fright. But he pulled through with Barbara's help, as she volunteered to work with him on his part after hours and on weekends. This was a very typical gesture of "the very atypical superstar." Holden has never forgotten her kindness and even now sends her roses every year commemorating the start of shooting of *Golden Boy.* Barbara is Lorna Moon, the hard-bitten girlfriend of fight-promoter Adolphe Menjou whose number one protégé (Holden) needs to be gently persuaded to give up his violin-playing ambitions in favor of becoming a fighter. In so doing, Lorna falls in love with the boy.

One of the most daring articles to appear in a fan magazine in the late Thirties was one that was published in the *Photoplay* issue of January 1939. Entitled "Hollywood's Unmarried Husbands and Wives" and written by Kirtley Baskette, it reveals, "Nowhere has domesticity, outside the marital state, reached such a full flower as in Hollywood. Nowhere are there so many famous unmarried husbands and wives." He continued, "To the outside world Clark Gable and Carole Lombard might as well be married. So might Bob Taylor and Barbara. Or George Raft and Virginia Pine, Charlie Chaplin and Paulette Goddard. Unwed couples they might be termed. But they go everywhere together; do everything in pairs. No hostess would think of inviting them separately, or pairing them with another. They solve one another's problems, handle each other's business affairs . . . Yet, to the world, their official status is 'just friends.' No more."

Focusing in on the Stanwyck-Taylor relationship, Baskette reported, "When Bob Taylor docked in New York from England and *A Yank at Oxford,* he waited around a couple of hours for a load of stuff he had bought over there to clear customs. Most of it was for—not Bob, but Barbara Stanwyck and her little son, Dion. . . . They've been practically a family since Bob bought his ranch estate in Northridge and built a house there. . . . Bob's house and Barbara's house stand now on ad-

With Barbara O'Neil in
Stella Dallas ('37).

With Joel McCrea and
Robert Preston in *Union
Pacific* ('39).

446

On the set of *Remember the Night* ('40) with director Mitchell Leisen and Fred MacMurray.

With William Holden and Adolphe Menjou in *Golden Boy* ('39).

joining knolls. The occupants ride together and work together and play there together in their time off. Bob trained and worked out for *The Crowd Roars* [MGM, 1938] on Barbara's ranch. Almost every evening, after work at the studio or on the ranch, he runs over for a plunge in her pool. . . . Even gifts and expressions of sentiment take on the practical, utilitarian aspect of old married folks' remembrances when these Hollywood single couples come across. . . . Bob Taylor presents Barbara Stanwyck with a tennis court on her birthday, with Barbara giving Bob a two-horse auto trailer for his!"

Writer Baskette concluded his daring (and it was very much that for its time when the studios controlled so much of the media) article with homey preaching, "For nobody, not even Hollywood's miracle men, has ever improved on the good old-fashioned satisfying institution of holy matrimony. And, until something better comes along, the best way to hunt happiness when you're in love in Hollywood or anywhere else—is with a preacher, a marriage license, and a bagful of rice."

The subjects of this broadside article and the stars' studios took the warning of future exposes to heart. With the exception of George Raft and Virginia Pine, the unmarried teams of Chaplin-Goddard, Gable-Lombard, and Stanwyck-Taylor would get to the church almost on time. On Saturday, May 13, 1939, Barbara and Robert Taylor drove to San Diego. They were eloping. At 12:30 A.M. on May 14 (to avoid a bad-luck jinx that might ensue from exchanging vows on May 13) they were married at the home of Thomas Whale, a friend, by justice of the peace Phillip Smith. Barbara was thirty-one; Taylor was twenty-seven. Marian Marx, wife of Zeppo, was Barbara's bridesmaid and Buck Mack was best man. Barbara was dressed in a navy blue silk crepe dress; Robert wore a brown business suit. At two o'clock that afternoon they announced their secret nuptials to reporters at the Victor Hugo Cafe in Beverly Hills where Barbara displayed her slender gold wedding band encircled with rubies and Robert's wedding gift to her of a gold St. Christopher's medal bearing the engraving

"God Protect Her Because I Love Her."

The next morning she was back to work on *Golden Boy* and Taylor resumed a love scene at MGM with Hedy Lamarr for *Lady of the Tropics* (1939). Taylor sold his one-bedroom ranch house and acreage and moved into Barbara's larger place shared with Dion and Buck Mack. A short time later, the quartet took up residence in a newly built home in Beverly Hills; there was no longer any need for discreet seclusion from the film community. In November 1939, the Taylors enjoyed a delayed honeymoon in New York City where reporters and fans were awed by her ruby ring, matching bracelet, and ruby spray worn in her "stylish turban." It was also observed that Taylor wore a cabochon ruby engagement ring. When asked by a newsman if they had had their first quarrel yet, Barbara responded, "We had that years ago. We pay no attention to little things like quarrels."

Barbara then began a schedule of filmmaking which one Hollywood writer properly termed "gruelling." During this hectic period when she made five successive features, the Taylors occupied separate bedrooms and saw each other only for a few hours each evening. There were those in Hollywood who insisted now, as they had before the marriage, that "Missy" Stanwyck was and only could be concerned with her film career, and that she had no intention of taking over from Bob's over-protective mother in trying to mold his career and status at MGM.

At Paramount, Barbara starred with Fred MacMurray in *Remember the Night* (1940) as a shoplifter whose trial is postponed until after Christmas. The Preston Sturges script has her placed in the care of assistant district attorney MacMurray so that the two Indianans may visit their respective homes for the Yuletide. On finding no welcome mat in place for her at her family address, MacMurray takes her with him to his family where she is welcomed by Beulah Bondi, Sterling Holloway, and Elizabeth Patterson. Naturally, the two stars fall in love and the lawman offers her a chance to escape, but she says, "I am guilty. When you make a mistake, you have to pay for it." She is sentenced to jail, with

Fred promising to wait for her release. It is a light comedy with touches of homeyness aptly supplied by the three top supporting players under the aegis of director Mitchell Leisen.

Also at Paramount she made what would be one of her best-liked comedies, *The Lady Eve* (1941). She is Jean Harrington, card-sharp daughter of "Colonel" Harrington (Charles Coburn) whose questionable profession also lies in the art of card shuffling. They are aboard a ship when they spot the ideal patsy, one Charles Pike (Henry Fonda) who is an ale-bottling millionaire. Golddigging Jean literally trips the naive playboy as he saunters past their table and then proceeds to seduce him. During her attempt at winning his complete confidence, she falls for his own personable ways and when daddy gets around to playing cards with the poor chump, she arranges for him to lose very little money. "Colonel" Harrington (Coburn) does hoodwink Charles out of $32,000, which infuriates Jean, and so he pretends to tear up Pike's payment check.

Meanwhile, the ship's purser informs Pike of the truth about father and daughter. Jean tries to explain but Pike claims that he had been wise to them all along which makes her angry. She vows to even the score. Sometime later, she runs into a fellow operator (Eric Blore) who happens to be a houseguest at the Pike estate in Connecticut. She persuades Sir Alfred (Blore) to introduce her as his British niece, Lady Eve Sidwich, and from then on the comedy (scripted and directed by Preston Sturges) really flies, including Barbara's fast dialogue and the pratfalls by Fonda. The hero is fascinated by the con girl's resemblance to Jean but refuses to believe they are the same person. He falls in love with Lady Eve and they marry. Her revenge occurs during their honeymoon train trip when she compares him to her many previous swains (all of whom are non-existent). *The Lady Eve,* released in February 1941, was chosen by the National Board of Review as one of 1941's ten best pictures. A diluted version of the film, entitled *The Birds and the Bees,* would be released in 1956 by RKO, starring a miscast

George Gobel, Mitzi Gaynor, and David Niven.

Barbara next tackled the role of Ann Mitchell, a cynical newswoman, in *Meet John Doe* (Warner Bros., 1941) directed by Frank Capra. It was the type of role that had done so much for Jean Arthur's career in the Thirties when Capra starred her in *Mr. Deeds Goes to Town* (1936) and *Mr. Smith Goes to Washington* (1939). The tough-nosed reporter sets out to exploit America's common man when she is fired from her job. She invents "John Doe" in her final column and states that the man will kill himself on Christmas Eve in protest of the country's corrupt atmosphere. The column generates reader reaction to the point where Ann, now rehired to her post, must produce a living John Doe. She finds him in the person of Long John Willoughby (Gary Cooper), a destitute one-time baseball pitcher whose pitching arm is no longer effective. John is put on radio, and fan clubs spring up around the nation. Dictator-like publisher D. B. Norton (Edward Arnold) encourages the Doe clubs and eventually holds a rally at which he wants John to nominate him as President of the United States. When Doe refuses, Norton exposes the truth about him and John is left alone on Christmas Eve to commit suicide as orginally outlined. Repentant and in love with him, Ann saves him from death at the final moment. The finale allowed for Barbara to display her fine ability to project hysteria, which was becoming her screen trademark. To quote the *New York World-Telegram*, "Barbara Stanwyck is supremely good as the columnist, lovely and talented."

On Wednesday, June 11, 1941, Barbara and Taylor gave their handprints to Sid Grauman in a block of cement at his Chinese Theatre on Hollywood Boulevard. Sharing the one block, Barbara wrote, "To Sid, We Love You," and they signed their names, with Barbara's on the left side.

In October 1941, Columbia presented *You Belong to Me* with Barbara reteamed with Henry Fonda. Despite a good script by Claude Binyon and top-flight direction by Wesley Ruggles, the lightweight comedy of a

449

lady doctor and her wealthy male patient whom she marries does not match the brilliance of *The Lady Eve.* It would be remade with less distinction by Columbia in 1950 as *Emergency Wedding* with Barbara Hale and Larry Parks featured.

The year ended on a merry note supplied by producer Samuel Goldwyn, director Howard Hawks, and writers Charles Brackett and Billy Wilder. In *Ball of Fire* (RKO) Barbara is a swinging burlesque stripper named Sugarpuss O'Shea who is temporarily in dutch with the police due to her connection with one Joe Lilac (Dana Andrews). For a hideout she picks the brownstone headquarters of eight stodgy university professors who are putting together an encyclopaedia. To Professor Bertram Potts (Gary Cooper), she is just what the doctor ordered to help him with his chapter on American slang.

In no time at all she has beguiled the handsome Ph.D's seven stuffy colleagues (Oscar Homolka, Henry Travers, S. Z. Sakall, Tully Marshall, Leonid Kinsky, Richard Haydn, Aubrey Mather) and even has them doing the conga. It is practically a foregone conclusion that she will soon have Professor Potts also under her shapely thumb. The *New York Times'* Bosley Crowther found her to be "strictly the Lady Eve with the same old apples to sell" in "an up-to-date version of *Snow White and the Seven Dwarfs.*" Howard Barnes of the *New York Herald-Tribune* wrote of Miss Stanwyck, "When she is playing a night-club stray with a heart of gold, she is better than any of her sisters in screen make-believe." Both critics liked the movie, with Barnes terming it a "rattling good comedy." The property would be remade in 1948 by Goldwyn as a musical entitled *A Song Is Born* with Danny Kaye and Virginia Mayo.

In January 1942, the nominations for the Academy Awards for 1941 were revealed and Barbara found that she was among those nominated in the Best Actress category, for *Ball of Fire.* Hers was the only comedy performance nominated from among the indestructible leading ladies that included Bette Davis (*The Little Foxes*—also for Samuel Goldwyn), Greer Garson (*Blossoms in the Dust*), Olivia de Havilland (*Hold Back the Dawn*), and Joan Fontaine (*Suspicion*). The surprise winner that evening of Wednesday, February 26, 1942, was Miss Fontaine; her sister Olivia had been the expected winner.

In *The Great Man's Lady* (Paramount, 1942), Barbara was required to age from a girl of sixteen to a wizened woman of 109. "I loved that film," she has said. "I was just crazy about it. I loved the challenge. But it was never very successful, and that kind of broke my heart." Directed by William A. Wellman, the film's chief fault is the script (by W. L. River) which fails to show us the greatness in the man Ethan Hoyt (Joel McCrea) that causes the woman Hannah Sempler (Barbara) to give him up so that he might prosper in politics. (Shades of the *Back Street* format once again!) It is Barbara's film all the way, with McCrea and Brian Donlevy (as her rejected suitor) in obligatory male support. The *New York Times* critic observed, "As the aged lady, Barbara Stanwyck does no violence to a marvelous makeup [by Robert Ewing] and she carries off the role of her younger self with spirit." Ewing, who was Barbara's soundstage makeup man for a decade, also painted several portraits of the star, two of which were from *The Great Man's Lady.* He said, "The mischievous twinkle in the eyes of the very old lady and the aura of impregnable dignity of the character as a mature woman are merely projections of the characteristics of the role as Barbara conceived, polished, then acted it."

In rapid succession came *The Gay Sisters* (Warner Bros., 1942), who are Fiona (Barbara), Evelyn (Geraldine Fitzgerald), and Susanna (Nancy Coleman), but, as *Newsweek* magazine found, "by no stretch of the imagination can any of the girls be described as gay." They are the Misses Gaylord of Manhattan's stately Fifth Avenue: they are proud, aggressive, and slowly becoming poorer through ill-fated marriages, children, and high living. Much of their lives is spent in courtrooms where, in one scene, the three show their unity by exiting arm-in-arm, with Fiona placing a well-aimed heel into the lens of a reporter's camera. George Brent portrays

Charles Barclay, a man who covets the Gaylord estate and land as the site for a Radio City type of edifice. Barclay appears to be the villain of the piece, but he is actually wiser than Fiona and wins her over (as unbelievable as it is). Perhaps one of her reasons is to provide parentage for her son who was fathered by Barclay some years before when they were young and indiscreet. *The Gay Sisters*, a frequent TV late-show entry, is the type of film now regarded as high camp. But, to its credit, it is rich in production values, musical scoring (Max Steiner), supporting players, and slick direction (Irving Rapper).

In February 1943, Barbara and Taylor went to court in Los Angeles to legally adopt their marquee names. Taylor's real monicker was Spangler Arlington Brugh. Also that same month, Robert was commissioned a lieutenant, junior grade, in the U.S. Navy and was a flying instructor at the Great Lakes Naval Training Station in Illinois. Barbara aided the war effort by helping out at the Hollywood Canteen and by donning scanty outfits in *Lady of Burlesque* (United Artists, 1943). Taken from Gypsy Rose Lee's novel, *The G-String Murders,* the film was produced by Hunt Stromberg. Barbara is said to have hated making this movie, but she seems to be having a good time as she sings, clowns with Pinky Lee, tosses innuendoes about with the chorines, and helps to solve the murder.

Also in 1943, she was seen in *Flesh and Fantasy* (Universal) in one of three episodes dealing with faith and destiny. She and Charles Boyer (the co-producer of the picture) star in the final segment. He is a circus aerialist who has a nightmare in which he is falling. The dream is punctuated by the screams of a woman (Barbara) wearing diamond earrings. He loses his nerve because of the recurring dream. Later, on an oceanliner, he meets his dream woman and falls in love with her. Although she is shrouded in mystery, she helps him to regain his confidence. He then has a second dream in which she is arrested. This dream comes true as they dock because she has stolen those diamond earrings. It is assumed that he will wait for her to serve whatever prison sentence she is to receive.

In March 1944, Barbara sold her interests in Marwyck Ranch. "Thank God," she said, "I won't have to answer any more questions on how to pick a winning race horse." The early months of 1944 also found her motorcycling to work because of the war-imposed gas rationing.

During the final days of 1943, she worked at Paramount for director Billy Wilder in his screen adaptation (with Raymond Chandler) of a James M. Cain short story. The film's release as *Double Indemnity* caused a sensation in April 1944. Wilder had to persuade Barbara to portray the murderess, Phyllis Dietrichson, as he had to persuade Fred MacMurray to assume the male lead after George Raft had rejected the project. In an unflattering, shoulder-length blonde wig, Barbara wears tight sweaters, tight skirts, and employs every body movement as an enticement. Her prey is insurance agent Walter Neff (MacMurray) whom she wants to help her kill her rich husband (Tom Powers) for the insurance. She professes her love for Neff. He believes her empty words and aids in the crime. A slick investigator (Edward G. Robinson), Neff's mentor and friend, suspects the duo of the deed. But before any arrests can be made, Neff kills the double-crossing Phyllis and is himself wounded and apprehended.

"In many ways *Double Indemnity* is really quite a gratifying and even a good movie," James Agee acknowledged in *The Nation*, "essentially cheap, I will grant, but smart and crisp and cruel. . . ." *Time* magazine labeled it "the season's nattiest, nastiest, most satisfying melodrama." The story would be remade in 1973 as an ABC-TV "Movie of the Week" with Samantha Eggar as Phyllis and Richard Crenna as the insurance man. The network would have done better to screen the 1944 classic.

In December 1943, Barbara had signed a contract with Warner Bros. and thus was back on the studio lot where she started sixteen years earlier. Bette Davis was now the ruling queen of the company, with such supporting rivals as Ida Lupino, Ann Sheridan, Joan Leslie, and the soon-to-arrive Lauren Bacall. Joan Crawford, who had left MGM, was

cooling her heels at Warner Bros. until she grabbed the Oscar-winning part in *Mildred Pierce* (1945). Olivia de Havilland, so much a part of the studio projects since her 1935 arrival at the Burbank facilities, was then embarking on a lawsuit to end the practice of studio extension of contracts when an employee lost time due to suspensions. Barbara remained on the Warners' lot for her next three films, beginning with *Hollywood Canteen* (1944), a salute to that organization of stars who so unselfishly devoted time and energies to entertaining servicemen. Barbara was among the Warner players who were seen briefly in various scenes in the picture.

She was Oscar-nominated a third time in January 1945 for her emoting in the sinister *Double Indemnity*. Again she was faced with tough competition: Ingrid Bergman (*Gas-*

With director Preston Sturges and Henry Fonda posing on the set of *The Lady Eve* ('41).

With Nancy Coleman and Geraldine Fitzgerald in *The Gay Sisters* ('42).

light), Bette Davis (*Mr. Skeffington*), Claudette Colbert (*Since You Went Away*), and Greer Garson (*Mrs. Parkington*). At a wartime, no-frills presentation on Thursday, March 15, 1945, at Grauman's Theatre, the Best Actress honors went to Miss Bergman. "I just feel like one of Crosby's horses," Barbara chuckled over her loss (meaning she was always an also-ran, but never a winner).

In early 1945, Barbara's hair began showing signs of gray, but she refused to touch it up. Also in that year, the Hollywood Women's Press Club named her as the town's most cooperative actress and the U.S. Treasury Department revealed that her 1944 fiscal year salary of $323,333 was only three thousand dollars less than that of America's top-paid woman, Deanna Durbin (of Universal Pictures). *Liberty* magazine reported that Bar-

As the aged Hannah Sempler in *The Great Man's Lady* ('42).

With Fred MacMurray in *Double Indemnity* ('44).

With Robert Hutton in
Hollywood Canteen
('44).

→

The glamour star of the
mid-Forties.

With Dennis Morgan in
*Christmas in
Connecticut* ('45).

455

bara had no secretary and preferred to answer her fan mail herself. She was generous with time and dollars to the Orthopedic Hospital in Los Angeles and was a benefactress of several orphanages. "I'm only buying my way past St. Peter," she offered in response to questions regarding such philanthropic ventures.

Although there were rumors that the woman's role in Paramount's *The Lost Weekend* (1945) would be built up to co-star Barbara with Ray Milland, it developed that Jane Wyman was signed for the distaff lead. Instead, Barbara was seen in just one 1945 release, *Christmas in Connecticut* (Warner Bros.), as Elizabeth Lane, who was declared by her employer, *Smart Housekeeping* magazine, as being America's best cook. For publicity sake, she has to pretend to be a housewife with a husband and child, all living in domestic bliss on a Connecticut farm. Actually, she is a bachelor girl in a Manhattan apartment who filches recipes for her readers' consumption from the owner-chef (S. Z. Sakall) of her favorite restaurant. "I don't have a farm," she admits. "I don't even have a window box." As a gimmick, her rotund boss (Sydney Greenstreet) who does not know the truth about her arranges for a rehabilitating war hero (Dennis Morgan) to spend Christmas with his popular lady editor and her "family." A husband (Reginald Gardiner), with a built-in Connecticut farm, is acquired, and a baby is brought in for the occasion. It is all great nostalgic fun and the film has become a traditional entry for TV showing at holiday time.

Robert Taylor returned to civilian life in November 1945 and resumed his screen career at MGM. Unfortunately, like so many other returning veterans, he was never able to generate the interest or popularity that he had enjoyed before the war.

Barbara's *My Reputation,* which had been completed in March 1944, was not released until 1946, a not too untypical practice in the saturated production-line filming of the war years. It was a sudsy drama of a Chicago widow's (Barbara) fight to have a boyfriend (George Brent) in spite of the prim wishes of her straight-laced mother (Lucile Watson)

and her two young sons (Scotty Beckett and Bobby Cooper). *Photoplay* labeled her performance as her "best work since *Double Indemnity,*" but the *New York Times* found that she "tried hard to act real, but the script seems to make her uncomfortable, except in a tight sweater in one scene."

She was then loaned to Paramount for *The Bride Wore Boots* (1946) which was given a one-star rating by *Photoplay* (which means "Good"), together with the critique, "A slapstick comedy that's supposed to be very funny, but unfortunately not even the expert presence of Robert Cummings, Barbara Stanwyck, and Diana Lynn can make sense out of this silly story." In short, Barbara's character, Sally Warren, likes horses, but husband Cummings does not and they quarrel. Into the tension strides southern gal Mary Lou Medford (Lynn) who thinks she wants Cummings as her own acquisition. This, to date, is Barbara's last screen comedy because "They don't write comedies like they used to."

She stayed on at Paramount for the Hal B. Wallis production, *The Strange Love of Martha Ivers* (1946). "Whisper her name," the trade ads suggested of Ivers who, like Phyllis Dietrichson of *Double Indemnity,* is a murderess and rotten to the core. As a youngster, she (Janis Wilson) accidentally murders her wealthy aunt (Judith Anderson) when she is prevented from running away with her boyfriend Sam Masterson (Darryl Hickman). A witness to the slaying is young Walter O'Neil (Mickey Kuhn), but an innocent man is charged and convicted of the misdeed. The years pass, and now Martha (Barbara) is the power of Iverstown, a status inherited from her aunt, along with the money. She is married to Walter (Kirk Douglas in his screen debut) who is a weakling now turned to alcohol in an effort to forget. When Sam Masterson (Van Heflin), now a gambler, returns to town, the duo is certain he has come back to expose them, which he has. Walter is scared and phones Sam to come over for a showdown. "I'll go and change," Martha says sarcastically. "I wouldn't want him to see me in the same dress twice." The confrontation occurs when Walter drunkenly falls to his death; later Martha kills herself. It is a gloomy film, but well-acted. It was directed by Lewis Milestone who has credited Barbara with being "a great trouper" and "wonderful to work with."

California (Paramount, 1946) represents another first for Barbara, her Technicolor debut. It is too bad it was not a more auspicious adventure. Heralded as the "first of Paramount's postwar outdoor epics," it is standard fare, described by *Newsweek* magazine as containing "every stock western situation except an attack by Indians with the hero saying 'I'll take the short cut and head them off [at the pass].'"

No story of California's early days could be filmed without the famed gold strike, and in this film it is what starts the action. The citizens want statehood but the local tyrant (George Coulouris) wants to control the state. His plans are thwarted by Jonathan Trumbo (Ray Milland), an Army deserter who is really a nice guy. As Lily Bishop, Barbara initially dislikes Trumbo. In fact, in a heated moment—and delivered only as Miss Stanwyck could—she blasts forth at Trumbo, "If I live long enough, and I will, I'm going to pull you off your fancy horse and shove your face in the mud." Eventually, she succumbs to his manly charms. *Newsweek* did concede, "There can be no complaint about the actors, everything considered. Ray Milland and Barbara Stanwyck are acceptable enough as the hero and heroine."

Two years after its completion—the studio considered its audience acceptance very problematic—*The Two Mrs. Carrolls* (Warner Bros.) was unveiled to movie audiences in April 1947. Filmed on the studio's Burbank lot, it has an English setting, complete with inclement weather. Geoffrey Carroll (Humphrey Bogart), an artist, poisons his first wife with ample doses in her nocturnal glass of milk. He then weds Sally Morton (Barbara) with whom he is content until Cecily Latham (Alexis Smith) happens along and he falls for her. It is now Sally's turn to get the poison-in-the-milk treatment, but Carroll's precocious daughter (Ann Carter) lets slip too

many coincidences and Sally is now aware of her husband's grisly plan. The climax comes with Sally barricaded in her room with a revolver as Carroll climbs a tree in the rain to gain entrance through a window. It is a suspenseful moment before the front door is broken open by Sally's all-time admirer (Patrick O'Moore) and Carroll swallows the poison he has saved for Sally rather than be taken to prison. Bogart was badly miscast as an artist, although he did supply several moments of leering villainy. Barbara is properly fearful as the overwrought heroine. (The play, by Martin Vale, had a Broadway run in 1943 with Elisabeth Bergner and Victor Jory.)

As Karen Duncan, a renowned pianist, in *The Other Love* (United Artists, 1947), Barbara is supposedly doomed from consumption (shades of *Camille*). She is found atop a glorious peak in Switzerland in a sanitarium where her doctor (David Niven) has more than a medical interest in her. Aside from being bone-thin, Karen seems robust enough, but when she learns that her life expectancy is short, she rejects the doctor's professed love because she is convinced that his feelings stem more from pity than love. She goes off to frolic in Monte Carlo with a playmate (Richard Conte) but the doctor locates her and convinces her that his affection is genuine. It is a gloomy, low-keyed soap opera, with Barbara at her dramatic best. The film is greatly aided by Miklos Rozsa's soundtrack music. Unfortunately, the downbeat tenor of the film plus the fact that United Artists had limited distribution facilities in comparison to the other major studios caused *The Other Love* to come and go rather quickly.

Back at Warner Bros., Barbara teamed with Errol Flynn in *Cry Wolf* (1947) in which she is menaced, so she believes, by the uncle (Flynn) of her dead spouse. After her husband's demise, she calls at the family estate to collect her inheritance but runs into objections from the uncle and is exposed to half-explained secrets which she is unable to comprehend. She endures several hair-raising moments when she climbs trees, lowers herself through a skylight, and ascends in a dumbwaiter to find the uncle's mysterious

457

With Ray Milland in
California ('46).

With Bobby Cooper and
Scotty Beckett in *My
Reputation* ('46).

With Errol Flynn in *Cry Wolf* ('47).

With Robert Taylor in the late Forties.

459

laboratory. The mystery is revealed when she encounters her "dead" husband (Richard Basehart) on the estate grounds and learns that he is insane. Later, the husband is killed accidentally and the uncle then explains that insanity is the family secret that he has tried to conceal. It was all weak material and as much a waste of Barbara's histrionic efforts as had been *The Two Mrs. Carrolls.* One can only wonder at the outcome of Barbara's career at this time if she had accepted the offer to play *Mildred Pierce,* the Warner Bros. film that won Joan Crawford an Oscar and earned her Jack L. Warner's favor and such other roles as *Humoresque* (1946) and *Possessed* (1947), parts Barbara could have played just as she could easily have assumed many of the roles then going to Bette Davis or Ann Sheridan.

Variety Girl (Paramount, 1947), like *Hollywood Canteen,* provided Barbara with a token, brief onscreen appearance as herself. In this tribute to the Variety Clubs of America, she was seen at the film's opening when she explains to Joan Caulfield the means by which the clubs originally got started. Most of the Paramount stock company appeared in this revue picture, and many of them performed vaudeville-type acts.

Barbara's salary for the fiscal year ending in 1947 was revealed by the U.S. Treasury Department to be $256,666. In January 1948 Hollywood press agent Helen Ferguson, a good friend of Barbara's, told fans through a multipage spread in *Motion Picture* magazine that Barbara was known as "The Queen" to her coworkers and friends, and that her idea of "howling" on Saturday night was a quiet dinner with her husband. Miss Ferguson wrote, "They see every movie Hollywood turns out," and "they share a consuming interest in their jobs and the industry." Barbara loved coffee and was considered by her friends as outspoken. One of the gestures that had delighted her most was the placement of a bronze plaque with her name inscribed on it in the Erasmus Hall High School in Brooklyn. Although Barbara never attended the school, she "enjoys the irony of that plaque, which lists the names of famous Erasmus graduates."

Along the way Warner Bros. had been persuaded to buy the screen rights to *The Fountainhead,* the blistering novel by Ayn Rand which was a best seller in 1943. Barbara and Humphrey Bogart were considered the ideal choices for the lead roles, but, due to filming costs, the production was shelved. It would be made by Warner Bros. in 1949 with Gary Cooper and Patricia Neal.

Instead Barbara made another MGM film, joining with Van Heflin in the cinema version of John P. Marquand's *B. F.'s Daughter* (1948). They are a good acting team, but the script by Luther Davis prevents them from letting loose. She is the millionaire daughter of Charles Coburn and married to idealist Heflin. She wants to buy his success while he would prefer to get to the top by his own merits. For the Depression-era setting, Barbara permitted her seventeen-inch-long tresses to be cut and shaped into a chic symphony of waves. In the words of critic Bosley Crowther *(New York Times)* with reference to the film "the only conclusion arrived is that money is not everything but it comes in mighty handy—a fact we presume the audience knows."

In most distinguished performers' working lives there is at least one vehicle which is so indelibly a part of their personae that it seems difficult to fathom anyone else in the part. Such was the case with the radio drama *Sorry, Wrong Number* written by Lucille Fletcher and which provided Agnes Moorehead with her greatest triumph. She was first heard in the part in 1943 and many times thereafter. When Hal B. Wallis acquired the screen rights to the thriller, many thought that only Miss Moorehead, already a distinguished "character" performer onscreen, could play the part. But Wallis already had made a commitment to Barbara and, realizing that the film required marquee value, assigned her to the role. Miss Moorehead rejected a supporting part in the film and later could only laugh that her recording of the melodrama was played constantly on the set as inspiration for the cast.

Sorry, Wrong Number, released in July 1948 by Paramount, proved to be Barbara's greatest screen triumph. Under Anatole Litvak's direction, the action takes place largely within the bedroom of hypochrondriac Leona Stevenson (Barbara), a neurotic, selfish, and possessive rich lady. To lessen the potential monotony of a one-set film, flashbacks are included in the storyline which broaden the characterization of Leona and show who she is and how she happened to become entangled in her present dilemma.

Within the story, her husband (Burt Lancaster) is her pawn. She has set him up professionally with her father's (Ed Begley) drug corporation and then complains because he spends more time on the job than with her. He becomes involved with a band of crooks to whom he is financially indebted. To make the requisite payoff to the underworld figures, he plans his wife's murder for the insurance money. Alone at night, Leona tries to make a telephone call, but gets spliced into a conversation between two men who are discussing the murder plans to liquidate a shut-in woman. She hangs up in concern and tries to phone for help but all her attempts are in vain. Through her frustration comes the realization that it is she who is to be the victim of this planned slaying. Near the climax, it develops that her murder is no longer necessary, but by the time the husband is able to telephone her, it is too late, and the killer picks up the receiver and mutters, "Sorry, wrong number."

The critics were jubilant over Barbara's intense performance. *Time* called it "her fattest role since *Double Indemnity,* and she makes the most of the pampered, petulant, terrified leading character." *Cue* found her giving "one of the finest performances of her career." The role of Leona Stevenson provided Barbara with a fourth Oscar nomination for Best Actress, but she again faced stiff adversaries in Olivia de Havilland *(The Snake Pit)* and Jane Wyman *(Johnny Belinda).* It was Warner Bros.' Miss Wyman who captured the elusive (for Barbara) statuette the night of Thursday, March 24, 1949. Notwithstanding her Oscar loss, Barbara's performance remains a landmark of exciting cinematic performing.

In October 1948, Barbara received the annual award for speech excellence given by the Linguaphone Institute of America for her "exceptional skill in the use of good English diction and intonation for conveying emotional nuances." Yet even long-standing fans of Miss Stanwyck admit that she had, and still has, a unique way of pronouncing the expression "I caaan't under-stannde," a weird mixture of Brooklynese and the Queen's English. She then went to Universal-International for *The Lady Gambles* (1949) which was not a remake of her 1934 Warner Bros. film *Gambling Lady.* At the start, she (as Joan Boothe) is happily wed to newsman Robert Preston. Then she is introduced to games of chance by a professional gambler (Stephen McNally). Once she is addicted to the gambling fever, it is emotion all the way.

Barbara did not stop working for a year, beginning in the summer of 1949. That was also the year columnist Earl Wilson observed about Barbara, "If she ever sues for alienation of affection, the defendant will be 'Missy'— her husband's airplane." Wilson claimed that Barbara told him, "Taylor lives in the airplane—lives in it. Oh, there are times when I go up with him with a tight grip and a tight lip to keep the family together. But it's his life and none of my business, and I wouldn't try to interfere."

"I was married to a man other women pursued!" Thus magazine ads introduced *East Side, West Side* (MGM, 1950), a Mervyn LeRoy production based on Marcia Davenport's best-selling novel. The cast, consisting of James Mason, Van Heflin, Ava Gardner, Cyd Charisse, Gale Sondergaard, and Barbara, is an impressive one of whom LeRoy in his casual 1974 autobiography, *Take One,* has said, "They were all pleasant and capable people, but, of them all, Barbara Stanwyck was the easiest. I suppose, if you took a vote among oldtimers on Hollywood crews for the most popular star, she would win the election by a landslide." Mr. LeRoy has also written, "She was a very earthy dame, and she could talk to the crew in their own language. They all loved her and—not that that was her motive—they would do anything to help her and make her look good."

Within the sophisticated Isobel Lennart scenario for *East Side, West Side,* Jessie Bourne (Barbara), rich and married to James

Mason, suffers grandly when she discovers he has a beautiful mistress, a model, played by Ava Gardner. She tries to persuade herself and a friend (Nancy Davis) that everything's okay, but we all know she is in torment. However, Mr. Heflin is present to give her solace during these trying times.

Once more Barbara worked for Hal B. Wallis in *The File on Thelma Jordan* (Paramount, 1950). She is the schizoid title character who is suspected of killing an elderly woman. Since her past is none too clean because of her affiliations with a gangster, she is condemned almost before her trial begins. She falls for the charms of the assistant district attorney (Wendell Corey) assigned to prosecute her, and he neatly arranges to lose the case. Once she has regained her freedom, we find that she was guilty all along. This film has interesting parallels to Joan Crawford's trio of tough underworld pictures at Warner Bros.: *Flamingo Road* (1949), *The Damned Don't Cry* (1950), and *This Woman Is Dangerous* (1952). Both of the superstars continued to prove in their gutsy roles oncamera that they had an abundance of staying power and revealed some of the enormous self-sufficiency that they utilized in their private and professional lives.

In *No Man of Her Own* (Paramount, 1950), Barbara was Helen Ferguson (no relation to her press-agent friend of the same name) who has been made pregnant by Lyle Bettger but is still unmarried. After Bettger kicks her out, she is involved in a train accident in which a woman is killed and Helen is identified mistakenly as that dead female. In need of a name for the baby and a roof over her head, she goes along with the error which is relatively easy to do since the late girl's husband, a war hero, is dead and his family has never met his wife. In her deception, she tumbles for the namesake's brother-in-law (John Lund). But their bliss is exchanged for tense moments when Bettger appears on the scene with intentions of blackmail. That villain is eradicated by an ex-flame, however, and Helen is now free to love the man of her choice. The film offered few of the light touches that used to distinguish the work of the picture's director, Mitchell Leisen.

The Furies (Paramount, 1950) finds Barbara wearing a long blonde wig again, but a better-coiffed one than she wore in *Double Indemnity.* She is Vance Jeffords, the lady and mistress of a vast cattle empire in the Arizona of the nineteenth century. She operates the spread for her aging and widowed father (Walter Huston) whom she idolizes. Her world is shattered when old dad brings home an equally aggressive woman (Judith Anderson) as his intended wife. It is a well-mounted Hal B. Wallis production which gains value from having been filmed in stark black and white.

To Please a Lady (MGM, 1950) brought Barbara together with Clark Gable after a period of nineteen years (their last picture together was *Night Nurse,* 1931). In this Clarence Brown-directed exercise, she is a renowned newspaper columnist, chic and tough, who publicly exposes the ruthlessness of a racing car driver (Gable) which results in his loss of career. In spite of her apparent dislike for the man, she keeps following him and the ending finds her in his arms. The total entertainment package is rather dull, although Barbara and Gable did complement each other physically.

While Robert Taylor was on location in Rome for *Quo Vadis* (MGM, 1951), Barbara visited him in the summer of 1950, having completed her work in *To Please a Lady.* But she found it somehow a betrayal of her own career to sit by while someone else did the acting. After a few weeks, she returned to Los Angeles. Then rumors filtered back from Rome that Mr. Taylor was squiring a lovely, young Italian extra. A few months later, when Taylor was returning to the States, he stopped over in London where his name was linked with ballerina Ludmilla Tcherina. Taylor returned to Los Angeles in December 1950 when he reportedly asked Barbara for his freedom and moved out of their home at 442 North Faring Road, West Los Angeles, on Friday, December 15.

Hardly anyone in Hollywood was too surprised at the splitup, but Louella Parsons wrote, "I could not have been more depressed," and added, "Of course, like everyone else on the inside, I had realized that things had not been all hearts and flowers between them for at least two years. But, because they are mature people, I had sincerely believed Bob and Barbara would see it through to steadier ground."

The celebrities' joint statement to the press included the following, "We are deeply disappointed but we could not solve our problems. We really tried." Both denied the existence of a third party responsible for their separation. On Wednesday, January 31, 1951, after selling the Stanwyck-Taylor home and moving into a smaller one with Uncle Buck Mack (Dion was away at Culver Military Academy), Barbara filed suit in Los Angeles to divorce her husband of eleven years. The divorce was granted on Wednesday, February 21 of that year in a three-minute hearing where Barbara, dressed in a "toast-colored suit with a matching hat perched on her gray curls," told Superior Judge Thurmond Clarke, "He [Taylor] said he had enjoyed his freedom during the months he was making a movie in Italy." Helen Ferguson was Barbara's witness at the short hearing. A reporter asked Barbara if she contemplated any new romances and she quickly answered, "No! I've had enough of that." After the divorce, columnist Erskine Johnson observed that although Barbara, whom he referred to as "gloomy Gussie," was trying to shake divorce blues, she "is a long way from kicking up her heels and making whoopee. Can she help it if she's not like the movie dolls who shrug a shoulder and say, 'Oh, well, just another husband'?"

Barbara was seen in only one 1951 film release. For MGM she was Lorna Bounty in *The Man with a Cloak.* It is a somber, early 1900s piece about Louis Calhern's housekeeper (Barbara) and butler (Joe De Santis) who plot to kill him for his riches. Their plans are halted by a mysterious stranger wearing a cloak (Joseph Cotten), who turns out to be Edgar Allen Poe. Barbara wore a black wig for this one, which was not becoming to her. Co-actor De Santis has praised her as "a pro" and "one of the few left and she don't take no guff from nobody."

Not only was Barbara vainly trying to manipulate a reconciliation with Robert Taylor (who had recently discovered the charms of actress Eleanor Parker), but she was struggling also to retain her star status in a film industry that had refocused on youth and fresh beauty in its attempt to survive the competition of television and the government break-up of the studio production and distribution combines. While other great stars such as Joan Crawford had only newly admitted oncamera to being mature women, Barbara had never hesitated to play her age oncamera. Yet, in the Fifties, there were fewer and fewer parts for dynamic personalities of her age.

The year 1952 recorded only one screen appearance for Barbara—at RKO in *Clash by Night,* directed by Fritz Lang. Taken from the Clifford Odets' play (briefly on Broadway in 1941 with Tallulah Bankhead), the film tells the story of Mae Doyle (Barbara), a cynical woman who once had big ideas. She returns home to a West Coast fishing village after an absence of ten years. Out of fatigue and loneliness, she marries Jerry D'Amato (Paul Douglas), an honest, likable fishing boat skipper whom she does not love. A while later, she meets Earl Pfeiffer (Robert Ryan), a movie-theater projectionist, with whom she has an affair. Jerry cannot comprehend her faithlessness and has a confrontation with Earl which results in Mae's returning to Jerry because she realizes that life is simpler with a simple man. The *Saturday Review* rated Barbara's acting as "a complete and convincing portrait," while the *New York Times* credited her as being "professionally realistic." During a fight scene between Douglas and Ryan, Barbara was accidentally pushed against a hot projection machine, but she continued the scene without interruption and later displayed a burned arm. More disruptive on the set was the male leads' quiet and not so quiet indignation about the enormous newspaper and photographer attention paid to relative newcomer Marilyn Monroe, playing the role of the girlfriend of Stanwyck's brother (Keith Andes). Generous, realistic, Barbara shrewdly realized that magnanimity not animosity was the needed ingredient, and convinced her co-players to give the rising star(let) her place in the soundstage sun.

In sharp contrast to the three previous

years, Barbara was seen in five movies during 1953. Earlier, she had asked her agent whether he thought she was finished in films because of the scarcity of offers. He replied that it was her asking price of $150,000 per picture that was keeping her from jobs. "Then cut it to $100,000, or to $50,000," she stormed, "I want to work." By this time, her hair was generously sprinkled with gray, but it photographed as blonde or soft brown, and she still refused to dye it. She freely admitted to her age (forty-five) and that she weighed 110 pounds. After the initial loneliness of single life, she became more or less accustomed to being husbandless. She read a great deal and continued to be active in civic and charitable affairs. Her close friends were few because of what Frank S. Nugent in *Colliers'*

In *The Lady Gambles* ('49).

With Paul Douglas and Robert Ryan in
Clash by Night ('52).

magazine of July 12, 1952, reported, "A certain Celtic directness of speech and thought."

Jeopardy (MGM, 1953), written for the screen by Mel Dinelli, is concerned with the rescue of Doug Stilwin (Barry Sullivan) by his wife Helen (Barbara). On a camping trip, the couple's son (Lee Aaker) is pinned down by the eroding timbers of a long-forgotten pier. In rescuing his son, Doug falls victim to the timbers which neither he nor Helen can remove. With the tide rising, Helen drives for help and encounters an escaped convict (Ralph Meeker). He agrees to help for certain material and physical benefits. He unpins the man but then leaves empty-handed because of Helen's fierce display of loyalty and tenacity. The John Sturges-directed feature was a brief sixty-nine minutes and, while a sturdy

As Vance Jeffords in *The Furies* ('50).

With Clifton Webb in *Titanic* ('53).

465

little vehicle, it might have been better suited to the small screen of television.

From *Titanic* (Twentieth Century-Fox, 1953), Barbara told Hedda Hopper, "I got two wonderful things—a great role and my friendships with Clifton [Webb] and Bob [Wagner]." Of course, the Charles Brackett, Walter Reisch, and Richard Breen screenplay which won them an Oscar is based on the April 15, 1912, sinking of the "invincible" luxury liner after hitting an iceberg on its England to America crossing.

In this, Fox's last major motion picture *not* shot in widescreen CinemaScope (let alone color), Barbara and Webb are a socially prominent couple with marital problems and two children (Audrey Dalton and Harper Carter). Wagner plays a college student romantically attuned to the daughter, with Thelma Ritter on hand as an "Unsinkable Molly Brown" type of character.

Barbara took no credit for her emotional scene during the sinking of the great ship. "The night we were making the scene of the dying ship in the outdoor tank at Twentieth, it was bitter cold. I was forty-seven feet up in the air in a lifeboat swinging on the davits. The water below was agitated into a heavy, rolling mass and it was thick with other lifeboats full of women and children. I looked down and thought: If one of those ropes snaps now, it's good-bye for you. Then I looked up at the faces lined along the rail—those left behind to die with the ship. I thought of the men and women who had been through this thing in our time. We were re-creating an actual tragedy and I burst into tears. I shook with great racking sobs and couldn't stop."

In cinema history, *Titanic* would be later overshadowed by the British-made *A Night to Remember* (1958) based on the Walter Lord book about the ocean disaster. For Barbara, *Titanic* held a special spot in her professional career. It was one of the last occasions in which she played the romantic lead in a major studio's major motion picture.

For Universal-International, Barbara was Naomi Murdoch, a woman who returns to visit her family and ex-husband (Richard Carlson), in *All I Desire* (1953). The inhabit-ants of the early 1900s small town are all set to ostracize her because of her past, but she proves that she is a good sort after all. *The Moonlighter* was a routine Western from Warner Bros. (1953) with the novelty of 3-D photography. She and co-star Fred MacMurray had done much more distinguished work in the past, but Westerns were popular in the mid-Fifties and the two very middle-aged performers gave their best to a cliché-saturated tale of rustlers and bank robbers. Barbara did much of her own stunt work, including a scene requiring her to slide down a waterfall. En route, she collided with rocks but director Roy Rowland said, "She received bruises, but she never complained or held up the picture in any way."

Fan magazines of the year had Miss Stanwyck cast in a real-life romance with Robert Wagner who was the same age as her son Dion who was in the U.S. Army in Europe. The gossips reported that Barbara and Wagner were seen holding hands at nightclubs and photographs were published to prove the point. "Those pictures . . . at cozy little dinners a deux are misleading," she confided to Hedda Hopper, a crusader for truth. "They were actually pictures of Bob and Clifton and me, but Clifton, who was sitting on my other side, was cut out of the published pictures. I suppose they thought it made a more exciting story."

One of Barbara's closest friends at this time was Nancy Sinatra, Sr., recently divorced from crooner Frank. "She is a great woman," Barbara said. "Her children are so talented it's frightening." Meanwhile, Robert Taylor in 1953 was the constant escort of actress Ursula Thiess, but Hollywood speculated that he would not marry the young actress until Barbara had first found a mate. Barbara and Taylor were now on the best of terms, but she had no inclination toward a third marriage with anyone.

In the meantime, she trekked to Mexico with director Hugo Fregonese and company to film *Blowing Wild* (Warner Bros., 1953), which brought her together again with Gary Cooper, another former co-star who had endured better projects. As Marina (a role rejected by Lauren Bacall), she is filled with

466

hatred toward her oil-digging husband (Anthony Quinn) and perks up only when her one-time suitor (Cooper) comes into the plot. He, however, refuses to rekindle their relationship and prefers the company of a showgirl (Ruth Roman). Marina eventually kills her husband with a timely push into the innards of an oil rig. Then she goes mad when she learns that Cooper despises her for her evil deed. The film is packed with emotional corn.

When asked by Louella Parsons why she was now making so many movies, Barbara replied truthfully that she liked to work. "Why shouldn't I love this business?" she asked. "As Ruby Stevens, a kid growing up in Brooklyn, I had nothing. . . . Hollywood has given me everything! In fact, most of the education I've acquired I got right here in this town." In December 1953, when news filtered into Wales about Barbara's refusal to dye her hair, *The Western Mail,* the national daily of Wales, accoladed her for her unique honesty. In an editorial, the newspaper stated, "Too many women have been twenty-nine too long. How refreshing therefore to read that the Hollywood film star is now without concealment going gray."

MGM's blockbuster of 1954 was *Executive Suite* with an all-star cast, headed by Fredric March, William Holden, Barbara, June Allyson, Walter Pidgeon, Shelley Winters, and Nina Foch. Produced by John Houseman, directed by Robert Wise, and based on the popular novel by Cameron Hawley, it relates the intra-company struggle for the presidency of a large furniture corporation after the firm's chief dies unexpectedly. Barbara is Julie Tredway, the mistress of the dead man. Her board of directors' vote gives the coveted job to Holden whose ideas for the future deserve more admiration than those proffered by his competitor (March). Barbara, who to children growing up in the Fifties seemed to be the cinema queen of hysteria, had a marvelous sequence in this feature. In one moment of near total emotional stress, she climbs out onto the ledge of the window outside the executive suite, threatening to jump and end her depression. All in all, *Executive Suite,* filmed in black and white, is an absorbing drama

and the characters, under Wise's direction, are three-dimensional.

Barbara's next film, described by the *New York Times* as "a workmanlike entertainment, but no landmark in its field," was *Witness to Murder* (United Artists, 1954). She is the witness who awakens in the middle of the night to see a man (George Sanders) in the apartment across the street strangle a girl. As in *Rear Window,* also 1954, no one believes her until the police investigator (Gary Merrill) suddenly senses merit in her story after finding certain flaws in the killer's insistence that he is innocent and that the witness is daft. Once again, Barbara had ample opportunity to display her talent for projecting heightened anxiety.

When Robert Taylor married Ursula Thiess in 1954, Barbara was was the first to telegraph her congratulations. With seventy-two feature films now to her credit, she, according to Sheilah Graham in November 1954, "has signed for six more." The actress told Miss Graham, "It's my hobby. I hate to sit still. It isn't work for me, it's fun."

She also confessed that the Western film was her favorite and, as if to prove the statement, she was seen in two successive oaters. *Cattle Queen of Montana* (RKO, 1954) co-starred her opposite Ronald Reagan, and the title pretty much tells the story of this Allan Dwan-directed vehicle shot in Glacier National Park in Montana. Of Miss Stanwyck, Dwan would recollect years later, "She's a very remarkable girl—terrific worker. . . . She was a real mixer, helped everybody." This was Barbara's first film in color since *California,* eight years earlier. *The Violent Men* (Columbia, 1955) provided her with better fare as Martha Wilkison, a blonde (wig) married to crippled rancher Edward G. Robinson, but in love with his younger and healthier brother (Brian Keith). As the Wilkisons' ranch house burns, she grabs her husband's crutches thinking he will be imprisoned within the flaming structure, but he escapes and she and Keith receive their just deserts.

These Westerns were followed by a box-office dud from RKO called *Escape to Burma* (1955) directed by Allan Dwan in Super-

Scope and color. Here, Barbara is the owner of a teak plantation and in love with surly Robert Ryan. The film has little to offer aside from scenery and animals and Barbara's comment was "the animals were better than the picture." In her quest to remain employed, it was obvious that Barbara was forsaking quality in filmmaking for quantity. She was capable of much better things, but the scripts were just barely, or even less than, standard fare.

On Sunday, September 18, 1955, Barbara made her television debut when she guest-starred on NBC-TV's "The Loretta Young Show." She returned to the anthology series a second time three weeks later. Obviously intrigued by the medium, she formed Barwyck Corp., her own independent production company, in March 1956, which was to handle a starring series for her. As it turned out, such a venture would be four years in the future.

There's Always Tomorrow (Universal, 1956), a remake of the 1934 studio film with Frank Morgan, Lois Wilson, and Binnie Barnes (in Barbara's role), offered Miss Stan-

wyck as a mature career woman who becomes the apex of a love triangle involving Fred MacMurray and his wife Joan Bennett. The latter couple are having domestic problems because he feels neglected and overlooked for the sake of the children (Gigi Perreau, William Reynolds, and Judy Nugent). Barbara's Norma Miller comes on the scene at just the right moment to provide him with the necessary interest. But she returns him to his proper place after confronting the wife and telling her, "Treat your man better, or next time you may lose him for good." The producer of this modest tearjerker was Ross Hunter who in years to come would specialize in overblown versions of this type of story.

While Barbara was appearing in lesser features, there were potential screen assignments in major productions. One of these talked-about jobs was the role of Vera Simpson, the society tramp in *Pal Joey*. Other contenders for the Columbia release were Mae West and Marlene Dietrich. However, when the 1957 feature went before the cameras, it was Columbia's contract glamour star Rita

With Fred MacMurray in *There's Always Tomorrow* ('56).

With Scott Brady and Barry Sullivan in *The Maverick Queen* ('56).

469

Hayworth who vied onscreen with Kim Novak for Frank Sinatra's affections.

Not one to sit idly by, Barbara was next *The Maverick Queen* (Republic, 1956), the owner of the Wyoming saloon bearing that name. She is also the feminine member of a gang headed by Butch Cassidy (Howard Petrie) and the Sundance Kid (Scott Brady). When Pinkerton detective Barry Sullivan enters the territory, she considers going straight but is later shot and dies in his arms. For some viewers this film is high camp, but it is nowhere near the same category as the Nicholas Ray-directed *Johnny Guitar* (Republic, 1954) starring Joan Crawford.

Barbara appeared with another old pro, James Cagney, in *These Wilder Years* (MGM, 1956), "a glum little tale about unwed mothers and unhappy tycoons" (*New York World-Telegram*). Originally, Debbie Reynolds was to have the pivotal role of Suzie, a part that went to Betty Lou Keim. Barbara appears as Ann Dempster, head of an adoption home, through whom wealthy Steve Bradford (Cagney) had placed his son for adoption. Now, years later, Bradford decides to find the son, but Ann opposes him. With the thorny issue entering a court of law, Bradford meets an unwed sixteen-year-old (Keim) who is pregnant and he adopts her with Ann's blessing. Homer Dickens in his *The Films of James Cagney* (1972) mentions that Barbara and Cagney hoofed it up between scenes with the Charleston, Black Bottom, and others. "It's a shame they didn't put one of their routines into the [black-and-white] film," wrote Dickens. "It might have helped."

In 1957, Dion Anthony Fay was married to a Las Vegas showgirl, Jan Porterfield. By this time, Barbara's relationship with her son had deteriorated to the point where she never talked of him nor saw him. Dion had said that he had not seen nor talked with his mother since 1952. A few years later, Dion was arrested in Los Angeles for selling pornographic pictures. Still later, Dion received the bulk of Frank Fay's estate when the latter died on September 25, 1961.

In her next film, *Crime of Passion* (United Artists, 1957), Barbara wants her lackadaisical policeman husband (Sterling Hayden) to rise above his status. In an effort to better his lot, the bored housewife attempts to seduce his boss (Raymond Burr) but kills him when he rejects her. The *New York Times* labeled the mini-film as "the most curiously misguided dramatic missile to hit town in some time."

Joel McCrea was Barbara's co-star for the sixth and (to date) final time in *Trooper Hook* (United Artists, 1957). She is Cora, a captive of Apache Indians until she is rescued by Hook (McCrea) and his cavalry. She is the mother of the Apache chief's (Rudolfo Acosta) son who is now five years old (played by Terry Lawrence). Hook returns her to her husband (John Dehner) but the latter refuses to accept the boy. When the Indian chief comes in search of his half-breed son, the husband and the redskin kill one another. Cora and the boy then face the future in the loving hands of Trooper Hook. Veteran Joel McCrea has gone on record in praising Barbara with, "She is, without reservations, the best I ever met. . . . She taught me a lot and I shall be ever grateful to her."

Forty Guns (Twentieth Century-Fox, 1957), filmed economically by cult-director-in-the-making Samuel Fuller, would be Barbara's last feature film for more than four years and her last Western motion picture to date. She is Jessica Drummond, the mean boss-lady of a band of forty gunmen who control a large part of Arizona until a peace officer (Barry Sullivan) is sent into the territory to clean it up. Jessica is uncontrollably attracted to him and slowly reforms. She is shot during a gun battle between her brother (John Ericson) and the brother (Gene Barry) of Sullivan, but she survives to express her feelings to Sullivan. *Forty Guns,* ignored by most critics and many filmgoers at the time of release, was just another example of how one-time film greats such as Barbara were reduced to appearing in drivel if they did not wish to absent themselves from the screen entirely.

In 1958, Barbara was seen on television in two episodes of "Zane Grey Theatre" (CBS), in an NBC-TV "Goodyear Theatre" presentation, and in an episode of NBC-TV's "Decision," all dramatic parts. As far back as 1955, she had tried to get a Western teleseries with herself in a continuing role, but no one would heed her concept. Then she tried to sell a series based on James D. Horan's book, *Desperate Women,* which recounted the lives of famous women of the West such as Belle Starr and Calamity Jane, but, again, no one was in the buying mood.

Then again, in August 1958, she tried to promote interest in a teleseries for herself, but admitted, "I don't even want to have the big-cheese role in the series. I'd have guest stars like they do on 'Wagon Train' [NBC-TV]." Ralph Edwards wanted her as the subject of his "This Is Your Life" video show, but she vetoed the idea as well as an invitation from Edward R. Murrow to appear on his "Person-to-Person" program. To the latter, she said, "Who am I? Why should I be on a program like that? It's ridiculous." When asked why she did not make movies anymore, she replied, "Because nobody asked me. They don't normally write parts for women my age, because America is now a country of youth." Hedda Hopper urged her to move to Europe because "I guarantee you wouldn't be over there twenty-four hours without having at least two offers for pictures." But Barbara would not budge from her two-story mansion in Holmby Hills where, reportedly, she was an avid book reader and watched old movies on television until "way into the night."

Then, in 1960, she obtained a half-hour NBC-TV anthology series entitled "The Barbara Stanwyck Show" styled much in the same vein as the earlier entries hostessed by Loretta Young and Jane Wyman. The opening episode on Monday, September 19, 1960, was *The Mink Coat* which the *New York Herald-Tribune* dismissed as "stereotyped, barely credible soap opera slush." Barbara's co-star in the opener was Stephen McNally. She won an Emmy Award for the series, which was (in typical video industry illogic) dropped for the next season. "As I understand it, from my producer, Lou Edelman," she voiced angrily, "'they' want action shows and have a theory

that women don't do action! The fact is, I'm the best action actress in the world. I can do horse drags, jump off buildings, and I have the scars to prove it."

For the following four years, she concentrated on television work and was seen twice on "Wagon Train" (NBC), twice on "The Untouchables" (ABC), and appeared in episodes of "Rawhide" (CBS) and the "Dick Powell Theatre" (NBC). She was reported to be romantically interested in Robert Stack—and he in her—but, again, this relationship was nothing more than a solid buddy friendship.

In 1961, she accepted the fifth-billed role in the Charles K. Feldman-produced *Walk on the Wild Side* (Columbia, 1962) as Jo Courtney, the lesbian madam of a New Orleans brothel. Hedda Hopper did not rate the role as "worthy of her," but Barbara said that "it was a chance to go back to pictures and see what would happen." The film, which was liked only for its Elmer Bernstein music and Saul Ban titles, was not a commercial success. But it did prove to be an interesting period study of offbeat characters, especially Barbara's as the "Doll House" proprietress with a legless husband and a yen for Capucine who is loved by Laurence Harvey but is afraid to return his affection. Others cast in this bizarre celluloid exercise were Jane Fonda as a tramp who becomes one of the bordello's girls and Anne Baxter as an inexplicably nice Mexican restaurant owner named Teresina Vidarverri.

Merle Miller and Evan Rhodes have chronicled their misadventures with CBS-TV in trying to translate a potential TV series, "County Agent," into a working reality in their perceptive, amusing, hard-to-believe book, *Only You, Dick Darling! Or How to Write One Television Script and Make $50,000,000* (1964). Jackie Cooper and Barbara were to star in the trouble-plagued project. Ex-child star Cooper would play the title role and Barbara would be a lady rancher who is "a man-killer, but Cooper likes her and goes to her for advice." After discussing Barbara's various professional pedigrees, Miller decided "It sounded as if Stanwyck would be natural in the role of the home agent." The project, eventually retitled "Calhoun," evolved so that Barbara Stanwyck's onscreen husband would be Howard Duff. What happened to the project that almost cost $400,000? It eventually got shelved and nothing happened—except for providing the basis for the best-selling *Only You, Dick Darling* book.

Meanwhile, in 1964, Barbara took a role rejected by Mae West in the Elvis Presley-starred *Roustabout* (Paramount). She welcomed the chance to work with rock 'n' roll star Presley and to be exposed to an entirely different type of audience. The 101-minute feature concerns a small carnival owned by Barbara which is on the brink of bankruptcy until she hires a singer (Presley) who attracts the big crowds. He is a born rebel and causes considerable trouble when not singing. Eventually, he grows up and becomes a decent fellow. Joan Freeman played Elvis' love interest while Barbara, looking trim and rugged, was relegated too often to the sidelines. Even her trademark sneer and piercing eyes were softened for this run-of-the-Presley screen venture.

Later in the year, Barbara played Irene Trent, a woman with recurring death dreams in *The Night Walker* (Universal, 1965). William Castle, one of filmdom's masters of suspense, was the producer and convinced Barbara to invest money in the venture. Their third partner, and Barbara's co-star in the picture, was Robert Taylor! Taylor remarked at the time, "Any actor who would turn down a chance to play opposite Barbara Stanwyck, under any circumstances, would have to be out of his head. Barbara and I have remained good friends. There's no reason why we shouldn't."

In the Robert Bloch-scripted scenario, Irene Trent has great difficulty in differentiating her dreams from reality. But, with the aid of an attorney (Taylor), the villain (Lloyd Bochner) is done in and she is able to return to normalcy. It is a much better motion picture than its lurid title suggests, and far better than some of the other scary items of the period such as *Strait-Jacket* (1964) and *Picture*

Mommy Dead (1966). Barbara helped sell the film with public appearances in New York, Boston, Toronto, and Chicago, where she made oblique references to a possible upcoming teleseries.

In the autumn of 1964, Robert Aldrich offered her a role in a film of Gothic mayhem in rural Louisiana called *Hush . . . Hush, Sweet Charlotte* (1964). At the time she was preoccupied with making a video series pilot which she considered far more important to her career. Mary Astor stepped in to play the role of Jewel Mayhew in this Bette Davis-Olivia de Havilland thriller.

The pilot was "The Big Valley" which was acquired by ABC-TV and premiered on Wednesday, September 15, 1965. In this sixty-minute color show, she is Victoria Barkley, a widow with three strapping sons (Peter Breck, Richard Long, and Lee Majors), a comely daughter (Linda Evans), and a vast ranch in California's San Joaquin Valley of the 1870s. The show ran for four television seasons. Critics took delight in referring to the program as a distaff "Bonanza" and to Barbara as "a Lorne Greene with skirts." When riled enough at the jibes to explain the show to the fourth estate, she stated that this was no female Cartright family show. "Our family is much tougher. My sons are strong. They're real men. This is not one of those 'Mother Knows Best' things. Hell, I wouldn't play one. Our family behaves like any normal family. We fight, argue, discuss things. We're not like some of the TV families today. I don't know where the hell these people are. I never see anybody like them in real life. The woman I'm playing has plenty of battles with her boys. She's a very vital person. So are her sons. They all have minds of their own."

Barbara thrived on the rugged production schedule and physical action demanded of her in the show. For those who knew her personally, they claimed "The Big Valley" became her way of life. Her friends were the cast and the crew of the show; with them she came alive. Detailing her daily routine for the teleseries, Barbara explained, "If we're shooting inside the studio, I get up at 4:30 in the morning and we start shooting at 8:00 and I get

472

home maybe 7:30 or 8:00 at night. If we're on location, which we are two days a week, that's 3:30 in the morning and maybe I get home around 8:30."

In 1966, Barbara received her second Emmy Award as Best Female Lead in a Series when Raymond Burr escorted her to the presentation. Also in 1966, she received the Screen Actors Guild Award for long-term excellence on the screen. California governor Ronald Reagan presented her with the award and a kiss. Barbara remarked, "That's the first time I've been kissed by a governor."

On Sunday, June 8, 1969, Robert Taylor died of lung cancer and, as Hollywood columnist Shirley Eder wrote in *Not This Time, Cary Grant* (1974), "Barbara was devastated." She attended the funeral at the request of Ursula Thiess Taylor, but wore a yellow suit because she did not feel privileged to wear mourning black. In *The Life of Robert Taylor* (1973), a Warner paperback original, authoress Jane Ellen Wayne paints an unflattering picture of Barbara throughout the book. The opening chapter discusses the funeral and Miss Wayne writes, "Those who watched Barbara Stanwyck that day said no one else showed the grief that she did so openly. . . . Her entrance was late and pitifully spectacular. She did nothing to cover up her red and swollen eyes except to wear a thin short black veil. Though she had been invited to sit with the family in private, she chose the main chapel. . . . She was outstanding by her late arrival in a bright-colored dress with two men holding her up, this frail and delicate woman portraying the widow—and perhaps that is how she felt. There was no doubt she knew what she was doing, though heavily sedated, for she had said many times, 'There will be no other man in my life.' She proved to the world that day she had never changed her mind." Miss Wayne later adds that during the services, "Barbara Stanwyck stood up in a faint and had to be carried out of the church but then managed to walk to her car." Later, at the Taylor-Thiess ranch, Barbara chatted with Ursula. "Barbara did all the talking. Ursula nodded and listened. The two stood for a while beneath a magnolia tree which had been

a gift from Bob to Ursula on their fifth wedding anniversary. . . . Their conversation will never be known. They had never been friendly and it is doubtful whatever was said bears importance, since Barbara was hardly herself that day. . . . It was a relief to everyone when she [Barbara] drove down the dusty driveway for home."

Still very anxious to work, Barbara agreed to appear in the ABC-TV "Movie-of-the-Week" entitled *The House That Wouldn't Die*, which was shown for the first time in October 1970. Her co-stars were Richard Egan, Michael Anderson, Jr., and Mabel Albertson. John Moxey, famed for his low-budget horror thrillers, helmed the project in an effective manner. Barbara's Ruth Bennett inherits an old house that is inhabited by restless spirits, and for the next seventy-three minutes colorful havoc reigns. A year later, she was in another telefeature for ABC-TV, *A Taste of Evil*, also directed by John Moxey. Here, she tries to drive her daughter (Barbara Parkins) crazy, hoping to gain possession of the money that was left the girl by her father. In the fall of 1971, sixty-four-year-old Barbara (looking far younger than her years) began work on a CBS-TV movie, *Fitzgerald and Pride*, playing a lawyer. After two days' work, she returned home with a severe pain in her left side. Unable to bear the pain, she telephoned Nancy Sinatra who rushed her to St. John's Hospital. The doctors readily diagnosed her problem as a ruptured kidney wall and an emergency operation was performed. She endured a lengthy recuperative period during which time letters, cards, and flowers were sent to her by concerned fans from all over the world. Susan Hayward, another Brooklyn red-head, replaced Barbara in the CBS telefeature which was retitled *Heat of Anger*.

Having finally recovered her strength, Barbara was anxious for more work. She appeared in one of three segments of *The Letters*, an ABC-TV "Movie-of-the-Week," as the older dominating sister of Dina Merrill and the individual who is murdered by money-hungry Leslie Nielsen. She had written her sister a letter before her death in which

she exposed Nielsen. This letter, when delivered a year later, is the tool which Merrill employs to keep Nielsen under control. Ex-hoofer and singer Gene Nelson directed Barbara's episode. Sadly, three key Stanwyck scenes had to be deleted to leave room for commercials.

In March 1974, Barbara, along with William Castle and John(ny) Green, was a recipient of an honorary award at the Thirty-Sixth Annual University of Southern California Chapter of Delta Kappa Alpha, the cin-

←

As Maggie Morgan in
Roustabout ('64).

Emmy award winner for TV's
"The Big Valley" ('66).

With Robert Taylor in *The Night Walker* ('65).

WHAT BECOMES A LEGEND MOST?

An exquisite extra-dark
natural mink
bred only by
the Great Lakes Mink men
and designed by Ben Kahn Salon.

BLACKGLAMA

With Michael Anderson, Jr., Kitty Winn, and Richard Egan in the telefeature *The House That Wouldn't Die* (ABC-TV, October 27, 1970).

←

The Living Legend.

Barbara Stanwyck of the Seventies.

ema fraternity. Two months later, she was inducted into the National Cowboy Hall of Fame in Oklahoma City. John Wayne was honored at the same time.

In July 1975, columnist Earl Wilson reported that producer Jimmy Nederlander wanted Barbara to return to Broadway in a "Ruby Keeler-Alice Faye type comeback," but in a straight play, rather than a musical. "Nederlander's got a great idea," Wilson wrote, "so great, it'll probably never happen." The journalist was correct.

In the mid-Seventies, it is a rare occasion when Barbara makes a public appearance. She was among those who attended the Hollywood Women's Press Club affair in December 1975, where she received a standing ovation in contrast to the hand of applause offered co-attendee Katharine Hepburn.

Thanks to the constant rescreening of her old movies and her "The Big Valley" teleseries, Barbara Stanwyck remains a familiar face and name to new generations. It can only be hoped that some astute film or television production will soon again take advantage of Barbara's vast reservoir of talent. Despite a very painful arthritic condition, she is still most eager and able to ply her craft, and to prove yet again what an indomitable lady she is.

FILMOGRAPHY

BROADWAY NIGHTS *(First National, 1927)* 6,765 feet.

Presenter, Robert Kane; director, Joseph C. Boyle; story, Norman Houston; adaptor, Forrest Halsey; camera, Ernest Haller.

Lois Wilson (Fannie Fanchette); Sam Hardy (Johnny Fay); Louis John Bartels (Baron); Philip Strange (Bronson); Barbara Stanwyck (Dancer); Bunny Weldon (Nightclub Producer); Sylvia Sidney (Herself); and Henry Sherwood, Georgette Duval, June Collyer.

THE LOCKED DOOR *(United Artists, 1929)* 74 min.

Presenter, Joseph P. Kennedy; director, George Fitzmaurice; based on the novel *The Sign on the Door* by Channing Pollock; screenplay, C. Gardner Sullivan; dialogue, George Scarborough; director of dialogue scenes, Earle Browne; camera, Ray June; editor, Hal Kern.

Rod La Rocque (Frank Devereaux); Barbara Stanwyck (Ann Carter); William "Stage" Boyd (Lawrence Reagan); Betty Bronson (Helen Reagan); Harry Stubbs (The Waiter); Harry Mestayer (District Attorney); Mack Swain (Hotel Proprietor); ZaSu Pitts (Telephone Girl); George Bunny (The Valet); Purnell Pratt (Police Officer); Fred Warren (Photographer); Charles Sullivan (Guest); Edgar Dearing (Cop); Mary Ashcraft, Violet Bird, Eleanor Fredericks, Martha Stewart, Virginia McFadden, Lita Chevret, Leona Leigh, Greta von Rue, Dorothy Gowan, Kay English (Girls on Rum Boat); and Edward Dillon.

MEXICALI ROSE *(Columbia, 1929)* 62 min.

Producer, Harry Cohn; director, Erle C. Kenton; story, Gladys Lehman; continuity, Norman Houston; dialogue, Lehman, Houston; dialogue director, James Seymour; assistant director, Sam Nelson; camera, Ted Tetzlaff; editor, Leon Barsha.

Barbara Stanwyck (Mexicali Rose); Sam Hardy (Happy Manning); William Janney (Bob Manning); Louis Natheaux (Joe, the Croupier); Arthur Rankin (Loco, the Halfwit); Harry Vejar (Ortiz); Louis King (Dad, the Drunk); Julia Beharano (Manuela).

LADIES OF LEISURE *(Columbia, 1930)* 98 min.

Producer, Harry Cohn; director, Frank Capra; based on the play *Ladies of the Evening* by Milton Herbert Gropper; screenplay, Jo Swerling; art director, Harrison Wiley; assistant director, David Selman; sound, John P. Livadary; camera, Joe Walker; editor, Maurice Wright.

Barbara Stanwyck (Kay Arnold); Ralph Graves (Jerry Strange); Lowell Sherman (Bill Standish); Marie Prevost (Dot Lamar); Nance O'Neil (Mrs. Strange); George Fawcett (Mr. Strange); Johnnie Walker (Charlie); Juliette Compton (Claire Collins).

ILLICIT *(Warner Bros., 1931)* 81 min.

Director, Archie Mayo; based on the play by Edith Fitzgerald, Robert Riskin; screenplay, Harvey Thew; costumes, Earl Luick; camera, Robert Kurrle; editor, William Holmes.

Barbara Stanwyck (Anne Vincent); James Rennie (Dick Ives); Ricardo Cortez (Price Baines); Natalie Moorhead (Margie True); Charles Butterworth (Evans); Joan Blondell (Helen "Duckie" Childers); Claude Gillingwater (Ives Sr.).

TEN CENTS A DANCE *(Columbia, 1931)* 80 min.

Producer, Harry Cohn; director, Lionel Barrymore; continuity, Dorothy Howell; screenplay, Jo Swerling; music, Abe Lyman & His Band; music director, C. Bakaleinikoff; song, Richard Rodgers and Lorenz Hart; art director, Edward Jewell; technical director, Edward Shulter; assistant director, Richard Rosson; sound, Russell Malmgren; camera, Ernest Haller and Gil Warrenton; editor, Arthur Huffsmith.

Barbara Stanwyck (Barbara O'Neil); Ricardo Cortez (Carlton); Monroe Owsley (Eddie Miller); Sally Blane (Molly); Blanche Frederici (Mrs. Blanchard); Martha Sleeper (Nancy); David Newell (Ralph Clark); Victor Potel (Smith, the Sailor); Sidney Bracy (Wilson, the Butler); Al Hill (Jones, the Sailor); Phyllis Crane (Eunice); Peggie Doner (Yvonne); Aggie Herring (Mrs. Crane); Harry Todd (Mr. Crane).

NIGHT NURSE *(Warner Bros., 1931)* 73 min.

Director, William A. Wellman; based on the novel by Dora Macy; screenplay, Oliver H. P. Garrett; additional dialogue, Charles Kenyon; costumes, Earl Luick; art director, Max Parker; camera, Barney McGill; editor, Edward M. McDermott.

Barbara Stanwyck (Lora Hart); Ben Lyon (Mortie); Joan Blondell (Maloney); Charles Winninger (Dr. Bell); Charlotte Merriam (Mrs. Richey); Edward Nugent (Eagan); Allan Lane (Intern); Blanche Frederici (Mrs. Maxwell); Vera Lewis (Miss Dillon); Ralfe Harolde (Dr. Ranger); Clark Gable (Nick); Walter McGrail (Drunk); Betty May (Nurse); Marcia Mae Jones (Nanny); Betty Jane Graham (Desney).

THE MIRACLE WOMAN *(Columbia, 1931)* 90 min.

Producer, Harry Cohn; director, Frank Capra; based on the play *Bless You Sister* by John Meehan, Robert Riskin; screenplay, Jo Swerling; continuity, Dorothy Howell; camera, Joseph Walker; editor, Maurice Wright.

Barbara Stanwyck (Florence Fallon); David Manners (John Carson); Sam Hardy (Hornsby); Beryl Mercer (Mrs. Higgins); Russell Hopton (Sam Welford); Charles Middleton (Simpson); Eddie Boland (Cullins); Thelma Hill (Cussie); Aileen Carlyle (Violet).

FORBIDDEN *(Columbia, 1932)* 85 min.

Producer, Harry Cohn; director/story Frank Capra; screenplay, Jo Swerling; camera, Joseph Walker; editor, Maurice Wright.

Barbara Stanwyck (Lulu Smith); Adolphe Menjou (Bob Grover); Ralph Bellamy (Al Holland); Dorothy Peterson (Helen); Thomas Jefferson (Winkinson) Charlotte Henry (Roberta); Tom Ricketts (Briggs); Halliwell Hobbes (Florist).

SHOPWORN *(Columbia, 1932)* 72 min.

Producer, Harry Cohn, director, Nicholas Grinde; story, Sarah Y. Mason; screenplay, Jo Swerling, Robert Riskin; camera, Joseph Walker; editor, Gene Havlick.

Barbara Stanwyck (Kitty Lane); Regis Toomey (David Livingston); ZaSu Pitts (Dot); Lucien Littlefield (Fred); Clara Blandick (Mrs. Livingston); Robert Alden (Toby); Oscar Apfel (Judge Forbes); Maude Turner Gordon (Mrs. Thorne); Albert Conti (Andre); Wallis Clark (Mr. Dean); Edwin Maxwell (Bierbatter).

SO BIG *(Warner Bros., 1932)* 80 min.

Producer, Jack L. Warner; director, William A. Wellman; based on the novel by Edna Ferber; screenplay, J. Grubb Alexander, Robert Lord; music, W. Franke Harling; costumes, Orry-Kelly; art director, Jack Okey; camera, Sid Hickox; editor, William Holmes.

Barbara Stanwyck (Selina Peake); George Brent (Roelf); Dickie Moore (Dirk as a Boy); Guy Kibbee (August Hemple); Bette Davis (Dallas O'Mara); Mae Madison (Julie Hemple); Hardie Albright (Dirk Peake); Robert Warwick (Jan Steen); Earle Foxe (Pervus Dejong); Alan Hale (Klaus Pool); Dorothy Peterson (Maartje); Dawn O'Day [Anne Shirley] (Selina as a Little Girl); Dick Winslow (Roelf as a Boy); Harry Beresford (Adam Oems); Eulalie Jensen (Mrs. Hemple); Elizabeth Patterson (Mrs. Tebbits); Rita LaRoy (Paula); Blanche Frederici (Widow Parrienburg); Willard Robertson (The Doctor); Harry Holman (Country Doctor); Lionel Belmore (Reverend Dekker).

THE PURCHASE PRICE *(Warner Bros., 1932)* 68 min.

Director, William A. Wellman; based on the story "The Mud Lark" by Arthur Stringer; screenplay, Robert Lord; art director, Jack Okey; camera, Sid Hickox; editor, William Holmes.

Barbara Stanwyck (Joan Gordon); George Brent (Jim Gilson); Lyle Talbot (Ed Fields); Hardie Albright (Don Leslie); David Landau (Bull McDowell); Murray Kinnell (Spike Forgan); Leila Bennett (Emily); Matt McHugh (Waco); Clarence Wilson (Justice of the Peace); Crauford Kent (Peters); Lucille Ward (Wife of Justice of the Peace); Dawn O'Day [Anne Shirley] (A Farmer's Daughter); Victor Potel (Clyde); Adele Watson (Mrs. Tipton); Snub Pollard (Joe).

THE BITTER TEA OF GENERAL YEN *(Columbia, 1933)* 89 min.

Producer, Walter Wanger; director, Frank Capra; based on the story by Grace Zaring Stone; sound, Edward L. Bernds; music, W. Franke Harling; costumes, Edward Stevenson; camera, Joseph Walker; editor, Edward Curtis.

Barbara Stanwyck (Megan Davis); Nils Asther (General Yen); Gavin Gordon (Dr. Robert Strike); Lucien Littlefield (Mr. Jacobson); Toshia Mori (Mah-Li); Richard Loo (Captain Li); Clara Blandick (Mrs. Jackson); Walter Connolly (Jones); Moy Ming (Dr. Lin); Robert Wayne (Reverend Bostwick); Knute Erickson (Dr. Hansen); Ella Hall (Mrs. Hansen); Arthur Millette (Mr. Pettis); Helen Jerome Eddy (Miss Reed); Martha Mattox (Miss Avery); Jessie Arnold (Mrs. Blake); Emmett Corrigan (Bishop Harkness).

LADIES THEY TALK ABOUT *(Warner Bros., 1933)* 69 min.

Directors, Howard Bretherton, William Keighley; based on the play *Women in Prison* by Dorothy Mackaye, Carlton Miles; screenplay, Sidney Sutherland, Brown Holmes; art director, Esdras Hartley; costumes, Orry-Kelly; camera, John Seitz; editor, Basil Wrangel.

Barbara Stanwyck (Nan Taylor); Preston Foster (David Slade); Lyle Talbot (Don); Dorothy Burgess (Susie); Lillian Roth (Linda); Maude Eburne (Aunt Maggie); Harold Huber (Lefty); Ruth Donnelly (Noonan); Robert Warwick (The Warden); Helen Ware (Miss Johnson); DeWitt Jennings (Tracy); Robert McWade (District Attorney); Cecil Cunningham (Mrs. Arlington); Helen Mann (Blondie); Grace Cunard (Marie); Mme. Sul-te-Wan (Mustard); Harold Healy (Dutch); Harry Gribbon (Bank Guard).

BABY FACE *(Warner Bros., 1933)* 70 min.

Director, Alfred E. Green; story, Mark Canfield; screenplay, Gene Markey, Kathryn Scola; art director, Anton Grot; costumes, Orry-Kelly; camera, James Van Trees; editor, Howard Bretherton.

Barbara Stanwyck (Lily Powers); George Brent (Mr. Trenholm); Donald Cook (Mr. Stevens); Arthur Hohl (Ed Sipple); John Wayne (Jimmy McCoy); Henry Kolker (Mr. Carter); James Murray (Brakeman); Robert Barrat (Nick Powers); Margaret Lindsay (Ann Carter); Douglass Dumbrille (Mr. Brody); Theresa Harris (Chico); Renee Whitney (The Girl); Nat Pendleton (Stolvich); Alphonse Ethier (Cragg); Harry Gribbon (Doorman); Arthur De Kuh (Lutza).

EVER IN MY HEART *(Warner Bros., 1933)* 68 min.

Director, Archie Mayo; story, Bertram Milhauser, Beulah Marie Dix; screenplay, Milhauser; art director, Anton Grot; costumes, Earl Luick; camera, Arthur Todd; editor, Owen Marks.

Barbara Stanwyck (Mary Archer); Otto Kruger (Hugo Wilbrandt); Ralph Bellamy (Jeff); Ruth Donnelly (Lizzie); Frank Albertson (Sam Archer); Florence Roberts (Eunice); Laura Hope Crews (Grandma); Clara Blandick (Anna); Ronnie Cosbey (Teddy Wilbrandt).

GAMBLING LADY *(Warner Bros., 1934)* 66 min.

Director, Archie Mayo; story, Doris Malloy; screenplay, Ralph Block, Malloy; art director, Anton Grot; costumes, Orry-Kelly; camera, George Barnes; editor, Harold McLernon.

Barbara Stanwyck (Lady Lee); Joel McCrea (Carry Madison); Pat O'Brien (Charlie Lang); C. Aubrey

Smith (Peter Madison); Claire Dodd (Sheila Aiken); Phillip Reed (Steve); Philip Faversham (Don); Robert Barrat (Mike Lee); Arthur Vinton (Fallin); Ferdinand Gottschalk (Cornelius); Robert Elliott (Graves); Arthur Treacher (Pryor); Margaret Morris (Operator); Willie Fung (Ching); Stanley Mack (Secretary); Renee Whitney (Baby Doll); Reverend Neal Dodd (Minister); Edward Keane (Duke); Wade Boteler (Cop); Willard Robertson (District Attorney); Bob Montgomery (Crooked Gambler); Milton Kibbee, Eddie Shubert, Ralph Brooks (Reporters).

A LOST LADY *(First National, 1934)* 61 min.

Director, Alfred E. Green; based on the novel by Willa Cather; screenplay, Gene Markey, Kathryn Scola; art director, Jack Okey; costumes, Orry-Kelly; camera, Sid Hickox; editor, Owen Marks.

Barbara Stanwyck (Marian Ormsby); Frank Morgan (Daniel Forrester); Ricardo Cortez (Ellinger); Lyle Talbot (Neil); Phillip Reed (Ned Montgomery); Hobart Cavanaugh (Robert); Rafaela Ottiano (Rosa); Henry Kolker (Ormsby); Walter Walker (Judge Hardy); Mary Forbes (Mrs. Hardy); Samuel S. Hinds (Jim Sloane); Jameson Thomas (Lord Verrington); Edward Keane (Man); Colin Kenny (Butler); Eddie Shubert Harry Seymour (Reporters); Joseph Crehan, Sam Godfrey (Doctors); Eulalie Jensen (Mrs. Sloane); Howard Hickman (Dr. Barlow).

THE SECRET BRIDE *(Warner Bros., 1935)* 64 min.

Director, William Dieterle; based on the play by Leonard Ide; screenplay, Tom Buckingham, F. Hugh Herbert, Mary McCall, Jr.; costumes, Orry-Kelly; art director, Anton Grot; camera, Ernest Haller; editor, Owen Marks.

Barbara Stanwyck (Ruth Vincent); Warren William (Robert Sheldon); Glenda Farrell (Hazel Normandie); Grant Mitchell (Willie Martin); Arthur Byron (Governor Vincent); Henry O'Neill (Jim Lansdale); Douglass Dumbrille (Dave Bredeen); Arthur Aylesworth (Lieutenant Nygard); William B. Davidson (Senator McPherson); Willard Robertson (Senator Grosvenor); Russell Hicks (Holdsteck); Vince Barnett (Drunk); Frank Darien (Justice of the Peace); Gordon "Bill" Elliott (Governor's Secretary); Spencer Charters (Messenger); Purnell Pratt (District Attorney); Mary Russell (Girl); Milton Kibbee (Judge's Secretary); Wallis Clark (Defense Attorney); Samuel S. Hinds (Clerk); Joseph Crehan (Senator).

THE WOMAN IN RED *(First National, 1935)* 68 min.

Director, Robert Florey; based on the novel *North Shore* by Wallace Irwin; screenplay, Mary McCall, Jr., Peter Milne; art director, Esdras Hartley; costumes, Orry-Kelly; camera, Sol Polito; editor, Terry Morse.

Barbara Stanwyck (Shelby Barrett); Gene Raymond (Johnnie Wyatt); Genevieve Tobin (Nikko—Mrs. Nicholas); John Eldredge (Gene Fairchild); Dorothy Tree (Olga); Phillip Reed (Dan McCall); Arthur Treacher

(Major Casserly); Doris Lloyd (Mrs. Casserly); Hale Hamilton (Wyatt Furness); Ann Shoemaker (Cora Furness); Nella Walker (Aunt Bettina); Claude Gillingwater, Sr. (Grandpa Furness); Brandon Hurst (Uncle Emlen); Jan Buckingham (Estella); Gordon "Bill" Elliott (Stuart Wyatt); Edward Keane (Ring Master); Jack Mulhall (Mr. Crozier); Evelyn Wynans (Woman); Edward Van Sloan (Foxall); Fredrik Vogeding (Erickson); George Chandler, Olive Jones, Franklin Parker (Reporters).

RED SALUTE (United Artists, 1935) 78 min.

Producer, Edward Small; director, Sidney Lanfield; story, Humphrey Pearson; screenplay, Pearson, Manuel Seff; art director, John Ducasse Schulze; camera, Robert Planck; editor, Grant Whytock.

Barbara Stanwyck (Drue Van Allen); Robert Young (Jeff); Hardie Albright (Arner); Cliff Edwards (Rooney); Ruth Donnelly (Mrs. Rooney); Gordon Jones (Lefty); Paul Stanton (Louise Martin); Purnell Pratt (General Van Allen); Nella Walker (Aunt Berty); Arthur Vinton (John Beal); Edward McWade (Baldy); Henry Kolker (Dean); Henry Otho (Border Patrolman); Lester Dorr (League Speaker); Jack Mower (Immigration Officer); Dave O'Brien, William Moore [Peter Potter], Fred Kohler, Jr. (Students at Rally); Edward Hearn (Border Patrolman); Chris-Pin Martin (Men's Room Attendant); Ben Hall (Student).

Reissue title: Her Enlisted Man.

ANNIE OAKLEY (RKO, 1935) 90 min.

Associate producer, Cliff Reid; director, George Stevens; story, Joseph A. Fields, Ewart Adamson; screenplay, Joel Sayre, John Twist; art directors, Van Nest Polglase, Perry Ferguson; music director, Alberto Columbo; camera, J. Roy Hunt; editor, Jack Hively.

Barbara Stanwyck (Annie Oakley); Preston Foster (Toby Walker); Melvyn Douglas (Jeff Hogarth); Moroni Olsen (Buffalo Bill); Pert Kelton (Vera Delmar); Andy Clyde (MacIvor); Chief Thundercloud (Sitting Bull); Margaret Armstrong (Mrs. Oakley); Delmar Watson (Wesley Oakley); Philo McCullough (Officer); Eddie Dunn, Ernie S. Adams (Wranglers); Harry Bowen (Father); Theodore Lorch (Announcer); Sammy McKin (Boy at Shooting Gallery).

A MESSAGE TO GARCIA (Twentieth Century-Fox, 1936) 86 min.

Producer, Darryl F. Zanuck; associate producer, Raymond Griffith; director, George Marshall; suggested by the essay by Elbert Hubbard and the book by Lieutenant Andrew S. Rowan; screenplay, W. P. Lipscomb, Gene Fowler; art directors, William Darling, Rudolph Sternad; set decorator, Thomas Little; music director, Louis Silver; camera, Rudolph Maté; editor, Herbert Levy.

Wallace Beery (Sergeant Dory); John Boles (Lieutenant Andrew Rowan); Barbara Stanwyck (Raphaelita Maderos); Herbert Mundin (Henry Piper); Martin

Garralaga (Rodriguez); Juan Torena (Luis Maderos); Alan Hale (Dr. Krug); Enrique Acosta (General Garcia); Jose Luis Tortosa (Pasquale Castova); Mona Barrie (Spanish Spy); Warren Hymer (Sailor); Andre Cuyas, Juan Duval (Sentries); Count Stefanelli (Raphaelita's Father); J. Betancourt (Bit); Fredrik Vogeding (German Stoker); Iris Adrian (Bit); Voice of John Carradine (President McKinley); Philip Morris (Army Officer).

THE BRIDE WALKS OUT (RKO, 1936) 81 min.

Producer, Edward Small; director, Leigh Jason; story, Howard Emmett Rogers; screenplay, P. J. Wolfson, Philip G. Epstein; art directors, Van Nest Polglase, Al Herman; costumes, Bernard Newman; music director, Roy Webb; camera, J. Roy Hunt; editor, Arthur Roberts.

Barbara Stanwyck (Carolyn Martin); Gene Raymond (Michael Martin); Robert Young (Hugh MacKenzie); Helen Broderick (Paulo Dodson); Vivien Oakland (Saleslady); Willie Best (Smokie); Robert Warwick (MacKenzie); Billy Gilbert (Donovan, the Bill Collector); Eddie Dunn (Milkman); Ward Bond (Taxi Driver); Edgar Dearing (Traffic Cop); Hattie McDaniel (Maime); James Farley (Store Detective).

HIS BROTHER'S WIFE (MGM, 1936) 90 min.

Producer, Lawrence Weingarten; director, W. S. Van Dyke, II; story, George Auerbach; screenplay, Leon Gordon, John Meehan; art directors, Cedric Gibbons, Harry McAfee, Edwin B. Willis; costumes, Dolly Tree; music, Franz Waxman; camera, Oliver T. Marsh; editor, Conrad A. Nervig.

Robert Taylor (Chris); Barbara Stanwyck (Rita Wilson); Jean Hersholt (Fahrenheim); Joseph Calleia (Fish Eye); George Eldredge (Tom); Samuel S. Hinds (Dr. Claybourne); Phyllis Clare (Clare); Edith Atwater (Mary); Jed Prouty (Billy Arnold); Rafael Storm (Captain Tantz); Orrin Burke (Dr. Claycious); Sherry Hall (Sam); William Stack (Winters); Edgar Edwards (Swede); George Davis (Milkman); Syd Saylor (Gambler); Frank Puglia (Hotel Clerk).

BANJO ON MY KNEE (Twentieth Century-Fox, 1936) 95 min.

Producer, Darryl F. Zanuck; associate producer, Nunnally Johnson; director, John Cromwell; based on the novel by Harry Hamilton; screenplay, Johnson; art director, Hans Peters; set decorator, Thomas Little; costumes, Gwen Wakeling; songs, Jimmy McHugh and Harold Adamson; music director, Arthur Lange; camera, Ernest Palmer; editor, Hansen Fritch.

Barbara Stanwyck (Pearl Holley); Joel McCrea (Ernie Holley); Helen Westley (Grandma); Buddy Ebsen (Buddy); Walter Brennan (Newt Holley); Katherine DeMille (Loota Long); Tony Martin (Chick Bean); Minna Gombell (Ruby); George Humbert (Jules); Walter Catlett (Warfield Scott); Spencer Charters (Judge Tope); Cecil Weston (Hattie); Louis Mason (Eph);

Hilda Vaughn (Gertha); Victor Kilian (Slade); Hall Johnson Choir (Themselves); Theresa Harris (Blues Singer); Eddy Waler (Truck Driver); Salty Holmes (Jug Blower); Davison Clark (Police Sergeant).

THE PLOUGH AND THE STARS (RKO, 1936) 72 min.

Associate producers, Cliff Reid, Robert Sisk; director, John Ford, assisted by Arthur Shields; based on the play by Sean O'Casey; screenplay, Dudley Nichols; art directors, Van Nest Polglase, Carroll Clark; set decorator, Darrell Silvera; costumes, Walter Plunkett; music, Roy Webb; music director, Nathaniel Shilkret; camera, Joseph August; editor, George Hively.

Barbara Stanwyck (Nora Clitheroe); Preston Foster (Jack Clitheroe); Barry Fitzgerald (Fluther Good); Dennis O'Dea (The Young Covey); Eileen Crowe (Bessie Burgess); Arthur Shields (Padraic Pearse); Erin O'Brien-Moore (Rosie Redmond); Brandon Hurst (Sergeant Tinley); F. J. McCormick (Captain Brennon); Una O'Connor (Maggie Corgan); Moroni Olsen (General Connolly); J. M. Kerrigan (Peter Flynn); Neil Fitzgerald (Lieutenant Kangon); Bonita Granville (Mollser Gogan); Cyril McLaglen (Corporal Stoddart); Robert Homans (Barman); Mary Gordon, Mary Quinn (Women); Lionel Pape (The Englishman); Michael Fitzmaurice (ICA); and Doris Lloyd.

INTERNES CAN'T TAKE MONEY (Paramount, 1937) 75 min.

Producer, Benjamin Glazer; director, Alfred Santell; based on the story by Max Brand; screenplay, Rian James, Theodore Reeves; art directors, Hans Dreier, Roland Anderson; costumes, Travis Banton; music, Gregory Stone; music director, Boris Morros; camera, Theodor Sparkuhl; editor, Doane Harrison.

Barbara Stanwyck (Janet Haley); Joel McCrea (Jimmie Kildare); Lloyd Nolan (Hanlon); Stanley Ridges (Innes); Lee Bowman (Interne Weeks); Barry Macollum (Stooly Martin); Irving Bacon (Jeff); Steve Gaylord Pendleton (Interne Jones); Pierre Watkin (Dr. Pearson); Charles Lane (Grate); James Bush (Haines); Nick Lukats (Interne); Frank Bruno (Eddie); Fay Holden (Sister Superior); Anthony Mace (Dr. Riley); Ellen Drew (Bit); Lillian Harmer (Mrs. Mooney); May Carlson (Ora); Jean Peterson (Frances); Pat Church (Chloe); Yvonne Dunkerley, Donna Staley (Girls); Priscilla Lawson (Nurse); Charles Sherlock (Man in Bookie's Office); Harvey Clark (Cashier); Charles Moore (Elevator Boy); Alexander Schonberg (Violinist).

British release title: You Can't Take Money.

THIS IS MY AFFAIR (Twentieth Century-Fox, 1937) 100 min.

Producer, Darryl F. Zanuck; associate producer, Kenneth Macgowan; director, William S. Seiter; screenplay, Allen Rivkin, Lamar Trotti; art director, Rudolph Sternad; costumes, Royer; songs, Mack Gordon and Harry Revel; music director, Arthur Lange; choreography, Jack Haskell; camera, Robert Planck; editor, Allen McNeil.

Robert Taylor (Lieutenant Richard L. Perry); Barbara Stanwyck (Lil Duryea); Victor McLaglen (Jock Ramsey); Brian Donlevy (Batiste Duryea); Sidney Blackmer (President Theodore Roosevelt); John Carradine (Ed); Alan Dinehart (Doc Keller); Douglas Fowley (Alec); Sig Rumann (Gus, the Boatman); Robert McWade (Admiral Dewey); Frank Conroy (President McKinley); Marjorie Weaver (Miss Blackburn); Douglas Wood (Henry V. Maxwell, the Bank Examiner); J. C. Nugent (Ernie); Tyler Brooke (Specialty); Willard Robertson (George Andrews); DeWitt Jennings (Bradley Wallace—Secret Service); Joseph Crehan (Priest); Dale Van Sickel (Officer at Ball); Tom London (Alec's Pal); Frank Moran (Guard); Lynn Bari, June Gale (Girls with Keller); Ethan Laidlaw (Barfly); Walter James (Friend); Ruth Gillette (Blonde); Edward Peil, Sr. (Secretary Hayes); John Quillan (Page Boy); Lee Shumway (Secret Service Man); Ben Taggart (Police Captain).

British release title: My Affair.

STELLA DALLAS (United Artists, 1937) 105 min.

Producer, Samuel Goldwyn; associate producer, Merritt Hulburd; director, King Vidor; based on the novel by Olive Higgins Prouty and the play by Harry Wagstaff Gribble, Gertrude Purcell; screenplay, Sarah Y. Mason, Victor Heerman; art director, Richard Day; costumes, Omar Kiam; music director, Alfred Newman; sound, Frank Maher; camera, Rudolph Maté; editor, Sherman Todd.

Barbara Stanwyck (Stella Martin Dallas); John Boles (Stephen Dallas); Anne Shirley (Laurel Dallas); Barbara O'Neil (Helen Morrison); Alan Hale (Ed Munn); Marjorie Main (Mrs. Martin); Edmund Elton (Mr. Martin); George Walcott (Charlie Martin); Gertrude Short (Carrie Jenkins); Tim Holt (Richard); Nella Walker (Mrs. Grosvenor); Bruce Saterlee (Con); Jimmy Butler (Con as an Adult); Jack Eggar (Lee); Dickie Jones (John); Ann Shoemaker (Miss Phillibrown).

BREAKFAST FOR TWO (RKO, 1937) 65 min.

Producer, Edward Kaufman; director, Alfred Santell; story, David Garth; screenplay, Charles Kaufman, Paul Yawitz, Viola Brothers Shore; art directors, Van Nest Polglase, Al Herman; set decorator, Darrell Silvera; costumes, Edward Stevenson; camera, J. Roy Hunt; editor, George Hively.

Barbara Stanwyck (Valentine Ransom); Herbert Marshall (Jonathan Blair); Glenda Farrell (Carol); Eric Blore (Butch); Frank M. Thomas (Sam Ransom); Donald Meek (Justice of the Peace); Etienne Girardot (Meggs); Pierre Watkin (Faraday).

ALWAYS GOODBYE (Twentieth Century-Fox, 1938) 75 min.

Producer, Darryl F. Zanuck; associate producer,

Raymond Griffith; director, Sidney Lanfield; story, Gilbert Emery, Douglas Doty; screenplay, Kathryn Scola, Edith Skouras; art directors, Bernard Herzbrun, Hans Peters; set decorator, Thomas Little; costumes, Royer; music director, Louis Silvers; camera, Robert Planck; editor, Robert Simpson.

Barbara Stanwyck (Margot Weston); Herbert Marshall (Jim Howard); Ian Hunter (Phillip Marshall); Cesar Romero (Count Giovanni Corini); Lynn Bari (Jessica Reid); Binnie Barnes (Harriet Martin); John Russell (Roddy); Mary Forbes (Martha Marshall); Albert Conti (Benoit); Marcelle Corday (Nurse); Franklin Pangborn (Bicycle Salesman); George Davis, Ben Welden (Taxi Driver); Eddy Conrad (Barber); Robert Lowery (Don); Rita Gould (Dowager); Eric Wilton (Butler); Eugene Borden (Purser); George Davis (Taxi Driver).

THE MAD MISS MANTON (RKO, 1938) 80 min.

Producer, Pandro S. Berman; associate producer, P. J. Wolfson; director, Leigh Jason; story, Wilson Collison; screenplay, Philip G. Epstein; art directors, Van Nest Polglase, Carroll Clark; set decorator, Darrell Silvera; costumes, Edward Stevenson; music, Roy Webb; camera, Nicholas Musuraca; editor, George Hively.

Barbara Stanwyck (Melsa Manton); Henry Fonda (Peter Ames); Sam Levene (Lieutenant Mike Brent); Frances Mercer (Helen Frayne); Stanley Ridges (Eddie Norris); Whitney Bourne (Pat James); Vicki Lester (Kit Beverly); Ann Evers (Lee Wilson); Catherine O'Quinn (Dora Fenton); Linda Terry (Myra Frost); Eleanor Hansen (Jane); Hattie McDaniel (Hilda); James Burke (Sergeant Sullivan); Paul Guilfoyle (Bat Regan); Penny Singleton (Frances Glesk); Leona Maricle (Sheila Lane); Kay Sutton (Gloria Hamilton); Miles Mander (Fred Thomas); John Qualen (Subway Watchman); Grady Sutton (District Attorney's Secretary); Olin Howland (Mister X [Joe, the Safecracker]); Mary Jo Desmond (Extra); Emory Parnell (Doorman); Eddy Chandler (Detective); George Magrill (Cop).

UNION PACIFIC (Paramount, 1939) 135 min.

Producer, Cecil B. DeMille; associate producer, William H. Pine; director, DeMille; story, Ernest Haycox; screenplay, Walter DeLeon, C. Gardner Sullivan, Jesse Lasky, Jr.; second unit director, Arthur Rosson; art directors, Hans Dreier, Roland Anderson; costumes, Natalie Visart; music, Sigmund Krumgold, John Leipold; camera, Victor Milner, Dewey Wrigley; editor, Anne Bauchens.

Barbara Stanwyck (Mollie Monahan); Joel McCrea (Jeff Butler); Akim Tamiroff (Fiesta); Robert Preston (Dick Allen); Lynne Overman (Leach Overmile); Brian Donlevy (Sid Campeau); Robert Barrat (Duke Ring); Anthony Quinn (Cordray); Stanley Ridges (Casement); Henry Kolker (Asa M. Barrows); Francis McDonald (Grenville M. Dodge); Willard Robertson (Oakes Ames); Harold Goodwin (Calvin); Evelyn Keyes (Mrs. Calvin); Richard Lane (Sam Reed); William Haade (Dusky Clayton); Regis Toomey (Paddy O'Rourke); J. M. Kerrigan (Monahan); Fuzzy Knight (Cookie); Harry Woods (Al Brett); Lon Chaney, Jr. (Dollarhide); Joseph Crehan (General U. S. Grant); Julia Faye (Mame); Sheila Darcy (Rose); Joe Sawyer (Shamus); Byron Foulger (Andrew Whipple); Jack Pennick (Harmonica Player); Dick Alexander, Max Davidson, Oscar G. Hendrian, Jim Pierce (Card Players); Walter Long (Irishman); Monte Blue (Indian); John Merton (Laborer); Jim Farley (Paddy); Buddy Roosevelt (Fireman); Richard Denning, David Newell (Reporters); Chief Thundercloud, Mala, Iron Eyes Cody, Sonny Chorre, Gregg Whitespear, Richard Robles, Tony Urchel (Indian Braves).

GOLDEN BOY (Columbia, 1939) 99 min.

Producer, William Perlberg; director, Rouben Mamoulian; based on the play by Clifford Odets; screenplay, Lewis Meltzer, Daniel Taradash, Sarah Y. Mason, Victor Heerman; art director, Lionel Banks; montages, D. W. Starling; costumes, Kalloch; music, Victor Young; music director, Morris Stoloff; camera, Nicholas Musuraca, Karl Freund; editor, Otto Meyer.

Barbara Stanwyck (Lorna Moon); Adolphe Menjou (Tom Moody); William Holden (Joe Bonaparte); Joseph Calleia (Eddie Puseli); Edward S. Brophy (Roxy Lewis); Don Beddoe (Bornac); Lee J. Cobb (Mr. Bonaparte); William H. Strauss (Mr. Carp); Sam Levene (Higgie); Beatrice Blinn (Anna); John Wray (Manager-Barker); Frank Jenks (Pepper White); Robert Sterling (Elevator Boy); Minerva Urecal (Customer); Irving "Big Gangi" Cohen (Ex-Pug); John Harmon, George Lloyd (Gamblers); Bruce Mitchell (Guard); Earl Askam (Cop); Gordon Armitage, Joe Gray, Mickey Golden (Fighters).

REMEMBER THE NIGHT (Paramount, 1940) 94 min.

Producer/director, Mitchell Leisen; screenplay, Preston Sturges; art directors, Hans Dreier, Roland Anderson; Miss Stanwyck's costumes, Edith Head; music, Frederick Hollander; camera, Ted Tetzlaff; editor, Doane Harrison.

Barbara Stanwyck (Lee Leander); Fred MacMurray (John Sargent); Beulah Bondi (Mrs. Sargent); Elizabeth Patterson (Aunt Emma); Willard Robertson (Francis X. O'Leary); Sterling Holloway (Willie); Charles Waldron (Judge—New York); Paul Guilfoyle (District Attorney); Charles Arnt (Tom); John Wray (Hank); Thomas W. Ross (Mr. Emery); Fred "Snowflake" Toones (Rufus); Tom Kennedy (Fat Mike); Georgia Caine (Lee's Mother); Virginia Brissac (Mrs. Emery); Spencer Charters (Judge at Rummage Sale); Chester Clute (Jewelry Salesman); Fuzzy Knight (Band Leader); Brooks Benedict (Court Spectator); Milton Kibbee, Pat O'Malley, Julia Faye, Avril Cameron, Joan Acker (Jury Members).

THE LADY EVE (Paramount, 1941) 97 min.

Producer, Paul Jones; director, Preston Sturges;

story, Monckton Hoffe; screenplay, Sturges; art directors, Hans Dreier, Ernst Fegte; costumes, Edith Head; music director, Sigmund Krumgold; camera, Victor Milner; editor, Stuart Gilmore.

Barbara Stanwyck (Jean Harrington); Henry Fonda (Charles Pike); Charles Coburn ("Colonel" Harrington); Eugene Pallette (Mr. Pike); William Demarest (Muggsy); Eric Blore (Sir Alfred McGlennon Keith); Melville Cooper (Gerald); Martha O'Driscoll (Martha); Janet Beecher (Mrs. Pike); Robert Greig (Burrows); Dora Clement (Gertrude); Luis Alberni (Pike's Chef); Frank C. Moran (Bartender at Party); Jimmy Conlin, Alan Bridge, Victor Potel (Stewards); Reginald Sheffield (Professor Jones); Robert Warwick (Manager in Bank); Wanda McKay, Ella Neal, Marcella Christopher (Daughters on Boat).

MEET JOHN DOE (Warner Bros., 1941) 123 min.

Producer/director, Frank Capra; story, Richard Connell, Robert Presnell; screenplay, Robert Riskin; art director, Stephen Goosson; costumes, Natalie Visart; music, Dmitri Tiomkin; music director, Leo F. Forbstein; choral arranger, Hall Johnson; montages, Slavko Vorkapich; camera, George Barnes; editor, Daniel Mandell.

Gary Cooper (John Doe [Long John Willoughby]); Barbara Stanwyck (Ann Mitchell); Edward Arnold (D. B. Norton); Walter Brennan (Colonel); James Gleason (Henry Connell); Spring Byington (Mrs. Mitchell); Gene Lockhart (Mayor Lovett); Rod La Rocque (Ted Sheldon); Irving Bacon (Beany); Regis Toomey (Bert Hansen); Aldrich Bowker (Pop Dwyer); Ann Doran (Mrs. Hansen); Warren Hymer (Angel Face); Mrs. Gardner Crane (Mrs. Brewster); Sterling Holloway (Dan); J. Farrell MacDonald (Sourpuss Smithers); Pat Flaherty (Mike Sanderson); Carlotta Jelm, Tina Thayer (Ann's Sisters); Bennie Bartlett (Red, the Office Boy); Hall Johnson Choir (Themselves); Stanley Andrews (Weston); Andrew Tombes (Spencer); Pierre Watkin (Hammett); Edward Earle (Radio M.C.); Mitchell Lewis (Bennett); Edmund Cobb, Jack Cheatham, Earl Bunn (Cops); Frank Moran (Man); Susan Peters, Maris Wrixon (Autograph Hounds); Vaughan Glaser (Governor); Knox Manning, Selmer Jackson, John B. Hughes (Radio Announcers at Convention).

YOU BELONG TO ME (Columbia, 1941) 94 min.

Producer/director, Wesley Ruggles; story, Dalton Trumbo; screenplay, Claude Binyon; art director, Lionel Banks; costumes, Edith Head; music, Frederick Hollander; music director, Morris Stoloff; camera, Joseph Walker; editor, Viola Lawrence.

Barbara Stanwyck (Helen Hunt); Henry Fonda (Peter Kirk); Edgar Buchanan (Billings); Roger Clark (Vandemer); Ruth Donnelly (Emma); Melville Cooper (Moody); Ralph Peters (Joseph); Maude Eburne (Ella); Renie Riano (Minnie); Ellen Lowe (Eva); Mary Treen (Doris); Gordon Jones (Robert Andrews); Fritz Feld (Desk Clerk); Paul Harvey (Barrows); Harold Wald-

ridge (Smithers); Lloyd Bridges, Stanley Brown (Ski Patrol); Jack Norton (Kuckel); Larry Parks (Blemish); Grady Sutton (Clerk); Georgia Caine (Necktie Woman).

BALL OF FIRE (RKO, 1941) 111 min.

Producer, Samuel Goldwyn; director, Howard Hawks; based on the story "From A to Z" by Billy Wilder and Thomas Monroe; screenplay, Charles Brackett, Wilder; art directors, Perry Ferguson, McClure Capps; set decorator, Howard Bristol; Miss Stanwyck's costumes, Edith Head; music, Alfred Newman; camera, Gregg Toland; editor, Daniel Mandell.

Gary Cooper (Professor Bertram Potts); Barbara Stanwyck (Sugarpuss O'Shea); Oscar Homolka (Professor Gurkakoff); Henry Travers (Professor Jerome); S. Z. Sakall (Professor Magenbruch); Tully Marshall (Professor Robinson); Leonid Kinskey (Professor Quintana); Richard Haydn (Professor Oddly); Aubrey Mather (Professor Peagram); Allen Jenkins (Garbage Man); Dana Andrews (Joe Lilac); Dan Duryea (Duke Pastrami); Ralph Peters (Asthma Anderson); Kathleen Howard (Miss Bragg); Mary Field (Miss Totten); Charles Lane (Larsen); Charles Arnt (McNeary); Elisha Cook (Waiter); Alan Rhein (Horseface); Eddie Foster (Pinstripe); Aldrich Bowker (Justice of the Peace); Addison Richards (District Attorney); Pat West (Bum); Kenneth Howell (College Boy); Will Lee (Benny, the Creep); Tim Ryan (Motor Cop); Tommy Ryan (Newsboy); Gene Krupa & His Orchestra (Themselves); Dick Rush, Ken Christy (Cops at Motor Court); June Horne, Ethelreda Leopold (Nursemaids in Park).

THE GREAT MAN'S LADY (Paramount, 1942) 90 min.

Producer/director, William A. Wellman; based on the story by Vina Delmar; screen story, Adela Rogers St. John, Seen Owen; screenplay, W. L. River; art directors, Hans Dreier, Earl Hedrick; makeup, Robert Ewing; costumes, Edith Head; music, Victor Young; special effects, Gordon Jennings; camera, William C. Mellor; editor, Thomas Scott.

Barbara Stanwyck (Hannah Sempler); Joel McCrea (Ethan Hoyt); Brian Donlevy (Steely Edwards); Katharine Stevens (Girl Biographer); Thurston Hall (Mr. Sempler); Lloyd Corrigan (Mr. Cadwallader); Etta McDaniel (Delilah); Frank M. Thomas (Senator Knobs); Lillian Yarbo (Mandy); Helen Lynd (Bettina); Mary Treen (Persis); Lucien Littlefield (City Editor); John Hamilton (Senator Grant); Fred "Snowflake" Toones (Fogey); Damian O'Flynn (Burns); Charles Lane (Pierce); Anna Q. Nilsson (Paula Wales); Milton Parsons (Froman); Fern Emmett (Secretary to City Editor); Irving Bacon (Parson); Monte Blue (Man at Hoyt City); Bob Perry (Miner).

THE GAY SISTERS (Warner Bros., 1942) 110 min.

Producer, Henry Blanke; director, Irving Rapper;

based on the novel by Stephen Longstreet; screenplay, Lenore Coffee; art director, Robert Haas; Miss Stanwyck's costumes by Edith Head; music, Max Steiner; orchestrator, Hugo Friedhofer; music director, Leo F. Forbstein; camera, Sol Polito; editor, Warren Low.

Barbara Stanwyck (Fiona Gaylord); George Brent (Charles Barclay); Geraldine Fitzgerald (Evelyn Gaylord); Nancy Coleman (Susanna Gaylord); Gig Young (Gig Young); Donald Crisp (Ralph Padlock); Gene Lockhart (Herschell Gibbon); Grant Mitchell (Gilbert Wheeler); Donald Woods (Penn Sutherland Gaylord); Larry Simms (Judge Barrows); William T. Orr (Dick Tone); George Lessey (Judge Barrows); Helene Thimig (Saakia); Anne Revere (Ida Orner); Charles Waldron (Mr. Van Rennsaeler); David Clyde (Benson); Mary Thomas (Fiona as a Child); Edward McNamara (Policeman); Dorothea Wolbert (Woman); Charles Drake, Bill Edwards (Clerks); Murray Alper (Elevator Operator); Hobart Bosworth (Clergyman); Creighton Hale (Simmons); Claire Du Brey (Matron).

LADY OF BURLESQUE *(United Artists, 1943)* 91 min.

Producer, Hunt Stromberg; director, William A. Wellman; based on the novel *The G-String Murders* by Gypsy Rose Lee; screenplay, James Gunn; art director, Bernard Herzbrun; Miss Stanwyck's costumes, Edith Head; other costumes, Natalie Visart; music, Arthur Lange; songs, Sammy Cahn and Harry Akst; choreography, Danny Dare; camera, Robert De Grasse; editor, James E. Newcomb.

Barbara Stanwyck (Dixie Daisy); Michael O'Shea (Biff Brannigan); J. Edward Bromberg (S. B. Foss); Iris Adrian (Gee Gee Graham); Gloria Dickson (Polly Baxter); Victoria Faust (Lolita La Verne); Stephanie Bachelor (Princess Nirvena); Charles Dingle (Inspector Harrigan); Marion Martin (Alice Angel); Eddie Gordon (Officer Pat Kelly); Frank Fenton (Russell Rogers); Pinky Lee (Mandy); Frank Conroy (Stacchi).

British release title: *Striptease Lady.*

FLESH AND FANTASY *(Universal, 1943)* 93 min.

Producers, Charles Boyer, Julien Duvivier; director, Duvivier; stories, Ellis St. Joseph, Oscar Wilde, Laslo Vadnay; screenplay, Ernest Pascal, Samuel Hoffenstein, St. Joseph; art directors, John B. Goodman, Richard Riedel, Robert Boyle; set decorators, R. A. Gausman, E. R. Robinson; Miss Stanwyck's costumes, Edith Head; other costumes, Vera West; music, Alexandre Tausman; music director, Charles Previn; camera, Paul Ivano, Stanley Cortez; editor, Arthur Hilton.

Edward G. Robinson (Marshall Tyler); Charles Boyer (Paul Gaspar); Barbara Stanwyck (Joan Stanley); Betty Field (Henrietta); Robert Cummings (Michael); Thomas Mitchell (Septimus Podgers); Charles Winninger (King Lamarr); Anna Lee (Rowena); Dame May Whitty (Lady Pamela Hardwick); C. Aubrey Smith (Dean of Chichester); Edgar Barrier (Stranger); David Hoffman (Davis); *Episode One Bits:* Leyland Hodgson (Cop); Edward Fielding (Sir Thomas);

Heather Thatcher (Lady Flora); Mary Forbes (Lady Thomas); Ian Wolfe (Librarian); Doris Lloyd (Mrs. Caxton); Clarence Muse (Jeff); Jack Gardner (Gunman); *Episode Two Bits:* Grace McDonald (Equestrienne); June Lang (Angel); Lane Chandler, Frank Mitchell (Acrobats); Neara Sanders, Beatrice Barrett (Chorus Girls); Frank Arnold (Clown); *Episode Three Bits:* George Lewis (Harlequin); Peter Lawford (Pierrot); Carl Vernell, Phil Warren, Sandra Morgan (Neighbors); Marjorie Lord (Justine).

DOUBLE INDEMNITY *(Paramount, 1944)* 107 min.

Producer, Joseph Sistrom; director, Billy Wilder; based on the short story by James M. Cain; screenplay, Wilder, Raymond Chandler; art directors, Hans Dreier, Hal Pereira; set decorator, Bertram Granger; costumes, Edith Head; music, Miklos Rozsa; process camera, Farciot Edouart; camera, John Seitz; editor, Doane Harrison.

Fred MacMurray (Walter Neff); Barbara Stanwyck (Phyllis Dietrichson); Edward G. Robinson (Barton Keyes); Porter Hall (Mr. Jackson); Jean Heather (Lola Dietrichson); Tom Powers (Mr. Dietrichson); Byron Barr (Nino Zachette); Richard Gaines (Mr. Norton); Fortunio Bonanova (Sam Gorlopis); John Philliber (Joe Peters); George Magrill (Bit); Bess Flowers (Norton's Secretary); Edmund Cobb (Train Conductor); Clarence Muse (Black Man); Judith Gibson (Pacific All-Risk Operator); Sam McDaniel (Garage Attendant).

HOLLYWOOD CANTEEN *(Warner Bros., 1944)* 123 min.

Producer, Alex Gottlieb; director/screenplay, Delmer Daves; art director, Leo Kuter; set decorator, Casey Roberts; music adaptor, Ray Heindorf; music director, Leo F. Forbstein; choreography, LeRoy Prinz; wardrobe, Milo Anderson; camera, Bert Glennon; editor, Christian Nyby.

Joan Leslie (Herself); Robert Hutton (Slim); Dane Clark (Sergeant); Janis Paige (Angela); Andrew Sisters, Jack Benny, Joe E. Brown, Eddie Cantor, Kitty Carlisle, Jack Carson, Joan Crawford, Helmut Dantine, Bette Davis, Faye Emerson, Victor Francen, John Garfield, Sydney Greenstreet, Alan Hale, Paul Henreid, Andrea King, Peter Lorre, Ida Lupino, Irene Manning, Nora Martin, Joan McCracken, Dolores Moran, Dennis Morgan, Eleanor Parker, William Prince, Joyce Reynolds, John Ridgely, Roy Rogers & Trigger, S. Z. Sakall, Alexis Smith, Zachary Scott, Barbara Stanwyck, Craig Stevens, Joseph Szigeti, Donald Woods, Jane Wyman, Jimmy Dorsey & His Band, Carmen Cavallaro & His Orchestra, Golden Gate Quartet, Rosario & Antonio, Sons of the Pioneers (Themselves); Mark Stevens, Dick Erdman (Soldiers on Deck); Kem Dibbs (Soldier); Robin Raymond (Blonde on Street); George Turner (Sailor); Chef Joseph Milani, Mary Gordon (Themselves); Betty Bryson, Willard Van Simons, William Alcorn, Jack Mattis, Jack Coffey (Dance Specialties); Dorothy Malone, Julie Bishop, Robert Shayne,

Colleen Townsend, Angela Greene, Paul Brinkman, Bill Kennedy (Themselves).

CHRISTMAS IN CONNECTICUT (Warner Bros., 1945) 101 min.

Producer, William Jacobs; director, Peter Godfrey; story, Aileen Hamilton; screenplay, Lionel Houser, Adele Commandini; art director, Stanley Fleischer; set decorator, Casey Roberts; costumes, Edith Head; music, Frederick Hollander; orchestrator, Jerome Moross; music director, Leo F. Forbstein; sound, Everett A. Brown; camera, Carl Guthrie; editor, Frank Magee.

Barbara Stanwyck (Elizabeth Lane); Dennis Morgan (Jefferson Jones); Sydney Greenstreet (Alexander Yardley); Reginald Gardiner (John Sloan); S. Z. Sakall (Felix Bassenak); Robert Shayne (Dudley Beecham); Una O'Connor (Norah); Frank Jenks (Sinkewicz); Joyce Compton (Mary Lee); Dick Elliott (Judge Crothers); Betty Alexander (Nurse Smith); Allen Fox (Postman); Lillian Bronson (Prim Secretary); Arthur Aylesworth (Sleigh Driver); Marke Blake, Charles Marsh, Pat Lane (Reporters); Olaf Hytten (Elkins).

British release title: Indiscretion.

MY REPUTATION (Warner Bros., 1946) 96 min.

Producer, Henry Blanke; director, Curtis Bernhardt; based on the novel Instruct My Sorrows by Clare Jaynes; screenplay, Catherine Turney; art director, Anton Grot; set decorator, George James Hopkins; Miss Stanwyck's costumes, Edith Head; other costumes, Leah Rhodes; music, Max Steiner; music director, Leo F. Forbstein; assistant director, Jesse Hibbs; sound, Everett A. Brown; special effects, Roy Davidson; camera, James Wong Howe; editor, David Weisbart.

Barbara Stanwyck (Jessica Drummond); George Brent (Scott Landis); Warner Anderson (Frank Everett); Lucile Watson (Mrs. Kimball); John Ridgely (Cary Abbott); Eve Arden (Ginna Abbott); Jerome Cowan (George Van Orman); Esther Dale (Anna); Scotty Beckett (Kim Drummond); Bobby Cooper (Keith Drummond); Leona Maricle (Riette Van Orman); Mary Servoss (Mary); Cecil Cunningham (Mrs. Thompson); Janis Wilson (Penny Boardman); Ann Todd (Gretchen Van Orman); Nancy Evans (Baby Hawks); Oliver Blake (Dave); Marjorie Hoshelle (Phyllis); Bruce Warren (Man in Bar); Sam McDaniel (Johnson); Dickie Humphreys, Marilyn Kaye, Shirley Doble, Dale Cornell (Jitterbuggers).

THE BRIDE WORE BOOTS (Paramount, 1946) 86 min.

Producer, Seton I. Miller; director, Irving Pichel; based the story by Dwight Michael Wiley and the play by Harry Segall; screenplay by Wiley; art directors, Hans Dreier, John Meehan; set decorators, Sam Comer, Jerry Welch; costumes, Edith Head; music, Frederick Hollander; assistant directors, Oscar Rudolph, Frank Permenter; sound, Ray Meadows, Don Johnson; special camera effects, Gordon Jennings; cam-

era, Stuart Thompson; editor, Ellsworth Hoagland.

Barbara Stanwyck (Sally Warren); Robert Cummings (Jeff Warren); Diana Lynn (Mary Lou Medford); Patric Knowles (Lance Gale); Peggy Wood (Grace Apley); Robert Benchley (Tod Warren); Willie Best (Joe); Natalie Wood (Carol Warren); Gregory Muradian (Johnnie Warren); Mary Young (Janet Doughton); Frank Orth (Judge); Myrtle Anderson (Florence); Charles Brown (Wells); Richard Gaines (Mallory—Jeff's Attorney); Alice Keating, Eula Guy, Gertrude Hoffman, Janet Clark, Ida Moore (Clubwomen); Minerva Urecal (Lady); Milton Kibbee (Hotel Manager).

THE STRANGE LOVE OF MARTHA IVERS (Paramount, 1946) 116 min.

Producer, Hal B. Wallis; director, Lewis Milestone; story, Jack Patrick; screenplay, Robert Rossen; art directors, Hans Dreier, John Meehan; set decorators, Sam Comer, Jerry Welch; costumes, Edith Head; music, Miklos Rozsa; assistant director, Robert Aldrich; sound, Harold Lewis, Walter Oberst; process camera, Farciot Edouart; camera, Victor Milner; editor, Archie Marshek.

Barbara Stanwyck (Martha Ivers); Van Heflin (Sam Masterson); Lizabeth Scott (Toni Marachek); Kirk Douglas (Walter O'Neil); Judith Anderson (Mrs. Ivers); Roman Bohnen (Mr. O'Neil); Darryl Hickman (Sam Masterson as a Boy); Janis Wilson (Martha Ivers as a Girl); Ann Doran (Secretary); Frank Orth (Hotel Clerk); James Flavin (Detective); Mickey Kuhn (Walter O'Neil as a Boy); Charles D. Brown (Special Investigator); Matt McHugh (Bus Driver); Walter Baldwin (Dempsey, the Garage Owner); Catherine Craig (French Maid); Harry Leonard, Sayre Dearing (Crap Shooters); Bert Roach, Ricky Ricardi, Billy Hurt, Gene Ashley (Men); Blake Edwards (Sailor); Tom Schamp, Kernan Cripps (Cops); Thomas Louden (Lynch, the Butler).

CALIFORNIA (Paramount, 1946) C-98 min.

Producer, Seton I. Miller; director, John Farrow; story, Boris Ingster; screenplay, Frank Butler, Theodore Strauss; art directors, Hans Dreier, Roland Anderson; set decorators, Sam Comer, Ray Moyer; women's costumes, Edith Head; Technicolor consultant, Natalie Kalmus; men's costumes, Gile Steele; music, Victor Young; songs, E. Y. Harburg and Earl Robinson; assistant director, Herbert Coleman; sound, Stanley Cooley, John Cope; camera, Ray Rennahan; editor, Eda Warren.

Ray Milland (Jonathan Trumbo); Barbara Stanwyck (Lily Bishop); Barry Fitzgerald (Michael Fabian); George Coulouris (Pharaoh Coffin); Albert Dekker (Mr. Pike); Anthony Quinn (Don Luis Rivera y Hernandez); Frank Faylen (Whitey); Gavin Muir (Booth Pennock); James Burke (Pokey); Eduardo Ciannelli (Padre); Roman Bohnen (Colonel Stuart); Argentina Brunetti (Elvira); Howard Freeman (Senator Creel); Julia Faye (Wagon Woman); Minerva Urecal (Emma-

Town Matron); Dook McGill (Coffin's Servant); Crane Whitley (Abe Clinton); Gertrude Hoffman (Old Woman); Ethan Laidlaw (Reb); Philip Van Zandt (Mr. Gunce); Lane Chandler, Ralph Dunn, Joe Whitemead, Russ Clark, Jeff Corey, William Hall (Men); Tony Paton, Frederic Santley, George Melford, Joe Whitemead (Delegates); Dick Wessel (Blacksmith); Will Wright (Chairman).

THE TWO MRS. CARROLLS *(Warner Bros., 1947)* 99 min.

Producer, Mark Hellinger; director, Peter Godfrey; based on the play by Martin Vale; screenplay, Thomas Job; art director, Anton Grot; set decorator, Budd Friend; music, Franz Waxman; orchestrator, Leonid Raab; music director, Leo F. Forbstein; assistant director, Claude Archer; camera, Peverell Marley; editor, Frederick Richards.

Humphrey Bogart (Geoffrey Carroll); Barbara Stanwyck (Sally Morton Carroll); Alexis Smith (Cecily Latham); Nigel Bruce (Dr. Tuttle); Isobel Elsom (Mrs. Latham); Pat O'Moore (Charles Pennington); Ann Carter (Beatrice Carroll); Anita Bolster (Christine); Barry Bernard (Mr. Bingdon); Colin Campbell (MacGregor); Peter Godfrey, Creighton Hale (Touts); Leyland Hodgson (Inspector).

THE OTHER LOVE *(United Artists, 1947)* 96 min.

Producer, Davis Lewis; director, Andre de Toth; based on the novel by Erich Maria Remarque; screenplay, Ladislas Fodor and Harry Brown; music, Miklos Rozsa; music director, Mort Glickman; assistant director, Joe Kramer; sound, William E. Clark; special effects, Howard and Theodore Lydecker; camera, Alfred Keller; editor, Walter Thompson.

Barbara Stanwyck (Karen Duncan); David Niven (Dr. Anthony Stanton); Maria Palmer (Roberta); Joan Lorring (Celestine); Richard Conte (Paul Clermont); Richard Hale (Professor Linnaker); Edward Ashley (Richard Shelton); Natalie Schafer (Dora Shelton); Lenore Aubert (Yvonne); Jimmy Horne (Pete); Mary Forbes (Mme. Gruen); Ann Codee (The Florist); Kathleen Williams (Florist's Assistant); Gilbert Roland (Croupier).

CRY WOLF *(Warner Bros., 1947)* 83 min.

Producer, Henry Blanke; director, Peter Godfrey; based on the novel by Marjorie Carleton; screenplay, Catherine Turney; art director, Carl Jules Weyl; set decorator, Jack McConaghy; music, Franz Waxman; orchestrator, Leonid Raab; music director, Leo F. Forbstein; assistant director, Claude Archer; sound, Charles Lang; camera, Carl Guthrie; editor, Folmar Blangsted.

Errol Flynn (Mark Caldwell); Barbara Stanwyck (Sandra Marshall); Richard Basehart (James Demarest); Geraldine Brooks (Julie Demarest); Jerome Cowan (Senator Caldwell); John Ridgely (Jackson Laidell); Patricia Barry (Angela); Rory Mallineon (Becket); Helene Thimig (Marta); Paul Stanton (Dav-

enport); Barry Bernard (Roberts, the Groom); John Elliott (Clergyman); Lisa Golm (Mrs. Laidell); Jack Mower (Watkins); Paul Panzer (Gatekeeper); Creighton Hale (Dr. Reynolds).

VARIETY GIRL *(Paramount, 1947)* 83 min.*

Producer, Daniel Dare; director, George Marshall; screenplay, Edmund Hartmann, Frank Tashlin, Robert Welch, Monte Brice; art directors, Hans Dreier, Robert Clatworthy; set decorators, Sam Comer, Ross Dowd; music director, Joseph J. Lilley; orchestrator, N. Van Cleave; music for puppetoon sequence, Edward Plumb; songs, Frank Loesser; assistant director, George Templeton; sound, Gene Merritt, John Cope; special effects, Gordon Jennings; process camera, Farciot Edouart; camera, Lionel Lindon, Stuart Thompson; editor, LeRoy Stone.

Mary Hatcher (Catherine Brown); Olga San Juan (Amber LaVonne); DeForest Kelley (Bob Kirby); William Demarest (Barker); Frank Faylen (Stage Manager); Frank Ferguson (J. R. O'Connell); Russell Hicks, Crane Whitley, Charles Coleman, Hal K. Dawson, Eddie Fetherstone (Men at Steambath); Catherine Craig (Secretary); Bing Crosby, Bob Hope, Gary Cooper, Ray Milland, Alan Ladd, Barbara Stanwyck, Paulette Goddard, Dorothy Lamour, Veronica Lake, Sonny Tufts, Joan Caulfield, William Holden, Lizabeth Scott, Burt Lancaster, Gail Russell, Diana Lynn, Sterling Hayden, Robert Preston, John Lund, William Bendix, Barry Fitzgerald, Cass Daley, Howard Da Silva, Billy De Wolfe, Macdonald Carey, Arleen Whelan, Patric Knowles, Mona Freeman, Cecil Kellaway, Johnny Coy, Virginia Field, Richard Webb, Stanley Clements, Cecil B. DeMille, Mitchell Leisen, Frank Butler, George Marshall, Roger Dann, Pearl Bailey, The Mulcays, Spike Jones & His City Slickers (Themselves); Ann Doran (Hairdresser); Jack Norton (Brown Derby Busboy); Eric Alden (Makeup Man); Frank Mayo (Director).

* Technicolor sequences.

B. F.'S DAUGHTER *(MGM, 1948)* 108 min.

Producer, Edwin H. Knopf; director, Robert Z. Leonard; based on the novel by John P. Marquand; screenplay, Luther Davis; art directors, Cedric Gibbons, Daniel B. Cathcart; set decorators, Edwin B. Willis, Jack D. Moore; women's costumes, Irene; music, Bronislau Kaper; music director, Charles Previn; assistant director, Bert Glazer; makeup, Jack Dawn; sound, Douglas Shearer, Charles E. Wallace; montage, Peter Ballbusch; special effects, Warren Newcombe; camera, Joseph Ruttenberg; editor, George White.

Barbara Stanwyck (Polly Fulton); Van Heflin (Thomas W. Brett); Richard Hart (Robert S. Tasmin); Charles Coburn (B. F. Fulton); Keenan Wynn (Martin Delwyn Ainsley); Margaret Lindsay (Apples Sandler); Spring Byington (Gladys Fulton); Marshall Thompson (Sailor); Barbara Laage (Eugenia Taris); Thomas E. Breen (Major Riley); Fred Nurney (Olaf); Edwin Cooper (Geneal Waldron); Tom Fadden (Mr. Holmquist); Davison Clark (Doorman); Anne O'Neal (Receptionist); Hal K. Dawson (Frederick X. Gibson); Laura Treadwell (Emily Lovelace); Bill Harbach (Co-Pilot); David Newell (Captain); Mary Jo Ellis, Lisa Kirby, Josette Deegan (Girls); Florence Wix, Major Sam Harris (Wedding Guests); Pierre Watkin (Joe Stewart); Mickey Martin, Gene Coogan, Jack Stenlino, Joe Recht (Soldiers).

British release title: *Polly Fulton.*

SORRY, WRONG NUMBER *(Paramount, 1948)* 89 min.

Producers, Hal B. Wallis, Anatole Litvak; director, Litvak; based on the radio play by Lucille Fletcher; screenplay, Fletcher; art directors, Hans Dreier, Earl Hedrick; set decorators, Sam Comer, Bertram Granger; costumes, Edith Head; Miss Stanwyck's jewelry, Ruser; music, Franz Waxman; makeup, Wally Westmore; assistant director, Richard McWhorter; sound, Gene Merritt, Walter Oberst; process camera, Farciot Edouart; special effects, Gordon Jennings; camera, Sol Polito; editor, Warren Low.

Barbara Stanwyck (Leona Stevenson); Burt Lancaster (Henry Stevenson); Ann Richards (Sally Lord Dodge); Wendell Corey (Dr. Alexander); Harold Vermilyea (Waldo Evans); Ed Begley (James Cotterell); Leif Erickson (Fred Lord); William Conrad (Morano); John Bromfield (Joe, the Detective); Jimmy Hunt (Jimmy Lord); Dorothy Neumann (Miss Jennings); Paul Fierro (Harpootlian); Kristine Miller (Dolly, Dr. Alexander's Girlfriend); Suzanne Dalbert (Cigarette Girl); Joyce Compton (Blonde); Tito Vuolo (Albert, the Waiter); Ashley Cowan (Clam Digger); Cliff Clark (Sergeant Duffy); Igor Dega, Grace Poggi (Dancers).

THE LADY GAMBLES *(Universal, 1949)* 99 min.

Producer, Michel Kraike; director, Michael Gordon; story, Lewis Meltzer, Oscar Saul; adaptor, Halsted Welles; screenplay, Roy Huggins; art director, Alexander Golitzen; set decorators, Russell Gausman, Ruby Levin; Miss Stanwyck's costumes, Orry-Kelly; music, Frank Skinner; assistant director, Frank Shaw; makeup, Bud Westmore, Bob Ewing; sound, Leslie I. Carey, Corson Jowett; camera, Russell Metty; editor, Milton Carruth.

Barbara Stanwyck (Joan Boothe); Robert Preston (David Boothe); Stephen McNally (Corrigan); Edith Barrett (Ruth Phillips); John Hoyt (Dr. Rojac); Elliott Sullivan (Barky); John Harmon (Frenchy); Phil Van Zandt (Chuck); Leif Erickson (Tony); Curt Conway (Bank Clerk); Houseley Stevenson (Pawnbroker); Don Beddoe (Mr. Sutherland); Nana Bryant (Mrs. Sutherland); Tony Curtis (Bellboy); Peter Leeds (Hotel Clerk); Frank Moran (Murphy); Esther Howard (Cross Lady); John Indrisano (Bert); Polly Bailey (Woman at Slot Machine); Francis McDonald (Trainer); Rex Lease (Guide); Kenneth Cutler (Clerk).

EAST SIDE, WEST SIDE *(MGM, 1950)* 108 min.

Producer, Voldemar Vetluguin; director, Mervyn LeRoy; based on the novel by Marcia Davenport; screenplay, Isobel Lennart; art directors, Cedric Gibbons, Randall Duell; set decorators, Edwin B. Willis, Arthur Krams; women's costumes, Helen Rose; music, Miklos Rozsa; assistant director, Howard Koch; makeup, Jack Dawn; sound, Douglas Shearer, A. N. Fenton; special effects, A. Arnold Gillespie; camera, Charles Rosher; editor, Harold F. Kress.

Barbara Stanwyck (Jessie Bourne); James Mason (Brandon Bourne); Van Heflin (Mark Dwyer); Ava Gardner (Isabel Morrison); Cyd Charisse (Rosa Senta); Nancy Davis (Helen Lee); Gale Sondergaard (Nora Kernan); Beverly Michaels (Felice Beckett); Raymond Greenleaf (Horace Ellcott Howland); Tom Powers (Owen Lee); Douglas Kennedy (Alec Dawning); Lisa Golm (Josephine); Paula Raymond (Joan Peterson); Jimmy Horne, Geraldine Farmer, Maria Reachi (Guests); Wesley Bly (Club Attendant); Wheaton Chambers (Doorman); Rita Lynn, Stella Soldi (Sistine Wives).

THE FILE ON THELMA JORDAN *(Paramount, 1950)* 100 min.

Producer, Hal B. Wallis; director, Robert Siodmak; based on the story by Marty Holland; screenplay, Ketti Frings; art directors, Hans Dreier, Earl Hedrick; set decorators, Sam Comer, Bertram Granger; costumes, Edith Head; music, Victor Young; process camera, Farciot Edouart; special effects, Gordon Jennings; camera, George Barnes; editor, Warren Low.

Barbara Stanwyck (Thelma Jordan); Wendell Corey (Cleve Marshall); Paul Kelly (Miles Scott); Joan Tetzel (Pamela Marshall); Stanley Ridges (Kingsley Willis); Richard Rober (Tony Laredo); Minor Watson (Judge Calvin Blackwell); Barry Kelley (District Attorney Pierce); Laura Eliot (Dolly); Basil Ruysdael (Judge Hancock); Jane Novak (Mrs. Blackwell); Gertrude Hoffman (Aunt Vera Edwards); Harry Antrim (Sidney); Theresa Harris (Esther); Kate Lawson (Clara); Byron Barr (McCary); Geraldine Wall (Matron); Jonathan Corey (Timmy Marshall); Robin Corey (Joan Marshall); Dorothy Klewer, Michael Ann Barrett, Fairy Cunningham, Geraldine Jordan (Girls in Jail); Jim Davies (Bailiff); Eric Alden, Gertrude Astor, Bill Meader (Reporters); Sam McDaniel (Porter).

NO MAN OF HER OWN *(Paramount, 1950)* 98 min.

Producer, Richard Maibaum; director, Mitchell Leisen; based on the novel *I Married a Dead Man* by William Irish (Cornell Woolrich); screenplay, Sally Benson, Catherine Turney; art directors, Hans Dreier, Henry Bumstead; set decorators, Sam Comer, Ray Moyer; costumes, Edith Head; music, Hugo Friedhofer; special effects, Gordon Jennings; process camera, Farciot Edouart; camera, Daniel L. Fapp; editor, Alma Macrorie.

Barbara Stanwyck (Helen Ferguson); John Lund (Bill

Harkness); Jane Cowl (Mrs. Harkness); Phyllis Thaxter (Patrice Harkness); Lyle Bettger (Stephen Morley); Henry O'Neill (Mr. Harkness); Richard Denning (Hugh Harkness); Carole Mathews (Blonde); Esther Dale (Josie); Milburn Stone (Plainclothesman); Griff Barnett (Dr. Parker); Harry Antrim (Ty Winthrop); Catherine Craig (Rosalie Baker); Georgia Backus (Nurse); Laura Eliot, Charles Dayton (Friends of the Family); Ivan Browning (Porter); Dooley Wilson (Dining Car Waiter); Willard Waterman (Jack Olsen); Summer Getchell (John Larrimore); Kathleen Freeman (Clara Larrimore); Gordon Nelson (Justice of the Peace); Esther Howard (Flowsy Woman at Boarding House); Stan Johnson, Steve Gaylord Pendleton (Policemen).

THE FURIES (Paramount, 1950) 109 min.

Producer, Hal B. Wallis; director, Anthony Mann; based on the novel by Niven Busch; screenplay, Charles Schnee; art directors, Hans Dreier, Henry Bumstead; set decorators, Sam Comer, Bertram Granger; costumes, Edith Head; music, Franz Waxman; special effects, Gordon Jennings; process camera, Farciot Edouart; camera, Victor Milner; editor, Archie Marshek.

Barbara Stanwyck (Vance Jeffords); Wendell Corey (Rip Darrow); Walter Huston (T. C. Jeffords); Judith Anderson (Florence Burnett); Gilbert Roland (Juan Herrera); Thomas Gomez (El Tigre); Beulah Bondi (Mrs. Anaheim); Albert Dekker (Reynolds); John Bromfield (Clay Jeffords); Wallace Ford (Scotty Hyslip); Blanche Yurka (Herrera's Mother); Louis Jean Heydt (Bailey); Frank Ferguson (Dr. Grieve); Lou Steele (Aguirre Herrera); Movita Castenada (Chiquita); Myrna Dell (Dallas Hart); Jane Novak (Woman); Arthur Hunnicutt, James Davies, Douglas Grange (Cowhands); Baron Lichter (Waiter).

TO PLEASE A LADY (MGM, 1950) 91 min.

Producer/director, Clarence Brown; screenplay, Barré Lyndon, Marge Decker; art directors, Cedric Gibbons, James Basevi; set decorators, Edwin B. Willis, Ralph S. Hurst; costumes, Helen Rose; music, Bronislau Kaper; special effects, A. Arnold Gillespie, Warren Newcombe; montage, Peter Ballbusch; camera, Harold Rosson; editor, Robert J. Kern.

Clark Gable (Mike Brannan); Barbara Stanwyck (Regina Forbes); Adolphe Menjou (Gregg); Will Geer (Jack Mackay); Roland Winters (Dwight Barrington); William C. McGaw (Joie Chitwood); Lela Bliss (Regina's Secretary); Emory Parnell (Mr. Wendell); Helen Spring (Janie); Frank Jenks (Newark Press Agent); Ted Husing (Indianapolis Announcer); Bill Hickman, Lew Smith (Mike's Mechanics); Richard Joy (Television Voice); William Welsh (Sports Announcer); John McGuire (Newark Referee); John Gallaudet (IMBA Promoter); Byron Foulger (Shoe Fitter); Arthur Loew, Jr. (Studio Production Man).

THE MAN WITH A CLOAK (MGM, 1951) 81 min.

Producer, Stephen Ames; director, Fletcher Markle; story, John Dickson Carr; screenplay, Frank Fenton; art directors, Cedric Gibbons, Arthur Lonergan; set decorators, Edwin B. Willis, Arthur Krams; women's costumes, Walter Plunkett; men's costumes, Gile Steele; music, David Raksin; camera, George Folsey; editor, Newell P. Kimlin.

Joseph Cotten (Dupin); Barbara Stanwyck (Lorna Bounty); Louis Calhern (Thevenet); Leslie Caron (Madeline Minot); Joe De Santis (Martin); Jim Backus (Flaherty); Margaret Wycherly (Mrs. Flynn); Richard Hale (Durand); Nicholas Joy (Dr. Roland); Roy Roberts (Policeman); Mitchell Lewis (Walter); Jean Inness (Landlady); Hank Worden (Driver); Charles Watts, Phil Dunham, James Logan, Cameron Grant (Quartet); Helyn Eby-Rock (Angry Woman); Francis Pierlot (Pharmacist).

CLASH BY NIGHT (RKO, 1952) 105 min.

Executive producers, Jerry Wald, Norman Krasna; producer, Harriet Parsons; director, Fritz Lang; based on the play by Clifford Odets; screenplay, Alfred Hayes; art directors, Albert S. D'Agostino, Carroll Clark; set decorators, Darrell Silvera, Jack Miles; costumes, Michael Woulfe; music, Roy Webb; music director, C. Bakaleinikoff; camera, Nicholas Musuraca; editor, George Amy.

Barbara Stanwyck (Mae Doyle); Paul Douglas (Jerry D'Amato), Robert Ryan (Earl Pfeiffer); Marilyn Monroe (Peggy); J. Carrol Naish (Uncle Vince); Keith Andes (Joe Doyle); Silvio Minciotti (Papa); Diane Stewart, Deborah Stewart (Twin Babies); Julius Tannen (Sad-Eyed Waiter); Tony Dante (Fisherman at Pier).

JEOPARDY (MGM, 1953) 69 min.

Producer, Sol Baer Fielding; director, John Sturges; story, Maurice Zimm; screenplay, Mel Dinelli; art directors, Cedric Gibbons, William Ferrari; set decorators, Edwin B. Willis, Fred MacLean; costumes, Helen Rose; music/music director, Dmitri Tiomkin; camera, Victor Milner; editor, Newell P. Kimlin.

Barbara Stanwyck (Helen Stilwin); Barry Sullivan (Doug Stilwin); Ralph Meeker (Lawson); Lee Aaker (Bobby Stilwin); Bud Wolfe (Lieutenant's Driver); Saul Gorss (Captain's Driver); Bob Castro (Machine Gunner); Natividad Vacio (Vendor); Louis Tomei, Ken Terrell (Barricade Officers); Rico Alaniz (Mexican Officer).

TITANIC (Twentieth Century-Fox, 1953) 98 min.

Producer, Charles Brackett; director, Jean Negulesco; screenplay, Charles Brackett, Walter Reisch, Richard Breen; art directors, Lyle Wheeler, Maurice Ransford; set decorator, Stuart Reiss; costumes, Dorothy Jeakins; music, Sol Kaplan; music director, Lionel Newman; orchestrator, Herbert Spencer; camera, Joe MacDonald; editor, Louis Loeffler.

Clifton Webb (Richard Sturges); Barbara Stanwyck

(Julia Sturges); Robert Wagner (Cliff Rogers); Audrey Dalton (Annette Sturges); Thelma Ritter (Maude Young); Brian Aherne (Captain E. J. Smith); Richard Basehart (George Healey); Allyn Joslyn (Earl Meeker); James Todd (Sandy Comstock); William Johnstone (John Jacob Astor); Charles FitzSimons (Chief Officer Wilde); Barry Bernard (First Officer Murdock); Harper Carter (Norman Sturges); Edmund Purdom (Second Officer Lightoller); Christopher Severn (Messenger); James Lilburn (Devlin); Frances Bergen (Mrs. John Jacob Astor); Guy Standing, Jr. (George D. Widener); Hellen Van Tuy (Mrs. Straus); Roy Gordon (Mr. Isidor Straus); Mae Marsh (Woman); Robin Camp (Messenger Boy); David Thursby (Seaman); Robin Hughes (Junior Officer); Pat Aherne (Seaman); Pat O'Moore (Relief Man); Elizabeth Flournoy (Woman with Baby).

ALL I DESIRE (Universal, 1953) 74 min.

Producer, Ross Hunter; director, Douglas Sirk; based on the novel *Stopover* by Carol Brink; adaptor, Gina Kaus; screenplay, James Gunn, Robert Blees; music director, Joseph Gershenson; song, David Lieberman; choreography, Kenny Williams; assistant director, Joseph E. Kenny; costumes, Rosemary Odell; art directors, Bernard Herzbrun, Alexander Golitzen; set decorators, Russell A. Gauman, Julia Heron; sound, Leslie I. Carey, Robert Pritchard; camera, Carl Guthrie; editor. Milton Carruth.

Barbara Stanwyck (Naomi Murdoch/ Narrator); Richard Carlson (Henry Murdoch); Lyle Bettger (Dutch Heineman); Marcia Henderson (Joyce Murdoch); Lori Nelson (Lily Murdoch); Richard Long (Russ Underwood); Maureen O'Sullivan (Sara Harper); Billy Gray (Ted Murdoch); Lotte Stein (Lena Engstrom); Fred Nurney (Hans Peterson); Dayton Lummis (Colonel Underwood); Brett Halsey (John Lexington in Play); Thomas E. Jackson (Dr. R. Tomlin); Virginia Brissac (Mrs. Tomlin); Lela Bliss (Belle Stanton); Guy Williams (Ticket Taker); Stuart Whitman (Dick in Play); Edmund Cobb (Hack Driver); Bobby Barber (Porch Loafer); Wheaton Chambers (Mr. Atkins).

THE MOONLIGHTER (Warner Bros., 1953) 77 min.

Producer, Joseph Bernhard; director, Roy Rowland; screenplay, Niven Busch; art director, Dan Hall; set decorator, Fred MacLean; costumes, Joe King, Ann Peck; music/music director, Heinz Roemheld; camera, Bert Glennon; editor, Terry Morse.

Barbara Stanwyck (Rela); Fred MacMurray (Wes Anderson); Ward Bond (Cole); William Ching (Tom Anderson); John Dierkes (Sheriff Daws); Morris Ankrum (Prince); Jack Elam (Strawboss); Charles Halton (Clem Usquebaugh); Norman Leavitt (Tidy); Sam Flint (Mr. Mott); Myra Marsh (Mrs. Anderson).

BLOWING WILD (Warner Bros., 1953) 90 min.

Producer, Milton Sperling; director, Hugo Fre-

gonese; screenplay, Philip Yordan; art director, Al Ybarra; set decorator, William Wallace; music, Dmitri Tiomkin; music director, Ray Heindorf; camera, Sid Hickox; editor, Alan Crosland, Jr.

Gary Cooper (Jeff); Barbara Stanwyck (Marina); Ruth Roman (Sal); Anthony Quinn (Paco); Ward Bond (Dutch); Ian MacDonald (Jackson); Richad Karlan (Henderson); Juan Garcia (El Gavilan).

EXECUTIVE SUITE (MGM, 1954) 104 min.

Producer, John Houseman; director, Robert Wise; based on the novel by Cameron Hawley; screenplay, Ernest Lehman; art directors, Cedric Gibbons, Edward Carfagno; set decorators, Edwin B. Willis, Emile Kuri; women's costumes, Helen Rose; special effects, A. Arnold Gillespie, Warren Newcombe; camera, George Folsey; editor, Ralph E. Winters.

William Holden (McDonald Walling); June Allyson (Mary Blemond Walling); Barbara Stanwyck (Julie Tredway); Fredric March (Loren Phineas Shaw); Walter Pidgeon (Frederick Y. Alderson); Shelley Winters (Eva Bardeman); Paul Douglas (Josiah Walter Dudley); Louis Calhern (George Nyle Caswell); Dean Jagger (Jesse Grimm); Nina Foch (Erica Martin); Tim Considine (Mike Walling); William Phipps (Bill Lundeen); Lucille Knoch (Mrs. George Nyle Caswell); Mary Adams (Sara Asenath Grimm); Virginia Brissac (Edith Alderson); Edgar Stehli (Julius Steigel); Harry Shannon (Ed Benedeck); Charles Wagenheim (Luigi Cassoni); Virginia Eiler (Western Union Operator); Jonathan Cott (Cop); Robin Camp (Mailroom Boy); Ray Mansfield (Alderson Secretary); A. Cameron Grant (Salesman); May McAvoy (Grimm's Secretary); John Doucette, Willis Bouchey (Morgue Officials); Esther Michelson (Woman News Dealer); David McMahon, Ralph Montgomery (Reporters); Raoul Freeman (Avery Bullard); Mike Lally (Spectator at Ball Game); Ann Tyrell (Shaw Secretary).

WITNESS TO MURDER (United Artists, 1954) 83 min.

Producer, Chester Erskine; director, Roy Rowland; screenplay, Erskine; art director, William Ferrari; set decorator, Alfred E. Spencer; costumes, Jack Masters, Irene Caine; music, Herschel Burke Gilbert; camera, John Alton; editor, Robert Swink.

Barbara Stanwyck (Cheryl Draper); George Sanders (Albert Richter); Gary Merrill (Lawrence Mathews); Jesse White (Eddie Vincent); Harry Shannon (Captain Donnelly); Clare Carleton (The Blonde); Lewis Martin (Psychiatrist); Dick Elliott (Apartment Manager); Harry Tyler (Charlie); Juanita Moore (Woman); Joy Hallward (Woman's Co-Worker); Gertrude Graner (Policewoman); Adeline DeWalt Reynolds (Old Lady).

CATTLE QUEEN OF MONTANA (RKO, 1954) C-88 min.

Producer, Benedict Bogeaus; director, Allan Dwan; story, Thomas Blackburn; screenplay, Howard Estabrook, Robert Blees; art director, Van Nest Polglase; set decorator, John Sturtevant; costumes, Gwen Wakeling; music, Louis Forbes; camera, John Alton; editor, Carl Lodato.

Barbara Stanwyck (Sierra Nevada Jones); Ronald Reagan (Farrell); Gene Evans (Tom McCord); Lance Fuller (Colorado); Anthony Caruso (Nachakos); Jack Elam (Yost); Yvette Dugay (Starfire); Morris Ankrum (J. I. "Pop" Jones); Chubby Johnson (Nat); Myron Healey (Hank); Rodd Redwing (Powhani); Paul Birch (Colonel Carrington); Byron Foulger (Land Office Employee); Burt Mustin (Dan); Roy Gordon (Bit).

THE VIOLENT MEN (Columbia, 1955) C-96 min.

Producer, Lewis J. Rachmil; director, Rudolph Maté; based on the novel by Donald Hamilton; screenplay, Harry Kleiner; art director, Carl Anderson; set decorator, Louis Diage; costumes, Jean Louis; music, Max Steiner; music director, Morris Stoloff; orchestrator, Murray Cutter; camera, Burnett Guffey, W. Howard Greene; editor, Jerome Thoms.

Glenn Ford (John Parrish); Barbara Stanwyck (Martha Wilkison); Edward G. Robinson (Lew Wilkison); Dianne Foster (Judith Wilkison); Brian Keith (Cole Wilkison); May Wynn (Caroline Vail); Warner Anderson (Jim McCloud); Basil Ruysdael (Tex Hinkleman); Lita Milan (Elena); Richard Jaeckel (Wade Matlock); James Westerfield (Magruder); Jack Kelly (De-Rosa); Willis Bouchey (Sheriff Martin Kenner); Harry Shannon (Purdue); Peter Hanson (George Menefee); Don Harvey (Jackson); Robo Bechi (Tony); Carl Andre (Dryer); James Anderson (Hank Purdue); Katharine Warren (Mrs. Vail); Tom Browne Henry (Mr. Vail); Bill Phipps (Bud Hinkleman); Edmund Cobb (Anchor Rider); Ethan Laidlaw (Barfly).

ESCAPE TO BURMA (RKO, 1955) C-88 min.

Producer, Benedict Bogeaus; director, Allan Dwan; based on the story "Bow Tamely to Me" by Kenneth Perkins; screenplay, Talbot Jennings, Hobart Donavan; art director, Van Nest Polglase; set decorator, Fay Babcock; costumes, Gwen Wakeling; music, Louis Forbes; camera, John Alton; editor, James Leicester.

Robert Ryan (Jim Brecan); Barbara Stanwyck (Gwen Moore); David Farrar (Cardigan); Murvyn Vye (Mekash); Robert Warwick (Sawbwa); Reginald Denny (Commissioner); Lisa Montell (Andora); Peter Coe (Guard Captain); Anthony Numkena (Kasha); Alex Montoya (Dacoit); Robert Cabal (Kumat); Lal Chand Mehra (Pookan); William Benegal Raw (Young Horn Player); John Mansfield (Sergeant); Gavin Muir (Astrologer); Roger (The Leopard); Neil (The Chimpanzee).

THERE'S ALWAYS TOMORROW (Universal, 1956) 84 min.

Producer, Ross Hunter; director, Douglas Sirk; based on the story by Ursula Parrott; screenplay, Bernard C. Schoenfeld; art directors, Alexander Golitzen, Eric Orborn; set decorators, Russell A. Gausman, Julia Heron; costumes, Jay Morley, Jr.; music, Herman Stein, Heinz Roemheld; camera, Russell Metty; editor, William M. Morgan.

Barbara Stanwyck (Norma Miller); Fred MacMurray (Clifford Groves); Joan Bennett (Marion Groves); Pat Crowley (Ann); William Reynolds (Vinnie Groves); Gigi Perreau (Ellen Groves); Race Gentry (Bob); Myrna Hansen (Ruth); Judy Nugent (Frankie Groves); Jane Darwell (Mrs. Rogers); Paul Smith (Bellboy); Jane Howard (Flower Girl); Louise Lorimer (Ohio Lady with Dog); Vonne Lester (Junior Executive); Dorothy Bruce (Sales Manager).

THE MAVERICK QUEEN (Republic, 1956) C-92 min.

Producer, Herbert J. Yates; associate producer/director, Joseph Kane; based on the novel by Zane Grey; screenplay, Kenneth Gamet, DeVallon Scott; art director, Walter Keller; set decorator, John McCarthy, Jr., Fay Babcock; costumes, Adele Palmer; music, Victor Young; song, Ned Washington and Young; special effects, Howard and Theodore Lydecker; camera, Jack Marta; editor, Richard L. Van Enger.

Barbara Stanwyck (Kit Banion); Barry Sullivan (Jeff); Scott Brady (Sundance); Mary Murphy (Lucy Lee); Wallace Ford (Jamie); Howard Petrie (Butch Cassidy); Jim Davis (A Stranger); Emile Meyer (Malone); Walter Sande (Sheriff Wilson); George Keymas (Muncie); John Doucette (Loudmouth); Taylor Holmes (Pete Callaher); Pierre Watkin (McMillan); Karen Scott, Carol Brewster (Girls); Tristram Coffin (Card Player).

THESE WILDER YEARS (MGM, 1956) 91 min.

Producer, John Schermer; director, Roy Rowland; based on the story by Ralph Wheelwright; screenplay, Frank Fenton; art directors, Cedric Gibbons, Preston Ames; set decorators, Edwin B. Willis, Edwin C. Boyle; costumes, Helen Rose; music, Jeff Alexander; makeup, William Tuttle; assistant director, Al Jennings; sound, Dr. Wesley C. Miller; camera, George J. Folsey; editor, Ben Lewis.

James Cagney (Steve Bradford); Barbara Stanwyck (Ann Dempster); Walter Pidgeon (James Rayburn); Betty Lou Keim (Suzie); Don Dubbins (Mark); Edward Andrews (Mr. Spottsford); Basil Ruysdael (Judge); Grandon Rhodes (Roy Oliphant); Will Wright (Old Cab Driver); Lewis Martin (Dr. Miller); Dorothy Adams (Aunt Martha); Dean Jones (Hardware Clerk); Herb Vigran (Traffic Cop); Ruth Lee (Miss Finch); William Forrest (Blount of Board of Directors); Michael Landon (Boy in Pool Room); Tom Laughlin (Football Player); Leon Tyler (Student Secretary); Russell Simpson (Farmer); Lillian Powell (Proprietress).

CRIME OF PASSION (United Artists, 1957) 84 min.

Executive producer, Bob Goldstein; producer, Herman Cohen; director, Gerd Oswald; screenplay, Jo Eisinger; art director, Leslie Thomas; set decorator, Morris Hoffman; costumes, Grace Houston; music, Paul Dunlap; camera, Joseph La Shelle; editor, Marjorie Fowler.

Barbara Stanwyck (Kathy); Sterling Hayden (Doyle); Raymond Burr (Inspector Pope); Fay Wray (Alice Pope); Royal Dano (Alidos); Virginia Grey (Sara); Dennis Cross (Detective Jules); Robert Griffin (Detective James); Jay Adler (Nalence); Malcolm Atterbury (Officer Spitz); S. John Launer (Chief of Police); Brad Trumbull (Detective Johns); Skipper McNally (Detective Jones); Robert Quarry (Reporter); Jean Howell (Mrs. Jules); Peg La Centra (Mrs. James); Nancy Reynolds (Mrs. Johns); Marjorie Owens (Mrs. Jones).

TROOPER HOOK (United Artists, 1957) 81 min.

Producer, Sol Baer Fielding; director, Charles Marquis Warren; story, Jack Schaefer; screenplay, Warren, David Victor, Herbert Little, Jr.; art director, Nick Remisoff; costumes, Voulee Giokaris; music/music director, Gerald Fried; assistant directors, Nathan Barragar, Nat Holt, Jr.; camera, Ellsworth Fredericks; editor, Fred Berger.

Barbara Stanwyck (Cora); Joel McCrea (Sergeant Hook); Earl Holliman (Jeff Bennett); John Dehner (Fred Sutliff); Royal Dano (Trude); Rudolfo Acosta (Nanchez); Edward Andrews (Charlie); Susan Kohner (Consuela); Celia Lovsky (Senora); Terry Lawrence (Quito).

FORTY GUNS (Twentieth Century-Fox, 1957) 80 min.

Producer/director/screenplay, Samuel Fuller; art director, John Mansbridge; set decorators, Walter M. Scott, Chester Bayhi; costumes, Charles LeMaire, Leah Rhodes; music/music director, Harry Sukman; assistant director, Harold E. Knox; camera, Joseph Biroc; editor, Gene Fowler, Jr.

Barbara Stanwyck (Jessica Drummond); Barry Sullivan (Griff Bonnell); Dean Jagger (Ned Logan); John Ericson (Brockie Drummond); Gene Barry (Wes Bonnell); Robert Dix (Chico Bonnell); "Jidge" Carroll (Barney Cashman); Gerald Milton (Shotgun Spangler); Eve Brent (Louvenia Spangler); Ziva Rodann (Rio); Hank Worden (John Chisum); Neyle Morrow (Wiley); Chuck Roberson (Howard Swain); Chuck Hayward (Charlie Savage); Sandra Wirth (Chico's Girl); Paul Dubov (Judge Macey); Eddie Parks (Sexton).

WALK ON THE WILD SIDE (Columbia, 1962) 114 min.

Producer, Charles K. Feldman; director, Edward Dmytryk; based on the novel by Nelson Algren; screenplay, John Fante, Edmund Morris; art director, Richard Sylbert; set decorator, William Kiernan; costumes, Charles LeMaire; titles, Saul Ban; music, Elmer Bernstein; orchestrators, Leo Shuken, Jack Hayes; camera, Joe MacDonald; editor, Harry Gerstad.

Laurence Harvey (Dove Linkhorn); Capucine

(Hallie); Jane Fonda (Kitty Twist); Anne Baxter (Teresina Vidarverri); Barbara Stanwyck (Jo Courtney); Joanna Moore (Miss Precious); Richard Rust (Oliver); Karl Swenson (Schmidt); Donald "Red" Barry (Dockery); Juanita Moore (Mama); John Anderson (Preacher); Ken Lynch (Frank Bonito); Todd Armstrong (Lieutenant Omar Stroud); Lillian Bronson (Amy Gerard); Adrienne Marden (Eva Gerard); Sherry O'Neil (Rebs); John Bryant (Spence); Kathryn Card (Landlady); Steve Benton, Nesdon Booth (Van Drivers); Murray Alper (Simon); Chester Jones (Black Waiter).

ROUSTABOUT (Paramount, 1964) C-101 min.

Producer, Hal B. Wallis; director, John Rich; story, Allan Weiss; screenplay, Anthony Lawrence, Weiss; art directors, Hal Pereira, Walter Tyler; set decorators, Sam Comer, Robert Benton; costumes, Edith Head; music/music director, Joseph J. Lilley; assistant director, D. Michael Moore; sound, Charles Grenzbach, John Carter; special camera effects, Paul K. Lerpae; process camera, Farciot Edouart; camera, Lucien Ballard; editor, Warren Low.

Elvis Presley (Charlie Rogers); Barbara Stanwyck (Maggie Morgan); Joan Freeman (Cathy Lean); Leif Erickson (Joe Lean); Sue Ann Langdon (Madame Mijanou); Pat Buttram (Harry Carver); Joan Staley (Marge); Dabbs Greer (Arthur Hielsen); Steve Brodie (Fred); Norman Grabowski (College Student); Jack Albertson (Lou); Jane Dulo (Hazel); Arthur Levy (Gus); Joel Fluellen (Cody); Ray Kellogg (Ernie); Beverly Adams (Cora); Billy Barty (Billy, the Midget); John Turk (Volcano Man); Raquel Welch (College Student); Katie Sweet (Little Girl).

THE NIGHT WALKER (Universal, 1965) 86 min.

Producer/director, William Castle; screenplay, Robert Bloch; art directors, Alexander Golitzen, Frank Arrigo; set decorators, John McCarthy, Julia Heron; costumes, Helen Colvig; music, Vic Mizzy; music director, Joseph Gershenson; camera, Harold E. Stine; editor, Edwin H. Bryant.

Robert Taylor (Barry Morland); Barbara Stanwyck (Irene Trent); Judi Meredith (Joyce Holliday); Hayden Rorke (Howard Trent); Rochelle Hudson (Hilda); Marjorie Bennett (Manager); Lloyd Bochner (The Dream); Jess Barker (Frank Malone); Paulle Clark (Pat); Tetsu Komai (Gardener); Kathleen Mulqueen (Customer); Teddy Durant (Narrator).

THE HOUSE THAT WOULDN'T DIE (ABC-TV, 1970) C-73 min.

Producer, Aaron Spelling; director, John Llewellyn Moxey; based on the novel Ammie, Come Home by Barbara Michaels; teleplay, Henry Farrell; art director, Tracy Bousman; music, Laurence Rosenthal; music director, George Duning; Miss Stanwyck's costumes, Nolan Miller; camera, Fleet Southcott; editor, Art Seid.

Barbara Stanwyck (Ruth Bennett); Richard Egan

(Pat McDougal); Michael Anderson, Jr. (Stan Whitman); Katherine "Kitty" Winn (Sara Dunning); Doreen Lang (Sylvia Wall); Mabel Albertson (Mrs. Delia McDougal).

A TASTE OF EVIL *(ABC-TV, 1971)* C-74 min.

Producer, Aaron Spelling; director, John Llewellyn Moxey; teleplay, Jimmy Sangster; art director, Paul Sylos; Miss Stanwyck's costumes, Nolan Miller; music, Robert Drasnin; camera, Arch Dalzell; editor, Art Seid.

Barbara Stanwyck (Miriam Jennings); Barbara Parkins (Susan Wilcox); Roddy McDowall (Dr. Michael Lomas); William Windom (Harold Jennings); Arthur O'Connell (John); Bing Russell (Sheriff); Dawn Frame (Young Susan).

THE LETTERS *(ABC-TV, 1973)* 74 min.

Executive producers, Aaron Spelling, Leonard Goldberg; producer, Paul Junger Witt; Miss Stanwyck's episode directed by Gene Nelson; based on a story by Ellis Marcus; teleplay, Marcus, Hal Sitowitz; art director, Tracy Bousman; Miss Stanwyck's costumes, Nolan Miller; music supervisor, Rocky Moriana; camera, Tim Southcott; editor, Carroll Sax.

Episode One: John Forsythe, Jane Powell, Lesley Warren; *Episode Two:* Dina Merrill (Penelope Parkington); Leslie Nielson (Derek Childs); Barbara Stanwyck (Geraldine Parkington); Gil Stuart (Michael); Orville Sherman (Minister); *Episode Three:* Ida Lupino, Ben Murphy, Pamela Franklin.

493

ABOUT THE STAFF

JAMES ROBERT PARISH, a New York-based freelance writer, was born in Cambridge, Massachusetts. He attended the University of Pennsylvania and graduated as a Phi Beta Kappa with a degree in English. A graduate of the University of Pennsylvania Law School, he was president of Entertainment Copyright Research Co., Inc. Later, he was a film reviewer and interviewer for entertainment trade papers. He is the author of such volumes as *The Great Movie Series, The Fox Girls, Actors' Television Credits, Hollywood's Great Love Teams,* and *The Jeanette MacDonald Story.* He is the co-author of *The MGM Stock Company, Liza!, The Great Western Pictures,* and *Film Directors Guide: The U.S.* Mr. Parish is also a film reviewer for national magazines.

DON E. STANKE in the past few years has interviewed more than forty personalities of American film and stage and has had career articles published on most of them in assorted cinema journals. Interviewing and writing is avocational, since Stanke is a full-time administrative manager with a San Francisco-based corporation. With Mr. Parish, he is the co-author of *The Glamour Girls, The Swashbucklers, The Debonairs,* and *The All-Americans,* and has contributed to the books *The Real Stars #2, The Tough Guys,* and *Hollywood Players: The Thirties.*

T. ALLAN TAYLOR, godson of the late Margaret Mitchell, has long been active in book publishing and is presently the production manager of one of the largest abstracting and technical indexing services in the United States. He was editor of such volumes as *The Fox Girls, The RKO Gals, The Great Spy Pictures, Hollywood's Great Love Teams,* and *Elvis!,* as well as others.

Since an early age, Brooklyn-born **JOHN ROBERT COCCHI** has been viewing and collating data on motion pictures and is now regarded as one of America's most energetic film researchers. He is the New York editor of *Boxoffice* Magazine. He was research associate on *The American Movies Reference Book: The Sound Era, The Fox Girls, Good Dames, The MGM Stock Company: The Golden Era,* and a contributing editor to *The Films of Jeanette MacDonald and Nelson Eddy.* He has written cinema history articles for such journals as *Film Fan Monthly* and *Screen Facts,* and is the author of a book on Western pictures. He is co-founder of one of New York City's leading film societies.

New York-born **FLORENCE SOLOMON** attended Hunter College and then joined Ligon Johnson's copyright research office. Later, she was appointed director for research at Entertainment Copyright Research Co., Inc., and is presently a reference supervisor at ASCAP's Index Division in New York City. Miss Solomon has collaborated on such tomes as *The American Movies Reference Book: The Sound Era, TV Movies, The Great Movie Series, The George Raft File, Film Directors Guide: Western Europe,* and several others. She is a niece of the noted sculptor, the late Sir Jacob Epstein.

Manhattanite **RICHARD WENTZLER**, having lived in all corners of the United States and Europe, has been involved in such diverse pursuits as acting, chess (he is rated in the "Expert" category), and filmmaking. He holds degrees in physics and earth-and-space sciences but now devotes his energies to writing, publicity, and film research. He is the author of a book on vitamins.

GERALD WEALES reviewed foreign films for the *Quarterly of Film, Radio, and Television* in the 1950s, before it was transmuted into *Film Quarterly,* and more recently has written on film for *The New York Times, Film Comment,* and *North American Review.* Winner of the George Jean Nathan Award for Dramatic Criticism, 1964-1965, he was drama critic for *The Reporter* and *Commonweal* and is the author of a number of books on the theater, including *The Jumping Off Place* and *Clifford Odets, Playwright.* He is Professor of English at the University of Pennsylvania in Philadelphia.

Index

Italicized numbers refer to picture pages.

499

Burke, Billie, 55, 132, 299, *355*
Burke, Edwin, 372
Burke, Johnny, 50
Burke, Paul, 150
Burlesque, 63, 426, 427
Burnell, Charles S., 303
Burnt Offerings, 248, *250*
Burr, Raymond, 470
Burton, Richard, 317, *318*
Busch, Mae, *40*
Bushell, Anthony, 186
Bushman, Francis X., Jr., 103–4
Butterworth, Charles, 186
Bye Bye Birdie, 67
Byington, Spring, 130, 296
Byron, Arthur, *195*
Byron, Walter, 185

Caan, James, *327,* 328
Cabin in the Cotton, 187, 188, 189 n, 253
Caesar, Sid, 382
Cagney, James, 20, 26–27, 28, 29, *30,* 37, 38, *41,*
    77, 186, 188, 192, 209 n, 216, 249, 275, 276,
    279, 294, 297, 405, 425, 470
Cain, James M., 133, 451
Calhern, Louis, 183, 188, 463
California, 457, *458,* 467
Call It a Day, 281, 284, 324
Call Me Madam, 63
Call Me Ziggy, 57
Calvet, Corinne, 386
Camille, 44, 457
Campbell, Marque, 162
Campos, Rafael, 328
Canadians, The, 367 n
Canary Murder Case, The, 357
Canby, Vincent, 333
Candida, 316
Caniff, Milton, 117
Cannes Film Festival, 317, 329
Cape Playhouse, 182, 183
Capital Films Exchange, 185
Capra, Frank, 238, 428, 429, 432, 433, 449
Captain Blood, 276–77, 280, 333
Capucine, 471
Caretakers, The, 152, 154
Carlisle, Mary, 43
Carlson, May, *443*
Carlson, Richard, 466, *468*
Carney, Art, 67
Carpenter, R. V., *62*
Carradine, John, *145*

Carrillo, Leo, 188
Carr, Larry, 102
Carroll, John, *371, 372*
Carroll, Leo G., *120*
Carroll, Madeleine, 141
Carroll, Nancy, 29, 425, 427
Carson, Jack, *135,* 137, *214, 294,* 296, 298, 302,
    381
Carter, Ann, 457
Carteret, George de, 272
Carter, Harper, 466
Carter, Marion, 432
Case of the Howling Dog, The, 192, 197
Casey, Ed, 352
Casino Murder Case, The, 357
Cassavetes, John, 76
Cassin, Billie. *See* Crawford, Joan
Cassin, Henry, 96, 97
Cass, Peggy, 394
Castle on the Hudson, 188
Castle, William, 72, 154, 472, 475
Catered Affair, The, 153, 233
Cather, Willa, 439
Cat on a Hot Tin Roof, 395
Cattle Queen of Montana, 467
Caulfield, Joan, 460
Cavanagh, Paul, 137
Cavanaugh, Hobart, *45*
CBS-TV, 77, 471
Cellist, The, 244
Center Door Fancy (J. Blondell), 20, 21, 73
Central Park, 35
Chained, 117
Champion, Gower, 67
Chandler, Helen, 184
Chandler, Jeff, 147
Chandler, Raymond, 451
Chanel (fashion designer), 34
Chanel, Coco, 404
Chaney, Lon, 104
Chaplin, Charlie, 220, 445, 448
Chapman, John, 316
Charge of the Light Brigade, The, 280–81
Charisse, Cyd, 461
Charles, Keith, 155
"Charlotte's Theme," 220
Charters, Spencer, *40*
Chase, Chris, 409
Chase, Ilka, *219,* 367
Chatterton, Ruth, 117, 185, 186, 187, 197, 282,
    308, 433, 438, 441
Chayefsky, Paddy, 233

Murfin, Jane, 367
Murphy, George, 51, *52*
Murray, James, 105
Murray, Mae, 102
Murrow, Edward R., 470
Mutiny on the Bounty, 276, 277
My Cousin Rachel, 317, *318,* 329
My First Hundred Years in Hollywood (Jack L. Warner), 186 n
My Girl Friday, 25
My Love Came Back, 293
My Reputation, 424, 456, *458*
My Sister Eileen, 350, 375, *377,* 387
My Ten Years in the Studio (Arliss), 186 n
My Way of Life (J. Crawford), 158
My Wicked, Wicked Ways (Flynn), 283

Nagel, Conrad, 141, 184, 367
Naked Genius, The, 56, 57, 60, 63
Nana (Zola), 205
Nanny, The, 241
Napoleon, 201
Nash Prize. *See* WAMPAS Achievement Trophy
Nathan, George Jean, 26
Natheaux, Louis, 105
National Board of Review, 449
National Council on the Arts, 405
National Enquirer, 409
National Film Theatre, 332
National Foundation for Infantile Paralysis, 381
Natwick, Mildred, 228
Neal, Patricia, 460
Nederlander, Jimmy, 478
Nelson, Ed, 332
Nelson, Gene, 475
Nelson, Harmon "Ham," 181, 187, 188, 192, 200 n, 201, *202,* 204, 207
Nelson, Ruth, 138
Never Wave at a WAC, 387, *389*
Nevinson, Nancy, 325
"New Dick Van Dyke Show, The," *75, 77*
Newell, David, 213
New Girl in Town, 67, 391
New School (New York), 245
Newsweek, 216, 226, 248, 298, 321, 325, 450, 457
Newton, Theodore, 189
New York Criticis Circle Award, 389
New York Daily Mirror, 37, 67, 129, 325
New York Daily News, 67, 441
New York Drama Critics Circle Award, 239
New Yorker, The, 241
New York Evening World, 104, 105

New York Film Critics Award, 229, 298, 312, 316
New York Foreign Language Press Film Critics Circle Award, 382, 383
New York Herald-Tribune, 132, 147, 153 n, 154, 328, 427, 471
New York Journal, 432
New York Post, 248
New York Sun, 362
New York Times, 38, 50, 51, 56, 67, 73, 113, 115, 132, 143, 147, 150, 162, 198, 249, 287, 298, 304, 308, 321, 324, 325, 362, 372, 382, 387, 395, 426, 427, 444, 450, 456, 463, 467, 470
New York World, 426
New York World-Telegram, 57, 444, 449, 470
Niblo, Fred, 21
Nichols, Dudley, 382
Nicholson, Kenyon, 113
Nielsen, Leslie, 473, 475
"Night Gallery," 155, *159*
Night in Spain, A, 426
Night Is Young, The, 357
Nightmare Alley, 59, 62, 76
Night Must Fall, 360, 362, 367
Night Nurse, 39, 429, *434,* 462
Night of the Iguana, The, 236, 238, 239
Night to Remember, A, 466
Night Walker, The, 472, 475
Niven, David, 292, 293, *294,* 387, 449, 457
Nixon, Richard M., 405
Nolan, Lloyd, 61, 441
No Man of Her Own, 462
No More Ladies, 119, *121,* 276
Noon Wine, 329, *330*
Noose, The, 426, 428
Norman, Maidie, 153
Norvell (astrologer), 45
Not as a Stranger, 320, *322*
No Time for Comedy, 291, 369, *370*
Notre Dame Convent (Belmont, Calif.), 273
Not This Time, Cary Grant (Eder), 473
Not Too Narrow, Not Too Deep (Sale), 128
Novak, Kim, 192 n, 386, 390, 470
Novarro, Ramon, 105, 357
Now, Voyager, 187, 217, *219,* 220, 248, 252
Nugent, Elliott, 298
Nugent, Frank S., 125, 208, 275, 293, 362, 464
Nugent, Judy, 468

Oakie, Jack, 46, 98
Oberon, Merle, 200, 208
O'Brien, Kate, 320
O'Brien-Moore, Erin, 205

523